cultural
anthropology

cultural anthropology

THIRTEENTH EDITION

CAROL R. EMBER

Human Relations Area Files

MELVIN EMBER

Human Relations Area Files

Prentice Hall

Boston   Columbus   Indianapolis   New York   San Francisco   Upper Saddle River
Amsterdam   Cape Town   Dubai   London   Madrid   Milan   Munich   Paris   Montréal   Toronto
Delhi   Mexico City   São Paulo   Sydney   Hong Kong   Seoul   Singapore   Taipei   Tokyo

Planet Friendly Publishing
✓ Made in the United States
✓ Printed on Recycled Paper
Text: 10%   Cover: 10%
Learn more: www.greenedition.org

At Pearson Education we're committed to producing books in an earth-friendly manner and to helping our customers make greener choices.
Manufacturing books in the United States ensures compliance with strict environmental laws and eliminates the need for international freight shipping, a major contributor to global air pollution.
And printing on recycled paper helps minimize our consumption of trees, water and fossil fuels. According to the Environmental Paper Network's Paper Calculator. The text of *Cultural Anthropology, Thirteenth Edition*, was printed on paper made with 10% post-consumer waste, and the cover was printed on paper made with 10% post-consumer waste. According to Environmental Paper Network's Paper Calculator, by using this innovative paper instead of conventional papers, we achieved the following environmental benefits:

Trees Saved: 61 • **Air Emissions Eliminated: 6,029 pounds**
Water Saved: 28,850 gallons • **Solid Waste Eliminated: 1,797 pounds**

For more information on our environmental practices, please visit us online at www.pearsonhighered.com/difference
Courier Corporation, the manufacturer of this book, owns the Green Edition Trademark.

VP, Editorial Director: Craig Campanella
Editor in Chief: Dickson Musslewhite
Publisher: Nancy Roberts
Editorial Assistant: Nart Varoqua
Assistant Editor: Vanessa Gennarelli
Director of Marketing: Brandy Dawson
Senior Marketing Manager: Laura Lee Manley
Marketing Assistant: Pat Walsh
Managing Editor: Maureen Richardson
Project Manager: Marianne Peters-Riordan
Copy Editor: Heather McElwain
Proofreader: David Heath
Senior Operations Supervisor: Mary Ann Gloriande
Operations Specialist: Cathleen Petersen
Senior Art Director: Nancy Wells

Art Director: Anne Bonanno Nieglos
Interior and Cover Designer: Ilze Lemesis
AV Project Manager: Maria Piper
Manager, Visual Research: Beth Brenzel
Manager, Rights and Permissions: Zina Arabia
Image Permission Coordinator: Frances Toepfer
Manager, Cover Visual Research & Permissions: Karen Sanatar
Cover Art: Jamie Marshall/Tribaleye Images/Image Bank/ Getty Images
Media Director: Brian Hyland
Senior Media Editor: David Alick
Media Project Manager: Diane Lombardo
Full-Service Project Management: Jill Traut
Composition: MPS Limited, A Macmillan Company
Printer/Binder and Cover Printer: Courier Companies, Inc.

 DK Maps designed and productioned by DK Education, a division of Dorling Kindersley Limited, 80 Strand, London WC2R ORL. DK and the DK logo are registered trademarks of Dorling Kindersley Limited.

This book was set in 10/11.5, Minion.

Credits and acknowledgments borrowed from other sources and reproduced, with permission, in this textbook appear on the appropriate page within the text (or on pages 389–390).

Library of Congress Cataloging-in-Publication Data

Ember, Carol R.
  Cultural anthropology / Carol Ember, Melvin Ember. — 13th ed.
    p. cm.
  ISBN-13: 978-0-205-71120-8 (pbk. : alk. paper)
  ISBN-10: 0-205-71120-0 (pbk. : alk. paper)
  1. Ethnology. I. Ember, Melvin. II. Title.
  GN316.E45 2010
  306—dc22

                    2009046599

10 9 8 7 6 5 4

Prentice Hall
is an imprint of

www.pearsonhighered.com

Student Edition
ISBN 10: 0-205-71120-0
ISBN 13: 978-0-205-71120-8

Exam Edition
ISBN 10: 0-205-71122-7
ISBN 13: 978-0-205-71122-2

A la Carte
ISBN 10: 0-205-82858-2
ISBN 13: 978-0-205-82858-6

For Mel–

Always the optimist, who believed that there were
laws governing human behavior that could be found if
you thought hard enough, worked hard enough, and
tested ideas against the anthropological record.

1933-2009

brief contents

contents

boxes

applied anthropology

current research and issues

migrants and immigrants

new perspectives on gender

preface

This thirteenth edition of *Cultural Anthropology* represents the most significant revision of the text since the tenth edition. The following are the four major changes:

- To emphasize the importance of applied or practicing anthropology in the profession of anthropology, we have included one applied anthropology box feature in every chapter and incorporated more applied work into the text itself.
- To highlight culture change and the impact of globalization, we now have a chapter near the beginning of the book called "Culture and Culture Change." We have also moved specific examples of culture change into their respective subject chapters.
- Third, to make it easier to use this text in a one semester course, we have shortened the number of chapters by two. As already explained, we have combined what was the "Concept of Culture" chapter with what was "Culture Change and Globalization." And what was a separate chapter on medical anthropology is now included with applied and practicing anthropology.
- Another major change is in our chapter on anthropological theory. Given the increasing importance of more integrated approaches to the understanding of culture, we have made our history of theory chapter reflect anthropological theory more broadly, incorporating a section on the evolution of evolution and on dramatic changes in "race" theory over time.

We have always tried to go beyond descriptions to explain not only *what* humans are and were like; but also *why* they got to be that way, in all their variety. This edition is no different. An important part of updating the text is finding new explanations, and we try to communicate the necessity to evaluate these new explanations logically as well as on the basis of the available evidence. Throughout the book, we try to communicate that no idea, including ideas put forward in textbooks, should be accepted even tentatively without supporting tests that could have gone the other way.

ORGANIZATION OF THE TEXT
Part I: Introduction to Anthropology

We see anthropology as a unified discipline that combines the insights of ethnographers, linguists, archaeologists, and physical anthropologists to create a holistic understanding of humans. In this section, we introduce the discipline of anthropology, outline its history and its major theoretical perspectives, and give an overview of the methods employed by anthropologists.

Chapter 1: What Is Anthropology? Chapter 1 introduces the students to anthropology. We discuss what we think is distinctive about anthropology in general, and about each of its subfields in particular. We outline how each of the subfields is related to other disciplines such as biology, psychology, and sociology. We direct attention to the increasing importance of applied anthropology and the importance of understanding others in today's more globalized world. This chapter has three boxes on individual anthropologists—an archaeologist, an ethnographer, and an applied anthropologist—and their work.

Chapter 2: Culture and Culture Change This extensively revised chapter emphasizes that culture is always changing. Our previous edition discussed culture change, ethnogenesis, and globalization near the end of the book. We have brought this material forward and integrated it into the present chapter. Particular aspects of culture change—economic, political, religious, and so on—are now included in their respective chapters. This chapter introduces the concept of culture and now includes a discussion of some of the controversies surrounding the concept. Rather than simply defining culture, we try to convey a feeling for what culture is. Throughout the chapter, we discuss individual variation and how such variation may be the beginning of new cultural patterns. We also discuss attitudes that hinder the study of culture, cultural relativism and the issue of human rights, patterning of culture, culture and adaptation, and mechanisms of culture change, before getting to the emergence of new cultures and the impact of globalization. The first box, on culture change and persistence in China, discusses what has changed because of government intervention and what has nevertheless persisted. The second box discusses an applied anthropologist's view of why Bedouin are reluctant to settle down. The third box discusses the increasing cultural diversity within countries of the world as a result of immigration and migration.

Chapter 3: History of Anthropological Theory This new chapter combines sections from several chapters in earlier editions to provide an introduction to major theoretical approaches used by anthropologists in the past and present. The chapter begins with a discussion of the evolution of evolutionary thinking—an approach that, at least in its later manifestations, underlies a considerable amount of the anthropological research we present in the text. We describe a number of older evolutionary and nonevolutionary approaches specific to anthropology. We then outline current theoretical approaches and explain how they influence anthropological research today. We explain how older approaches are not necessarily discarded. Some older approaches, particularly with regard to evolution, have withstood the test of time. The first box uses a research question about the Abelam of New Guinea to illustrate how different theoretical approaches suggest different types of answers. The second, a new applied box, describes the relationship between theory and practice to illustrate how anthropologists employ theory to solve research problems.

Chapter 4: Explanation and Evidence In this chapter, we begin by discussing what it means to explain and what kinds of evidence are needed to evaluate an explanation. We then describe the major types of study in anthropology—ethnography, within-culture comparisons, regional comparisons, worldwide cross-cultural comparisons, and historical research. We follow this with a discussion of ethics in fieldwork. We have added a new section on ethnographer disagreements that incorporates some of the material in a previous box on how to know what is true in fieldwork. A box on applied anthropology, "There Is Nothing Like Evidence to Shake Mistaken Beliefs," describes how cross-cultural research on potato farming around the world helped change applied work on potato production. Another box explores the differences between scientific and humanistic understanding and points out that the different approaches are not really incompatible.

Part II: Cultural Variation

In most of the chapters that follow, we try to convey the range of cultural variation with ethnographic examples from all over the world. Wherever we can, we discuss possible explanations of why societies may be similar or different in regard to some aspect of culture. If anthropologists have no explanation as yet for the variation, we say so. But if we have some idea of the conditions that may be related to a particular kind of variation, even if we do not know yet why they are related, we discuss that too. If we are to train students to go beyond what we know now, we have to tell them what we do not know, as well as what we think we know.

Chapter 5: Communication and Language We begin by discussing communication in humans and other animals. We have expanded our discussion of nonverbal human communication to include kinesics and paralanguage. We describe the debate about the degree of difference between human and nonhuman primate language abilities. We discuss the origins of language and how creoles and children's language acquisition may help us understand the origins. We have expanded our section on creoles to discuss pidgin languages as well. We describe the fundamentals of descriptive linguistics and the processes of linguistic divergence. After discussing the interrelationships between language and other aspects of culture, we discuss the ethnography of speaking and the differences in speech by status, gender, and ethnicity. We discuss interethnic or intercultural communication, indicating how linguists can play a role in helping people improve their cross-cultural communication. At the end of the chapter, we discuss writing and literacy. The first box, an applied box, discusses language extinction and what some anthropologists are doing about it. The second box, discusses why some immigrant groups retain their "mother tongues" longer than others. And to stimulate thinking about the possible impact of language on thought, we ask

in the last box whether the English language promotes sexist thinking.

Chapter 6: Getting Food Chapter 6 discusses how societies vary in getting their food, how they have changed over time, and how the variation seems to affect other kinds of cultural variation—including variation in economic systems, social stratification, and political life. We include a discussion of "market foragers" to emphasize that most people in a modern market economy are not in fact producers of food. We have expanded our discussion of complex foragers for this edition. Although it is commonly thought that industrialization is mainly to blame for negative developments in the environment, our first box explores where particular foods came from and how different foods and cuisines spread around the world as people migrated. Our second box, an applied box, deals with the negative effects in preindustrial times of irrigation, animal grazing, and overhunting.

Chapter 7: Economic Systems In this extensively revised chapter, we emphasize recent change by incorporating material that used to be in a separate chapter on culture change. We now discuss commercialization by way of migratory labor and remittances, nonagricultural commercial production, supplementary cash crops, and commercial and industrial agriculture. Chapter 7 begins with a discussion of how societies vary in the ways they allocate resources (what is "property" and what ownership may mean), convert or transform resources through labor into usable goods, and distribute and perhaps exchange goods and services. We have added new research on the effects of money on sharing and a discussion of informal banking systems (*hawala* brokers).

The first extensively updated box addresses the controversy over whether communal ownership leads to economic disaster. The second box discusses the impact of working abroad and sending money home. The third updated applied box illustrates the impact of the world system on local economies, with special reference to the deforestation of the Amazon.

Chapter 8: Social Stratification: Class, Ethnicity, and Racism This chapter explores the variation in degree of social stratification and how the various forms of social inequality may develop. We discuss how egalitarian societies work hard to prevent dominance, and the controversy about whether pastoral societies with individual ownership of animals are egalitarian. We then discuss the recognition of social class and how people in the United States generally deny the existence of class. We have expanded our section on caste, adding a discussion of occupational caste in Africa. The discussion of Rwanda is extensively revised to convey the sometimes complex relationship between class, caste, and ethnicity. We end with an extensive discussion of "race," racism, and ethnicity and how they often relate to the inequitable distribution of resources. We have added a new discussion of the very different concepts of "race" in Latin America. The updated first box discusses social stratification on the global level—how the gap between rich and poor countries has been widening, and what may account for that trend. The second box discusses possible reasons for disparities in death by disease between African Americans and European Americans.

Chapter 9: Culture and the Individual

Anthropology, with its focus on culture, may seem to ignore the individual. In this extensively revised chapter (formerly "Psychology and Culture"), we discuss how understanding individuals and psychological processes is vital to anthropological understanding, including understanding culture change. We open with a discussion of some of the universals of psychological development, emphasizing the need for psychological research to incorporate research on humans the world over. In a new section on the anthropology of childhood, we discuss the importance of the long period in which the young are dependent on parents for learning as well as nonparental figures, and how important it is to look at children, too often ignored, as agents. We identify some larger processes that may influence personality, such as the native theories ("ethnotheories"), adaptation, as well as possible genetic or physiological influences. We then turn to understanding more specific variation in childrearing, including a new section on parent-child play. After discussing some differences in perception, cognition, and behaviors in adults, we turn to how understanding psychological processes may help us understand cultural variation. The chapter closes with a new section on the individual as an agent of culture change. The applied anthropology box refers to a comparison of preschools in Japan, China, and the United States, discussing how schools may consciously and unconsciously teach values. The second box discusses the idea that women may have a different sense of themselves than men have, and therefore a different sense of morality.

Chapter 10: Sex, Gender, and Culture

In the first part of Chapter 10, we open with a section on culturally varying gender concepts, including cultures that have more than two genders. We also add a discussion of transgender. We discuss how and why sex and gender differences vary cross-culturally. In addition to discussing the gender division of labor in primary and secondary subsistence, we have added additional material on women hunters and discuss what impact it has on theories about the gender division of labor. In the second part of the chapter, we discuss variation in sexual attitudes and practices. Following revised sections on marital sex and extramarital sex, there is an expanded discussion of homosexuality, including female-female relationships. In the first box, we examine cross-cultural research about why some societies allow women to participate in combat. A second box discusses research on why women's political participation may be increasing in some Coast Salish communities of western Washington State and British Columbia, now that they have elected councils. The last is a new applied anthropology box that examines the impact of economic development on women's status.

Chapter 11: Marriage and the Family

We have revised our section on the universality of marriage with a new discussion of the Na exception in China. After discussing various theories about why marriage might be universal, we move on to discuss variation in how one marries, restrictions on marriage, whom one should marry, and how many one should marry. We close with a discussion of variation in family form. We introduce recent research on the Hadza that supports one of the theories about marriage. We then discuss the phenomenon of couples choosing to live together, and we have updated our discussion of polygyny and polyandry, referring to new research. We have also added a new section on adoption. To better prepare students for understanding kinship charts in the chapter that follows, we have introduced a new diagram explaining different types of family structures. The first box discusses arranged marriage and how it has changed among South Asian immigrants in England and the United States. To introduce topics regarding the husband-wife relationship that are only beginning to be investigated, the second box discusses variation in love, intimacy, and sexual jealousy. The third updated box discusses why one-parent families are on the increase in countries like ours. The fourth box, a new applied box, discusses extended families and social security.

Chapter 12: Marital Residence and Kinship

This chapter has been rearranged so that explanations of all types of residence can be found together. We hope the discussion of kinship now flows more smoothly. In addition to explaining the variation that exists in marital residence, kinship structure, and kinship terminology, this chapter emphasizes how understanding residence is important for understanding social life. We have revised our artwork on kinship terminology in a way we hope will make that subject easier to understand. The first box discusses the possible relationship between neolocality and adolescent rebellion. The second box discusses the role that Chinese lineages play in supporting migration and making a living in the diaspora. The third box is on how variation in residence and kinship affects the lives of women. The new applied box discusses how cross-cultural research on the floor area of residences in matrilocal versus patrilocal societies can be used to help archaeologists make inferences about the past.

Chapter 13: Associations and Interest Groups

We discuss the importance of associations in many parts of the world, distinguishing them on whether they are nonvoluntary (common in more egalitarian societies) or voluntary, increasingly important in the modern world. Associations also vary in the degree to which they are based on universally ascribed characteristics (like age and sex), variably ascribed characteristics (like ethnicity), or achieved characteristics. The first box, which is a new applied box, looks at the importance of NGOs in bringing about change at the local and international levels. The second updated box addresses the question of whether separate women's associations increase women's status and power. The third box discusses why street gangs develop and why they often become violent. The last box discusses the role of ethnic associations in Chinatowns in North America.

Chapter 14: Political Life: Social Order and Disorder

We look at how societies have varied in their levels of political organization, the various ways people become leaders, the degree to which they participate in the political process, and the peaceful and violent methods of resolving conflict. We have added new material on different types of states, ranging from the more autocratic to the less autocratic that rely more on collective action and where leaders avoid personal aggrandizement. We have also expanded our discussion of peaceful societies. We discuss how colonialization has transformed legal systems and ways of making decisions, and we have expanded our discussion of states as empires. The first box discusses the role of migrants in the growth of cities. The second box, an applied box, deals with the cross-national and cross-cultural relationship between economic development and democracy. The third box deals with how new local courts among the Abelam of New Guinea are allowing women to address sexual grievances.

Chapter 15: Religion and Magic

Consistent with increasing the visibility of culture change, we have added a major section in this chapter on religious change, with an expanded discussion of the possible causes of religious conversion. We also discuss revitalization and fundamentalist movements. After discussing why religion may be culturally universal, we discuss variation in religious belief and practice with extensive examples. We discuss how humans tend to anthropomorphize in the face of unpredictable events. We have expanded our sections on life after death, divination, and our discussion of why women may predominate in possession trances before moving onto religious change. The new applied box raises the question of whether and to what degree religion promotes moral behavior, cooperation, and harmony. The second discusses the role of colonialism in religious change. The last box discusses the emergence of new religions and points out that nearly all the major churches or religions in the world began as minority sects or cults.

Chapter 16: The Arts

After discussing how art might be defined and the appearance of the earliest art, we discuss variation in the visual arts, music, and folklore, and review how some of those variations might be explained. In regard to how the arts change over time, we discuss the myth that the art of "simpler" peoples is timeless, and how arts have changed as a result of European contact. We address the role of ethnocentrism in studies of art with a section on how Western museums and art critics look at the visual art of less complex cultures. In the section on body adornment, we discuss how permanent or nonpermanent body markings may relate to variation in political systems. The first box, on applied anthropology, explores ancient and more recent rock art and the methods that can be used to help preserve it. The second box, dealing with universal symbolism in art, reviews recent research on the emotions displayed in masks. The last box discusses the global spread of popular music.

Part III: Using Anthropology

Anthropology is not a discipline that focuses on pure research; rather, most anthropologists believe their work is truly valuable only if it can be used to improve the lives of others. In this section, we examine how anthropological knowledge is used in a variety of settings and toward a variety of ends.

Chapter 17: Applied, Practicing, Anthropology, and Medical Anthropology

This extensively revised chapter now integrates medical anthropology. The field of applied or practicing anthropology is very diverse. In this chapter, we first focus on general issues: ethics, evaluating the effects of planned change, and the difficulties in implementing change. In the course of this discussion, we cover a variety of projects, mostly development projects. We then turn to several other kinds of application: *cultural resource management*, the "social impact" studies required in connection with many government or private programs, and *forensic anthropology*—the use of physical anthropology to help identify human remains and assist in solving crimes. The forensic section is considerably revised to deal with identification difficulties associated with age, sex, and "race." The previous box on reforestation in Haiti is now incorporated into the text. The chapter concludes with an extensive discussion of the application of anthropological knowledge to the study of health and illness. The three applied boxes discuss how anthropologists have been able to help in business, evaluating why an applied medical project didn't work, and the last explores eating disorders, biology, and the cultural construction of beauty.

Chapter 18: Global Problems

In this chapter, we discuss the relationship between basic and applied research, and how research may suggest possible solutions to various global social problems, including natural disasters and famines, homelessness, crime, family violence, war, and terrorism. The section on family violence has been updated with new research on corporal punishment and the effects of television on children. This chapter has four boxes. One updated box is on global warming and our dependence on oil. The second is a new applied box about the problem of corporal punishment of children and what might be done to discourage it. The third is on ethnic conflicts and whether or not they are inevitable. The last box describes how the problem of refugees has become a global problem.

FEATURES NEW TO THIS EDITION

Applied Anthropology Boxes in Each Chapter

Anthropology is not a discipline focused on pure research. Most anthropologists want their work to be actively used to help others. In our increasingly interconnected world, it would seem that anthropological knowledge would become increasingly valuable for understanding others. For these reasons, we decided to emphasize applied anthropology in this revision of our text. Adding an applied anthropology box to each chapter, we hope, will provide students a better understanding of the vast range of issues to which anthropological knowledge can be usefully applied.

Features Retained in This Edition

Current Research and Issues Boxes. These boxes deal with current research, topics students may have heard about in the news, and research controversies in anthropology. Examples include variation in love, intimacy, and sexual jealousy in the husband-wife relationship, whether inequality between countries is increasing, whether ethnic conflicts are ancient hatreds, and human rights versus cultural relativity.

New Perspectives on Gender Boxes. These boxes involve issues pertaining to sex and gender, both in anthropology and everyday life. Examples are sexism in language, separate women's associations and women's status and power, and morality in women versus men.

Migrants and Immigrants Boxes. These boxes deal with humans on the move, and how migration and immigration have impacted recent and contemporary social life. Examples include why some immigrant groups retained their "mother tongues" longer than others, the spread of foods in recent times, arranging marriages in the diaspora, and the problem of refugees.

Dorling Kindersley Maps. To emphasize important themes, we have adapted maps originally produced by Dorling Kindersley—a leading publisher of educational maps.

Map Table of Contents:

Map 1. The First Hominids
Map 2. The Emergence of Modern Humans
Map 3. The Spread of Modern Humans
Map 4. The Spread of Agriculture
Map 5. The First Civilizations
Map 6. Trade, Crops, and the Spread of Disease, 500–1500 A.D.
Map 7. Trading in Human Lives
Map 8. The Industrial Revolution and the Spread of Technology
Map 9. Western Imperialism
Map 10. Migration in the 19th Century
Map 11. Biological Exchanges
Map 12. European Expansion in the 16th Century

Student-Friendly Pedagogy

Readability. We derive a lot of pleasure from trying to describe research findings, especially complicated ones, in ways that introductory students can understand. Thus, we try to minimize technical jargon, using only those terms students must know to appreciate the achievements of anthropology and to take advanced courses. We think readability is important, not only because it may enhance the reader's understanding of what we write, but also because it should

make learning about anthropology more enjoyable! When new terms are introduced, which of course must happen sometimes, they are set off in boldface type and defined in the text (and in the Glossary at the end of the book).

Glossary. At the end of each chapter, we list the new terms that have been introduced; these terms were identified by boldface type and are defined in the text. We deliberately do not repeat the definitions at the end of the chapter to allow students to ask themselves if they know the terms. However, we do provide page numbers to find the definitions, and we also provide all the definitions again in the Glossary at the end of the book.

Summaries. In addition to the outline provided at the beginning of each chapter, a detailed summary at the end of each chapter will help students review the major concepts and findings discussed.

Critical Questions. We provide three or four questions at the end of each chapter that will stimulate thinking about the implications of the chapter. The questions do not ask for repetition of what is in the text. We want students to imagine, to go beyond what we know or think we know.

End of Book Notes. Because we believe in the importance of documentation, we think it essential to tell our readers, both professionals and students, what our conclusions are based on. Usually the basis is published research. The abbreviated notes in this edition provide information to find the complete citation in the bibliography at the end of the book.

SUPPLEMENTS

This textbook is part of a complete teaching and learning package that has been carefully created to enhance the topics discussed in the text.

PEARSON
myanthrolab *MyAnthroLab* is an interactive and instructive multimedia site designed to help students and instructors save time and improve results. It offers access to a wealth of resources geared to meet the individual teaching and learning needs of every instructor and student. Combining an ebook, video, audio, multimedia simulations, research support, and assessment, MyAnthroLab engages students and gives them the tools they need to enhance their performance in the course. Please see your Pearson sales representative for more information about **MyAnthroLab** or visit the website at www.myanthrolab.com.

Instructor's Resource Manual with Tests (0-205-71124-3). For each chapter in the text, this valuable resource provides a detailed outline, list of objectives, discussion questions, and classroom activities. In addition, test questions in multiple-choice and short-answer formats are available for each chapter; the answers to all questions are page-referenced to the text. For easy access, this manual is available within the instructor section of MyAnthroLab for *Cultural Anthropology,* Thirteenth Edition, or at www.pearsonhighered.com/irc.

MyTest (0-205-71148-0). This computerized software allows instructors to create their own personalized exams, to edit any or all of the existing test questions and to add new questions. Other special features of this program include random generation of test questions, creation of alternate versions of the same test, scrambling question sequence, and test preview before printing. For easy access, this software is available within the instructor section of MyAnthroLab for *Cultural Anthropology,* Thirteenth Edition, or at www.pearsonhighered.com/irc.

PowerPoint™ Presentation Slides (0-205-71125-1). These PowerPoint slides combine text and graphics for each chapter to help instructors convey anthropological principles in a clear and engaging way. In addition, Classroom Response System (CRS) In-Class Questions allow instant, class-wide responses to chapter-specific questions during a lecture to gauge student comprehension. For easy access, they are available within the instructor section of MyAnthroLab for *Cultural Anthropology,* Thirteenth Edition, or at www.pearsonhighered.com/irc.

Strategies in Teaching Anthropology, Sixth Edition (0-205-71123-5).   Unique in focus and content, this book focuses on the "how" of teaching anthropology across all four fields and provides a wide array of associated learning outcomes and student activities. It is a valuable single-source compendium of strategies and teaching "tricks of the trade" from a group of seasoned teaching anthropologists, working in a variety of teaching settings, who share their pedagogical techniques, knowledge, and observations.

EthnoQuest® (0-13-185013-X). This interactive multimedia simulation includes a series of 10 ethnographic encounters with the culture of a fictional Mexican village set in a computer-based learning environment. It provides students with a realistic problem-solving experience and is designed to help students experience the fieldwork of a cultural anthropologist. Please see your Pearson sales representative for more information about **EthnoQuest®**.

The Dorling Kindersley/Prentice Hall Atlas of Anthropology. Beautifully illustrated by Dorling Kindersley, with narrative by leading archaeological author Brian M. Fagan, this striking atlas features 30 full-color maps, timelines, and illustrations to offer a highly visual but explanatory geographical overview of topics from all four fields of anthropology. Please contact your Prentice Hall representative for ordering information.

ACKNOWLEDGMENTS

We thank the people at Prentice Hall for all their help, and particularly Nancy Roberts, Publisher for Anthropology; Marianne Peters-Riordan and Jill Traut for seeing the manuscript through the production process, and Beth Brenzel for photo research.

We want to thank the following for reviewing our chapters and making suggestions about them:

Gary Burbridge, *Grand Rapids Community College*
Garrett Cook, *Baylor University*
Jennifer Fillion, *Mott Community College*
Kendi Howells Douglas, *Great Lakes Christian College*
Sheperd Jenks, *Albuquerque TVI Community College*
Robert Jorgensen, *Utah Valley University*
Pat Judd, *Three Rivers Community College*
Daniel R. Maher, *University of Arkansas-Fort Smith*
Linda Matthei, *Texas A&M University-Commerce*
Barbara Mueller, *Casper College*

Thank you all, named and unnamed, who gave us advice.

Carol R. Ember and Melvin Ember

about the authors

Carol R. Ember started at Antioch College as a chemistry major. She began taking social science courses because some were required, but she soon found herself intrigued. There were lots of questions without answers, and she became excited about the possibility of a research career in social science. She spent a year in graduate school at Cornell studying sociology before continuing on to Harvard, where she studied anthropology primarily with John and Beatrice Whiting.

For her PhD dissertation, she worked among the Luo of Kenya. While there, she noticed that many boys were assigned "girls' work," such as babysitting and household chores, because their mothers (who did most of the agriculture) did not have enough girls to help out. She decided to study the possible effects of task assignment on the social behavior of boys. Using systematic behavior observations, she compared girls, boys who did a great deal of girls' work, and boys who did little such work. She found that boys assigned girls' work were intermediate in many social behaviors, compared with the other boys and girls. Later, she did cross-cultural research on variation in marriage, family, descent groups, and war and peace, mainly in collaboration with Melvin Ember, whom she married in 1970. All of these cross-cultural studies tested theories on data for worldwide samples of societies.

From 1970 to 1996, she taught at Hunter College of the City University of New York. She has served as president of the Society of Cross-Cultural Research and was one of the directors of the Summer Institutes in Comparative Anthropological Research, which were funded by the National Science Foundation. She is president-elect of the Society for Anthropological Sciences. Since 1996, she has served as executive director of the Human Relations Area Files, Inc., a nonprofit research agency at Yale University. She is currently acting president of that organization.

After graduating from Columbia College, Melvin Ember went to Yale University for his PhD. His mentor at Yale was George Peter Murdock, an anthropologist who was instrumental in promoting cross-cultural research and building a full-text database on the cultures of the world to facilitate cross-cultural hypothesis testing. This database came to be known as the Human Relations Area Files (HRAF) because it was originally sponsored by the Institute of Human Relations at Yale. Growing in annual installments and now distributed in electronic format, the HRAF database currently covers more than 385 cultures, past and present, all over the world.

Melvin Ember did fieldwork for his dissertation in American Samoa, where he conducted a comparison of three villages to study the effects of commercialization on political life. In addition, he did research on descent groups and how they changed with the increase of buying and selling. His cross-cultural studies focused originally on variation in marital residence and descent groups. He has also done cross-cultural research on the relationship between economic and political development, the origin and extension of the incest taboo, the causes of polygyny, and how archaeological correlates of social customs can help us draw inferences about the past.

After four years of research at the National Institute of Mental Health, he taught at Antioch College and then Hunter College of the City University of New York. He has served as president of the Society for Cross-Cultural Research. From 1987 until his death in September 2009, he was president of the Human Relations Area Files, Inc., a nonprofit research agency at Yale University.

Carol R. Ember and
Melvin Ember

cultural anthropology

What Is Anthropology?

nthropology, by definition, is a discipline of infinite curiosity about human beings. The term comes from the Greek *anthropos* for "man, human" and *logos* for "study." Anthropologists seek answers to an enormous variety of questions about humans. They are interested in both universals and differences in human populations. They want to discover when, where, and why humans appeared on the earth, how and why they have changed since then, and how and why modern human populations vary in their biological and cultural features. Anthropology has a practical side too. Applied and practicing anthropologists put anthropological methods, information, and results to use, in efforts to solve practical problems.

Defining anthropology as the study of human beings is not complete, however, for such a definition would appear to incorporate a whole catalog of disciplines: sociology, psychology, political science, economics, history, human biology, and perhaps even the humanistic disciplines of philosophy and literature. Needless to say, practitioners of the many other disciplines concerned with humans would not be happy to be regarded as being in subbranches of anthropology. After all, most of those disciplines have existed longer than anthropology, and each is somewhat distinctive. There must, then, be something unique about anthropology—a reason for its having developed as a separate discipline and for its having retained a separate identity over the last 100 years.

● ○ ●

THE SCOPE OF ANTHROPOLOGY

Anthropologists are generally thought of as individuals who travel to little-known corners of the world to study exotic peoples or who dig deep into the earth to uncover the fossil remains or the tools and pots of people who lived long ago. These views, though clearly stereotyped, do indicate how anthropology differs from other disciplines concerned with humans. Anthropology is broader in scope, both geographically and historically. Anthropology is concerned explicitly and directly with all varieties of people throughout the world, not just those close at hand or within a limited area. Anthropologists are also interested in people of all periods. Beginning with the immediate ancestors of humans, who lived a few million years ago, anthropology traces the development of humans until the present. Every part of the world that has ever contained a human population is of interest to anthropologists.

Anthropologists have not always been as global and comprehensive in their concerns as they are today. Traditionally, they concentrated on non-Western cultures and left the study of Western civilization and similarly complex societies, with their recorded histories, to other disciplines. In recent years, however, this division of labor among the disciplines has begun to disappear. Now anthropologists work in their own and other complex societies.

What induces anthropologists to choose so broad a subject for study? In part, they are motivated by the belief that any suggested generalization about human beings, any possible explanation of some characteristic of human culture or biology, should be shown to apply to many times and places of human existence. If a generalization or explanation does not prove to apply widely, anthropologists are entitled or even obliged to be skeptical about it.

The skeptical attitude, in the absence of persuasive evidence, is our best protection against accepting invalid ideas about humans.

For example, when American educators discovered in the 1960s that African American schoolchildren rarely drank milk, they assumed that lack of money or education was the cause. But evidence from anthropology suggested a different explanation. Anthropologists had known for years that people do not drink fresh milk in many parts of the world where milking animals are kept; rather, they sour it before they drink it, or they make it into cheese. Why they do so is now clear. Many people lack the enzyme lactase that is necessary for breaking down lactose, the sugar in milk. When such people drink regular milk, it actually interferes with digestion. Not only is the lactose in milk not digested, but other nutrients are less likely to be digested as well; in many cases, drinking milk will cause cramps, stomach gas, diarrhea, and nausea. Studies indicate that milk intolerance is found in many parts of the world.[1] The condition is common in adulthood among Asians, southern Europeans, Arabs and Jews, West Africans, Inuit (Eskimos), and North and South American native peoples, as well as African Americans. Because anthropologists are acquainted with human life in an enormous variety of geographic and historical settings, they are often able to correct mistaken beliefs about different groups of people.

THE HOLISTIC APPROACH

In addition to the worldwide as well as historical scope of anthropology, another distinguishing feature of the discipline is its **holistic,** or multifaceted, approach to the study of human beings. Anthropologists study not only all varieties of people but many aspects of human experience as well. For example, when describing a group of people, an anthropologist might discuss the history of the area in which the people live, the physical environment, the organization of family life, the general features of their language, the group's settlement patterns, political and economic systems, religion, and styles of art and dress. The goal is not just to understand these aspects separately, but to understand the connections between different aspects of physical and social life. Throughout this book, we will see that patterns of traits regularly co-occur. We not only want to identify those patterns or regularities; we want to explain them.

In the past, individual anthropologists tried to cover as many subjects as possible. Today, as in many other disciplines, so much information has been accumulated that anthropologists tend to specialize in one topic or area. Thus, one anthropologist may investigate the physical characteristics of some of our prehistoric ancestors. Another may study the biological effect of the environment on a human population over time. Still another will concentrate on many customs of a particular group of people. Despite this specialization, however, the discipline of anthropology retains its holistic orientation in that its many different specialties, taken together, describe many aspects of human existence, both past and present.

THE ANTHROPOLOGICAL CURIOSITY

Thus far, we have described anthropology as being broader in scope, both historically and geographically, and more holistic in approach than other disciplines concerned with human beings. But this statement again implies that anthropology is the all-inclusive human science. How, then, is anthropology really different from the other disciplines? We suggest that anthropology's distinctiveness lies principally in the kind of curiosity it arouses.

In studying a human population, anthropologists tend to focus on *typical* characteristics (traits, customs) of that population: People in many societies depend on agriculture. Why? And where and when did people first start to farm? Why do some populations have lighter skin than others? Why do some languages contain more terms for color than others? Why do some societies have more political participation than others? Individuals may provide information to anthropologists, but the anthropological curiosity mostly focuses on the typical characteristics of human groups and how to understand and explain them. For example, whereas economists take a monetary system for granted and study how it operates, anthropologists would ask how frequently monetary systems are found, why they vary, and why only some societies during the last few thousand years used money. This is not to imply that anthropologists are not interested in variation within human groups. In understanding a political system, anthropologists might want to know why certain people tend to be leaders, or why rural communities operate differently than urban ones. Or, variation in a physical trait might be related to susceptibility to a particular disease. Rather, a focus on typical characteristics of human groups—how and why populations and their characteristics have varied around the globe and throughout the ages—is what mainly distinguishes anthropology from other disciplines.

FIELDS OF ANTHROPOLOGY

Different anthropologists concentrate on different characteristics of societies. Some are concerned primarily with *biological* or *physical characteristics* of human populations; others are interested principally in what we call *cultural characteristics.* Hence, there are two broad classifications of subject matter in anthropology: **biological (physical) anthropology** and **cultural anthropology.** Biological anthropology is one major field of anthropology. Cultural anthropology is divided into three major subfields—archaeology, linguistics, and ethnology. Ethnology, the study of recent cultures, is now usually referred to by the parent name, cultural anthropology (see Figure 1–1). Crosscutting these four fields is a fifth, **applied** or **practicing anthropology.**

Biological Anthropology

Biological (physical) anthropology seeks to answer two distinct sets of questions. The first set includes questions

FIGURE 1–1 The Subdivisions of Anthropology
The four major subdisciplines of anthropology (in bold letters) may be classified according to subject matter (biological or cultural) and according to the period with which each is concerned (distant past versus recent past and present). There are applications of anthropology in all four subdisciplines.

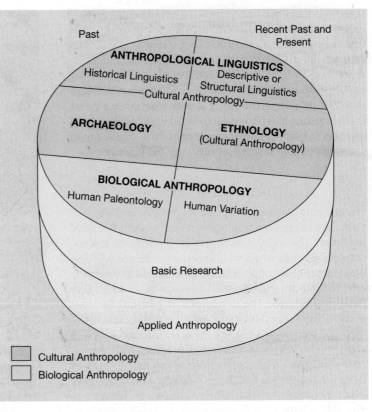

about the emergence of humans and their later evolution (this focus is called **human paleontology** or **paleoanthropology**). The second set includes questions about how and why contemporary human populations vary biologically (this focus is called **human variation**).

To reconstruct human evolution, human paleontologists search for and study the buried, hardened remains or impressions—known as **fossils**—of humans, prehumans, and related animals. Paleontologists working in East Africa, for instance, have excavated the fossil remains of humanlike beings that lived more than 4 million years ago. These findings have suggested the approximate dates when our ancestors began to develop two-legged walking, very flexible hands, and a larger brain.

In attempting to clarify evolutionary relationships, human paleontologists may use not only the fossil record but also geological information on the succession of climates, environments, and plant and animal populations. Moreover, when reconstructing the past of humans, paleontologists are also interested in the behavior and evolution of our closest relatives among the mammals—the prosimians, monkeys, and apes, which, like ourselves, are members of the order of **Primates.** Anthropologists, psychologists, and biologists who specialize in the study of primates are called **primatologists.** The various species of primates are observed in the wild and in the laboratory. One especially popular subject of study is the chimpanzee, which bears a close resemblance to humans in behavior and physical appearance, has a similar blood chemistry, and is susceptible to many of the same diseases. It now appears that chimpanzees share 99 percent of their genes with humans.[2]

Birute Galdikas works with two orangutans in Borneo.

From primate studies, biological anthropologists try to discover characteristics that are distinctly human, as opposed to those that might be part of the primate heritage. With this information, they may be able to infer what our prehistoric ancestors were like. The inferences from primate studies are checked against the fossil record. The evidence from the earth, collected in bits and pieces, is correlated with scientific observations of our closest living relatives. In short, biological anthropologists piece together bits of information obtained from different sources. They construct theories that explain the changes observed in the fossil record and then attempt to evaluate their theories by checking one kind of evidence against another. Human paleontology thus overlaps disciplines such as geology, general vertebrate (and particularly primate) paleontology, comparative anatomy, and the study of comparative primate behavior.

The second major focus of biological anthropology, the study of human variation, investigates how and why contemporary human populations differ in biological or physical characteristics. All living people belong to one species, **Homo sapiens,** for all can successfully interbreed. Yet, much varies among human populations. Investigators of human variation ask such questions as: Why are some peoples taller than others? How have human populations adapted physically to their environmental conditions? Are some peoples, such as Inuit (Eskimos), better equipped than other peoples to endure cold? Does darker skin pigmentation offer special protection against the tropical sun?

To understand better the biological variations observable among contemporary human populations, biological anthropologists use the principles, concepts, and techniques of at least three other disciplines: human genetics (the study of human traits that are inherited), population biology (the study of environmental effects on, and interaction with, population characteristics), and epidemiology (the study of how and why diseases affect different populations in different ways). Research on human variation, therefore, overlaps research in other fields. Biological anthropologists, however, are concerned most with human populations and how they vary biologically.

Cultural Anthropology

Cultural anthropology is concerned with how and why cultures vary or are similar in the past and present. But what is culture? The concept of culture is so central to anthropology, we will devote a whole chapter to the concept and how culture changes. Briefly, the term *culture* refers to the customary ways that a particular population or society thinks and behaves. The culture of a social group includes many things—from the language that people speak, the way children are brought up, the roles assigned to males and females, religious beliefs and practices, and preferences in music. Anthropologists are interested in all of these and other learned behaviors and ideas that have come to be widely shared or customary in the group. The three main branches of cultural anthropology are **archaeology** (the study of past cultures, primarily through their material remains), **anthropological linguistics** (the anthropological study of languages), and **ethnology** (the study of existing and recent cultures), now usually referred to by the parent name, *cultural anthropology*.

Archaeology   Archaeologists seek not only to reconstruct the daily life and customs of peoples who lived in the past but also to trace cultural changes and to offer possible explanations for those changes. This concern is similar to that of historians, but archaeologists reach much farther back in time. Historians deal only with societies that left written records and are therefore limited to the last 5,000 years of human history. Human societies, however, have existed for more than a million years, and only a small proportion in the last 5,000 years had writing. For all those past societies lacking a written record, archaeologists serve as historians. Lacking written records for study, archaeologists must try to reconstruct history from the remains of human cultures. Some of these remains are as grand as the Mayan temples discovered at Chichén Itzá in Yucatán, Mexico. More often, they are as ordinary as bits of broken pottery, stone tools, and garbage heaps.

Most archaeologists deal with **prehistory,** the time before written records. But a specialty within archaeology, called **historical archaeology,** studies the remains of recent peoples who left written records. This specialty, as its name implies, employs the methods of both archaeologists and historians to study recent societies for which there is both archaeological and historical information.

In trying to understand how and why ways of life have changed through time in different parts of the world, archaeologists collect materials from sites of human

In urban areas before new construction begins, archaeologists may be called upon to excavate and record information on historical sites, as here in New York City.

occupation. Usually, these sites must be unearthed. On the basis of materials they have excavated and otherwise collected, they then ask various questions: Where, when, and why did the distinctive human characteristic of toolmaking first emerge? Where, when, and why did agriculture first develop? Where, when, and why did people first begin to live in cities?

To collect the data they need to suggest answers to these and other questions, archaeologists use techniques and findings borrowed from other disciplines, as well as what they can infer from anthropological studies of recent and contemporary cultures. For example, to guess where to dig for evidence of early toolmaking, archaeologists rely on geology to tell them where sites of early human occupation are likely to be found, because of erosion and uplifting, near the surface of the earth. To infer when agriculture first developed, archaeologists date the relevant excavated materials by a process originally developed by chemical scientists. To try to understand why cities first emerged, archaeologists may use information from historians, geographers, and others about how recent and contemporary cities are related economically and politically to their hinterlands. If we can discover what recent and contemporary cities have in common, we can speculate on why cities developed originally. Thus, archaeologists use information from the present and recent past in trying to understand the distant past.

Anthropological Linguistics   Anthropological linguistics is another branch of cultural anthropology. Linguistics, or the study of languages, is a somewhat older discipline than anthropology, but the early linguists concentrated on the study of languages that had been written for a long time—languages such as English that had been written for nearly a thousand years. Anthropological linguists began to do fieldwork in places where the language was not yet written. This meant that anthropologists could not consult a dictionary or grammar to help them learn the language. Instead, they first had to construct a dictionary and grammar. Then they could study the structure and history of the language.

new perspectives on gender

Researcher at Work: Elizabeth M. Brumfiel

Now a professor of anthropology at Northwestern University, Elizabeth M. Brumfiel became interested in the origins of social inequality when she was an undergraduate. Archaeologists had known for some time that substantial wealth differences between families developed only recently (archaeologically speaking), that is, only after about 6,000 years ago. The archaeological indicators of inequality are fairly clear—elaborate burials with valuable goods for some families and large differences in houses and possessions. However, why the transformation occurred was not so clear. When she was in graduate school at the University of Michigan, Brumfiel says, she didn't accept the then-current explanation that inequality provided benefits to the society (e.g., the standard of living of most people improved as the leaders got richer). Consequently, for her PhD research in central Mexico, she began to test the "benefit" explanation in an area that had been independent politically at first and then became part of the Aztec Empire. She studied the surface material remains in the area and historical documents written by Europeans and Aztec nobility. Her findings contradicted the benefit explanation of social inequality; she found little improvement in the standard of living of the local people after the Aztec Empire had absorbed them.

Another important part of her research agenda was understanding the lives of women. How were they affected by the expansion of the Aztec Empire? Did their work change? How were women portrayed in art? In the Aztec capital of

Dona Maria (right) interpreting during the meeting of Cortez and Montezuma II in 1519. Women like Dona Maria apparently held high status in Aztec culture.

Tenochtitlán, images of militarism and masculinity became increasingly important with the growth of the empire, and sculptures showed women in positions of work (e.g., kneeling). However, the images of women in the area of Brumfiel's fieldwork did not change. For example, most of the sculptures after the Aztecs had taken over still showed women standing, not kneeling.

Like many anthropologists, Brumfiel asked herself how she could contribute to the community in which she did her fieldwork. She decided to design an exhibit to display the successes of the people who had lived in the area for 1,200 years. The exhibit tells the people of Xaltocan what she found out from her studies.

As she continues to explore issues about the origins of inequality and the position of women, Brumfiel is quite comfortable with knowing that someone will think that she has "gotten it wrong, and will set out on a lifetime of archaeological research to find her own answers."

Source: Brumfiel 2009.

Like biological anthropologists, linguists study changes that have taken place over time, as well as contemporary variation. Some anthropological linguists are concerned with the emergence of language and also with the divergence of languages over thousands of years. The study of how languages change over time and how they may be related is known as **historical linguistics.** Anthropological linguists are also interested in how contemporary languages differ, especially in their construction. This focus of linguistics is generally called **descriptive** or **structural linguistics.** The study of how language is used in social contexts is called **sociolinguistics.**

In contrast with human paleontologists and archaeologists, who have physical remains to help them reconstruct change over time, historical linguists deal only with languages—and usually unwritten ones at that. (Remember

current research and issues

Researcher at Work: Terence E. Hays

Books and articles often report research in a straightforward manner: here's the problem, here's the answer—that kind of thing. However, many researchers know from experience that knowledge does not always come in a straightforward manner. A professor at Rhode Island College, Terence E. Hays has reflected on the twists and turns in his fieldwork among the Ndumba in the Eastern Highlands province of Papua New Guinea. He first started studying whether different types of people (e.g., women and men) had different types of plant knowledge and whether they classified plants differently. (The interest in plant and animal classification, *ethnobiology*, is closely connected with linguistic research.) In the course of his first fieldwork, in 1972, he witnessed an initiation ceremony for 10- to 12-year-old males—a dramatic and traumatic rite of passage ceremony that included the physical trauma of nosebleeding as well as the social traumas of "attacks" by women and seclusion in the forest. The ceremony was full of symbolism of why the sexes needed to avoid each other. Although he collected stories and myths about plants for his research on ethnobiology, he kept uncovering themes in the stories about the danger of men associating with women.

Hays's curiosity was aroused about these ceremonies and myths. How

Terence Hays during fieldwork in New Guinea.

important are myths in perpetuating cultural themes? Do other societies that have separate men's houses have similar myths? He realized when he returned home from the field that many societies have similar stories. Are these stories generally linked to initiation rites and to physical segregation of the sexes? Answering these questions required comparison, so he embarked on collecting myths and folktales from colleagues who worked in other New Guinea Highland societies. In the course of collecting these comparative materials, he realized he didn't have all

the ethnographic information he needed, so he went back to the field to get it. As Hays remarked, "As an ethnographer I was continually faced with the question, How do you know it's true? But even when I could reach a (hard-won) conviction that something was true for the Ndumba, the second question awaited: How do you know it's generally true, which you can't know without comparison?"

Source: Hays 2009.

---

that writing is only about 5,000 years old, and most languages since then have not been written.) Because unwritten languages must be heard to be studied, they do not leave any trace once speakers have died. Linguists interested in reconstructing the history of unwritten languages must begin in the present, with comparisons of contemporary languages. On the basis of these comparisons, they draw inferences about the kinds of change in language that may have occurred in the past and that may account for similarities and differences observed in the present. Historical linguists typically ask such questions as these: Did two or more contemporary languages diverge from a common ancestral language? If they are related, how far back in time did they begin to differ?

Unlike historical linguists, the descriptive (or structural) linguists are typically concerned with discovering and recording the principles that determine how sounds and words are put together in speech. For example, a structural description of a particular language might tell us that the sounds *t* and *k* are interchangeable in a word without causing a difference in meaning. In American Samoa, one could say *Tutuila* or *Kukuila* as the name of the largest island, and everyone, except perhaps newly arrived anthropologists who know little about the Samoan language yet, would understand that the same island was being mentioned.

Sociolinguists are interested in the social aspects of language, including what people speak about and how they interact conversationally, their attitudes toward speakers of other dialects or languages, and how people speak differently in different social contexts. In English, for example, we do not address everyone we meet in the same way. "Hi, Sandy" may be the customary way a person greets a friend. But we would probably feel uncomfortable addressing a doctor by a first name; instead, we would probably say, "Good morning, Dr. Brown." Such variations in language use, which are determined by the social status of the people being addressed, are significant for sociolinguists.

Ethnology (Cultural Anthropology)   Ethnologists, or cultural anthropologists, try to understand how and why peoples today and in the recent past differ or are similar in their customary ways of thinking and acting. Also, how and why do cultures develop and change? How does one aspect of culture affect others? Cultural anthropologists ask questions such as: Why is the custom of marriage nearly universal in all cultures? What explains why families live with or near their kin in some societies, but not in other societies? What changes result from the introduction of money to a previously noncommercial economy? When family members move far away to work, what are the impacts on social relationships? What happens when a society is severely stressed because of natural disasters or violent conflicts? The aim of ethnologists is largely the same as that of archaeologists. However, ethnologists generally use data collected through observation and interviews of living peoples. Archaeologists, on the other hand, must work with fragmentary remains of past cultures, on the basis of which they can only make inferences about the customs of prehistoric peoples.

One type of ethnologist, **ethnographers,** usually spend a year or so living with, talking to, and observing the people whose customs they are studying. This fieldwork provides the data for a detailed description (an **ethnography**) of customary behavior and thought. Ethnographers vary in the degree to which they strive for completeness in their coverage of cultural and social life. Earlier ethnographers tended to strive for holistic coverage; more recent ethnographers have tended to specialize or focus on narrower realms such as ritual healing or curing, interaction with the environment, effects of modernization or globalization, or gender issues. Ethnographies often go beyond description; they may address current anthropological issues or try to explain some aspect of culture.

Many cultures have undergone extensive change in the recent past so trying to understand what life was like in earlier times is important. Ethnographers can ask older people what life was like when they were young, and information about the past may be contained in historical documents usually not written by anthropologists. An **ethnohistorian** studies how the ways of life of a particular group of people have changed over time. Ethnohistorians investigate written documents such as missionary accounts, reports by traders and explorers, and government records, to try to establish the cultural changes that have occurred. Unlike ethnographers, who rely mostly on their own observations and interviewing, ethnohistorians rely on the reports of others. Often, they must attempt to piece together and make sense of widely scattered, and even apparently contradictory, information. Thus, the ethnohistorian's research is very much like that of a historian, except that ethnohistorians are usually concerned with the history of a people who did not themselves leave written records. Ethnohistorians try to reconstruct the recent history of a people and may also suggest why certain changes in their way of life took place.

Ethnographic and ethnohistorical research is very time-consuming, and it is a rare for one person to study more than a few cultures. The **cross-cultural researcher** (who may be a cultural anthropologist or some other kind of social scientist,) is interested in discovering general patterns about cultural traits—what is universal, what is variable, why traits vary, and what the consequences of the variability might be. Why, for example, is there more gender inequality in some societies than in others? Is family violence related to aggression in other areas of life? What are the effects of living in a very unpredictable environment? In testing possible answers to such questions, cross-cultural researchers use data from samples of cultures (usually described initially by ethnographers) to try to arrive at explanations or relationships that hold across cultures. Archaeologists may find the results of cross-cultural research useful for making inferences about the past, particularly if they can discover material indicators of cultural variation.

Because ethnologists may be interested in many aspects of customary behavior and thought—from economic behavior to political behavior to styles of art, music, and religion—ethnology overlaps with disciplines that concentrate on some particular aspect of human existence, such as sociology, psychology, economics, political science, art, music, and comparative religion. But the distinctive feature of cultural anthropology is its interest in how all these aspects of human existence vary from society to society, in all historical periods, and in all parts of the world.

Applied Anthropology

All knowledge may turn out to be useful. In the physical and biological sciences, it is well understood that technological breakthroughs like DNA splicing, spacecraft docking in outer space, and the development of miniscule computer chips could not have taken place without an enormous amount of basic research to uncover the laws of nature in the physical and biological worlds. If we did not understand fundamental principles, the technological achievements we are so proud of would not be possible. Researchers are often simply driven by curiosity, with no thought to where the research might lead, which is why such research is sometimes called *basic research*. The same is true of the social sciences. If a researcher finds out that societies with combative sports tend to have more wars, it may lead to other inquiries about the relationships between one kind of aggression and another. The knowledge acquired may ultimately lead to discovering ways to correct social problems, such as family violence and war.

applied anthropology

Getting Development Programs to Notice Women's Contributions to Agriculture

When Anita Spring first did fieldwork in Zambia in the 1970s, she was not particularly interested in agriculture. Rather, medical anthropology was her interest. Her work focused on customary healing practices, particularly involving women and children. She was surprised at the end of the year when a delegation of women came to tell her that she didn't understand what it meant to be a woman. "To be a woman is to be a farmer," they said. She admits that it took her a while to pay attention to women as farmers, but then she began to participate in efforts to provide technical assistance to them. Like many others interested in women in development, Spring realized that all too often development agents downplay women's contributions to agriculture.

How does one bring about change in male-centered attitudes and practices? One way is to document how much women actually contribute to agriculture. Beginning with the influential writing of Ester Boserup in *Woman's Role in Economic Development* (1970), scholars began to report that in Africa south of the Sahara, in the Caribbean, and in parts of Southeast Asia, women were the principal farmers or agricultural laborers. Moreover, as agriculture became more complex, it required more work time in the fields, so the women's contribution to agriculture increased. In addition, men increasingly went away to work, so women had to do much of what used to be men's work on the farms.

In the 1980s, Spring designed and directed the Women in Agricultural Development Project in Malawi, funded by the Office of Women in the U.S. Agency for International Development. Rather than focusing just on women, the project aimed to collect data on both female and male agriculturalists and how development agents treated them. The project did more than collect information; mini-projects were set up and evaluated so that successful training techniques could be passed on to development agents in other regions. Spring points out that the success of the program was due not just to the design of the project. Much of the success depended on the interest and willingness of Malawi itself to change. It didn't hurt that the United Nations and other donor organizations increasingly focused attention on women. It takes the efforts of many to bring about change. Increasingly, applied anthropologists like Anita Spring are involved in these efforts from beginning to end, from the design stage to implementation and evaluation.

Source: Spring 1995; 2000b.

Whereas basic research may ultimately help to solve practical problems, applied research is more explicit in its practical goals. Today, more than half of all professional anthropologists are applied, or practicing, anthropologists.[3] Applied or practicing anthropology is explicit in its concern with making anthropological knowledge useful.[4] Applied anthropologists may be trained in any or all of the subfields of anthropology. In contrast to basic researchers, who are almost always employed in colleges, universities, and museums, applied anthropologists are commonly employed in settings outside traditional academia, including government agencies, international development agencies, private consulting firms, businesses, public health organizations, medical schools, law offices, community development agencies, and charitable foundations.

Biological anthropologists may be called upon to give forensic evidence in court, or they may work in public health, or design clothes and equipment to fit human anatomy. Archaeologists may be involved in preserving and exhibiting artifacts for museums and in doing contract work to find and preserve cultural sites that might be damaged by construction or excavation. Linguists may work in bilingual educational training programs or may work on ways to improve communication. Ethnologists may work in a wide variety of applied projects ranging from community development, urban planning, health care, and agricultural improvement to personnel and organizational management and assessment of the impact of change programs on people's lives.[5] We discuss applied anthropology in boxes in almost all chapters and more fully in the last part of this book "Using Anthropology."

SPECIALIZATION

As disciplines grow, they tend to develop more and more specialties. This trend is probably inevitable because, as knowledge accumulates and methods become more advanced, there is a limit to what any one person can reasonably keep track of. So, in addition to the general divisions we have outlined already, particular anthropologists tend to identify themselves with a variety of specializations. Anthropologists commonly have a geographic specialty, which may be as broad as Old World or New World or as narrow as the southwestern United States. Those who study the past (archaeologists or human paleontologists) may also specialize in different time periods. Ethnologists often specialize in more specific subject

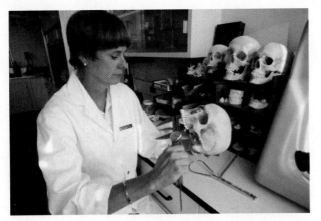

Forensic anthropology is one kind of applied anthropology. Kathy Reichs is a forensic anthropologist working in a medical examiner's office.

matters in addition to one or two cultural areas. Just as most of the chapters in this book refer to broad subject specialties, so do some ethnologists identify themselves as *economic anthropologists, political anthropologists,* or *psychological anthropologists.* Others may identify themselves by theoretical orientations, such as *cultural ecologists,* who are concerned with the relationship between culture and the physical and social environments. These specialties are not mutually exclusive, however. A cultural ecologist, for example, might be interested in the effects of the environment on economic behavior, political behavior, or how people bring up their children.

Does specialization isolate an anthropologist from other kinds of research? Not necessarily. Some specialties have to draw on information from several fields, inside and outside anthropology. For example, *medical anthropologists* study the cultural and biological contexts of human health and illness. Thus, they need to understand the economy, diet, and patterns of social interaction, as well as attitudes and beliefs regarding illness and health. In addition, they may need to draw on research in human genetics, public health, and medicine.

THE RELEVANCE OF ANTHROPOLOGY

Anthropology is a comparatively young discipline. Anthropologists only began to go to live with people in far-away places in the late 1800s. Compared to our knowledge of the physical laws of nature, we know much less about people, about how and why they behave as they do. That anthropology and other sciences dealing with humans began to develop only relatively recently is not in itself a sufficient reason for our knowing less than in the physical sciences. Why, in our quest for knowledge of all kinds, did we wait so long to study ourselves? Leslie White suggests that those phenomena most remote from us and least significant as determinants of human behavior were the first to be studied. The reason, he surmises, is that humans like to think of themselves as citadels of free will, subject to no

laws of nature. Hence, there is no need to see ourselves as objects to be explained.[6]

The idea that it is impossible to account for human behavior scientifically, either because our actions and beliefs are too individualistic and complex or because human beings are understandable only in otherworldly terms, is a self-fulfilling notion. We cannot discover principles explaining human behavior if we neither believe such principles exist nor bother to look for them. The result is assured from the beginning. People who do not believe in principles of human behavior will be reinforced by their finding none. If we are to increase our understanding of human beings, we first have to believe it is possible to do so.

If we aim to understand humans, it is essential that we study humans in all times and places. We must study ancient humans and modern humans. We must study their cultures and their biology. How else can we understand what is true of humans generally or how they are capable of varying? If we study just our own society, we may come up only with explanations that are culture-bound, not general or applicable to most or all humans. Anthropology is useful, then, to the degree that it contributes to our understanding of human beings everywhere.

In addition, anthropology is relevant because it helps us avoid misunderstandings between peoples. If we can understand why other groups are different from ourselves, we might have less reason to condemn them for behavior that appears strange to us. We may then come to realize that many differences between peoples are products of physical and cultural adaptations to different environments. For example, someone who first finds out about the !Kung as they lived in the Kalahari Desert of southern Africa in the 1950s might assume that the !Kung were "backward." (The exclamation point in the name *!Kung* signifies one of the clicking sounds made with the tongue by speakers of the !Kung language.) The !Kung wore little clothing, had few possessions, lived in meager shelters, and enjoyed none of our technological niceties like radio and computers. But let us reflect on how a typical North American community might react if it awoke to find itself in an environment similar to that in which the !Kung lived. The people would find that the arid land makes both agriculture and animal husbandry impossible, and they might have to think about adopting a nomadic existence. They might then discard many of their material possessions so that they could travel easily, to take advantage of changing water and food supplies. Because of the extreme heat and the lack of extra water for laundry, they might find it more practical to be almost naked than to wear clothes. They would undoubtedly find it impossible to build elaborate homes. For social security, they might start to share the food brought into the group. Thus, if they survived at all, they might end up looking and acting far more like the !Kung looked than like typical North Americans.

Physical differences, too, may be seen as results of adaptations to the environment. For example, in our society, we admire people who are tall and slim. If these same

A large number of emigrants from the former Soviet Union, particularly from Black Sea cities and towns such as Odessa, live in the Brighton Beach neighborhood of Brooklyn. Migrant and immigrant communities, such as "Little Odessa," are an increasing focus of anthropological study.

individuals were forced to live above the Arctic Circle, however, they might wish they could trade their tall, slim bodies for short, compact ones, because stocky physiques conserve body heat more effectively and may therefore be more adaptive in cold climates.

Exposure to anthropology might help to alleviate some of the misunderstandings that arise between people of different cultural groups from subtle causes operating below the level of consciousness. For example, different cultures have different conceptions of the gestures and interpersonal distances that are appropriate under various circumstances. Arabs consider it proper to stand close enough to other people to smell them.[7] On the basis of the popularity of deodorants in our culture, we can deduce that Americans prefer to keep the olfactory dimension out of interpersonal relations. We may feel that a person who comes too close is being too intimate. We should remember, however, that this person may only be acting according to a culturally conditioned conception of what is proper in a given situation. If our intolerance for others results in part from a lack of understanding of why peoples vary, then the knowledge that anthropologists accumulate may help lessen that intolerance.

As the world becomes increasingly interconnected or globalized, the importance of understanding and trying to respect cultural and physical differences becomes more and more important. Minor misunderstandings can escalate quickly into more serious problems. Even when powerful countries think they are being helpful, they may convey that other countries are inferior. They may also unknowingly promote behaviors that are not in the best interest of the people they are trying to help. At the extreme, misunderstandings can lead to violent confrontations. In today's world, going to war with modern weapons of mass destruction can kill more people than ever before.

Is understanding and respecting cultural and biological differences enough? Although education is undoubtedly useful, many anthropologists think that more explicit attention has to be paid toward solving real world problems

at both the global and local levels. At the global level, we have to deal with many types of violent conflict, the degradation of the environment, the growing inequality between rich and poor countries, and major threats to health. At the local level, we have to grapple with whether particular development plans are advantageous and how to improve nutrition and health of particular societies. One solution does not necessarily fit all—what's good for some may not be good for others in different circumstances. To find out if some change will be advantageous requires careful study. Many ethical issues arise. Is it ethical to try to interfere with other people's lives? Is it ethical not to, if they are suffering or ask for help?

Knowledge of our past may bring both a feeling of humility and a sense of accomplishment. If we are to attempt to deal with the problems of our world, we must be aware of our vulnerability so that we do not think that problems will solve themselves. But we also have to think enough of our accomplishments to believe that we can find solutions to problems. Much of the trouble we get into may be a result of feelings of self-importance and invulnerability—in short, our lack of humility. Knowing something about our evolutionary past may help us to understand and accept our place in the biological world. Just as for any other form of life, there is no guarantee that any particular human population, or even the entire human species, will perpetuate itself indefinitely. The earth changes, the environment changes, and humanity itself changes. What survives and flourishes in the present might not do so in the future.

Yet, our vulnerability should not make us feel powerless. We have many reasons to feel confident about the future. Consider what we have accomplished so far. By means of tools and weapons fashioned from sticks and stones, we were able to hunt animals larger and more powerful than ourselves. We discovered how to make fire, and we learned to use it to keep ourselves warm and to cook our food. As we domesticated plants and animals, we gained greater control over our food supply and were able to establish more permanent settlements. We mined and smelted ores to fashion more durable tools. We built cities and irrigation systems, monuments and ships. We made it possible to travel from one continent to another in a single day. We conquered some illnesses and prolonged human life.

In short, human beings and their cultures have changed considerably over the course of history. Human populations have often been able to adapt to changing circumstances. Let us hope that humans continue to adapt to the challenges of the present and future.

SUMMARY ● ○ ○

1. Anthropology is literally the study of human beings. It differs from other disciplines concerned with people in that it is broader in scope. It is concerned with humans in all places of the world (not simply those places close to us), and it traces human evolution and cultural development from millions of years ago to the present day.

2. Another distinguishing feature of anthropology is its holistic approach to the study of human beings. Anthropologists study not only all varieties of people but also all aspects of those peoples' experiences and how different aspects of life relate to each other.

3. Anthropologists are commonly concerned with identifying and explaining typical characteristics (traits and customs) of particular human populations.

4. Biological or physical anthropology is one of the major fields of the discipline. Biological anthropology studies the emergence of humans and their later physical evolution (the focus called human paleontology). It also studies how and why contemporary human populations vary biologically (the focus called human variation).

5. Another broad area of concern to anthropology is cultural anthropology. Its three subfields—archaeology, anthropological linguistics, and ethnology (now usually referred to by the parent name, *cultural anthropology*)—all deal with aspects of human culture, that is, with the customary ways of thinking and behaving of particular societies.

6. Archaeologists seek not only to reconstruct the daily life and customs of prehistoric peoples but also to trace cultural changes and offer possible explanations for those changes. Therefore, archaeologists try to reconstruct history from the remains of human cultures.

7. Anthropological linguists are concerned with the emergence of language and with the divergence of languages over time (a subject known as historical linguistics). They also study how contemporary languages differ, both in construction (descriptive or structural linguistics) and in actual speech (sociolinguistics).

8. Ethnologists (now often called simply cultural anthropologists) seek to understand how and why peoples of today and the recent past differ or are similar in their customary ways of thinking and acting. One type of ethnologist, the ethnographer, usually spends a year or so living with and talking to a particular population and observing their customs. Later, ethnographers may prepare a detailed description (an ethnography) of many or some aspects of cultural and social life. Another type of ethnologist, the ethnohistorian, investigates written documents to determine how the ways of life of a particular group of people have changed over time. A third type of ethnologist, the cross-cultural researcher, studies data collected by ethnographers and ethnohistorians for a sample of cultures and attempts to discover which explanations of particular customs may be generally applicable.

9. In all four major subdisciplines of anthropology are applied anthropologists, people who apply anthropological knowledge to achieve more practical goals, usually in the service of an agency outside the traditional academic setting.

10. Anthropology may help people to be more tolerant. Anthropological studies can show us why other people are the way they are, both culturally and physically. Customs or actions that appear improper or offensive to us may be other peoples' adaptations to particular environmental and social conditions.

11. Anthropology is also valuable in that knowledge of our past may bring us both a feeling of humility and a sense of accomplishment. Like any other form of life, we have no guarantee that any particular human population will perpetuate itself indefinitely. Yet, knowledge of our achievements in the past may give us confidence in our ability to solve the problems of the future.

GLOSSARY TERMS ○ ● ○

anthropological linguistics 6
anthropology 2
applied (practicing) anthropology 4
archaeology 6
biological (physical) anthropology 4
cross-cultural researcher 9
cultural anthropology 4
descriptive (structural) linguistics 7
ethnographer 9
ethnography 9
ethnohistorian 9
ethnology 6
fossils 5
historical archaeology 6
historical linguistics 7
holistic 4
Homo sapiens 5
human paleontology 5
human variation 5
paleoanthropology 5
prehistory 6
Primates 5
primatologists 5
sociolinguistics 7

CRITICAL QUESTIONS ○ ○ ●

1. Why study anthropology? What are its goals, and how is it useful?

2. How does anthropology differ from other fields of study you've encountered that deal with humans? (Compare with psychology, sociology, political science, history, or biology, among others.)

3. What do you think about the suggestion that anthropology is the fundamental discipline studying humans?

PEARSON
myanthrolab

Read the chapter by Terence E. Hays, "From Ethnographer to Comparativist and Back Again," on MyAnthroLab, and answer the following questions:

1. Many researchers find that their interests change when they go to the field. What did Hays start out studying? What did he get more interested in?

2. Explain why Hays thinks that you need both ethnography and comparison.

Culture and Culture Change

e all consider ourselves to be unique individuals with our own set of personal opinions, preferences, habits, and quirks. Indeed, all of us are unique; and yet most of us also share many feelings, beliefs, and habits with most of the people who live in our society. If we live in North America, we are likely to have the feeling that eating dogs is wrong, have the belief that bacteria or viruses cause illness, and have the habit of sleeping on a bed. Most people hardly ever think about the ideas and customs they share with other people in their society, assuming them to be "natural." These ideas and behaviors are part of what we mean by *culture*. We only begin to become aware that our culture is different when we become aware that other peoples have different feelings, different beliefs, and different habits from ours. So most North Americans would never even think of the possibility of eating dog meat if they did not know that people in some other societies commonly do so. They would not realize that their belief in germs was cultural if they were not aware that people in some societies think that witchcraft or evil spirits causes illness. They might not become aware that it is their custom to sleep on beds if they were not aware that people in many societies sleep on the floor or on the ground. Only when we compare ourselves with people in other societies may we become aware of cultural differences and similarities. This is, in fact, the way that anthropology as a profession began. When Europeans began to explore and move to faraway places, they were forced to confront the sometimes striking facts of cultural variation.

Most of us are aware that "times have changed," especially when we compare our lives with those of our parents. Some of the most dramatic changes have occurred in attitudes about sex and marriage, changes in women's roles, and changes in technology. But such culture change is not unusual. Throughout history, humans have replaced or altered customary behaviors and attitudes as their needs have changed. Just as no individual is immortal, no particular cultural pattern is impervious to change. Anthropologists want to understand how and why such change occurs. Culture change may be gradual or rapid. Although there has always been contact between different societies, contact between faraway cultures through exploration, colonization, trade, and more recently multinational business has accelerated the pace of change within the last 600 years or so. Globalization has made the world more and more interconnected. We conclude this chapter with a discussion of the future of cultural diversity.

● ○ ●

DEFINING CULTURE

In everyday usage, the word *culture* refers to a desirable quality we can acquire by attending a sufficient number of plays and concerts and visiting art museums and galleries. Anthropologists, however, have a different definition, as Ralph Linton explained:

Culture refers to the total way of life of any society, not simply to those parts of this way which the society regards as higher or more desirable. Thus culture, when applied to our own way of life, has nothing to do with playing the piano or reading Browning. For the social scientist such activities are simply elements within the totality of our culture. This totality also includes such mundane activities as washing dishes or driving an automobile, and for the purposes of cultural studies these stand quite on a par with "the finer things of life." It follows that for the social scientist there are no uncultured societies or even individuals. Every society has a culture, no matter how simple this culture may be, and every human being is cultured, in the sense of participating in some culture or other.[1]

Culture, then, refers to innumerable aspects of life, including many things we consider ordinary. Linton emphasized common habits and behaviors in what he considered culture, but the totality of life also includes not just what people do, but also how they commonly think and feel. As we define it here, **culture** is the set of learned behaviors and ideas (including beliefs, attitudes, values, and ideals) that are characteristic of a particular society or other social group. Behaviors can also produce products or *material culture*—things like houses, musical instruments, and tools that are the products of customary behavior.

Different kinds of groups can have cultures. People come to share behaviors and ideas because they communicate with and observe each other. Although groups from families to societies share cultural traits, anthropologists have traditionally been concerned with the cultural characteristics of *societies*. Many anthropologists define **society** as a group of people who occupy a particular territory and speak a common language not generally understood by neighboring peoples. By this definition, societies may or may not correspond to countries. There are many countries, particularly newer ones, that have within their boundaries different peoples speaking mutually unintelligible languages. By our definition of society, such countries are composed of many different societies and therefore many cultures. Also, by our definition of society, some societies may even include more than one country. For example, we would have to say that Canada and the United States form a single society because the two groups generally speak English, live next to each other, and share many common ideas and behaviors. That is why we refer to "North American culture" in this chapter. The terms *society* and *culture* are not synonymous. Society refers to a group of people; culture refers to the learned and shared behaviors, ideas, and characteristic of those people. As we will discuss shortly, we also have to be careful to describe culture as of particular time period; what is characteristic of one time may not be characteristic of another.

Culture Is Commonly Shared

If only one person thinks or does a certain thing, that thought or action represents a personal habit, not a pattern of culture. For a thought or action to be considered cultural, some social group must commonly share it. We usually share many behaviors and ideas with our families and friends. We commonly share cultural characteristics with those whose ethnic or regional origins, religious affiliations, and occupations are the same as or similar to our own. We share certain practices and ideas with most people in our society. We also share some cultural traits with people beyond our society who have similar interests (such as rules for international sporting events) or similar roots (as do the various English-speaking nations).

When we talk about the commonly shared customs of *a* society, which constitute the traditional and central concern of cultural anthropology, we are referring to *a* culture. When we talk about the commonly shared customs of a group within a society, which are a central concern of sociologists and increasingly of concern to anthropologists, we are referring to a **subculture.** (A subculture is not necessarily the same as an ethnic group; we discuss the concept of ethnicity further in the chapter on social stratification, ethnicity, and racism.) When we study the commonly shared customs of some group that includes different societies, we are talking about a phenomenon for which we do not have a single word—for example, as when we refer to *Western culture* (the cultural characteristics of societies in or derived from Europe) or the *culture of poverty* (the presumed cultural characteristics of poor people the world over).

We must remember that, even when anthropologists refer to something as cultural, there is always individual variation, which means that not everyone in a society shares a particular cultural characteristic of that society. For example, it is cultural in North American society for adults to live apart from their parents. But not all adults in our society do so, nor do all adults wish to do so. The custom of living apart from parents is considered cultural because

A daughter braids her doll's hair, imitating what her mother is doing.

most adults practice that custom. In every society studied by anthropologists—in the simplest as well as the most complex—individuals do not all think and act the same.[2] Indeed, individual variation is a major source of new culture.[3]

Culture Is Learned

Not all things shared generally by a group are cultural. Typical hair color is not cultural, nor is eating. For something to be considered cultural, it must be learned as well as shared. A typical hair color (unless dyed) is not cultural because it is genetically determined. Humans eat because they must; but what and when and how they eat are learned and vary from culture to culture. Most North Americans do not consider dog meat edible, and indeed the idea of eating dogs horrifies them. But in China, as in some other societies, dog meat is considered delicious. In North American culture, many people consider a baked ham to be a holiday dish. In several societies of the Middle East, however, including those of Egypt and Israel, eating the meat of a pig is forbidden by sacred writings.

To some extent, all animals exhibit learned behaviors, some of which most individuals in a population may share and may therefore consider cultural. But different animal species vary in the degree to which their shared behaviors are learned or are instinctive. The sociable ants, for instance, despite all their patterned social behavior, do not appear to have much, if any, culture. They divide their labor, construct their nests, form their raiding columns, and carry off their dead—all without having been taught to do so and without imitating the behavior of other ants. Our closest biological relatives, the monkeys and the apes, not only learn a wide variety of behaviors on their own, they also learn from each other. Some of their learned responses are as basic as those involved in maternal care; others are as frivolous as the taste for candy. Frans de Waal reviewed seven long-term studies of chimpanzees and identified at least 39 behaviors that were clearly learned from others.[4] If shared and socially learned, these behaviors could be described as cultural.

The proportion of an animal's life span occupied by childhood roughly reflects the degree to which the animal depends on learned behavior for survival. Monkeys and apes have relatively long childhoods compared to other animals. Humans have by far the longest childhood of any animal, reflecting our great dependence on learned behavior. Although humans may acquire much learned behavior by trial and error and imitation, as do monkeys and apes, most human ideas and behaviors are learned from others. Much of it is probably acquired with the aid of spoken, symbolic language. We will have much more to say about language in a later chapter. Using language, a human parent can describe a snake and tell a child that a snake is dangerous and should be avoided. If symbolic language did not exist, the parent would have to wait until the child actually saw a snake and then, through example, show the child that such a creature is to be avoided. Without language, we probably could not transmit or receive information so efficiently and rapidly, and thus would not be heir to so rich and varied a culture.

To sum up, we may say that something is cultural if it is a learned behavior or idea (belief, attitude, value, ideal) that the members of a society or other social group generally share.

Controversies About the Concept of Culture

Although we have explained what we mean by culture and we have tried to give the definition most anthropologists use, some would disagree with the definition. One of the disagreements is whether the concept of culture should refer just to the rules or ideas behind behavior,[5] or should also include the behaviors or the products of behavior, as is our choice here.

Cognitive anthropologists are most likely to say that culture refers to rules and ideas behind behavior, and therefore that culture resides in people's heads.[6]

Every individual will have slightly different constructs that are based in part on their own unique experiences. Because many people in a society share many of the same experiences, they will share many ideas—those shared ideas anthropologists describe as culture. This view allows for individual differences within a society, and also suggests that individual variation is the source of new culture.

Observers of human life often point to the seeming force of "culture," the profound effect on individuals of living in social groups. As we will see shortly in the section on cultural constraints, these social constraints suggest that culture exists outside of individuals. In the strongest view, one that was more acceptable in the past, culture is thought of as having a "life" of its own that could be studied without much regard for individuals at all.[7] According to this view, people are born blank slates, which culture can put its stamp on in each generation. Individuals may acquire their culture in the course of growing up, but understanding culture does not require understanding psychological processes.

There are a number of problems if we view culture as having a "life" of its own. First, where does it reside exactly? Second, if individuals do not matter, what are the mechanisms of culture change? And lastly, if psychological processes are irrelevant, how is it that there is considerable similarity across cultures?

As we will see in the next section, people do behave differently in social groups in ways that they might not even imagine ahead of time. Mob behavior is an extreme, but telling example. Therefore, we think we should look at behavior as well as rules or ideas in people's heads in describing a culture. It is not necessary to postulate that culture has a "life" of its own to explain why people sometimes behave differently in social groups. Humans are social beings and respond to others. So, in contrast to many cognitive anthropologists, we include behavior and the products of behavior in describing culture. But like cognitive anthropologists, we believe that one must consider individual variation in describing culture to sort out what is individual and what is shared. Those commonly shared and learned behaviors as well as ideas are the stuff of culture.

CULTURAL CONSTRAINTS

The noted French sociologist Émile Durkheim stressed that culture is something *outside* us, exerting a strong coercive power on us. We do not always feel the constraints of our culture because we generally conform to the types of conduct and thought it requires. Social scientists refer to standards or rules about what is acceptable behavior as **norms.** The importance of a norm usually can be judged by how members of a society respond when the norm is violated.

Cultural constraints are of two basic types, *direct* and *indirect.* Naturally, the direct constraints are the more obvious. For example, if you choose to wear a casual shorts outfit to a wedding, you will probably be subject to some ridicule and a certain amount of social isolation. But if you choose to wear nothing, you may be exposed to a stronger, more direct cultural constraint—arrest for indecent exposure.

Although indirect forms of cultural constraint are less obvious than direct ones, they are no less effective. Durkheim illustrated this point when he wrote, "I am not obliged to speak French with my fellow-countrymen, nor to use the legal currency, but I cannot possibly do otherwise. If I tried to escape this necessity, my attempt would fail miserably."[8] In other words, if Durkheim had decided he would rather speak Icelandic than French, nobody would have tried to stop him. But hardly anyone would have understood him either. And although he would not have been put into prison for trying to buy groceries with Icelandic money, he would have had difficulty convincing the local merchants to sell him food.

In a series of classic experiments on conformity, Solomon Asch revealed how strong social pressure can be. Asch coached the majority of a group of college students to give deliberately incorrect answers to questions involving visual stimuli. A "critical subject," the one student in the room who was not so coached, had no idea that the other participants would purposely misinterpret the evidence presented to them. Asch found that, in one-third of the experiments, the critical subjects consistently gave incorrect answers, seemingly allowing their own correct perceptions to be distorted by the obviously incorrect statements of the others. And in another 40 percent of the experiments, the critical subject yielded to the opinion of the group some of the time.[9] These studies have been replicated in the United States and elsewhere. Although the degree of conformity appears to vary in different societies, most studies still show conformity effects.[10] Many individuals still do not give in to the wishes of the majority, but a recent study using MRIs has shown that perceptions can actually be altered if participants consciously alter their answers to conform to others.[11]

ATTITUDES THAT HINDER THE STUDY OF CULTURES

Many of the Europeans who first traveled to faraway places were revolted or shocked by customs they observed. Such reactions are not surprising. People commonly feel that their own behaviors and attitudes are the correct ones and that people who do not share those patterns are immoral or inferior.[12] People who judge other cultures solely in terms of their own culture are **ethnocentric**—that is, they hold an attitude called **ethnocentrism.** Most North Americans would think that eating dogs or insects is disgusting, but most do not feel the same way about eating beef. Similarly, they would react negatively to child betrothal or digging up the bones of the dead.

Our own customs and ideas may appear bizarre or barbaric to an observer from another society. Hindus in

Because we are ethnocentric about many things, it is often difficult to criticize our own customs, some of which might seem shocking to a member of another society. The elderly in America often spend their days alone. In contrast, the elderly in Japan often live in a three-generational family.

India, for example, would consider our custom of eating beef disgusting. In their culture, the cow is a sacred animal and may not be slaughtered for food. In many societies, a baby is almost constantly carried by someone, in someone's lap, or asleep next to others.[13] People in such societies may think it is cruel of us to leave babies alone for long periods of time, often in devices that resemble cages (cribs and playpens). Even our most ordinary customs—the daily rituals we take for granted—might seem thoroughly absurd when viewed from an outside perspective. An observer of our society might justifiably take notes on certain strange behaviors that seem quite ordinary to us, as the following description shows:

> The daily body ritual performed by everyone includes a mouth-rite. Despite the fact that these people are so punctilious about the care of the mouth, this rite involves a practice which strikes the uninitiated stranger as revolting. It was reported to me that the ritual consists of inserting a small bundle of hog hairs into the mouth, along with certain magical powders, and then moving the bundle in a highly formalized series of gestures. In addition to the private mouth-rite, the people seek out a holy-mouth man once or twice a year. These practitioners have an impressive set of paraphernalia, consisting of a variety of augers, awls, probes, and prods. The use of these objects in the exorcism of the evils of the mouth involves almost unbelievable ritual torture of the client. The holy-mouth man opens the client's mouth and, using the above-mentioned tools, enlarges any holes which decay may have created in teeth. Magical materials are put into these holes. If there are no naturally occurring holes in the teeth, large sections of one or more teeth are gouged out so that the supernatural substance can be applied. In the client's view, the purpose of these ministrations is to arrest decay and to draw friends. The extremely sacred and traditional character of the rite is evident in the fact that the natives return to the holy-mouth man year after year, despite the fact that their teeth continue to decay.[14]

We are likely to protest that to understand the behaviors of a particular society—in this case, our own—the observer must try to find out what the people in that society say about why they do things. For example, the observer might find out that periodic visits to the "holy-mouth man" are for medical, not magical, purposes. Indeed, the observer, after some questioning, might discover that the "mouth-rite" has no sacred or religious connotations whatsoever. Actually, Horace Miner, the author of the passage on the "daily rite ritual," was not a foreigner. An American, he described the "ritual" the way he did to show how the behaviors involved might be interpreted by an outside observer.

Ethnocentrism hinders our understanding of the customs of other people and, at the same time, keeps us from understanding our own customs. If we think that everything we do is best, we are not likely to ask why we do what we do or why "they" do what "they" do.

We may not always glorify our own culture. Other ways of life may sometimes seem more appealing. Whenever we are weary of the complexities of civilization, we may long for a way of life that is "closer to nature" or "simpler" than our own. For instance, a young North American whose parent is holding two or three jobs just to provide the family with bare necessities might briefly be attracted to the lifestyle of the !Kung of the Kalahari Desert in the 1950s. The !Kung shared their food and therefore were often free to engage in leisure activities during the greater part of the day. They obtained all their food by men hunting animals and women gathering wild plants. They had no facilities for refrigeration, so sharing a large freshly killed animal was clearly more sensible than hoarding meat that would soon rot. Moreover, the sharing provided a kind of social security system for the !Kung. If a hunter was unable to catch an animal on a certain day, he could obtain food for himself and his family from someone else in his band. Then, at some later date, the game he caught would provide food for the family of another, unsuccessful hunter. This system of sharing also ensured that people too young or too old to help with collecting food would still be fed.

Could we learn from the !Kung? Perhaps we could in some respects, but we must not glorify their way of life either or think that their way of life might be easily imported into our own society. Other aspects of !Kung life would not appeal to many North Americans. For example, when the nomadic !Kung decided to move their camps, they had to carry all the family possessions, substantial amounts of food and water, and all young children below age 4 or 5. This is a sizable burden to carry for any distance. The nomadic !Kung traveled about 1,500 miles in a single year and families had few possessions.[15] It is unlikely that most North Americans would find the !Kung way of life enviable in all respects.

Both ethnocentrism and its opposite, the glorification of other cultures, hinder effective anthropological study.

CULTURAL RELATIVISM

As we discuss in the chapter on the history of theory in anthropology, early evolutionists tended to think of Western cultures as being at the highest or most progressive stage of evolution. Not only were these early ideas based on very poor evidence of the details of world ethnography, they could also be ethnocentric glorifications of Western culture.

But Franz Boas and many of his students—like Ruth Benedict, Melville Herskovits, and Margaret Mead—felt otherwise.[16] They stressed that the early evolutionists did not sufficiently understand the details of the cultures they theorized about, nor did they understand the context in which these customs appeared. Challenging the attitude that Western cultures were obviously superior, the Boasians insisted that a society's customs and ideas should be described objectively and understood in the context of that society's problems and opportunities. This attitude is known as **cultural relativism.** Does cultural relativism mean that the actions of another society, or of our own, should not be judged? Does our insistence on objectivity mean that anthropologists should not make moral judgments about the cultural phenomena they observe and try to explain? Does it mean that anthropologists should not try to bring about change? Not necessarily. Although the concept of cultural relativism remains an important anthropological tenet, anthropologists differ in their interpretation of the principle of cultural relativism.

Many anthropologists are uncomfortable with the strong form of cultural relativism that suggests that all patterns of culture are equally valid. What if the people practice slavery, violence against women, torture, or genocide? If the strong doctrine of relativism is adhered to, then these cultural practices are not to be judged, and we should not try to eliminate them. A weaker form of cultural relativism asserts that anthropologists should strive for objectivity in describing a people and should be wary of superficial or quick judgment in their attempts to understand the reasons for cultural behavior. Tolerance should be the basic mode unless there is strong reason to behave otherwise.[17] The weak version of cultural relativity does not preclude anthropologists from making judgments or from trying to change behavior they think is harmful. But judgments need not, and should not, preclude accurate description and explanation.

Human Rights and Relativism

The news increasingly reports behaviors that Western countries consider to be violations of human rights. Examples range from jailing people for expressing certain political ideas to ethnic massacre. But faced with criticism from the West, people in other parts of the world are saying that the West should not dictate its ideas about human rights to other countries. Indeed, many countries say they have different codes of ethics. Are the Western countries being ethnocentric by taking their own cultural ideas and applying them to the rest of the world? Should we instead rely on the strong version of the concept of cultural relativism, considering each culture on its own terms? If we do that, it may not be possible to create a universal standard of human rights.

What we do know is that all cultures have ethical standards, but they do not emphasize the same things. For example, some cultures emphasize individual political rights; others emphasize political order. Some cultures emphasize protection of individual property; others emphasize the sharing or equitable distribution of resources. People in the United States may have freedom to dissent, but they can be deprived of health insurance or of food if they lack the money to buy them. Cultures also vary markedly in the degree to which they have equal rights for minorities and women. In some societies, women are killed when a husband dies or when they disobey a father or brother.

Some anthropologists argue strongly against cultural relativism. For example, Elizabeth Zechenter says that cultural relativists claim there are no universal principles of morality, but insist on tolerance for all cultures. If tolerance is one universal principle, why shouldn't there be others? In addition, she points out that the concept of cultural relativism is often used to justify traditions desired by the dominant and powerful in a society. She points to a case in 1996, in Algeria, where two teenage girls were raped and murdered because they violated the fundamentalist edict against attending school. Are those girls any less a part of the culture than the fundamentalists? Would it make any difference if most Algerian women supported the murders? Would that make it right? Zechenter does not believe that international treaties such as the Universal Declaration of Human Rights impose uniformity among diverse cultures. Rather, they seek to create a floor below which no society is supposed to fall.[18]

Can the concept of cultural relativism be reconciled with the concept of an international code of human rights? Probably not completely. Paul Rosenblatt recognizes the dilemma but nonetheless thinks that something has to be done to stop torture and "ethnic cleansing," among other practices. He makes the case that "to the extent that it is easier to persuade people whose viewpoints and values one understands, relativism can be a tool for change . . . a relativist's awareness of the values and understanding of the elite makes it easier to know what arguments would be persuasive. For example, in a society in which the group rather than the individual has great primacy, it might be persuasive to show how respect for individual rights benefits the group."[19]

DESCRIBING A CULTURE

If all individuals are unique and all cultures have some internal variation, how do anthropologists discover what may be cultural? Understanding what is cultural involves two parts—separating what is shared from what is very individually variable, and understanding whether common behaviors and ideas are learned.

To understand better how an anthropologist might make sense of diverse behaviors, let us examine the diversity at a professional football game in the United States. When people attend a football game, various members of the crowd behave differently while "The Star-Spangled Banner" is being played. As they stand and listen, some people remove their hats; a child munches popcorn; a veteran of the armed forces stands at attention; a teenager searches the crowd for a friend; and the coaches take a final opportunity to intone secret chants and spells designed to sap the strength of the opposing team. Yet, despite these individual variations, most of the people at the game respond in a basically similar manner: Nearly everyone stands silently, facing the flag. Moreover, if you go to several football games, you will observe that many aspects of the event are notably similar. Although the plays will vary from game to game, the rules of the game are never different, and although the colors of the uniforms of the teams are different, the players never appear on the field dressed in swimsuits.

In deciding what is cultural behavior, anthropologists look for commonalities, understanding that there is always considerable variation. In North American culture, unmarried couples are allowed and even encouraged to spend time with each other, but how they spend their time varies.

Although the variations in individual reactions to a given stimulus are theoretically limitless, in fact they tend to fall within easily recognizable limits. A child listening to the anthem may continue to eat popcorn but will probably not do a rain dance. Similarly, the coaches will unlikely react to that same stimulus by running onto the field and embracing the singer. Variations in behavior, then, are confined within socially acceptable limits, and part of the anthropologists' goals is to find out what those limits are. They may note, for example, that some limitations on behavior have a practical purpose: A spectator who disrupts the game by wandering onto the field would be required to leave. Other limitations are purely traditional. In our society, it is considered proper for a man to remove his overcoat if he becomes overheated, but others would undoubtedly frown upon his removing his trousers even if the weather were quite warm. Using observation and interviewing, anthropologists discover the customs and the ranges of acceptable behavior that characterize the society under study.

Similarly, anthropologists interested in describing courtship and marriage in our society would encounter a variety of behaviors. Dating couples vary in where they go (coffee shops, movies, restaurants, bowling alleys), what

behaviors they engage in on dates, how long they date before they split up or move on to more serious relationships. If they decide to marry, ceremonies may be simple or elaborate and involve either religious or secular rituals. Despite this variability, the anthropologists would begin to detect certain regularities in courting practices. Although couples may do many different things on their first and subsequent dates, they nearly always arrange the dates by themselves; they try to avoid their parents when on dates; they often manage to find themselves alone at the end of a date; they put their lips together frequently; and so forth. After a series of more and more closely spaced encounters, a man and woman may decide to declare themselves publicly as a couple, either by announcing that they are engaged or by revealing that they are living together or intend to do so. Finally, if the two of them decide to marry, they must in some way have their union recorded by the civil authorities.

In our society, a person who wishes to marry cannot completely disregard the customary patterns of courtship. If a man saw a woman on the street and decided he wanted to marry her, he could conceivably choose a quicker and more direct form of action than the usual dating procedure. He could get on a horse, ride to the woman's home, snatch her up in his arms, and gallop away with her. In Sicily, until the last few decades, such a couple would have been considered legally married, even if the woman had never met the man before or had no intention of marrying. But in North American society, any man who acted in such a fashion would be arrested and jailed for kidnapping and would probably have his sanity challenged. Although individual behaviors may vary, most social behavior falls within culturally acceptable limits.

In the course of observing and interviewing, anthropologists also try to distinguish actual behavior from the ideas about how people in particular situations ought to feel and behave. In everyday terms, we speak of these ideas as *ideals;* in anthropology, we refer to them as *ideal cultural traits*. Ideal cultural traits may differ from actual behavior because the ideal is based on the way society used to be. (Consider the ideal of "free enterprise," that industry should be totally free of governmental regulation.) Other ideals may never have been actual patterns and may represent merely what people would like to see as correct behavior. Consider the idealized belief, long cherished in North America, that everybody is "equal before the law," that everybody should be treated in the same way by the police and courts. Of course, we know that this is not always true. The rich, for example, may receive less jail time and be sent to nicer prisons. Nevertheless, the ideal is still part of our culture; most of us continue to believe that the law should be applied equally to all.

When dealing with customs that are overt or highly visible within a society—for example, the custom of sending children to school—an investigator can determine the existence of such practices by direct observation and by interviewing a few knowledgeable people. But when dealing with a domain of behavior that may include many individual variations, or when the people studied are

Distance between people conversing varies cross-culturally. The faces of the Rajput Indian men on the left are much closer than the faces of the American women on the right.

There, the characteristic being measured is plotted on the horizontal axis (in this case, the distance between conversational pairs), and the number of times each distance is observed (its frequency) is plotted on the vertical axis. If we were to plot how a sample of North American casual conversational pairs is distributed, we would probably get a bell-shaped curve that peaks at around 3 feet.[21] Is it any wonder, then, that we sometimes speak of keeping others "at arm's length"?

Although we may be able to discover by interviews and observation that a behavior, thought, or feeling is widely shared within a society, how do we establish that something commonly shared is learned, so that we can call it cultural? Establishing that something is or is not learned may be difficult. Because children are not reared apart from adult caretakers, the behaviors they exhibit as part of their genetic inheritance are not clearly separated from those they learn from others around them. We suspect that particular behaviors and ideas are largely learned if they vary from society to society. We also suspect genetic influences when particular behaviors or ideas are found in all societies. For example, as we will see in the chapter on language, children the world over seem to acquire language at about the same age, and the structure of their early utterances seems to be similar. These facts suggest that human children are born with an innate grammar. However, although early childhood language seems similar the world over, the particular languages spoken by adults in different societies show considerable variability. This variability suggests that particular

unaware of their pattern of behavior and cannot answer questions about it, the anthropologist may need to collect information from a larger sample of individuals to establish what the cultural trait is.

One example of a cultural trait that most people in a society are not aware of is how far apart people stand when they are having a conversation. Yet there is considerable reason to believe that unconscious cultural rules govern such behavior. These rules become obvious when we interact with people who have different rules. We may experience considerable discomfort when another person stands too close (indicating too much intimacy) or too far (indicating unfriendliness). Edward Hall reported that Arabs customarily stand quite close to others, close enough, as we have noted, to be able to smell the other person. In interactions between Arabs and North Americans, then, the Arabs will move closer at the same time that the North Americans back away.[20]

If we wanted to arrive at the cultural rule for conversational distance between casual acquaintances, we could study a sample of individuals from a society and determine the *modal response,* or *mode.* The mode is a statistical term that refers to the most frequently encountered response in a given series of responses. So, for the North American pattern of casual conversational distance, we would plot the actual distance for many observed pairs of people. Some pairs may be 2 feet apart, some 2.5, and some 4 feet apart. If we count the number of times every particular distance is observed, these counts provide what we call a *frequency distribution.* The distance with the highest frequency is the *modal pattern.* Very often the frequency distribution takes the form of a *bell-shaped curve,* as shown in Figure 2–1.

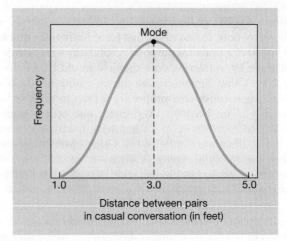

FIGURE 2–1 **Frequency Distribution Curve**

languages have to be learned. Similarly, if the courtship patterns of one society differ markedly from those of another, we can be fairly certain that those courtship patterns are learned and therefore cultural.

CULTURE IS PATTERNED

Anthropologists have always known that culture is not a hodgepodge of unrelated behaviors and ideas—that a culture is mostly integrated. In saying that a culture is mostly *integrated,* we mean that the elements or traits that make up that culture are not just a random assortment of customs but are mostly adjusted to or consistent with one another.

A culture may also tend to be integrated for psychological reasons. The ideas of a culture are stored in the brains of individuals. Research in social psychology has suggested that people tend to modify beliefs or behaviors that are not cognitively or conceptually consistent with other information.[22] We do not expect cultures to be completely integrated, just as we do not expect individuals to be completely consistent. But if a tendency toward cognitive consistency is found in humans, we might expect that at least some aspects of a culture would tend to be integrated for that reason alone. How this pressure for consistency works is not hard to imagine. Children, for example, seem to be very good at remembering *all* the things their parents say. If they ask for something and the parents say no, they may say, "But you said I could yesterday." This pressure for consistency may even make parents change their minds! Of course, not everything one wants to do is consistent with the rest of one's desires, but there surely is pressure from within and without to make it so.

Humans are also capable of rational decision making; they can usually figure out that certain things are not easy to do because of other things they do. For example, if a society has a long postpartum sex (a custom in which couples abstain from sex for a year or more after the birth of a baby), we might expect that most people in the society could figure out that it would be easier to observe the taboo if husband and wife did not sleep in the same bed. Or if people drive on the left side of the road, as in England, it is easier and less dangerous to drive a car with a steering wheel on the right because that placement allows you to judge more accurately how close you are to cars coming at you from the opposite direction.

Consistency or integration of culture traits may also be produced by less conscious psychological processes. As we discuss in the chapters on culture and the individual, religion and magic, and the arts, people may generalize (transfer) their experiences from one area of life to another. For example, where children are taught that it is wrong to express anger toward family and friends, it turns out that folktales parallel the childrearing; anger and aggression in the folktales tend to be directed only toward strangers, not toward family and friends. It seems as if the expression of anger is too frightening to be expressed close to home, even in folktales.

Adaptation to the environment is another major reason for traits to be patterned. Customs that diminish the survival chances of a society are not likely to persist. Either the people clinging to those customs will become extinct, taking the customs with them, or the customs will be replaced, thereby possibly helping the people to survive. By either process, **maladaptive customs**—those that diminish the chances of survival and reproduction—are likely to disappear. The customs of a society that enhance survival and reproductive success are **adaptive customs** and are likely to persist. Hence, we assume that if a society has survived long enough to be described in the annals of anthropology (the "ethnographic record"), much, if not most, of its cultural repertoire is adaptive, or was at one time.

When we say that a custom is adaptive, however, we mean it is adaptive only with respect to a specific physical and social environment. What may be adaptive in one environment may not be adaptive in another. Therefore, when we ask why a society may have a particular custom, we really are asking if that custom makes sense as an adaptation to that society's particular environmental conditions. If certain customs are more adaptive in particular settings, then those "bundles" of traits will generally be found together under similar conditions. For example, the !Kung, as we have mentioned, subsisted by hunting wild animals and gathering wild plants. Because wild game is mobile and different plants mature at different times, a nomadic way of life may be an adaptive strategy. That food-getting strategy cannot support that many people in one area, so small social groups make more sense than large communities. Because people move frequently, it is probably more adaptive to have few material possessions. As we will see, these cultural traits usually occur together when people depend on hunting and gathering for their food.

We must remember that not all aspects of culture are consistent, nor is a society forced to adapt its culture to changing environmental circumstances. Even in the face of changed circumstances, people may choose not to change their customs. For example, the Tapirapé of central Brazil did not alter their custom of limiting the number of births, even though they suffered severe population losses after contact with Europeans and their diseases. The Tapirapé population fell to fewer than 100 people from over 1,000. Clearly, they were on the way to extinction, yet they continued to value small families. Not only did they believe that a woman should have no more than three children, but they took specific steps to achieve this limitation. They practiced infanticide if twins were born, if the third child was of the same sex as the first two children, and if the possible fathers broke certain taboos during pregnancy or in the child's infancy.[23]

Of course, it is also possible that a people will behave maladaptively, even if they try to alter their behavior. After all, although people may alter their behavior according to what they perceive will be helpful to them, what they perceive to be helpful may not prove to be adaptive. The tendency for a culture to be integrated or patterned, then, may be cognitively and emotionally, as well as adaptively, induced.

HOW AND WHY CULTURES CHANGE

When you examine the history of a society, it is obvious that its culture has changed over time. Some of the shared behaviors and ideas that were common at one time are modified or replaced at another time. That is why, in describing a culture, it is important to understand that a description pertains to a particular time period. (Moreover, in many large societies, the description may only be appropriate for a particular subgroup.) For example, the !Kung of the 1950s were mostly dependent on the collection of wild plants and animals and moved their campsites frequently, but later they became more sedentary to engage in wage labor. Whether we focus on some aspect of past behavior or on contemporary behavior depends on what question we want to answer. If we want to maximize our understanding of cultural variation, such as variation in religious belief and practice, it may be important to focus on the earliest descriptions of a group before they were converted to a major world religion. On the other hand, if we want to understand why a people adopted a new religion or how they altered their religion or resisted change in the face of pressure, we need to examine the changes that occurred over time.

In the remainder of this chapter, we will discuss how and why cultures change and briefly review some of the widespread changes that have occurred in recent times. In general, the impetus for change may come from within the society or from without. From within, the unconscious or conscious pressure for consistency will produce culture change if enough people adjust old behavior and thinking to new. And change can also occur if people try to invent better ways of doing things. Michael Chibnik suggests that people who confront a new problem conduct mental or small "experiments" to decide how to behave. These experiments may give rise to new cultural traits.[24] A good deal of culture change may be stimulated by changes in the external environment. For example, if people move into an arid area, they will either have to give up farming or develop a system of irrigation. In the modern world, changes in the social environment are probably more frequent stimuli for culture change than changes in the physical environment. Many North Americans, for example, started to think seriously about conserving energy and about using sources of energy other than oil only after oil supplies from the Middle East were curtailed in 1973 and 1974. As we noted earlier, a significant amount of the radical and rapid culture change that has occurred in the last few hundred years has been due to the imperial expansion of Western societies into other areas of the world. Native Americans, for instance, were forced to alter their lifestyles drastically when they were driven off their lands and confined to reservations.

Discovery and Invention

Discoveries and inventions, which may originate inside or outside a society, are ultimately the sources of all culture change. But they do not necessarily lead to change. If an invention or discovery is ignored, no change in culture results. Only when society accepts an invention or discovery and uses it regularly can we begin to speak of culture change.

The new thing discovered or invented, the innovation, may be an object—the wheel, the plow, the computer—or it may involve behavior and ideas—buying and selling, democracy, monogamy. According to Ralph Linton, a discovery is any addition to knowledge, and an invention is a new application of knowledge.[25] Thus, a person might discover that children can be persuaded to eat nourishing food if the food is associated with an imaginary character that appeals to them. And then someone might exploit that discovery by inventing a character named Popeye who appears in a series of animated cartoons, acquiring miraculous strength by devouring cans of spinach.

Unconscious Invention In discussing the process of invention, we should differentiate between various types of inventions. One type is the consequence of a society's setting itself a specific goal, such as eliminating tuberculosis or placing a person on the moon. Another type emerges less intentionally. This second process of invention is often referred to as *accidental juxtaposition* or *unconscious invention*. Linton suggested that some inventions, especially those of prehistoric days, were probably the consequences of literally dozens of tiny initiatives by "unconscious" inventors. These inventors made their small contributions, perhaps over many hundreds of years, without being aware of the part they were playing in bringing one invention, such as the wheel or a better form of hand ax, to completion.[26] Consider the example of children playing on a fallen log, which rolls as they walk and balance on it, coupled with the need at a given moment to move a slab of granite from a cave face. The children's play may have suggested the use of logs as rollers and thereby set in motion a series of developments that culminated in the wheel.

In reconstructing the process of invention in prehistoric times, however, we should be careful not to look back on our ancestors with a smugness generated by our more highly developed technology. We have become accustomed to turning to the science sections of our magazines and newspapers and finding, almost daily, reports of miraculous new discoveries and inventions. From our point of view, it is difficult to imagine such a simple invention as the wheel taking so many centuries to come into being. We are tempted to surmise that early humans were less intelligent than we are. But the capacity of the human brain has been the same for perhaps 100,000 years; there is no evidence that the inventors of the wheel were any less intelligent than we are.

Intentional Innovation Some discoveries and inventions arise out of deliberate attempts to produce a new idea or object. It may seem that such innovations are obvious responses to perceived needs. For example, during the Industrial Revolution, there was a great demand for inventions that would increase productivity. James Hargreaves, in 18th-century England, is an example of an inventor

current research and issues

Culture Change and Persistence in China

In the years since the 1949 Communist takeover in China, the central government has initiated a variety of changes in family life. Many of these changes were literally forced; people who resisted them were often resettled or jailed. Ancestor worship and lineage organization were attacked or declared illegal. Most private property was abolished, undermining family loyalties. Why participate in family activities if there could be no economic reward? Still, the actions of the central government did not completely change family life. Even coercion has its limits.

The government may have wanted to restrict the family and kinship, but its investments in public health and famine relief reduced mortality, thereby strengthening family ties. Fewer infants died, more children lived long enough to marry, old age became more common—all of these developments allowed people in all social classes to have larger and more complex networks of kin than were possible before 1949. To be sure, government policies undercut the power and authority of extended family patriarchs. But the new healthier conditions were conducive to large, multigenerational households with economic as well as social ties to other kin.

As China became more accessible to anthropologists and other researchers from abroad, many investigators came to study the variability and similarity in Chinese family life. Most of these studies focused on the dominant Han Chinese (the Han constitute about 95 percent of the total population of China); investigators have also studied many of the 55 "recognized" minority cultures in China. Burton Pasternak, a U.S. anthropologist, Janet Salaff, a Canadian sociologist, and Chinese sociologists studied four communities of Han who had moved outside the Great Wall to colonize the Inner Mongolian frontier (Inner Mongolia is part of China). The results of their study suggest that, despite strong pressures from the government, what changes or persists in a culture mainly reflects what is possible ecologically and economically. A tradition of intensive agriculture cannot persist in the absence of sufficient watering. The government's insistence on one child per family cannot withstand a family's need for more children.

Han farmers who crossed the Great Wall were searching for a better life. They found difficulties in climate and soil that forced many to return home. But many adjusted to the grasslands and remained. Some continued to depend on farming on the fringes of the grasslands. Others farther out on the grasslands became herders. The Han who switched to herding are now in many respects more like the native Mongol herders than like Han or Mongol farmers. The gender division of labor among the Han pastoralists became much sharper than among the Han farmers because men are often far away with the herds. Pastoralist children, not that useful in herding because mistakes can be very costly, are more likely than farm children to stay in school for a long time. Perhaps because of the greater usefulness of children on the farm, Han farm families have more children than Han pastoralists. But both groups have more than one child per family. Herdsmen are less likely than farmers to need cooperative labor, so Han pastoralists are more likely to live as an independent family living apart from kin than as an extended family (which was traditional). In short, the adjustment of the Han to the grasslands seems to be explained more by ecological requirements than by ethnic traditions.

Although an increasing number of Han have become more like Mongols in their pastoral adaptations, many Mongols have adopted an urban way of life and moved away from their pastoral life. The Chinese government was initially responsible for encouraging non-Mongols to move into Inner Mongolia, particularly into its new capital, Hohhot. At the same time, many Mongols moved from the grasslands and into the capital city. Chinese government policy was intended to make each non-Han ethnic group a minority in its traditional land, but the government paradoxically also tried to encourage minority ethnic pride in their traditional culture. So the city of Hohhot is filled with images of the traditional herding culture in its buildings and monuments.

As described by anthropologist William Jankowiak, who studied the Mongols in the capital city of Hohhot, the results were not what the Chinese government intended. In many ways, to be sure, the urban Mongols had abandoned their traditional culture and assimilated to the dominant Han culture. But we see the force of ecology more than the hand of tradition in the outcome. Many Mongols in the city no longer speak the Mongol language. Parents find it difficult to get children to speak Mongol when they live among Han. The scarcity of housing makes it difficult for the Mongols to form an ethnic enclave, or even live near kin as they did in the past. In contrast to life in the rural areas, which revolves around kinship, city life requires interacting with strangers as well as relatives. Indeed, nonkin are often more important to you than kin. As one person said to Jankowiak, "We hide from our cousins but not our friends."

Sources: Davis and Harrell 1993; Pasternak 2009; Jankowiak 2004.

who responded to an existing demand. Textile manufacturers were clamoring for such large quantities of spun yarn that cottage laborers, working with foot-operated spinning wheels, could not meet the demand. Hargreaves, realizing that prestige and financial rewards would come to the person who invented a method of spinning large quantities of yarn in a short time, set about the task and developed the spinning jenny.

But perceived needs and the economic rewards that may be given to the innovator do not explain why only some people innovate. We know relatively little about why some people are more innovative than others. The ability to innovate may depend in part on individual characteristics such as high intelligence and creativity. And creativity may be influenced by social conditions.

A study of innovation among Ashanti artist carvers in Ghana suggests that creativity is more likely in some socioeconomic groups than in others.[27] Some carvers produced only traditional designs; others departed from tradition and produced "new" styles of carving. Two groups were found to innovate the most—the wealthiest and the poorest carvers. These two groups of carvers may tolerate risk more than the middle socioeconomic group. Innovative carving entails some risk because it may take more time and it may not sell. Wealthy carvers can afford the risk, and they may gain some prestige as well as income if their innovation is appreciated. The poor are not doing well anyway, and they have little to lose by trying something new.

Some societies encourage innovativeness more than others, and this can vary substantially over time. Patricia Greenfield and her colleagues describe the changes in weaving in a Mayan community in the Zinacantán region of Chiapas, Mexico.[28] In 1969 and 1970, innovation was not valued. Rather, tradition was; there was the old "true way" to do everything, including how one dressed. There were only four simple weaving patterns, and virtually all males wore ponchos with the same pattern. By 1991, virtually no poncho was the same and the villagers had developed elaborate brocaded and embroidered designs. In a period of 20 years, innovation had increased dramatically.

Two other things had also changed. The economy was more commercialized; textiles as well as other items were now bought and sold. The other change was a shift to a much less directed teaching style. Earlier, mothers would give highly structured instruction to their daughters, often with "four hands" on the loom. Later, girls were allowed to learn more by themselves, by trial and error, and they produced more abstract and varied designs.

Who Adopts Innovations? Once someone discovers or invents something, there is still the question of whether others will adopt the innovation. Many researchers have studied the characteristics of "early adopters." Such individuals tend to be educated, high in social status, upwardly mobile, and, if they are property owners, have large farms and businesses. The individuals who most need technological improvements—those who are less well off—are generally the last to adopt innovations. The theory is that only the wealthy can afford to take the substantial risks associated with new ways of doing things. In periods of rapid technological change, therefore, the gap between rich and poor is likely to widen because the rich adopt innovations sooner, and benefit more from them, than the poor.[29]

Does this imply that the likelihood of adopting innovations is a simple function of how much wealth a possible adopter possesses? Not necessarily. Frank Cancian reviewed several studies and found that upper-middle-class individuals show more conservatism than lower-middle-class individuals. Cancian suggested that, when the risks are unknown, the lower-middle-class individuals are more receptive to innovation because they have less to lose. Later on, when the risks are better known—that is, as more people adopt the innovation—the upper-middle class catches up to the lower-middle class.[30] So the readiness to accept innovation, like the likelihood of creativity among Ashanti carvers, may not be related to socioeconomic position in a linear way.

The speed of accepting an innovation may depend partly on how new behaviors and ideas are typically

A Mayan woman from San Martin Jilotepeque working on a hip-strap loom. Designs became more individual and complex by the 1990s.

transmitted in a society. In particular, is a person exposed to many versus few "teachers"? If children learn most of what they know from their parents or from a relatively small number of elders, then innovation will be slow to spread throughout the society, and culture change is likely to be slow. Innovations may catch on more rapidly if individuals are exposed to various teachers and other "leaders" who can influence many in a relatively short time. And the more peers we have, the more we might learn from them.[31] Perhaps this is why the pace of change appears to be so quick today. In societies like our own, and increasingly in the industrializing world, it is likely that people learn in schools from teachers, from leaders in their specialties, and from peers.

Costs and Benefits An innovation that is technologically superior is not necessarily going to be adopted. There are costs as well as benefits for both individuals and large-scale industries. Take the computer keyboard. The keyboard used most often on computers today is called the QWERTY keyboard (named after the letters on the left side of the line of keys below the row of number keys). This keyboard was actually invented to slow typing speed down! Early typewriters had mechanical keys that jammed if the typist went too fast.[32] Computer keyboards don't have that problem, so an arrangement of keys that allowed faster typing would probably be better. Different keyboard configurations have been invented, but they haven't caught on. Most people probably would find it too hard or too time-consuming to learn a new style of typing, so the original style of keyboard persists.

In large-scale industries, technological innovations may be very costly to implement. A new product or process may require revamping a manufacturing or service facility and retraining workers. Before a decision is made to change, the costs of doing so are weighed against the potential benefits. If the market is expected to be large for a new product, the product is more likely to be produced. If the market is judged small, the benefits may not be sufficient inducement to change. Companies may also judge the value of an innovation by whether competitors could copy it. If the new innovation can be easily copied, the inventing company may not find the investment worthwhile. Although the market may be large, the inventing company may not be able to hold onto market share if other companies could produce the product quickly without having to invest in research and development.[33]

Diffusion

The source of new cultural elements in a society may also be another society. The process by which cultural elements are borrowed from another society and incorporated into the culture of the recipient group is called **diffusion.** Borrowing sometimes enables a group to bypass stages or mistakes in the development of a process or institution. For example, Germany was able to accelerate its program of industrialization in the 19th century because it was able to avoid some of the errors its English and Belgian competitors made by taking advantage of technological borrowing. Japan did the same somewhat later. Indeed, in recent years, some of the earliest industrialized countries have fallen behind their imitators in certain areas of production, such as automobiles, televisions, cameras, and computers.

In a well-known passage, Linton conveyed the far-reaching effects of diffusion by considering the first few hours in the day of an American man in the 1930s. This man

> . . . awakens in a bed built on a pattern which originated in the Near East but which was modified in northern Europe before it was transmitted to America. He throws back covers made from cotton, domesticated in India, or linen, domesticated in the Near East, or silk, the use of which was discovered in China. All of these materials have been spun and woven by processes invented in the Near East. . . . He takes off his pajamas, a garment invented in India, and washes with soap invented by the ancient

A Masai man in Kenya can call home or around the world from the plains of Kenya.

Gauls. He then shaves, a masochistic rite which seems to have derived from either Sumer or ancient Egypt.

Before going out for breakfast he glances through the window, made of glass invented in Egypt, and if it is raining puts on overshoes made of rubber discovered by the Central American Indians and takes an umbrella, invented in southeastern Asia. . . .

On his way to breakfast he stops to buy a paper paying for it with coins, an ancient Lydian invention. . . . His plate is made of a form of pottery invented in China. His knife is of steel, an alloy first made in southern India, his fork a medieval Italian invention, and his spoon a derivative of a Roman original. . . . After his fruit (African watermelon) and first coffee (an Abyssinian plant), . . . he may have the egg of a species of bird domesticated in Indo-China, or thin strips of the flesh of an animal domesticated in eastern Asia which have been salted and smoked by a process developed in northern Europe. . . .

While smoking (an American Indian habit), he reads the news of the day, imprinted in characters invented by the ancient Semites upon a material invented in China by a process invented in Germany. As he absorbs the accounts of foreign troubles he will, if he is a good conservative citizen, thank a Hebrew deity in an Indo-European language that he is 100 percent American.[34]

Patterns of Diffusion The following are the three basic patterns of diffusion: direct contact, intermediate contact, and stimulus diffusion.

1. **Direct contact.** Elements of a society's culture may first be taken up by neighboring societies and then gradually spread farther and farther afield. The spread of the use of paper (a sheet of interlaced fibers) is a good example of extensive diffusion by direct contact. The invention of paper is attributed to the Chinese Ts'ai Lun in A.D. 105. Within 50 years, paper was being made in many places in central China. Although the art of papermaking was kept secret for about 500 years, paper was distributed as a commodity to much of the Arab world through the markets at Samarkand. But when Samarkand was attacked by the Chinese in A.D. 751, a Chinese prisoner was forced to set up a paper mill. Paper manufacture then spread to the rest of the Arab world; it was first manufactured in Baghdad in A.D. 793, Egypt about A.D. 900, and Morocco about A.D. 1100. Papermaking was introduced as a commodity in Europe by Arab trade through Italian ports in the 12th century. The Moors built the first European paper mill in Spain about 1150. The technical knowledge then spread throughout Europe, with paper mills built in Italy in 1276, France in 1348, Germany in 1390, and England in 1494.[35] In general, the pattern of accepting the borrowed invention was the same in all cases: Paper was first imported as a luxury, then in ever-expanding quantities as a staple product. Finally, and usually within one to three centuries, local manufacture began.

2. **Intermediate contact.** Diffusion by intermediate contact occurs through the agency of third parties. Frequently, traders carry a cultural trait from the society that originated it to another group. As an example of diffusion through intermediaries, Phoenician traders spread the alphabet—which may have been invented by another Semitic group—to Greece. At times, soldiers serve as intermediaries in spreading a culture trait. European crusaders, such as the Knights Templar and the Knights of St. John, acted as intermediaries in two ways: They carried Christian culture to Muslim societies of North Africa and brought Arab culture back to Europe. In the 19th century, Western missionaries in all parts of the world encouraged natives to wear Western clothing. Hence, in Africa, the Pacific Islands, and elsewhere, native peoples can be found wearing shorts, suit jackets, shirts, ties, and other typically Western articles of clothing.

3. **Stimulus diffusion.** In stimulus diffusion, knowledge of a trait belonging to another culture stimulates the invention or development of a local equivalent. A classic example of stimulus diffusion is the Cherokee syllabic writing system created by a Native American named Sequoya so that his people could write down their language. Sequoya got the idea from his contact with Europeans. Yet, he did not adopt the English writing system; indeed, he did not even learn to write English. What he did was utilize some English alphabetic symbols, alter others, and invent new ones. All the symbols he used represented Cherokee syllables and in no way echoed English alphabetic usage. In other words, Sequoya took English alphabetic ideas and gave them a new, Cherokee form. The stimulus originated with Europeans; the result was peculiarly Cherokee.

The Selective Nature of Diffusion Although there is a temptation to view the dynamics of diffusion as similar to a stone sending concentric ripples over still water, this would be an oversimplification of the way diffusion actually occurs. Not all cultural traits are borrowed as readily as the ones we have mentioned, nor do they usually expand in neat, ever-widening circles. Rather, diffusion is a selective process. The Japanese, for instance, accepted much from Chinese culture, but they also rejected many traits. Rhymed tonal poetry, civil service examinations, and foot binding, which the Chinese favored, were never adopted in Japan. The poetry form was unsuited to the structure of the Japanese language; the examinations were unnecessary in view of the entrenched power of the Japanese aristocracy; and foot binding was repugnant to a people who abhorred body mutilation of any sort.

Not only would we expect societies to reject items from other societies that are repugnant, we would also expect them to reject ideas and technology that do not satisfy some psychological, social, or cultural need. After all, people are not sponges; they don't automatically soak up the things around them. If they did, the amount of cultural variation in the world would be extremely small, which is clearly not the case. Diffusion is also selective because cultural traits differ in the extent to which they can be communicated. Elements of material culture, such as mechanical processes and techniques, and other traits, such as physical sports and the like, are not especially difficult to demonstrate. Consequently, they are accepted or rejected on their merits. But the moment we move out of the material context, we encounter real difficulties. Linton identified the problem in these words:

> Although it is quite possible to describe such an element of culture as the ideal pattern for marriage . . . it is much less complete than a description of basketmaking. . . . The most thorough verbalization has difficulty in conveying the series of associations and conditioned emotional responses which are attached to this pattern [marriage] and which gave it meaning and vitality within our own society. . . . This is even more true of those concepts which . . . find no direct expression in behavior aside from verbalization. There is a story of an educated Japanese who after a long discussion on the nature of the Trinity with a European friend . . . burst out with: "Oh, I see now, it is a committee."[36]

Finally, diffusion is selective because the overt form of a particular trait, rather than its function or meaning, frequently seems to determine how the trait will be received. For example, the enthusiasm in women for bobbed hair (short haircuts) that swept through much of North America in the 1920s never caught on among the Native Americans of northwestern California. To many women of European ancestry, short hair was a symbolic statement of their freedom. To Native American women, who traditionally cut their hair short when in mourning, it was a reminder of death.[37]

In the process of diffusion, then, we can identify a number of different patterns. We know that cultural borrowing is selective rather than automatic, and we can describe how a particular borrowed trait has been modified by the recipient culture. But our current knowledge does not allow us to specify when one or another of these outcomes will occur, under what conditions diffusion will occur, and why it occurs the way it does.

Acculturation

On the surface, the process of change called **acculturation** seems to include much of what we have discussed under the label of diffusion, because acculturation refers to the changes that occur when different cultural groups come into intensive contact. As in diffusion, the source of new cultural items is the other society. But more often than not, anthropologists use the term *acculturation* to describe a situation in which one of the societies in contact is much more powerful than the other. Thus, acculturation can be seen as a process of extensive cultural borrowing in the context of superordinate-subordinate relations between societies.[38] There is probably always some borrowing both ways, but generally the subordinate or less powerful society borrows the most.

External pressure for culture change can take various forms. In its most direct form—conquest or colonialization—the dominant group uses force or the threat of force to try to bring about culture change in the other group. For example, in the Spanish conquest of Mexico, the conquerors forced many of the native groups to accept Catholicism. Although such direct force is not always exerted in conquest situations, dominated peoples often have little choice but to change. Examples of such indirectly forced change abound in the history of Native Americans in the United States. Although the federal government made few direct attempts to force people to adopt American culture, it did drive many native groups from their lands, thereby obliging them to give up many aspects of their traditional ways of life. To survive, they had no choice but to adopt many of the dominant society's traits. When Native American children were required to go to schools, which taught the dominant society's values, the process was accelerated.

A subordinate society may acculturate to a dominant society even in the absence of direct or indirect force. Perceiving that members of the dominant society enjoy more secure living conditions, the dominated people may identify with the dominant culture in the hope that they will be able to share some of its benefits by doing so. Or, they may elect to adopt cultural elements from the dominant society because they perceive that the new element has advantages. For example, in Arctic areas, many Inuit and Lapp groups seemed eager to replace dog sleds with snowmobiles without any coercion.[39] There is evidence that the Inuit weighed the advantages and disadvantages of the snowmobile versus the dog sled and that its adoption was gradual. Similarly, rifles were seen as a major technological improvement, increasing the success rate in hunting, but the Inuit did not completely abandon their former ways of hunting. More recently the Inuit are trying out GPS devices for navigating.[40]

Acculturation processes vary considerably depending upon the wishes of the more powerful society, the attitudes of the less powerful, and whether there is any choice. More powerful societies do not always want individuals from another culture to assimilate or "melt into" the dominant culture completely; instead, they may prefer and even actively promote a *multicultural* society. Multiculturalism can be voluntary or it may arise out of deliberate segregation. Then too, even though the less powerful group may be pressured by the dominant group to acquire some of their culture traits, they may resist or even reject those cultural elements, at least for a considerable length of time.

Many millions of people, however, never had a chance to acculturate after contact with Europeans. They simply died, sometimes directly at the hands of the conquerors, but probably more often as a result of the new diseases the Europeans inadvertently brought with them. Depopulation because of measles, smallpox, and tuberculosis was particularly common in North and South America and on the islands of the Pacific. Those areas had previously been isolated from contact with Europeans and from the diseases of that continuous landmass we call the Old World—Europe, Asia, and Africa.[41] (See the DK Map

applied anthropology

Why the Bedouin Do Not Readily Settle Down

Most countries of the world today want to "develop." They want to increase their crop yields and their exports, build major roads and irrigation projects, and industrialize. Anthropologists interested in development have pointed out that many development schemes have failed in part because they do not adequately consider the culture of the people whose lives they affect. Thus, the international agencies that lend money have increasingly turned for advice to anthropologists to help plan and evaluate development projects.

Governments often view traditional ways of life negatively and fail to recognize that the old ways of life may be adaptive. Because culture is integrated, people cannot be expected to change an aspect of culture that is central to their lives. It is not that people do not want to change, but change is unlikely if it doesn't integrate well with other aspects of their lifestyle.

In many countries of the Middle East, governments want the Bedouin—people who herd animals over vast stretches of semiarid grassland—to settle down. Governments have tried to settle them by force or by enticements, but settlement schemes have failed time after time. In retrospect, such failures are not surprising. The Bedouin continue to try to herd animals near newly constructed settlements, but such grazing often results in human-made deserts near the settlements, so the settlements are abandoned. The traditional Bedouin pattern of herding animals depends on mobility. When the animals eat the tops of the grasses in a particular place, the people need to move on. When water starts drying up in one location, the herds need to be moved. Overgrazing near a settlement and plowing land in a semiarid environment can lead to quick erosion of the soil and the loss of plant cover. After the failure of many settlement schemes, governments may try to encourage a return to more traditional methods of grazing.

It is not that the Bedouin are reluctant to change in all respects. Many Bedouin readily gave up relying on camels for transport in favor of trucks. Trucks are a modern adaptation, yet they still allow mobility. Now the Bedouin are able to get water from wells and transport water to their animals by truck. The adoption of trucks led to other changes in Bedouin life. Small animals can be more readily transported to new pastures by truck, so many Bedouin have given up their dependence on camels and shifted to sheep and goat herding. Money is required to buy trucks and pay for gasoline and repairs, so more time is spent working for wages in temporary jobs.

In the 1980s, Dawn Chatty was asked by the government of the Middle Eastern country of Oman to help design a project to extend basic social services to the Bedouin without coercing them to alter their way of life. It isn't often that governments fund in-depth studies to understand the needs of the people being affected, but Chatty was able to persuade the Oman government that such a study was necessary as a first step. With United Nations funding, she began a study of the Harasiis pastoralists of southern Oman to evaluate their needs. The government wanted some action right away, so the project soon incorporated a mobile health unit that could begin a program of primary care as well as immunization against measles, whooping cough, and polio. After a period of evaluation, the project team also recommended an annual distribution of tents, the establishment of dormitories so children could live at schools, a new system of water delivery, and veterinary and marketing assistance.

Unfortunately, a development project often ends without any guarantee that health and other services will continue to be provided. As Chatty found out, long-term change is not as easy to achieve as short-term change. Along with other applied anthropologists, she continues to push for what Michael Cernea called "putting people first."

Sources: Chatty 1996; Cernea 1991, 7.

"Biological Exchanges" in the back of the book.) The story of Ishi, the last surviving member of a group of Native Americans in California called the Yahi, is a moving testimonial to the frequently tragic effect of contact with Europeans. In the space of 22 years, the Yahi population was reduced from several hundred to near zero. The historical record on this episode of depopulation suggests that European Americans murdered 30 to 50 Yahi for every European American murdered, but perhaps 60 percent of the Yahi died in the 10 years following their initial exposure to European diseases.[42]

Nowadays, many powerful nations—and not just Western ones—may seem to be acting in more humanitarian ways to improve the life of previously subjugated as well as other "developing" peoples. For better or worse, these programs, however, are still forms of external pressure. The tactic used may be persuasion rather than force, but most of the programs are nonetheless designed to bring about acculturation in the direction of the dominant societies' cultures. For example, the introduction of formal schooling cannot help but instill new values that may contradict traditional cultural patterns. Even health care programs may alter traditional ways of life by undermining the authority of shamans and other leaders and by increasing population beyond the number that can be supported in traditional ways. Confinement to "reservations" or other kinds of direct force are not the only ways a dominant society can bring about acculturation.

The process of acculturation also applies to immigrants, most of whom, at least nowadays, choose to leave one country for another. Immigrants are almost always a minority in the new country and therefore are in a subordinate position. If the immigrant's culture changes, it is almost always in the direction of the dominant culture. Immigrant groups vary considerably in the degree and speed with which they adopt the new culture and the social roles of the new society in which they live. An important area of research is explaining the variation in acculturation and assimilation. (*Assimilation* is a concept very similar to acculturation, but *assimilation* is a term more often used by sociologists to describe the process by which individuals acquire the social roles and culture of the dominant group.) Why do some immigrant groups acculturate or assimilate faster than others? As we will see in the chapter on language, a comparative study by Robert Schrauf assessed the degree to which immigrant groups coming to North America retained their native language over time. He looked at whether they lived in tightly knit communities, retained religious rituals, had separate schools and special festivals, visited their homeland, did not intermarry, or worked with others of their ethnic group. All of these factors might be expected to lead to retention of the native language (and presumably other cultural patterns), but only living in tightly knit communities and retaining religious rituals strongly predicted retaining the native language over a long period of time.[43]

CULTURE CHANGE AND ADAPTATION

Earlier in this chapter when we discussed the fact that culture is patterned, we indicated that adaptation to the environment is one reason why certain culture traits will cluster, because more than one trait is likely to be *adaptive* in a particular environment. We make the assumption that most of the customary behaviors of a culture are probably *adaptive*, or at least not maladaptive, in that environment. Even though customs are learned and not genetically inherited, cultural adaptation may resemble biological adaptation in one major respect. The frequency of certain genetic alternatives is likely to increase over time if those genetic traits increase their carriers' chances of survival and reproduction. Similarly, the frequency of a new learned behavior will increase over time and become customary in a population if the people with that behavior are most likely to survive and reproduce.

One of the most important differences between cultural evolution and genetic evolution is that individuals often can decide whether or not to accept and follow the way their parents behave or think, whereas they cannot decide whether or not to inherit certain genes. When enough individuals change their behavior and beliefs, we say that the culture has changed. Therefore, it is possible for culture change to occur much more rapidly than genetic change.

A dramatic example of intentional cultural change was the adoption and later elimination of the custom of *sepaade* among the Rendille, a pastoral population that herds camels, goats, and sheep in the desert in northern Kenya. According to the *sepaade* tradition, some women had to wait to marry until all their brothers were married. These women could well have been over 40 by the time they married. The Rendille say that this tradition was a result of intense warfare between the Rendille and the Borana during the mid-19th century. Attacked by Borana on horseback, the male warriors had to leave their camels unattended and the frightened camels fled. The daughters of one male age-set were appointed to look after the camels, and the *sepaade* tradition developed. In 1998, long after warfare with the Borana ceased, the elders decided to free the *sepaade* from their obligation to postpone their own marriages. Interviews with the Rendille in the 1990s revealed that many individuals were fully aware of the reason for the tradition in the first place. Now, they said, there was peace, so there was no longer any reason for the *sepaade* tradition to continue.[44]

The adoption of the *sepaade* is an example of culture change in a changing environment. But what if the environment is stable? Is culture change more or less likely? Robert Boyd and Peter Richerson have shown mathematically that, when the environment is relatively stable and individual mistakes are costly, staying with customary modes of behavior (usually transmitted by parents) is probably more adaptive than changing.[45] But what happens when the environment, particularly the social environment, is changing? There are plenty of examples in the modern world: People have to migrate to new places for work; medical care leads to increased population so that land is scarcer; people have had land taken away from them and are forced to make do with less land; and so on.

It is particularly when circumstances change that individuals are likely to try ideas or behaviors that are different from those of their parents. Most people would want to adopt behaviors that are more suited to their present circumstances, but how do they know which behaviors are better? There are various ways to find out. One way is by experimenting, trying out various new behaviors. Another way is to evaluate the experiments of others. If a person who tries a new technique seems successful, we would expect that person to be imitated, just as we would expect people to stick with new behaviors they have personally tried and found successful. Finally, one might choose to do what most people in the new situation decide to do.[46]

Why one choice rather than another? In part, the choice may be a function of the cost or risk of the innovation. It is relatively easy, for example, to find out how long it takes to cut down a tree with an introduced steel ax, as compared with a stone ax. Not surprisingly, innovations such as a steel ax catch on relatively quickly because comparison is easy and the results clear-cut. But what if the risk is very great? Suppose the innovation involves adopting a whole new way of farming that you have never practiced before. You can try it, but you might not have any food if you fail. As we discussed earlier, risky innovations are likely to be tried only by those individuals who can afford the risk. Other people may then evaluate their success and adopt the new strategy if it looks promising. Similarly, if you migrate

Revolutionary leaders are often from high-status backgrounds. Here we see a depiction of Patrick Henry giving his famous speech to the aristocratic landowners in the Virginia General Assembly on March 23, 1775. Urging the Virginians to fight the British, Henry said that the choice was "liberty or death."

Source: Currier & Ives, "Give Me Liberty or Give Me Death!", 1775. Lithograph, 1876. c. The Granger Collection, New York.

to a new area, say, from a high-rainfall area to a drier one, it may pay to look around to see what most people in the new place do; after all, the people in the drier area probably have customs that are adaptive for that environment.

We can expect, then, that the choices individuals make may often be adaptive ones. But it is important to note that adopting an innovation from someone in one's own society or borrowing an innovation from another society is not always or necessarily beneficial, either in the short or the long run. First, people may make mistakes in judgment, especially when some new behavior seems to satisfy a physical need. Why, for example, have smoking and drug use diffused so widely even though they are likely to reduce a person's chances of survival? Second, even if people are correct in their short-term judgment of benefit, they may be wrong in their judgment about long-run benefit. A new crop may yield more than the old crop for five consecutive years, but the new crop may fail miserably in the sixth year because of lower-than-normal rainfall or because the new crop depleted soil nutrients. Third, people may be forced by the more powerful to change, with few if any benefits for themselves.

Whatever the motives for humans to change their behavior, the theory of natural selection suggests that new behavior is not likely to become cultural or remain cultural over generations if it has harmful reproductive consequences, just as a genetic mutation with harmful consequences is not likely to become frequent in a population.[47] Still, we know of many examples of culture change that seem maladaptive—the switch to bottle-feeding rather than nursing infants, which may spread infection because contaminated water is used, or the adoption of alcoholic beverages, which may lead to alcoholism and early death.

Revolution

Certainly the most drastic and rapid way a culture can change is as a result of **revolution**—replacement, usually violent, of a country's rulers. Historical records, as well as our daily newspapers, indicate that people frequently rebel

against established authority. Rebellions, if they occur, almost always occur in state societies, where there is a distinct ruling elite. They take the form of struggles between rulers and ruled, between conquerors and conquered, or between representatives of an external colonial power and segments of the native society. Rebels do not always succeed in overthrowing their rulers, so rebellions do not always result in revolutions. And even successful rebellions do not always result in culture change; the individual rulers may change, but customs or institutions may not. The sources of revolution may be mostly internal, as in the French Revolution, or partly external, as in the Russian-supported 1948 revolution in Czechoslovakia and the United States-supported 1973 revolution against President Allende in Chile.

The American War of Independence toward the end of the 18th century is a good example of a colonial rebellion, the success of which was at least partly a result of foreign intervention. The American rebellion was a war of neighboring colonies against the greatest imperial power of the time, Great Britain. In the 19th century and continuing into the middle and later years of the 20th century, there would be many other wars of independence, in Latin America, Europe, Asia, and Africa. We don't always remember that the American rebellion was the first of these anti-imperialist wars in modern times, and the model for many that followed. And just like many of the most recent liberation movements, the American rebellion was also part of a larger worldwide war, involving people from many rival nations. Thirty thousand German-speaking soldiers fought, for pay, on the British side; an army and navy from France fought on the American side. There were volunteers from other European countries, including Denmark, Holland, Poland, and Russia.

One of these volunteers was a man named Kosciusko from Poland, which at the time was being divided between Prussia and Russia. Kosciusko helped win a major victory for the Americans, and subsequently directed the fortification of what later became the American training school for army officers, West Point. After the war, he returned to Poland and led a rebellion against the Russians, which was only briefly successful. In 1808, he published the *Manual on the Maneuvers of Horse Artillery*, which was used for many years by the American army. When he died, he left money to buy freedom and education for American slaves. The executor of Kosciusko's will was Thomas Jefferson.

As in many revolutions, those who were urging revolution were considered "radicals." At a now-famous debate in Virginia in 1775, delegates from each colony met at a Continental Congress. Patrick Henry put forward a resolution to prepare for defense against the British armed forces. The motion barely passed, by a vote of 65 to 60. Henry's speech is now a part of American folklore. He rose to declare that it was insane not to oppose the British and that he was not afraid to test the strength of the colonies against Great Britain. Others might hesitate, he said, but he would have "liberty or death." The "radicals" who supported Henry's resolution included many aristocratic landowners, two of whom, George Washington and Thomas Jefferson, became the first and third occupants of the highest political office in what became the United States of America.[48]

Not all peoples who are suppressed, conquered, or colonialized eventually rebel against established authority. Why this is so, and why rebellions and revolts are not always successful in bringing about culture change, are still open questions. But some possible answers have been investigated. One historian who examined the classic revolutions of the past, including the American, French, and Russian revolutions, suggested some conditions that may give rise to rebellion and revolution:

1. **Loss of prestige of established authority,** often as a result of the failure of foreign policy, financial difficulties, dismissals of popular ministers, or alteration of popular policies. France in the 18th century lost three major international conflicts, with disastrous results for its diplomatic standing and internal finances. Russian society was close to military and economic collapse in 1917, after three years of World War I.

2. **Threat to recent economic improvement.** In France, as in Russia, those sections of the population (professional classes and urban workers) whose economic fortunes had only shortly before taken an upward swing were "radicalized" by unexpected setbacks, such as steeply rising food prices and unemployment. The same may be said for the American colonies on the brink of their rebellion against Great Britain.

3. **Indecisiveness of government,** as exemplified by lack of consistent policy, which gives the impression of being controlled by, rather than in control of, events. The frivolous arrogance of Louis XVI's regime and the bungling of George III's prime minister, Lord North, with respect to the problems of the American colonies are examples.

4. **Loss of support of the intellectual class.** Such a loss deprived the prerevolutionary governments of France and Russia of any avowed philosophical support and led to their unpopularity with the literate public.[49]

The classic revolutions of the past occurred in countries that were industrialized only incipiently at best. For the most part, the same is true of the rebellions and revolutions in recent years; they have occurred mostly in countries we call "developing." The evidence from a worldwide survey of developing countries suggests that rebellions have tended to occur where the ruling classes depended mostly on the produce or income from land, and therefore were resistant to demands for reform from the rural classes that worked the land. In such agricultural economies, the rulers are not likely to yield political power or give greater economic returns to the workers, because to do so would eliminate the basis (landownership) of the rulers' wealth and power.[50]

Finally, a particularly interesting question is why revolutions sometimes, perhaps even usually, fail to measure up to the high hopes of those who initiate them. When rebellions succeed in replacing the ruling elite, the result is often the institution of a military dictatorship even more restrictive and repressive than the government that existed before. The new ruling establishment may merely substitute one set of repressions for another, rather than bring any real change to the nation. On the other hand, some revolutions have resulted in fairly drastic overhauls of societies.

The idea of revolution has been one of the central myths and inspirations of many groups both in the past and in the present. The colonial empire building of countries such as England and France created a worldwide situation in which rebellion became nearly inevitable. In numerous technologically underdeveloped lands, which have been exploited by more powerful countries for their natural resources and cheap labor, a deep resentment has often developed against the foreign ruling classes or their local clients. Where the ruling classes, native or foreign, refuse to be responsive to those feelings, rebellion becomes the only alternative. In many areas, it has become a way of life.

GLOBALIZATION: PROBLEMS AND OPPORTUNITIES

Investment capital, people, and ideas are moving around the world at an ever faster rate.[51] Transportation now allows people and goods to circle the globe in days; telecommunications and the Internet make it possible to send a message around the world in seconds and minutes. Economic exchange is enormously more global and transnational. The word **globalization** is often used nowadays to refer to "the massive flow of goods, people, information, and capital across huge areas of the earth's surface."[52] The process of globalization has resulted in the worldwide spread of cultural features, particularly in the domain of economics and international trade. We buy from the same companies (that have factories all over the world), we sell our products and services for prices that are set by world market forces. We can eat pizza, hamburgers, curry, or sushi in most urban centers. In some ways, cultures are changing in similar directions. They have become more

Television has dramatically enhanced world communication. We can see what's happening on the other side of the world almost in real time. People in Niger watch television powered by another important invention, solar panels.

commercial, more urban, and more international. The job has become more important, and kinship less important, as people travel to and work in other countries, and return just periodically to their original homes. Ideas about democracy, the rights of the individual, and alternative medical practices and religions have become more widespread; people in many countries of the world watch the same TV shows, wear similar fashions, and listen to the same or similar music. In short, people are increasingly sharing behaviors and beliefs with people in other cultures, and the cultures of the world are less and less things "with edges," as Paul Durrenberger says.[53]

Globalization began in earnest about A.D. 1500, with exploration by and expansion of Western societies.[54] (See the DK Map "European Expansion in the 16th century in the back of the book.) In the last few decades, globalization has greatly intensified such that there are very few places in the world that have not been affected.[55] Thus, much of the culture change in the modern world has been externally induced, if not forced. This is not to say that cultures are changing now only because of external pressures; but externally induced changes have been the changes that anthropologists and other social scientists most frequently study. Most of the external pressures have come from Western societies, but not all. Far Eastern societies, such as Japan and China, have also stimulated culture change. And the expansion of Islamic societies after the 8th century A.D. made for an enormous amount of culture change in the Near East, Africa, Europe, and Asia.

But diffusion of a culture trait does not mean that it is incorporated in exactly the same way, and the spread of certain products and activities through globalization does not mean that change happens in the same way everywhere. For example, the spread of multinational fast-food restaurants like McDonald's or Kentucky Fried Chicken has come to symbolize globalization. But the behavior of the Japanese in such restaurants is quite different from behavior in the United States. Perhaps the most surprising difference is that the Japanese in McDonald's actually have more familial intimacy and sharing than in more traditional restaurants. We imagine that establishments like

McDonald's promote fast eating. But Japan has long had fast food—noodle shops at train stations, street vendors, and boxed lunches. Sushi, which is usually ordered in the United States at a sit-down restaurant, is usually served in Japan at a bar with a conveyor belt—individuals only need to pluck off the wanted dish as it goes by. Observations at McDonald's in Japan suggest that mothers typically order food for the family while the father spends time with the children at a table, a rare event since fathers often work long hours and cannot get home for dinner often. Food, such as French fries, is typically shared by the family. Even burgers and drinks are passed around, with many people taking a bite or a sip. Such patterns typify long-standing family practices. Japan has historically borrowed food, such as the Chinese noodle soup, now called ramen. Indeed, in a survey, ramen was listed as the most representative Japanese food. The burger was the second most-often listed. McDonald's has become Japanese—the younger generation does not even know that McDonald's is a foreign company—they think it is Japanese.[56]

Globalization is not new. The world has been global and interdependent since the 16th century.[57] What we currently call "globalization" is a more widespread version of what we used to call by various other names—diffusion, acculturation, colonialism, imperialism, or commercialization. But globalization is now on a much grander scale; enormous amounts of international investment fuel world trade. Shifts in the world marketplace may drastically affect a country's well-being more than ever before. For example, 60 percent of Pakistan's industrial employment is in textile and apparel manufacturing, but serious unemployment resulted when that manufacturing was crippled by restrictive American import policies and fears about war between India and Afghanistan.[58]

As we have seen in this chapter, there are many negative effects of colonialism, imperialism, and globalization. Many native peoples in many places lost their land and have been forced to work for inadequate wages in mines and plantations and factories that foreign capitalists own. Frequently, there is undernutrition if not starvation. Global travel has resulted in the quick spread of diseases such as HIV and severe acute respiratory syndrome (SARS), and increasing deforestation has led to a spread of malaria.[59] But are there any positive consequences? The "human development indicators" collected by the United Nations suggest an improvement in many respects, including increases in life expectancy and literacy in most countries. Much of the improvement in life expectancy is undoubtedly due to the spread of medicines developed in the advanced economies of the West. There is generally less warfare as colonial powers enforced pacification within the colonies that later became independent states. Most important, perhaps, has been the growth of middle classes all over the world, whose livelihoods depend on globalizing commerce. The middle classes in many countries have become strong and numerous enough to pressure governments for democratic reforms and the reduction of injustice.

World trade is the primary engine of economic development. Per capita income is increasing. Forty years ago, the countries of Asia were among the poorest countries in the world in terms of per capita income. Since then, because of their involvement in world trade, their incomes have risen enormously. In 1960, South Korea was as poor as India. Now its per capita income is 20 times higher than India's. Singapore is an even more dramatic example. In the late 1960s, its economy was a disaster. Today, its per capita income is higher than Britain's.[60] Mexico used to be a place where North Americans built factories to produce garments for the North American market. Now its labor is no longer so cheap. But because it has easy access to the North American market and because its plentiful labor is acquiring the necessary skills, Mexico is now seeing the development of high-tech manufacturing with decent salaries.[61]

There is world trade also in people. Many countries of the world now export people to other countries. Mexico has done so for a long time. Virtually every family in a Bangladesh village depends on someone who works overseas and sends money home. Without those remittances, many would face starvation. The government encourages people to go abroad to work. Millions of people from Bangladesh are now overseas on government-sponsored work contracts.[62]

But does a higher per capita income mean that life has improved generally in a country? Not necessarily. As we will see in the chapter on social stratification, inequality within countries can increase with technological improvements because the rich often benefit the most. In addition, economic wealth is increasingly concentrated in a relatively small number of countries. Obviously, then, not everyone is better off even if most countries are doing better on average. Poverty has become more common as countries have become more unequal.

Although many of the changes associated with globalization seem to be driven by the economic and political power of the richer countries, the movement of ideas, art, music, and food is more of a two-way process. A large part of that process involves the migration of people who bring their culture with them. As we will see in the box titled "Migrants and Immigrants," movements of people have played a large role in the entry of food such as tortilla chips and salsa, sushi, and curries into the United States, music like reggae and many types of dance music from Latin America, and African carvings and jewelry such as beaded necklaces. Recently there has even been increased interest in acquiring indigenous knowledge of plants, the knowledge of indigenous healers, and learning about shamanistic trances. As indigenous knowledge comes to be viewed as potentially valuable, shamans have been able to speak out on national and international issues. In Brazil, shamans have organized to speak out against "biopiracy"—what is perceived as the unethical appropriation of biological knowledge for commercial purposes. In a more globalized world, shamans and other indigenous activists can be heard by more people than ever before. Despite the fact that indigenous people constitute less than one percent of the Brazilian population, some activist groups have been able to keep in touch with international environmentalists, using tape recorders and video cameras to convey information about their local situation.[63]

It is probably not possible to go back to a time when societies were not so dependent on each other, not so interconnected through world trade, not so dependent on commercial exchange. Even those who are most upset with globalization find it difficult to imagine that it is possible to return to a less connected world. For better or worse, the world is interconnected and will remain so. The question now is whether the average economic improvements in countries will eventually translate into economic improvements for most individuals.

ETHNOGENESIS: THE EMERGENCE OF NEW CULTURES

Many of the processes that we have discussed—the expansion and domination by the West and other powerful nations, the deprivation of the ability of peoples to earn their livelihoods by traditional means, the imposition of schools or other methods to force acculturation, the attempts to convert people to other religions, and globalization—have led to profound changes in culture. But if culture change in the modern world has made cultures more alike in some ways, it has not eliminated cultural differences. Indeed, people are still very variable culturally from one place to the next. New differences have also emerged. Often, in the aftermath of violent events such as depopulation, relocation, enslavement, and genocide by dominant powers, deprived peoples have created new cultures in a process called **ethnogenesis**.[64]

Some of the most dramatic examples of ethnogenesis come from areas where escaped slaves (called Maroons) created new cultures. Maroon societies emerged in the past few hundred years in a variety of New World locations, from the United States to the West Indies and northern parts of South America. One of the new cultures, now known as Aluku, emerged when slaves fled from coastal plantations in Suriname to the swampy interior country

migrants and immigrants

Increasing Cultural Diversity within the Countries of the World

The modern world is culturally diverse in two ways. There are native cultures in every part of the world, and today most countries have people from different cultures who have arrived relatively recently. Recent arrivals may be migrants coming for temporary work, or they may be refugees, forced by persecution or genocide to migrate, or they may be immigrants who voluntarily come into a new country. Parts of populations have moved away from their native places since the dawn of humanity. The first modern-looking humans moved out of Africa only in the last 100,000 years. People have been moving ever since. The people we call Native Americans were actually the first to come to the New World; most anthropologists think they came from northeast Asia. In the last 200 years, the United States and Canada have experienced extensive influxes of people (see the DK map "Migration in the 19th Century".) As is commonly said, they have become nations of migrants and immigrants, and Native Americans are now vastly outnumbered by the people and their descendants who came from Europe, Africa, Asia, Latin America, and elsewhere. North America not only has native and regional subcultures, but also ethnic, religious, and occupational subcultures, each with its own distinctive set of culture traits. Thus, North American culture is partly a "melting pot" and partly a mosaic of cultural diversity. Many of us, not just anthropologists, like this diversity. We like to go to ethnic restaurants regularly. We like salsa, sushi, and spaghetti. We compare and enjoy the different geographic varieties of coffee. We like music and artists from other countries. We often choose to wear clothing that may have been manufactured halfway around the world. We like all of these things not only because they may be affordable. We like them mostly, perhaps, because they are different.

Many of the population movements in the world today, as in the past, are responses to persecution and war. The word *diaspora* is often used nowadays to refer to these major dispersions. Most were and are involuntary; people are fleeing danger and death. But not always. Scholars distinguish different types of diaspora, including "victim," "labor," "trade," and "imperial" diasporas. The Africans who were sold into slavery, the Armenians who fled genocide in the early 20th century, the Jews who fled persecution and genocide in various places over the centuries, the Palestinians who fled to the West Bank, Gaza, Jordan, and Lebanon in the mid-20th century, and the Rwandans who fled genocide toward the end of the 20th century may have mostly been victims. The Chinese, Italians, and the Poles may have mostly moved to take advantage of job opportunities, the Lebanese to trade, and the British to extend and service their empire. Often these categories overlap; population movements can and have occurred for more than one reason. Some of the recent diasporas are less one-way than in the past. People are more "transnational," just as economics and politics are more "globalized." The new global communications have facilitated the retention of homeland connections—socially, economically, and politically. Some diasporic communities play an active role in the politics of their homelands, and some nation-states have begun to recognize their far-flung emigrants as important constituencies.

As cultural anthropologists increasingly study migrant, refugee, and immigrant groups, they focus on how the groups have adapted their cultures to new surroundings, what they have retained, how they relate to the homeland, how they have developed an ethnic consciousness, and how they relate to other minority groups and the majority culture.

Sources: M. Ember et al. 2005; Levinson and M. Ember 1997.

---

along the Cottica River. After a war with the Dutch colonists, this particular group moved to French Guiana. The escaped slaves, originating from widely varying cultures in Africa or born on Suriname plantations, organized themselves into autonomous communities with military headmen.[65] They practiced slash-and-burn cultivation, with women doing most of the work. Although settlements shifted location as a way of evading enemies, coresidence in a community and collective ownership of land became important parts of the emerging identities. Communities took on the names of the specific plantations from which their leaders had escaped. Principles of inheritance through the female line began to develop, and full-fledged matriclans became the core of each village. Each village had its own shrine, the *faaka tiki*, where residents invoked the clan ancestors, as well as a special house where the deceased were brought to be honored and feted before being taken to the forest for burial. Clans also inherited avenging spirits with whom they could communicate through mediums.

The Aluku case is a clear example of ethnogenesis because the culture did not exist 350 years ago. It emerged and was created by people trying to adapt to circumstances not of their own making. In common with other cases of emerging ethnic identity, the Aluku came not only to share new patterns of behavior but also to see themselves as having a common origin (a common ancestor), a shared history, and a common religion.[66]

The emergence of the Seminole in Florida is another case of ethnogenesis. The early settlers who moved to what is now Florida and later became known as Seminole largely derived from the Lower Creek Kawita chiefdom.

Osceola, a Seminole chief, born of a British father and a Creek mother. He led his people against the settlers in the Seminole Wars but was captured and died in confinement at Fort Moultrie, South Carolina.

The Kawita chiefdom, like other southeastern Muskogean chiefdoms, was a large, complex, multiethnic paramount chiefdom. Its ruler, Kawita, relied on allegiance and tribute from outlying districts; ritual and linguistic hegemony was imposed by the ruler.[67]

A combination of internal divisions among the Lower Creek, vacant land in northern Florida, and weak Spanish control over northern Florida apparently prompted dissidents to move away and settle in three different areas in Florida. Three new chiefdoms were established, essentially similar to those the settlers left and still under the supposed control of Kawita.[68] But the three chiefdoms began to act together under the leadership of Tonapi, the Talahassi chief. After 1780, over a period of 40 or so years, the three Seminole chiefdoms formally broke with Kawita. Not only was geographic separation a factor, but the political and economic interests of the Creek Confederacy and of the Seminole had diverged. For example, the Creek supported neutrality in the American Revolution, but the Seminole took the side of the British. During this time, the British encouraged slaves to escape by promising freedom in Florida. These Maroon communities allied themselves with the emerging Seminole. The composition of the Seminole population again changed dramatically after the War of 1812 and the Creek War of 1814.[69] First, a large number of Creek refugees, mostly Upper Creek Talapusa (who spoke a different Muskogean language), became Seminole. Second, the Seminole ranks were also expanded by a large number of escaped slaves and Maroons who fled when the Americans destroyed a British fort in 1816. Larger-scale political events continued to influence Seminole history. When the Americans conquered Florida, they insisted on dealing with one unified Seminole council, they removed the Seminole to a reserve in Florida, and later, after the second Seminole war, removed most of them to Oklahoma.[70]

It would seem from this and other cases that cultural identities can be shaped and reshaped by political and economic processes.

CULTURAL DIVERSITY IN THE FUTURE

Measured in terms of travel time, the world today is much smaller than it has ever been. It is possible now to fly halfway around the globe in the time it took people less than a century ago to travel to the next state. In the realm of communication, the world is even smaller. We can talk to someone on the other side of the globe in a matter of minutes, we can send that person a message (by fax or Internet) in seconds, and through television we can see live coverage of events in that person's country. More and more people are drawn into the world market economy, buying and selling similar things and, as a consequence, altering the patterns of their lives in sometimes similar ways. Still, although modern transportation and communication facilitate the rapid spread of some cultural characteristics to all parts of the globe, it is highly unlikely that all parts of the world will end up the same culturally. Cultures are bound to retain some of their original characteristics or develop distinctive new adaptations. Even though television has diffused around the world, local people continue to prefer local programs when they are available. And even when people all over the world watch the same program, they may interpret it in very different ways. People are not just absorbing the messages they get; they often resist or revise them.[71]

Until recently, researchers studying culture change generally assumed that the differences between people of different cultures would become minimal. But in the last 30 years or so, it has become increasingly apparent that, although many differences disappear, many people are affirming ethnic identities in a process that often involves deliberately introducing cultural difference.[72] Eugeen Roosens describes the situation of the Huron of Quebec, who in the late 1960s seemed to have disappeared as a distinct culture. The Huron language had disappeared and the lives of the Huron were not obviously distinguishable from those of the French Canadians around them. The Huron then developed a new identity as they actively worked to promote the rights of indigenous peoples like themselves. That their new defining cultural symbols bore no resemblance to the past Huron culture is beside the point.

One fascinating possibility is that ethnic diversity and ethnogenesis may be a result of broader processes. Elizabeth Cashdan found that ethnic diversity appears to be related to environmental unpredictability, which is associated with greater distance from the equator.[73] There appear to be many more cultural groups nearer to the equator than in very northern and southern latitudes. Perhaps, Cashdan suggests, environmental unpredictability in the north and south necessitates wider ties between social groups to allow cooperation in case local resources fail. This may minimize the likelihood of cultural divergence, that is, ethnogenesis. Hence, there will be fewer cultures further from the equator.

Future research on culture change should increase our understanding of how and why various types of change are occurring. If we can increase our understanding of culture change in the present, we should be better able to understand similar processes in the past. We may be guided in our efforts to understand culture change by the large number of cross-cultural correlations that have been discovered between a particular cultural variation and its presumed causes.[74] All cultures have changed over time; variation is the product of differential change. Thus, the variations we see are the products of change processes, and the discovered predictors of those variations may suggest how and why the changes occurred. The task of discovering which particular circumstances favor which particular patterns is a large and difficult one. In the chapters that follow, we hope to convey the main points of what anthropologists think they know about aspects of cultural variation, culture change, and what they do not know.

SUMMARY ● ○ ○

1. Despite individual differences, the members of a particular society share many behaviors and ideas that constitute their culture.

2. Culture may be defined as the set of learned behaviors and ideas (including beliefs, attitudes, values, and ideals) that are characteristic of a particular society or other social group.

3. The type of group within which cultural traits are shared can vary from a particular society or a segment of that society to a group that transcends national boundaries. When anthropologists refer to *a* culture, they usually are referring to the cultural patterns of a particular society—that is, a particular territorial population speaking a language not generally understood by neighboring territorial populations. Although other animals exhibit some cultural behavior, humans are unusual in the number and complexity of the learned patterns that they transmit to their young. And they have a unique way of transmitting their culture: through spoken, symbolic language.

4. Ethnocentrism, judging other cultures in terms of your own, and its opposite—the glorification of other cultures—impede anthropological inquiry. An important tenet in anthropology is the principle of cultural relativism: the attitude that a society's customs and ideas should be studied objectively and understood in the context of that society's culture. But when it comes to some cultural practices such as violence against women, torture, slavery, or genocide, most anthropologists can no longer adhere to the strong form of cultural relativism that asserts that all cultural practices are equally valid.

5. Anthropologists seek to discover the customs and ranges of acceptable behavior that constitute the culture of a society under study. In doing so, they focus on general or shared patterns of behavior rather than on individual variations. When dealing with practices that are highly visible, or with beliefs that are almost unanimous, the investigator can rely on observation on or interviewing off a few knowledgeable people. With less obvious behaviors or attitudes, anthropologists must collect information from a sample of individuals. The mode of a frequency distribution can then be used to express the cultural pattern.

6. Cultures have patterns or clusters of traits. They tend to be integrated for psychological and adaptive reasons.

7. Culture is always changing. Because culture consists of learned patterns of behavior and belief, cultural traits can be unlearned and learned anew as human needs change. The sources of change may be external and/or internal.

8. Discoveries and inventions, though ultimately the sources of all culture change, do not necessarily lead to change. Only when society accepts an invention or discovery and uses it regularly can culture change be said to have occurred. Some inventions are probably the result of dozens of tiny, perhaps accidental, initiatives over a period of many years. Other inventions are consciously intended. Why some people are more innovative than others is still only incompletely understood. There is some evidence that creativity and a readiness to adopt innovations may be related to socioeconomic position.

9. The process by which cultural elements are borrowed from another society and incorporated into the culture of the recipient group is called diffusion. Cultural traits do not necessarily diffuse; that is, diffusion is a selective, not automatic, process. A society accepting a foreign cultural trait is likely to adapt it in a way that effectively harmonizes it with the society's own traditions.

10. When a group or society is in contact with a more powerful society, the weaker group is often obliged to acquire cultural elements from the dominant group. This process of extensive borrowing in the context of superordinate-subordinate relations between societies is called acculturation. Acculturation processes vary considerably depending upon the wishes of the more powerful society, the attitudes of the less powerful, and whether there is any choice.

11. Even though customs are not genetically inherited, cultural adaptation may be similar to biological adaptation in one major respect. Traits (cultural or genetic) that are more likely to be reproduced (learned or inherited) are likely to become more frequent in a population over time. Particularly when the environment changes, individuals may try out ideas and behaviors that are different than their parents.

12. Perhaps the most drastic and rapid way a culture can change is by revolution—a usually violent replacement

of the society's rulers. Rebellions occur primarily in state societies, where there is a distinct ruling elite. However, not all peoples who are suppressed, conquered, or colonized eventually rebel or successfully revolt against established authority.

13. Globalization—the widespread flow of people, information, technology, and capital over the earth's surface—has minimized cultural diversity in some respects, but it has not eliminated it.

14. Ethnogenesis is the process by which new cultures are created.

GLOSSARY TERMS ○ ● ○

acculturation **29**	ethnogenesis **35**
adaptive customs **23**	globalization **33**
cultural relativism **19**	maladaptive customs **23**
culture **16**	norms **18**
diffusion **27**	revolution **32**
ethnocentric **18**	society **16**
ethnocentrism **18**	subculture **16**

CRITICAL QUESTIONS ○ ○ ●

1. Would it be adaptive for a society to have everyone adhere to the cultural norms? Explain your answer.

2. Some anthropologists think of culture as being "outside" individuals; others think of culture as being "inside" individuals in the form of individual cognitive maps as to how people should behave. How would these different views affect research methods and the resultant cultural descriptions? How would these views affect the understanding of culture change?

3. Not all people faced with external pressure to change do so or do so at the same rate. What factors might explain why some societies rapidly change their culture?

4. Does the concept of cultural relativism promote international understanding, or does it hinder attempts to have international agreement on acceptable behavior, such as human rights?

PEARSON myanthrolab

Read the chapter by Regina Smith Oboler, "Nandi: From Cattle-Keepers to Cash-Crop Farmers," on MyAnthroLab, and answer the following questions:

1. Who are the Nandi? Give a brief description of them, and include the time period and community being described by Oboler.

2. As you read about the Nandi, you may be surprised by some of their customs. Indicate which specific customs surprise you. Describe whether you think you are reacting simply because their customs are different from your customs, whether you are being ethnocentric, or if you prefer their customs.

3. Anthropologists have to learn not to judge behavior in another culture in terms of their own culture. Give an example from Regina Smith Oboler's fieldwork among the Nandi.

History of Theory in Anthropology

istorians of anthropology often trace the birth of the discipline to the 16th-century encounters between Europeans and native peoples in Africa and the Americas. For Europeans, these peoples and their practices often seemed bizarre or irrational, yet to live and work with them, it was important to understand their cultures. This need for cross-cultural understanding was one of the roots of anthropology. The other was the emerging focus on evolution. The recognition that species were not stable but changed over time emerged in parallel with the idea that societies changed over time. Together, these ideas launched the notion that other cultures could be changed, that they could and should be "civilized." The movement by Europeans to "civilize" others between the 16th and 19th centuries destroyed some of the world's cultural diversity, but the field of anthropology emerged out of those efforts. As we shall see, we have knowledge of those cultures that were changed or destroyed by the "civilizing" efforts of European explorers and colonists largely because of the efforts of early anthropologists.

While anthropology may have been born out of its largely colonialist background, anthropologists are now overwhelmingly inclined to support the value of other ways of life and try to support the needs of peoples formerly colonized or dominated by powerful nation-states.

As we review the history of anthropological ideas, keep in mind that, although many of the early points of view were later rejected and replaced, not all ideas suffer the same fate. Evolutionary theory, for example, has been modified substantially over the years, but much of the theory of natural selection put forward by Darwin in the mid-1800s has been supported by empirical evidence and has withstood the test of time. Also keep in mind that some of the ideas we discuss are more properly *theoretical orientations* rather than theories. A **theoretical orientation** is a general idea about how phenomena are to be explained; *theories*, as we discuss more fully in the next chapter, are more specific explanations that can be tested with empirical evidence. ● ○ ●

THE EVOLUTION OF EVOLUTION

Older Western ideas about nature's creatures were very different from Charles Darwin's theory of *evolution*, which suggested that different species developed, one from another, over long periods of time. In the 5th millennium B.C., the Greek philosophers Plato and Aristotle believed that animals and plants form a single, graded continuum going from more perfection to less perfection. Humans, of course, were at the top of this scale. Later Greek philosophers added the idea that the creator gave life or "radiance" first to humans, but some of that essence was lost at each subsequent creation.[1] Macrobius, summarizing the thinking of Plotinus, used an image that was to persist for centuries, the image of what

came to be called the "chain of being": "The attentive observer will discover a connection of parts, from the Supreme God down to the last dregs of things, mutually linked together and without a break. And this is Homer's golden chain, which God, he says, bade hand down from heaven to earth."[2]

Belief in the chain of being was accompanied by the conviction that an animal or plant species could not become extinct. In fact, all things were linked to one another in a chain, and all links were necessary. Moreover, the notion of extinction threatened people's trust in God; it was unthinkable that a whole group of God's creations could simply disappear.

The idea of the chain of being persisted through the years, but philosophers, scientists, poets, and theologians did not discuss it extensively until the 18th century. Those discussions prepared the way for evolutionary theory. Ironically, although the chain of being did not allow for evolution, its idea that nature had an order of things encouraged studies of natural history and comparative anatomical studies, which stimulated the development of the idea of evolution. People were also now motivated to look for previously unknown creatures. Moreover, humans were not shocked when naturalists suggested that humans were close to apes. This notion was perfectly consistent with the idea of a chain of being; apes were simply thought to have been created with less perfection.

Early in the 18th century, an influential scientist, Carolus Linnaeus (1707–1778), classified plants and animals in a *systema naturae,* which placed humans in the same order (Primates) as apes and monkeys. Linnaeus did not suggest an evolutionary relationship between humans and apes; he mostly accepted the notion that all species were created by God and fixed in their form. Not surprisingly, then, Linnaeus is often viewed as an anti-evolutionist. But Linnaeus's hierarchical classification scheme, in descending order from kingdom to class, order, **genus** (a group of related species), and species, provided a framework for the idea that humans, apes, and monkeys had a common ancestor.

Others did not believe that species were fixed in their form. According to Jean-Baptiste Lamarck (1744–1829), acquired characteristics could be inherited and therefore species could evolve; individuals who in their lifetime developed characteristics helpful to survival would pass those characteristics on to future generations, thereby changing the physical makeup of the species. For example, Lamarck explained the long neck of the giraffe as the result of successive generations of giraffes stretching their necks to reach the high leaves of trees. The stretched muscles and bones of the necks were somehow transmitted to the offspring of the neck-stretching giraffes, and eventually all giraffes came to have long necks. But because Lamarck and later biologists failed to produce evidence to support the hypothesis that acquired characteristics can be inherited, this explanation of evolution is now generally dismissed.[3]

By the 19th century, some thinkers were beginning to accept evolution whereas others were trying to refute it. For example, Georges Cuvier (1769–1832) was a leading opponent of evolution. Cuvier's theory of catastrophism proposed that a quick series of catastrophes accounted for changes in

The giraffe's long neck is adaptive for eating tree leaves high off the ground. When food is scarce, longer-necked giraffes would get more food and reproduce more successfully than shorter-necked giraffes; in this environment, natural selection would favor giraffes with longer necks.

the earth and the fossil record. Cataclysms and upheavals such as Noah's flood had killed off previous sets of living creatures, which each time were replaced by new creations.

Major changes in geological thinking occurred in the 19th century. Earlier, geologist James Hutton (1726–1797) had questioned catastrophism, but his work was largely ignored. In contrast, Sir Charles Lyell's (1797–1875) volumes of the *Principles of Geology* (1830–1833), which built on Hutton's earlier work, received immediate acclaim. Their concept of *uniformitarianism* suggested that the earth is constantly being shaped and reshaped by natural forces that have operated over a vast stretch of time. Lyell also discussed the formation of geological strata and paleontology. He used fossilized fauna to define different geological epochs. Lyell's works were read avidly by Charles Darwin before and during Darwin's now-famous voyage on the *Beagle.* The two corresponded and subsequently became friends.

After studying changes in plants, fossil animals, and varieties of domestic and wild pigeons, Charles Darwin (1809–1882) rejected the notion that each species was created at one time in a fixed form. The results of his investigations pointed clearly, he thought, to the evolution of species through the mechanism of natural selection. While Darwin was completing his book on the subject, naturalist

Alfred Russel Wallace (1823–1913) sent him a manuscript that came to conclusions about the evolution of species that matched Darwin's own.[4] In 1858, the two men presented the astonishing theory of natural selection to their colleagues at a meeting of the Linnaean Society of London.[5]

In 1859, when Darwin published *The Origin of Species by Means of Natural Selection*,[6] he wrote, "I am fully convinced that species are not immutable; but that those belonging to what are called the same genera are lineal descendants of some other and generally extinct species, in the same manner as the acknowledged varieties of any one species."[7] His conclusions outraged those who believed in the biblical account of creation, and the result was bitter controversy that continues to this day.[8]

Although Darwin's idea of evolution by natural selection was strongly challenged when first published (particularly, as illustrated here, the idea that humans and primates shared a common ancestor), it has withstood rigorous testing and is the foundation of many anthropological theories.

Until 1871, when his *The Descent of Man* was published, Darwin avoided stating categorically that humans were descended from nonhuman forms, but the implications of his theory were clear. People immediately began to take sides. In June 1860, at the annual meeting of the British Association for the Advancement of Science, Bishop Wilberforce saw an opportunity to attack the Darwinists. Concluding his speech, he faced Thomas Huxley, one of the Darwinists' chief advocates, and inquired, "Was it through his grandfather or his grandmother that he claimed descent from a monkey?" Huxley responded,

> If . . . the question is put to me would I rather have a miserable ape for a grandfather than a man highly endowed by nature and possessing great means and influence and yet who employs those faculties and that influence for the mere purpose of introducing ridicule into a grave scientific discussion—I unhesitatingly affirm my preference for the ape.[9]

Although Huxley's retort to Bishop Wilberforce displays both humor and quick wit, it does not answer the bishop's question very well. A better answer, and one we pursue in the chapter on genetics and evolution, is that Darwinists would claim that we descended from monkeys neither through our grandmother or our grandfather, but that both we and monkeys are descended from a common ancestor who lived long ago. Darwinists would further argue that natural selection was the process through which the physical and genetic form of that common ancestor diverged to become both monkey and human.

EARLY ANTHROPOLOGICAL THEORY

In anthropology, as in any discipline, there is a continual ebb and flow of ideas. One theoretical orientation will arise and may grow in popularity until another is proposed in opposition to it. Often, one orientation will capitalize on those aspects of a problem that a previous orientation ignored or played down. In our survey of many of the orientations that have developed since the emergence of anthropology as a professional discipline, we follow an approximate historical sequence. As we discuss each school of thought, we will indicate what kinds of information or phenomena it emphasizes (if it does) as explanatory factors. Some of these orientations have passed into history by now; others continue to attract adherents.

Early Evolutionism

In the early years of anthropology, Darwinism had a strong impact on theory. The prevailing view was that culture generally develops (or evolves) in a uniform and progressive manner, just as Darwin argued species did. It was thought that most societies pass through the same series of stages, to arrive ultimately at a common end. The sources of culture change were generally assumed to be embedded within the culture from the beginning, and therefore the ultimate course of development was thought to be internally determined. Two 19th-century anthropologists whose writings exemplified the theory that culture generally evolves uniformly and progressively were Edward B. Tylor (1832–1917) and Lewis Henry Morgan (1818–1881).

Tylor maintained that culture evolved from the simple to the complex and that all societies passed through three basic stages of development: from savagery through barbarism to civilization.[10] "Progress" was therefore possible for all. To account for cultural variation, Tylor and other early evolutionists postulated that different contemporary societies were at different stages of evolution. According to this view, the "simpler" peoples of the day had not yet reached "higher" stages. Tylor believed there was a kind of psychic unity among all peoples that explained parallel evolutionary sequences in different cultural traditions. In other words, because of the basic similarities common to all peoples, different societies often find the same solutions to the same problems independently. But Tylor also noted that cultural traits may spread from one society to another by simple *diffusion*—the borrowing by one culture of a trait belonging to another as the result of contact between the two.

Another 19th-century proponent of uniform and progressive cultural evolution was Lewis Henry Morgan. A lawyer in upstate New York, Morgan became interested in the local Iroquois Indians and defended their reservation in a land-grant case. In gratitude, the Iroquois "adopted" Morgan.

In his best-known work, *Ancient Society,* Morgan postulated several sequences in the evolution of human culture. For example, he speculated that the family evolved through six stages. Human society began as a "horde living in promiscuity," with no sexual prohibitions and no real family structure. Next was a stage in which a group of brothers was married to a group of sisters and brother-sister matings were permitted. In the third stage, group marriage was practiced, but brothers and sisters were not allowed to mate. The fourth stage was characterized by a loosely paired male and female who still lived with other people. Then came the husband-dominant family, in which the husband could have more than one wife simultaneously. Finally, the stage of civilization was distinguished by the monogamous family, with just one wife and one husband who were relatively equal in status.[11] However, Morgan's postulated sequence for the evolution of the family is not supported by the enormous amount of ethnographic data that has been collected since his time. For example, no recent society generally practices group marriage or allows brother-sister mating. (In the chapter on marriage and the family, we discuss how recent cultures have varied in regard to marriage customs.)

The evolutionism of Tylor, Morgan, and others of the 19th century is largely rejected today. For one thing, their theories cannot satisfactorily account for cultural variation. The "psychic unity of mankind" or "germs of thought" that were postulated to account for parallel evolution cannot also account for cultural differences. Another weakness in the early evolutionist theories is that they cannot explain why some societies have regressed or even become extinct. Finally, although other societies may have progressed to "civilization," some of them have not passed through all the stages. Thus, early evolutionist theory cannot explain the details of cultural evolution and variation as anthropology now knows them.

"Race" Theory

Evolutionism also influenced another branch of anthropological theory, one that posited that the reason human cultures differed in their behaviors was because they represented separate subspecies of humans, or "races." This idea was also influenced by the fact that, by the 19th century at least, it became clear that few cultures were being "civilized" in the way Europeans expected. Rather than attribute this to the strength of cultural tradition, some attributed it to the innate capabilities of the people—in other words, to their "race." Members of "uncivilized

The 19th-century belief that progress was a universal in social change had a profound impact on early anthropological theorists such as Edward B. Tylor and Lewis Henry Morgan.

THE PROGRESS OF THE CENTURY.

races" were, by their very nature, incapable of being "civilized." Such ideas were widely held and supported during the late 19th and early 20th centuries and, as we shall see, American anthropology played a large role in showing that "race" theory was unsupported in a variety of contexts. Unfortunately, "race" theory persists in some disciplines.

The roots of "race" theory are fairly easy to trace.[12] As discussed earlier, the classification of plants and animals into distinct biological groups began with the work of Linneaus. In his *systema natura,* humans are classified into four distinct "races" (American, European, Asiatic, and African), each defined not only by physical characteristics but also by emotional and behavioral ones. Similarly, Johann Blumenbach (1752–1840), a founder of the field of biological anthropology, divided humans into five "races" (Caucasian, Mongolian, Malayan, Ethiopian, and American). Interestingly, each of his races relates to peoples of recently colonized areas, and Blumenbach makes clear that the purpose of his division of humanity is to help classify the variety of humans that European colonists were encountering at the time.

Samuel Morton (1799–1851), a Philadelphia physician, was the first to explicitly link "race" with behavior and intelligence. Morton collected and measured the skulls of Native Americans, and, in *Crania Americana* (1839), concluded that not only were Native Americans a separate "race," but their behavioral differences from European Americans were rooted in the physical structures of their brains. Expanding his study, he examined skulls of ancient Egyptians, and, in *Crania Aegyptiaca* (1844), concluded that "race" differences were ancient and unchanging.

The presumed fixity of these "race" differences was essential, not only to justify the exploitive relationships of

colonialism and slavery, but also to fight against Darwin's idea of evolution. If God created the world in a fixed and stable form, then "races" should be fixed as well. Thus, not surprisingly, one of the 19th century's strongest critics of evolution, Harvard naturalist Louis Agassiz (1807–1873), was also one of the century's most outspoken supporters of "race" theory. Between 1863 and 1865, Agassiz measured thousands of Civil War soldiers, and used the data he collected to argue that significant and stable differences existed between people of African versus European descent. He implied that these differences illustrated God's creation of human "races."

By the turn of the 20th century, "race" theory was being used in attempts to shape the structure of society. Eminent British scientist Francis Galton (1822–1911) promoted a social and political movement aimed at manipulating "races" by selectively breeding humans with desirable characteristics and preventing those with undesirable ones from having offspring. **Eugenics**, as this movement was called, was widely accepted in Europe, and had strong supporters in the United States, support that continues to this day. For example, in *The Bell Curve* (1994), Richard Herrnstein and Charles Murray assert that there are "race" differences in IQ (and, consequently, success in life), and suggest that social policies should discourage "races" deemed to have low IQs from having many children.

The scholarly use of "race" theory declined precipitously following World War II, when the Nazi genocide against "races" that they viewed as inferior exposed the idea's dangerous potential. At the same time, advances in biological anthropology began to demonstrate that "race" itself was an analytical concept with very little utility. By the 1970s, biologists were able to show that purely genetic races of humans are not clearly identifiable, and therefore

Race theory was used to justify the exploitive relationships of slavery and colonialism. In this 19th-century advertisement, a slave gathers cocoa beans to be made into chocolate for European consumption.

not applicable to humans.[13] Still, "race" theory has not disappeared completely.[14]

Diffusionism

In the late 19th and early 20th centuries, although the cultural evolutionism of Tylor and Morgan was still popular and "race" theory was at its height, diffusionism began to take hold among anthropologists in several parts of the world. The two main schools with a diffusionist viewpoint were the British and the German-Austrian.

The main spokesmen for the British school of diffusionism were G. Elliott Smith, William J. Perry, and W. H. R. Rivers. Smith and Perry stated that most aspects of higher civilization were developed in Egypt (which was relatively advanced because of its early development of agriculture) and were then diffused throughout the world as other peoples came into contact with the Egyptians.[15] People, they believed, are inherently uninventive and invariably prefer to borrow the inventions of another culture rather than develop ideas for themselves. This viewpoint was never widely accepted, and it has now been abandoned completely.

Inspired by Friedrich Ratzel, Fritz Graebner and Father Wilhelm Schmidt led the early 20th-century German-Austrian diffusionist school. This school also held that people borrow from others because they are basically uninventive. In contrast to Smith and Perry of the British school, who assumed that all cultural traits originated in one place (Egypt) and filtered out to cultures throughout the world, the German-Austrian school suggested the existence and diffusion of several different cultural complexes (*Kulturkreise,* plural in German).[16] Like the British diffusionists, however, the *Kulturkreis* (singular) school provided little documentation for the historical relationships it assumed.

A separate American diffusionist school of thought, led by Clark Wissler and Alfred Kroeber, also arose in the first few decades of the 20th century, but it was more modest in its claims. The American diffusionists attributed the characteristic features of a culture area to a geographical *culture center,* where the traits were first developed and from which they then diffused outward. This theory led Wissler to formulate his age-area principle: If a given trait diffuses outward from a single culture center, it follows that the most widely distributed traits found to exist around such a center must be the oldest traits.[17]

Although most anthropologists today acknowledge the spread of traits by diffusion, few try to account for most aspects of cultural development and variation in terms of diffusion. For one thing, the diffusionists dealt only in a very superficial way with the question of how cultural traits are transferred from one society to another. The failing was a serious one, because one of the things we want to explain is why a culture accepts, rejects, or modifies a trait that one of its neighbors has. Also, even if it could be demonstrated how and why a trait diffused outward from a cultural center, we would still be no closer to an explanation of how or why the trait developed within that center in the first place.

LATER ANTHROPOLOGICAL THEORY

The beginning of the 20th century brought the end of evolutionism's reign in cultural anthropology. Its leading opponent was Franz Boas (1858–1942), whose main disagreement with the evolutionists involved their assumption that universal laws governed all human culture. Boas pointed out that these 19th-century individuals lacked sufficient data (as did Boas himself) to formulate many useful generalizations. Boas also strongly opposed "race" theory, and made significant contributions to the study of human variation that demonstrated how supposedly "racial," and supposedly biological, characteristics actually varied depending on where a person grew up. Boas almost single-handedly brought about the decline of "race" theory in America, as well as trained the first generation of American anthropologists, including (among others) Alfred Kroeber, Robert Lowie, Edward Sapir, Melville Herskovits, and Margaret Mead.[18]

Historical Particularism

Boas stressed the apparently enormous complexity of cultural variation, and perhaps because of this complexity he believed it was premature to formulate universal laws. He felt that single cultural traits had to be studied in the context of the society in which they appeared. In 1896, Boas published an article entitled "The Limitation of the Comparative Method of Anthropology,"[19] which dealt with his objections to the evolutionist approach. In it, he stated that anthropologists should spend less time developing theories based on insufficient data. Rather, they should devote their energies to collecting as much data as possible, as quickly as possible, before cultures disappeared (as so many already had, after contact with foreign societies). He asserted that valid interpretations could be made and theories proposed only after this body of data was gathered.

Boas expected that, if a tremendous quantity of data was collected, the laws governing cultural variation would emerge from the mass of information by themselves. According to the method he advocated, the essence of science is to mistrust all expectations and to rely only on facts. But, the "facts" that are recorded, even by the most diligent observer, will necessarily reflect what that individual considers important. Collecting done without some preliminary theorizing, without ideas about what to expect, is meaningless, for the facts that are most important may be ignored whereas irrelevant ones may be recorded. Although it was appropriate for Boas to criticize previous "armchair theorizing," his concern with innumerable local details did not encourage a belief that it might be possible to explain the major variations in culture that anthropologists observe.

Psychological Approaches

In the 1920s, some American anthropologists began to study the relationship between culture and personality.

Although there are varying opinions about how the culture-and-personality school got started, the writings of Sigmund Freud and other psychoanalysts were undoubtedly influential. Edward Sapir, one of Boas's earliest students, reviewed psychoanalytical books and seems to have influenced two other students of Boas—Ruth Benedict and Margaret Mead—who became early proponents of a psychological orientation.[20]

In seminars at Columbia University in the 1930s and 1940s, Ralph Linton, an anthropologist, and Abram Kardiner, a psychoanalyst, developed important ideas for culture-and-personality studies. Kardiner suggested that there is a *basic personality* in every culture that is produced by *primary institutions* (such as type of household, subsistence, and childrearing practices). In other words, just as children's later personalities may be shaped by their earlier experiences, the personalities of adults in a society should be shaped by common cultural experiences. In turn, the *basic personality* gives rise to other institutions (such as art, folklore, and religion), called *secondary institutions*, which are viewed as projections from basic personality. John Whiting and Irvin Child independently put forward a similar and somewhat more elaborated theoretical framework somewhat later.[21] If similar primary institutions exist, it follows that similar personality outcomes and similar secondary institutions should be predicted. Indeed, as we will see in the chapter on culture and the individual, many subsequent cross-cultural studies have supported these connections.

The presence or absence of fathers has important consequences for psychological development, and some societies have much more father presence than others. This Tongan father in the South Pacific is shown with his family.

As time went on, the focus of the psychological approach broadened and diversified. There was more interest in diversity of personality within societies and in universals across human societies. Through this focus on universals, human development from infancy through adolescence, as well as thought processes and emotional responses, was examined to understand human nature. The interest in cultural differences did not disappear but focused more on particular societies—particularly their ethnopsychologies (native psychological concepts and theories), or concepts of the self and emotion.[22]

To generalize about the psychological approach to cultural anthropology, then, we may say that it explicitly employs psychological concepts and methods to help understand cultural differences and similarities.[23] In the chapter on culture and the individual, we discuss psychological approaches in more detail.

Functionalism

In Europe, the reaction against evolution was not as dramatic as in the United States, but a clear division between the diffusionists and those who came to be known as *functionalists* emerged by the 1930s. **Functionalism** in social science looks for the part (function) that some aspect of culture or social life plays in maintaining a cultural system. Two quite different schools of functionalism arose in conjunction with two British anthropologists—Bronislaw Malinowski (1884–1942) and Arthur Reginald Radcliffe-Brown (1881–1955).

Malinowski's version of functionalism assumes that all cultural traits serve the needs of *individuals* in a society; that is, they satisfy some *basic* or *derived need* of the members of the group. Basic needs include nutrition, reproduction, bodily comfort, safety, relaxation, movement, and growth. Some aspects of the culture satisfy these basic needs and give rise to derived needs that must also be satisfied. For example, culture traits that satisfy the basic need for food give rise to the secondary, or derived, need for cooperation in food collection or production. Societies will in turn develop forms of political organization and social control that guarantee the required cooperation. How did Malinowski explain such things as religion and magic? He suggested that, because humans always live with a certain amount of uncertainty and anxiety, they need stability and continuity. Religion and magic are functional in that they serve those needs.[24]

Unlike Malinowski, Radcliffe-Brown felt that the various aspects of social behavior *maintain* a *society's social structure* rather than satisfying individual needs. By social structure, he meant the total network of existing social relationships in a society.[25] The phrase *structural-functionalism* is often used to describe Radcliffe-Brown's approach. To explain how different societies deal with the tensions that are likely to develop among people related through marriage, Radcliffe-Brown suggested that societies do one of two things: They may develop strict rules forbidding the people involved ever to interact face-to-face (as do the Navajos, for example, in requiring a man to avoid his mother-in-law). They may also allow mutual disrespect and teasing between the in-laws. Radcliffe-Brown suggested that avoidance is likely to occur between in-laws of different generations, whereas disrespectful teasing is likely between in-laws of the same generation.[26] Both avoidance and teasing, he suggested, are ways to avoid real conflict and help maintain the social structure. (American mother-in-law jokes may also help relieve tension.)

The major objection to Malinowski's functionalism is that it cannot readily account for cultural variation. Most of the needs he identified, such as the need for food, are universal: All societies must deal with them if they are to survive. Thus, although the functionalist approach may tell us why all societies engage in food-getting, it cannot tell why different societies have different food-getting practices. In other words, functionalism does not explain why certain specific cultural patterns arise to fulfill a need that might be fulfilled just as easily by any of a number of alternative possibilities.

A major problem of the structural-functionalist approach is that it is difficult to determine whether a particular custom is in fact functional in the sense of contributing to the maintenance of the social system. In biology, the contribution an organ makes to the health or life of an animal can be assessed by removing it. But we cannot subtract a cultural trait from a society to see if the trait really does contribute to the maintenance of that group. It is conceivable that certain customs within a society may be neutral or even detrimental to its maintenance. Moreover, we cannot assume that all of a society's customs are functional merely because the society is functioning at the moment. Even if we are able to assess whether a particular custom is functional, this theoretical orientation fails to deal with the question of why a particular society chooses to meet its structural needs in a particular way. A given problem does not necessarily have only one solution. We must still explain why one of several possible solutions is chosen.

Neoevolution

The evolutionary approach to cultural variation did not die with the 19th century. Beginning in the 1940s, Leslie A. White (1900–1975) attacked the Boasian emphasis on historical particularism and championed the evolutionist orientation.

Though quickly labeled a neoevolutionist, White rejected the term, insisting that his approach did not depart significantly from the theories adopted in the 19th century. What White did add to the classical evolutionist approach was a conception of culture as an energy-capturing system. According to his "basic law" of cultural evolution, "other factors remaining constant, *culture evolves as the amount of energy harnessed per capita per year is increased or as the efficiency of the instrumental means of putting the energy to work is increased.*"[27] In other words, a more advanced technology gives humans control over more energy (human, animal, solar, and so on), and cultures expand and change as a result.

White's orientation has been criticized for the same reasons that the ideas of Tylor and Morgan were. In

describing what has happened in the evolution of human culture, he assumed that cultural evolution is determined strictly by conditions (preeminently technological ones) inside the culture. That is, he explicitly denied the possibility of environmental, historical, or psychological influences on cultural evolution. The main problem with such an orientation is that it cannot explain why some cultures evolve whereas others either do not evolve or become extinct. White's theory of energy capture sidesteps the question of why only some cultures are able to increase their energy capture.

Julian H. Steward (1902–1972), another later evolutionist, divided evolutionary thought into three schools: unilinear, universal, and multilinear.[28] Steward believed that Morgan and Tylor's theories exemplified the unilinear approach to cultural evolution, the classical 19th-century orientation that attempted to place particular cultures on the rungs of a sort of evolutionary ladder. Universal evolutionists such as Leslie White, on the other hand, were concerned with culture in the broad sense, rather than with individual cultures. Steward classified himself as a multilinear evolutionist: one who deals with the evolution of particular cultures and only with demonstrated sequences of parallel culture change in different areas.

Steward was concerned with explaining specific cultural differences and similarities. Consequently, he was critical of White's vague generalities and his disregard of environmental influences. White, on the other hand, asserted that Steward fell into the historical-particularist trap of paying too much attention to particular cases.

Marshall Sahlins (born 1930) and Elman Service (1915–1996), who were students and colleagues of both White and Steward, combined the views of those two individuals by recognizing two kinds of evolution—specific and general.[29] **Specific evolution** refers to the particular sequence of change and adaptation of a particular society in a given environment. **General evolution** refers to a general progress of human society, in which higher forms (having higher-energy capture) arise from and surpass lower forms. Thus, specific evolution is similar to Steward's multilinear evolution, and general evolution resembles White's universal evolution. Although this synthesis does serve to integrate the two points of view, it does not give us a way of explaining why general evolutionary progress has occurred. But, unlike the early evolutionists, some of the later evolutionists did suggest a mechanism to account for the evolution of particular cultures—namely, adaptation to particular environments.

Structuralism

Claude Lévi-Strauss (1908–2009) was the leading proponent of an approach to cultural analysis called **structuralism.** Lévi-Strauss's structuralism differs from that of Radcliffe-Brown. Whereas Radcliffe-Brown concentrated on how the elements of a society function as a system, Lévi-Strauss concentrates more on the origins of the systems themselves. He sees culture, as expressed in art, ritual, and the patterns of daily life, as a surface representation of the underlying structure of the human mind. Consider, for example, how he tries to account for what anthropologists call a *moiety system*. Such a system is said to exist if a society is divided into two large intermarrying kin groups (each called a *moiety*, probably derived from the French word *moitié*, meaning "half"). Lévi-Strauss says that moiety systems reflect the human mind's predisposition to think and behave in terms of *binary oppositions* (contrasts between one thing and another).[30] Clearly, a moiety system involves a binary opposition: You are born into one of two groups and you marry someone in the other. The problem with Lévi-Strauss's explanation of moieties is that he is postulating a constant—the human mind's supposed dualism—to account for a cultural feature that is not universal. Moiety systems are found in only a relatively small number of societies, so how could something that is universal explain something else that is not?

Lévi-Strauss's interpretations of cultural phenomena (which tend to be far more involved and difficult to follow than the example just described) have concentrated on the presumed cognitive processes of people, the ways in which people supposedly perceive and classify things in the world around them. In studies such as *The Savage Mind* and *The Raw and the Cooked*, he suggested that even technologically simple groups often construct elaborate systems of classification of plants and animals, not only for practical purposes but also out of a need for such intellectual activity.[31]

Structuralism has influenced thinking not only in France; Britain too has been receptive. But the British structuralists, such as Edmund Leach, Rodney Needham, and Mary Douglas, do not follow Lévi-Strauss in looking for panhuman or universal principles in the human mind. Rather, they concentrate on applying structural analysis to particular societies and particular social institutions.[32] For example, Mary Douglas discusses an argument that took place in her home over whether soup is an "appropriate" supper. She suggests that meals (in her household and in culturally similar households) have certain structural principles. They have contrasts—hot and cold, bland and spiced, liquid and semiliquid—and various textures. They must incorporate cereals, vegetables, and animal protein. Douglas concludes that, if the food served does not follow these principles, it cannot be considered a meal.[33]

Some structuralist writings have been criticized for their concentration on abstruse, theoretical analysis at the expense of observation and evidence. For example, it is not always clear how Lévi-Strauss derived a particular structuralist interpretation, and in the absence of any systematically collected supporting evidence, readers must decide whether the interpretation seems plausible. Thus, Lévi-Strauss's studies have come to be regarded by many as vague and untestable, as self-contained intellectual constructs with little explanatory value. Moreover, even if some universal patterns underlie cultural phenomena, universals or constants cannot explain cultural differences.

Ethnoscience and Cognitive Anthropology

Lévi-Strauss's structuralist approach involves intuitively grasping the rules of thought that may underlie a given culture. An ethnographic approach known as **ethnoscience** attempts to derive these rules from a logical analysis of ethnographic data that are kept as free as possible from contamination by the observer's own cultural biases. Rather than collecting data according to a predetermined set of anthropological categories (referred to as an *etic* view), ethnoscientists seek to understand a people's world from their point of view (an *emic* view). Studying their language using systematic elicitation techniques, ethnoscientists try to formulate the rules that underlie the cultural domains. The rules are believed to be comparable to the grammatical rules that generate the correct use of the language. Research commonly focuses on kinship terms, plant and animal taxonomies, and disease classification. Ethnoscience was an early kind of *cognitive anthropology*.[34] Later researchers developed techniques to test whether the rules presumably uncovered were being followed by other members of the society and how much "cultural consensus" there was on these rules. (As we will see later, techniques for evaluating cultural consensus also provide ways of choosing the best people to interview, who are likely to be most knowledgeable about the culture.) Cognitive anthropologists also branched out to studying decision making, cultural goals and motivations, and discourse analysis.[35]

Many ethnoscientists think that, if we can discover the rules that generate cultural behavior, we can explain much of what people do and why they do it. Probably individuals do generally act according to the conscious and unconscious rules they have internalized. But we still need to understand why a particular society has developed the particular cultural rules it has. Just as a grammar does not explain how a language came to be what it is, an ethnoscientific discovery of a culture's rules does not explain why those rules developed.

Cultural Ecology

Some anthropologists are concerned mostly with the influence of environment on culture. Julian Steward was one of the first to advocate the study of **cultural ecology**—the analysis of the relationship between a culture and its environment. Steward felt that the explanation for some aspects of cultural variation could be found in the adaptation of societies to their particular environments. But rather than merely hypothesize that the environment did or did not determine cultural variation, Steward wished to resolve the question *empirically*—that is, he wanted to carry out investigations to evaluate his viewpoint.[36]

Steward felt, however, that cultural ecology must be separated from *biological ecology*, the study of the relationships between organisms and their environment. Later cultural ecologists, such as Andrew Vayda and Roy Rappaport, wished to incorporate principles of biological ecology into the study of cultural ecology to make a

The European colonization of the Americas began in the sixteenth century. This miniature from 1533-1534 depicts the landing of a trading ship in Venezuela. The containers of goods next to the native populations may be gold or another valued commodity that the Spaniards, in particular, exported from South America.

single science of ecology.[37] In their view, cultural traits, just like biological traits, can be considered adaptive or maladaptive. Cultural ecologists assume that cultural adaptation involves the mechanism of *natural selection—* the more frequent survival and reproduction of the better adapted. Environment, including the physical and social environments, affects the development of culture traits in that "individuals or populations behaving in certain different ways have different degrees of success in survival and reproduction and, consequently, in the transmission of their ways of behaving from generation to generation."[38]

Consider how culture and environment may interact among the Tsembaga, who live in the interior of New Guinea.[39] The Tsembaga live mainly on the root crops and greens they grow in home gardens; they also raise pigs. The pigs are seldom eaten; instead, they keep residential areas clean by consuming garbage, and they help prepare the soil for planting by rooting in it. Small numbers of pigs are easy to keep and require little care; they run free all day, returning at night to eat whatever substandard tubers are found in the course of their owners' harvesting of their daily rations. But problems arise when the pig herd grows large. Often there are not enough substandard tubers, and then the pigs must be fed human rations. Also, a large herd is likely to intrude upon garden crops. If one person's pig invades a neighbor's garden, the garden owner often retaliates by killing the offending pig. In turn, the dead animal's owner may kill the garden owner, the garden owner's wife, or one of his pigs. As the number of such feuds increases, people begin to put as much distance as possible between their pigs and other people's gardens.

Rappaport suggests that, to cope with the problem of pig overpopulation, the Tsembaga developed an elaborate cycle of rituals involving the slaughter of large numbers of surplus pigs. The cultural practice of ritual pig feasts can be viewed as a possible adaptation to environmental factors that produce a surplus pig population. But it is hard to know if the ritual pig feasts are more adaptive than other possible solutions to the problem of pig overpopulation. For example, it might be more adaptive to slaughter and eat pigs regularly so that pig herds never get too large. Without being able to contrast the effects of alternative solutions, a cultural ecologist studying a single society may find it difficult to obtain evidence that a custom already in place is more adaptive than other possible solutions to the problem.

More recent ecological anthropologists have criticized the earlier ecologists for having an overly narrow view of a bounded culture in an isolated environment and have considered the environment in a broader context—moving well beyond the local ecosystem to national and even international levels.[40] As we will discuss shortly, hardly any people on earth are unaffected by larger political, social, and environmental forces.

Political Economy

Like cultural ecology, the school of thought known as **political economy** assumes that external forces explain the way a society changes and adapts. But it is not the natural environment, or the social environment in general, that is central to the approach of political economy. What is central is the social and political impact of those powerful state societies (principally Spain, Portugal, Britain, and France) that transformed the world by colonialism and imperialism after the mid-1400s, and fostered the development of a worldwide economy or world system.[41] Scholars now realize that imperialism is at least 5,000 years old; most, if not all, of the first civilizations were imperialistic. Imperialistic expansion of the first state societies was linked to expanding commercialization, the growth of buying and selling.[42] Today, of course, the entire world is linked commercially. Not surprisingly, the political economy orientation grew in importance as the global reach of capitalism accelerated.

Some of the earliest figures associated with the political economy approach in anthropology were trained at Columbia University when Julian Steward was a professor there. For those students, Steward's cultural ecology was insufficiently attentive to recent world history. For example, Eric Wolf and Sidney Mintz argued that the communities they studied in Puerto Rico developed as they did because of colonialism and the establishment of plantations to supply sugar and coffee to Europe and North America.[43] And Eleanor Leacock, who studied the Montagnais-Naskapi Indians of Labrador, suggested that their system of family hunting territories was not an old characteristic, present before European contact, but developed instead out of the Indians' early involvement in the European-introduced fur trade.[44]

Central to the later and continuing intellectual development of political economy in anthropology are the writings, published in the 1960s and 1970s, of two political sociologists, André Gunder Frank and Immanuel Wallerstein. Frank suggested that the development of a region (Europe, for example) depended on the suppression of development or underdevelopment of other regions (for example, the New World, Africa). He argued that, if we want to understand why a country remains underdeveloped, we must understand how developed nations exploit it.[45] Frank is concerned with what happened in the underdeveloped world. Wallerstein is more concerned with how capitalism developed in the privileged countries and how the expansionist requirements of the capitalist countries led to the emergence of the world system.[46]

The political economy or world-system view has inspired many anthropologists to study history more explicitly and to explore the impact of external political and economic processes on local events and cultures in the underdeveloped world. In the past, when anthropologists first started doing fieldwork in the far corners of the world, they could imagine that the cultures they were studying or reconstructing could be investigated as if those cultures were more or less isolated from external influences and forces. In the modern world, such isolation hardly exists. The political economy approach has reminded us that the world, every part of it, is interconnected, for better or worse.

RECENT DEVELOPMENTS IN ANTHROPOLOGICAL THEORY

In recent years, anthropology has seen a range of new approaches incorporated into anthropological theory. Many of these approaches have been adopted from other disciplines, such as evolutionary biology and literary criticism. They are providing anthropology with an increasing breadth of thought from which to address the many questions of interest to anthropologists today.

Evolutionary Ecology Approaches

The various approaches discussed here share the idea that natural selection can operate on the behavioral or social characteristics of populations, not just on their physical traits. If so, some of the human behavior we observe, including those behaviors that vary by society, might be explained by evolutionary principles. Two important works by biologists introduced these ideas to anthropology: Edward O. Wilson's book *Sociobiology: The New Synthesis* and Richard D. Alexander's article "The Search for a General Theory of Behavior."[47] **Sociobiology** was the term for this evolutionary approach. More recently, scholars have introduced varying theoretical modifications. The main theoretical perspectives are **behavioral ecology**, **evolutionary psychology**, and **dual-inheritance theory**.[48]

Before looking at how these orientations differ from each other, let us first see how evolutionary ecological theories, particularly behavioral ecology and evolutionary psychology, differ from cultural ecology. Although both orientations assume the importance of natural selection in cultural evolution, they differ in important ways. Cultural ecology focuses mostly on what biologists would call **group selection**: Cultural ecologists talk mostly about how a certain behavioral or social characteristic may be adaptive for a group or society in a given environment. (A newly emergent behavioral or social trait that is adaptive is likely to be passed on to future generations by cultural transmission.) In contrast, evolutionary ecology focuses more on what biologists call **individual selection**: Evolutionary ecologists talk mostly about how a certain characteristic may be adaptive for an individual in a given environment.[49] *Adaptive* means the ability of individuals to get their genes into future generations. This viewpoint implies that behavior is transmitted in some way (by genes or learning) to people who share your genes (usually offspring).[50] If a certain behavior is adaptive for individuals in a particular environment (or a particular historical context in which these individuals are able to reproduce more than others), it should become more widespread in future generations as the individuals with those traits increase in number. Whereas a cultural ecologist such as Rappaport might consider how ritual pig feasts were adaptive for the Tsembaga as a whole, evolutionary ecologists would insist that to speak of adaptation it must be shown how the pig feasts benefited individuals and their closest kin.

Behavioral ecology typically tries to understand the relationship of human behavior to the environment.[51] In addition to the principle of individual selection, behavioral ecologists point to the importance of analyzing economic tradeoffs because individuals have limited time and resources. As we will see later in the economics chapter, the theory of *optimal foraging* is used to explain the decision-making behavior of recent hunter-gatherers. Evolutionary psychology, on the other hand, is more interested in universal human psychology. It is argued that human psychology was primarily adapted to the environment that characterized most of human history—our hunting-gathering way of life.[52] Dual-inheritance theory, in contrast to the other evolutionary perspectives, gives much more importance to culture as part of the evolutionary process. Dual inheritance refers to both genes and culture playing different but nonetheless important and interactive roles in transmitting traits to future generations.[53]

The behavioral ecological approaches have led to an active program of research in anthropology. However, these approaches have aroused considerable controversy, particularly from those cultural anthropologists who do not believe that biological considerations have much to do with understanding culture.

Feminist Approaches

Women have played an important role in the history of anthropology. Margaret Mead, Ruth Benedict, and Mary Douglas are just a few of the women who have made lasting contributions to the discipline. Yet the study of women and women's roles in other cultures was relatively rare, and, by the 1960s, women anthropologists began asking why women were not a more important focus of research. It was not accidental that this movement

Women have recently become a more important focus of research in anthropology. A Trobriand Island woman in Papua New Guinea stacks yams during the yam harvest festival.

coincided with the "women's movement" in the United States. One group of scholars argued that women were in subservient positions in all cultures, and hence were largely "invisible" to anthropologists studying those cultures. Another group argued that, although women historically held positions of power and authority in many cultures, the impact of colonization and capitalism had moved them into subservient positions. In either case, it became clear to these scholars that a focused effort on studying the roles of women was necessary, and feminist anthropology was born.

Feminist anthropology is a highly diverse area of research. Feminist anthropologists share an interest in the role of women in culture, but vary widely in how they approach this common interest. Some feminist anthropologists take an overtly political stance, seeing their task as identifying ways in which women are exploited and working to overcome them. Others simply try to understand women's lives and how they differ from those of men. Despite the diversity, feminist anthropology shares a critical assessment of traditional scholarship and understanding the importance of power.[54] In these ways, feminist anthropology shares a good deal with the political economy perspective as well as postmodernism, which we discuss shortly. In some cases, entirely new understandings of other cultures have come from feminist scholarship. For example, Annette Weiner studied the same culture that Malinowski had, in the Trobriand Islands, and found that Malinowski had overlooked an entire women-run economic system.[55] Similarly, Sally Slocum pointed out that, although hunting was a focus for paleoanthropologists interested in human origins, the gathering of wild foods, typically a female activity, was hardly discussed at all, even though gathered foods are more important than hunted foods in the diets of some recent foragers. Slocum's work forced paleoanthropologists to consider the role of gathered foods and, consequently, of women, in human evolution.[56]

One of the most important effects feminist research has had on anthropology is the recognition that perceptions of other cultures are shaped by the observer's culture and how the observer behaves in the field. Male researchers may not be able to ask about or observe some women's roles, just as women may not be able to ask about or observe some men's roles. More broadly, feminist scholarship suggested that the scientific approach was only one way of studying other cultures, and that different ways of studying other cultures might lead to different understandings. From this insight grew two powerful theoretical agendas that continue to affect anthropology today.

One agenda stemming from feminist scholarship is that science is inherently male in its orientation and that its impact on the world has been to further the subjugation of women. But female scientists would strongly disagree: Science is neither male nor female. A second agenda, less radical than the first, is to experiment with alternative ways of studying and describing other

applied anthropology

The Relationship Between Theory and Practice

Applied anthropology in the United States goes back to the late 1800s, when the government focused on "applied ethnology" to help with the administration of programs dealing with Native Americans, but it was only during and after the Great Depression and World War II that applied anthropological work increased significantly. Applied work during this earlier time usually involved research and consultation, with no active role in bringing about change. However, by the 1950s and afterward, applied anthropologists began to be more involved in directed social change.

Applied anthropology came to maturity at the same time that anthropology was re-discovering the importance of theory. As the influence of Boas and historical particularism waned, American anthropologists began to explore new areas of theory, and began to collaborate with ecologists, economists, and others to develop the variety of theoretical perspectives that populate the discipline today. In putting anthropology to use, applied anthropologists draw upon theoretical orientations and specific theories within those orientations. To illustrate this, we will draw upon examples from nutritional anthropology, a field that involves anthropologists from all the major subdisciplines.

Applied nutritional anthropologists are actively engaged in matters of public health, such as how infants are fed and grow, gender inequality in access to food, dietary insufficiencies, and serious malnutrition and starvation. Three of the most important theoretical perspectives involve ecology, evolutionary adaptation, and political economy. The ecological perspective not only emphasizes the effects of the physical and social environment on what people grow, the technology they use, and their patterns of consumption, but also considers the effects of these patterns on the environment. Adaptation can involve genetic changes, such as the ability of some populations to digest raw milk, or cultural adaptations such as developing processing techniques to make certain plants edible (i.e., bitter manioc that contains toxic amounts of cyanide prior to processing). The political economy perspective points to inequalities in nutrition due to class and status differences within societies and the increasing disparity between the developed and undeveloped societies around the world. In working on change programs to improve nutrition, applied anthropologists have to be pragmatic—to try to find theories that may help understand and therefore help solve some problem. They often work with practitioners from different fields and are not likely to be dogmatic about which theoretical orientation to draw upon.

Applied anthropologists do not see themselves as simply borrowing theory; they see their work as central to the task of theory building. For one thing, the work of applied anthropologists provides a "natural laboratory" for evaluating theory, where hypotheses can be tested empirically. Further, in applying new aspects of or challenges to the theory, ones not encountered in more academic or pure research settings, are often brought to light. Finally, because theory is closely linked to methods (as the information that a theory identifies as being important will shape the way researchers collect information), applied anthropologists are often at the forefront of methodological innovation.

Sources: Eddy and Partridge 1987; C. Hill 2000; Himmelgreen and Crooks 2005; Pelto et al. 2000; Van Willigen 2002, 25–30.

cultures, ways that give more voice to the people being studied and that allow for the feelings, opinions, and insights of the observer to be openly expressed in anthropological writing. Many of these feminist anthropologists have used personal narratives, storytelling, and even poetry as ways to express their understanding of the cultures they have studied.[57]

Interpretive Approaches

The "literary turn" in anthropology, in which anthropologists began to experiment with fiction, personal insights, and even poetry as forms of ethnography, did not come solely out of feminist anthropology. Since the 1960s, writers in the field of literary criticism have influenced the development of a variety of "interpretive" approaches in cultural anthropology, particularly with respect to ethnography.[58] Clifford Geertz (1926–2006) popularized the idea that a culture is like a literary text that can be analyzed for meaning, as the ethnographer interprets it. According to Geertz, ethnographers choose to interpret the meaning of things in their field cultures that are of interest to themselves. Then they try to convey their interpretations of cultural meaning to people of their own culture. Thus, according to Geertz, ethnographers are a kind of selective intercultural translator.[59]

For many interpretive anthropologists, the goal of anthropology is to understand what it means to be a person living in a particular culture, rather than to explain why cultures vary. The task of understanding meaning, these scholars claim, cannot be achieved scientifically, but can only be approached through forms of literary analysis. Among the most important of these is **hermeneutics**—the study of meaning. Using hermeneutics, anthropologists might examine a particular behavior, closely examining the interactions of people, the language they use, and the symbols they employ (both physical and linguistic) to derive what that behavior means to the people engaged in it. One of the most famous examples is Geertz's analysis of cockfighting on the Indonesian island of Bali, which he suggests reflects, and thus allows us to comprehend, the Balinese worldview.[60]

A key facet of interpretive analyses is that they are openly subjective and personal. Geertz's interpretation of the Balinese cockfight is neither right nor wrong—it is simply his. Another anthropologist viewing the same phenomenon might come to a completely different interpretation. Interpretive anthropologists accept this as part of the nature of being human. They suggest that no human sees the world in quite the same way, so that no interpretation of human behavior can or should be the same. Anthropology, then, becomes a reflection of the anthropologist as much as it is a description of other peoples. For many anthropologists, this self-centered approach makes interpretive anthropology very unappealing; for others, it is the only truthful way to work.

Some anthropologists think that interpretation is the only achievable goal in cultural anthropology because they do not believe it is possible to describe or measure cultural phenomena (and other things involving humans) in objective or unbiased ways. Scientific anthropologists do not agree. To be sure, interpretive ethnographies might provide insights. But we do not have to believe what an interpretation suggests, no matter how eloquently it is stated. (We are rarely given objective evidence to support the interpretation.) Scientific researchers have developed many techniques for minimizing bias and increasing the objectivity of measurement. Thus, interpretive anthropologists who deny the possibility of scientific understanding of human behavior and thinking may not know how much has been achieved so far by scientific studies of cultural phenomena, which we try to convey in the chapters that follow.

As Dan Sperber has suggested, the task of interpretation in cultural anthropology is clearly different from the task of explanation.[61] The goal of interpretation is to convey intuitive understanding of human experiences in a *particular* culture (intuitive in the sense of not requiring conscious reasoning or systematic methods of inquiry). Thus, interpretative ethnographers are like novelists (or literary critics). In contrast, the goal of explanation is to provide causal and general understanding of cultural phenomena (causal in the sense of mechanisms that account for why something comes to be shared in a population, and general in the sense of applying to a number of similar cases).

Does the goal (interpretation vs. explanation) preclude or invalidate the other? We don't think so. We share Sperber's view that interpretation and explanation are not opposed goals: They are just different kinds of understanding. Indeed, an intuitive interpretation described in causal and general terms might turn out, when scientifically tested, to be a powerful explanation.

Postmodernist Approaches

Postmodernism in its broadest sense rejects "modernism." There are many postmodern movements—in the arts, in literature, in philosophy, in history, and in anthropology, among others. In anthropology, *post-structuralism* is a closely related term. It is difficult to summarize what postmodernism is in anthropology because postmodernism itself rejects authoritative definitions and any one narrative of events.[62] Not only is all knowledge subjective in the postmodern view, it is also actively shaped by the political powers-that-be. One of the most influential postmodern theorists is the French philosopher Michel Foucault (1926–1984). Foucault argued that those in political power were able to shape the way accepted truths were defined. In the modern age, truth is defined through science, and science, in turn, is controlled by Western political and intellectual elites.[63] Science, then, is not only a way of understanding the world, it is a way of controlling and dominating it. Many of the others who had an influence on post-structuralism or postmodernism also were important French intellectuals—for example, Pierre Bourdieu, Roland Barthes, Jacques Lacan, and Jacques Derrida. Whereas structuralism was implicitly comparative—looking for similarities in underlying structure—post-structuralism emphasizes extreme relativity, not only between, but also within cultures.

Postmodernism questions the whole enterprise of ethnography. Ethnography is viewed as being "constructed," almost as a work of fiction.[64] For anthropologists who accept the postmodern view of science, anthropology is just another tool used by dominant powers to control others. By studying others "objectively," we dehumanize the people being studied. Turning people into objects for study allows them to become objects that can be molded and used by the political powers-that-be. Postmodern anthropologists have not given up writing about other cultures, but have experimented with different styles of ethnography, such as having a variety of different people speak for themselves.[65]

Not surprisingly, the postmodern movement in anthropology, which effectively questioned all the descriptive work from the past and present, as well as all the attempts to test and evaluate theory, created an enormous schism in anthropology, one that is still present today. How can anthropology continue to exist if its efforts contribute to the domination and control of others? Postmodern scholars answer that anthropology must transform itself into a purely activist discipline that seeks to express the voices of the dominated rather than to study or interpret them. Anthropology should be a conduit for the disenfranchised and subjugated to be heard. Even so, does that preclude anthropology from being scientific?

▶current research and issues

Evaluating Alternative Theories

In working among the Abelam of New Guinea, Richard Scaglion was puzzled why they invest so much energy in growing giant ceremonial yams, sometimes more than 10 feet long. As well, why do they abstain from sex for six months while they grow them? Of course, to try to understand, we need to know much more about the Abelam way of life. Scaglion had read about them, lived among them, and talked to them, but, as many ethnographers have discovered, answers to *why* questions don't just leap out at you. Answers, at least tentative ones, often come from theoretical orientations that suggest how or where to look for answers. Scaglion considers several possibilities. As Donald Tuzin had suggested for a nearby group, the Plains Arapesh, yams may be symbols of, or stand for, shared cultural understandings. (Looking for the meanings of symbols is a kind of interpretative

approach to ethnographic data.) The Abelam think of yams as having souls that appreciate tranquillity. Yams also have family lines; at marriage, the joining of family lines is symbolized by planting different yam lines in the same garden. During the yam-growing cycle (remember that yams appreciate tranquillity), lethal warfare and conflict become channeled mostly into competitive but nonlethal yam-growing contests. So yam growing may be functional in the sense that it helps to foster harmony.

Then again, ceremonial yam growing may have adaptive ecological consequences. Just as the Tsembaga pig feasts seemed to keep human population in line with resources, Scaglion thinks that ceremonial yam growing did too. Growing pig populations damage gardens and create conflicts, but pigs are also given away during competitive yam ceremonies, so the pig population declines. Wild

animals that are hunted also have a chance to replenish themselves because hunting is frowned upon during the yam-growing cycle.

As Scaglion's discussion illustrates, theoretical orientations help researchers derive explanations. They do not have to be "rival" explanations, in the sense that one has to be right and others wrong; more than one theory may help explain some phenomenon. But we can't assume that a theory is correct and helps us to understand just because it sounds good. The important point is that we need something more to evaluate theory. As we discuss in the next chapter, we have to find ways to test a theory against evidence. Until we do that, we really don't know how many, or if indeed any, of the theories available are helpful.

Source: Scaglion 2009a.

The Pragmatic Approach

Many, perhaps most, anthropologists do not have a particular theoretical orientation that drives their research agenda. In the interest of being honest about our own orientations, we consider ourselves to be in this category. We do believe that anthropology can strive for humanistic understanding and be scientific at the same time. The important priority for us is the research question. Whatever the research question you ask, it is important to see what others have said about that question. The various theories may come from different orientations, but the important thing is not where ideas come from, but where they lead you and what you can predict. Similarly, for us, there is also no one correct method of conducting research. Different strategies have advantages and disadvantages, and progress is most likely by examining theoretical ideas from different vantage points. To be sure, it is not likely that any one researcher will be completely open to all points of view. It is all the more important then for different researchers with different perspectives to tackle the same research questions.

To a great extent, the scientific study of human behavior depends upon the belief that it is possible to find answers to puzzling questions about humans. If you do not

believe that there are answers, you will not waste your time looking. Our belief that the scientific study of humans and their cultures is possible is bolstered by the many patterns we have already discovered. Although postmodern, interpretive, and some feminist approaches have challenged the very foundations of anthropology, anthropology as a discipline continues to thrive. In part, this is because anthropologists have learned important lessons from the work of feminist, interpretive, and postmodern scholars. No anthropologist working today could ignore women's roles, for example. It is no longer possible to ignore half of humanity. Understanding meaning, along with explaining variation, is now a parallel goal of anthropology. Anthropologists realize that their knowledge of others is possibly subjective and imperfect, but that doesn't mean it is impossible to study humans and their cultures scientifically.

The Future

It is difficult to predict what anthropological theory will be like in the future. Some ideas are likely to be discarded or ignored, and others revised. Scholarly disciplines and theories are very much the products of their times, and understanding how and why ideas have changed is part of what we need to understand. But some theoretical approaches and theories lead to greater understanding because they are more predictive of the world around us. In the next chapter, we examine the logic of explanation and evidence and how theory can be tested by anthropological research.

SUMMARY ● ○ ○

1. Which aspects of life anthropologists concentrate on usually reflects their theoretical orientation, subject interest, or preferred method of research.

2. A theoretical orientation is usually a general attitude about how cultural phenomena are to be explained.

3. Ideas about evolution took a long time to take hold because they contradicted the biblical view of events; species were viewed as fixed in their form by the creator. But in the 18th and early 19th centuries, increasing evidence suggested that evolution was a viable theory. In geology, the concept of uniformitarianism suggested that the earth is constantly subject to shaping and reshaping by natural forces working over vast stretches of time. A number of thinkers during this period began to discuss evolution and how it might occur.

4. The prevailing theoretical orientation in anthropology during the 19th century was based on a belief that culture generally evolves in a uniform and progressive manner; that is, most societies were believed to pass through the same series of stages, to arrive ultimately at a common end. Two proponents of this early theory of cultural evolution were Edward B. Tylor and Lewis Henry Morgan.

5. The diffusionist approach, popular in the late 19th and early 20th centuries, was developed by two main schools—the British and the German-Austrian. In general, diffusionists believed that most aspects of high civilization had emerged in culture centers from which they then diffused outward.

6. During the early 20th century, the leading opponent of evolutionism was Franz Boas, whose historical particularism rejected the way in which early evolutionists had assumed that universal laws governed all human culture. Boas stressed the importance of collecting as much anthropological data as possible, from which the laws governing cultural variation would supposedly emerge by themselves.

7. The psychological orientation in anthropology, which began in the 1920s, seeks to understand how psychological factors and processes may help us explain cultural practices.

8. Functionalism in social science looks for the part (function) that some aspect of culture or social life plays in maintaining a cultural system. There are two quite different schools of functionalism. Malinowski's version of functionalism assumes that all cultural traits serve the needs of *individuals* in a society. Radcliffe-Brown's felt that the various aspects of social behavior maintain a *society's social structure* rather than satisfying individual needs.

9. In the 1940s, Leslie A. White revived the evolutionary approach to cultural development. White believed that technological development, or the amount of energy harnessed per capita, was the main driving force creating cultural evolution. Anthropologists such as Julian H. Steward, Marshall Sahlins, and Elman Service have also presented evolutionary viewpoints.

10. Claude Lévi-Strauss was the leading proponent of structuralism. Lévi-Strauss saw culture, as it was expressed in art, ritual, and the patterns of daily life, as a surface representation of the underlying patterns of the human mind.

11. Whereas Lévi-Strauss's structuralist approach involves intuitively grasping the rules of thought that may underlie a given culture, an ethnographic approach known as ethnoscience attempts to derive these rules from a logical analysis of data—particularly the words people use to describe their activities. In this way, ethnoscientists try to formulate the rules that generate acceptable behavior in a given culture. Cognitive anthropology has its roots in ethnoscience.

12. Cultural ecology seeks to understand the relationships between cultures and their physical and social environments. Cultural ecologists ask how a particular culture trait may be adaptive in its environment.

13. The theoretical orientation called political economy focuses on the impact of external political and economic processes, particularly as connected to colonialism and imperialism, on local events and cultures in the underdeveloped world. The political economy approach has reminded us that all parts of the world are interconnected for better or worse.

14. Evolutionary ecology involves the application of biological evolutionary principles to the social behavior of animals, including humans.

15. Feminist approaches were born from the realization that the study of women and women's roles in other cultures was relatively rare. Some feminist anthropologists take an overtly political stance, seeing their task as identifying ways in which women are exploited and working to overcome them. Others simply try to understand women's lives and how they differ from those of men.

16. For many interpretive anthropologists, the goal of anthropology is to understand what it means to be a person living in a particular culture, rather than to explain why cultures vary. The task of understanding meaning, these scholars claim, cannot be achieved scientifically, but can only be approached through forms of literary analysis.

17. Postmodernists take the interpretative idea that all knowledge is subjective, further arguing that knowledge is actively shaped by the political powers-that-be.

18. There are anthropologists who do not follow any particular theoretical orientation or prefer any particular subject matter or method of research. These anthropologists think of themselves as having a pragmatic orientation, using different methods and theories to answer different research questions.

GLOSSARY TERMS ○ ● ○

behavioral ecology **51**
cultural ecology **49**
dual-inheritance
    theory **51**
ethnoscience **49**
eugenics **45**
evolutionary
    psychology **51**
functionalism **47**
general evolution **48**

genus **42**
group selection **51**
hermeneutics **54**
individual selection **51**
political economy **50**
sociobiology **51**
specific evolution **48**
structuralism **48**
theoretical
    orientation **40**

CRITICAL QUESTIONS ○ ○ ●

1. Does a theoretical orientation enhance one's way of looking at the world, or does it blind one to other possibilities? Explain your answer.

2. In anthropology, as in many other fields, one theoretical orientation will arise and may grow in popularity until another is proposed in opposition to it. Is this kind of rejection healthy for a discipline? If so, why? If not, why not?

3. Although anthropology is holistic in including the study of humans as both biological organisms and as cultural or social organisms, cultural and biological theories are rarely considered together. Why do you think? Explain why you think that this helps or hinders anthropology.

PEARSON
myanthrolab

Read Richard Scaglion, "Abelam: Giant Yams and Cycles of Sex, Warfare and Ritual" on MyAnthroLab and answer the following questions:

1. Describe what Scaglion means by the "ethnographic present." Does using that concept allow for studying cultural change?

2. Pick two of the theoretical orientations you have read about in this chapter, then indicate how they might point toward an explanation of some aspects of the yam-growing cycle."

Explanation and Evidence

Anthropologists in the field try to arrive at accurate answers to descriptive questions. How do the people make a living? How do they marry? What gods do they believe in? But as important as accurate description is, it is not the ultimate goal of anthropology. Anthropologists want to understand—to know why people have certain customs or beliefs, not just to see that they do have them. As difficult as the how and what questions are to answer, the why questions are even harder. Why questions deal with explanations, which are harder to generate and harder to evaluate. In science, to understand is to explain, and so the major goal of science is to arrive at trustworthy explanations.[1]

For many anthropologists, the plausibility or persuasiveness of an explanation cannot be considered a sufficient reason to accept it. The explanation must also be tested and supported by objective evidence that could conceivably have falsified it. Even when it is supported, there still may be grounds for skepticism. According to the scientific orientation, all knowledge is uncertain and therefore is subject to increasing or decreasing confirmation as new tests are made. If this is true—and it may be uncomfortable to acknowledge—it means that we will never arrive at absolute truth. On the other hand, and this is encouraging, we should be able to achieve more reliable understanding if we keep testing our theories.

This chapter is concerned largely with scientific understanding—what it means to explain, and what kinds of evidence are needed to evaluate an explanation. We also discuss the various types of research that are conducted in cultural anthropology, from ethnography and ethnohistory to cross-cultural and other types of comparisons.

● ○ ●

EXPLANATIONS

An **explanation** is an answer to a why question. There are many types of explanations, some more satisfying than others. For example, suppose we ask why a society has a long postpartum sex taboo. We could guess that the people in that society want to abstain from sex for a year or so after the birth of a baby. Is this an explanation? Yes, because it does suggest that people have a purpose in practicing the custom; it therefore partly answers the why question. But such an explanation would not be very satisfying because it does not specify what the purpose of the custom might be. How about the idea that people have a long postpartum sex taboo because it is their tradition? Yes, that too is an explanation, but it is not satisfactory for a different reason. It is a tautology; that is, the thing to be explained (the taboo) is being explained by itself, by its prior existence. To explain something in terms of tradition is to say that people do it because they already do it, which is not informative. What kinds of explanations are more satisfactory, then? In science, investigators try to achieve two kinds of explanations: associations and theories.

An American anthropologist working with four Kenyan research assistants in Katheri, Kenya.

Associations or Relationships

One way of explaining something (an observation, an action, a custom) is to say how it conforms to a general principle or relationship. So to explain why the water left outside in the basin froze, we say that it was cold last night and that water freezes at 32°F (0°C). The statement that water solidifies (becomes ice) at 32°F is a statement of a relationship or association between two **variables**—things or quantities that vary. In this case, variation in the state of water (liquid vs. solid) is related to variation in the temperature of the air (above 32°F vs. below 32°F). The truth of the relationship is suggested by repeated observations. In the physical sciences, such relationships are called **laws** when almost all scientists accept them.

We find such explanations satisfactory because they allow us to predict what will happen in the future or to understand something that has happened regularly in the past.

In the social sciences, associations are usually stated *probabilistically;* that is, we say that two or more variables tend to be related in a predictable way, which means that there are usually some exceptions. For example, to explain why a society has a long postpartum sex taboo, we can point to the association (or correlation) that John Whiting found in a worldwide sample of societies: Societies with apparently low-protein diets tend to have long postpartum sex taboos.[2] We call the relationship between low-protein diets and the sex taboo a **statistical association,** which means that the observed relationship is unlikely to be due to chance.

The statement that water becomes ice at 32 degrees Fahrenheit (0 degrees Celsius) defines an association between two variables, water and temperature. A theory explains why an association exists.

Theories

Even though laws and statistical associations explain by relating what is to be explained to other things, we want to know more: why those laws or associations exist. Why does water freeze at 32°F? Why do societies with low-protein diets tend to have long postpartum sex taboos? Therefore, scientists try to formulate theories that will explain the observed relationships (laws and statistical associations).[3]

Theories—explanations of laws and statistical associations—are more complicated than the observed relationships they are intended to explain. It is difficult to be precise about what a theory is. By way of example, let us return to the question of why some societies have long postpartum sex taboos. We have already seen that a known statistical association can be used to help explain it. In general (but not always), if a society has a low-protein diet, it will have a long postpartum sex taboo. But most people would ask additional questions: Why does a low-protein diet explain the taboo? What is the mechanism by which a society with such a diet develops the custom of a long postpartum sex taboo? A theory is intended to answer such questions.

John Whiting theorized that a long postpartum sex taboo may be an adaptation to tropical environments, particularly where the major food staples are low in protein. In such environments babies are vulnerable to the protein-deficiency disease called kwashiorkor. But if a baby could continue to nurse for a long time, it might have more of a chance to survive. The postpartum sex taboo might be adaptive, Whiting's theory suggests, because it increases the likelihood of a baby's survival. That is, if a mother puts off having another baby for a while, the first baby might have a better chance to survive because it can be fed mother's milk for a longer time. Whiting suggests that parents may be aware, whether unconsciously or consciously, that having another baby too soon might jeopardize the survival of the first baby, and so they might decide that it would be a good idea to abstain from intercourse for more than a year after the birth of the first baby.

As this example of a theory illustrates, there are differences between a theory and an association. A theory is more complicated, containing a series of statements. An association usually states quite simply that there is a relationship between two or more measured variables. Another difference is that, although a theory may mention some things that are observable, such as the presence of a long postpartum sex taboo, parts of it are difficult or impossible to observe directly. For example, with regard to Whiting's theory, it would be difficult to find out if people had deliberately or unconsciously decided to practice a long postpartum sex taboo because they recognized that babies would thereby have a better chance to survive. Then, too, the concept of adaptation—that some characteristic promotes greater reproductive success—is difficult to verify because it is difficult to find out whether different individuals or groups have different rates of reproduction because they do or do not practice the supposedly adaptive custom. Thus, some concepts or implications in a theory are unobservable (at least at the present time), and only some aspects may be observable. In contrast, statistical associations or laws are based entirely on observations.[4]

WHY THEORIES CANNOT BE PROVED

Many people think that the theories they learned in physics or chemistry courses have been proved. Unfortunately, many students get that impression because their teachers present "lessons" in an authoritative manner. Scientists and philosophers of science now generally agree that, although some theories may have considerable evidence supporting them, no theory can be said to be proved or unquestionably true. This is because many of the concepts and ideas in theories are not directly observable and therefore are not directly verifiable. For example, scientists may try to explain how light behaves by postulating that it consists of particles called photons, but photons cannot be observed, even with the most powerful microscope. So exactly what a photon looks like and exactly how it works remain in the realm of the unprovable. The photon is a **theoretical construct,** something that cannot be observed or verified directly. Because all theories contain such constructs, theories cannot be proved entirely or with absolute certainty.[5]

Why should we bother with theories, then, if we cannot prove that they are true? Perhaps the main advantage of a theory as a kind of explanation is that it may lead to new understanding or knowledge. A theory can suggest new relationships or imply new predictions that new research might support or confirm. For example, Whiting's theory about long postpartum sex taboos has implications that researchers could investigate. Because the theory discusses how a long postpartum sex taboo might be adaptive, we would expect that certain changes would result in the

▶current research and issues

Science and Humanism

This chapter deals largely with the scientific view of understanding, but there are anthropologists who question whether the scientific approach is desirable or possible. They often describe themselves as humanists who use the human capacity to intuit, empathize, evoke, interpret, and illuminate as ways to understand. This orientation offers a very different kind of understanding because, compared with that offered by science, it does not insist on objectivity, nor does it insist on putting insights to empirical tests as science does. This is not to say that scientists do not intuit or interpret. They often do in the process of deriving theories, which involves creative leaps of imagination. Scientists, like anyone else, may empathize with the plight of the people they study. But the crucial difference between the humanistic and scientific orientations lies in the end result. For humanists, interpretation or evocation is the goal; for scientists, the goal is testing interpretations to see if they may be wrong.

Is objectivity possible? Or, because we are humans observing other humans, can we only be subjective? Objectivity requires trying to get at the truth despite the observer's subjective desires or needs. Is that possible? Can any human be unbiased? In an absolute sense, no one can be completely free of bias. But science has ways to strive for objectivity; it does not need to assume that every human is completely unbiased. Remember

that, even when humans engage in physical science, they are often the observers or the creators of the instruments that do the observation. When an instrument points to a number, two people may get slightly different readings because they look at the instrument from different angles. But neither person will be far off the mark, and the average of readings by two or more individuals will be very close to a "true" score.

Do we see other people objectively? Undoubtedly, some things about them are harder to "see" than others. It is easier to know objectively that wives and husbands usually sit down to dinner together, harder to "see" how they feel about one another. Suppose you are in a society where you never observe any obvious expression of affection between husbands and wives. At first, your own cultural bias might lead you to think that such couples don't care for each other much. Such an observation might indeed be biased (and not objective) if it turned out that couples privately express affection to each other but avoid public expressions. It might also be that couples communicate their affection for each other in ways you didn't notice. But that doesn't mean that you wouldn't be able to figure this out eventually. In trying to understand the meaning of female-male relationships, you might very well try to establish close, personal relationships with some families. You might then ask people to tell

you stories to try to see how they portrayed relations between husband and wife. In short, a humanistic approach might help you understand how couples really feel about each other. But a scientist might also go through the same procedure to come to a tentative understanding.

As this example illustrates, humanistic understanding and science are really not incompatible. Both the scientist and the humanist would agree on the need to convey what a culture is like (e.g., with regard to how couples feel about each other). But scientists would insist on more. First, they would try to verify, perhaps by systematic interviewing, how commonly a feeling is shared in the culture; second, they would want to explain why this feeling is common in some cultures but not in others. Therefore, they would have to create a theory to explain the variation and then collect evidence to test the theory to see if it might be wrong.

If humans are always biased observers, how can humanists convey the meaning behind other cultures? Aren't humanists trying to get close to the "truth" too? The poet Marianne Moore wrote that poetry gives us "imaginary gardens with real toads in them." Can imagination, humanistic or scientific, be meaningful without at least some real toads?

Sources: Lett 1996. The quote from Marianne Moore is from Timpane 1991, 128. ◣◣◣

---

taboo's disappearance. For example, suppose people adopted either mechanical birth control devices or began to give supplementary high-protein foods to babies. With birth control, a family could space births without abstaining from sex, so we would expect the custom of postpartum abstinence to disappear. We would also expect it to disappear with protein supplements for babies, because kwashiorkor would then be less likely to afflict babies. Whiting's ideas might also prompt investigators to try to find out whether parents are consciously or unconsciously aware of the problem of close birth spacing in areas with low supplies of protein.

Although theories cannot be proved, they are rejectable. The method of **falsification,** which shows that a theory seems to be wrong, is the main way that theories are judged.[6] Scientists derive implications or predictions that should be true if the theory is correct. So, for example, Whiting predicted that societies with long postpartum sex taboos would be found more often in the tropics than in temperate regions and that they would be likely to have low-protein food supplies. Such predictions of what might be found are called **hypotheses.** If the predictions turn out not to be correct, the researcher is obliged to conclude that something may be wrong with the theory or something

Yanomamö Indians of Brazil depend on root crops and thus have a relatively low-protein diet, while the Inuit of Nunavut depend largely on sea mammals and fish and thus have a relatively high-protein diet.

wrong with the test of the theory. Theories that are not falsified are accepted for the time being because the available evidence seems to be consistent with them. But remember that, no matter how much the available evidence seems to support a theory, we can never be certain it is true. There is always the possibility that some implication of it, some hypothesis derivable from it, will not be confirmed in the future.

GENERATING THEORIES

In the previous chapter, we discussed theoretical orientations that are popular in anthropology. Most orientations merely suggest where to look for answers to questions; they do not by themselves suggest particular explanations for particular phenomena. You cannot directly deduce a theory from a theoretical orientation. For example, an anthropologist with an ecological theoretical orientation is likely to say that some particular custom exists because it is or used to be adaptive. But exactly how a particular custom may be adaptive must still be specified; the theoretical orientation does not automatically suggest the mechanism of its adaptiveness. Whiting's theory suggests specific conditions under which the long postpartum sex taboo might be adaptive. The theory does not just say that the taboo is adaptive. How, then, does an anthropologist develop an explanation or theory for some particular phenomenon?

It is difficult to specify any one procedure that is guaranteed to produce a theory, because developing a theory requires creative imagination, and no discovery procedure by itself necessarily generates creativity. Too much dependence on a particular theoretical orientation may, in fact, be detrimental, because it may blind the investigator to other possibilities. A more important factor in generating a theory may be the investigator's belief that it is possible to do so. A person who believes that something is explainable will be more apt to notice possibly connected facts, as well as to recall possibly relevant considerations, and put them all together in some explanatory way.

We can point to two types of procedures that have helped anthropologists produce explanations of cultural phenomena: *single-case analysis* and a *comparative study*.

In analyzing a single case, an anthropologist may be interested in explaining a particular custom. While in the field, ethnographers may ask informants why they practice (or think they practice) the custom. Sometimes such inquiries will elicit a plausible explanation. But more often than not, the informants merely answer, "We have always done it that way." The investigator may then make a kind of mental search through other features of the society or its environment that may be connected with the custom. If possible, the anthropologist may try to view the situation historically, to see if the custom appeared rather recently. If it did, what possible explanatory conditions appeared just before the custom?

An anthropologist may also generate an explanation by comparing different societies that share this characteristic to determine what other characteristics regularly occur along with it. Societies in which the characteristic is lacking would also be considered, because a possible cause of that characteristic should be absent in those societies. If a characteristic occurs regularly in different cultures along with certain other features, we can be reasonably certain that the possible causes of that characteristic have been narrowed down. It must be remembered, however, that the investigator is not a computer. It is not necessary to search through all the characteristics that different cultures might share. The investigator usually looks only at those traits that can plausibly be connected. Here is where an individual's theoretical orientation generally comes into play, because that orientation usually points to the possible importance of one particular set of factors over others.

EVIDENCE: TESTING EXPLANATIONS

In any field of investigation, theories are generally the most plentiful commodity, apparently because of the human predisposition to try to make sense of the world. It is necessary, then, for us to have procedures that enable us to select those theories that are more likely to be correct from among the many available. "Just as mutations arise naturally but are not all beneficial, so hypotheses [theories] emerge naturally but are not all correct. If progress is to occur, therefore, we require a superfluity of hypotheses and also a mechanism of selection."[7] In other words, generating a theory or interpretation is not enough. We need some reliable method of testing whether or not that interpretation is likely to be correct. If an interpretation is not correct, it may detract from our efforts to achieve understanding by misleading us into thinking the problem is already solved.

The strategy in all kinds of testing in science is to predict what one would expect to find if a particular interpretation were correct, and then to conduct an investigation to see if the prediction is generally consistent with the data. If the prediction is not supported, the investigator is obliged to accept the possibility that the interpretation is wrong. If, however, the prediction holds true, then the investigator is entitled to say that evidence supports the theory. Thus, conducting research designed to test expectations derived from theory allows researchers to eliminate some interpretations and to accept others, at least tentatively.

Operationalization and Measurement

We test predictions derived from a theory to see if the theory may be correct, to see if it is consistent with observable events or conditions in the real world. A theory and the predictions derived from it are not useful if there is no way to measure the events or conditions mentioned in the predictions. If there is no way of relating the theory to observable events, it does not matter how good the theory sounds; it is still not a useful scientific theory.[8] To transform theoretical predictions into statements that might be verified, a researcher provides an **operational definition** of each of the concepts or variables mentioned in the prediction. An operational definition is a description of the procedure that is followed to measure the variable.[9]

Whiting predicted that societies with a low-protein diet would have a long postpartum sex taboo. Amount of protein in the diet is a variable; some societies have more, others have less. Length of the postpartum sex taboo is a variable; a society may have a short taboo or a long taboo. Whiting operationally defined the first variable, *amount of protein,* in terms of staple foods.[10] For example, if a society depended mostly on root and tree crops (cassava, bananas), Whiting rated the society as having low protein. If the society depended mostly on cereal crops (wheat, barley, corn, oats), he rated it as having moderate protein, because cereal crops have more protein by weight than root and tree crops. If the society depended mostly on hunting, fishing, or herding for food, he rated it as having high protein. The other variable in Whiting's prediction, *length of postpartum sex taboo,* was operationalized as follows: A society was rated as having a long taboo if couples customarily abstained from sex for more than a year after the birth of a baby; abstention for a year or less was considered a short taboo.

Specifying an operational definition for each variable is extremely important because it allows other investigators to check a researcher's results.[11] Science depends on *replication,* the repetition of results. Only when many

researchers observe a particular association can we call that association or relationship a law. Providing operational definitions is also extremely important because it allows others to evaluate whether a measure is appropriate. Only when we are told exactly how something was measured can we judge whether the measure reflects what it is supposed to reflect. Specifying measures publicly is so important in science that we are obliged to be skeptical of any conclusions offered by a researcher who fails to say how variables were measured.

To **measure** something is to say how it compares with other things on some scale of variation.[12] People often assume that a measuring device is always a physical instrument, such as a scale or a ruler, but physical devices are not the only way to measure something. *Classification* is also a form of measurement. When we classify people as male or female or employed versus unemployed, we are dividing them into *sets.* Deciding which set they belong to is a kind of measurement. We can also measure things by deciding which cases or examples have more or less of something (e.g., more or less protein in the diet). The measures employed in physical science are usually based on scales that allow us to assign numbers to each case; we measure height in meters and weight in grams, for example. However we measure our variables, the fact that we can measure them means that we can test our hypotheses to see if the predicted relationships actually exist, at least most of the time.

Sampling

After deciding how to measure the variables in some predicted relationship, an investigator must decide how to select which cases to study to see if the predicted relationship holds. If the prediction is about the behavior of people, the sampling decision involves which people to observe. If the prediction is about an association between societal customs, the sampling decision involves which societies to study. Investigators must decide not only which cases to choose but also how many to choose. No researcher can investigate all the possible cases, so choices must be made. Some choices are better than others. In the chapter on the concept of culture, we talked about the advantages of random sampling. A random sample is one in which all cases selected had an equal chance of being included in the sample. Almost all statistical tests used to evaluate the results of research require random sampling, because only results based on a random sample can be assumed to be probably true for some larger set or universe of cases.

Before researchers can sample randomly, they must specify the **sampling universe,** that is, the list of cases to be sampled from. Suppose an anthropologist is doing fieldwork in a society. Unless the society is very small, it is usually not practical to use the whole society as the sampling universe. Because most fieldworkers want to remain in a community for a considerable length of time, the community usually becomes the sampling universe. If a cross-cultural researcher wants to test an explanation, it is necessary to sample the world's societies. But we do not have descriptions of all the societies, past and present, that have existed in the world. So samples are usually drawn from published lists of described societies that have been classified or coded according to standard cultural variables,[13] or they are drawn from the Human Relations Area Files (HRAF) Collection of Ethnography, an indexed, annually growing collection of original ethnographic books and articles on more than 400 societies around the world, past and present.[14]

Random sampling is not often employed in anthropology, but a nonrandom sample might still be fairly representative if the investigator has not personally chosen the cases for study. We should be particularly suspicious of any sample that may reflect the investigator's own biases or interests. For example, if investigators pick only the people with whom they are friendly, the sample is suspicious. If cross-cultural researchers select sample societies because ethnographies on them happen to be on their own bookshelves, such samples are also suspicious. A sampling procedure should be designed to get a fair representation of the sampling universe, not a biased selection. If we want to increase our chances of getting a representative sample, we have to use a random sampling procedure. To do so, we conventionally number the cases in the statistical universe and then use a table of random numbers to draw our sample cases.

Statistical Evaluation

When researchers have measured the variables of interest for all the sample cases, they are ready to see if the predicted relationship actually exists in the data. Remember, the results may not turn out to be what the theory predicts. Sometimes researchers construct a *contingency table,* like that shown in Table 4–1, to see if the variables are associated as predicted. In Whiting's sample of 172 societies, each case is assigned to a box, or cell, in the table, depending on how the society is measured on the two variables of interest. For example, a society that has a long postpartum sex taboo and a low-protein diet is placed in the third row of the Long Duration column (Whiting's sample [see Table 4–1] has 27 such societies). A society that has a short postpartum sex taboo and a low-protein diet is placed in the third row in the Short Duration column (the sample has 20 such societies). The statistical question is: Does the

way the cases are distributed in the six central cells of the table generally support Whiting's prediction? If we looked just at the table, we might not know what to answer. Many cases appear to be in the expected places. For example, most of the high-protein cases (47 of 62) have short taboos, and most of the low-protein cases (27 of 47) have long taboos. But there are also many exceptions (e.g., 20 cases have low-protein diets and a short taboo). So, although many cases appear to be in the expected places, there are also many exceptions. Do the exceptions invalidate the prediction? How many exceptions would compel us to reject the hypothesis? Here is where we resort to *statistical tests of significance.*

Statisticians have devised various tests that tell us how "perfect" a result has to be for us to believe that there is probably an association between the variables of interest, that one variable generally predicts the other. Essentially, every statistical result is evaluated in the same objective way. We ask: What is the chance that this result is purely accidental, that there is no association at all between the two variables? Although some of the mathematical ways of answering this question are complicated, the answer always involves a **probability value** (or **p-value**)—the likelihood that the observed result or a stronger one could have occurred by chance. The statistical test Whiting uses gives a p-value of less than .01 ($p < .01$) for the observed result. In other words, there is less than 1 chance out of 100 that the relationship observed (the distribution of cases) is purely accidental. A p-value of less than .01 is a fairly low probability; most social scientists conventionally agree to call any result with a p-value of .05 or less (5 or fewer chances out of 100) a **statistically significant,** or probably true, result. When we describe relationships or associations in the rest of this book, we are almost always referring to results that have been found to be statistically significant.

But why should a probably true relationship have any exceptions? If a theory is really correct, shouldn't *all* the cases fit? There are many reasons why we can never expect a perfect result. First, even if a theory is correct (e.g., if a low-protein diet really does favor the adoption of a long postpartum sex taboo), there may still be other causes that we have not investigated. Some of the societies could have a long taboo even though they have high protein. For example, societies that depend mostly on hunting for their food, and would therefore be classified as having a high-protein diet, may have a problem carrying infants from one campsite to another and may practice a long postpartum sex taboo so that two infants will not have to be carried at the same time.

Exceptions to the predicted relationship might also occur because of *cultural lag.*[15] Cultural lag occurs when change in one aspect of culture takes time to produce change in another aspect. Suppose that a society recently changed crops and is now no longer a low-protein society but still practices a long postpartum sex taboo. This society would be an exception to the predicted relationship, but it might fit the theory if it stopped practicing the taboo in a few years. Measurement inaccuracy is another source of exceptions. Whiting's measure of protein, which is based on the major sources of food, is not a very precise

Availability of Protein	Duration of Postpartum Sex Taboo		
	Short (0–1 Year)	Long (More Than 1 Year)	Total
High	47	15	62
Medium	38	25	63
Low	20	27	47
Total	105	67	172

TABLE 4–1 Association Between Availability of Protein and Duration of Postpartum Sex Taboo

Source: Based on Whiting 1964, 520.

measure of protein in the diet. It does not take into account the possibility that a "tree crop" society might get a lot of protein from fishing or raising pigs. So it might turn out that some supposedly low-protein societies have been misclassified, which may be one reason why 20 cases are in the lowest cell in the left-hand column of Table 4–1. Measurement error usually produces exceptions.

Significant statistical associations that are predictable from a theory offer tentative support for the theory. But much more is needed before we can be fairly confident about the theory. Replication is needed to confirm whether other researchers can reproduce the predictions using other samples. Other predictions should be derived from the theory to see if they too are supported. The theory should be pitted against alternative explanations to see which theory works better. We may have to combine theories if the alternative explanations also predict the relationship in question. The research process in science thus requires time and patience. Perhaps most important, it requires that researchers be humble. No matter how wonderful one's own theory seems, it is important to acknowledge that it may be wrong. If we don't acknowledge that possibility, we can't be motivated to test our theories. If we don't test our theories, we can never tell the difference between a better or worse theory, and we will be saddled forever with our present ignorance. In science, knowledge or understanding is explained variation. Thus, if we want to understand more, we have to keep testing our beliefs against sets of objective evidence that could contradict our beliefs.

TYPES OF RESEARCH IN CULTURAL ANTHROPOLOGY

Cultural anthropologists use several methods to conduct research. Each has certain advantages and disadvantages in generating and testing explanations. The types of research in cultural anthropology can be classified according to two criteria. One is the spatial scope of the study—analysis of a single society, analysis of societies in a region, or analysis of a worldwide sample of societies. The other criterion is the temporal scope of the study—historical versus nonhistorical. Combinations of these criteria are shown in Table 4–2.

Ethnography

Around the beginning of the 20th century, anthropologists realized that they would have to study their subject in depth if they were to produce anything of scientific value.

To describe cultures more accurately, they started to live among the people they were studying. They observed, and even took part in, the important events of those societies and carefully questioned the people about their native customs. This method is known as **participant-observation.** Participant-observation always involves **fieldwork,** which is firsthand experience with the people being studied, but fieldwork may also involve other methods, such as conducting a census or a survey.[16]

Participant-observation, the cornerstone of modern anthropology, is the means by which most anthropological information is obtained. Regardless of other methods that anthropologists may use, participant-observation is regarded as fundamental, usually for a year or more. In contrast to the casual descriptions of travelers and adventurers, anthropologists' descriptions record, describe, analyze, and eventually formulate a picture of the culture, or at least part of it.[17] After doing fieldwork, an anthropologist may prepare an *ethnography,* a description and analysis of a single society.

Hardly any cultural anthropologist disputes the value of fieldwork in another culture, both for what it contributes to understanding others and for what it contributes to understanding yourself and your own culture. Probably the immersion does it. Living with other people (participant-observation) allows anthropologists to see things they would not otherwise notice. At the same time, they cannot help but realize how the smallest habitual things they do, which they may have thought were just natural, are just wrong in the field site. At the beginning, anthropologists have culture shock because they don't comprehend so much. At the end, anthropologists have culture shock when they return home. All of a sudden, many things in their own society now may seem strange. Indeed, the experience is so profound that most cultural anthropologists feel that fieldwork provides them with the "deepest" kind of knowledge. Not just deep, but real.

How an anthropologist goes about doing long-term participant-observation in another culture—and, more important, doing it well—is not so straightforward. Much of it depends on the person, the culture, and the interaction between the two. Without a doubt, the experience is physically and psychologically demanding, comparable often to a rite of passage. Although it helps enormously to learn the local language before one goes, often it is not possible to do so, and so most anthropologists find themselves struggling to communicate in addition to trying to figure out how to behave properly. Participant-observation carries its own dilemma. Participation implies living

TABLE 4–2 Types of Research in Cultural Anthropology		
Scope	Nonhistorical	Historical
Single society	Ethnography/fieldwork Within-culture comparison	Ethnohistory Within-culture comparison
Region	Controlled comparison	Controlled comparison
Worldwide sample	Cross-cultural research	Cross-historical research

Anthropologist Margaret Kieffer conducts an ethnographic interview with a Mayan woman in Guatemala.

like the people you have come to study, and trying to understand subjectively what they think and feel by doing what they do, whereas observation implies a certain amount of objectivity and detachment.[18] Because participant-observation is such a personal experience, it is not surprising that anthropologists have begun to realize that *reflecting* on their experiences and their personal interaction with the people they live with is an important part of understanding the enterprise.

An essential part of the participant-observation process is finding some knowledgeable people who are willing to work with you (anthropologists call them *informants*), to help you interpret what you observe and tell you about aspects of the culture that you may not have a chance to see, or may not be entitled to see. For example, it is not likely that you will see many weddings in a village of 200 people in a year or two of fieldwork. So how can you know who will be a good informant? It is obviously important to find people who are easy to talk to and who understand what information you need. But how do you know who is knowledgeable? You can't just assume that the people you get along with have the most knowledge. (Besides, knowledge is often specialized; one person may know a whole lot more about some subjects than others.) At a minimum, you have to try out a few different people to compare what they tell you about a subject. What if they disagree? How do you know who is more trustworthy or accurate? Fortunately, formal methods have been developed to help select the most knowledgeable informants. One method called the "cultural consensus model" relies on the principle that those things that most informants agree on are probably cultural. After you establish which things appear to be cultural by asking a sample of informants the same questions about a particular cultural domain, it will be easy to discover which informants are very likely to give answers that closely match the cultural consensus. These individuals are your best bets to be the most knowledgeable in that domain.[19] It may seem paradoxical,

but the most knowledgeable and helpful individuals are not necessarily "typical" individuals. Many anthropologists have pointed out that key informants are likely to feel somewhat marginal in their culture. After all, why would they want to spend so much time with the visiting anthropologist?[20]

Participant-observation is valuable for understanding some aspects of culture, particularly the things that are the most public, readily talked about, and most widely agreed upon. But more systematic methods are important too: mapping, house-to-house censuses, behavior observations (e.g., to determine how people spend their time), as well as focused interviews with a sample of informants.

Ethnographies and ethnographic articles on particular topics provide much of the essential data for all kinds of studies in cultural anthropology. To make a comparison of societies in a given region or worldwide, an anthropologist would require ethnographic data on many societies. With regard to the goal of generating theory, ethnography, with its in-depth, firsthand, long-term observation, provides an investigator with a wealth of descriptive material covering a wide range of phenomena. Thus, it may stimulate interpretations about the way different aspects of the culture are related to each other and to features of the environment. The ethnographer in the field has the opportunity to get to know the context of a society's customs by directly asking the people about those customs and by observing the phenomena that appear to be associated with those practices. In addition, the ethnographer who develops a possible explanation for some custom can test that hunch by collecting new information related to it. In this sense, the ethnographer is similar to a physician who is trying to understand why a patient has certain symptoms of illness.

Although ethnography is extremely useful for generating explanations, a field study of a single site does not generally provide sufficient data to test a hypothesis. For example, an ethnographer may think that a particular society practices *polygyny* (one man married to two or more women simultaneously) because it has more women than men. But the ethnographer could not be reasonably sure that this explanation was correct unless the results of a comparative study of a sample of societies showed that most polygynous societies have more women than men. After all, the fact that one society has both these conditions could be a historical accident rather than a result of some necessary connection between the two conditions.

Ethnographer Disagreements   Although few people doubt the value of fieldwork, there have been challenges about its veracity. Consider the controversy over the fieldwork of Margaret Mead, who lived on a small island in American Samoa in the 1920s and wrote about the sexual freedom of adolescents in *Coming of Age in Samoa*.[21] Derek Freeman, who worked in Western Samoa largely in the 1960s, wrote a scathing critique of Mead's fieldwork in his *Margaret Mead and Samoa: The Making and Unmaking of an Anthropological Myth*. Essentially, Freeman said that Mead got most things wrong. For example, he stated that the Samoans are puritanical in their sexuality.[22] If both did fieldwork, and fieldwork gives us real, deep knowledge, shouldn't they both be right? But how can they be? Was one a good fieldworker and the other not? How can we know what is true?

Paul Shankman suggests that both might be partly right if we recognize several things. First, he points out that we can speak of sexual permissiveness and sexual restrictiveness only in comparative terms. We need to understand that Mead did her fieldwork at a time when premarital sex was uncommon in the United States, but sex patterns changed subsequently. So, in contrast with American girls during Mead's time, Samoan girls may have seemed more sexually free.[23] Second, Samoa changed a great deal over time with missionization, colonialization, World War II, and commercialization. Third, Samoa was variable—American Samoa versus Western Samoa, rural versus urban. So, what the two fieldworkers experienced may have been quite different, and therefore they could both be right.[24] But, in fact, Shankman suggests that, if we ignore Mead's and Freeman's conclusions about permissive or restrictive sexuality, if we separate ideal from actual behavior, and if we look at actual data on individual sexual behavior as collected by both Mead and Freeman, the two fieldworkers are not all that different: Samoans are in the middle of the worldwide range of cultures in regard to the occurrence of premarital sex.[25]

What do we conclude from this controversy? As many anthropologists are now pointing out, it is important to reflect on the possible influences of the context of the fieldwork, the qualities of the people doing it, how those people interact with the people they live with, and the kinds of methods used to try to verify conclusions. Others point out that reflection, although important, is not enough. If we want to be more sure that we are understanding correctly, it is not sufficient to assume that the traditional style of fieldwork (participant-observation and interviewing of a few selected informants by one person) can always discover the truth in a field situation. Particularly for those behaviors that are private, or more variable, or not easily verbalized, anthropological fieldworkers should consider interviewing a representative sample of people and using tests of informant accuracy. More than one fieldworker, particularly different types of fieldworkers, may be important too. Particularly in societies where women and men live very segregated lives, female-male teams, usually a married couple, can successfully gain rapport with members of their own gender. Ethnographers who go to the field with children report that they can thereby learn more about child socialization and children's lives; even their children, if old enough, can provide valuable information about their play and interactions with other children.[26] Besides, going with family is often an asset because the ethnographer is considered more "normal."

Ethics in Fieldwork   Anthropologists have many ethical obligations—to the people they study, their anthropological colleagues, to the public and world community, and even to their employers and their own and host countries. But anthropologists agree that, should a conflict arise in ethical obligations, the most important obligation is to protect the interests of the people they study. According to the profession's code of ethics, anthropologists should tell people in the field site about the research, and they should respect the right of people to remain anonymous if they so choose.[27] For this reason, informants are often given "pseudonyms" or fake names; many anthropologists have extended this principle to using a fake name for the community as well. But the decision to create a fake name for a community is questionable in many circumstances.[28] First, anthropologists "stick out" and it is not hard for anyone interested to figure out where they lived and worked. Governments may have to be asked for research clearance, which means that they know where the anthropologist is going to do the fieldwork. Second, people who are studied are often proud of their place and their customs and they may be insulted if their community is called something else. Third, important geographic information is often vital to understanding the community. You have to reveal if it is located at the confluence of two major rivers, or if it is the trading center of the region. Lastly, it may be difficult for a future anthropologist to conduct a follow-up study if the community is disguised. Of course, if a community were truly in danger, there would be no question that an anthropologist has an obligation to try to protect it.

Honest, objective reporting is also an obligation to the anthropological profession, to the public at large, and to the observed community. But suppose a custom or trait that appears perfectly reasonable to the observed community is considered objectionable by outsiders. Such customs could range from acts that outsiders consider criminal, such as infanticide, to those that are considered repugnant, such as eating dogs. An anthropologist may believe that publication of the information could bring harm to the population. Kim Hill and Magdalena Hurtado faced this situation when they realized that infanticide rates were high in the group they studied in South America.

They did not want to play up their findings, nor did they want to dissimulate. After they met with community leaders to discuss the situation, they agreed not to publish their findings in Spanish to minimize the possibility that the local media or neighboring groups might learn of their findings.[29]

Everyday decisions like how to compensate people for their time are not easy either. Nowadays, many if not most informants expect to be paid or receive gifts. But in the early days of anthropology, in places where money was not an important part of the native economy, the decision to pay people was not a clear ethical choice. If money is rare, paying people increases the importance of money in that economy. Even nonmonetary gifts can increase inequalities or create jealousies. On the other hand, doing nothing by way of compensation doesn't seem right either. As an alternative, some anthropologists try to find some community project that they can help with—that way, everyone benefits. This is not to say that the anthropologist is necessarily a burden on the community. People often like to talk about their customs, and they may want others to appreciate their way of life. Anthropologists are also often amusing. They may ask "funny" questions, and when they try to say or do customary things, they often do them all wrong. Every anthropologist has probably been laughed at sometimes in the field.

Within-Culture Comparisons

Ethnographers could test a theory within one society if they decide to compare individuals, families, households, communities, or districts. The natural variability that exists can be used to create a comparison. Suppose we want to verify Whiting's assumption that in a society with a low-protein diet, longer postpartum taboos enhance the survival of babies. Although almost all couples might practice a long postpartum sex taboo because it is customary, some couples might not adhere to the taboo consistently and some couples might not conceive quickly after the taboo is lifted. So we would expect some variation in spacing between births. If we collected information on the births of each mother and the survival outcome of each birth, we would be able to compare the survival rates of children born a short time after the mother's last pregnancy with those of children born after longer intervals. A significantly higher survival rate for the births after longer intervals would support Whiting's theory. What if some communities within the society had access to more protein than others? If Whiting's theory is correct, those communities with more protein should also have a higher survival rate for babies. If there were variation in the length of the postpartum sex taboo, the communities with more protein should have shorter taboos.

Whether or not we can design intracultural tests of hypotheses depends on whether we have sufficient variability in the variables in our hypotheses. More often than not we do, and we can make use of that variation to test hypotheses within a culture.

Regional Controlled Comparisons

In a regional controlled comparison, the anthropologist compares ethnographic information obtained from societies found in a particular region—societies that presumably have similar histories and occupy similar environments. The anthropologist who conducts a regional comparison is apt to be familiar with the complex of cultural features associated with that region. These features may provide a good understanding of the context of the phenomenon that is to be explained. An anthropologist's knowledge of the region under study, however, is probably not as great as the ethnographer's knowledge of a single society. Still, the anthropologist's understanding of local details is greater in a regional comparison than in a worldwide comparison. The worldwide comparison is necessarily so broad that the investigator is unlikely to know a great deal about any of the societies being compared.

The regional controlled comparison is useful not only for generating explanations but also for testing them. Because some of the societies being compared will have the characteristic that is to be explained and some will not, the anthropologist can determine whether the conditions hypothesized to be related are in fact related, at least in that region. We must remember, however, that two or more conditions may be related in one region for reasons peculiar to that region. Therefore, an explanation supported in one region may not fit others.

Cross-Cultural Research

Anthropologists can generate interpretations on the basis of worldwide comparisons by looking for differences between those societies having and those lacking a particular characteristic. But the most common use of worldwide comparisons has been to test explanations. An example is Whiting's test of his theory about the adaptive functions of a long postpartum sex taboo. Recall that Whiting hypothesized that, if his theory were correct, variation in protein supplies in the adult diet should predict variation in the duration of the postpartum sex taboo. Cross-cultural researchers first identify conditions that should generally be associated if a particular theory is correct. Then they look at a worldwide sample of societies to see if the expected association generally holds true. As we indicated in the sampling section, most cross-culturalists choose a published sample of societies that was not constructed for any specific hypothesis test. Two of the most widely used samples are the Standard Cross-Cultural (SCCS) Sample of 186 societies and the annually growing HRAF Collection of Ethnography. Because HRAF actually contains full-text ethnographies that are subject-indexed by paragraph, a researcher can fairly quickly find information to code a new variable across a large number of societies. In contrast, the SCCS sample contains pointers to ethnography, not ethnographies themselves. However, other researchers have now coded thousands of variables for this sample, so researchers who want to use data coded by others tend to use this sample.[30]

The advantage of cross-cultural research is that the conclusion drawn from it is probably applicable to most

applied anthropology

There Is Nothing Like Evidence to Shake Mistaken Beliefs

Potatoes are widely grown in the Andean highlands of South America, and they may have been domesticated there or close by. It is often assumed therefore that the highlands are the best place to grow potatoes. But some scientists were skeptical (after all, potatoes have been grown successfully at low altitudes elsewhere). Perhaps, the scientists reasoned, potatoes are grown in the Andean highlands because other crops such as corn are not suited to the highlands. Potatoes grow in the ground, and the short Andean growing season or a frost won't kill them. They can stay in the ground for some time without rotting. Other crops such as corn could be grown in the highlands, but they grow more safely and productively in the warmer lowlands, which have a longer growing season and less risk of untimely frost. Also, corn would be the crop of choice in the lowlands, particularly if there is adequate rainfall or the crop can be irrigated (as in the coastal river valleys of Peru that empty into the Pacific). Corn agriculture would leave little room for

growing potatoes in the lowlands. By default, then, potatoes might have become the crop of choice in the highlands because little else could produce as many edible calories.

For many years, the International Potato Center in Lima, Peru, has employed anthropologists to conduct research on how to increase potato production while protecting the environment and preserving biodiversity. To explore the possibilities, the anthropologists decided to investigate how and where potatoes were grown around the world, adopting the strategy of comparative research that was pioneered by the Human Relations Area Files (HRAF) to document cross-cultural variation and to test hypotheses about it. Data on potato production were obtained from 132 countries. Surprisingly, the data showed that the bulk of potatoes produced in developing countries were not grown in the tropical highlands, where the Potato Center had targeted most of its work, but rather in the lowland subtropical zones of Asia, where potatoes are typically rotated with rice or wheat. The Center

discovered from its comparative study that its own development projects in tropical hilly areas of Asia (the Philippines, Indonesia, Thailand, Sri Lanka) and Africa (Rwanda, Burundi) had disadvantageous consequences. They had degraded the environment because potatoes leave the slopes precariously exposed during periods of high rainfall. Furthermore, potatoes are often grown as a luxury crop for fast food restaurants, tourist hotels, and airlines—not as food for the poor. Who would have thought that the potato could be a luxury crop?

The worldwide comparative research by the Potato Center's anthropologists became a model for other agricultural centers and programs that work on how to increase sustainable and safe production of other important world crops, such as rice, corn, wheat, and peanuts. Applied anthropology can "open eyes" and suggest possibilities because it looks worldwide at the human condition.

Sources: Rhoades 2005, 61–85; Rhoades 2001.

---

societies, if the sample used for testing has been more or less randomly selected and therefore is representative of the world. In other words, in contrast with the results of a regional comparison, which may or may not be applicable to other regions, the results of a cross-cultural study are probably applicable to most societies and most regions.

As we have noted, the greater the number of societies examined in a study, the less likely it is that the investigator will have detailed knowledge of the societies involved. So if a cross-cultural test does not support a particular explanation, the investigator may not know enough about the sample societies to know how to modify the interpretation or come up with a new one. In this situation, the anthropologist may reexamine the details of one or more particular societies to stimulate fresh thinking on the subject. Another limitation of cross-cultural research, as a means of both generating and testing explanations, is that only those explanations for which the required information is generally available in ethnographies can be tested. An investigator interested in explaining something that has not been generally described must resort to some other research strategy to collect data.

Historical Research

Ethnohistory consists of studies based on descriptive materials about a single society at more than one point in time. It provides the essential data for historical studies of all types, just as ethnography provides the essential data for all nonhistorical types of research. Ethnohistorical data may consist of sources other than the ethnographic reports prepared by anthropologists—accounts by explorers, missionaries, traders, and government officials. Ethnohistorians, like historians, cannot simply assume that all the documents they find are simply descriptions of fact; they were written by very different kinds of people with very different goals and purposes. So they need to separate carefully what may be fact from what may be speculative interpretation. To reconstruct how a culture changed over hundreds of years, where the natives left few or no written accounts, anthropologists have to seek out travelers' accounts and other historical documents that were written by non-natives. Mary Helms had to do this when she decided to do fieldwork among the Miskito of Nicaragua, to reconstruct how their life had changed under the conditions of European colonialism. She was particularly

The manner of their fishing.

Ethnohistorians need to analyze pieces of information from a variety of sources such as the accounts of European explorers. Pictured here is a group of Roanoke Native Americans fishing in the late 1500s. It provides the ethnohistorian good information on how these people harvested fish.

Source: John White/Copyright The British Museum.

interested in discovering why the Miskito were able to preserve a lot of political independence.[31]

In terms of generating and testing hypotheses, studies of single societies over time tend to be subject to the same limitations as studies of single societies confined to a single period. Like their nonhistorical counterparts, studies that concentrate on a single society observed through time are likely to generate more than one hypothesis, but they do not generally provide the opportunity to establish with reasonable certainty which of those hypotheses is

correct. Cross-cultural historical studies (of which we have only a few examples thus far) suffer from the opposite limitation. They provide ample means of testing hypotheses through comparison, but they are severely constrained, because of the necessity of working with secondhand data, in their ability to generate hypotheses derived from the available data.

There is, however, one advantage to historical studies of any type. The goal of theory in cultural anthropology is to explain variation in cultural patterns, that is, to specify what conditions will favor one cultural pattern rather than another. Such specification requires us to assume that the supposed causal, or favoring, conditions antedated the pattern to be explained. Theories or explanations, then, imply a sequence of changes over time, which are the stuff of history. Therefore, if we want to come closer to an understanding of the reasons for the cultural variations we are investigating, we should examine historical sequences. They will help us determine whether the conditions we think caused various phenomena truly antedated those phenomena and thus might more reliably be said to have caused them. If we can examine historical sequences, we may be able to make sure that we do not put the cart before the horse.

The major impediment to historical research is that collecting and analyzing historical data—particularly when they come from the scattered accounts of explorers, missionaries, and traders—tends to be very time-consuming. It may be more efficient to test explanations nonhistorically first, to eliminate some interpretations. Only when an interpretation survives a nonhistorical test should we look to historical data to test the presumed sequence.

In the chapters that follow, we discuss not only what we strongly suspect about the determinants of cultural variation but also what we do not know or only dimly suspect. We devote a lot of our discussion to what we do not know—what has not yet been the subject of research that tests hypotheses and theories—because we want to convey a sense of what cultural anthropology might discover in the future.

SUMMARY ● ○ ○

1. Scientists try to achieve two kinds of explanations—associations (observed relationships between two or more variables) and theories (explanations of associations).

2. A theory is more complicated than an association. Some concepts or implications in a theory are unobservable; an association is based entirely on observations.

3. Theories can never be proved with absolute certainty. There is always the possibility that some implication, some derivable hypothesis, will not be confirmed by future research.

4. A theory may be rejectable through the method of falsification. Scientists derive predictions that should be true if the theory is correct. If the predictions turn out to be incorrect, scientists are obliged to conclude that something may be wrong with the theory.

5. To make a satisfactory test, we have to specify operationally how we measure the variables involved in the relationships we expect to exist, so that other researchers can try to replicate, or repeat, our results.

6. Tests of predictions should employ samples that are representative. The most objective way to obtain a representative sample is to select the sample cases randomly.

7. The results of tests are evaluated by statistical methods that assign probability values to the results. These values allow us to distinguish between probably true and probably accidental results.

8. Cultural anthropologists use several different methods to conduct research. Each has certain advantages and disadvantages in generating and testing explanations. The types of research in cultural anthropology can be classified according to two criteria: the spatial scope of the study (analysis of a single society, analysis of several or more societies in a region, or analysis of a worldwide sample of societies) and the temporal scope of the study (historical vs. nonhistorical). The basic research methods, then, are ethnography and ethnohistory, historical and nonhistorical regional controlled comparisons, and historical and nonhistorical cross-cultural research.

GLOSSARY TERMS ○ ● ○

explanation **58**
falsification **61**
fieldwork **65**
hypotheses **61**
laws **59**
measure **63**
operational
    definition **63**
participant-
    observation **65**
probability value
    (*p*-value) **64**
sampling universe **63**
statistical association **59**
statistically
    significant **64**
theoretical
    construct **60**
theories **60**
variables **59**

CRITICAL QUESTIONS ○ ○ ●

1. Are theories important? Explain why or why not.

2. Can a unique event be explained? Explain your answer.

3. How does measurement go beyond observation?

4. Why is scientific understanding always uncertain?

5. If two ethnographers describing the same culture disagree, how do we decide who's right?

PEARSON
myanthrolab

Read the chapter by Carol R. Ember and Melvin Ember, "On Cross Cultural Research" on MyAnthroLab and answer the following questions:

1. Give a few examples of questions that can be answered by cross-cultural research.

2. What are the basic assumptions and steps in a cross-cultural study?

Communication and Language

ew of us can remember when we first became aware that words signified something. Yet that moment was a milestone for us, not just in the acquisition of language but in becoming acquainted with all the complex, elaborate behavior that constitutes our culture. Without language, the transmission of complex traditions would be virtually impossible, and each person would be trapped within his or her own world of private sensations.

Helen Keller, left deaf and blind by illness at the age of 19 months, gives a moving account of the afternoon she first established contact with another human being through words:

> [My teacher] brought me my hat, and I knew I was going out into the warm sunshine. This thought, if a wordless sensation may be called a thought, made me hop and skip with pleasure.
>
> We walked down the path to the well house, attracted by the fragrance of the honeysuckle with which it was covered. Someone was drawing water and my teacher placed my hand under the spout. As the cool stream gushed over one hand she spelled into the other the word water, first slowly, then rapidly. Suddenly I felt a misty consciousness as of something forgotten—a thrill of returning thought; and somehow the mystery of language was revealed to me. I knew then that w-a-t-e-r meant the wonderful cool something that was flowing over my hand. That living word awakened my soul, gave it light, hope, joy, set it free! There were barriers still, it is true, barriers that could in time be swept away.
>
> I left the well house eager to learn. Everything had a name, and each name gave birth to a new thought. As we returned to the house every object which I touched seemed to quiver with life. That was because I saw everything with the strange, new sight that had come to me.[1]

● ○ ●

COMMUNICATION

Against all odds, Helen Keller had come to understand the essential function that language plays in all societies—namely, that of communication. The word *communicate* comes from the Latin verb *communicare*, "to impart," "to share," "to make *common*." We communicate by agreeing, consciously or unconsciously, to call an object, a movement, or an abstract concept by a common name. For example, speakers of English have agreed to call the color of grass *green*, even though we have no way of comparing precisely how two people actually experience this color. What we share is the agreement to call similar sensations *green*. Any system of language consists of publicly accepted symbols by which individuals try to share private experiences. Spoken or vocal language is probably the major transmitter of culture, allowing us to share and pass on our complex configuration of attitudes, beliefs, and patterns of behavior.

Nonverbal Human Communication

As we all know from experience, the spoken word does not communicate all that we know about a social situation. We can usually tell when someone says, "It was good to meet you," whether he or she really means it. We can tell if people are sad from their demeanor, even if they just say, "I'm fine," in response to the question "How are you?"

Obviously, our communication is not limited to spoken language. We communicate directly through facial expression, body stance, gesture, and tone of voice and indirectly through systems of signs and symbols, such as writing, algebraic equations, musical scores, dancing, painting, code flags, and road signs. As Anthony Wilden put it, "every act, every pause, every movement in living and social systems is also a message; silence is communication; short of death it is impossible for an organism or person not to communicate."[2] How can silence be a communication? Silence may reflect companionship, as when two people work side by side on a project, but silence can also communicate unfriendliness. An anthropologist can learn a great deal from what people in a society do not talk about. For example, in India, sex is not supposed to be talked about. HIV infection is spreading very fast in India, so the unwillingness of people to talk about sex makes it extraordinarily difficult for medical anthropologists and health professionals to do much to reduce the rate of spread.[3]

Some nonverbal communication appears to be universal in humans. For example, humans the world over appear to understand facial expression in the same way; that is, they are able to recognize a happy, sad, surprised, angry, disgusted, or afraid face. How the face is represented in art appears to evoke similar feelings in many different cultures. As we explore later in the arts chapter, masks intended to be frightening have sharp, angular features and inward- and downward-facing eyes and eyebrows.

Nonverbal communication is also culturally variable. In the chapter on the culture and culture change, we discussed how the distance between people standing together is culturally variable. In the realm of facial expression, different cultures have different rules about the emotions that are acceptable to express. One study compared how Japanese and Americans express emotion. Individuals from both groups were videotaped while they were shown films intended to evoke feelings of fear and disgust. When the subjects saw the films by themselves, without other people present, they showed the same kinds of facial expressions of fear and disgust. But there was a cultural effect too. When an authority figure was present during the videotaping, the Japanese subjects tried to mask their negative feelings with a half-smile more often than did the Americans.[4] Many gestures are culturally variable. In some cultures, an up and down nod of the head means "yes," in others it means "no."

Kinesics is the study of communication by nonverbal or nonvocal means, including posture, mannerisms, body movement, facial expressions, and signs and gestures. Informally, we may refer to nonverbal communication as "body language." As noted previously, some aspects of body language, such as facial expressions of emotion, may be human universals. Specific signs and gestures are often culturally variable and the cause of cultural misunderstandings. Nonverbal communication can even involve the voice. Consider how we might know that a person is not fine even though she just said "I'm fine." We can tell a lot by tone of voice. A depressed person might speak very quietly and use a flat tone of voice. If a person thought about explaining what was really wrong but thought better of it, a significant pause or silence might come before the words, "I'm fine." Even a person's **accent** (differences in pronunciation) can tell a lot about the person's background, such as place of origin and education. There are also nonverbal (nonword) sounds that people make—grunts, laughs, giggles, moans, and sighs. **Paralanguage** refers to all the optional vocal features or silences that communicate meaning apart from the language itself. Although body language and some forms of paralanguage enable humans to communicate without spoken language, language spoken by humans probably never occurs without kinetic communication and paralanguage.[5]

Nonhuman Communication

Systems of communication are not unique to human beings, nor is communication by sound. Other animal species communicate in a variety of ways. One way is by sound. A bird may communicate by a call that "this is my territory"; a squirrel may utter a cry that leads other squirrels to flee from danger. Another means of animal

Apes lack the human capacity for speech, so researchers have explored the capacity of chimpanzees and other apes to communicate with hand gestures. Researcher Joyce Butler teaches Nim, a chimpanzee, a sign for "drink." A family employs sign language to communicate with a deaf child.

communication is odor. An ant releases a chemical when it dies, and its fellows then carry it away to the compost heap. Apparently the communication is highly effective; a healthy ant painted with the death chemical will be dragged to the funeral heap again and again. Bees use another means of communication, body movement, to convey the location of food sources. Karl von Frisch discovered that the black Austrian honeybee—by choosing a round dance, a wagging dance, or a short, straight run—can communicate not only the precise direction of the source of food but also its distance from the hive.[6]

One of the biggest scholarly debates is the degree to which nonhuman animals, particularly nonhuman primates, differ from humans in their capacity for language. Some scholars see so much discontinuity that they postulate that humans must have acquired (presumably through mutation) a specific genetic capability for language. Others see much more continuity between humans and nonhuman primates and point to research that shows much more cognitive capacity in nonhuman primates than previously thought possible. They point out that the discontinuity theorists are constantly raising the standards for the capacities thought necessary for language.[7] For example, in the past, only human communication was thought to be symbolic. But recent research suggests that some monkey and ape calls in the wild are also symbolic.

When we say that a call, word, or sentence is **symbolic communication,** we mean at least two things. First, the communication has meaning even when its referent (whatever is referred to) is not present. Second, the meaning is arbitrary; the receiver of the message could not guess its meaning just from the sound(s) and does not know the meaning instinctively. In other words, symbols have to be learned. There is no compelling or "natural" reason that the word *dog* in English should refer to a smallish four-legged omnivore.

Vervet monkeys in Africa are not as closely related to humans as are African apes. Nevertheless, scientists who have observed vervet monkeys in their natural environment consider at least three of their alarm calls to be symbolic because each of them *means* (refers to) a different kind of predator—eagles, pythons, or leopards—and monkeys react differently to each call. For example, they look up when they hear the "eagle" call. Experimentally, in the absence of the referent, investigators have been able to evoke the normal reaction to a call by playing it back electronically. Another indication that the vervet alarm calls are symbolic is that infant vervets appear to need some time to learn the referent for each. When they are very young, infants apply a particular call to more animals than adult vervets apply the call to. So, for example, infant vervets will often make the eagle warning call when they see any flying bird. The infants learn the appropriate referent apparently through adult vervets' repetition of infants' "correct" calls; in any case, the infants gradually learn to restrict the call to eagles. This process is probably not too different from the way a North American infant in an English-speaking family first applies the "word" *dada* to all adult males and gradually learns to restrict it to one person.[8] Or to how the Embers' daughter Kathy said "dog"

to all pictures of four-footed animals, including elephants, when she was 18 months old.

All of the nonhuman vocalizations we have described so far enable individual animals to convey messages. The sender gives a signal that is received and "decoded" by the receiver, who usually responds with a specific action or reply. How is human vocalization different? Because monkeys and apes appear to use symbols at least some of the time, it is not appropriate to emphasize symbolism as the distinctive feature of human language. However, there is a significant quantitative difference between human language and other primates' systems of vocal communication. All human languages employ a much larger set of symbols.

Another often-cited difference between human and nonhuman vocalizations is that the other primates' vocal systems are *closed*—that is, different calls are not combined to produce new, meaningful utterances. In contrast, human languages are *open* systems, governed by complex rules about how sounds and sequences of sounds can be combined to produce an infinite variety of meanings.[9] For example, an English speaker can combine *care* and *full* (*careful*) to mean one thing, then use each of the two elements in other combinations to mean different things. *Care* can be used to make *carefree, careless,* or *caretaker; full* can be used to make *powerful* or *wonderful*. And because language is a system of shared symbols, it can be re-formed into an infinite variety of expressions and be understood by all who share these symbols. In this way, for example, T. S. Eliot could form a sentence never before formed—"In the room the women come and go/talking of Michelangelo"[10]—and all speakers of English could understand the sense of his sentence, though not necessarily his private meaning.

Although no primatologist disputes the complexity and infinite variety with which human languages can combine sounds, other primates (cotton-top tamarins, pygmy marmosets, capuchin monkeys, and rhesus macaques) also combine calls in orderly sequences,[11] but not nearly as much as humans do.

Another trait thought to be unique to humans is the ability to communicate about past or future events. But Sue Savage-Rumbaugh has observed wild bonobos leaving what appear to be messages to other bonobos to follow a trail. They break off vegetation where trails fork and point the broken plants in the direction to follow.

Perhaps most persuasive are the successful attempts to teach apes to communicate with humans and with each other using human-created signs. These successes have led many scholars to question the traditional assumption that the gap between human and other animal communication is enormous. Even a parrot, which has a small brain, has been taught to communicate with a human trainer in ways once thought impossible. Alex (the parrot) could correctly answer questions in English about what objects were made of, how many objects of a particular type there were, and even what made two objects the same or different.[12] When he is not willing to continue a training session, Alex says, "I'm sorry . . . Wanna go back."[13]

Chimpanzees Washoe and Nim and the gorilla Koko were taught hand signs based on American Sign Language (ASL; used by the hearing impaired in the United States).

The chimpanzee Sarah was trained with plastic symbols. Subsequently, many chimpanzees were trained on symbol keyboards connected to computers. Some of the best examples of linguistic ability come from a chimpanzee named Kanzi. In contrast to other apes, Kanzi initially learned symbols just by watching his mother being taught, and he spontaneously began using the computer symbols to communicate with humans, even indicating his intended actions. Kanzi did not need rewards or to have his hands put in the right position. And he understood a great deal of what was spoken to him in English. For example, when he was 5 years old, Kanzi heard someone talk about throwing a ball in the river, and he turned around and did so. Kanzi has come close to having a primitive English grammar when he strings symbols together.[14] If chimpanzees and other primates have the capacity to use non-spoken language and even to understand spoken language, then the difference between humans and nonhumans may not be as great as people used to think.

Are these apes really using language in some minimal way? Many investigators do agree about one thing—nonhuman primates have the ability to "symbol," to refer to something (or a class of things) with an arbitrary "label" (gesture or sequence of sounds).[15] For example, Washoe originally learned the sign *dirty* to refer to feces and other soil and then began to use it insultingly, as in "dirty Roger," when her trainer Roger Fouts refused to give her things she wanted.

When we discuss the structure of sounds (phonology) later in this chapter, we will see that every human language has certain ways of combining sounds and ways of not combining those sounds. Apes do not have anything comparable to linguistic rules for allowed and disallowed combinations of sounds. In addition, humans have many kinds of discourse. We make lists and speeches, tell stories, argue, and recite poetry. Apes do none of these things.[16] But apes do have at least some of the capacities for language. Therefore, understanding their capacities may help us better understand the evolution of human language.

THE ORIGINS OF LANGUAGE

How long humans have had spoken language is not known. Some think that the earliest *Homo sapiens*, perhaps 100,000 years ago, may have had the beginnings of language. Others believe that language developed only after 100,000 years ago, with the emergence of modern humans. Because the only unambiguous remains of language are found on written tablets, and the earliest stone tablets date back only about 5,000 years,[17] pinpointing the emergence of earliest languages remains speculative. Theories about when language developed are based on nonlinguistic information such as when cranial capacity expanded dramatically, when complex technology and symbolic artifacts (such as art) started to be made, and when the anatomy of the throat, as inferred from fossil remains, began to resemble what we see in modern humans.

Noam Chomsky and other theoreticians of grammar suggest that there is an innate *language-acquisition device* in the human brain, as innate to humans as call systems

are to other animals.[18] If humans are unique in having an innate capacity for language, then some mutation or series of mutations had to be favored in human evolution, not before the human line separated from apes. Whether such a mechanism in fact exists is not clear. But we do know that the actual development of individual language is not completely biologically determined; if it were, all human beings would speak the same brain-generated language. Instead, about 4,000 to 5,000 mutually unintelligible languages have been identified. More than 2,000 of them were still spoken as of recently, most by peoples who did not traditionally have a system of writing.

Can we learn anything about the origins of language by studying the languages of nonliterate (without writing) and technologically simpler societies? The answer is no, because such languages are not simpler or less developed than ours. The sound systems, vocabularies, and grammars of technologically simpler peoples are in no way inferior to those of peoples with more complex technology.[19] Of course, people in other societies, and even some people in our own society, will not be able to name the sophisticated machines used in our society. All languages, however, have the potential for doing so. As we will see later in this chapter, all languages possess the amount of vocabulary their speakers need, and all languages expand in response to cultural changes. A language that lacks terminology for some of our conveniences may have a rich vocabulary for events or natural phenomena that are of particular importance to the people in that society.

If there are no primitive languages, and if the earliest languages have left no traces that would allow us to reconstruct them, does that mean we cannot investigate the origins of language? Some linguists think that understanding the way children acquire language, which we discuss shortly, can help us understand the origins of language. Other linguists have suggested that an understanding of how Creole languages develop will also tell us something about the origins of language.

Pidgin and Creole Languages

In many contact situations where one group is much more powerful than the other, people shift to the dominant language, and their native language gradually becomes lost (see the boxes "Can Languages Be Kept from Extinction?" and "Why Are 'Mother Tongues' Retained, and for How Long?"). However, some contact situations led to a different result—the development of a new language, different from the dominant language or the previous native languages.

Some languages developed where European colonial powers established commercial enterprises that relied on imported labor, generally slaves. The laborers in one place often came from many different societies and, in the beginning, would speak with their masters and with each other in some kind of simplified way, using linguistic features of one or more of the languages. Often, most of the vocabulary is drawn from the masters' language.[20] These *pidgin languages* become a new way of communicating. Pidgins are simplified languages and lack many of the building blocks found in the languages of whole societies,

applied anthropology

Can Languages Be Kept from Extinction?

Not only animal and plant species are endangered; many peoples and their languages are too. In the last few hundred years, and continuing in some places today, Western expansion and colonization have led to the depopulation and extinction of many native societies, mainly as a result of introduced disease and campaigns of extermination. Thus, many languages disappeared with the peoples that spoke them. More than 50 of approximately 200 aboriginal languages in Australia disappeared relatively quickly as a result of massacre and disease.

Today, native languages are endangered more by the fact that they are not being passed on to children. Political and economic dominance by speakers of Western languages undoubtedly play an enormous role in this process. First, schooling is usually conducted in the dominant language. Second, when another culture is dominant, the children may prefer (often with the encouragement of their parents) to speak in the language perceived to have higher prestige.

Almost all the languages of aboriginal Australia are now gone. This is a worldwide trend. Michael Krauss, a linguist who tracks disappearing languages, estimates that 90 percent of the world's languages are endangered in the current century. A common estimate of the number of existing languages is 6,000. If the 90 percent endangered estimate is correct, only 600 human languages will be left at the end of this century.

What can be done? For a long time, linguists have worked on describing languages that are endangered, often working closely with the few remaining speakers. Although description is essential to language preservation, linguists are increasingly engaging actively in efforts to revitalize endangered languages by participating in community programs

and by playing active roles in organizations that are preserving, often in digitized archives, endangered languages and recordings of speech. After all, without speakers or any written records, languages are truly lost. The following are a few examples of "dead" languages being brought back to life. Kaurna, a language of Australia, abandoned for over a century, is now used in songs, ritual events, public speeches, and everyday greetings. It has moved from no use to some use. Hebrew is an often-cited example of a "dead" language that was brought back to life because more than 5 million people now speak it. However, Hebrew, like Latin, was never really "dead" in the same sense as Kaurna. Hebrew has been used in religious contexts for over 16 centuries and had extensive written literature. But the Hebrew case indicates something fundamental—for successful revitalization to occur, a community of people must be strongly motivated to revive it. Anthropological linguists may help design and implement revitalization programs, but they are unlikely to be successful without the interest of the community.

Total immersion programs are probably the most likely to work, but they are the most costly and difficult to implement. School programs employing total immersion during the school day beginning with preschool have had considerable success among the Maori of New Zealand, as well as among Hawaiians of the United States and the Mohawk of Canada. Bilingual programs are perhaps the most popular programs, but they use only partial immersion. Krauss, who is particularly interested in preserving native Alaskan languages, developed materials on native languages with help from the state government of Alaska to assist teachers in bilingual programs. UNESCO favors a very different

approach, to teach adults first, who can then teach their children naturally.

Computer technology provides new avenues for revitalizing languages. H. Russell Bernard believes that "to keep a language truly alive we must produce authors." With the help of computer technology, which allows reconfiguring a keyboard to produce special characters for sounds, Bernard has taught native speakers to write their native languages directly on computers. These texts then become the basis for dictionaries. So far, more than 80 people, speaking 12 endangered languages, have become authors in Mexico and South America. Although these authors may not be using the standardized characters linguists use to represent sounds, they are producing "written" materials that might otherwise be lost forever. These texts provide more than just information about language. In their works, the authors convey ideas about curing illness, acquiring food, raising children, and settling disputes. On a broader scale, the Web provides a way for far-flung people to access language materials, pick up advice for teaching languages, and even feel more part of a "community" with those whose language is shared.

We are not sure when humans first developed spoken language. But the enormous linguistic diversity on this planet took a long time to develop. As Krauss points out, "Each language is a unique repository of facts and knowledge about the world that we can ill afford to lose" (quoted in Kolbert 2005). Unfortunately, it may take only a short time for that diversity to become a thing of the past.

Sources: Crystal 2000, 4, 142, 154; Holmes 2001, 65–71; Grenoble and Whaley 2006; Kolbert 2005; Shulman 1993.

building blocks such as prepositions (*to, on,* and so forth) and auxiliary verbs (designating future and other tenses). If a pidgin language is used merely as system of communicating in a limited setting, it may not develop into a fully developed language. However, children may begin to use pidgin as their first language. The pidgin language may expand and become more complex grammatically.[21] Many pidgin languages developed into and were replaced by so-called *creole languages,* which incorporate much of the vocabulary of another language (often the masters' language) but also have a grammar that differs from it and from the grammars of the laborers' native languages.[22]

Derek Bickerton argues that there are striking grammatical similarities in creole languages throughout the world. This similarity, he thinks, is consistent with the idea that some grammar is inherited by all humans. Creole languages, therefore, may resemble early human languages. All creoles use intonation instead of a change in word order to ask a question. The creole equivalent of the question "Can you fix this?" would be "You can fix this?" The Creole version puts a rising inflection at the end; in contrast, the English version reverses the subject and verb without much inflection at the end. All creoles express the future and the past in the same grammatical way, by the use of particles (such as the English *shall*) between subject and verb, and they all employ double negatives, as in the Guyana English Creole "Nobody no like me."[23]

It is possible that many other things about language are universal, that all languages are similar in many respects, because of the way humans are "wired" or because people in all societies have similar experiences. For example, names for frogs may usually contain *r* sounds because frogs make them.[24]

Children's Acquisition of Language

Apparently a child is equipped from birth with the capacity to reproduce all the sounds used by the world's languages and to learn any system of grammar. Research on 6-month-old infants finds that they can distinguish sounds of approximately 600 consonants and 200 vowels—all the sounds of all the languages of the world. But, by about the time of their first birthdays, babies become better at recognizing the salient sounds and sound clusters of their parents or caretakers and become less adept at distinguishing those of other languages.[25]

Children's acquisition of the structure and meaning of language has been called the most difficult intellectual achievement in life. If that is so, it is pleasing to note that they accomplish it with relative ease and vast enjoyment. As we have noted, many believe that this "difficult intellectual achievement" may in reality be a natural response to the capacity for language that is one of humans' genetic characteristics. All over the world, children begin to learn language at about the same age, and in no culture do children wait until they are 7 or 10 years old. By 12 or 13 months of age, children are able to name a few objects and actions, and by 18 to 20 months, they can make one key word stand for a whole sentence: "Out!" for "Take me out for a walk right now"; "Juice!" for "I want some juice

now." Evidence suggests that children acquire the concept of a word as a whole, learning sequences of sounds that are stressed or at the ends of words (e.g., "raffe" for giraffe). Even children with hearing impairments who are learning signs in ASL tend to acquire and use signs in a similar fashion.[26]

Children the world over tend to progress to two-word sentences at about 18 to 24 months of age. In their sentences, they express themselves in "telegraph" form—using nounlike words and verblike words but leaving out the seemingly less important words. So a two-word sentence such as "Shoes off" may stand for "Take my shoes off," or "More milk" may stand for "Give me more milk, please."[27] They do not utter their two words in random order, sometimes saying "off" first, other times saying "shoes" first. If children say, "Shoes off," then they will also say, "Clothes off" and "Hat off." They seem to select an order that fits the conventions of adult language, so they are likely to say, "Daddy eat," not "Eat Daddy." In other words, they tend to put the subject first, as adults do. And they tend to say "Mommy coat" rather than "Coat Mommy" to indicate "Mommy's coat."[28] Adults do not utter sentences such as "Daddy eat," so children seem to know a lot about how to put words together with little or no direct teaching from their caretakers. Consider the 5-year-old who, confronted with the unfamiliar "Gloria in Excelsis," sings quite happily, "Gloria eats eggshells." To make the words fit the structure of English grammar is more important than to make the words fit the meaning of the Christmas pageant.

If there is a basic grammar imprinted in the human mind, we should not be surprised that children's early and later speech patterns seem to be similar in different languages. We might also expect children's later speech to be similar to the structure of creole languages. And it is, according to Derek Bickerton.[29] The "errors" children make in speaking are consistent with the grammar of creoles. For example, English-speaking children 3 to 4 years old tend to ask questions by intonation alone, and they tend to use double negatives, such as "I don't see no dog," even though the adults around them do not speak that way and consider the children's speech "wrong."

But some linguists argue that the evidence for an innate grammar is weak because children the world over do not develop the same grammatical features at similar ages. For example, word order is a more important determinant of meaning in English than in Turkish; the endings of words are more important in Turkish. The word at the beginning of the sentence in English is likely to be the subject. The word with a certain ending in Turkish is the likely subject. Consistent with this difference, English-speaking children learn word order earlier than Turkish children do.[30]

Future research on children's acquisition of language and on the structure of creole languages may bring us closer to an understanding of the origins of human language. But, even if much of grammar is universal, we still need to understand how and why the thousands of languages in the world vary, which brings us to the conceptual tools linguists have had to invent to study languages.

migrants and immigrants

Why Are "Mother Tongues" Retained, and for How Long?

The longer an immigrant group lives in another country, the more they incorporate the culture of their new home. At some point, the original language is no longer even partially understood. Consider people who originally came from Wales, the region west of England in Great Britain. In that region, until about 100 years ago, most people spoke the Welsh language, which belongs to the Celtic subfamily of Indo-European along with Irish and Scottish Gaelic and Breton. (Celtic is a different subfamily from the one English belongs to, which is Germanic.) In 1729, the Welsh in Philadelphia established the Welsh Society, the oldest ethnic organization in the United States. Many of the members, if not all, spoke Welsh in addition to English at that time. But, by the 20th century, hardly any of their descendants did.

If immigrant groups eventually lose their "mother tongues" in many if not most countries, this doesn't mean that the process occurs at the same speed in every group. Why is that? Why do some immigrant groups lose their language faster than others? Is it because they do not live in tightly knit ethnic enclaves? Or because they marry outside their ethnic group? Or because they do not have traditional festivals or celebrations marking their separate identity? A comparative study by Robert Schrauf discovered the most likely reasons. First, Schrauf assessed the degree to which immigrant groups coming to North America retained their native language over time. The greatest retention was defined as when the third generation (the grandchildren of immigrants) continued to use the native language. Examples were Chicanos, Puerto Ricans, Cubans, and Haitians. On the other hand, the third generation in some groups had no compre-hension of the native language except for isolated words. Even the second generation (the children of immigrants) mostly spoke and understood only English. Examples were Italians, Armenians, and Basques. Chinese and Koreans were in the middle, with some evidence that the third generation understands a little of the native language. Schrauf then measured seven social factors that might explain longer versus shorter retention of the mother tongue. He looked at whether the group lived in tightly knit communities, retained religious rituals from the old country, had separate schools and special festivals, visited their homeland, did not intermarry, or worked with others of their ethnic group.

Schrauf used data on 11 North American ethnic groups drawn from the HRAF Collection of Ethnography. The major advantage of the HRAF materials is that ethnographies written for more general purposes, or for purposes other than linguistic ones, contain a wealth of information concerning sociocultural features of ethnic groups that may be tested for their possible effects on language retention and loss.

We might suspect that all of the factors Schrauf measured would lead people to retain their native language (and presumably other native cultural patterns). But not all do, apparently. Only living in tightly knit communities and retaining religious rituals strongly predict retention of the mother tongue in the home into the third generation. Why? Possibly because living in an ethnic community and religious rituals are experienced early in life: Conditions associated with early socialization might have more lasting effects than conditions experienced later in life, such as schooling, visits to the homeland, marriage, and work. Participation in celebrations and festi-vals is probably important too, but it does not have quite as strong an effect, perhaps because celebrations and festivals are not everyday experiences.

As always, in the case of research, this study raises questions for future research. Would the same effects be found outside of North America? Would the results be the same if we looked also at other immigrant groups in North America? Does frequent travel back to the homeland help language retention? Do some immigrant groups live in close-knit communities because of discrimination or choice? If choice, are some groups more interested in assimilating than others? And if so, why?

Sources: Caulkins 1997; Schrauf 1999.

Living in an ethnic neighborhood as in San Francisco's Chinatown encourages retention of the mother tongue.

A lot of language instruction occurs by pointing to something and saying what it is called.

DESCRIPTIVE LINGUISTICS

In every society, children do not need to be taught "grammar" to learn how to speak. They begin to grasp the essential structure of their language at a very early age, without direct instruction. If you show English-speaking children a picture of one "gork" and then a picture of two of these creatures, they will say there are two "gorks." Somehow they know that adding an *s* to a noun means more than one. But they do not know this consciously, and adults may not either. One of the most surprising features of human language is that meaningful sounds and sound sequences are combined according to rules that the speakers often do not consciously know.

These rules should not be equated with the "rules of grammar" you were taught in school so that you would speak "correctly." Rather, when linguists talk about rules, they are referring to the patterns of speaking that are discoverable in actual speech. Needless to say, there is some overlap between the actual rules of speaking and the rules taught in school. But there are rules that children never hear about in school, because their teachers are not linguists and are not aware of them. When linguists use the term *grammar*, they are *not* referring to the prescriptive rules that people are supposed to follow in speaking. Rather, *grammar* to the linguist consists of the actual, often unconscious principles that predict how most people talk. As we have noted, young children may speak two-word sentences that conform to a linguistic rule, but their speech is hardly considered "correct."

Discovering the mostly unconscious rules operating in a language is a very difficult task. Linguists have had to invent special concepts and methods of transcription (writing) to permit them to describe: (1) the rules or principles that predict how sounds are made and how they are used (slightly varying sounds are often used interchangeably in words without creating a difference in meaning—this aspect of language is called **phonology**); (2) how sound sequences (and sometimes even individual sounds) convey meaning and how meaningful sound sequences are strung together to form words (this aspect is called **morphology**);

and (3) how words are strung together to form phrases and sentences (this aspect is called **syntax**).

Understanding the language of another people is an essential part of understanding the culture of that people. Although sometimes what people say is contradicted by their observed behavior, there is little doubt that it is hard to understand the beliefs, attitudes, values, and worldview of a people without understanding their language and the nuances of how that language is used. Even behavior, which theoretically one can observe without understanding language, usually cannot be readily understood without interpretation. Imagine that you see people go by a certain rock and seemingly walk out of their way to avoid it. Suppose they believe that an evil spirit resides there. How could you possibly know that without being able to ask and to understand their answer?

Phonology

Most of us have had the experience of trying to learn another language and finding that some sounds are exceedingly difficult to make. Although the human vocal tract theoretically can make a very large number of different sounds—**phones,** to linguists—each language uses only some of them. It is not that we cannot make the sounds that are strange to us; we just have not acquired the habit of making those sounds. And until the sounds become habitual for us, they continue to be difficult to make.

Finding it difficult to make certain sounds is only one of the reasons we have trouble learning a "foreign" language. Another problem is that we may not be used to combining certain sounds or making a certain sound in a particular position in a word. Thus, English speakers find it difficult to combine *z* and *d*, as Russian speakers often do (because we never do so in English), or to pronounce words in Samoan, a South Pacific language, that begin with the sound English speakers write as *ng*, even though we have no trouble putting that sound at the end of words, as in the English *sing* and *hitting*.

To study the patterning of sounds, linguists who are interested in *phonology* have to write down speech utterances as sequences of sound. This task would be almost impossible if linguists were restricted to using their own alphabet (say, the one we use to write English), because other languages use sounds that are difficult to represent with the English alphabet or because the alphabet we use in English can represent a particular sound in different ways. (English writing represents the sound *f* by *f* as in *food*, but also as *gh* in *tough* and *ph* in *phone*.) In addition, in English, different sounds may be represented by the same letter. English has 26 letters but more than 40 significant sounds (sounds that can change the meaning of a word).[31] To overcome these difficulties in writing sounds with the letters of existing writing systems, linguists have developed systems of transcription with special alphabets in which each symbol represents only one particular sound.

Once linguists have identified the sounds or phones used in a language, they try to identify which sounds affect meaning and which sounds do not. One way is to start with a simple word like *lake* and change the first sound to *r* to make the word *rake*. A linguist will ask if this new combination of sounds means the same thing. An English speaker would say *lake* means something completely different from *rake*. These minimal contrasts enable linguists to identify a **phoneme** in a language—a sound or set of sounds that makes a difference in meaning in that language.[32] So the sound *l* in *lake* is different phonemically from the sound *r* in *rake*. The ways in which sounds are grouped together into phonemes vary from language to language. We are so used to phonemes in our own language that it may be hard to believe that the contrast between *r* and *l* may not make a difference in meaning in some languages. For example, in Samoan, *l* and *r* can be used interchangeably in a word without changing the meaning (therefore, these two sounds belong to the same phoneme in Samoan). So Samoan speakers may say "Leupena" sometimes and "Reupena" at other times when they are referring to someone who in English would be called "Reuben."

English speakers may joke about languages that "confuse" *l* and *r*, but they are not usually aware that we do the same thing with other sets of sounds. For example, in English, the word we spell *and* may be pronounced quite differently by two different English speakers without changing the meaning, and no one would think that a different word was spoken. We can pronounce the *a* in *and* as in the beginning of the word *air,* or we can pronounce it as the *a* in *bat.* If you say those varying *a* sounds and try to think about how you are forming them in your mouth, you will realize that they are two different sounds. English speakers might recognize a slight difference in pronunciation but pay little or no attention to it because the two ways to pronounce the *a* in *and* do not change the meaning. Now think about *l* and *r*. If you form them in your mouth, you will notice that they are only slightly different with respect to how far the tongue is from the ridge behind the upper front teeth. Languages do tend to consider sounds that are close as belonging to the same phoneme, but why they choose some sounds and not others to group together is not yet fully understood.

Some recent research suggests that infants may learn early to ignore meaningless variations of sound (those that are part of the same phoneme) in the language they hear at home. It turns out that, as early as 6 months of age, infants "ignore" sound shifts within the same phoneme of their own language, but they "hear" a sound shift within the phoneme of another language. Researchers are not sure how babies learn to make the distinction, but they seem to acquire much of the phonology of their language very early indeed.[33]

After discovering which sounds are grouped into phonemes, linguists can begin to discover the sound sequences that are allowed in a language and the usually unconscious rules that predict those sequences. For example, words in English rarely start with three nonvowel sounds. But when they do, the first sound or phone is always an *s,* as in *strike* and *scratch*.[34] (Some other words in English may start with three consonants but only two sounds are involved, as in *chrome,* where the *ch* stands for the sound in *k*.) Linguists' descriptions of the patterning of sounds

(phonology) in different languages may allow them to investigate why languages vary in their sound rules.

Why, for example, are two or more consonants strung together in some languages, whereas in other languages, vowels are *almost* always put between consonants? The Samoan language now has a word for "Christmas" borrowed from English, but the borrowed word has been changed to fit the rules of Samoan. In the English word, two consonants come first, *k* and *r*, which we spell as *ch* and *r*. The Samoan word is *Kerisimasi* (pronounced as if it were spelled Keh-ree-see-mah-see). It has a vowel after each consonant, or five consonant-vowel syllables.

Why do some languages like Samoan alternate consonants and vowels more or less regularly? Recent cross-cultural research suggests three predictors of this variation. One predictor is a warmer climate. Where people live in warmer climates, the typical syllable is more likely to be a consonant-vowel syllable. Linguists have found that consonant-vowel syllables provide the most contrast in speech. Perhaps when people converse outdoors at a distance, which they are likely to do in a warmer climate, they need more contrast between sounds to be understood. A second predictor of consonant-vowel alternation is literacy. Languages that are written have fewer consonant-vowel syllables. If communication is often in written form, meaning does not have to depend so much on contrast between adjacent sounds. A third (indeed the strongest) predictor of consonant-vowel alternation is the degree to which babies are held by others. Societies with a great deal of baby-holding have a lot of consonant-vowel syllables. Later, in the chapter on the arts, you will read about research that relates baby-holding to a societal preference for regular rhythm in music. The theory is that, when babies are held on a person much of the day, they begin to associate regular rhythm with pleasurable experiences. The baby senses the regular rhythm of the caretaker's heartbeats or the caretaker's rhythmic work, and the reward value of that experience generalizes to a preference for all regular rhythms in adult life, including apparently a regular consonant-vowel alternation in adult speech. Compare the rhythm of the Samoan word *Kerisimasi* with the English word *Christmas*.[35]

Morphology

A phoneme in a language usually does not mean something by itself. Usually phonemes are combined with other phonemes to form a meaningful sequence of sounds. *Morphology* is the study of sequences of sounds that have meaning. Often these meaningful sequences of sounds make up what we call *words,* but a word may be composed of a number of smaller meaningful units. We take our words so much for granted that we do not realize how complicated it is to say what words are. People do not usually pause very much between words when they speak; if we did not know our language, a sentence would seem like a continuous stream of sounds. This is how we first hear a foreign language. Only when we understand the language and write down what we say do we separate (by spaces) what we call words. But a word is really only an arbitrary sequence of sounds that has a meaning; we would not "hear" words as separate units if we did not understand the language spoken.

Because anthropological linguists traditionally investigated unwritten languages, sometimes without the aid of interpreters, they had to figure out which sequences of sounds conveyed meaning. And because words in many languages can often be broken down into smaller meaningful units, linguists had to invent special words to refer to those units. Linguists call the smallest unit of language that has a meaning a **morph.** Just as a phoneme may have one or more phones, one or more morphs with the same meaning may make up a **morpheme.** For example, the prefix *in-*, as in *indefinite,* and the prefix *un-*, as in *unclear,* are morphs that belong to the morpheme meaning *not.* Although some words are single morphs or morphemes (e.g., *for* and *giraffe* in English), many words are a combination of morphs, generally prefixes, roots, and suffixes. Thus *cow* is one word, but the word *cows* contains two meaningful units—a root (*cow*) and a suffix (pronounced like *z*) meaning more than one. The **lexicon** of a language, which a dictionary approximates, consists of words and morphs and their meanings.

It seems likely that the intuitive grasp children have of the structure of their language includes a recognition of morphology. Once they learn that the morph */-z/* added to a noun-type word indicates more than one, they plow ahead with *mans, childs;* once they grasp that the morpheme class pronounced */-t/* or */-d/* or */-ed/* added to the end of a verb indicates that the action took place in the past, they apply that concept generally and invent *runned, drinked, costed.* They see a ball roll near*er* and near*er,* and they transfer that concept to a kite, which goes upp*er* and upp*er.* From their mistakes as well as their successes, we can see that children understand the regular uses of morphemes. By the age of 7, they have mastered many of the irregular forms as well—that is, they learn which morphs of a morpheme are used when.

The child's intuitive grasp of the dependence of some morphemes on others corresponds to the linguist's recognition of free morphemes and bound morphemes. A *free* morpheme has meaning standing alone—that is, it can be a separate word. A *bound* morpheme displays its meaning only when attached to another morpheme. The morph pronounced */-t/* of the bound morpheme meaning *past tense* is attached to the root *walk* to produce *walked;* but the */-t/* cannot stand alone or have meaning by itself.

In English, the meaning of an utterance (containing a subject, verb, object, and so forth) usually depends on the order of the words. "The dog bit the child" is different in meaning from "The child bit the dog." But in many other languages, the grammatical meaning of an utterance does not depend much, if at all, on the order of the words. Rather, meaning may be determined by how the morphs in a word are ordered. For example, in Luo, a language of East Africa, the same bound morpheme may mean the subject or object of an action. If the morpheme is the prefix to a verb, it means the subject; if it is the suffix to a verb, it means the object. Another way that grammatical meaning may be conveyed is by altering or adding a bound morpheme to a

word to indicate what part of speech it is. For example, in Russian, when the subject of a sentence, the word for *mail* is pronounced something like *pawchtah.* When *mail* is used as the object of a verb, as in "I gave her the mail," the ending of the word changes to *pawchtoo.* And if I say, "What was in the mail?" the word becomes *pawchtyeh.*

Some languages have so many bound morphemes that they might express as a complex but single word what is considered a sentence in English. For example, the English sentence, "He will give it to you" can be expressed in Wishram, a Chinookan dialect that was spoken along the Columbia River in the Pacific Northwest, as *acimluda* (a-c-i-m-l-ud-a, literally "will-he-him-thee-to-give-will"). Note that the pronoun *it* in English is gender-neutral; Wishram requires that *it* be given a gender, in this case, "him."[36]

Syntax

Because language is an open system, we can make up meaningful utterances that we have never heard before. We are constantly creating new phrases and sentences. Just as they do for morphology, speakers of a language seem to have an intuitive grasp of *syntax*—the rules that predict how phrases and sentences are generally formed. These "rules" may be partly learned in school, but children know many of them even before they get to school. In adulthood, our understanding of morphology and syntax is so intuitive that we can even understand a nonsense sentence, such as this famous one from Lewis Carroll's *Through the Looking-Glass:*

> 'Twas brillig, and the slithy toves
> Did gyre and gimble in the wabe

Simply from the ordering of the words in the sentence, we can surmise which part of speech a word is, as well as its function in the sentence. *Brillig* is an adjective; *slithy,* an adjective; *toves,* a noun and the subject of the sentence; *gyre* and *gimble,* verbs; and *wabe,* a noun and the object of a prepositional phrase. Of course, an understanding of morphology helps too. The *-y* ending in *slithy* is an indication that the latter is an adjective, and the *-s* ending in *toves* tells us that we most probably have more than one of these creatures. In addition to producing and understanding an infinite variety of sentences, speakers of a language can tell when a sentence is not "correct" without consulting grammar books. For example, an English speaker can tell that "Child the dog the hit" is not an acceptable sentence but "The child hit the dog" is fine. There must, then, be a set of rules underlying how phrases and sentences are constructed in a language.[37] Speakers of a language know these implicit rules of syntax but are not usually consciously aware of them. The linguist's description of the syntax of a language tries to make these rules explicit.

HISTORICAL LINGUISTICS

The field of **historical linguistics** focuses on how languages change over time. Written works provide the best data for establishing such changes. For example, the following brief passage from Chaucer's *Canterbury Tales,* written in the English of the 14th century, has recognizable elements but is different enough from modern English to require a translation.

> *A Frere ther was, a wantowne and a merye,*
> *A lymytour, a ful solempne man.*
> *In alle the ordres foure is noon that kan*
> *So muche of daliaunce and fair language.*
> *He hadde maad ful many a mariage*
> *Of yonge wommen at his owene cost.*

> *A Friar there was, wanton and merry,*
> *A limiter [a friar limited to certain districts], a*
> * very important man.*
> *In all the orders four there is none that knows*
> *So much of dalliance [flirting] and fair*
> * [engaging] language.*
> *He had made [arranged] many a marriage*
> *Of young women at his own cost.*[38]

In this passage, we can recognize several changes. Many words are spelled differently today, and in some cases, meaning has changed: *Full,* for example, would be translated today as *very.* What is less evident is that changes in pronunciation have occurred. For example, the *g* in

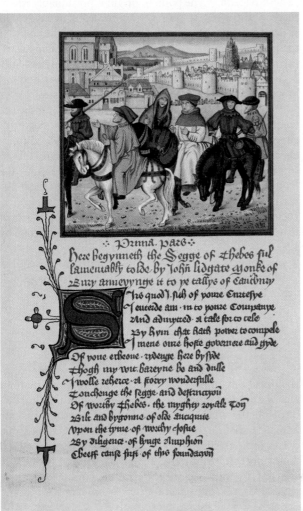

An illustration accompanies the ornate script text on a page from Chaucer's famed *The Canterbury Tales.*

mariage (marriage) was pronounced *zh,* as in the French from which it was borrowed, whereas now it is usually pronounced like either *g* in *George.*

Because languages spoken in the past leave no traces unless they were written, and most of the languages known to anthropology were not written by their speakers, you might think that historical linguists can study linguistic change only by studying written languages such as English. But that is not the case. Linguists can reconstruct changes that have occurred by comparing contemporary languages that are similar. Such languages show phonological, morphological, and syntactical similarities because they usually derive from a common ancestral language. For example, Romanian, Italian, French, Spanish, and Portuguese have many similarities. On the basis of these similarities, linguists can reconstruct what the ancestral language was like and how it changed into what we call the Romance languages. Of course, these reconstructions can easily be tested and confirmed because we know from many surviving writings what the ancestral language, Latin, was like; we also know from documents how Latin diversified as the Roman Empire expanded. Thus, common ancestry is frequently the reason why neighboring, and sometimes even separated, languages show patterns of similarity.

But languages can be similar for other reasons too. Contact between speech communities, often with one group dominant over another, may lead one language to borrow from the other. For example, English borrowed a lot of vocabulary from French after England was conquered by the French-speaking Normans in A.D. 1066. Languages may also show similarities even though they do not derive from a common ancestral language and even though there has been no contact or borrowing between them. Such similarities may reflect common or universal features of human cultures or human brains or both. (As we noted earlier in the chapter, the grammatical similarities exhibited by creole languages may reflect how the human brain is "wired.") Finally, even unrelated and separated languages may show some similarities because of the phenomenon of convergence; similarities can develop because some processes of linguistic change may have only a few possible outcomes.

Language Families and Culture History

Latin is the ancestral language of the Romance languages. We know this from documentary (written) records. But if the ancestral language of a set of similar languages is not known from written records, linguists still can reconstruct many features of that language by comparing the derived languages. (Such a reconstructed language is called a **protolanguage.**) That is, by comparing presumably related languages, linguists can become aware of the features that many of them have in common, features that were probably found in the common ancestral language. The languages that derive from the same protolanguage are called a *language family.* Most languages spoken today can be grouped into fewer than 30 families. The language family that English belongs to is called *Indo-European,* because it includes most of the languages of Europe and some of the languages of India. (Persian, spoken in Iran, and Kurdish also belong to this family.) About 50 percent of the world's population (now more than 6 billion people) speak Indo-European languages.[39] Another very large language family, now spoken by more than a billion people, is Sino-Tibetan, which includes the languages of northern and southern China as well as those of Tibet and Burma.[40]

The field of historical linguistics got its start in 1786, when a British scholar living in India, Sir William Jones, noticed similarities between Sanskrit, a language spoken and written in ancient India, and classical Greek, Latin, and more recent European languages.[41] In 1822, Jakob Grimm, one of the brothers Grimm of fairy tale fame, formulated rules to describe the sound shifts that had occurred when the various Indo-European languages diverged from each other. So, for example, in English and the other languages in the Germanic branch of the Indo-European family, *d* regularly shifted to *t* (compare the English *two* and *ten* with the Latin *duo* and *decem*), and *p* regularly shifted to *f* (compare the English *father* and *foot,* to Latin's *pater* and *pes*). Scholars generally agree that the Indo-European languages derive from a language spoken 5,000 years to 6,000 years ago.[42] The ancestral Indo-European language, many of whose features have now been reconstructed, is called *proto-Indo-European,* or *PIE* for short.

Where did PIE originate? Some linguists believe that the approximate location of a protolanguage is suggested by the words for plants and animals in the derived languages. More specifically, among these different languages, the words that are **cognates**—that is, words that are similar in sound and meaning—presumably refer to plants and animals that were present in the original homeland. So, if we know where those animals and plants were located 5,000 years to 6,000 years ago, we can guess where PIE people lived. Among all the cognates for trees in the Indo-European languages, Paul Friedrich has identified 18 that he believes were present in the eastern Ukraine in 3000 B.C. On this basis, he suggests that the eastern Ukraine was the PIE homeland.[43] Also consistent with this hypothesis is the fact that the Balto-Slavic subfamily of Indo-European, which includes most of the languages in and around the former Soviet Union, has the most tree names (compared with other subfamilies) that are similar to the reconstructed form in proto-Indo-European.[44]

Marija Gimbutas thinks we can even identify the proto-Indo-Europeans archaeologically. She believes that the PIE people were probably the people associated with what is known as the Kurgan culture (5000 B.C. to 2000 B.C.), which spread out from the Ukraine around 3000 B.C. The Kurgan people were herders, raising horses, cattle, sheep, and pigs. They also relied on hunting and grain cultivation. Burials suggest differences in wealth and special status for men.[45] Why the Kurgan and linguistically similar people were able to expand to many places in Europe and the Near East is not yet clear. Some have suggested that horses and horse-drawn wagons and perhaps horseback riding provided important military advantages.[46] In any case, it is clear that many Kurgan cultural elements were distributed after 3000 B.C. over a wide area of the Old World.

Colin Renfrew disagrees with the notion that the Ukraine was the homeland of PIE. He thinks that PIE is 2,000 years to 3,000 years older than Kurgan culture and that the PIE people lived in a different place. Renfrew locates the PIE homeland in eastern Anatolia (Turkey) in 7000 B.C. to 6000 B.C., and he suggests, on the basis of archaeological evidence, that the spread of Indo-European to Europe and what is now Iran, Afghanistan, and India accompanied the spread of farming to those areas.[47]

Just as some historical linguists and archaeologists have suggested when and where the PIE people may have lived originally and how they may have spread, other linguists and archaeologists have suggested culture histories for other language families. For example, the Bantu languages in Africa (spoken by perhaps 100 million people) form a subfamily of the larger Niger-Congo family of languages. Bantu speakers currently live in a wide band across the center of Africa and down the eastern and western sides of southern Africa. All of the Bantu languages presumably derive from people who spoke proto-Bantu. But where was their homeland?

As in the case of proto-Indo-European, different theories have been proposed. But most historical linguists now agree with Joseph Greenberg's suggestion that the origin of Bantu was in what is now the Middle Benue area of eastern Nigeria.[48] The point of origin is presumably where there is the greatest diversity of related languages and *dialects* (varying forms of a language); it is assumed that the place of origin has had the most time for linguistic diversity to develop, compared with an area only recently occupied by a related language. For example, England has more dialect diversity than New Zealand or Australia.

Why were the Bantu able to spread so widely over the last few thousand years? Anthropologists have only begun to guess.[49] Initially, the Bantu probably kept goats and practiced some form of agriculture and thereby were able to spread, displacing hunter-gatherers in the area. As the Bantu speakers expanded, they began to cultivate certain cereal crops and herd sheep and cattle. Around this time, after 1000 B.C., they also began to use and make iron tools, which may have given them significant advantages. In any case, by 1,500 years to 2,000 years ago, Bantu speakers had spread throughout central Africa and into the northern reaches of southern Africa. But speakers of non-Bantu languages still live in eastern, southern, and southwestern Africa.

THE PROCESSES OF LINGUISTIC DIVERGENCE

Historical or comparative linguists hope to do more than record and date linguistic divergence. Just as physical anthropologists may attempt to develop explanations for human variation, so linguists investigate the possible causes of linguistic variation. Some of the divergence undoubtedly comes about gradually. When groups of people speaking the same language lose communication with one another because they become separated, either physically or socially, they begin to accumulate small changes in phonology, morphology, and syntax (which occur continuously in any language). These variant forms of language are considered **dialects** when the differences in phonology, morphology, and syntax are not great enough to produce unintelligibility. (Dialects should not be confused with accents, which are merely differences in pronunciation.) Eventually, if the separation continues, the former dialects of the same language will become separate languages; that is, they will become mutually unintelligible, as German and English now are. Just as culture change originates from individual changes, language change originates from individual speakers, either from spontaneous innovation or from borrowing. Only when innovative speech patterns are picked up by others does linguistic change occur.[50]

Geographic barriers, such as large bodies of water, deserts, and mountains, may separate speakers of what was once the same language, but distance by itself can also produce divergence. For example, if we compare dialects of English in the British Isles, it is clear that the regions farthest away from each other are the most different linguistically (compare the northeast of Scotland and London).[51] In northern India, hundreds of semi-isolated villages and regions developed hundreds of local dialects. Today, the inhabitants of each village understand the dialects of the surrounding villages and, with a little more difficulty, the dialects of the next circle of villages. But slight dialect shifts accumulate village by village, and it seems as if different languages are being spoken at the opposite ends of the region, which are separated by more than a thousand miles.[52]

Even where there is little geographic separation, there may still be a great deal of dialect differentiation because of social distance. So, for example, the spread of a linguistic feature may be halted by religious, class, or other social differences that inhibit communication.[53] In the village of Khalapur in northern India, John Gumperz found substantial differences in speech between the Untouchables and other groups. Members of the Untouchables have work contacts with members of other groups but no friend-

The Fledermaus cabaret bar in Vienna uses some English words in its sign out front.

ships.[54] Without friendships and the easy communication between friends, dialect differentiation can readily develop.

Whereas isolation brings gradual divergence between speech communities, contact results in greater resemblance. This effect is particularly evident when contact between mutually unintelligible languages introduces borrowed words, which usually name some new item borrowed from the other culture—*tomato, canoe, sushi,* and so on. Bilingual groups within a culture may also introduce foreign words, especially when the mainstream language has no real equivalent. Thus, *salsa* has come into English, and *le weekend* into French.

Conquest and colonization often result in extensive and rapid borrowing, if not linguistic replacement. The Norman conquest of England introduced French as the language of the new aristocracy. It was 300 years before the educated classes began to write in English. During this time, the English borrowed words from French and Latin, and the two languages—English and French—became more alike than they would otherwise have been. About 50 percent of the English general vocabulary originated in French. As this example suggests, different social classes may react to language contact differently. For example, English aristocrats eventually called their meat "pork" and "beef" (derived from the French words), but the people who raised the animals and prepared them for eating continued (at least for a while) to refer to the meat as "pig" and "bull," the original Anglo-Saxon words.

In those 300 years of extensive contact, the grammar of English remained relatively stable. English lost most of its inflections or case endings, but it adopted little of the French grammar. In general, the borrowing of words, particularly free morphemes,[55] is much more common than the borrowing of grammar.[56] As we might expect, borrowing by one language from another can make the borrowing language more different from its *sibling languages* (those derived from a common ancestral language) than it would otherwise be. Partly as a result of the French influence, the English vocabulary looks quite different from the languages to which it is actually most similar in terms of phonology and grammar—German, Dutch, and the Scandinavian languages.

RELATIONSHIPS BETWEEN LANGUAGE AND CULTURE

Some attempts to explain the diversity of languages have focused on the possible interactions between language and other aspects of culture. On the one hand, if it can be shown that a culture can affect the structure and content of its language, then it would follow that linguistic diversity derives at least in part from cultural diversity. On the other hand, the direction of influence between culture and language might work in reverse: Linguistic features and structures might affect other aspects of the culture.

Cultural Influences on Language

One way a society's language may reflect its corresponding culture is in **lexical content,** or vocabulary. Which experiences, events, or objects are singled out and given words may be a result of cultural characteristics.

Basic Words for Colors, Plants, and Animals

Early in the 20th century, many linguists pointed to the lexical domain (vocabulary) of color words to illustrate the supposed truth that languages vary arbitrarily or without apparent reason. Different languages not only had different numbers of basic color words (from 2 to 12 or so; for example, the words *red, green,* and *blue* in English), but they also, it was thought, had no consistency in the way they classified or divided the colors of the spectrum. But findings from a comparative (cross-linguistic) study contradicted these traditional presumptions about variation in the number and meaning of basic color words. On the basis of their study of at first 20 and later over 100 languages, Brent Berlin and Paul Kay found that languages did not encode color in completely arbitrary ways.[57]

Although different languages do have different numbers of basic color words, most speakers of any language are very likely to point to the same color chips as the best representatives of particular colors. For example, people the world over mean more or less the same color when they are asked to select the best "red." Moreover, there appears to be a nearly universal sequence by which basic color words are added to a language.[58] If a language has just two basic color words, its speakers will always refer to "black" (or dark) hues and "white" (or light) hues. If a language has three basic color words, the third word will nearly always be "red." The next category to appear is either "yellow" or "grue" (green/blue), then different words for green and blue, and so on. To be sure, we usually do not see the process by which basic color words are added to a language. But we can infer the usual sequence because, for example, if a language has a word for "yellow," it will almost always have a word for "red," whereas having a word for "red" does not mean that the language will have a word for "yellow."

What exactly is a *basic* color word? All languages, even the ones with only two basic color terms, have many different ways of expressing how color varies. For example, in English, we have words such as turquoise, blue-green, scarlet, crimson, and sky blue. Linguists do not consider these to be basic color words. In English, the basic color words are *white, black, red, green, yellow, blue, brown, pink, purple, orange,* and *gray.* One feature of a basic color word is that it consists of a single morph; it cannot include two or more units of meaning. This feature eliminates combinations such as *blue-green* and *sky blue.* A second feature of a basic color word is that the color it represents is not generally included in a higher-order color term. For example, scarlet and crimson are usually considered variants of red, turquoise a variant of blue. A third feature is that basic terms tend to be the first-named words when people are asked for color words. Finally, for a word to be considered a basic color word, many individual speakers of the language have to agree on the central meaning (in the color spectrum) of the word.[59]

Why do different societies (languages) vary in number of basic color terms? Berlin and Kay suggest that the number of basic color terms in a language increases with technological specialization as color is used to decorate and distinguish objects.[60] Cross-linguistic variation in the number of basic color terms does not mean that some languages make more color distinctions than others. Every language could make a particular distinction by combining words (e.g., "fresh leaf" for green); a language need not have a separate basic term for that color.

There may also be many basic color terms because of a biological factor.[61] Peoples with darker (more pigmented) eyes seem to have more trouble distinguishing colors at the dark (blue-green) end of the spectrum than do peoples with lighter eyes. It might be expected, then, that peoples who live nearer the equator (who tend to have darker eyes, presumably for protection against damaging ultraviolet radiation) would tend to have fewer basic color terms. And they do.[62] Moreover, it seems that both cultural and biological factors are required to account for cross-linguistic variation in the number of basic color terms. Societies tend to have six or more such terms (with separate terms for blue and green) only when they are relatively far from the equator and only when their cultures are more technologically specialized.[63] As we will see in later chapters, technological specialization tends to go with larger communities, more centralized governments, occupational specialization, and more social inequality. Societies with such traits are often referred to in a shorthand way as more "complex," which should not be taken to mean "better."

Echoing Berlin and Kay's finding that basic color terms seem to be added in a more or less universal sequence, Cecil Brown has found what seem to be developmental sequences in other lexical domains. Two such domains are general, or *life-form,* terms for plants and for animals. Life-form terms are higher-order classifications. All languages have lower-order terms for specific plants and animals. For example, English has words such as *oak, pine, sparrow,* and *salmon.* English speakers make finer distinctions too—*pin oak, white pine, white-throated sparrow,* and *red salmon.* But why, in some languages, do people have a larger number of general terms such as *tree, bird,* and *fish?* It seems that these general terms show a universal developmental sequence too. That is, general terms seem to be added in a somewhat consistent order. After "plant" comes a term for "tree"; then one for "grerb" (small, green, leafy, nonwoody plant); then "bush" (for plants between tree and grerb in size); then "grass"; then "vine."[64] The life-form terms for animals also seem to be added in sequence; after "animal" comes a term for "fish," then "bird," then "snake," then "wug" (for small creatures other than fish, birds, and snakes—for example, worms and bugs), then "mammal."[65]

More complex societies tend to have a larger number of general, or life-form, terms for plants and animals than do simpler societies, just as they tend to have a larger number of basic color terms. Why? And do all realms or domains of vocabulary increase in size as social complexity increases? If we look at the total vocabulary of a language (as can be counted in a dictionary), more complex societies do have larger vocabularies.[66] But we have to remember that complex societies have many kinds of specialists, and dictionaries will include the terms such specialists use. If we look instead at the nonspecialist, **core vocabulary** of languages, it seems that all languages have a core vocabulary of about the same size.[67] Indeed, although some domains increase in size with social complexity, some remain the same and still others decrease. An example of a smaller vocabulary domain in complex societies is that of specific names for plants. Urban North Americans may know general terms for plants, but they know relatively few names for specific plants. The typical individual in a small-scale society can commonly name 400 to 800 plant species; a typical person in our own and similar societies may be able to name only 40 to 80.[68] The number of life-form terms is larger in societies in which ordinary people know less about particular plants and animals.[69]

The evidence now available strongly supports the idea that the vocabulary of a language reflects the everyday distinctions that are important in the society. Those aspects of environment or culture that are of special importance will receive greater attention in the language.

Grammar Most of the examples we could accumulate would show that a culture influences the names of things visible in its environment. Evidence for cultural influence on the grammatical structure of a language is less extensive. Harry Hoijer draws attention to the verb categories in the language of the Navajo, a traditionally nomadic people. These categories center mainly in the reporting of events, or "eventings," as he calls them. Hoijer notes that, in "the reporting of actions and events, and the framing of substantive concepts, Navajo emphasizes movement and specifies the nature, direction, and status of such movement in considerable detail."[70] For example, Navajo has one category for eventings that are in motion and another for eventings that have ceased moving. Hoijer concludes that the emphasis on events in the process of occurring reflects the Navajo's nomadic experience over the centuries, an experience also reflected in their myths and folklore.

A linguistic emphasis on events may or may not be generally characteristic of nomadic peoples; as yet, no one has investigated the matter cross-culturally or comparatively. But there are indications that systematic comparative research would turn up other grammatical features that are related to cultural characteristics. For example, many languages lack the possessive transitive verb we write as "have," as in "I have." Instead, the language may say something such as "it is to me." A cross-cultural study has suggested that a language may develop the verb "have" after the speakers of that language have developed a system of private property or personal ownership of resources.[71] As we shall see later, in the chapter on economic systems, the concept of private property is far from universal and tends to occur only in complex societies with social inequality. In contrast, many societies have some kind of communal ownership, by kin groups or communities. How people talk about owning seems to reflect how they own; societies that lack a concept of private property also lack the verb "have."

Linguistic Influences on Culture: The Sapir-Whorf Hypothesis

There is general agreement that culture influences language. But there is less agreement about the opposite possibility—that language influences other aspects of culture. Edward Sapir and Benjamin Lee Whorf suggested that language is a force in its own right, that it affects how individuals in a society perceive and conceive reality. This suggestion is known as the *Sapir-Whorf hypothesis*.[72] In comparing the English language with Hopi, Whorf pointed out that English-language categories convey discreteness with regard to time and space, but Hopi does not. English has a discrete past, present, and future, and things occur at a definite time. Hopi expresses things with more of an idea of ongoing processes without time being apportioned into fixed segments. According to Ronald Wardhaugh, Whorf believed that these language differences lead Hopi and English speakers to see the world differently.[73]

As intriguing as that idea is, the relevant evidence is mixed. Linguists today do not generally accept the view that language coerces thought, but some suspect that particular features of language may facilitate certain patterns of thought.[74] The influences may be clearest in poetry and metaphors, where words and phrases are applied to other than their ordinary subjects, as in "all the world's a stage."[75] One of the serious problems in testing the Sapir-Whorf hypothesis is that researchers need to figure out how to separate the effects of other aspects of culture from the effects of language.

One approach that may reveal the direction of influence between language and culture is to study how children in different cultures (speaking different languages) develop concepts as they grow up. If language influences the formation of a particular concept, we might expect that children will acquire that concept earlier in societies where the languages emphasize that concept. For example, some languages make more of gender differences than others. Do children develop gender identity earlier when their language emphasizes gender? (Very young girls and boys seem to believe they can switch genders by dressing in opposite-sex clothes, suggesting that they have not yet developed a stable sense that they are unchangeably girls or boys.) Alexander Guiora and his colleagues have studied children growing up in Hebrew-speaking homes (Israel), English-speaking homes (the United States), and Finnish-speaking homes (Finland). Hebrew has the most gender emphasis of the three languages; all nouns are either masculine or feminine, and even second-person and plural pronouns are differentiated by gender. English emphasizes gender less, differentiating by gender only in the third-person singular (*she* or *her* or *hers; he* or *him* or *his*). Finnish emphasizes gender the least; although some words, such as *man* and *woman,* convey gender, differentiation by gender is otherwise lacking in the language. Consistent with the idea that language may influence thought, Hebrew-speaking children acquire the concept of stable gender identity the earliest on the average, Finnish-speaking children the latest.[76]

Another approach is to predict from language differences how people may be expected to perform in experiments. Comparing the Yucatec Mayan language and English, John Lucy predicted that English speakers might recall the *number* of things presented more than Yucatec Mayan speakers. For most classes of nouns, English requires a linguistic way of indicating whether something is singular or plural. You cannot say "I have dog" (no indication of number), but must say "I have a dog," "I have dogs," or "I have one (two, three, several, many) dogs." Yucatec Maya, like English, can indicate a plural, but allows the noun to be neutral with regard to number. For example, the translated phrase there-is-dog-over-there (*yàan pèek té'elo'*) can be left ambiguous about whether there is one or more than one dog. In English, the same ambiguity would occur in the sentence "I saw deer over there," but English does not often allow ambiguity for animate or inanimate nouns.[77] In a number of experiments, Yucatec Mayan and American English speakers were equally likely to recall the objects in a picture, but they differed in how often they described the number of a particular object in the picture. Yucatec Mayan speakers did so less often, consistent with their language's lack of insistence on indicating number.[78] So the salience of number in the experiments was probably a consequence of how the languages differ. Of course, it is possible that salience of number is created by some other cultural feature, such as dependence on money in the economy.

THE ETHNOGRAPHY OF SPEAKING

Traditionally, linguists concentrated on trying to understand the structure of a language, the usually unconscious rules that predict how the people of a given society typically speak. In recent years, many linguists have begun to study how people in a society vary in how they speak. This type of linguistic study, *sociolinguistics,* is concerned with the *ethnography of speaking*—that is, with cultural and subcultural patterns of speech variation in different social contexts.[79] The sociolinguist might ask, for example, what kinds of things one talks about in casual conversation with a stranger. A foreigner may know English vocabulary and grammar well but may not know that one typically chats with a stranger about the weather or where one comes from, and not about what one ate that day or how much money one earns. A foreigner may be familiar with much of the culture of a North American city, but if that person divulges the real state of his or her health and feelings to the first person who says, "How are you?" he or she has much to learn about "small talk" in North American English.

Similarly, North Americans tend to get confused in societies where greetings are quite different from ours. People in some other societies may ask as a greeting, "Where are you going?" or "What are you cooking?" Some Americans may think such questions are rude; others may try to answer in excruciating detail, not realizing that only vague answers are expected, just as we don't really expect a detailed answer when we ask people how they are.

Social Status and Speech

That a foreign speaker of a language may know little about the small talk of that language is but one example of the sociolinguistic principle that what we say and how we say it are not wholly predictable by the rules of our language.

Strangers shake hands when they meet; friends may touch each other more warmly. How we speak to others also differs according to the degree of friendship.

Who we are socially and whom we are talking to may greatly affect what we say and how we say it.

In a study interviewing children in a New England town, John Fischer noted that, in formal interviews, children were likely to pronounce the ending in words such as *singing* and *fishing,* but in informal conversations, they said "*singin'*" and "*fishin'.*" Moreover, he noted that the phenomenon also appeared to be related to social class; children from higher-status families were less likely to drop the ending than were children from lower-status families. Subsequent studies in English-speaking areas tend to support Fischer's observations with regard to this speech pattern. Other patterns are observed as well. For example, in Norwich, England, lower classes tend to drop the *h* in words such as *hammer,* but in all classes, the pattern of dropping the *h* increases in casual situations.[80] With respect to grammatical differences, in inner-city Detroit, lower class African Americans are more likely to use double negatives as in "It ain't nobody's business," in contrast to middle-class African Americans who usually say "It isn't anybody's business."[81]

Research has shown that English people from higher-class backgrounds tend to have more *homogeneous* speech, conforming more to what is considered standard English (the type of speech heard on television or radio), whereas people from lower-class backgrounds have very *heterogeneous* speech, varying in their speaking according to the local or dialect area they come from.[82] In some societies, social status differences may be associated with more marked differentiation of words. Clifford Geertz, in his study of Javanese, showed that the vocabularies of the three rather sharply divided groups in Javanese society—peasants, townspeople, and aristocrats—reflect their separate positions. For example, the concept *now* is expressed differently in these three groups. A peasant will use *saiki* (considered the lowest and roughest form of the word); a townsman will use *saniki* (considered somewhat more elegant); and an aristocrat will use *samenika* (the most elegant form).[83]

Status relationships between people can also influence the way they speak to each other. Terms of address are a good example. In English, forms of address are relatively simple. One is called either by a first name or by a title (such as *Doctor, Professor, Ms.,* or *Mister*) followed by a last name. A study by Roger Brown and Marguerite Ford indicates that terms of address in English vary with the nature of the relationship between the speakers.[84] The reciprocal use of first names generally signifies an informal or intimate relationship between two people. A title and last name used reciprocally usually indicates a more formal or businesslike relationship between individuals who are roughly equal in status. Nonreciprocal use of first names and titles in English is reserved for speakers who recognize a marked difference in status between them. This status difference can be a function of age, as when a child refers to her mother's friend as Mrs. Miller and is in turn addressed as Sally, or can be due to occupational hierarchy, as when a person refers to his boss as Ms. Ramirez and is in turn addressed as Joe. In some cases, generally between boys and between men, the use of the last name alone represents a middle ground between the intimate and the formal usages.

Gender Differences in Speech

In many societies, the speech of men differs from the speech of women. The variation can be slight, as in our own society, or more extreme, as with the Carib Indians in the Lesser Antilles of the West Indies, among whom women and men use different words for the same concepts.[85] In Japan, males and females use entirely different words for numerous concepts (e.g., the male word for water is *mizu;* the female version is *ohiya*), and females often add the polite prefix *o-* (females will tend to say *ohasi* for chopsticks; males will tend to say *hasi*).[86] In the United States and other Western societies, there are differences in the speech of females and males, but they are not as dramatic as in the Carib and Japanese cases. For example, earlier we noted the tendency for the *g* to be dropped in words such as *singing* when the situation is informal and when the social class background is lower. But there is also a gender difference. Women are more likely than men to keep the *g* sound and less likely than men to drop the *h* in words such as *happy*. In Montreal,

women are less likely than men to drop the *l* in phrases such as *il fait* ("he does") or in the idiom *il y a* ("there is/are").[87] And in Detroit, in each social class, African American women are less likely than men to use double negatives.[88]

Gender differences occur in intonation and in phrasing of sentences as well. Robin Lakoff found that, in English, women tend to answer questions with sentences that have rising inflections at the end instead of a falling intonation associated with a firm answer. Women also tend to add questions to statements, such as "They caught the robber last week, didn't they?"[89]

One explanation for the gender differences, particularly with regard to pronunciation, is that women in many societies may be more concerned than men with being "correct."[90] (This is not in the linguist's sense; it is important to remember that linguists do not consider one form of speech more correct than another, just as they do not consider one dialect superior to another. All are equally capable of expressing a complex variety of thoughts and ideas.) In societies with social classes, what is considered more correct by the average person may be what is associated with the upper class. In other societies, what is older may be considered more correct. For example, in the Native American language of Koasati, which used to be spoken in Louisiana, males and females used different endings in certain verbs. The differences seemed to be disappearing in the 1930s, when the research on Koasati was done. Young girls had begun to use the male forms and only older women still used the female forms. Koasati men said that the women's speech was a "better" form of speech.[91] Gender differences in speech may parallel some of the gender differences noted in other social behavior (as we will see in the chapter on sex, gender, and culture): Girls are more likely than boys to behave in ways that are acceptable to adults.

There are not enough studies to know just how common it is for women to exhibit more linguistic "correctness." We do know of some instances where it is not the case. For example, in a community in Madagascar where people speak Merina, a dialect of Malagasy, it is considered socially correct to avoid explicit directives. So, instead of directly ordering an action, a Merina speaker will try to say it indirectly. Also, it is polite to avoid negative remarks, such as expressing anger toward someone. In this community, however, women, not men, often break the rules; women speak more directly and express anger more often.[92] This difference may be related to the fact that women are more involved in buying and selling in the marketplace.

Some researchers have questioned whether it is correctness that is at issue. Rather, we may be dealing in these examples with unequal prestige and power. Women may try to raise their status by conforming more to standard speech. When they answer a question with a rising inflection, they may be expressing uncertainty and a lack of power. Alternatively, perhaps women want to be more cooperative conversationalists. Speaking in a more "standard" fashion is consistent with being more likely to be understood by others. Answering a question with another question leads to continued conversation.[93]

new perspectives on gender

Does the English Language Promote Sexist Thinking?

Does English promote sexist thinking, or does the language merely reflect gender inequalities that already exist? For those who wish to promote gender equality, the answers to these questions are important because, if language influences thought (along the lines put forward by Edward Sapir and Benjamin Whorf), then linguistic change will be necessary to bring about change in the culture of gender. If it is the other way around, that is, if language reflects inequality, then social, economic, and political changes have to come before we can expect substantial linguistic change to occur.

Leaving aside for the moment which changes first, how does English represent gender inequity? Consider the following written by Benjamin Lee Whorf: "Speech is the best show man puts on. . . . Language helps man in his thinking." Although *man* in English technically refers to all humans and *his* technically refers to the thinking of a single person of either gender, the frequent use of such words could convey the idea that males are more important. Similarly, do the words *chairman, policeman, businessman,* and *salesman* convey that males are supposed to have those jobs? What is conveyed when there are two words for the two genders, as in *actor* and *actress* and *hero* and *heroine*? Usually the base word is male and the suffix is added for the female form. Does the suffix convey that the female form is an afterthought or less important?

It is not just the structure of the language that may convey gender inequality. How come in the pairs *sir/madam, master/mistress, wizard/witch,* the female version has acquired negative connotations? Men might be called animal names, such as wolves, rats, or pigs. But more animal images seem to be applied to women. They can be *chicks, henpeckers, cows, dogs, bitches, kittens,* or *birds.* Coming back to the original questions, how would we know whether language promotes sexism or sexism influences language? One way to find out is to do experimental studies, such as the one conducted by Fatemeh Khosroshashi. Some individuals were asked to read texts written with *man, he,* and *his* referring to people; others were asked to read texts with more gender-neutral phrasing. Individuals were subsequently asked to draw pictures to go with the texts. The ones who read the texts with more male terminology drew more accompanying pictures of men, strongly suggesting that the use of the terms *man, he,* and *his* conveyed the thought that the people in the text were men, not women, *because* of the vocabulary used. We need more such studies to help address the intellectual question of which comes first, linguistic or nonlinguistic culture.

It would be important to know whether societies with more "male-oriented" language are more male-dominated than are societies without such distinctions. We don't have that kind of comparative research yet. But one study by Robert and Ruth Munroe looked at the *proportion* of female and male nouns in ten languages (six Indo-European, four other than Indo-European) in which nouns have gender. Although none of those societies could be described as having a female bias, the Munroes were able to ask whether those societies with less male bias in social customs (e.g., all children are equally likely to inherit property) have a higher proportion of female nouns than male nouns (more female than male nouns). The answer appears to be yes. Although this study does not reveal what came first, studies like it are important if we want to discover how language differences may be related to other aspects of culture. If male-oriented languages are not related to male dominance, then it is not likely that sexist thinking is a consequence of language.

On the assumption that language may influence thought, many are pushing for changes in the way English is used, if not structured. It is hard to get English speakers to adopt a gender-neutral singular pronoun to replace *he*. Attempts to do so go back to the 18th century and include suggestions of *tey, thon, per,* and *s/he*. Although these efforts have not succeeded, the way English is written and spoken has begun to change. Words or phrases such as *chair* (or *chairperson*), *police officer,* and *sales assistant* (*salesperson*) have begun to replace their former *man* versions. If Whorf were writing his sentence now, it probably would be written: "Speech is the best show humans put on. . . . Language helps people think."

Sources: Holmes 2001, 305–16; Khosroshashi 1989; Lakoff 1973; Munroe and Munroe 1969; Romaine 1994, 105–16; Wardhaugh 2002, 317.

Men and women typically differ in what they talk about, or do not talk about. Deborah Tannen offers some examples. When women hear about someone else's troubles, they are likely to express understanding of the other's feelings; in contrast, men are likely to offer solutions. Men tend not to ask for directions; women do. Women tend to talk a lot in private settings; men talk more in public settings. These and other differences can cause friction and misunderstanding between the genders. When women express their troubles and men offer solutions, women feel that their feelings are not understood; men are frustrated that the women do not take their solutions seriously. Men may prefer to sit at home quietly and feel put upon to have to engage in conversation; women feel slighted when men avoid extended conversations with them. Why these differences? Tannen suggests that misunderstanding between men and women arises because boys and girls grow up in somewhat different cultures. Girls typically play in small groups, talk frequently, and are intimate with others. Boys more often play in large groups in which jockeying for status and attention are more of a concern. Higher-status individuals give directions and solutions; they do not seek directions or solutions. So asking for directions is like acknowledging lower status. But large play groups resemble public settings, and so later in life, men feel more comfortable speaking in public. Women, in contrast, are more comfortable speaking in small, intimate groups.[94]

Multilingualism and Code-Switching

For many people, the ability to speak more than one language is a normal part of life. One language may be spoken at home and another in school, the marketplace, or government. Or more than one language may be spoken at home if family members come from different cultures and still other languages are spoken outside. Some countries explicitly promote multilingualism. For example, Singapore has four official languages—English, Mandarin (one of the Chinese languages), Tamil, and Malay. English is stressed for trade, Mandarin as the language of communication with most of China, Malay as the language of the general region, and Tamil as the language of an important ethnic group. Moreover, most of the population speaks Hokkien, another Chinese language. Education is likely to be in English and Mandarin.[95]

What happens when people who know two or more languages communicate with each other? Very often you find them **code-switching,** using more than one language in the course of conversing.[96] Switching can occur in the middle of a Spanish-English bilingual sentence, as in "No van a bring it up in the meeting" ("They are not going to bring it up in the meeting").[97] Or switching can occur when the topic or situation changes, such as from social talk to schoolwork. Why do speakers of more than one language sometimes switch? Although speakers switch for a lot of different reasons, what is clear is that the switching is not a haphazard mix that comes from laziness or ignorance. Code-switching involves a great deal of knowledge of two or more languages and an awareness of what is considered appropriate or inappropriate in the community. For example, in the Puerto Rican community in New York City, code-switching within the same sentence seems to be common in speech among friends, but if a stranger who looks like a Spanish speaker approaches, the language will shift entirely to Spanish.[98]

Although each community may have its own rules for code-switching, variations in practice may need to be understood in terms of the broader political and historical context. For example, German speakers in Transylvania, where Romanian is the national language, hardly ever code-switch to Romanian. Perhaps the reason is that, before the end of World War II, German speakers were a privileged economic group who looked down upon landless Romanians and their language. Under socialism, the German speakers lost their economic privilege, but they continued to speak German among themselves. In the rare cases that Romanian is used among German speakers, it tends to be associated with low-status speech, such as singing bawdy songs. The opposite situation occurred in a Hungarian region of German-speaking Austria. The people of this agricultural region, annexed to Austria in 1921, were fairly poor peasant farmers. After World War II, business expansion began to attract labor from rural areas, so many Hungarians eagerly moved into jobs in industry. Younger generations saw German as a symbol of higher status and upward mobility; not surprisingly, code-switching between Hungarian and German became part of their conversations. Indeed, in the third generation, German has become the language of choice, except when speaking to the oldest Hungarians. The Hungarian-Austrian situation is fairly common in many parts of the world, where the language of the politically dominant group ends up being "linguistically dominant."[99]

WRITING AND LITERACY

Most of us have come to depend on writing for so many things that it is hard to imagine a world without it. Yet humans spent most of their history on earth without written language and many, if not most, important human achievements predate written language. Parents and other teachers passed on their knowledge by oral instruction and

Children do not need help learning the language spoken in their homes. However, reading and writing cannot usually be learned without instruction. Nowadays, children in most cultures are expected to learn to read and write in school. These Trobriand children from Papua New Guinea are allowed to wear their traditional clothes to school once a week.

demonstration. Stories, legends, and myths abounded—the stuff we call oral literature—even in the absence of writing. This is not to say that writing is not important. Far more information and far more literature can be preserved for a longer period of time with a writing system. The earliest writing systems are only about 6,000 years old and are associated with early cities and states. Early writing is associated with systematic record-keeping—keeping of ledgers for inventorying goods and transactions. In early times, probably only the elite could read and write—indeed only recently has universal literacy (the ability to read and write) become the goal of most countries. But in most countries, the goal of universal literacy is far from achieved. Even in countries with universal education, the quality of education and the length of education varies considerably between subcultures and genders. Just as some ways of speaking are considered superior to others, a high degree of literacy is usually considered superior to illiteracy.[100] But literacy in what language or languages? As we discussed in the box on endangered languages, recent efforts to preserve languages have encouraged writing of texts in languages that were only spoken previously. Obviously, there will be few texts in those languages; other languages have vast numbers of written texts. As more accumulated knowledge is written and stored in books, journals, and databases, attainment of literacy in those written languages will be increasingly critical to success. And texts do not only convey practical knowledge—they may also convey attitudes, beliefs, and values that are characteristic of the culture associated with the language in which the texts are written.

SUMMARY ● ○ ○

1. The essential function language plays in all societies is that of communication. Although human communication is not limited to spoken language, such language is of overriding importance because it is the primary vehicle through which culture is shared and transmitted.

2. Systems of communication are not unique to humans. Other animal species communicate in a variety of ways—by sound, odor, body movement, and so forth. The ability of chimpanzees and gorillas to learn and use sign language suggests that symbolic communication is not unique to humans. Still, human language is distinctive as a communication system in that its spoken and symbolic nature permits an infinite number of combinations and recombinations of meaning.

3. Nonverbal human communication includes posture, mannerisms, body movement, facial expressions, and signs and gestures. Nonverbal human communication also includes tone of voice, accent, nonword sounds, and all the optional vocal features that communicate meaning apart from the language itself.

4. Descriptive (or structural) linguists try to discover the rules of phonology (the patterning of sounds), morphology (the patterning of sound sequences and words), and syntax (the patterning of phrases and sentences) that predict how most speakers of a language talk.

5. By comparative analysis of cognates and grammar, historical linguists test the notion that certain languages derive from a common ancestral language, or protolanguage. The goals are to reconstruct the features of the protolanguage, to hypothesize how the offspring languages separated from the protolanguage or from each other, and to establish the approximate dates of such separations.

6. When two groups of people speaking the same language lose communication with each other because they become separated either physically or socially, they begin to accumulate small changes in phonology, morphology, and syntax. If the separation continues, the two former dialects of the same language will eventually become separate languages—that is, they will become mutually unintelligible.

7. Whereas isolation brings about divergence between speech communities, contact results in greater resemblance. This effect is particularly evident when contact between people who speak mutually unintelligible languages introduces borrowed words, most of which name some new item borrowed from the other culture.

8. Some attempts to explain the diversity of languages have focused on the possible interaction between language and other aspects of culture. On the one hand, if it can be shown that a culture can affect the structure and content of its language, then it would follow that linguistic diversity derives at least in part from cultural diversity. On the other hand, the direction of influence between culture and language might work in reverse; the linguistic structures might affect other aspects of the culture.

9. In recent years, some linguists have begun to study variations in how people actually use language when speaking. This type of linguistic study, called sociolinguistics, is concerned with the ethnography of speaking—that is, with cultural and subcultural patterns of speaking in different social contexts.

10. In bilingual or multilingual populations, code-switching (using more than one language in the course of conversing) has become increasingly common.

11. Written language dates back only about 6,000 years, but writing and written records have become increasingly important; literacy is now a major goal of most countries.

GLOSSARY TERMS ○ ● ○

accent **74**	morpheme **82**
code-switching **91**	morphology **80**
cognates **84**	paralanguage **74**
core vocabulary **86**	phoneme **81**
dialects **85**	phones **80**
historical linguistics **82**	phonology **80**
kinesics **74**	protolanguage **83**
lexical content **85**	syntax **80**
lexicon **82**	symbolic
morph **82**	communication **75**

CRITICAL QUESTIONS ○ ○ ●

1. Why might natural selection have favored the development of true language in humans but not in apes?

2. Would the world be better off with many different languages spoken or with just one universal language? Why do you think so?

3. Discuss some new behavior or way of thinking that led people to adopt or invent new vocabulary or some new pattern of speech.

4. How does some aspect of your speech differ from your parents or others of the previous generation? Why do you think it has changed?

PEARSON
myanthrolab

Read the chapter by Jane H. Hill, "Do Apes Have Language?" on MyAnthroLab and answer the following questions.

1. Jane Hill raises the question of whether apes have language. Briefly, what is her answer to the question?

2. Chimpanzees have learned signs from American Sign Language but they have not been able to learn to speak words. Why not?

Getting Food

or most people in our society, getting food consists of a trip to the supermarket. Within an hour, we can gather enough food from the shelves to last us a week. Seasons don't daunt us. Week after week, we know food will be there. But we do not think of what would happen if the food were not delivered to the supermarket. We wouldn't be able to eat, and without eating for a while, we would die. Despite the old adage "Man [or woman] does not live by bread alone," we could not live at all without bread or the equivalent. Food-getting activities, then, take precedence over other activities important to survival. Reproduction, social control (the maintenance of peace and order within a group), defense against external threat, and the transmission of knowledge and skills to future generations—none could take place without energy derived from food. But it is not merely energy that is required for survival and long-term reproduction. Food-getting strategies need to provide the appropriate combination of nutrients throughout varying seasons and changing environmental conditions. Food-getting activities are also important because the way a society gets its food strongly predicts other aspects of a culture, from community size and permanence of settlement to type of economy and degree of inequality and type of political system, and even art styles and religious beliefs and practices.

In contrast with our own and similar societies, most societies have not had food-getting specialists. Rather, almost all able-bodied adults were largely engaged in getting food for themselves and their families. Such economies are described as **subsistence economies.** For millions of years, humans obtained their food by gathering wild plants, hunting or scavenging wild animals, and fishing. Agriculture is a relatively recent phenomenon, dating back only about 10,000 years. And industrial or mechanized agriculture is hardly more than a century old. Harvesting machines have been used a little bit longer, but self-propelled machines had to wait for the internal combustion engine and the rise of the oil industry.

In this chapter, we look at the ways different societies get food and discuss some of the features associated with the different patterns. We ask why societies vary in their food-getting strategies. We shall see that the physical environment by itself has only a limited or restraining effect on how a society gets most of its food. To explain the variation more fully, we discuss at the end of the chapter why societies in the prehistoric past switched from collecting wild food resources to cultivating plants and raising animals. ● ○ ●

FORAGING

Foraging or *food collection* may be generally defined as a food-getting strategy that obtains wild plant and animal resources through gathering, hunting, scavenging, or fishing. Although this was the way humans got their food for most of human history, foragers in the world today, also commonly referred to as **hunter-gatherers,** are not very numerous, and most of them live in what have been called the *marginal areas* of the earth—deserts, the

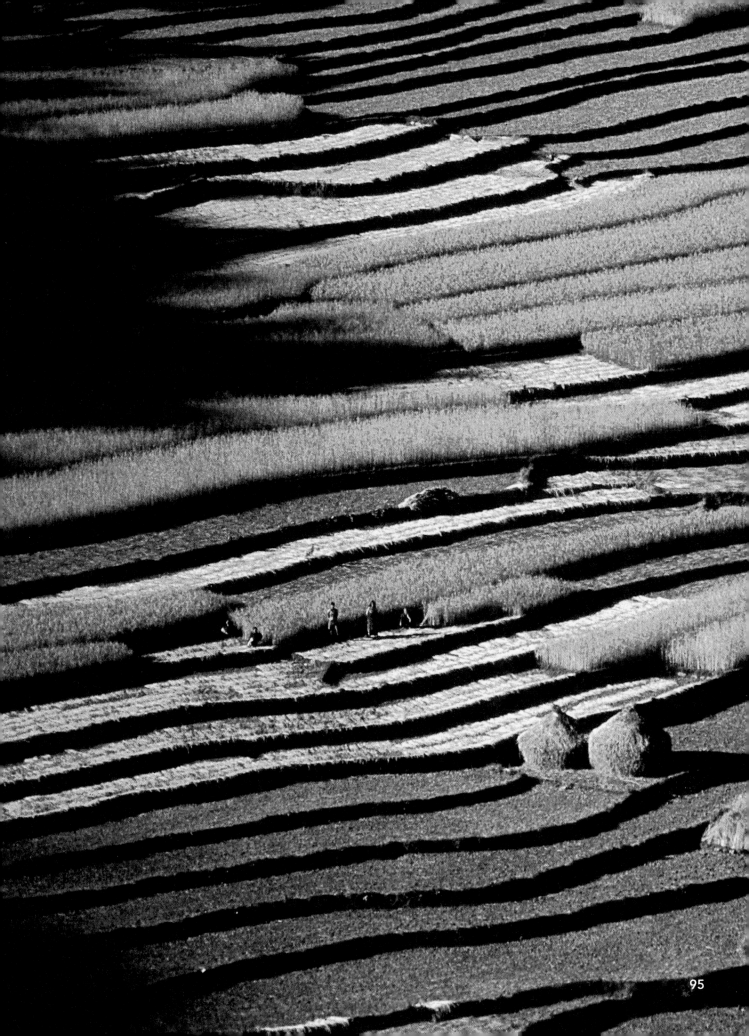

Arctic, and dense tropical forests—habitats that do not allow easy exploitation by modern agricultural technologies. In the last few hundred years, only about 5 million people are or were foragers.[1]

Anthropologists are interested in studying the relatively few foraging societies still available for observation because these groups may help us understand some aspects of human life in the past, when all people were foragers. But we must be cautious in drawing inferences about the past from our observations of recent and contemporary foragers, for three reasons. First, early foragers lived in almost all types of environments, including some very bountiful ones. Therefore, what we observe among recent and contemporary foragers, who generally live in deserts, the Arctic, and tropical forests, may not be comparable to what would have been observable in more favorable environments in the past.[2] Second, contemporary foragers are not relics of the past. Like all contemporary societies, they have evolved and are still evolving. Indeed, recent research reveals considerable variation in economic behavior as well as in social structure in foraging groups that share common ancestry; this implies that recent foragers have responded to differences in local environmental conditions.[3] Third, recent and contemporary foragers have been interacting with kinds of societies that did not exist until after 10,000 years ago—agriculturalists, pastoralists, and intrusive, powerful state societies.[4] For example, evidence from South Asia and Southeast Asia suggests that trade with agriculturalists was probably an important component of foragers' economic strategies for millennia.[5] And, in the recent past, foraging people have increasingly depended on agriculture and commercial activities as well as trade. In short, what we see recently may be very different from the distant past when foraging was the only means of subsistence.

Let us examine two areas of the world with very different environments where recent foragers lived: Australia and the North American Arctic.

Australian Aborigines

Before Europeans came to the Australian continent, all the aboriginal people who lived there depended on foraging. Although the way of life of Australian aborigines is now considerably altered, we consider the life of the Ngatatjara as described by Richard Gould in the 1960s, when they still lived by gathering wild plants and hunting wild animals in the Gibson Desert of western Australia.[6] (We mostly use the present tense in our discussion because that is the custom in ethnographic writing, but readers should remember that we are referring to aboriginal life in the 1960s.)

The desert environment of the Ngatatjara averages less than 8 inches of rain per year, and the temperature in summer may rise to 118°F. The few permanent water holes are separated by hundreds of square miles of sand, scrub, and rock. Even before Europeans arrived in Australia, the area was sparsely populated—fewer than one person per 35 to 40 square miles. Now there are even fewer people, because the aboriginal population was decimated by introduced diseases and mistreatment after the Europeans arrived.

On a typical day, the camp begins to stir just before sunrise, while it is still dark. Children are sent to fetch water, and the people breakfast on water and food left over from the night before. In the cool of the early morning, the adults talk and make plans for the day. The talking goes on for a while. Where should they go for food—to places they have been to recently or to new places? Sometimes there are other considerations. For example, one woman may want to search for plants whose bark she needs to make new sandals. When the women decide which plants they want to gather and where they think those plants are most likely to be found, they take up their digging sticks and set out with large wooden bowls of drinking water on their heads. Their children ride on their hips or walk alongside. Meanwhile, the men may have decided to hunt emus, 6-foot-tall ostrichlike birds that do not fly. The men go to a creek bed where they will wait to ambush any game that may come along. They lie patiently behind a screen of brush they have set up, hoping for a chance to throw a spear at an emu or even a kangaroo. They can throw only once, because the game will run away if they miss.

By noon, the men and women are usually back at camp, the women with their wooden bowls each filled with up to 15 pounds of fruit or other plant foods, the men more often than not with only some small game, such as lizards and rabbits. The men's food-getting is less certain of success than the women's, so most of the Ngatatjara aborigines' diet is plant food. The daily cooked meal is eaten toward evening, after an afternoon spent resting, gossiping, and making or repairing tools.

The aborigines traditionally were nomadic, moving their campsites fairly frequently. The campsites were isolated and inhabited by only a small number of people, or they were clusters of groups including as many as 80 people. The aborigines never established a campsite right next to a place with water. If they were too close, their presence would frighten away game and might cause tension with neighboring bands, who would also wait for game to come to the scarce watering spots.

Today, many aborigines live in small settled villages. For example, in the 1980s, Victoria Burbank worked in a village she calls "Mangrove" in the Northern Territory of Australia. The once-nomadic aborigines now live in a village of about 600, which was founded in the 1950s around a Protestant mission. Their houses have stoves, refrigerators, toilets, washing machines, and even television sets. Their children attend school full-time, and there is a health clinic for their medical needs. They still do some foraging, but most of their food comes from the store. Some earn wages, but many subsist on government welfare checks.[7]

The Inuit (Eskimo)

The diet of the Australian aborigines was mainly wild plant foods. But for the Inuit (Eskimo) peoples, who live year-round in the North American Arctic, plants are too scarce to be the most important part of the diet. From Greenland and Labrador in the east to Alaska in the west,

Inupiaq hunters bringing two caribou home.

the Inuit used to depend almost entirely on sea and land mammals and fish. (The term *Eskimo* is used widely in the West, but it is not a word in any of the native languages in that area. Many of the native Arctic groups, particularly those now living in Canada, prefer to be called Inuit.) We focus here on the traditional life of the north Alaskan Inupiaq in the beginning of the 19th century, as reconstructed by Ernest Burch (the "ethnographic present" in the following discussion).[8] Northern Alaska is relatively "warm" for its latitude but not for most of us farther south; little sun and below-zero temperatures for a month or so in the winter are hardly warm. Rivers and lakes freeze in October and do not thaw until May. Even the ocean freezes for part of the winter.

What the Inupiaq get for food depends mostly on the season, but the critical resources are sea mammals (ranging in size from whales to seals), fish, and caribou or wild reindeer. The usual technique for hunting sea mammals is to hurl a toggle harpoon into the animal from a kayak. It is very difficult to kill a moving sea mammal, so hunters attach a line to the animal with the harpoon; on the other end of the line is a sealskin float that indicates where the harpooned sea mammal can be located. The sea mammal gets more and more tired pulling the float until the hunter is able to kill it with a lance. One man alone can manage to hunt smaller sea mammals, but groups of men are needed to hunt whales. In the winter, when the sea ice is frozen, hunters use a different hunting technique. Hunters must locate a breathing hole and then wait, immobile and attentive, for hours or sometimes days until a seal comes up for air. The instant a seal surfaces, the hunters must aim perfectly with the harpoon.

The women butcher the animal, prepare it for eating or storage, and process the skin. Women sew all of the skin clothing. They also hunt small animals, such as hares, and do much of the fishing. Various techniques are used for fishing—hook and line, spearing, and ambushing with nets and dams. Women make the fishing nets, and it takes the better part of a year to make one. Although there are not many plants to gather, the women do that too.

Related families usually live together and move camp by boat or sled to be in the best place to intercept the migratory animals and fish. For instance, caribou migrate, so the Inupiaq try to catch them by building a corral in a place through which they are expected to pass. A network

of interrelated families lives and moves in a territory of thousands of square miles, moving outside it only when they have made arrangements with other groups to do so.

Much has changed since the time just described. Now the Inupiaq live in villages or towns with many modern conveniences. In the village of Kivalina, there are permanent houses with electricity, telephones, and television sets. Dog teams have been replaced by all-terrain vehicles and snowmobiles. There are powerful outboard motors rather than skin boats. Many men and women have full-time wage-paying jobs. But even though the people may buy most of their food, there is still a preference for traditional foods, so the Inupiaq still hunt and fish on the weekends.

General Features of Foragers

Despite the differences in terrain and climate under which they live and the different food-collecting technologies they use, Australian aborigines, Inuit, and most other recent foragers have certain characteristic cultural patterns (see Table 6–1). Most live in small communities in sparsely populated territories and follow a nomadic lifestyle, forming no permanent settlements. As a rule, they do not recognize individuals' land rights. Their communities generally do not have different classes of people and tend to have no specialized or full-time political officials.[9] Division of labor in foraging societies is based largely on age and gender: Men exclusively hunt large marine and land animals and usually do most of the fishing, and women usually gather wild plant foods.[10] Foragers must decide what plants or animals to target. Optimal foraging theory, which we discuss in the next chapter, helps explain some of the decisions foragers make.

Is there a typical pattern of food-getting among foragers? Many anthropologists have assumed that foragers typically get their food more from gathering than from hunting, and that women contribute more than men to subsistence, because women generally do the gathering.[11] Although gathering is the most important food-getting activity for some foragers (e.g., the Ngatatjara aborigines and the !Kung of southern Africa), this is not true for most food-collecting societies known to us. A survey of 180 such societies indicates that there is a lot of variation with regard to which food-getting activity is most important to the society. Gathering is the most important activity for 30 percent of the surveyed societies, hunting for 25 percent, and fishing for 38 percent. (That is why we prefer the term *foragers* rather than the often-used *hunter-gatherers*; the term "foragers" allows us to recognize the importance of fishing.) In any case, because men generally do the fishing as well as the hunting, the men usually contribute more to food-getting than do the women among recent foragers.[12]

Because foragers move their camps often and walk great distances, it may seem that the food-collecting way of life is difficult. Although we do not have enough quantitative studies to tell us what is typical of most foragers, studies of two Australian aborigine groups[13] and of one !Kung group[14] indicate that those foragers do not spend many hours getting food. For example, !Kung adults spend an average of about 17 hours per week collecting food. Even

TABLE 6–1   **Variation in Food-Getting and Associated Features**

| | Food Collectors | | Food Producers | |
	Foragers	Horticulturalists	Pastoralists	Intensive Agriculturalists
Population density	Lowest	Low to moderate	Low	Highest
Maximum community size	Small	Small to moderate	Small	Large (towns and cities)
Nomadism/ permanence of settlements	Generally nomadic or seminomadic	More sedentary: communities may move after several years	Generally nomadic or seminomadic	Permanent communities
Food shortages	Infrequent	Infrequent	Frequent	Frequent
Trade	Minimal	Minimal	Very important	Very important
Full-time craft specialists	None	None or few	Some	Many (high degree of craft specialization)
Individual differences in wealth	Generally none	Generally minimal	Moderate	Considerable
Political leadership	Informal	Some part-time political officials	Part- and full-time political officials	Many full-time political officials

when you add the time spent making tools (about 6 hours a week) and doing housework (about 19 hours a week), the !Kung seem to have more leisure time than many agriculturalists, as we discuss later.

Complex Foragers

When we say that foragers tend to have certain traits, this does not mean that all of them have those traits. There is considerable variability among societies that depend on foraging. Foraging societies that depend heavily on fishing (such as on the Pacific Coast of the northwestern United States and Canada or on the south coast of New Guinea) are more likely to have bigger and more permanent communities and more social inequality than foraging societies elsewhere who mostly depend on game and plants.[15] The Pacific Coast and New Guinea coastal people also tend to have higher population densities, food storage,[16] occupational specialization, resource ownership, slavery, and competitiveness.[17] Two foraging groups that depended heavily on annual salmon runs were the Tlingit of southeastern Alaska and the Nimpkish of British Columbia. Both groups had a three-tiered class system with a high class, commoners, and slaves. The high-status individuals were obliged to stage competitive elaborate feasts and distributions of valuables.[18] This type of inequality and competitiveness was very different from what we find in typical foragers, who generally show little social differentiation. In a worldwide study of foragers, those societies that were more dependent on fishing also tended to have more fighting between communities, compared with other foragers. Perhaps this is because some fishing sites were more predictable than others and people were willing to fight to defend them.[19]

In New Guinea, about 40 societies depend almost exclusively on foraging. Wild sago provides most of the carbohydrates for these foragers, but they vary considerably on how they obtain animal protein. Paul Roscoe has found that the amount of dependence upon fishing is strongly associated with density of population and settlement size. For example, societies with more than 75 percent dependence upon fishing have average community sizes of about 350 people, as compared with community size of about 50 for those with less than 25 percent dependence upon fishing. Some villages were much larger. One Asmat village had over 1,400 people and a Waropen village over 1,700.

FOOD PRODUCTION

Beginning about 10,000 years ago, certain peoples in widely separated geographic locations made the revolutionary changeover to **food production.** That is, they began to cultivate and then domesticate plants and animals. (Domesticated plants and animals are different from the ancestral wild forms.) With domestication of these food sources, people acquired control over certain natural processes, such as animal breeding and plant seeding. Today, most peoples in the world depend for their food on some combination of domesticated plants and animals.

Anthropologists generally distinguish three major types of food production systems—horticulture, intensive agriculture, and pastoralism.

Horticulture

The word **horticulture** may conjure up visions of people with "green thumbs" growing orchids and other flowers in greenhouses. But to anthropologists, the word means the growing of crops of all kinds with relatively simple tools and methods, in the absence of permanently cultivated fields. The tools are usually hand tools, such as the digging stick or hoe, not plows or other equipment pulled by animals or tractors. And the methods used do not include fertilization, irrigation, or other ways to restore soil fertility after a growing season.

There are two kinds of horticulture. The more common one involves a dependence on **extensive (shifting) cultivation**. The land is worked for short periods and then left idle for some years. During the years when the land is not cultivated, wild plants and brush grow; when the fields are later cleared by *slash-and-burn techniques*, nutrients are returned to the soil. The other kind of horticulture involves a dependence on long-growing tree crops. The two kinds of horticulture may be practiced in the same society, but in neither case is there permanent cultivation of field crops.

Most horticultural societies do not rely on crops alone for food. Many also hunt or fish; a few are nomadic for part of the year. For example, the Kayapo of the Brazilian Amazon leave their villages for as long as three months at a time to trek through the forest in search of game. The entire village participates in a trek, carrying large quantities of garden produce and moving their camp every day.[20] Other horticulturalists raise domestic animals, but these are usually not large animals, such as cattle and camels.[21] More often than not, horticulturalists raise smaller animals, such as pigs, chickens, goats, and sheep.

Let us look now at two horticultural societies, the Yanomamö of the Brazilian-Venezuelan Amazon and the Samoans of the South Pacific.

The Yanomamö Dense tropical forest covers most of Yanomamö territory. From the air, the typical village is located in a forest clearing and looks like a single, large, circular lean-to with its inner side open to the central plaza. Each individual family has its own portion of the lean-to under the common roof. Each family's portion of the lean-to has a back wall (part of the closed back wall around the circular village structure), but the portions are open on the sides to each other as well as onto the central plaza of the village. The Yanomamö get most of their calories from garden produce, but according to Raymond Hames, the Yanomamö actually spend most of their time foraging.[22]

Before the people can plant, the forest must be cleared of trees and brush. Like most shifting cultivators, the Yanomamö use a combination of techniques: slashing the undergrowth, felling trees, and using controlled burning to clear a garden spot—in other words, **slash-and-burn** horticulture. Before the 1950s, the Yanomamö had only stone axes, so felling trees was quite difficult. Now they have steel machetes and axes given or traded to them by missionaries.

Because of the work involved in clearing a garden, the Yanomamö prefer to make use of forest patches that have little thorny brush and not too many large trees.[23] After the ground is cleared, the Yanomamö plant plantains, manioc, sweet potatoes, taro, and a variety of plants for medicine, condiments, and craft materials. Men do the heavy clearing work to prepare a garden, and they as well as women plant the crops. Women usually go to the gardens daily to weed and harvest. After two or three years, the yields diminish and the forest starts growing back, making continued cultivation less desirable and more difficult, so they abandon the garden and clear a new one. If they can, they clear adjacent forest, but if gardens are far from the village, they will move the village to a new location. Villages are moved about every five years because of gardening needs and warfare. There is a great deal of intervillage raiding, so villages are often forced to flee to another location.

Extensive cultivation requires a lot of territory because new gardens are not cleared until the forest grows back. What is often misunderstood is why it is so important to shift gardens. Not only is a burned field easier to plant, but the organic matter that is burned provides necessary nutrients for a good yield. If horticulturalists come back too quickly to a spot with little plant cover, a garden made there will not produce a satisfactory yield.

The Yanomamö crops do not provide much protein, so hunting and fishing are important to their diet. Men hunt birds, peccaries, monkeys, and tapir with bows and arrows. Women, men, and children enjoy fishing. They catch fish by hand, with small bows and arrows, and by stream poisoning. Everybody gathers honey, hearts of palm, Brazil nuts, and cashews, although the men usually climb trees to shake down the nuts. Much of the foraging is done from the village base, but the Yanomamö, like the Kayapo, may go on treks to forage from time to time.

The Samoans The Samoans numbered about 56,000 people in 1839, soon after European missionaries arrived.[24] The islands of Samoa, which are about 2,300 miles south of the Hawaiian Islands, are volcanic in origin, with central ridges and peaks as high as 6,000 feet. Though the land is generally steep, the islands have a lush plant cover watered by up to 200 inches of rain a year (about five times the amount of rain that falls on New York City in a year). All that rain does not interfere much with outdoor activity, because the torrential showers do not last long and the water disappears quickly into the porous volcanic soil. The temperature is relatively constant, rarely falling

A Yanomamö boy peels cassava.

below 70°F or rising above 88°F. Strong cooling trade winds blow most of the year, generally from the east or southeast, and on the coasts one hears a continuous low rumble from the huge Pacific swells that break upon the fringing coral reefs offshore.

Samoan horticulture involves mostly three tree crops requiring little work except in harvesting. Once planted, and with hardly more than a few years of waiting, the breadfruit tree continues to produce about two crops a year for up to a half century. Coconut trees may continue to produce for a hundred years. And banana trees make new stalks of fruit, each weighing more than 50 pounds, for many years; merely cutting down one stalk induces the plant to grow another. Young men do most of the harvesting of tree crops. Women do the occasional weeding.

The Samoans also practice some shifting cultivation; men periodically clear small patches of land for taro, a root crop that is a staple food. The taro patches can produce a few crops before they must be allowed to revert to bush so that soil fertility can be restored. But even taro cultivation does not require much work; planting requires nothing more than slightly burying the top sliced off a root just harvested. Young men do most of the planting and harvesting. The taro patches are weeded infrequently, mostly by women. This kind of casual farming behavior prompted Captain Bligh, of *Mutiny on the Bounty* fame, to describe the Tahitians as lazy.[25] Captain Bligh's attitude was ethnocentric. South Pacific islanders such as the Samoans and Tahitians cannot weed as often as European farmers without risking the erosion of their soil, because, in contrast with European farmlands, which are generally flat or only slightly sloping, the land of Samoa and Tahiti is mostly steep. The Samoan and Tahitian practice of not weeding crops and growing them in glorious and messy confusion minimizes soil erosion; the deep and shallow root structures of the various plants growing together prevent the loose volcanic soil from being washed away by the torrential showers.

The Samoans keep chickens and pigs, which they eat only occasionally. The major source of animal protein in the Samoan diet is fish, caught inside and outside the reef.

The islands of American Samoa have very little flat land for cultivation. To prevent soil erosion, crops are interspersed among the naturally occurring brush. If land were completely cleared and single-cropped, the frequent torrential rains would quickly wash away the loose volcanic topsoil.

Younger men may swim in the deep sea outside the reef and use a sling to spear fish; older men are more likely to stand on the reef and throw a four-pointed spear at fish swimming inside the reef. For many years, people in the villages of Samoa have sold copra, the sun-dried meat of the ripe coconut, to the world market for coconut oil. Men generally cut the copra from the shells after the ripe coconuts fall by themselves to the ground. With the cash earned from the sale of copra, people buy imported items such as machetes, kerosene, and flour. People in most villages still produce most of the foods they eat, but many have migrated to towns on the bigger islands and to cities in Hawaii and on the U.S. mainland to find wage-paying jobs.

General Features of Horticulturalists In most horticultural societies, simple farming techniques have tended to yield more food from a given area than is generally available to foragers. Consequently, horticulture is able to support larger, more densely populated communities. The way of life of horticulturalists is more sedentary than that of foragers, although communities may move after some years to farm a new series of plots. (Some horticulturalists have permanent villages because they depend mostly on food from trees that keep producing for a long time.) In contrast with most recent food-collecting groups, horticultural societies exhibit the beginnings of social differentiation. For example, some individuals may be part-time craftworkers or part-time political officials, and certain members of a kin group may have more status than other individuals in the society.

Intensive Agriculture

People engaged in **intensive agriculture** use techniques that enable them to cultivate fields permanently. Essential nutrients may be put back in the soil through the use of fertilizers, which may be organic material (most commonly dung from humans or other animals) or inorganic (chemical) fertilizers. But there are other ways to restore nutrients. The Luo of western Kenya plant beans around corn plants. Bacteria growing around the roots of the bean plant replace lost nitrogen, and the corn plant conveniently provides a pole for the bean plant to wind around as it grows. Some intensive agriculturalists use irrigation from streams and rivers to ensure an adequate supply of waterborne nutrients. Crop rotation and plant stubble that has been plowed under also restore nutrients to the soil.

In general, the technology of intensive agriculturalists is more complex than that of horticulturalists. Plows rather than digging sticks are generally employed. But there is enormous variation in the degree to which intensive agriculturalists rely on mechanization rather than hand labor. In some societies, the most complex machine is an animal-drawn plow; in the corn and wheat belts of the United States, huge tractors till, seed, and fertilize 12 rows at a time.[26]

Let's look at two groups of intensive agriculturalists, those of rural Greece and those of the Mekong Delta in Vietnam.

Rural Greece The village of Vasilika is situated at the foot of Mount Parnassus on the Boeotian plain. As described by Ernestine Friedl in the 1950s, its population was about 220 inhabitants.[27] Grapevines and wheat are cultivated for domestic use. The agricultural year begins in March with pruning of the vines and hoeing of the fields, tasks regarded as men's work. Winemaking begins in September, after the grain harvest, and involves the whole family. Men, women, and children talk and joke as they pick the grapes and put them into large baskets. After they remove the leaves and stems, the men trample the fruit, and the newly pressed grape juice, or *must*, is transferred to barrels. After adding whatever sugar and alcohol are needed, farmers also add resin to give the wine its characteristic flavor.

The villagers use horses to plow their wheat fields in October, and in November, they sow the seed by hand. The wheat crop is harvested the following summer, usually by machine. Wheat constitutes the staple village food and is eaten as bread, as a cereal (called *trakhana*), or as noodles. It is also commonly bartered for other food items, such as fish, olive oil, and coffee.

Cotton and tobacco are the main **cash crops**—that is, crops raised for sale. In this dry plains country, the success of the cotton crop depends on irrigation, and the villagers use efficient diesel pumps to distribute water. The real work in the cotton fields begins after the spring plowing and seeding have been completed. Then the young plants must be hoed and mulched, a task done mostly by women. The season of cotton cultivation is especially hard on women, who must do all the cooking and household chores in addition to working in the cotton fields. Irrigation, which begins in July, is men's work. It is usually done three times a season and involves the clearing of shallow ditches, the mounting of pumps, and the channeling of water. Cotton picking, which starts in October, is considered women's work. For picking, as well as hoeing and harvesting, a farmer owning more than five acres usually hires women from the same village or neighboring villages and sometimes even from distant towns. The cotton ginning is carried out by centrally located contractors, who are paid on the spot with 6 percent of each farmer's crop. Most of the seed reclaimed in the ginning is used for the next year's planting. The remainder is pressed into cakes to serve as supplementary food for ewes at lambing time. Tobacco yields a larger cash income than cotton, and the tobacco crop fits well into what would otherwise be slack periods in cultivation.

Raising animals plays a relatively minor role in the villagers' economic life. Each farmer has a horse or two for heavy draft work, a mule or donkey, about two dozen sheep, and some fowl.

Farmers at Vasilika are responsive to modern developments; they are prepared to experiment to a certain extent, especially with mechanization. Where the amount of acreage under cultivation warrants the expense, tractors are hired for plowing. Specialists are regularly called in to handle harvesting, cotton ginning, and similar tasks. Indeed, the Greek farmer is content to be a farmer and to rely on the skills of others to repair his roof, maintain his water pump, and provide the mechanical know-how for crop production.

Rural Vietnam: The Mekong Delta The village of Khanh Hau, situated along the flat Mekong Delta, comprised about 600 families when Gerald Hickey described it in the late 1950s, before the Vietnam War.[28] The delta area has a tropical climate, with a rainy season that lasts from May to November. As a whole, the area has been made habitable only through extensive drainage.

Wet rice cultivation is the principal agricultural activity of Khanh Hau. It is part of a complex, specialized arrangement that involves three interacting components: (1) a complex system of irrigation and water control; (2) a variety of specialized equipment, including plows, waterwheels, threshing sledges, and winnowing machines; and (3) a clearly defined set of socioeconomic roles—from those of landlord, tenant, and laborer to those of rice miller and rice merchant.

In the dry season, the farmer decides what sort of rice crop to plant, whether of long (120 days) or short (90 days) maturation. The choice depends on the capital at his disposal, the current cost of fertilizer, and the anticipated demand for rice. The seedbeds are prepared as soon as the rains have softened the ground in May. The soil is turned over (plowed) and broken up (harrowed) as many as six separate times, with two-day intervals for "airing" between operations. During this time, the rice seeds are soaked in water for at least two days to stimulate sprouting. Before the seedlings are planted, the paddy is plowed once more and harrowed twice in two directions at right angles.

Planting is a delicate, specialized operation that must be done quickly and is performed most often by hired male laborers. But efficient planting is not enough to guarantee a good crop. Proper fertilization and irrigation are equally important. In the irrigating, steps must be taken to ensure that the water level remains at exactly the proper depth over the entire paddy. Water is distributed by means of scoops, wheels, and mechanical pumps. Successive crops of rice ripen from late September to May; all members of the family may be called upon to help with the harvest. After each crop is harvested, it is threshed, winnowed, and dried. Normally, the rice is sorted into three portions: one is set aside for use by the household in the following year; one is for payment of hired labor and other services (such as loans from agricultural banks); and one is for cash sale on the market. Aside from the harvesting,

Vietnamese farmers in the Mekong Delta working in a flooded rice paddy. Much of the delta was originally tropical forest.

women do little work in the fields, spending most of their time on household chores. In families with little land, however, young daughters help in the fields and older daughters may hire themselves out to other farmers.

The villagers also cultivate vegetables, raise pigs, chickens, and the like, and frequently engage in fishing. The village economy usually supports three or four implement makers and a much larger number of carpenters.

General Features of Intensive Agricultural Societies

Societies with intensive agriculture are more likely than horticulturalists to have towns and cities, a high degree of craft specialization, complex political organization, and large differences in wealth and power. Studies suggest that intensive agriculturalists work longer hours than horticulturalists.[29] For example, men engaged in intensive agriculture average nine hours of work a day, seven days a week; women average almost 11 hours of work per day. Most of the work for women in intensive agricultural societies involves food processing and work in and around the home, but they also spend a lot of time working in the fields. We discuss some of the implications of the work patterns for women in the chapter on sex, gender, and culture.

Intensive agricultural societies are more likely than horticultural societies to face famines and food shortages, even though intensive agriculture is generally more productive than horticulture.[30] Why, if more food can be produced per acre, is there more risk of shortage among intensive agriculturalists? Intensive agriculturalists may be more likely to face food shortages because they are often producing crops for a market. Producing for a market pushes farmers to cultivate plants that give them the highest yield rather than cultivating plants that are drought-resistant or that require fewer nutrients. Farmers producing for a market also tend to concentrate on one crop. Crop diversity is often a protection against total crop failure because fluctuations in weather, plant diseases, or insect pests are not likely to affect all the crops. There are also fluctuations in market demand. If the market demand drops and the price falls for a particular crop, farmers may not have enough cash to buy the other food they need.

The Commercialization and Mechanization of Agriculture

Some intensive agriculturalists produce very little for sale; most of what they produce is for their own use. But there is a worldwide trend for intensive agriculturalists to produce more and more for a market. This trend is called **commercialization,** which may occur in any area of life and which involves increasing dependence on buying and selling, usually with money as the medium of exchange. Some of the push toward commercialization comes from external pressures, from governments that impose taxes that must be paid by money. But some of the shift occurs when subsistence farmers choose to plant a cash crop to earn money for various reasons. For example, the Malaiyali farmers of India grow a cash crop, tapioca (cassava), as a way of responding to unpredictable rainfall. Tapioca is fairly drought-tolerant, grows in poor soils, and can be planted later in the year when the rainfall has become more predictable.[31]

The increasing commercialization of agriculture is associated with several other trends. One is that farm work is becoming more mechanized as hand labor becomes scarce, because of migration to industrial and service jobs in towns and cities, or because hired hand labor has become too expensive. A second trend is the emergence and spread of *agribusiness,* large corporation-owned farms that may be operated by multinational companies and worked entirely by hired, as opposed to family, labor. For example, consider how cotton farming has changed in the southeastern United States. In the 1930s, tractors replaced mules and horses used in plowing. This change allowed some landowners to evict their sharecroppers and expand their holdings. After World War II, mechanical cotton pickers replaced most of the harvest laborers. But a farmer had to have a good deal of money to acquire those machines, each of which cost many tens of thousands of dollars.[32] So the mechanization of cotton farming sent many rural farm laborers off to the cities of the North in search of employment, and the agricultural sector increasingly became big business. A third trend associated with the commercialization of agriculture, including animal raising, is a reduction in the proportion of the population engaged in food production. In the United States today, for example, less than 2 percent of the total population work on farms.[33] A fourth trend is that much of what people produce for sale nowadays is shipped to or received from markets in other countries. For example, in the summer months, fruits and vegetables are often shipped to markets where consumers have little local fresh produce. The spread of different kinds of food is not new (see the box "Food on the Move") but is accelerating in today's world. In the next chapter on economics, we discuss more fully some of the apparent consequences of the worldwide changeover to commercial or market economies.

"Market Foraging" in Industrial Societies

Food in countries such as the United States and Canada comes largely from intensive agriculture and animal husbandry practiced by a small proportion of the population. Those food specialists make their living by selling animal and plant products to marketers, distributors, and food processors. Indeed, most people know very little about how to grow crops or raise animals. Food appears in markets or supermarkets already processed by other specialists. It comes in paper or plastic packages, looking far different from how it originally looked in the field or on the feedlot. Thus, most of us are "market foragers," collecting our food from stores. In some ways, as we shall see in the chapter on culture and the individual, we behave very much like foragers of wild plants and animals. But there are also enormous differences between our kind of foraging and the original kind. If our society did not have very productive intensive agriculture and animal husbandry, we would not have towns and cities, thousands of different full-time occupations (hardly any of which are involved in food-getting), a centralized government, or many of our other characteristics.

Pastoralism

Most agriculturalists keep and breed some animals (practice animal husbandry), but a small number of societies

migrants and immigrants

Food on the Move

People in North America get most of their food from stores. Most people do not know where the food comes from originally—where it was first grown or raised. This is partly because relatively few are directly involved in food-getting (less than 2 percent of the workers in the United States). Even when you count all the activities related to food-getting, such as marketing and transportation, only 14 percent of U.S. workers have anything to do with the production and distribution of food. But nowadays, many of the foods we buy in markets—tacos, salsa, bagels, pasta, pizza, sausage, soy sauce, and teriyaki—have become mainstream "North American" food. Where did these foods come from? Originally, they were eaten only by ethnic and immigrant minorities who came to the United States and Canada. Some, but not all, of their foods caught on and became widely consumed. They became, in short, as "American" as apple pie.

The ingredients in many of these food items resulted from previous movements of people even further back in time. Consider the ingredients in pizza, a favorite food now for many of us. The dough is made from wheat flour, which was first grown in the Middle East, perhaps as much as 10,000 years ago. How do anthropologists know that? Archaeologists have discovered wheat kernels that old in Middle Eastern sites, and they have found flat stones and stone rolling pins from that time that we know were used to grind kernels into flour (we can tell from microscopic analysis of the residue on the stone). What about other ingredients that may be found in pizza? Cheese was first made in the Middle East too, at least 5,000 years ago (we have writings from that time that mention cheese). Tomatoes were first grown in South America, probably several thousand years ago. They got to Italy, the birthplace of the tomato pie (which became transformed into pizza), less than 200 years ago. Just 100 years ago, tomatoes (the key ingredient in pizza for some) were so new in eastern Europe that people

were afraid to eat them because their leaves are poisonous to humans and some other animals. Another food we associate with Italian cuisine, spaghetti-type noodles, came to Italy (from China) less than 500 years ago. So the major ingredients of pizza, just like round-noodle pasta, are all not native to Italy.

The amazing thing about foods is that they so often travel far and wide, generally carried by the people who like to eat them. And some of our foods, when alive, also travel widely. For example, the bluefin tuna (which can weigh more than a thousand pounds) swims thousands of miles from feeding to breeding grounds in the North Atlantic, Mediterranean, and Caribbean. This largest of all existing fishes is being hunted into extinction because its meat is so prized for what the Japanese call *sushi*, a kind of food that has spread from Japan throughout the world.

Sources: Diament 2005, A32–34; Revkin 2005, F1, F4.

---

depend mostly for their living on domesticated herds of animals that feed on natural pasture.[34] We call such a system **pastoralism.** We might assume that pastoralists breed animals to eat their meat, but most do not. Pastoralists more often get their animal protein from live animals in the form of milk, and some pastoralists regularly take blood, which is rich in protein, from their animals to mix with other foods. The herds often indirectly provide food because many pastoralists trade animal products for plant foods and other necessities. In fact, a large proportion of their food may actually come from trade with agricultural groups.[35] For example, some pastoral groups in the Middle East derive much of their livelihood from the sale of what we call oriental rugs, which are made from the wool of their sheep on hand looms. Two pastoral societies we shall examine are the Basseri of southern Iran and the Lapps of Scandinavia.

The Basseri The Basseri, described by Fredrik Barth as of the 1960s, are a tribe of about 16,000 tent-dwelling nomads.[36] Their herds consist principally of sheep and goats, though donkeys and camels are raised for pulling or carrying, and the wealthier men have horses for riding. Theirs is

a dry, arid habitat, with rainfall averaging no more than 10 inches a year. The Basseri's pastoral way of life is based on a regular, migratory exploitation of the grazing lands within their territory, which measures about 15,000 square miles in all. In winter, when the mountains to the north are covered with snow, the plains and foothills to the south offer extensive pasturage. During the spring, grazing is excellent on a plateau near the center of the territory. By summer, when most of the lower-lying pastures have dried up, sufficient food for the herds can be found in the mountains at an altitude of nearly 6,000 feet.

Annual migrations are so important to the economies of the Basseri and other pastoralist societies of that region that they have developed the concept of *il-rah,* or "tribal road." A major pastoral tribe such as the Basseri has a traditional route and schedule. The route, consisting of the localities in the order in which each is visited, follows existing passes and lines of communication. The schedule, which regulates the length of time each location will be occupied, depends on the maturation of different pastures and the movements of other tribes. The *il-rah* is regarded, in effect, as the property of the tribe. Local populations and authorities recognize the tribe's right to pass along roads and cultivated lands, to draw water from the public wells, and to pasture flocks on public land.

The Basseri herd sheep and goats together, with one shepherd (a boy or unmarried man) responsible for a flock of 300 to 400 animals. Children of both sexes are usually responsible for herding the baby animals (lambs and kids). Milk and its by-products are the most important commodities, but wool, hides, and meat are also important to the economy of the Basseri. Both wool and hides are traded, but they are even more useful within the tribe. The Basseri, especially the women, are skilled spinners and weavers, and much of their time is spent at these activities. Saddlebags and pack bags are woven on horizontal looms from homespun wool and hair, as are carpets, sleeping rugs, and the characteristic black tents made of panels of woven goat hair. Woven goat hair provides an exceptionally versatile cloth. For winter use, it retains heat and repels water; in the summer, it insulates against heat and permits free circulation of air. Lambskin hides also serve many purposes. When plucked and turned inside out, they are made into storage bags to hold water, buttermilk, sour milk, and other liquids.

Most of the Basseri must trade for the necessities and luxury items they do not produce within the community. The staple items they sell are butter, wool, lambskins, rope, and occasionally livestock.

The Lapps

The Lapps or Saami practice reindeer herding in northwestern Scandinavia where Finland, Sweden, and Norway share common frontiers. It is a typical Arctic habitat: cold, windswept, with long, dark days for half the year. Considerable change has occurred recently, so we first discuss the food-getting strategy in the 1950s, as described by Ian Whitaker and T. I. Itkonen.[37]

The Lapps herd their reindeer either intensively or, more often, extensively. In the *intensive system,* the herd is constantly under observation within a fenced area for the whole year. Intensively herded reindeer and other animals are accustomed to human contact. Hence, the summer corralling of the females for milking and the breaking in of the ox-reindeer for use as work animals are not difficult tasks. The *extensive system* involves allowing the animals to migrate over a large area. It requires little surveillance and encompasses large herds. Under this system, the reindeer

are allowed to move through their seasonal feeding cycles watched by only one or two scouts. The other Lapps stay with the herd only when it has settled in its summer or winter habitat. But milking, breaking in, and corralling are harder in the extensive than in the intensive system because the animals are less accustomed to humans.

Even under the extensive system, which theoretically permits Lapps to engage in subsidiary economic activities such as hunting and fishing, the reindeer herd is the essential, if not the only, source of income. A family might possess as many as 1,000 reindeer, but usually the figure is half that number. Studies show 200 to be the minimum number of reindeer needed to provide for a family of four or five adults. Women may have shared the herding chores in the past under the intensive system, but now, under the extensive system, men do the herding. Women still do the milking. The Lapps eat the meat of the bull reindeer; the female reindeer are kept for breeding purposes. Bulls are slaughtered in the fall, after the mating season. Meat and hides are frequently sold or bartered for other food and necessities.

Reindeer are still herded nowadays, but snowmobiles, all-terrain vehicles, and even helicopters have replaced sleds for herding. Ferries move reindeer to and from different pastures, and the herders communicate by field telephones. With faster transportation, many Lapps now live in permanent homes and can still get to their herds in hours. Lapp children spend much of their time in school and, consequently, do not learn much of the herding ways. The Norwegian government now regulates pastoralism, licensing pastoralists and trying to limit the number of reindeer they can herd.[38] And many Lapps (they prefer to call themselves Saami) no longer have reindeer.

General Features of Pastoralism

In recent times, pastoralism has been practiced mainly in grassland and other semiarid habitats that are not especially suitable for cultivation without some significant technological input such as irrigation. Most pastoralists are nomadic, moving camp fairly frequently to find water and new pasture for their herds. But other pastoralists have somewhat more sedentary lives. They may move from one settlement to another in different seasons, or they may send some people out to travel with the herds in different seasons. Pastoral communities are usually small, consisting of a group of related families.[39] Individuals or families may own their own animals, but the community makes decisions about when and where to move the herds.

As we have noted, there is a great deal of interdependence between pastoral and agricultural groups. That is, trade is usually necessary for pastoral groups to survive. Like agriculturalists, pastoralists are more vulnerable than foragers and horticulturalists to famine and food shortages. Pastoralists usually inhabit drought-prone regions, but recent pastoralists have had their access to grazing lands reduced, and political pressures have pushed them to decrease their movement over large areas. Mobility kept the risk of overgrazing to a minimum, but overgrazing in small territories has increased the risk of desertification.[40]

A Saami reindeer herder feeds two of her animals in the snow.

applied anthropology

The Effect of Food-Getting on the Environment

Many people are now aware of industrial pollution—the dumping of industrial wastes in the ground or into rivers, the spewing of chemicals into the air through smokestacks—but we don't often realize how much humans have altered the environment by the ways they collect and produce food. Consider irrigation. Irrigation has made agriculture productive in arid or unpredictable rainfall environments. There are various ways to capture water for irrigation. Water can be channeled from rivers; rainwater can be caught in terraces carved out of hillsides; ancient water can be pumped up from vast underground reservoirs called aquifers. But much of the water use is wasteful, seeping into the channels or evaporating into the air before reaching the plants. Plants absorb water and leave behind the salts. But the extensive evaporation of water during irrigation mostly leads to higher concentration of minerals and salts. If drainage is poor and if the water table rises, the salt concentrations are not washed away. Often, the more a piece of land has been irrigated, the saltier the ground becomes. Eventually, the soil becomes too salty to grow crops effectively and crops have to be grown elsewhere.

Some archaeologists have suggested that the accumulation of toxic salts in the soil at least partly explains the doom or decline of various groups in the past. For example, salinization probably contributed to the decline of Sumer, an early empire in Mesopotamia, and other early states in what is now southern Iraq and southwestern Iran. Over time,

the concentration of people shifted from the lower portion of the Tigris-Euphrates river system to the upper portion as irrigated land lower down became unusable for farming. Today, much of the soil is still too salty for cultivation. Recent irrigation schemes during Saddam Hussein's regime have seriously degraded the downstream Iraqi marshes. Less than 10 percent of the marsh wetlands remain, putting over 60 bird species at risk. In addition, the loss of the marshlands has reduced the ability of the marshland to filter the water before it reaches the Persian Gulf, which has led to declines in productivity of the coastal fisheries. The severity of the degradation in the region has been compared with the deforestation of the Amazon.

The lessons of history have not been learned yet. The San Joaquin Valley of California, perhaps the most productive agricultural area in the world, now has a serious salinization problem. One solution in many of the areas of the Great American Desert is to pump water up from underground. Indeed, in many places there is a great deal of water underground. For example, the Ogallala aquifer, which underlies parts of Nebraska, Kansas, Texas, Oklahoma, Colorado, and New Mexico, contains water left from the ice ages. But the pumping solution, if it is a solution, is only a short-term fix, for the huge Ogallala aquifer is also the fastest-disappearing aquifer. The only question is how long it will take to disappear totally.

Too many people raising too many animals can also have serious effects on the environment. We can easily

imagine how the possibility of profit might inspire people to try to raise more animals than the land will support. For example, 300 years ago the Great American Desert was a vast grassland. It supported large herds of buffalo, which were all but exterminated by overhunting in the next 200 years. The European-American settlers soon discovered they could raise cattle and sheep on this grassland, but many parts of it were overgrazed. It took the swirling dust storms of the 1930s to make people realize that overgrazing as well as poor farming practices could be disastrous. The problems are not just recent ones. The Norse colonized Greenland and Iceland around A.D. 800; but overgrazing of pasture undoubtedly contributed to soil erosion and the disappearance or decline of the colonies by A.D. 1500.

Are environmental problems associated only with food production? Although food producers may be the worst offenders, there is reason to think that foragers may also have sometimes overfished, overgathered, or overhunted. For example, some scholars suspect that the movement of humans into the New World was mainly responsible for the disappearance of the mammoth. Unfortunately, there is little evidence that humans have been good conservers in the past. That does not mean that humans cannot do better in the future—but they have to want to.

Source: Los Angeles Times 1994; Reisner 1993; Hillel 2000; Curtis et al. 2005; Dirks 2009.

ENVIRONMENTAL RESTRAINTS ON FOOD-GETTING

Of great interest to anthropologists is why different societies have different methods of getting food. Archaeological evidence suggests that major changes in food-getting, such as the domestication of plants and animals, have been independently invented in at least several areas of the world. Yet, despite these comparable inventions and their

subsequent spread by diffusion and migration, there is still wide diversity in the means by which people obtain food.

How much does the physical environment affect food-getting? Anthropologists have concluded that the physical environment by itself has a restraining, rather than a determining, effect on the major types of subsistence. Because they have very short growing seasons, cold regions of the earth are not particularly conducive to growing plants. No society we know of has practiced agriculture in the Arctic; instead, people who live there rely primarily on animals for

Areas that have practiced irrigation for long time periods begin to suffer from salinization and become unsuitable for agriculture as in parts of Alberta, Canada.

food. But both foraging (as among the Inuit) and food production (as among the Lapps) can be practiced in cold areas. Indeed, cross-cultural evidence indicates that neither foraging nor food production is significantly associated with any particular type of habitat.[41]

We know that foraging has been practiced at one time or another in almost all areas of the earth. The physical environment does seem to have some effect on what kind of foraging is practiced, that is, on the extent to which foragers will depend on plants, animals, or fish. Farther away from the equator, foragers depend much less on plants for food and much more on animals and fish.[42] Lewis Binford argues that fishing becomes increasingly important in cold climates because foragers need nonportable housing in severe winters to protect themselves from the cold. Therefore, they cannot rely on large animals, which usually have to feed themselves by moving over considerable distances in the winter. Fishing is more localized than hunting, and therefore foragers who rely on fishing can stay in their nonportable houses in winter.[43]

There is one habitat that may have precluded foraging until recent times. If it were not for the nearness of food producers, particularly agriculturalists, recent foragers such as the Mbuti of central Africa could probably not have supported themselves in the tropical forest habitats where they now live.[44] Tropical forests are lush in plants, but they do not provide much in the way of reachable fruits, seeds, and flowers that humans can eat. Animals are available in tropical forests, but typically they are lean and do not provide humans with sufficient carbohydrates or fat. Like the Mbuti groups who hunt and gather in the forest, many tropical foragers trade for agricultural products; other collectors cultivate some crops in addition to hunting and gathering. It would seem, then, that foragers could not survive in tropical forests were it not for the carbohydrates they obtain from agriculturalists.

When we contrast horticulture and intensive agriculture, the physical environment appears to explain some of the variation. Approximately 80 percent of all societies that practice horticulture or simple agriculture are in the

tropics, whereas 75 percent of all societies that practice intensive agriculture are not in tropical forest environments.[45] Tropical forests have abundant rainfall. But despite the attractiveness of lush vegetation and brilliant coloring, tropical forestlands do not usually offer favorable environments for intensive agriculture. Perhaps the heavy rainfall quickly washes away certain minerals from cleared land. Also, the difficulty of controlling insect pests and weeds, which abound in tropical forests,[46] may make intensive agriculture less productive.

But difficulty is not impossibility. Today, there are some areas, for instance, the Mekong Delta in Vietnam, whose tropical forests have been cleared and prevented from growing again by the intensive cultivation of rice in paddies. And, although cultivation is not normally possible in dry lands, because of insufficient natural rainfall to sustain crops, agriculture can be practiced where there are oases—small, naturally watered areas where crops can be grown with a simple technology—or rivers that can be tapped by irrigation, one of the techniques used with intensive agriculture.

The animals that pastoralists raise depend primarily on grass for food, so it is not surprising that pastoralism is typically practiced in grassland regions of the earth. These regions may be **steppes** (dry, low grass cover), **prairies** (taller, better-watered grass), or **savannas** (tropical grasslands). The grassland habitat favors large game and hence supports both hunting and pastoral technologies, except where machine technology makes intensive agriculture possible, as in parts of the United States, Canada, and Ukraine.

Very different strategies of food-getting have been practiced in the same environment over time. A dramatic illustration is the history of the Imperial Valley in California. The complex systems of irrigation now used in that dryland area have made it a very productive region. Yet, about 400 years ago, this same valley supported only hunting and gathering groups who subsisted on wild plants and animals.

It is evident from the Imperial Valley example and many others like it that the physical environment does not

This area of Montana is cultivated now. In the past, only foraging was practiced.

by itself account for the system of food-getting in an area. Even a polar environment could have agriculture with heated greenhouses, though it would be too expensive. Technological advances as well as enormous capital investment in irrigation, labor, and equipment have made intensive agriculture possible in the Imperial Valley. But the agriculture there is precarious, depending on sources of water and power from elsewhere. In a prolonged drought, it may be difficult or too expensive to obtain the needed water. And should the prices for vegetables fall, the farming businesses in the Imperial Valley could find themselves unable to finance the investment and borrowing of capital that they need to continue. So technological, social, and political factors rather than environmental factors mostly determine what kind of food-getting can be practiced in a given environment.

THE ORIGIN OF FOOD PRODUCTION

During the period from about 40,000 to about 15,000 years ago, which we know best archaeologically for Europe, people seem to have gotten most of their food from hunting the available migratory herds of large animals, such as wild cattle, antelope, bison, and mammoths. These hunter-gatherers were probably highly mobile to follow the migrations of the animals. Beginning about 14,000 years ago, people in some regions began to depend less on big game hunting and more on relatively stationary food resources, such as fish, shellfish, small game, and wild plants. Saltwater and freshwater food supplies may have become more abundant in many areas after the glaciers withdrew. As the ice melted, the level of the oceans rose and formed inlets and bays where crabs, clams, and sea mammals could be found. In some areas, particularly Europe and the Near East, the exploitation of local and relatively permanent resources may have supported an increasingly settled way of life.

We see the first evidence of a changeover to food production—the cultivation and domestication of plants and animals—in the Near East about 8000 B.C. This shift occurred, probably independently, in other areas as well. There is evidence of cultivation some time

around 6000 B.C. in China, Southeast Asia (what is now Malaysia, Thailand, Cambodia, and Vietnam), and Africa. In the New World, there appear to have been several places of original cultivation and domestication. The highlands of Mexico (about 7000 B.C.) and the central Andes around Peru (by about 6000 B.C.) were probably the most important in terms of food plants used today.

Most peoples today are food producers rather than foragers. But why did people start to produce their food? We know that an economic transformation occurred in widely separate areas of the world beginning about 10,000 years ago, as people began to domesticate plants and animals. But why did domestication occur? And why did it occur independently in different places within a period of a few thousand years? (Considering that people depended only on wild plants and animals for millions of years, the differences in exactly when domestication first occurred in different parts of the world seem small.)

There are many theories of why food production developed; most have tried to explain the origin of domestication in the Near East. Lewis Binford and Kent Flannery suggested that some change in external circumstances, not necessarily environmental, must have induced or favored the changeover to food production.[47] As Flannery pointed out, there is no evidence of a great economic incentive for hunter-gatherers to become food producers. In fact, as we have seen, some contemporary hunter-gatherers may actually obtain adequate nutrition with far less work than many agriculturalists.

Binford and Flannery thought that the incentive to domesticate animals and plants may have been a desire to reproduce what was wildly abundant in the most bountiful or optimum hunting and gathering areas. Because of population growth in the optimum areas, people might have moved to surrounding areas containing fewer wild resources. In those marginal areas, people would have turned to food production to reproduce what they used to have.

The Binford-Flannery model seems to fit the archaeological record in the Levant, the southwestern part of the Fertile Crescent, where population increase did precede the first signs of domestication.[48] But as Flannery admitted, in some regions, such as southwestern Iran, the optimum hunting and gathering areas do not show population increase before the emergence of domestication.[49]

The Binford-Flannery model focuses on population pressure in a small area as the incentive to turn to food production. Mark Cohen theorized that population pressure on a global scale explains why so many of the world's peoples adopted agriculture within the span of a few thousand years.[50] He argued that hunter-gatherers all over the world gradually increased in population, so that the world was more or less filled with foragers by about 10,000 years ago. Thus, people could no longer relieve population pressure by moving to uninhabited areas. To support their increasing populations, they would have had to exploit a broader range of less desirable wild foods; that is, they would have had to switch to broad-spectrum collecting, or they would have had to increase the yields of the most desirable wild plants by weeding, protecting them from animal pests, and perhaps deliberately planting the most productive among them. Cohen suggested that people might have tried a variety of these strategies to support themselves but would generally have ended up depending on cultivation because that would have been the most efficient way to allow more people to live in one place.

Recently, some archaeologists have returned to the idea that climatic change played a role in the emergence of agriculture. It seems clear from the evidence now available that the climate of the Near East about 13,000 years to 12,000 years ago became more seasonal; the summers got hotter and drier, and the winters became colder. These climatic changes may have favored the emergence of annual species of grain that archaeologically we see proliferating in many areas of the Near East.[51] Some foragers intensively exploited the seasonal grains, developing an elaborate technology for storing and processing the grains and giving up their previous nomadic existence to do so. The transition to agriculture may have occurred when sedentary foraging no longer provided sufficient resources for the population. This change could have happened for a number of reasons. First, sedentarization itself may have led to shortages of resources, either because population increased with sedentarization[52] or because people in permanent villages depleted the local wild resources nearby.[53] Second, climate change may have reduced the available stands of wild grain. In at least one area of the Near East, the onset of drier and cooler weather may have led foragers to try to cultivate their food supplies.[54] Change to a more seasonal climate might also have led to a shortage of certain nutrients for foragers. In the dry seasons, certain nutrients would have been less available. For example, grazing animals become lean when grasses are not plentiful, and so meat from hunting would have been in short supply in the dry seasons. Although it may seem surprising, some recent hunter-gatherers have starved when they had to rely on lean meat. If they could have somehow increased their carbohydrate or fat intake, they might have been more likely to get through the periods of lean game.[55] So it is possible that some wild foragers in the past thought of planting crops to get them through the dry seasons when hunting, fishing, and gathering did not provide enough carbohydrates and fat for them to avoid starvation.

THE SPREAD AND INTENSIFICATION OF FOOD PRODUCTION

Whatever the reasons for the switch to food production, we still need to explain why food production has supplanted foraging as the primary mode of subsistence. We cannot assume that collectors would automatically adopt production as a superior way of life once they understood the process of domestication. After all, as we have noted, domestication may entail more work and provide less security than the food-collecting way of life.

The spread of agriculture may be linked to the need for territorial expansion. As a sedentary, food-producing population grew, it may have been forced to expand into new territory. Some of this territory may have been vacant, but foragers probably already occupied much of it. Although food production is not necessarily easier than collection, it is generally more productive per unit of land. Greater productivity enables more people to be supported in a given territory. In the competition for land between the faster-expanding food producers and the foragers, the food producers may have had a significant advantage: They had more people in a given area. Thus, the foraging groups may have been more likely to lose out in the competition for land. Some groups may have adopted cultivation, abandoning the foraging way of life to survive. Other groups, continuing as foragers, may have been forced to retreat into areas not desired by the cultivators. Today, as we have seen, the small number of remaining foragers inhabit areas not particularly suitable for cultivation—dry lands, dense tropical forests, and polar regions.

Just as prior population growth might account for the origins of domestication, further population growth and ensuing pressure on resources at later periods might also at least partly explain the transformation of horticultural systems into intensive agricultural systems. Ester Boserup suggested that intensification of agriculture, with a consequent increase in yield per acre, is not likely to develop naturally out of horticulture because intensification requires much more work.[56] She argued that people will be willing to intensify their labor only if they have to. Where emigration is not feasible, the prime mover behind intensification may be prior population growth. The need to pay taxes or tribute to a political authority may also stimulate intensification.

Boserup's argument about intensification is widely accepted. However, her assumption that more work is required with intensive agriculture has recently been questioned. Comparing horticultural (swidden or shifting) rice production with rice produced on permanent fields using irrigation, Robert Hunt found that *less,* not more, labor is required with irrigation.[57] Still, population increase may generally provide the impetus to intensify production to increase yields to support the additional people.

Intensive agriculture has not yet spread to every part of the world. Horticulture continues to be practiced in certain tropical regions, and there are still some pastoralists and foragers. Some environments may make it somewhat more difficult to adopt certain subsistence practices. For example, intensive agriculture cannot supplant horticulture in some tropical environments without tremendous investments in chemical fertilizers and pesticides, not to mention the additional labor required.[58] And enormous amounts of water may be required to make agriculturalists out of foragers and pastoralists who now exploit semiarid environments. However, difficulty is not impossibility. Anna Roosevelt points out that, although horticulture was a common food-getting strategy in Amazonia in recent times, archaeological evidence indicates that there were complex societies practicing intensive agriculture on raised, drained fields in the past.[59] The physical environment does not completely control what can be done with it.

SUMMARY ● ○ ○

1. Foraging—hunting, gathering, and fishing—depends on wild plants and animals and is the oldest human food-getting technology. There is a lot of variation with regard to which food-getting activity is most important to the society. Recent foragers depended most on fishing, followed by gathering and hunting. Today, only a small number of societies depend largely on foraging and they tend to inhabit marginal environments.

2. Foragers can be found in various physical habitats. Most foragers are nomadic, and population density is low. Usually, the small bands consist of related families, with the division of labor along age and gender lines only. Personal possessions are limited, individuals' land rights are seldom recognized, and people are not differentiated by class.

3. Beginning about 10,000 years ago, certain peoples in widely separated geographic locations began to make the revolutionary changeover to food production—the cultivation and raising of plants and animals. Over the centuries, food production began to supplant food collection as the predominant mode of subsistence.

4. Horticulturalists farm with relatively simple tools and methods and do not cultivate fields permanently. Their food supply is sufficient to support larger, more densely populated communities than can be fed by foraging. Their way of life is sedentary, although communities may move after some years to farm a new series of plots.

5. Intensive agriculture is characterized by techniques such as fertilization and irrigation that allow fields to be cultivated permanently. In contrast with horticultural societies, intensive agriculturalists are more likely to have towns and cities, a high degree of craft specialization, large differences in wealth and power, and more complex political organization. They are also more likely to face food shortages. In the modern world, intensive agriculture is increasingly mechanized and geared to production for a market.

6. Pastoralism is a subsistence technology involving principally the raising of large herds of animals. It is generally found in low-rainfall areas. Pastoralists tend to be nomadic, to have small communities consisting of related families, and to depend significantly on trade because they do not produce items (including certain types of food) they need.

7. Anthropologists generally agree that the physical environment normally exercises a restraining rather than a determining influence on how people in an area get their food; technology as well as social and political factors may be more important.

8. We see the first evidence of a changeover to food production in the Near East about 8000 B.C. Theories about why food production originated remain controversial, but most archaeologists think that certain conditions must have pushed people to switch from collecting to producing food. Some possible causal factors include (1) population growth in regions of bountiful wild resources, which may have pushed people to move to marginal areas where they tried to reproduce their former abundance; (2) global population growth, which filled most of the world's habitable regions and may have forced people to utilize a broader spectrum of wild resources and to domesticate plants and animals; and (3) the emergence of hotter and drier summers and colder winters, which may have favored sedentarization near seasonal stands of wild grain; population growth in such areas may have forced people to plant crops and raise animals to support themselves.

9. Because food producers can support more people in a given territory than foragers can, they may have had a competitive advantage in confrontations with foragers.

GLOSSARY TERMS ○ ● ○

cash crops **101**	intensive agriculture **100**
commercialization **102**	pastoralism **103**
extensive (shifting) cultivation **99**	prairie **106**
	savanna **106**
food production **98**	slash-and-burn **99**
foraging **94**	steppe **106**
horticulture **98**	subsistence economies **94**
hunter-gatherers **94**	

CRITICAL QUESTIONS ○ ○ ●

1. Why might meat be valued more than plant foods in many societies?

2. Why might foragers be less likely than intensive agriculturalists to suffer from food shortages?

3. Why do certain foods in a society come to be preferred?

PEARSON
myanthrolab

Read the chapter by Burton Pasternak, "Han: Pastoralists and Farmers on a Chinese Frontier," on MyAnthroLab and answer the following questions.

1. The Han Chinese traditionally depended on intensive agriculture. The Mongols traditionally depended on pastoralism. What happened to the Han when they moved beyond the Great Wall to a grassland environment?

2. How has the change to more pastoralism affected marriage and family among the Han?

3. How have the Mongols changed?

Economic Systems

hen we think of economics, we think of things and activities involving money. We think of the costs of goods and services, such as food, rent, haircuts, and movie tickets. We may also think of factories, farms, and other enterprises that produce the goods and services we need, or think we need. In industrial societies, workers may stand before a moving belt for eight hours, tightening identical bolts that glide by. For this task, they are given bits of paper that may be exchanged for food, shelter, and other goods or services. But many societies—indeed, most that are known to anthropology—did not have money or the equivalent of the factory worker until relatively recently. Still, all societies have economic systems, whether or not they involve money. All societies have customs specifying how people gain access to natural resources; customary ways of transforming or converting those resources, through labor, into necessities and other desired goods and services; and customs for distributing and perhaps exchanging goods and services.

In the earlier days of anthropology, it was easier to study the economic system of a people in relative isolation from other societies. But now, almost every area of the earth has been affected by global political and economic forces—colonialism, imperialism, the spread of capitalism, and involvement in a world market system. Most people had no choice about becoming part of that system, but there is considerable variation in how and to what degree change was accepted or resisted. Even for people who resisted, many aspects of traditional economic systems have altered over the last few centuries. In the sections that follow, we describe the traditional economic system first and then turn to some of the more recent changes.

As we shall see in this chapter, a great deal of the cross-cultural variation in economic systems is related to how a society primarily gets its food. However, other aspects of the culture also affect the economies. These other influences, which we cover in subsequent chapters, include the presence or absence of social (class and gender) inequality, family and kinship groups, and the political system.

● ○ ●

THE ALLOCATION OF RESOURCES

Natural Resources: Land

Every society has access to natural resources—land, water, plants, animals, minerals—and every society has cultural rules for determining who has access to particular resources and what can be done with them. In societies like the United States, where land and many other things may be bought and sold, land is divided into precisely measurable units, the borders of which may be visible or invisible. Individuals usually own relatively small plots of land and the resources on them. Large plots of land are generally owned collectively. The owner may be a government agency, such as the National Park Service, which owns land on behalf of the entire population of the United States (referred to as public ownership). Or the owner may be a corporation—a private collective of shareholders. In the United States, property ownership entails a more or less exclusive right to use land or other resources (called *usufruct*) in whatever ways the owner wishes, including the right to withhold or

prevent use by others. In the United States and many other societies, property ownership also includes the right to "alienate" property—that is, to sell, give away, bequeath, or destroy the resources owned. This type of property ownership by individuals, families, or private corporations is often referred to as a *private property* system.

Society specifies what is considered property and the rights and duties associated with that property.[1] These specifications are social in nature, for they may be changed over time. For example, France declared all its beaches to be public, thereby stating, in effect, that the ocean shore is not a resource that an individual can own. As a result, all the hotels and individuals that had fenced-off portions of the best beaches for their exclusive use had to remove the barriers. Even in countries with private property, such as the United States, people cannot do anything that they want with their property. Federal, state, and local governments have adopted legislation to prevent the pollution of the air and the water supply. Such regulation may be new, but the rights of ownership in the United States have been limited for some time. For example, government may take land for use in the construction of a highway; compensation is paid, but the individual cannot prevent confiscation. Similarly, people are not allowed to burn their houses or to use them as brothels or munitions arsenals. In short, even with an individualistic system of ownership, property is not entirely private.

How societies differ in their rules for access to land and other natural resources seems to be related in part to how they differ in food-getting. Let us now examine how foragers, horticulturalists, pastoralists, and intensive agriculturalists structure rights to land in different ways. We look at traditional patterns first. As we shall see later, traditional rights to land have been considerably affected by state societies that have spread to and colonized native societies in the New World, Africa, and Asia.

Foragers Members of food-collecting societies generally do not have private ownership of land. If there is collective ownership, it is always by groups of related people (kinship groups) or by territorial groups (bands or villages). Land is not bought and sold.

The reason is probably that land itself generally has no intrinsic value for foragers; what is of value is the presence of game and wild plant life on the land. If game moves away or food resources become less plentiful, the land is less valuable. Therefore, the greater the possibility that the wild food supply in a particular locale will fluctuate, the less desirable it is to parcel out small areas of land to individuals and the more advantageous it is to make land ownership communal. The Hadza of Tanzania, for example, do not believe that they have exclusive rights over the land on which they hunt. Members of the group can hunt, gather, or draw water wherever they like.[2] This is not to say that private ownership of land does not exist among foragers. Among foragers heavily dependent on fishing in rivers, individual or family ownership is more common,[3] perhaps because the fishing in rivers is more predictable than other kinds of foraging. And, in some foraging societies, individuals and families have private rights to trees.[4] Although foragers generally do not have private ownership of important land resources, there is considerable

variation in the extent of communal ownership. In some societies, such as the Hadza, groups do not claim or defend particular territories. In fact, the Hadza do not even restrict use of their land to members of their own language group. But the Hadza are somewhat unusual. It is more common in food-collecting societies for a group of individuals, usually kin, to "own" land. To be sure, such ownership is not usually exclusive; typically some degree of access is provided to members of neighboring bands.[5]

At the other extreme, local groups try to maintain exclusive rights to particular territories. Why have some foragers been more territorial than others? One suggestion is that, when the plants and animals collected are predictably located and abundant, groups are more likely to be sedentary and to try to maintain exclusive control over territories. In contrast, when plant and animal resources are unpredictable in location or amount, territoriality will tend to be minimal.[6] Territorial foragers appear to have predictably located resources *and* more permanent villages, so it is hard to know which factor is more important in determining whether territory will be defended.

Horticulturalists Like foragers, most horticulturalists do not have individual or family ownership of land. This may be because rapid depletion of the soil necessitates letting some of the land lie fallow for a period of years or abandoning an area after a few years and moving to a new location. There is no reason for individuals or families to claim permanent access to land that, given available technology, is not usable permanently. But, in contrast to foragers, horticulturalists are more likely to allocate particular plots of land to individuals or families for their use, although these individuals or families do not commonly own the land in our sense of potentially permanent ownership.

Among the Mundurucú of Brazil, the village controls the rights to use land. People in the community can hunt and fish where they like, and they have the right to clear a garden plot wherever land belonging to the community is not being used. Gardens can be cultivated for only two years before the soil is exhausted; then the land reverts to the community. The Mundurucú distinguish between the land and the produce on the land, so that a person who cultivates the land owns the produce. Similarly, the person who kills an animal or catches a fish owns it, no matter where it was obtained. But because all food is shared with others, it does not really matter who owns it. Rights to land became more individualized when Mundurucú men began to tap rubber trees for sale. Rights to a particular path in the forest where trees were tapped could not be bought and sold, but the rights could be inherited by a son or son-in-law.[7]

Pastoralists The territory of pastoral nomads usually far exceeds that of most horticultural societies. Because their wealth ultimately depends on mobile herds, uncultivated pasture for grazing, and water for drinking, pastoralists often combine the adaptive potential of both foragers and horticulturalists. Like foragers, they generally need to know the potential of a large area of land. The Basseri, described in the last chapter, moved over an area of 15,000 square miles to obtain supplies of grass and water. And, like horticulturalists, pastoralists must move on when a resource

current research and issues

Does Communal Ownership Lead to Economic Disaster?

In a paper called "The Tragedy of the Commons," Garrett Hardin suggested that, if animals are grazed on common land, it is economically rational for individual animal owners to graze as many animals as possible, because they do not incur the pasture costs. According to Hardin, tragedy results because pasture is degraded by overgrazing, and productivity falls. Similarly, why shouldn't a fisher take as much fish as possible from the ocean, a kind of commons, and not worry about the consequences? On the other hand, if the resource is privately owned, individuals might try to conserve their resources because degrading those resources will cost them in the long run by decreasing their yields. The theory, then, is that private owners will find it rational to conserve their resources to minimize costs and maximize yields.

Is it really true that communal ownership tends to result in overexploitation of resources and lower yields, and private ownership tends to result in conservation of resources and higher yields? This is an active area of research in economic anthropology. We do know about instances where communal grazing lands have been more productive than private grazing lands in comparable climates. For example, the Borana of Ethiopia, who have communal grazing, produce more animal protein per acre at lower cost than Australian cattle ranches, although their climates are similar. And there are instances, such as the overgrazing in the Great American Desert (described in the box "The Effect of Food-Getting on the Environment" in the preceding chapter), where private ownership did lead to degradation of the environment.

Commercialization may be more important than private versus communal ownership in explaining overgrazing or overfishing, at least initially. In the Micronesian islands of Palau, which had traditional conservation practices, serious overfishing became a problem apparently only when

Fishing people often have communal rights to places to fish as in this area of Zaire.

people started to sell fish to Japanese colonists for imported trade goods. Some of those goods (nets and motors) helped to make fishing easier. Eventually, overfishing resulted in reduced catches and increased costs of fishing, and the Palauans had to buy much of their fish in imported cans.

It may also be that sustainability requires some regulation by political authorities. Before 1995, the halibut fishery in Alaska was facing collapse. Competing fishers rushed to fill their holds, no matter how dangerous the weather. Because the fishers often overshot the industry quota, regulators shortened the fishing season to just a few days. And when the boats returned after a few days with a year's worth of fish, the market was flooded and prices fell. In 1995, business became better and safer after a system of "catch shares" was adopted. The fishers were each allocated a transferable quota that they could use to catch fish or sell to others. The quotas are a percentage of the total allowable catch, which regulators set each year. The results: Captains could plan when to fish without worrying about weather or being beaten to the schools of fish by other fishers, regulators

could extend the fishing season, and prices for halibut climbed. The new regulatory system was a success. The halibut fishery was sustained and the fishers were better off. But regulation does not always work, judging by the "groundfishing" (fishing for fish, like cod, that feed off the ocean bottom) industry off the New England coast. In contrast to lobster fisherman who have accepted regulation, groundfishers have not. Perhaps this is because the groundfishing industry did not play a role in creating the regulations, nor do they have a cohesive community that can police itself.

Is there a lesson here for sustaining and even enhancing resources in general? So, which is more likely to lead to conservation, communal ownership or private ownership? We cannot say yet with any confidence. We need more comparisons of cases to tell us. It may be that conservation can be fostered in either type of system, if the people involved are so motivated.

Sources: Hardin 1968; Johannes 1981; Dirks 2009; Stokstad 2008; Acheson 2006.

A Surui village in the Amazon with cleared land for horticulture in the foreground and the surrounding rain forest in the background.

is exhausted (in this case, until grass renews itself). Also like horticulturalists, they depend for subsistence on human manipulation of a natural resource—animals—as opposed to the horticulturalists' land.

Because land is only good if there is sufficient pasture and water, there would be considerable risk to individuals or families to own land that did not predictably have grass and water. So, like most foragers and horticulturalists, community members generally have free access to pasture land.[8] Although grazing land tends to be communally held, it is customary for pastoralist individuals to own animals.[9] Fredrik Barth argued that, if animals were not so owned, the whole group might be in trouble because the members might be tempted to eat up their productive capital—their animals—in bad times. When animals are owned individually, a family whose herd drops below the minimum number of animals necessary for survival can drop out of nomadic life, at least temporarily, and work for wages in sedentary agricultural communities. But, in so doing, such a family does not jeopardize other pastoral families. On the other hand, if the fortunate were to share their herds with the unfortunate, all might approach bankruptcy. Thus, Barth argued, individual ownership is adaptive for a pastoral way of life.[10]

John Dowling questioned that interpretation. As he pointed out, pastoral nomads are not the only ones who have to save some of their "crop" for future production. Horticulturalists also must save some of their crop, in the form of seeds or tubers, for future planting. But horticulturalists generally lack private ownership of productive resources, so the necessity to save for future production cannot explain private ownership of animals in pastoral societies. Dowling suggested that private ownership will develop only in pastoral societies that depend on selling their products to nonpastoralists.[11] Thus, it may be the opportunity to sell their products as well as their labor that explains both the possibility of dropping out of nomadic life and the private ownership of animals among most pastoralists.

As among hunter-gatherers, pastoralists vary in how much a group actually has ownership rights to the territories through which they move their animals. The Basseri have rights to pass through certain areas, including agricultural areas and even cities, but they do not own the entire territory. The Baluch, another pastoralist group in the border region between Iran, Pakistan, and Afghanistan, claim a "tribal" territory, which they defend by force, if necessary.[12]

Intensive Agriculturalists Individual ownership of land resources—including the right to use the resources and the right to sell or otherwise dispose of them—is common among intensive agriculturalists. The development of such ownership is partly a result of the possibility of using land season after season, which gives the land more or less permanent value. But the concept of individual ownership is also partly a political and social matter. So, for example, the occupation and cultivation of frontier land in the United States was transformed by law into individual ownership. Under the Homestead Act of 1862, if a person cleared a 160-acre piece of land and farmed it for five years, the federal government would consider that person the owner of the land. This practice is similar to the custom in some societies by which a kin group, a chief, or a community is obligated to assign a parcel of land to anyone who wishes to farm it. The difference is that, once the American homesteader had become the owner of the land, the laws of the country gave the homesteader the right to dispose of it at will by selling or giving it away. Once individual ownership of land has become established, property owners may use their economic, and hence political, power to pass laws that favor themselves. In the early years of the United States, only property owners could vote.

Private individual ownership is usually associated with intensive agriculture, but not always. As we mentioned in the preceding chapter, intensive agriculture is usually associated with more complex political systems and with differences in wealth and power, so we need to understand the larger political and social context to understand particular systems of land allocation. Some communist and socialist nations with intensive agriculture formed agricultural collectives. For example, after World War II, the small farm holdings in a village in Bulgaria named Zamfirovo were incorporated into a village cooperative.

Most of the villagers worked as laborers on the new cooperative, but the cooperative allocated to every household a small plot on which to grow its own grain, vegetables, and grapes. These plots were fairly productive, and Westerners often attributed their productivity to private enterprise. But the cooperative provided much of the labor needed to plant and plow these plots, so they could hardly be considered private property. In 1989, after the overthrow of the communist regime, the cooperative was dissolved, and the land was divided and sold to private owners.[13]

Colonialism, the State, and Land Rights

Almost universally around the world, colonial conquerors and settlers have taken land away from the natives or aborigines. Even if the natives were given other land in exchange, as in Brazil and the United States, these reservations were often, if not always, poorer in potential than the original land. (If the reservation land hadn't been poorer in quality, the settlers would have taken it for themselves.) For example, in the 19th century, the land of the pastoral Maasai stretched from the Lake Turkana area of northern Kenya down to northern Tanzania. The British pushed the Maasai onto a reserve in the southern part of Kenya, south of the Mombasa-Uganda railway, and gave some of their prime grazing lands and water resources to Europeans for farming and ranching near Nairobi as well as near the Naivasha and Nakuru lakes. The Maasai grazing land was reduced by about 60 percent and the Maasai were also forbidden to graze in the areas where game parks were established by the British for tourism.[14] Europeans, who constituted less than 1 percent of the population in Kenya, acquired access to or control of 20 percent of the land, mostly in the highlands, where there was the greatest potential for commercial production of tea and coffee.[15]

In addition, the new centralized governments often tried to change how the natives owned the land, almost always in the direction of individual or private ownership. If kin groups or larger social entities owned the land, it would be more difficult for the settlers to get the natives to give it up, either by sale or threat. Individual owners could be dispossessed more easily.[16]

The newcomers who benefited from these forced changes were not always people of European background, but they were commonly people from expanding state societies. Beginning in the late 15th century, the expanding groups came mostly from western Europe. But in recent times, as well as in the millennia before and after the time of Christ, conquerors and settlers have come from India, China, Japan, Arabia, Scandinavia, Russia, and other countries. This is not to say that native peoples in Africa, Asia, and the New World were never guilty of conquering and exploiting others on their continents or elsewhere. They were. The Aztecs in Mexico and Central America, the native kingdoms in West Africa after about 800 years ago, and the Arabs after the rise of Islam were just some of the expanding state societies of the past, before the rise of the West. Wherever there have been "civilized" (urban) societies, there have been imperialism and colonialism. In North America, the British recognized the principle that lands not ceded to the crown would be native hunting grounds, but such recognition of rights by the British and then by the United States remained in force only as long as the various native groups remained numerous enough to constitute a threat to the settlers. President Andrew Jackson, for example, called for removal of all eastern Native American groups to "permanent" settlements west of the Mississippi. Some 90,000 people were removed. But, as settlers moved west, the reservations were often reduced in size.[17] In much of colonial Africa, governments ceded land to European-owned companies for development. Reserves were established for large native populations, who then were invariably forced to work as laborers on European-owned plantations and in European-owned mines.[18]

The taking of land by state authorities does not just happen with colonialism and imperialism. Indigenous revolutionary movements have collectivized land, as in Russia, or broken up large private landholdings, as in Mexico. Typically, state authorities do not like communal land-use systems. State authorities particularly view mobile pastoralists unfavorably, because their mobility makes them difficult to control. Governments usually try to settle pastoralists or break up communally held pasture into small units.[19] In Kenya, after independence from the British, the pastoral Maasai continued to lose grazing territory. The national government strongly promotes tourism, for which game parks are vital, and development, such as the construction of greenhouses growing flowers for the European market. With the advice of international development agencies, the Kenyan government pushed for privatization of grazing land. But grazing on individual-owned plots requires capital to grow or buy food for cattle, pay for medicines, and to get cattle to market.[20]

Technology

To convert resources to food and other goods, every society makes use of a technology, which includes tools, constructions (such as fish traps), and required skills (such as how and where to set up a fish trap). Societies vary considerably in their technologies and in the way access to technology is allocated. For example, foragers and pastoralists typically have fairly small tool kits. They must limit their tools, and their material possessions in general, to what they can comfortably carry with them. As for access to

Colonial governments have often taken land away from the natives to establish plantations. A family in Guatemala works on a coffee plantation.

technology, foragers and horticulturalists generally allow equal opportunity. In the absence of specialization, most individuals have the skills to make what they need. But in an industrial society like our own, the opportunity to acquire or use a particular technology (which may be enormously expensive as well as complex) is hardly available to all. Most of us may be able to buy a drill or a hammer, but few of us can buy the factory that makes it.

The tools foragers most need are weapons for the hunt, digging sticks, and receptacles for gathering and carrying. Of all foragers, the Inuit probably had the most sophisticated weapons, including harpoons, compound bows, and ivory fishhooks. Yet the Inuit also had relatively fixed settlements with available storage space and dog teams and sleds for transportation.[21]

Among foragers, tools are considered to belong to the person who made them. There is no way of gaining superiority over others through possession of tools, because whatever resources for toolmaking are available to one are available to all. In addition, the custom of sharing applies to tools as well as to food. For example, Elizabeth Thomas, speaking of the !Kung, said, "The few possessions that Bushmen have are constantly circulating among the members of their groups."[22]

Pastoralists, like foragers, are somewhat limited in their possessions, for they too are nomadic. But pastoralists can use their animals to carry some possessions. Each family owns its own tools, clothes, and perhaps a tent, as well as its own livestock. The livestock are the sources of other needed articles, for the pastoralists often trade their herd products for the products of the townspeople. Horticulturalists, on the other hand, are more self-sufficient than pastoralists. Their principal farming tools are the knife for slashing and the hoe or stick for digging. What a person makes is considered his or her own, yet everyone is often obligated to lend tools to others. In Chuuk society, the owner of a canoe has first use of it; the same is true for farming implements. Yet, if a close relative needs the canoe and finds it unused, the canoe may be taken without permission. A distant relative or neighbor must ask permission to borrow any tools, but the owner may not refuse. If owners were to refuse, they would risk being scorned and refused if they were to need tools later.

Societies with intensive agriculture and industrialized societies are likely to have tools made by specialists, which means that tools must be acquired by trade or purchase. Probably because complex tools cost a considerable amount of money, they are less likely than simple tools to be shared except by those who contributed to the purchase price. For example, a diesel-powered combine requires a large amount of capital for its purchase and upkeep. The person who has supplied the capital is likely to regard the machine as individual private property and to regulate its use and disposal. The owner must then use the machine to produce enough surplus to pay for its cost and upkeep as well as for its replacement. The owner may rent the machine to neighboring farmers during slack periods to obtain a maximum return on the investment.

Expensive equipment, however, is not always individually owned in societies with intensive agriculture or industrialized economies. Even in capitalist countries, there may be collective ownership of machines by cooperatives or co-ownership with neighbors.[23] Governments often own very expensive equipment or facilities such as airports, highways, and dams. Such resources are owned collectively by the whole society. Rights of use depend on the facility. Anyone can use a highway, but only contributing municipalities can draw upon the water in a dam. Other productive resources in industrial societies, such as factories or service companies, may be owned jointly by shareholders, who purchase a portion of a corporation's assets in return for a proportionate share of its earnings. The proportion of technology and facilities owned by various levels of government also reflects the type of political-economic system—socialist and communist countries have more public ownership than do capitalist countries.

THE CONVERSION OF RESOURCES

In all societies, resources have to be transformed or converted through labor into food, tools, and other goods. These activities constitute what economists call *production*. In this section, after briefly reviewing different types of production, we examine what motivates people to work, how societies divide up the work to be done, and how they organize work. As we shall see, some aspects of the conversion of natural resources are culturally universal, but there is also an enormous amount of cultural variation.

Types of Economic Production

At the times they were first described, most of the societies known to anthropology had a *domestic*—family or kinship—mode of production. People labored to get food and to produce shelter and implements for themselves and their kin. Usually families had the right to exploit productive resources and control the products of their labor. Even part-time specialists, such as potters, could still support themselves without that craft if they needed to. At the other extreme are *industrial* societies, where much of the work is based on mechanized production, as in factories but also in mechanized agriculture. Because machines and materials are costly, only some individuals (capitalists), corporations, or governments can afford the expenses of production. Therefore, most people in industrial societies labor for others as wage earners. Although wages can buy food, people out of work lose their ability to support themselves, unless they are protected by welfare payments or unemployment insurance. Then there is the *tributary* type of production system, found in nonindustrial societies in which most people still produce their own food but an elite or aristocracy controls a portion of production (including the products of specialized crafts). The feudal societies of medieval western Europe were examples of tributary production, as was czarist Russia under serfdom.[24]

Many people have suggested that our own and other developed economies are now moving from *industrialism* to *postindustrialism*. In many areas of commerce, computers have radically transformed the workplace. Computers "drive" machines and robots, and much of the manual work required in industry is disappearing. Businesses are

In postindustrial economies, computers and robots rather than people do much of the work in factories. There are few people in this Bavarian brewery.

now more knowledge- and service-oriented. Information is more accessible with telecommunication, so much so that *telecommuting* has entered our vocabulary to describe how people can now work (for wages) at home. This economic transformation has important implications for both home life and the workplace. With inexpensive home computers and speedy data transmission by telephone and other means, more people are able to work at home. In addition, when information and knowledge become more important than capital equipment, more people can own and have access to the productive resources of society.[25] If "who owns what" partly determines who has political and other influence, the wider ownership of resources that is possible in postindustrial society may eventually translate into new, more democratic political forms and processes.

Incentives for Labor

Why do people work? Probably all of us have asked ourselves this question. Our concern may not be why other people are working, but why we have to work. Clearly, part of the answer is that work is necessary for survival. Although there are always some able-bodied adults who do not work as much as they should and rely on the labor of others, no society would survive if most able-bodied adults were like that. In fact, most societies probably succeed in motivating most people to want to do (and even enjoy) what they have to do. But are the incentives for labor the same in all societies? Anthropologists think the answer is both yes and no. One reason people may work is because they must. But why do people in some societies apparently work *more* than they must?

We can be fairly certain that a particular and often-cited motive—the profit motive, or the desire to exchange something for more than it costs—is not universal or always the dominant motive. There can be no profit motive among people who produce food and other goods primarily for their own consumption, as do most foragers, most horticulturalists, and even some intensive agriculturalists. Such societies have what we call a *subsistence economy,* not a money or commercial economy. Anthropologists have noticed that people in subsistence economies (with a domestic mode of production) often work less than people in

commercial economies (with tributary or industrial modes of production). Indeed, foragers appear to have a considerable amount of leisure time, as do many horticulturalists. It has been estimated, for example, that the men of the horticultural Kuikuru tribe in central Brazil spent about three and a half hours a day on subsistence. It appears that the Kuikuru could have produced a substantial surplus of manioc, their staple food, by working 30 minutes more a day.[26] Yet, they and many other peoples do not produce more than they need. Why should they? They cannot store a surplus for long because it would rot; they cannot sell it because there is no market nearby; and they do not have a political authority that might collect it for some purpose. Although we often think "more is better," a food-getting strategy with such a goal might even be disastrous, especially for foragers. The killing of more animals than a group could eat might seriously jeopardize the food supply in the future, because overhunting could reduce reproduction among the hunted animals.[27] Horticulturalists might do well to plant a little extra, just in case part of the crop failed, but a great deal extra would be a tremendous waste of time and effort.

It has been suggested that, when resources are converted primarily for household consumption, people will work harder if they have more consumers in the household. That is, when there are few able-bodied workers and a proportionately large number of consumers (perhaps because there are many young children and elderly people), the workers have to work harder. But when there are proportionately more workers, they can work less. This idea is called *Chayanov's rule.*[28] Alexander Chayanov found this relationship in data on rural Russians before the Russian Revolution.[29] But it appears to work in other places too. Paul Durrenberger and Nicola Tannenbaum collected data in Thailand in several villages and found general support for Chayanov's rule.[30] And Michael Chibnik found support for Chayanov's rule when he compared data from 12 communities in five areas of the world. The communities ranged in complexity from New Guinea horticulturalists to commercial Swiss farmers. Although Chayanov restricted his theory to farmers who mostly produced food for their own consumption and did not hire labor, Chibnik's analysis suggests that Chayanov's rule applies even for hired labor.[31] However, Durrenberger and Tannenbaum found that political and social factors explained some of the variability in household production. For example, in the villages that lacked social classes, families with a high ratio of workers to consumers produced less, apparently to avoid doing much better than other families. In contrast, in the villages that had social classes, households with a high ratio of workers to consumers produced more, and gained prestige from their efforts.[32]

There appear to be many societies in which some people work harder than they need to just for their own families' subsistence. What motivates them to work harder? Sharing and other transfers of food and goods often go well beyond the household, sometimes including the whole community or even groups of communities, as we will see later in this chapter. In such societies, social rewards come to those who are generous, who give things away. Thus, people who work harder than they have to for subsistence may be motivated to do so because they thereby gain respect or esteem.[33] In many societies too, as we shall see in subsequent chapters, extra food and goods may be needed at times for special purposes and occasions; goods and services may be needed to arrange and celebrate marriages, to form alliances, and to perform rituals and ceremonies (including what we would call sporting events). Thus, how the culture defines what one works for and what is needed may go beyond what is necessary.

In commercial economies such as our own—where foods, other goods, and services are sold and bought—people seem to be motivated to keep any extra income for themselves and their families. Extra income is converted into bigger dwellings, more expensive furnishings and food, and other elements of a "higher" standard of living. But the desire to improve one's standard of living is probably not the only motive operating. Some people may work partly to satisfy a need for achievement,[34] or because they find their work enjoyable. In addition, just as in precommercial societies, some people may work partly to gain respect or influence by giving some of their income away. Not only do we respect philanthropists and movie stars for giving to charities; our society encourages such giving by making it an allowable tax deduction. Still, the emphasis on giving in commercial societies is clearly less developed than in subsistence economies. We consider charity by the religious or rich appropriate and even admirable, but we would think it foolish or crazy for people to give so much away that they become poverty-stricken.

Forced and Required Labor

Thus far, we have mostly discussed *voluntary labor*—voluntary in the sense that no formal organization within the society compels people to work and punishes them for not working. Social training and social pressure are powerful enough to persuade an individual to perform some useful task. In both food-collecting and horticultural societies, individuals who can stand being the butt of jokes about laziness will still be fed. At most, the other members of the group will ignore them. There is no reason to punish them and no way to coerce them to do the work expected of them.

More complex societies have ways of forcing people to work for the authorities, whether those authorities are kings or presidents. An indirect form of forced labor is taxation. The average tax in the United States (local, state, and federal) is about 33 percent of income, which means that the average person works four months out of the year for the various levels of government. If a person decides not to pay the tax, the money will be taken forcibly or the person may be put in prison.

Money is the customary form of tax payment in a commercial society. In a politically complex but nonmonetary society, people may pay their taxes in other ways—by performing a certain number of hours of labor or by giving up a certain percentage of what they produce. The **corvée**, a system of required labor, existed in the Inca Empire in the central Andes before the Spanish conquest. Each male commoner was assigned three plots of land to work: a temple plot, a state plot, and his own plot. The enormous stores of food that went into state warehouses were used to

The Great Wall of China, like many monumental works in ancient societies, was built with forced labor.

supply the nobles, the army, the artisans, and all other state employees. If labor became overabundant, the people were still kept occupied; it is said that one ruler had a hill moved to keep some laborers busy. In addition to subsistence work for the state, Inca commoners were subject to military service, to duty as personal servants for the nobility, and to other "public" service.[35] Elderly villagers in the Chiang Mai area of Thailand describe corvée this way: "Villagers had to work one *rai* [*rai myong* or 0.1 acre] per person for them for nothing. And one had to do it properly. The lord's underlings would take a banana tree trunk and stick it upright in the field after it was plowed. If it fell over, that meant it was well plowed. Otherwise, one would have to keep on plowing until the ground was soft."[36]

Conscription or the draft, or compulsory military service, is also a form of corvée, in that a certain period of service is required, and failure to serve can be punished by a prison term or involuntary exile. Emperors of China had soldiers drafted to defend their territory and to build the Great Wall along the northern borders of the empire. The wall extends over 1,500 miles, and thousands were drafted to work on it. Slavery is the most extreme form of forced work, in that slaves have little control over their labor. Because slaves constitute a category or class of people in many societies, we discuss slavery more fully in the chapter on social stratification.

Division of Labor

All societies have some division of labor, some customary assignment of different kinds of work to different kinds of people. Universally, males and females and adults and children do not do the same kinds of work. In a sense, then, division of labor by gender and age is a kind of universal specialization of labor. Many societies known to anthropology divide labor only by gender and age; other societies have more complex specialization.

By Gender and Age All societies make use of gender differences to some extent in their customary assignment

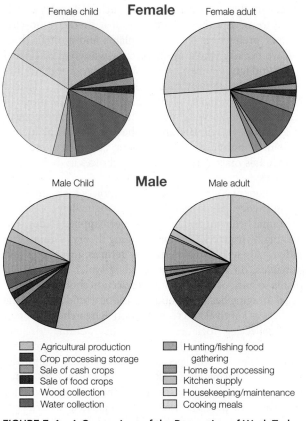

Female

Female child   Female adult

Male

Male Child   Male adult

- ▢ Agricultural production
- ▢ Crop processing storage
- ▢ Sale of cash crops
- ▢ Sale of food crops
- ▢ Wood collection
- ▢ Water collection
- ▢ Hunting/fishing food gathering
- ▢ Home food processing
- ▢ Kitchen supply
- ▢ Housekeeping/maintenance
- ▢ Cooking meals

FIGURE 7–1   A Comparison of the Proportion of Work Tasks Done by Adults and Children

Source: From J. Levine et al. 2002.

of labor. In the chapter on sex, gender, and culture, we discuss the division of labor by gender in detail.

Age is also a universal basis for division of labor. Clearly, children cannot do work that requires a great deal of strength. But, in many societies, girls and boys contribute much more in labor than do children in our own society. For example, they help in animal tending, weeding, and harvesting and do a variety of domestic chores such as child care, fetching water and firewood, and cooking and cleaning. In agricultural communities in the Ivory Coast, children's tasks mirror the tasks of same-sex adults (see Figure 7–1). In some societies, a child that is 6 years old is considered old enough to be responsible for a younger sibling for a good part of the day.[37] Animal tending is often important work for children. Children in some societies spend more time at this task than adults.[38]

Why do children do so much work in some societies? If adults, particularly mothers, have heavy workloads, and children are physically and mentally able to do the work, a good part of the work is likely to be assigned to children.[39] As we have seen, food producers probably have more work than foragers, so we would expect that children would be likely to work more where there is herding and farming. Consistent

with this expectation, Patricia Draper and Elizabeth Cashdan found differences in children's work between nomadic and settled !Kung. Even though recently settled !Kung have not switched completely from foraging to food production, children's as well as adults' activities have changed considerably. The children living in nomadic camps had virtually no work at all; adults did all the gathering and hunting. But the settled children were given lots of chores, ranging from helping with animals to helping with the harvest and food processing.[40]

What we have said about the !Kung should not imply that children in foraging societies always do little work. For example, among the Hadza of Tanzania, children between the ages of 5 and 10 are able to get one-third to one-half of their calories as they forage with their mothers. The Hadza also have more children than the !Kung.[41] Is there a relationship between children's work and fertility? When children in a society do a great deal of work, parents may value them more and may consciously want to have more children.[42] This may be one of the reasons why birth rates are especially high in intensive agricultural societies where workloads are very high.[43]

Beyond Gender and Age   In societies with relatively simple technologies, there is little specialization of labor beyond that of gender and age. But as a society's technology becomes more complex and it is able to produce large quantities of food, more of its people are freed from subsistence work to become specialists in some other tasks.

In contrast with foragers, horticultural societies may have some part-time specialists. Some people may devote special effort to perfecting a particular skill or craft—pottery making, weaving, house building, doctoring—and in return for their products or services be given food or other gifts. Among some horticultural groups, the entire village may specialize part-time in making a particular product, which can then be traded to neighboring people.

With the development of intensive agriculture, full-time specialists—potters, weavers, blacksmiths—begin to appear. The trend toward greater specialization reaches its

These Haitian women specialize in making and selling baskets for sale.

peak in industrialized societies, where workers develop skills in one small area of the economic system. Full-time specialization makes people dependent on the necessity to sell their labor or products to make a living. In societies with full-time occupational specialization, different jobs are usually associated with differences in prestige, wealth, and power, as we shall see in the chapter on social stratification.

The Organization of Labor

The degree to which labor has to be organized reaches its peak in industrial societies, which have great occupational specialization and complex political organization. The coordination required to produce an automobile on an assembly line is obvious; so is the coordination required to collect taxes from every wage earner.

In many food-collecting and horticultural societies, there is little formal organization of work. Work groups tend to be organized only when productive work requires it and to dissolve when they are no longer needed. Furthermore, the groups so organized often have changing composition and leadership; participation tends to be individualistic and voluntary.[44] Perhaps this flexibility is possible because, when virtually everyone has the same work to do, little instruction is needed, and almost anyone can assume leadership. Still, some types of work require more organization than others. Hunting big game usually requires coordinated efforts by a large number of hunters; so might catching fish in large nets. For example, on Moala, a Fijian island in the Pacific, net fishing is a group affair. A party of 20 to 30 women wades out on the reef and makes a semicircle of nets. At a signal from an experienced woman, usually the chief's wife, the women move together at the ends, forming a circle. After the fish are caught in the nets, the women bite them on the backs of their heads to kill them and put them in baskets that they carry ashore. Around Christmas, the village, or several villages, undertakes a larger fish drive. The day before, more than 100 people make a "sweep," some 1,600 yards long, from coconut fronds. The next day, the men, women, and children all participate in the surround, catching thousands of fish.[45]

Kinship ties are an important basis for work organization, particularly in nonindustrial societies. For example, among the horticultural Kapauku of western New Guinea, the male members of a village are a kin group, and all work together to build drainage ditches, large fences, and bridges.[46] With increasing technological complexity, the basis of work organization begins to shift to more formally organized groups.[47] In modern industrial societies, the predominant basis of organization is the *contract*—the agreement between employers and employees whereby the latter perform a specified amount of work for a specified amount of wages. Although the arrangement may be entered into voluntarily, laws and the power of the state enforce the obligation of the parties to abide by the contract.

Making Decisions About Work

Foragers ignore many of the plant and animal species in their environment, choosing to go after only some. Why? The people may say that some animals are taboo whereas others are delicious. But where do such customary beliefs come from? Are they adaptive? And if there are no customary preferences for certain plants and animals, how can we explain why a food collector will go after certain foods and ignore others on a particular day? Food producers also make choices constantly. For example, a farmer has to decide when to plant, what to plant, how much to plant, when to harvest, how much to store, and how much to give away or sell. Researchers have tried to explain why certain economic decisions become customary and why individuals make certain economic choices in their everyday lives.

A frequent source of ideas about choices is **optimal foraging theory,** which was developed originally by students of animal behavior and which has been applied to decision making by foragers. Optimal foraging theory assumes that individuals seek to maximize the returns, in calories and nutrients, on their labor in deciding which animals and plants to hunt or collect. Natural selection should favor optimal foraging because "good" decisions would increase the chances of survival and reproduction. Research in different food-collecting societies supports the optimal foraging model.[48] For example, the Aché of eastern Paraguay consistently prefer to hunt peccaries (wild piglike mammals) rather than armadillos. Although peccaries take much longer to find and are harder to kill than armadillos, a day spent hunting peccaries yields more than 4,600 calories per hour of work, whereas hunting armadillos yields only about 1,800 calories an hour.[49] Other factors in addition to calorie yield, such as predictability of resources, may also influence which foods are collected. For example, the !Kung of the Kalahari Desert depend largely on mongongo nuts, even though these nuts yield fewer calories per hour of work than does meat. But mongongo nuts in season are more dependable than game is. Once a group of !Kung hikes to a grove of ripe mongongo nuts, they know they can obtain food there until the supply is exhausted; they are not as certain of getting game when they seek it.[50] Similarly on Ifaluk, an atoll in the Federated States of Micronesia where fishing is the main source of animal protein, men most often choose to fish in the place where there is the highest return on average. But they do not always fish there; if the return on a previous day was lower than average, they tend to choose other spots.[51]

How does a farmer decide whether to plant a particular crop and how much land and labor to devote to it? Christina Gladwin and others suggested that farmers make decisions in steps, with each choice point involving a yes or no answer. For example, in the high-altitude region of Guatemala, farmers could choose to plant about eight crops, or combinations of them, such as corn and beans, which grow together well. A farmer will quickly exclude some choices because of the answers to certain questions: Can I afford the seed and fertilizer? Can this crop be watered adequately? Is the altitude appropriate? And so on. If any of the answers is no, the crop is not planted. By a further series of yes-or-no decisions, farmers presumably decide which of the remaining possibilities will be planted.[52]

Individuals may not always be able to state clearly their rules for making decisions, nor do they always have complete knowledge about the various possibilities, particularly when some of the possibilities are new. That does not mean, however, that researchers cannot predict or explain economic choices. For example, Michael Chibnik found that men in two villages in Belize and in Central America were not able to say why they devoted more or less time to working for wages versus growing crops. But their behavior was still predictable. Older men grew crops because wage labor was more physically demanding; and in the village with a higher cost of living, men were more likely to work for wages.[53]

THE DISTRIBUTION OF GOODS AND SERVICES

Goods and services are distributed in all societies by systems that, however varied, can be classified under three general types: reciprocity, redistribution, and market or commercial exchange.[54] The three systems often coexist in a society, but one system usually predominates. The predominant system seems to be associated with the society's food-getting technology and, more specifically, its level of economic development.

Reciprocity

Reciprocity consists of giving and taking without the use of money; it mainly takes the form of gift giving or generalized reciprocity. There may also be exchanges of equal value (barter or nonmonetary trade) or balanced reciprocity, without the use of money.[55]

Generalized Reciprocity When goods or services are given to another, without any apparent expectation of a return gift, we call it **generalized reciprocity.** Generalized reciprocity sustains the family in all societies. Parents give food, clothing, and labor to children because they want to or perhaps feel obliged to, but they do not usually calculate exactly how their children will reciprocate years later. These gifts are one-way transfers. In this sense, all societies have some kind of generalized reciprocity. But some societies depend on it almost entirely to distribute goods and services.

Lorna Marshall recounted how the !Kung divided an eland brought to a site where five bands and several visitors were camping—more than 100 people in all. The owner of the arrow that had first penetrated the eland was, by custom, the owner of the meat. He first distributed the forequarters to the two hunters who had aided him in the kill. After that, the distribution depended on kinship: Each hunter shared with his wives' parents, wives, children, parents, and siblings, and they in turn shared with their kin. Sixty-three gifts of raw meat were recorded, after which further sharing of raw and cooked meat was begun. The !Kung distribution of large game—clearly, generalized reciprocity—is common among foragers. But giving away is not limited to game. For example, when Marshall left the band that had sponsored her in 1951, she gave each woman in the band a present of enough cowrie shells to make a necklace—one large shell and 20 small ones. When

The Inuit of Baffin Island, Canada are collecting their shares of whale meat. Hunting societies commonly share meat from larger animals.

she returned in 1952, she found no cowrie shell necklaces and hardly a single shell among the people in the band. Instead, the shells appeared by ones and twos in the ornaments of the people of neighboring bands.[56]

Although generalized reciprocity may seem altruistic or unselfish, researchers have suggested that giving may in fact benefit the givers in various ways. For example, parents who help their children may not only perpetuate their genes (the ultimate biological benefit) but may also be likely to receive care and affection from their grown-up children when the parents are old. And giving parents may be happier and enjoy life more than nongiving parents. So, in the shorter as well as the longer run, givers may derive economic and psychological benefits, in addition to reproductive benefits.

Parent-child giving may seem easy to understand, but why do some societies rely more on generalized reciprocity than others, particularly beyond the family? Sharing may be most likely if resources are unpredictable. So a !Kung band may share its water with other bands because they may have water now but not in the future. A related group in the Kalahari, the G//ana,[57] has been observed to share less than other groups. It turns out that the resources available to the G//ana are more predictable, because the G//ana supplement their hunting and gathering with plant cultivation and goat herding. Cultivated melons (which store water) appear to buffer the G//ana against water shortages, and goats buffer them against shortages of game. Thus, whereas the !Kung distribute the meat right after a kill, the G//ana dry it and then store it in their houses.[58]

The idea that unpredictability favors sharing may also explain why some foods are more often shared than others. Wild game, for example, is usually unpredictable; when hunters go out to hunt, they cannot be sure that they will come back with meat. Wild plants, on the other hand, are more predictable; gatherers can be sure when they go out that they will come back with at least some plant foods. In any case, it does appear that foragers tend to share game much more than wild plant foods.[59] Even among people who depend largely on horticulture, such as the Yanomamö of Venezuela and Brazil, food items that are less predictably obtained (hunted game and fish) are shared more often than the more predictably obtained garden produce.[60] But, although meat is shared more than plant food, horticulturalists often share foraged or cultivated plants. Why? Sharing plant food may be advantageous to horticulturalists who are some distance from their gardens because they may not have to go as often. And sharing may solidify a social relationship so that other families will help in times of need, such as sickness or accident, when it may be hard to work.[61] Does food sharing increase the food supply for an individual? Calculations for the Aché of eastern Paraguay, who get most of their food from hunting when they go on food-collecting trips, suggest that the average individual gets more food when food is shared. Even the males who actually do the hunting get more, although the benefits are greater for the females and children on the trip.[62] Mathematically, the risk that an individual food collector will not find enough food on a particular day will be appreciably reduced if at least six to eight adult collectors share the food they collect. Food-collecting bands may often contain only 25 to 30 people, which is about the size that is needed to ensure that there are six to eight adult collectors.[63]

Although giving things to others may be expected in some societies, this does not necessarily mean that everyone does so willingly or without some social pressure. For example, the !Kung call "far-hearted" anyone who does not give gifts, and they express their disapproval openly.

Day-to-day unpredictability is one thing; more prolonged scarcity is another. What happens to a system of generalized reciprocity when resources are scarce because of a drought or other disaster? Does the ethic of giving break down? Evidence from a few societies suggests that the degree of sharing may actually *increase* during the period of food shortage.[64] For example, in describing the Netsilik Inuit, Asen Balikci said, "Whenever game was abundant, sharing among non-relatives was avoided, since every family was supposedly capable of obtaining the necessary catch. In situations of scarcity, however, caribou meat was more evenly distributed throughout camp."[65] Sharing may increase during mild scarcity because people can minimize their deprivation, but generalized reciprocity may be strained by extreme scarcity such as famine.[66]

Researchers generally have difficulty explaining sharing because they assume that, other things being equal, individuals would tend to be selfish. But experimental evidence suggests that sharing is likely even with people who do not know each other or who have no expectation of any return in the future from that person. Experimenters set up "games" in which they can control for or eliminate certain responses. For example, in one game, a particular player is given a certain amount of money and the player decides how much of the money to offer to the second player in the game. The second player can accept or reject the offer. If the division is rejected, no one gets any money. If the division is accepted, both players receive the proposed division. If selfishness were normal, one would expect that the proposer of the division would try to give away as little as possible and the second player should always accept whatever is offered because otherwise nothing is gained.

Surprisingly, equal divisions are commonly proposed and low offers are commonly rejected because they are viewed as unfair. If a person views the offer as unfair and forfeits any money, that player seems willing to "punish" the greedy individual. Although such experiments were mostly done at first in Western societies, we now have results from over 15 other societies that largely confirm the earlier results.[67] And there is now evidence suggesting that cooperation may even evoke pleasure. Researchers studying brain activity in women, who are playing a game allowing either cooperative or greedy strategies, found to their surprise that cooperation made certain areas of the brain light up. These areas are normally associated with pleasure, such as when eating desserts. So cooperation may be more "natural" than some people think.[68]

Balanced Reciprocity   **Balanced reciprocity** is explicit and short term in its expectations of return. In contrast to generalized reciprocity or a one-way transfer, which has no expectation of a return, balanced reciprocity involves either an immediate exchange of goods or services or an agreed-upon exchange over a limited period of time. *Barter* is the term used most often for this type of nonmonetary exchange of goods and services. The !Kung, for instance, trade with the Tswana Bantu: a gemsbok hide for a pile of tobacco, five strings of beads made from ostrich eggshells for a spear, or three small skins for a good-sized knife.[69] In the 1600s, the Iroquois of the North American Northeast traded deerskin to Europeans for brass kettles, iron hinges, steel axes, woven textiles, and guns.[70] The !Kung and Iroquois acquired trade goods by balanced reciprocity, but such exchanges were not crucial to their economies.

In contrast, some societies depend much more heavily on balanced reciprocity. For example, the Efe, who hunt and gather in the Ituri forest of central Africa, get most of their calories from manioc, peanuts, rice, and plantains grown by another group—the agricultural Lese. Efe men and women provide labor to the Lese, and in exchange, receive a portion of the harvest as well as goods such as metal pots and spears.[71] Pastoralists, too, are rarely self-sufficient, as we mentioned in the preceding chapter. They have to trade their pastoral products to agriculturalists to get the grain and other things they need.

Balanced reciprocity may mostly involve labor. Cooperative work parties usually exchange or balance gifts of labor. A cooperative work party, or *kuu,* among the Kpelle of Liberia may number from 6 to 40 people, all of whom are generally relatives or friends. In addition to promising return work on a particular date, each farmer rewards the work party's hard day's labor by providing a feast and sometimes rhythmic music to work by.[72] When we say that an exchange is balanced, we do not mean to imply that the things exchanged are exactly equivalent in value or that the exchange is purely economic. In the absence of a money economy, where there is no explicit standard by which value can be judged, there is no way to assess value objectively. The point is that the parties in balanced reciprocity are freely giving each other the respective goods and services they each want; they are not coerced into doing so, so presumably they are not conceiving of the exchange as unbalanced.[73] And when something is valued, it may be valued for other than economic reasons. The exchange itself may also be fun, adventuresome, or aesthetically pleasing, or it may enhance social relationships.

Because exchanges can have different motivations, they can have different meanings. Consequently, some economic anthropologists now want to distinguish between gift and commodity exchanges. *Gift exchanges* are personal and involve the creation or perpetuation of some kind of enduring relationship between people and groups. In our society, the exchange of dinner invitations or Christmas gifts is motivated by social considerations; we are not interested only in the actual food or objects received. In contrast, *commodity exchanges,* which can occur even in the absence of money, focus on the objects or services received—the transaction itself is the motive. When the transaction is completed, the relationship between the parties involved usually ends.[74]

*The **Kula** Ring*   The horticultural Trobriand Islanders, who live off the eastern coast of New Guinea, worked out an elaborate scheme for trading ornaments, food, and other necessities with the people of neighboring islands. The exchange of goods between far-flung islands is essential, for some of the islands are small and rocky and cannot produce enough food to sustain their inhabitants, who specialize instead in canoe building, pottery making, and other crafts. Other islanders produce far more yams, taro, and pigs than they need. However, the practical side of the trade is hidden beneath a complex ceremonial exchange, called the *kula* ring, an exchange of valued shell ornaments across a set of far-flung islands.[75]

Two kinds of ornaments are involved in the ceremonial exchanges—white shell armbands (*mwali*), which are given only in a counterclockwise direction, and red shell necklaces (*soulava*), which are given only in a clockwise direction. The possession of one or more of these ornaments allows a man to organize an expedition to the home of one of his trading partners on another island. The high point of an expedition is the ceremonial giving of the valued *kula* ornaments. During the two- to three-day visit, the trading of necessities goes on. Some of the exchange takes the form of gift giving between trading partners. By the time the visitors leave, they have accomplished a year's trading, without seeming to do so.

But the practical advantages of the *kula* ring are not the only gains. There may be purely social ones, for goods are traded with ease and enjoyment. A trading expedition takes on the flavor of adventure rather than of business. Many of the traditions of the islands are kept alive: Myth, romance, ritual, and history are linked to the circulating ornaments, especially the larger, finer pieces, which are well known and recognized as heirlooms. A man is able to possess many valued things within his lifetime, each for a year or so. Each object, when it is received, arouses enthusiasm in a way that one lifelong possession could not.[76] The *kula* ring continued to be an important institution after Papua New Guinea became an independent country. For example, active participation in the *kula* ring helped candidates in the 1960s and the 1970s to be elected to the national parliament.[77]

The *kula* is not the only form of exchange in Trobriand life. For example, on the two days following a burial, the kin of the deceased give yams, taro, and valuables to those who helped care for the deceased before death, to those who participated in the burial ceremonies, and to those who came to mourn the deceased. After these initial exchanges, the hamlet settles into mourning. Women from other hamlets bring food to the people in mourning, and the mourning women prepare bundles of banana leaves and weave skirts of banana fiber for later distribution. Husbands help their wives accumulate valuables to "buy" extra bundles of banana leaves. Then the women's mortuary ceremony is held. It is very competitive—each of the mourning women tries to distribute the most bundles and skirts. As many as 5,000 bundles and 30 skirts might be distributed by one mourning woman in a single day. Each of these giveaways completes a balanced reciprocity: The giver is reciprocating for gifts of goods and services received in the past. A woman's brothers gave her yams and taro during the year. She gives her brothers' wives bundles or skirts, which are also given to those who helped make the special mourning skirts and to those who brought or cooked food during the mourning period.[78]

Sometimes the line between generalized and balanced reciprocity is not so clear. Consider our gift giving at Christmas. Although such gift giving may appear to be generalized reciprocity, and it often is in the case of gift giving from parents to children, there may be strong expectations of balance. Two friends or relatives may try to exchange presents of fairly equal value, based on calculations of what last year's gift cost. If a

Men perform the *kula* dance at an interisland exchange celebration in the Trobriand Islands, Papua New Guinea.

person receives a $5 present when he or she gave a $25 present, that person may be hurt and perhaps angry. On the other hand, a person who receives a $500 present when he or she gave a $25 present may well also be dismayed. But Christmas giving, like the Trobriand *kula* ring, also illustrates that exchanges are not simply economic, but serve many other purposes, including fun.

Kinship Distance and Type of Reciprocity

Most food-collecting and horticultural societies depend on some form of reciprocity for the distribution of goods and labor. Marshall Sahlins suggested that the form of the reciprocity depends largely on the kinship distance between people. Generalized reciprocity may be the rule for family members and close kinsmen. Balanced reciprocity may be practiced among equals who are not closely related. People who would consider it inappropriate to trade with their own families will trade with neighboring groups.[79] In general, the importance of reciprocity declines with economic development.[80] In societies with intensive agriculture, and even more so in industrialized societies, reciprocity distributes only a small proportion of goods and services.

Reciprocity as a Leveling Device

Reciprocal gift giving may do more than equalize the distribution of goods within a community, as in the !Kung's sharing. It may also tend to equalize the distribution of goods between communities.

Many Melanesian societies in and near New Guinea have the custom of holding pig feasts in which 50, 100, or even 2,000 pigs are slaughtered. Andrew Vayda, Anthony Leeds, and David Smith suggested that these enormous feasts, though apparently wasteful, are just one of the outcomes of a complex of cultural practices that are highly advantageous. The people of these societies cannot accurately predict how much food they will produce during the year. Some years they will have bumper crops and other years, very poor crops because of fluctuations in the weather. So it might be wise to overplant just in case the yield is poor. Yet overplanting results in overproduction during average and exceptionally good years. What can be done with this extra food? Root crops such as yams and taro do not keep well over long periods, so any surplus is fed to pigs, which become, in effect, food-storing repositories. Pigs are then available for needed food during lean times. But if there are several years of surpluses, pigs can become too much of a good thing. Pigs wanting food can destroy yam and taro patches. When the pig population grows to menacing proportions, a village may invite other villages to a gigantic feast that results in a sharp reduction of the pig population and keeps the fields from being overrun. Over the years, the pig feasts serve to equalize the food consumption, and especially the protein consumption, of all the villages that participate in the feasts.[81] Thus, the custom of pig feasts may be a way for villages to "bank" surplus food by storing up "social credit" with other villages, which will return that credit in subsequent feasts.

In some Melanesian societies, the pig feasts foster an element of competition among the men who give them. "Big men" may try to bolster their status and prestige by the size of their feasts. A reputation is enhanced not by keeping wealth but by giving it away. A similar situation existed among many Native American groups of the Pacific Northwest, where a chief might attempt to enhance his status by holding a **potlatch.** At a potlatch, a chief and his group would give away blankets, pieces of copper, canoes, large quantities of food, and other items to their guests. The host chief and his group would later be invited to other potlatches.

The competitive element in the potlatch appears to have intensified after contact with Europeans. Because of the fur trade, the number of trade goods increased, and so more items could be given away. Possibly more important was the population decline among the Indians, caused by diseases such as smallpox that European traders introduced. Distant relatives of chiefs who had no direct heirs might compete for the right to the title, each attempting to give away more than the others.[82] Chiefs may also have attempted to attract men to their half-empty villages by spectacular giveaways.[83] Decimated groups might have coalesced to maintain the potlatching. For example, when the Tlingit population declined to a low in the 1910s, kin groups coalesced to assemble enough resources for a potlatch.[84] Although the potlatch system seems wasteful in that goods were often destroyed in the competition, the system probably also served to equalize the distribution of goods among competing groups.

On one level of analysis, the Melanesian pig feasts, and the Pacific Northwest potlatches were all reciprocal exchanges between communities or villages. But these exchanges were not just intercommunity versions of reciprocal gift giving between individuals. Because these feasts were organized by people who collected goods, they also involved another mode of distribution, which anthropologists call *redistribution*.

Redistribution

Redistribution is the accumulation of goods or labor by a particular person, or in a particular place, for the purpose of subsequent distribution. Although redistribution is found in all societies, it becomes an important mechanism only in societies that have political hierarchies—that is, chiefs or other specialized officials and agencies. In all societies, there is some redistribution, at least within the family. Members of the family pool their labor, products, or income for the common good. But in many societies, there is little or no redistribution beyond the family. It seems that redistribution on a territorial basis emerges when there is a political apparatus to coordinate centralized collection and distribution of goods or to mobilize labor for some public purpose.

In the African state of Bunyoro, in western Uganda, for example, the king (called the *mukama*) retained much of the wealth for himself and his close kin. The *mukama* had the authority to grant the use of land and all other natural resources to his subordinate chiefs, and they in turn granted it to the common people. In return, everyone was required to give the *mukama* large quantities of food, crafts, and even labor services. The *mukama* then redistributed these goods and services, in theory at least, to all the people. The *mukama* was praised with names that emphasized his generosity: *Agutamba* ("he who relieves distress") and *Mwebingwa* ("he to whom the people run for help"). But it is clear that much of what the king redistributed did not find its way back to the common people, who produced the bulk of the goods. Instead, the wealth was distributed largely according to rank within the state.[85]

Other redistribution systems are more equal. For example, among the Buin of Melanesia, "the chief is housed, dressed, and fed exactly like his bondsman."[86] Even though the chief owns most of the pigs, everyone shares equally in the consumption of the wealth. In general, where redistribution is important, as in societies with higher levels of productivity, the wealthy are more likely than the poor to benefit from the redistributions.[87]

Why do redistribution systems develop? Elman Service suggested that they develop in agricultural societies that contain subregions suited to different kinds of crops or natural resources. Foragers can take advantage of environmental variation by moving to different areas. With agriculture, the task is more difficult; it might be easier to move different products across different regions.[88] If the demand for different resources or products becomes too great, reciprocity between individuals might become awkward. So it might be more efficient to have someone—a chief, perhaps—coordinate the exchanges.

Marvin Harris agreed that redistribution becomes more likely with agriculture, but for a somewhat different reason. He argued that competitive feasting, as in New Guinea, is adaptive because it encourages people to work harder to produce somewhat more than they need. Why would this feature be adaptive? Harris argued that, with agriculture, people really have to produce more than they need so that they can protect themselves against crises such as crop failure. The groups that make feasts may be indirectly ensuring themselves against crises by storing up social credit with other villages, who will reciprocate by making feasts for them in the future. On the other hand, inducements to collect more than they need may not be advantageous to food-collecting groups, who might lose in the long run by overcollecting.[89]

Market or Commercial Exchange

When we think of markets, we usually think of bustling, colorful places where goods are bought and sold. The exchanges usually involve money. In our own society, we have supermarkets and the stock market and other places for buying and selling that we call shops, stores, and malls. In referring to **market** or **commercial exchange**, economists and economic anthropologists are referring to exchanges or transactions in which the "prices" are subject to supply and demand, whether or not the transactions actually occur in a marketplace.[90] Market exchange involves not only the exchange (buying and selling) of goods but also transactions of labor, land, rentals, and credit.

On the surface, many market exchanges resemble balanced reciprocity. One person gives something and receives something in return. How, then, does market exchange differ from balanced reciprocity? It is easy to

distinguish market exchange from balanced reciprocity when money is directly involved, because reciprocity is defined as not involving money. But market exchange need not always involve money directly.[91] For example, a landowner grants a tenant farmer the right to use the land in exchange for a portion of the crop. So, to call a transaction market exchange, we have to ask whether supply and demand determine the price. If a tenant farmer gave only a token gift to the landowner, we would not call it market exchange, just as a Christmas gift to a teacher is not payment for teaching. If tenants, however, are charged a large portion of their crops when the supply of land is short, or if landowners lower their demands when few people want to tenant-farm, then we would call the transactions market or commercial exchange. The forces of supply and demand create considerable risk for those dependent on monetary exchange for life's necessities. A wage earner who loses a job may not be able to afford food or shelter; a farmer relying on a cash crop may not get a price sufficient to support the family. Societies with monetary exchange usually have considerable inequities in wealth and power.

Kinds of Money   Although market exchange need not involve money, most commercial transactions, particularly nowadays, do involve what we call money. Some anthropologists define money according to the functions and characteristics of the **general-purpose money** used in our own and other complex societies, for which nearly all goods, resources, and services can be exchanged. According to this definition, money performs the basic functions of serving as an accepted medium of exchange, a standard of value, and a store of wealth. As a medium of exchange, it allows all goods and services to be valued in the same objective way; we say that an object or service is worth so much money. Also, money is nonperishable, and therefore savable or storable, and almost always transportable and divisible, so transactions can involve the buying and selling of goods and services that differ in value.

Although money can technically be anything, the first money systems used rare metals such as gold and silver. These metals are relatively soft and therefore can be melted and shaped into standard sizes and weights. The earliest standardized coins we know of are said to have been made by the Lydians in Asia Minor and the Chinese, in the 7th century A.D. It is important to realize that money has little or no intrinsic value; rather, it is society that determines its value. In the United States today, paper bills, bank checks, and credit and debit cards are fully accepted as money, and money is increasingly transferred electronically.

General-purpose money is used both for commercial transactions (buying and selling) and for noncommercial transactions (payment of taxes or fines, personal gifts, contributions to religious and other charities). General-purpose money provides a way of condensing wealth: Gold dust or nuggets are easier to carry around than bushels of wheat; paper bills, a checkbook, and plastic cards are handier than a herd of sheep or goats.

In many societies, money is not an all-purpose medium of exchange. Many peoples whose food production per capita is not sufficient to support a large population of nonproducers of food have **special-purpose money.** This consists of objects of value for which only some goods and services can be exchanged on the spot or through balanced reciprocity. In some parts of Melanesia, pigs are assigned value in terms of shell money—lengths of shells strung together in units each roughly as long as the distance covered by a man's outstretched arms. According to its size, a pig will be assigned a value in tens of such units up to 100.[92] But shell money cannot be exchanged for all the goods or services a person might need. Similarly, a Pacific Northwest native could exchange food, but not most other goods and services, for a "gift of wealth," such as blankets. The gift was a "receipt" that entitled the person to receive an equal amount of food, but little else, later.

Degrees of Commercialization

Most societies were not commercialized at all, or only barely so, when first described in the ethnographic record by explorers, missionaries, and anthropologists. That is, most societies as first described did not rely on market or commercial exchange to distribute goods and services. But commercial exchange has become the dominant form of distribution in the modern world. Most societies of the ethnographic past are now incorporated into larger nation-states; for example, the Trobriand Islanders and other societies in Melanesia are now districts in the nation of Papua New Guinea. Selling today goes far beyond the nation-state. The world is now a multinational market.[93]

But there is considerable variation in the degree to which societies today depend on market or commercial exchange. Many societies still allocate land without purchase and distribute food and other goods primarily by reciprocity and redistribution, participating only peripherally in market exchange. These are societies in transition; their traditional subsistence economies are becoming commercialized. Among the Luo of western Kenya, for example, most rural families still have land that their kin groups allocated to them. The food they eat they mostly produce themselves. But many men also work for wages—some nearby, others far away in towns and cities, where they spend a year or two. These wages are used to pay government taxes, to pay for children's schooling, and to buy commercially produced items, such as clothes, kerosene lamps, radios, fish from Lake Nyanza, tea, sugar, and coffee. Occasionally, families sell agricultural surpluses or craft items such as reed mats. Economies such as that of the rural Luo are not fully commercialized, but they may become so in the future.

What anthropologists call *peasant economies* are somewhat more commercialized than transitional subsistence economies such as that of the Luo. Although **peasants** also produce food largely for their own consumption, they regularly sell part of their surplus (food, other goods, or labor) to others, and land is one of the commodities they buy, rent, and sell. But, although their production is somewhat commercialized, peasants are still not like the fully commercialized farmers in industrialized societies, who rely on the market to exchange all or almost all of their crops for all or almost all of the goods and services they need.

In fully commercialized societies such as our own, market or commercial exchange dominates the economy; prices and wages are regulated, or at least significantly affected, by the forces of supply and demand. A modern industrial or postindustrial economy may involve international as well as national markets in which everything—natural resources, labor, goods, services, prestige items, religious and ceremonial items—has a price, stated in the same money terms. Reciprocity is reserved for family members and friends or remains behind the scenes in business transactions. Redistribution, however, is an important mechanism. It is practiced in the form of taxation and the use of public revenue for transfer payments and other benefits to low-income families—welfare, Social Security, health care, and so on. But commercial exchange is the major way goods and services are distributed.

Why Do Money and Market Exchange Develop?

Most economists think that money is invented in a society, or copied from another society, when trade increases and barter becomes increasingly inefficient. The more important or frequent trade is, the more difficult it is to find a person who can give something you want and wants something you have to give. Money makes it easy to trade. It is a valuable that may be exchanged for *anything,* and so it is an efficient medium of exchange when trade becomes important. In contrast, many anthropologists do not link the origins of money or market exchange to the necessities of trade. Instead, they link the origins of money to various noncommercial "payments," such as the *kula* valuables and the taxes that have to be paid to a political authority. All of the available explanations of money suggest that money will be found mostly in societies at higher levels of economic development; and indeed it is. When simpler societies have money, dominant and more complex societies have usually introduced it.[94] In the next major section, we discuss more fully the impact of colonialism and global markets on societies that were not so long ago subsistence economies.

Most theories about the development of money and market exchange assume that producers have regular surpluses they want to exchange. But why do people produce surpluses in the first place? Perhaps they are motivated to produce extra only when they want to obtain goods from a distance and the suppliers of such goods are not well known to them, making reciprocity less likely as a way to obtain those goods. So some theorists suggest that market exchange begins with external, or intersocietal, trade; kin would not likely be involved, so transactions would involve bargaining, and therefore are market exchange, by definition. Finally, some argue that, as societies become more complex and more densely populated, social bonds between individuals become less kinlike and friendly, and therefore reciprocity becomes less likely.[95] Perhaps this is why traders in developing areas are often foreigners or recent immigrants.[96]

In any case, Frederic Pryor's cross-cultural research supports the notion that all types of market exchange—goods, labor, land, and credit—are more likely with higher levels of economic productivity. Pryor also found that

Fiesta sponsors spend a great deal of money for food and drink as well as for musicians and dancers. Here we see a fiesta in Oaxaca, Mexico.

market exchange of goods appears at lower levels of economic development than market exchange of labor and credit; market exchange of land, probably because it is associated with private property (individual ownership), appears mostly at the highest levels of productivity. Perhaps surprisingly, smaller societies tend to have more market exchange or trade with other societies. Larger societies can presumably get more of what they need from inside the society; for example, until recently, China had relatively little foreign trade throughout much of its history.[97]

Possible Leveling Devices in Commercial Economies   As we will see in the next chapter, societies that depend substantially on market or commercial exchange tend to have marked differences in wealth among the people. Nonetheless, there may be mechanisms that lessen the inequality, that act at least partially as leveling devices. Some anthropologists have suggested that the fiesta complex in highland Indian communities of Latin America may be a mechanism that tends to equalize income.[98] In these peasant villages, fiestas are held each year to celebrate important village saints. The outstanding feature of this system is the extraordinary amount of money and labor a sponsoring family must contribute. Sponsors must hire ritual specialists, pay for church services, musicians, and costumes for dancers, and cover the complete cost of food and drink for the entire community. The costs incurred can very easily amount to a year's wages.[99]

Some anthropologists have suggested that, although the richer Indians who sponsor fiestas are clearly distributing a good deal of wealth to the poorer members of their own and other communities, the fiestas do not really level

wealth at all. First, true economic leveling would entail the redistribution of important productive resources such as land or animals; the fiesta only temporarily increases the general level of consumption. Second, the resources the sponsors expend are usually extra resources that have been accumulated specifically for the fiesta, which is why the sponsors are always appointed in advance. Third, and perhaps most important, the fiestas do not seem to have reduced long-term wealth distinctions within the villages.[100]

In nations such as ours, can the income tax and the social-assistance programs it pays for, such as welfare and disaster relief, be thought of as leveling devices? Theoretically, our tax system is supposed to work that way, by taxing higher incomes at higher rates. But we know that, in fact, it doesn't. Those in higher income brackets can often deduct an appreciable amount from their taxable incomes and therefore pay taxes at a relatively low rate. Our tax system may help some to escape extreme poverty, but, like the fiesta system, it has not eliminated marked distinctions in wealth.

THE WORLDWIDE TREND TOWARD COMMERCIALIZATION

One of the most important changes resulting from the expansion of Western societies and the capitalist system is the increasingly worldwide dependence on commercial exchange. The borrowed customs of buying and selling may at first be supplementary to traditional means of distributing goods in a society. But, as the new commercial customs take hold, the economic base of the receiving society alters. Inevitably, this alteration is accompanied by other changes, which have broad social, political, and even biological and psychological ramifications.

In examining contemporary patterns of change, however, we should bear in mind that commercialization has occurred in many parts of the world in the ancient past. The Chinese, Persians, Greeks, Romans, Arabs, Phoenicians, and Hindus were some of the early state societies that pushed commercial enterprises in other areas. We may cast some light on how and why earlier cultures changed when we consider several questions: How, and why, does a contemporary society change from a subsistence to a commercial economic base? What are the resultant cultural changes? Why do they occur?

In general, the limited evidence available suggests that a previously noncommercial people may begin to sell and buy things simply to live, not just because they may be attracted by goods they can obtain only by commercial exchange. If the resources available to a group have been significantly reduced per person—because the group has been forced to resettle on a small "reservation" or because population has increased—the group may be likely to take advantage of any commercial opportunities that become available, even if such opportunities require considerably more work, time, and effort.[101]

Many anthropologists have noted that, with the introduction of money, customs of sharing seem to change dramatically. Money, perhaps because it is nonperishable and largely hideable, tends to invoke feelings of not wanting to share. The plight of a man from the central highlands of New Guinea is typical. He agrees that it is not good manners to refuse a request from a relative or village friend; nonetheless, to keep his income from being "eaten," he tries to conceal some of his income. Some of the strategies include opening a savings account into which his pay is deposited, purchasing a semipermanent house, or joining a revolving credit association.[102] A recent series of experiments in the United States, where money has always been fundamental to the economic system, suggests that even the mere reminder of money causes people to behave more independently and to be less helpful to others.[103]

Migratory Labor

One way commercialization can occur is for some members of a community to move to a place that offers the possibility of working for wages. This happened in Tikopia, an island near the Solomon Islands in the South Pacific. In 1929, when Raymond Firth first studied the island, its economy was still essentially noncommercial—simple, self-sufficient, and largely self-contained.[104] Some Western goods were available but, with the exception of iron and steel in limited quantities, not sought after. Their possession and use were associated solely with Europeans. This situation changed dramatically with World War II. During the war, military forces occupied neighboring islands, and people from Tikopia migrated to those islands to find employment. In the period following the war, several large commercial interests extended their activities in the Solomons, thus creating a continued demand for

labor. As a result, when Firth revisited Tikopia in 1952, he found the economic situation already significantly altered. More than 100 Tikopians had left the island to work for varying periods. The migrants wanted to earn money because they aspired to standards of living previously regarded as appropriate only to Europeans. Already, living conditions on Tikopia were changing. Western cooking and water-carrying utensils, mosquito nets, kerosene storm lamps, and so forth had come to be regarded as normal items in a Tikopia household.

The introduction of money into the economy of Tikopia not only altered the economic system but also affected other areas of life. Compared with the situation in 1929, land was under more intensive cultivation in 1952, with introduced manioc and sweet potatoes supplementing the old principal crop, taro. Pressures on the food supply resulting from improved living standards and an increased population seem to have weakened the ties of extended kinship. For example, the nuclear families constituting the extended family (the landholding and land-using unit in 1929) were not cooperating as much in 1952. In many cases, in fact, the land had actually been split up among the constituent nuclear families; land rights had become more individualized. People were no longer as willing to share with members of their extended family, particularly with respect to the money and goods acquired by working in the Solomons.

In many areas of the world, the money sent back home has become a major factor in the economy (see the box "Working Abroad to Send Money Home"). Often remittances are not sent through the formal banking system, but rather through an informal network of brokers. In the Middle East and South Asia, the system is called *hawala* and is based on an honor system. For instance, the Hazara, the third largest ethnic group in Afghanistan, have migrated throughout the 20th century to cities in Afghanistan as well as to Pakistan and Iran. The banks in Afghanistan are not functioning and the Hazara often do not have official identification papers, so they use *hawala* brokers to transfer money back home.[105] The money from remittances often far exceeds the money spent by development efforts.[106] But unlike development efforts, usually supported by wealthier countries, money received by remittances can be channeled where families want. Migration becomes part of a family's economic strategy. Of course, not all families can employ that strategy—the poorest families cannot afford the costs of long-distance migration.[107]

Nonagricultural Commercial Production Commercialization can also occur when a self-sufficient society comes to depend more and more on trading for its livelihood. Such a change is exemplified by the Mundurucú of the Amazon Basin, who largely abandoned general horticulture for commercial rubber production. A similar change may also be seen in the Montagnais of northeastern Canada, who came to depend increasingly on commercial fur trapping, rather than hunting, for subsistence. Robert Murphy and Julian Steward found that, when modern goods from industrialized areas became available through trade, both the Mundurucú and the Montagnais devoted their energies

migrants and immigrants

Working Abroad to Send Money Home

Throughout recorded history, people have been going to other places to make a living. They do it not just because they need jobs to support themselves, but also to support their families back home. Indeed, the people left behind might suffer terribly, or even starve, without the money sent back to them (which economists call "remittances"). Going to another country to work temporarily generated more than $100 billion in remittances in 2003. In the 19th century, men from China were recruited to come to North America to build the transcontinental railroads, and Italians were recruited to work on building the railroads in New York State, New Jersey, Connecticut, and Massachusetts. In the years after World War II, when West German businesses were short of labor because so many people had been killed in the war, men from Turkey were recruited to come to Germany to fill the available jobs. Now, 30 to 40 years later, they make up a sizeable proportion of the population. Most if not all of the labor-short countries in western Europe (including England and France, the Netherlands, Sweden, Norway, Italy, and Spain) have attracted considerable numbers of immigrants in recent years. Indeed, much like the United States before them, the countries of western Europe are now becoming quite diverse culturally.

We may think that many if not most immigrants want to stay in the countries they have moved to. But this was not always true in the past, and it is not always true today. Many in the past just wanted to stay a few years. They wanted to earn money to help relatives back home, and maybe (if they were lucky) they could earn enough money to return home themselves and buy a farm or other small business. They often didn't become citizens in the new country because they didn't intend to stay. But until recently, most immigrants never went home again, and by the second or third generation, they had lost their native languages. In the last few decades, people who move to other countries to work often go home again—and again and again. They have become "transnationals," fluent in at least two languages, and comfortable living in different countries alternately. They may even retain two (or more) citizenships. Consider how different this is from many past immigrants who were highly motivated to "pass." It is not clear yet what explains why some people are more comfortable now with not passing. Could it be that some places are less ethnocentric than in the past? If so, why is that?

Not all moves to another country turn out well for the migrants. Consider the poor young women from Sri Lanka who are recruited to work as housemaids in other countries. They may be burned or beaten if their work is deemed unacceptable, and they may return home with no money saved from their work time abroad. One in every 19 citizens of Sri Lanka now works abroad, most of them as housemaids. For a country like Sri Lanka, migration has become a safety valve for the economy. The Sri Lankan economy may be advantaged by the remittances received, but not without suffering for some of the migrants.

Sources: M. Ember et al. 2005; Waldman 2005.

---

to producing specialized cash crops or other trade items. They did this to obtain other industrially made objects.[108] The primary socioeconomic change that occurred among the Mundurucú and the Montagnais was a shift from cooperative labor and community autonomy to individualized economic activity and a dependence on an external market.

Among the Mundurucú, for example, before close trading links were established, the native population and the Europeans had been in contact for some 80 years without the Mundurucú way of life being noticeably altered. The men did give up their independent military activities to perform as mercenaries for the Brazilians, but they continued to maintain their horticultural economy. Some trading took place with Brazilians, with the chief acting as agent for the village. Barter was the method of exchange. Traders first distributed their wares, ranging from cheap cottons to iron hatchets, trinkets, and so on; they returned about three months later to collect manioc, India rubber, and beans from the Mundurucú. At this time (1860), however, rubber was only a secondary item of commerce.

The rapidly growing demand for rubber from the 1860s onward increased the importance of Mundurucú-trader

Navajo women weave rugs for sale.

relationships. Traders now openly began to appoint agents, called *capitoes,* whose job it was to encourage greater rubber production. *Capitoes* were given economic privileges and hence power, both of which began to undercut the position of the traditional chief. In addition, the process of rubber collection itself began to alter Mundurucú social patterns by moving people away from their jungle-based communities.

Wild rubber trees are found only along rivers, which are often a considerable distance from the jungle habitat of the Mundurucú and can be exploited only during the dry season (late May to December). So the Mundurucú man who elected to gather rubber had to separate himself from his family for about half the year. Furthermore, rubber collecting is a solitary activity. Each tapper must daily work his territory, consisting of about 150 trees, and he must live close to his trees because the work lasts all day. Therefore, the tapper usually lives alone or in a small group except during the rainy season, when he returns to his village.

At this stage in the commercialization process, the Mundurucú became increasingly dependent on goods the trader supplied. Firearms were useless without regular quantities of gun powder and lead or shot; clothing required needles and thread for repairs. But these items could be earned only through increased rubber production, which in turn led to greater dependency on the outside world. Inevitably, the ability to work with traditional materials and the desire to maintain traditional crafts disappeared. Metal pots took the place of clay ones, and manufactured hammocks replaced homemade ones. Gradually, the village agricultural cycle ceased to be followed by all in the community so that rubber production would not suffer. The authority of the traditional chiefs was weakened as that of the *capitoes* was enhanced.

The point of no return was reached when significant numbers of Mundurucú abandoned the villages for permanent settlements near their individual territories of trees. These new settlements lacked the unity, the sense of community, of former village life. Nuclear families held and carefully maintained property in the interest of productivity.

With the discovery of gold, many Mundurucú young men have turned to panning for gold in rivers. The required equipment is simple, and gold is easier to transport and trade than rubber. Because gold can be sold for cash, which is then used for purchases, trading relationships are no longer so important. Cash is now used to buy transistor radios, tape recorders, watches, bicycles, and new kinds of clothing, in addition to firearms, metal pots, and tools. With money as a medium of exchange, the traditional emphasis on reciprocity has declined. Even food may now be sold to fellow Mundurucú, a practice that would have been unthinkable in the 1950s.[109]

Supplementary Cash Crops

A third way commercialization occurs is when people cultivating the soil produce a surplus above their subsistence requirements, which is then sold for cash. In many cases, this cash income must be used to pay rent or taxes. Under

Apricots laid out in flat baskets are drying in the Himalayan sun and are sold to the world market.

these circumstances, commercialization may be said to be associated with the formation of a peasantry.

Peasants first appeared with the emergence of state and urban civilizations about 5,000 years to 6,000 years ago, and they have been associated with civilization ever since.[110] To say that peasants are associated with urban societies perhaps needs some qualification. The contemporary, highly industrialized urban society has little need of peasants. Their scale of production is small and their use of land "uneconomic." A highly industrialized society with a large population of nonfood producers requires mechanized agriculture. As a result, the peasant has passed, or is passing, out of all but the most peripheral existence in industrial countries.

What changes does the development of a peasantry entail? In some respects, there is little disturbance of the cultivator's (now peasant's) former way of life. The peasant still has to produce enough food to meet family needs, to replace what has been consumed, to cover a few ceremonial obligations (e.g., the marriage of a child, village festivals, and funerals). But in other respects, the peasant's situation is radically altered. For, in addition to the traditional obligations—indeed, often in conflict with them—the peasant now has to produce extra crops to meet the requirements of a group of outsiders—landlords or officials of the state. These outsiders expect to be paid rent or taxes in produce or currency, and they are able to enforce their expectations because they control the military and the police.

Introduction of Commercial and Industrial Agriculture

Commercialization can come about through the introduction of commercial agriculture, cultivation for sale rather than personal consumption. The system of agriculture may come to be industrialized. In other words, some of the production processes, such as plowing, weeding, irrigation, and harvesting, can be done by machine. Commercial agriculture is, in fact, often as mechanized as any manufacturing industry. Land is worked for the maximum return it will yield, and labor is hired and fired just as impersonally as in other industries.

applied anthropology

Impact of the World System—Deforestation of the Amazon

When we speak of the economic system of a people, we must keep in mind that probably no group has ever been completely isolated from outside economic, political, social, or environmental events. In the modern world, with the expanding demand and opportunity of a growing world market economy, even the most self-sufficient groups cannot avoid the effects of their connections to the outside world. Consider the great rain forest drained by the Amazon River and its tributaries. Covering more than a billion acres, it is not only the home to many largely self-sufficient indigenous cultures; it also supports about 20 percent of all the earth's plant and animal species.

The Amazon forest is a very important part of the earth's ecosystem. The vast forests absorb CO_2, which helps to reduce global warming. The forest also puts moisture into the atmosphere through evaporation—about 8 trillion tons of water a year. The less forest, the less water moves into the atmosphere. The forest, in turn, is affected by natural changes in climate. For example, warming will lead to reduced rainfall, putting stress on the ability of the forest to grow or the existing trees to survive. And drier climates will lead to more natural fires.

Human behavior is seriously affecting the extent of the Amazon forest and the global weather system. The Amazon forest and other tropical forests are disappearing at an alarming rate because of the accelerated clearing of forest by humans, primarily for ranching and farming. By 2001, about 13 percent of the Amazon forests had been cleared. Some have suggested that the world demand for wood, hamburger, and gold is largely responsible for the diminution of the Amazon forest. A new threat is the increased use of land to grow crops to produce biofuels. Burning the forest is the main method of clearing land after large trees are felled or after plant matter has grown up after fallowing. Pollution from fires both because of land clearing and from fires that escape control contribute to increased greenhouse gases and global warming.

Like many tropical forests, the Amazon has large numbers of desirable hardwood trees. Forests in Africa and Asia are already largely depleted, so the demand for wood from the Amazon has grown considerably. In addition, the Amazon Development Agency in Brazil has offered incentives to clear forest for cattle ranching, which can provide hamburger to fast-food restaurants. There is little concern that a few seasons of overgrazing can make it impossible even for grasses to grow in the soils of the former forest. And cattle ranching has increased the need to grow forage or soybeans to feed the animals.

The indigenous people often find themselves in a land squeeze, with loggers, cattle ranchers, and miners trying to encroach on their territory. With less land, food-getting and traditional economic practices are in jeopardy. But it is naive to assume that the indigenous people are interested only in maintaining their traditional economies. They often accept the dilemma of economic development: They might lose some land, but selling rights to loggers and miners brings in money, which they can use to buy things they need and want. And, indigenous people themselves, although they contribute relatively little to the direct deforestation that is occurring, are increasingly involved in the world market economy, which means that they may contribute more to deforestation in the future. Researchers studying the Tsimane' of the Bolivian lowlands, mainly foragers who also farm, have found that those who grow a cash crop are most likely to clear more forest. Development experts and applied anthropologists are searching for ways to achieve development without destroying or degrading the environment. For example, indigenous groups are encouraged to gather Brazil nuts, a wild but renewable resource, for sale. Others are encouraged to harvest latex (natural rubber) and hearts of palm. Medicinal plants have economic value to multinational pharmaceutical and biotechnical companies, which have discovered that the conservation of biodiversity may be economically advantageous to themselves as well as to the local people and to scientists who want to study the diversity. The countries with large portions of Amazon forest have played an important role in encouraging development, but have worked to reduce deforestation with international pressure. For example, in Brazil, the annual rate of forest clearing has declined since 2004, because of the intervention of the Brazilian government. The international community is also working on a plan that would encourage countries to reduce deforestation, perhaps in exchange for monetary credits.

Can development be sustainable? Whether we like it or not, economic development and the desire for it are not going to go away. But we need to do more than applaud or bemoan economic development. In particular, we need more research that reveals what impact particular changes will have on people, other animals, plants, and the environment. Most of all, for the sake of human rights, we need to listen to the people whose lives will be most affected, to understand their needs as well as those of the developers.

Sources: Holloway 1993; Moran 1993; Winterbottom 1995, 60–70; Betts et al. 2008; Nepstad et al. 2008; Vadez et al. 2008.

E. J. Hobsbawm noted some of the developments that accompanied the introduction of commercial agriculture in 18th-century England and in continental Europe somewhat later.[111] The close, near-familial relationship between farmer and farm laborer disappeared, as did the once-personal connection between landlord and tenant. Land came to be regarded as a source of profit rather than a way of life. Fields were merged into single units and enclosed, and local grazing and similar privileges were reduced. Labor was hired at market rates and paid in wages. Eventually, as the emphasis on large-scale production for a mass market increased, machines began to replace farmers.

The introduction of commercial agriculture brings several important social consequences. Gradually, a class polarization develops. Farmers and landlords become increasingly separated from laborers and tenants, just as the employer in town becomes socially separated from the employees. Gradually, too, manufactured items of all sorts are introduced into rural areas. Laborers migrate to urban centers in search of employment, often meeting even less sympathetic conditions there than exist in the country.

The changeover to commercial agriculture may result in an improved standard of living in the short and long run. But sometimes the switch is followed by a decline in the standard of living if the market price for the commercial crop declines. For example, the changeover of the farmer-herders of the arid *sertão* region of northeastern Brazil after 1940 to the production of sisal (a plant whose fibers can be made into twine and rope) seemed to be a move that could provide a more secure living in their arid environment. But when the world price for sisal dropped and the wages of sisal workers declined, many workers were forced to curtail the caloric intake of their children. The poorer people were obliged to save their now more limited food supplies for the money earners, at the expense of the children.[112]

Commercialization can start in various ways: People can begin to sell and buy because they begin to work near home or away for wages, or because they begin to sell nonagricultural products, surplus food, or cash crops (crops grown deliberately for sale). One type of commercialization does not exclude another; all types can occur in any society. However commercialization begins, it seems to have predictable effects on traditional economics. The ethic of generalized reciprocity declines, particularly with respect to giving away money. (Perhaps because it is nonperishable and hideable, money seems more likely than other goods to be kept for one's immediate family rather than shared with others.) Property rights become individualized rather than collective when people begin to buy and sell. Even in societies that were previously egalitarian, commercialization usually results in more unequal access to resources and hence a greater degree of social stratification.

SUMMARY ● ○ ○

1. All societies have economic systems, whether or not these involve the use of money. All societies have customs specifying access to natural resources; customary ways of transforming or converting those resources, through labor, into necessities and other desired goods and services; and customs for distributing and perhaps exchanging goods and services.

2. Regulation of access to natural resources is a basic factor in all economic systems. The concept of individual or private ownership of land—including the right to use its resources and the right to sell or otherwise dispose of them—is common among intensive agriculturalists. In contrast, foragers, horticulturalists, and pastoralists generally lack individual ownership of land. Among pastoral nomads, however, animals are considered family property and are not usually shared.

3. Every society makes use of a technology, which includes tools, constructions, and required skills. Even though foragers and horticulturalists tend to think of tools as "owned" by the individuals who made them, the sharing of tools is so extensive that individual ownership does not have much meaning. Among intensive agriculturalists, toolmaking tends to be a specialized activity. Tools tend not to be shared, except mainly by those who have purchased them together.

4. Incentives for labor vary cross-culturally. Many societies produce just for household consumption; if there are more consumers, producers work harder. In some subsistence economies, people may work harder to obtain the social rewards that come from giving to others. Forced labor generally occurs only in complex societies.

5. Division of labor by gender is universal. In many nonindustrial societies, large tasks are often accomplished through the cooperative efforts of a kinship group. Such cooperation is not as prevalent in industrialized societies. In general, the more technically advanced a society is, the more surplus food it produces and the more some of its members engage in specialized work.

6. The organization of labor reaches its peak in complex societies; work groups tend to be formally organized, and sometimes there is an enforced obligation to participate. In food-collecting and horticultural societies, in contrast, there is little formal organization of work.

7. Goods and services are distributed in all societies by systems that can be classified under three types: reciprocity, redistribution, and market or commercial exchange. Reciprocity is giving and taking without the use of money and generally assumes two forms: generalized reciprocity and balanced reciprocity. Generalized reciprocity is gift giving without any immediate or planned return. In balanced reciprocity, individuals exchange goods and services immediately or in the short term.

8. Redistribution is the accumulation of goods or labor by a particular person, or in a particular place, for the purpose of subsequent distribution. It becomes an important mechanism of distribution only in societies with political hierarchies.

9. Market or commercial exchange, where "prices" depend on supply and demand, tends to occur with increasing levels of economic productivity. Especially nowadays, market exchange usually involves an all-purpose medium of exchange—money. Most societies today

are at least partly commercialized; the world is becoming a single market system.

10. Many of the cultural changes observed in the modern world have been generated, directly or indirectly, by the dominance and expansion of Western societies. One of the principal changes resulting from the expansion of Western culture is the increasing dependence of much of the world on commercial exchange—that is, the proliferation of buying and selling in markets, usually accompanied by the use of money as the medium of exchange. The borrowed custom of buying and selling may at first be supplementary to traditional means of distributing goods, but as the new commercial customs take hold, the economic base of the receiving society alters. Inevitably, this alteration is accompanied by other changes, which have broad social, political, and even biological and psychological ramifications.

11. One way commercialization can occur is for members of a community to become migratory workers, traveling to a place nearby that offers the possibility of working for wages. Commercialization can also occur when a simple, self-sufficient hunting or agricultural society comes to depend more on trading for its livelihood. A third way commercialization occurs is when those cultivating the soil produce more than they require for subsistence. The surplus is then sold for cash. In many instances, this cash income must be used to pay rent or taxes; under such circumstances, commercialization may be said to be associated with the formation of a peasantry. A fourth way in which commercialization can come about is through the introduction of commercial agriculture, in which all the cultivated commodities are produced for sale rather than for personal consumption. Along with this change, the system of agriculture may be industrialized, with some of the production processes being done by machine.

GLOSSARY TERMS ○ ● ○

balanced reciprocity **122**
corvée **118**
generalized
  reciprocity **121**
general-purpose
  money **125**
market or commercial
  exchange **125**

optimal foraging
  theory **120**
peasants **126**
potlatch **124**
reciprocity **121**
redistribution **124**
special-purpose
  money **126**

CRITICAL QUESTIONS ○ ○ ●

1. What conditions might enable us to achieve a world of sustainable resources?
2. What are the possible effects of a postindustrial economy in which a large proportion of the population has inexpensive access to computers and information?
3. Do you expect any appreciable change in the amount of resources privately owned in the future? State your reasons.
4. We tend to emphasize the negative consequences of the worldwide trend toward commercialization. Have there been any beneficial consequences?
5. Why might an increasing understanding of cultural variation also provide an increasing understanding of culture change?

myanthrolab

Read "Yanomamö: Varying Adaptations of Foraging Agriculturalists" by Raymond B. Hames on MyAnthroLab and answer these case study questions:

1. Why does Hames refer to the Yanomamö as "foraging horticulturalists"?
2. Customary behavior in all societies varies somewhat over time as well as over space. What kinds of differences did Hames find in food-getting and economy between lowland and highland groups?
3. Hames measured how people spend their time during the day. What differences did he find between women and men's work? Which gender generally worked more? Does the conclusion change depending on how work is defined?

Social Stratification: Class, Ethnicity, and Racism

long-enduring value in the United States is the belief that "all men are created equal." These famous words from the American Declaration of Independence do not mean that all people are equal in wealth or status but rather that all (including women nowadays) are supposed to be equal before the law. Equality before the law is the ideal. But the ideal is not always the actuality. Some people have advantages in legal treatment, and they generally also tend to have advantages of other kinds, including economic advantages. Without exception, recent and modern industrial and postindustrial societies such as our own are *socially stratified*—that is, they contain social groups such as families, classes, or ethnic groups that have unequal access to important advantages such as economic resources, power, and prestige.

Hasn't such inequality always existed? Anthropologists, based on first-hand observations of recent societies, would say not. To be sure, even the simplest societies (in the technological sense) have some differences in advantages based on age, ability, or gender—adults have higher status than children, the skilled more than the unskilled, men more than women (we discuss this topic in the chapter on sex, gender, and culture). But anthropologists would argue that *egalitarian* societies exist where *social groups* (e.g., families) have more or less the same access to rights or advantages. As we noted in the last chapter, the economic systems of many food collectors and horticulturalists promote equal access to economic resources for all families in the community. Moreover, such societies also tend to emphasize the sharing of food and other goods, which tends to equalize any small inequalities in resources between families. Until about 10,000 years ago, all human societies depended on food they hunted, gathered, and/or fished. And so we might expect that egalitarianism characterized most of human history. That is indeed what archaeologists suggest. Substantial inequality generally appears only with permanent communities, centralized political systems, and intensive agriculture, which are cultural features that began to appear in the world only in the last 10,000 years. Before that time, then, most societies were probably egalitarian. In the world today, egalitarian societies have all but disappeared because of two processes—the global spread of commercial or market exchange and the voluntary or involuntary incorporation of many diverse people into large, centralized political systems. In modern societies, some groups have more advantages than others. These groups may include *ethnic* groups. That is, ethnic diversity is almost always associated with differential access to advantages. When ethnic diversity is also associated with differences in physical features such as skin color, the social stratification may involve *racism*, the belief that some "racial" groups are inferior.

Systems of social stratification are strongly linked to the customary ways in which economic resources are allocated, distributed, and converted through labor into goods and services. So we would not expect much inequality if all people had relatively equal access to economic resources. But stratification cannot be understood solely in terms of economic resources; there are other benefits such as prestige and power that may be unequally distributed. We first examine how societies vary in their systems of stratification. Then we turn to possible explanations of why they vary.

● ○ ●

VARIATION IN DEGREE OF SOCIAL INEQUALITY

Societies vary in the extent to which social groups, as well as individuals, have unequal access to advantages. In this chapter, we are concerned with differential or unequal access to three types of advantages: (1) wealth or economic resources, (2) power, and (3) prestige. **Economic resources** are things that have value in a culture; they include land, tools and other technology, goods, and money. **Power,** a second but related advantage, is the ability to make others do what they do not want to do; power is influence based on the threat of force. When groups in a society have rules or customs that give them unequal access to wealth or resources, they generally also have unequal access to power. So, for example, when we speak of a "company town" in the United States, we are referring to the fact that the company that employs most of the residents of the town usually has considerable control over them. Finally, there is the advantage of **prestige.** When we speak of prestige, we mean that someone or some group is accorded particular respect or honor. Even if it is true that there is always unequal access by individuals to prestige (because of differences in age, gender, or ability), some societies in the ethnographic record have no social groups with unequal access to prestige.

Thus, anthropologists conventionally distinguish three types of society in terms of the degree to which different social groups have unequal access to advantages: *egalitarian, rank,* and *class societies* (see Table 8–1). Some societies in the ethnographic record do not fit easily into any of these three types; as with any classification scheme,

some cases seem to straddle the line between types.[1] **Egalitarian societies** contain no social groups with greater or lesser access to economic resources, power, or prestige. **Rank societies** do not have very unequal access to economic resources or to power, but they do contain social groups with unequal access to prestige. Rank societies, then, are partly stratified. **Class societies** have unequal access to all three advantages—economic resources, power, and prestige.

EGALITARIAN SOCIETIES

Egalitarian societies can be found not only among foragers such as the !Kung, Mbuti, Australian aborigines, Inuit, and Aché, but also among horticulturalists such as the Yanomamö and pastoralists such as the Lapps. An important point to keep in mind is that egalitarian does not mean that all people within such societies are the same. There will always be differences among individuals in age and gender and in such abilities or traits as hunting skill, perception, health, creativity, physical prowess, attractiveness, and intelligence. According to Morton Fried, egalitarian means that, within a given society, "there are as many positions of prestige in any given age/sex grade as there are persons capable of filling them."[2] For instance, if a person can achieve high status by fashioning fine spears, and if many people in the society fashion such spears, then many acquire high status as spear makers. If high status is also acquired by carving bones into artifacts, and if only three people are considered expert carvers of bones, then only those three achieve high status as carvers. But the next generation might produce eight spear makers and 20 carvers. In an egalitarian society, the number of prestigious positions is adjusted to fit the number of qualified candidates. We would say, therefore, that such a society is not socially stratified.

There are, of course, differences in position and prestige arising out of differences in ability. Even in an egalitarian society, differential prestige exists. But, although some people may be better hunters or more skilled artists than others, there is still *equal access* to status positions for people of the same ability. Any prestige gained by achieving high status as a great hunter, for instance, is neither transferable nor inheritable. Because a man is a great hunter, it is not assumed that his sons are also great hunters. There also may be individuals with more influence, but it cannot be inherited, and there are no groups with appreciably more influence over time. An egalitarian society keeps inequality at a minimal level.

	SOME SOCIAL GROUPS HAVE GREATER ACCESS TO:			
Type of Society	**Economic Resources**	**Power**	**Prestige**	**Examples**
Egalitarian	No	No	No	!Kung, Mbuti, Australian aborigines, Inuit, Aché, Yanomamö
Rank	No	No	Yes	Samoans, Tahiti, Trobriand Islands, Ifaluk
Class/caste	Yes	Yes	Yes	United States, Canada, Greece, India, Inca

TABLE 8–1   Stratification in Three Types of Societies

Any differences in prestige that do exist are not related to economic differences. Egalitarian groups depend heavily on *sharing,* which ensures equal access to economic resources despite differences in acquired prestige. For instance, in some egalitarian communities, some members achieve higher status through hunting. But even before the hunt begins, how the animal will be divided and distributed among the members of the band has already been decided according to custom. The culture works to separate the status that members achieve—recognition as great hunters—from actual possession of the wealth, which in this case would be the slain animal.

Just as egalitarian societies do not have social groups with unequal access to economic resources, they also do not have social groups with unequal access to power. As we will see later in the chapter on political life, unequal access to power by social groups seems to occur only in state societies, which have full-time political officials and marked differences in wealth. Egalitarian societies use a number of customs to keep leaders from dominating others. Criticism and ridicule can be very effective. The Mbuti of central Africa shout down an overassertive leader. When a Hadza man (in Tanzania) tried to get people to work for him, other Hadza made fun of him. Disobedience is another strategy. If a leader tries to command, people just ignore the command. In extreme cases, a particularly domineering leader may be killed by community agreement; this behavior was reported among the !Kung and the Hadza. Finally, particularly among more nomadic groups, people may just move away from a leader they don't like. The active attempts to put down upstarts in many egalitarian societies prompts Christopher Boehm to suggest that dominance comes naturally to humans. Egalitarian societies work hard to reverse that tendency.[3] The Mbuti provide an example of a society almost totally equal: "Neither in ritual, hunting, kinship nor band relations do they exhibit any discernible inequalities of rank or advantage."[4] Their hunting bands have no leaders, and recognition of the achievement of one person is not accompanied by privilege of any sort. Economic resources such as food are communally shared, and even tools and weapons are frequently passed from person to person. Only within the family are rights and privileges differentiated.

Foraging societies with extensive sharing of resources are more readily labeled egalitarian as compared with some pastoral societies where households may vary considerably in the number of animals they own. Should we consider a pastoral society with unequal distribution of animals egalitarian? Here there is controversy. One important issue is whether unequal ownership persists through time—that is, inherited. If vagaries of weather, theft, and gifts of livestock to relatives make livestock ownership fluctuate over time, wealth differences may mostly be temporary. A second important issue is whether the inequalities in livestock ownership make any difference in the ease of acquiring other "goods," such as prestige and political power. If wealth in livestock is ephemeral and is not associated with differential access to prestige and power, then some anthropologists would characterize such pastoral societies as egalitarian.[5] It is easy to imagine how an egalitarian society with some wealth differences, as opposed to one with no wealth differences, could become a rank or a class society. All you would need is a mechanism for retaining more wealth in some families over time.

RANK SOCIETIES

Most societies with social *ranking* practice agriculture or herding, but not all agricultural or pastoral societies are ranked. Ranking is characterized by social groups with unequal access to prestige or status but *not* significantly unequal access to economic resources or power. Unequal

In egalitarian societies, such as among the Mbuti hunter-gatherers, houses tend to look the same.

access to prestige is often reflected in the position of chief, a rank which only some members of a specified group in the society can achieve.

Unusual among rank societies were the 19-century Native Americans who lived along the northwestern coast of the United States and the southwestern coast of Canada. An example were the Nimpkish, a Kwakiutl group.[6] These societies were unusual because their economy was based on food collecting. But huge catches of salmon—which were preserved for year-round consumption—enabled them to support fairly large and permanent villages. These societies were similar to food-producing societies in many ways, not just in their development of social ranking. Still, the principal means of proving one's high status was to give away wealth. The tribal chiefs celebrated solemn rites by grand feasts called *potlatches,* at which they gave gifts to every guest.[7]

In rank societies, the position of chief is at least partly hereditary. The criterion of superior rank in some Polynesian societies, for example, was genealogical. Usually the eldest son succeeded to the position of chief, and different kinship groups were differentially ranked according to their genealogical distance from the chiefly line. In rank societies, chiefs are often treated with deference by people of lower rank. For example, among the Trobriand Islanders of Melanesia, people of lower rank must keep their heads lower than a person of higher rank. So, when a chief is standing, commoners must bend low. When commoners have to walk past a chief who happens to be sitting, he may rise and they will bend. If the chief chooses to remain seated, they must crawl.[8]

Although there is no question that chiefs in a rank society enjoy special prestige, there is some controversy over whether they really do not also have material advantages. Chiefs may sometimes look as if they are substantially richer than commoners, for they may receive many gifts and have larger storehouses. In some instances, the chief may even be called the "owner" of the land. However, Marshall Sahlins maintains that the chief's storehouses only house temporary accumulations for feasts or other redistributions. And although the chief may be designated the "owner" of the land, others have the right to use the land. Furthermore, Sahlins suggests that the chief in a rank society lacks power because he usually cannot make people give him gifts or force them to work on communal projects. Often the chief can encourage production only by working furiously on his own cultivation.[9]

This picture of economic equality in rank societies is beginning to be questioned. Laura Betzig studied patterns of food sharing and labor on Ifaluk, a small atoll in the Western Carolines.[10] Chiefly status is inherited geneaologically in the female line, although most chiefs are male. (In the chapter on sex, gender, and culture, we discuss why political leaders are usually male, even in societies structured

In societies with rank and class, deference is usually shown to political leaders, as in the case of this Fon chief in the lowlands of Cameroon, Africa.

around women.) As in other chiefly societies, Ifaluk chiefs are accorded deference. For example, during collective meals prepared by all the island women, chiefs were served first and were bowed to. The Ifaluk chiefs are said to control the fishing areas. Were the catches equitably distributed? Betzig measured the amount of fish each household got. All the commoners received an equal share, but the chiefs got extra fish; their households got twice as much per person as other households. Did the chiefs give away more later?

Theoretically, generosity is supposed to even things out, but Betzig found that the gifts from chiefs to other households did not equal the amount the chiefs received from others. Furthermore, although everyone gave to the chiefs, the chiefs gave mostly to their close relatives. On Ifaluk, the chiefs did not work harder than others; in fact, they worked less. Is this true in other societies conventionally considered to be rank societies? We do not know. However, we need to keep in mind that the chiefs in Ifaluk were not noticeably better off either. If they lived in palaces with servants, had elaborate meals, or were dressed in fine clothes and jewelry, we would not need measures of food received or a special study to see if the chiefs had greater access to economic resources, because their wealth would be obvious. But rank societies may not have had as much economic equality as we used to think.

CLASS SOCIETIES

In class societies, as in rank societies, there is unequal access to prestige. But, unlike rank societies, class societies are characterized by groups of people that have substantially greater or lesser access to economic resources and power. That is, not every social group has the same opportunity to obtain land, animals, money, or other economic benefits or the same opportunity to exercise power that other groups have. Fully stratified or class societies range from somewhat open to virtually closed class, or *caste*, systems.

Open Class Systems

A **class** is a category of people who all have about the same opportunity to obtain economic resources, power, and prestige. Different classes have differing opportunities. We call class systems *open* if there is some possibility of moving from one class to another. Since the 1920s, there have been many studies of classes in towns and cities in the United States. Researchers have produced profiles of these different communities—known variously as Yankee City, Middletown, Jonesville, and Old City—all of which support the premise that the United States has distinguishable, though somewhat open, social classes. Both W. Lloyd Warner and Paul Lunt's Yankee City study[11] and Robert and Helen Lynd's Middletown study[12] concluded that the social status or prestige of a family is generally correlated with the occupation and wealth of the head of the family. Class systems are by no means confined to the United States. They are found in all nations of the modern world.

Although class status is not fully determined at birth in open class societies, there is a high probability that most people will stay close to the class into which they were born and will marry within that class. Classes tend to perpetuate themselves through the inheritance of wealth. John Brittain suggested that, in the United States, the transfer of money through bequests accounts for much of the wealth of the next generation. As we might expect, the importance of inheritance seems to increase at higher levels of wealth. That is, the wealth of richer people comes more from inheritance than does the wealth of not-so-rich people.[13]

Other mechanisms of class perpetuation may be more subtle, but they are still powerful. In the United States, many institutions make it possible for an upper-class person to have little contact with other classes. Private day and boarding schools put upper-class children in close contact mostly with others of their class. Attending these schools makes it more likely they will get into universities with higher prestige. Debutante balls and exclusive private parties ensure that young people meet the "right people." Country clubs, exclusive city clubs, and service in particular charities continue the process of limited association. People of the same class also tend to live in the same neighborhoods. Before 1948, explicit restrictions kept certain groups out of particular neighborhoods, but after the U.S. Supreme Court ruled such discrimination unconstitutional, more subtle methods were developed. For instance, zoning restrictions may prohibit multiple-family dwellings in a town or neighborhood and lots below a certain acreage.[14]

Identification with a social class begins early in life. In addition to differences in occupation, wealth, and prestige, social classes vary in many other ways, including religious

People of the same social class tend to socialize together, where they live, where they vacation, or through shared activities. Debutantes and their escorts are presented at the Krewe of Rex ball during Mardi Gras in New Orleans.

affiliation, closeness to kin, ideas about childrearing, job satisfaction, leisure-time activities, style of clothes and furniture, and (as noted in the chapter on communication and language) even in styles of speech.[15] People from each class tend to be more comfortable with those from the same class; they talk similarly and are more likely to have similar interests and tastes.

Class boundaries, though vague, have been established by custom and tradition; sometimes they have been reinforced by the enactment of laws. Many of our laws serve to protect property and thus tend to favor the upper and upper-middle classes. The poor, in contrast, seem to be disadvantaged in our legal system. The crimes the poor are most likely to commit are dealt with harshly by the courts, and poor people rarely have the money to secure effective legal counsel.

In open class systems, it is not always clear how many classes there are. In Stanley Barrett's study of "Paradise," Ontario, some people thought that there were only two classes in the past. One person said, "There was the hierarchy, and the rest of us." Another said that there were three classes: "The people with money, the in-between, and the ones who didn't have anything." Many said there were four: "The wealthy businessmen, the middle class, blue collar workers, and the guys that were just existing."[16] A few insisted that there were five classes. With the breakdown of the old rigid class structure, there are more people in the middle.[17]

Degree of Openness Some class systems are more open than others; that is, it is easier in some societies to move from one class position to another. Social scientists typically compare the class of people with the class of their parent or parents to measure the degree of mobility. Although most people aspire to move up, mobility also includes moving down. Obtaining more education, particularly a university education, is one of the most effective ways to move upward in contemporary societies. For example, in the United States, individuals with a college bachelor's degree average 75 percent more income than those with only a high school diploma. And individuals with professional degrees earn on average 119 percent more than those with a bachelor's degree.[18] In many countries, educational attainment predicts one's social class better than parents' occupation does.[19]

How do the United States and Canada compare with other countries in degree of class mobility? Canada, Finland, and Sweden have more mobility than the United States and Britain. Mexico and Peru have less mobility than the United States and Brazil, and Colombia considerably less.[20]

Class openness also varies over time. In "Paradise," Ontario, Barrett found that the rigid stratification system of the 1950s opened up considerably as new people moved into the community. No one disputed who belonged to the elite in the past. They were of British background, lived in the largest houses, had new cars, and vacationed in Florida. Moreover, they controlled all the leadership positions in the town. By the 1980s, though, the leaders came mostly from the middle and working classes.[21]

Degree of Inequality Degree of class mobility, however, is not the same as degree of economic inequality. For example, Japan, Italy, and Germany have less mobility than the United States, but less inequality (see later). Degree of inequality can vary considerably over time. In the United States, inequality has fluctuated considerably from the 1900s to the present. The greatest inequality was just before the 1929 stock market crash, when the top 1 percent had 42.6 percent of all the wealth. The least inequality was in the mid-1970s, after the stock market declined by 42 percent. Then the top 1 percent controlled 17.6 percent of the wealth.

Change over time in the degree of inequality sometimes appears to have economic causes; for example, the 1929 crash made the wealthy less wealthy. But some of the change over time is due to shifts in public policy. During the New Deal of the 1930s, tax changes and work programs shifted more income to ordinary people; in the 1980s, tax cuts for the wealthy helped the rich get richer. In the 1990s, the rich continued to get richer and the poor got poorer.[22] By 2006, inequality was more concentrated at the top than since the 1929 crash. Only since the severe recession between 2007 and 2009 have the rich gotten somewhat poorer.[23] One way of calculating the disparity between rich and poor is to use the ratio of income held by the top fifth of the households divided by the income held by the bottom fifth. Comparatively speaking, the United States presently has more inequality than any of the countries in western Europe, with a ratio of 8.5 to 1 (see Figure 8–1). That is, the top 20 percent of U.S. households controls 8.5 times the wealth controlled by the bottom 20 percent. Norway, on the other hand, has a ratio of about 4 to 1. And Germany has a ratio of about 4.3 to 1. The degree of inequality in the United States exceeds that of India, with a ratio of about 4.7 to 1. Brazil is one of the most unequal countries, with ratios of 32 to 1.

Recognition of Class

Societies that have open class systems vary in the degree to which members of the society recognize that there are classes, albeit somewhat open classes. The United States is unusual in that, despite objective evidence of multiple social classes, many people deny their existence. The ideology that hard work and strong character can transform anyone into a success appears to be so powerful that it masks the realities of social inequality.[24] A recent poll found that more people in the United States now believe that the chance of moving up has improved in the last few decades, when in reality mobility has declined.[25] When we were growing up, we were told that "Anyone can be President of the United States." As "proof," people pointed to a few individuals who rose from humble beginnings. But consider the odds. How many presidents have come from poor families? How many were not European in background? How many were not Protestant? (And, as we discuss in the chapter on sex, gender, and culture, how many were not male?) So far, almost all of the presidents of the United States have been mainly

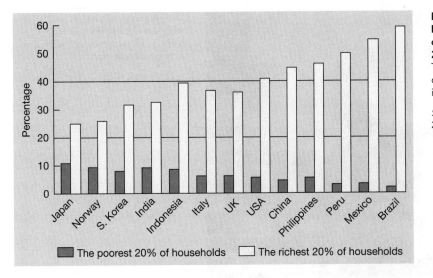

FIGURE 8–1 Proportion of National Income Earned by the Richest 20 Percent of Households Compared with the Poorest 20 Percent: Selected Country Comparisons. The countries are ordered by their Gini coefficients, a widely used measure of degree of income inequality.

Source: These data are abstracted from World Bank 2004, 60–62.

European in ancestry, all but one have been Protestant, and all have been male. And only a handful came from humble beginnings. The paradox of an open class system is that, to move up in the social ladder, people seem to have to believe that it is possible to do so. However, it is one thing to believe in mobility; it is another thing to deny the existence of classes. Why might people need to deny that classes exist?

Caste Systems

Some societies have classes (called castes) that are virtually closed. A **caste** is a ranked group in which membership is determined at birth, and marriage is restricted to members of one's own caste. The only way you can belong is by being born into the group; and because you cannot marry outside the group, your children cannot acquire another caste status either. In India, for example, there are several thousand hereditary castes. Although the precise ranking of these thousands of groups is not clear, there appear to be four main levels of hierarchy. The castes in India are often thought to be associated with different occupations, but that is not quite true. Most Indians live in rural areas and have agricultural occupations, but their castes vary widely.[26]

Castes may exist in conjunction with a more open class system. Indeed, in India today, members of a low caste who can get wage-paying jobs, chiefly those in urban areas, may improve their social standing in the same ways available to people in other class societies. In general, however, they still cannot marry someone in a higher caste, so the caste system is perpetuated.

Questions basic to all stratified societies, and particularly to a caste society, were posed by John Ruskin, a 19th-century British essayist: "Which of us . . . is to do the hard and dirty work for the rest—and for what pay? Who is to do the pleasant and clean work, and for what pay?"[27] In India, those questions have been answered by the caste system, which mainly dictates how goods and services are exchanged, particularly in rural areas.[28] Who is to do the hard and dirty work for the rest of society is clearly established: A large group of Untouchables forms the bottom of

the hierarchy. Among the Untouchables are subcastes such as the Camars, or leatherworkers, and the Bhangis, who traditionally are sweepers. At the top of the hierarchy, performing the pleasant and clean work of priests, are the Brahmans. Between the two extremes are thousands of castes and subcastes.[29] In a typical village, a potter makes clay drinking cups and large water vessels for the entire village population. In return, the principal landowner gives him a house site and supplies him twice yearly with grain. Some other castes owe the potter their services: The barber cuts his hair; the sweeper carries away his rubbish; the washer washes his clothes; the Brahman performs his children's weddings. The barber serves every caste in the village except the Untouchables; he, in turn, is served by half of the others. He has inherited the families he works for, along with his father's occupation. All castes help at harvest and at weddings for additional payment, which sometimes includes a money payment.

This description is, in fact, an idealized picture of the caste system of India. In reality, the system operates to the advantage of the principal landowning caste—sometimes the Brahmans and sometimes other castes. Also, it is not carried on without some resentment; signs of hostility are shown toward the ruling caste by the Untouchables and other lower castes. The resentment does not appear to be against the caste system as such. Instead, the lower castes exhibit bitterness at their own low status and strive for greater equality. For instance, one of the Camars' traditional services is to remove dead cattle; in return, they can have the meat to eat and the hide to tan for their leatherworking. Because handling dead animals and eating beef are regarded as unclean acts, the Camars of one village refused to continue this service. Thus, they lost a source of free hides and food in a vain attempt to escape unclean status.

Since World War II, the economic basis of the caste system in India has been undermined somewhat by the growing practice of giving cash payment for services. For instance, the son of a barber may be a teacher during the week, earning a cash salary, and confine his haircutting to weekends. But he still remains in the barber caste (Nai) and must marry within that caste.

Caste is somewhat less important in India, but has not disappeared. In Mumbai, the washers of the Dhobi caste process laundry.

Perpetuation of the caste system is ensured by the power of those in the upper castes, who derive three main advantages from their position: economic, prestige, and sexual gains. The economic gain is the most immediately apparent. An ample supply of cheap labor and free services is maintained by the threat of sanctions. Lower-caste members may have their use of a house site withdrawn; they may be refused access to the village well or to common grazing land for animals; or they may be expelled from the village. Prestige is also maintained by the threat of sanctions; people in the higher castes expect deference and servility from those in the lower castes. The sexual gain is less apparent but equally real. The high-caste male has access to two groups of females, those of his own caste and those of lower castes. High-caste females are kept free of the "contaminating" touch of low-caste males because low-caste males are allowed access only to low-caste women. Moreover, the constant reminders of ritual uncleanness serve to keep those of the lower castes "in their place." People in higher castes do not accept water from Untouchables, sit next to them, or eat at the same table with them.

Japan also had a caste group within a class society. Now called *burakumin* (instead of the pejorative *eta*), this group traditionally had occupations that were considered unclean.[30] Comparable to India's Untouchables, they were a hereditary, endogamous (in-marrying) group. Their occupations were traditionally those of farm laborer, leatherworker, and basket weaver; their standard of living was very low. The burakumin are physically indistinguishable from other Japanese.[31] Despite that, the burakumin were considered a separate "race" by some for centuries.[32] The Japanese government officially abolished discrimination against the burakumin in 1871, but the burakumin did not begin organizing to bring about change until the 20th century. As of 1995, 73 percent of burakumin marriages were with non-burakumin. In public opinion polls, two-thirds of burakumin now said

that they had not encountered discrimination. However, most burakumin still live in segregated neighborhoods where unemployment, crime, and alcoholism rates are high.[33]

In a considerable number of sub-Saharan African societies, some occupational specialties are only performed by certain castes. The specialties usually involve metalworking, pottery, woodworking, leatherworking, playing musical instruments, and praise-singing. There may be different castes for different specialties or one caste for many specialties. In some cases, the caste consists of people who traditionally hunted and gathered. In almost all cases, the specialists had to marry within their own group and their social position was inherited. These castes usually constituted only a small minority of the society's population and were not the lowest ranking groups in society. Only slaves had a lower rank. Some of the castes took on additional tasks, such as go-betweens for arranging marriages, messengers, and circumcisers. The caste vocational distinctions have weakened in recent times as people have become more educated.[34]

In Rwanda, long before the ethnic division arose between the Hutu and Tutsi (see discussion later in the ethnicity section), the Twa, who comprised less than 1 percent of the population, were subject to serious discrimination. Their bodies were viewed as dangerous and polluting and they were avoided whenever possible. For example, if a Twa were present while others were eating or drinking, separate utensils were reserved only for Twa. The Twa traditional occupations were foraging, making pottery, entertaining, and serving as torturers or executioners for the Rwandan king. Mutton was considered a Twa food and other Rwandans would not eat mutton.[35]

In the United States, African Americans used to have more of a castelike status determined partly by the inherited characteristic of skin color. Until recently, some states had laws prohibiting an African American from marrying a European American. When interethnic marriage did

current research and issues

The Gap Between Poor and Rich Countries

When people support themselves by what they collect and produce themselves, as most people did until a few thousand years ago, it is difficult to compare the standards of living of different societies because we cannot translate what people have into market or monetary value. Only where people are at least partly involved in the world market economy can we measure the standard of living in monetary terms. Today, this comparison is possible for most of the world. Many people in most societies depend on buying and selling for a living; and the more people who depend on international exchange, the more possible it is to compare them in terms of standard economic indicators. We do not have such indicators for all the different societies, but we do have them for many countries. Those indicators suggest that the gap between the rich and poor countries in the world is not only very substantial but has generally increased in the last couple of decades.

To convey just how economically unequal the world has become, let us compare economic data for the years 1960, 1978, and 2000. In 1960, about a third of 126 countries (41) were classified as rich, and 17 percent were in the next lower rank—contenders to be rich. By 1978, about one-quarter (or 11) of the rich countries slipped down into the ranks of the contenders and about 7 percent (three) moved into the Third World category. By 2000, an additional five rich countries

slipped down. During the same time frame, only four countries moved up to join the rich—Singapore, Hong Kong, Taiwan, and South Korea. During the same time periods, almost all of the poorest countries stayed at the bottom, and if there was movement among the non-rich countries, it was mostly downward. Western countries increased their hold on the world's wealth during this period. Of the 41 originally rich countries in 1960, almost half (19) were non-Western. In 2000, there were fewer rich countries—only 31—but only 30 percent (nine) were non-Western.

If the world as a whole is seeing improvements in technology and economic development, why is the gap between the rich and poor countries increasing? As we saw in the chapter on culture and culture change, often the rich within a society benefit most from new technology, at least initially. They are not only the most likely to be able to afford it, they also are the only ones who can afford to take the risks that it involves. The same may be true for nations. Those that already have capital are more likely than the poorer nations to take advantage of improvements in technology. In addition, the poorer countries generally have the highest rates of population growth, so income per capita can fall if population increases faster than the rate of economic development. Economists tell us that a developing country may, at least initially, experience

an increase in inequality, but the inequality often decreases over time. Will the inequalities among countries also decrease as the world economy develops further?

If it is true that the disparity between rich and poor countries has increased in recent years, it is also true that the world has seen improvement in some respects. The United Nations has computed a "human development index" for 177 countries, combining measures of life expectancy, literacy, and a measure of per capita purchasing power. According to this index, most countries, including developing countries, have improved substantially between 1990 and 2005. For example, Bangladesh, China, and Uganda have increased their ranking by about 20 percent between 1990 and 2005. Some countries are doing worse—most of these are in sub-Saharan Africa or had been parts of the former Soviet Union. World leaders at the United Nations Millennium Declaration have committed themselves to a number of goals by the year 2015, including halving the proportion of people living in extreme poverty and halving the proportion of people suffering from hunger. Even if those goals are achieved, much more will remain to be done if we are to achieve a more equal world.

Sources: United Nations Development Programme 2007; UN News Centre 2005; Milanovic 2005.

occur, children of the union were often regarded as having lower status than European American children, even though they may have had blond hair and light skin. In the South, where treatment of African Americans as a caste was most apparent, European Americans refused to eat with African Americans or sit next to them at lunch counters, on buses, and in schools. Separate drinking fountains and toilets reinforced the idea of ritual uncleanness. The economic advantages and gains in prestige that European Americans enjoyed are well documented.[36]

In the following sections on slavery, racism, and inequality, we discuss the social status of African Americans in more detail.

Slavery

Slaves are people who do not own their own labor, and as such they represent a class. We may associate slavery with a few well-known examples, such as ancient Egypt, Greece, and Rome or the southern United States, but slavery has existed in some form in almost every part of the world at one time or another, in simpler as well as in more complex societies. Slaves are often obtained from other cultures directly: kidnapped, captured in war, or given as tribute. Or they may be obtained indirectly as payment in barter or trade. Slaves sometimes come from the same culture; one became a slave as payment of a debt, as a punishment for a crime, or even as a chosen alternative to poverty. Slave societies vary in the degree to which it is possible to become freed from slavery.[37] Sometimes the slavery system has been a closed class, or caste, system, sometimes a relatively open class system. In different slave-owning societies, slaves have had different, but always some, legal rights.[38]

In ancient Greece, slaves often were conquered enemies. Because city-states were constantly conquering one another or rebelling against former conquerors, slavery was a threat to everyone. After the Trojan War, the transition of Hecuba from queen to slave was marked by her cry, "Count no one happy, however fortunate, before he dies."[39] Nevertheless, Greek slaves were considered human beings, and they could even acquire some higher-class status along with freedom. Andromache, Hecuba's daughter-in-law, was taken as a slave and concubine by one of the Greek heroes. When his legal wife produced no children, Andromache's slave son became heir to his father's throne. Although slaves had no rights under law, once they were freed, either by the will of their master or by purchase, they and their descendants could become assimilated into the dominant group. In other words, slavery in Greece was not seen as the justified position of inferior people. It was regarded, rather, as an act of fate—"the luck of the draw"—that relegated one to the lowest class in society.

Among the Nupe, a society in central Nigeria, slavery was of quite another type.[40] The methods of obtaining slaves—as part of the booty of warfare and, later, by purchase—were similar to those of Europeans, but the position of the slaves was very different. Mistreatment was rare. Male slaves were given the same opportunities to earn money as other dependent males in the household—younger brothers, sons, or other relatives. A slave might be given a garden plot of his own to cultivate, or he might be given a commission if his master was a craftsman or a tradesman. Slaves could acquire property, wealth, and even slaves of their own. But all of a slave's belongings went to the master at the slave's death.

Manumission—the granting of freedom to slaves—was built into the Nupe system. If a male slave could afford the marriage payment for a free woman, the children of the resulting marriage were free; the man himself, however, remained a slave. Marriage and concubinage were the easiest ways out of bondage for a slave woman. Once she had produced a child by her master, both she and the child had free status. The woman, however, was only figuratively free; if a concubine, she had to remain in that role. As might be expected, the family trees of the nobility and the wealthy were liberally grafted with branches descended from slave concubines.

The most fortunate slaves among the Nupe were the house slaves. They could rise to positions of power in the household as overseers and bailiffs, charged with law enforcement and judicial duties. (Recall the Old Testament story of Joseph, who was sold into slavery by his brothers. Joseph became a household slave of the pharaoh and rose to the position of second in the kingdom because he devised an ingenious system of taxation.) There was even a titled group of Nupe slaves, the Order of Court Slaves, who were trusted officers of the king and members of an elite. Slave status in general, though, placed one at the bottom of the social ladder. In the Nupe system, few slaves, mainly princes from their own societies, ever achieved membership in the titled group. Nupe slavery was abolished at the beginning of the 20th century.

In the United States, slavery originated as a means of obtaining cheap labor, but the slaves soon came to be regarded as deserving of their low status because of their alleged inherent inferiority. Because the slaves were from Africa and were dark-skinned (see the DK map "Trading in Human Lives" at the back of the book), some European Americans justified slavery and the belief in "black" people's inferiority by quoting scripture out of context ("They shall be hewers of wood and drawers of water"). Slaves could not marry or make any other contracts, nor could they own property. In addition, their children were also slaves, and the master had sexual rights over the female slaves. Because the status of slavery was determined by birth in the United States, slaves constituted a caste. During the days of slavery, therefore, the United States had both a caste and a class system. It is widely assumed that slavery occurred only in the southern United States, but although not on as large a scale, slavery existed in the northern states as well. New Jersey was the last northern state to legally give up slavery around the time of the U.S. Civil War.[41]

Even after the abolition of slavery, as we have noted, some castelike elements remained. It is important to note that these castelike elements were not limited to the American South where slavery had been practiced. For example, although Indiana was established as a "free" state in 1816, in its first constitution, "negros" did not have the right to vote nor could they intermarry with "whites." In the constitution of 1851, Indiana did not allow "negros" to come into the state, nor did it allow the existing African American residents to attend public schools even though they had to pay school taxes.[42] In Muncie, Indiana, in the first half of the 20th century, there was customary segregation in shows, restaurants, and parks. Not until the 1950s was the public swimming pool desegregated.[43]

As for why slavery may have developed in the first place, cross-cultural research is as yet inconclusive. We do know, however, that slavery is not an inevitable stage in economic development, contrary to what some have assumed. In other words, slavery is not found mainly in certain economies, such as those dependent on intensive agriculture. Unlike the United States until the Civil War, many societies with intensive agriculture did not develop any variety of slavery. Also, the hypothesis that slavery develops where available resources are plentiful but labor is scarce is not supported by the cross-cultural evidence. All we can say definitely is that slavery does not occur in developed or industrial economies; either it disappears or it was never present in them.[44]

RACISM AND INEQUALITY

Racism is the belief that some "races" are inferior to others. In a society composed of people with noticeably different physical features, such as differences in skin color, racism is almost invariably associated with social stratification. Those "races" considered inferior make up a larger proportion of the lower social classes or castes. Even in more open class systems, where individuals from all backgrounds can achieve higher status positions, individuals from groups deemed inferior may be subject to discrimination in housing or may be more likely to be searched or stopped by the police.

In some societies, such as the United States, the idea that humans are divided into "races" is taken so much for granted that people are asked for their "race" on the census. Most Americans probably assume that the classification of people into categories such as "white" or "black" reflects important biological categories. But that is not so. We now know from genetic research that there is enormous genetic diversity within the African continent, in fact, more than between Africa and any other continent.[45] There is no clear boundary where one trait is present or absent. For example, in the area around Egypt, there is a gradient of skin color as you move from north to south in the Nile Valley. Nose shape varies with humidity, but its gradient is not the same as the gradient for skin color, so the two distributions are quite different. Both of these characteristics make it impossible to draw discrete boundaries between groups on the basis of external traits such as skin color and nose shape. The genetic diversity within Africa is consistent with the fossil evidence that the African continent is where both early humans and modern humans emerged. This is as you may remember, parallel to linguistic diversity—English developed in England, and there we find the most dialect diversity. Modern humans emerged first in Africa, so it is accurate to say that we are all African, and members of the "human race."

You may have noticed that we put "race" in quotes to reflect the fact that most anthropologists are now persuaded that the biological concept of "race" is not scientifically useful when applied to humans. However, "race" is a social concept that is important as a classifier in some societies.

Race as a Social Category

Racial classifications are social categories to which individuals are assigned, by themselves and others, to separate "our" group from others. We have seen that people tend to be *ethnocentric,* to view their culture as better than other cultures. Racial classifications may reflect the same tendency to divide "us" from "them," except that the divisions are supposedly based on biological differences.[46] The "them" are almost always viewed as inferior to "us."

We know that racial classifications have often been, and still are, used by certain groups to justify discrimination, exploitation, or genocide. The "Aryan race" was supposed to be the group of blond-haired, blue-eyed, white-skinned people whom Adolf Hitler wanted to dominate the world, to which end he and others attempted to destroy as many members of the Jewish "race" as they could. (An estimated 6 million Jews and others were murdered in what is now called the Holocaust.[47]) But who were the Aryans? Technically, Aryans are any people, including the German-speaking Jews in Hitler's Germany, who speak one of the Indo-European languages. The Indo-European languages include such disparate modern tongues as Greek, Spanish, Hindi, Polish, French, Icelandic, German, Gaelic, and English. And many Aryans speaking these languages have neither blond hair nor blue eyes. Similarly, all kinds of people may be Jews, whether or not they descend from the

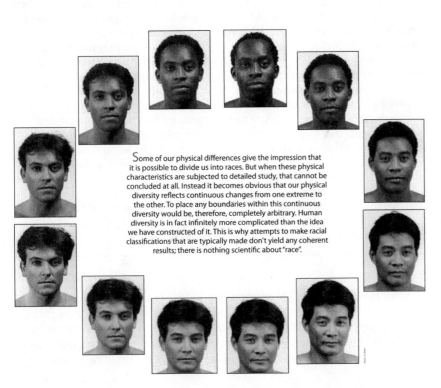

Some of our physical differences give the impression that it is possible to divide us into races. But when these physical characteristics are subjected to detailed study, that cannot be concluded at all. Instead it becomes obvious that our physical diversity reflects continuous changes from one extreme to the other. To place any boundaries within this continuous diversity would be, therefore, completely arbitrary. Human diversity is in fact infinitely more complicated than the idea we have constructed of it. This is why attempts to make racial classifications that are typically made don't yield any coherent results; there is nothing scientific about "race".

It is an illusion that there are races. The diversity of human beings is so great and so complicated that it is impossible to classify the 5.8 billions of individuals into discrete "races."

applied anthropology

Unequal in Death: African Americans Compared with European Americans

Everyone dies of something. Yet, if you consider cardiovascular disease, the leading cause of death in the United States, it turns out that after controlling for the effects of age and gender, African Americans die more often from that disease than European Americans. The same kind of disparity occurs also with almost every other major cause of death—cancer, cirrhosis of the liver, kidney disease, diabetes, injuries, infant mortality, and homicide. Medical anthropologists and health policy researchers want to know why. Without such understanding, it is hard to know how to reduce the disparity.

One reason may be subtle discrimination by the medical profession itself. For example, a European American with chest pain in the United States is more likely than an African American to be given an angiogram, a medical procedure that injects radioactive dye into the heart to look for deficits in blood flow through the coronary arteries that supply blood to the heart. And even if coronary heart disease is detected by an angiogram, an African American is less likely to receive bypass surgery. Thus, the death rate from cardiovascular disease may be higher for African Americans than for European Americans because of unequal medical care. Seeing a patient physically appears to make a difference. When heart specialists reviewed cases to make decisions about subsequent treatment after catheterization, recommendations did not differ by "race" when the doctors did not know the "race" of the patient.

Yet, although some difference in mortality may be due to disparity in medical treatment, this could only be part of the picture. African Americans may be more prone to cardiovascular disease because they are about twice as likely as European Americans to have high rates of hypertension (high blood pressure). But, why the disparity in hypertension? Three possible explanations, not mutually exclusive, are discussed in the research literature. The first is a possible difference in genetics. The second is a difference in lifestyle. The third is class difference.

Most of the Africans that came to the Americas were forcibly taken as slaves between the 16th and 19th centuries, largely from West Africa. In one comparative study of hypertension, African Americans had much higher blood pressure than Africans in Nigeria and Cameroon, even in urban areas. People with African ancestry in the Caribbean were in the middle of the range. Lifestyle differences were also vast—the West Africans had plenty of exercise, were lean, and ate low-fat and low-salt diets. Any possible difference in genes would seem to be insignificant. Jared Diamond has suggested that individuals who could retain salt would have been most likely to survive the terrible conditions of the sailing ships that brought slaves to the New World. Many died from diarrhea and dehydration (salt-depleting conditions) on those voyages. Retention of salt would have been a genetic advantage then, but disadvantageous in places such as the United States with high-salt, high-fat diets. Critics of this theory suggest that salt-depleting diseases were not the leading causes of death in the slave voyages; tuberculosis and violence were more frequent causes of death. Furthermore, critics say that the slave ship theory would predict little genetic diversity in African American populations with respect to hypertension, but in fact there is great diversity.

Hypertension could be related also to differences in lifestyle and wealth. As we noted in the section on racism and inequality, African Americans in the United States are disproportionately poorer. Study after study has noted that healthier lifestyle habits are generally correlated with higher positions on the socioeconomic ladder. Moreover, individuals from higher social positions are more likely to have health insurance and access to care in superior hospitals. But even after correcting for factors such as obesity, physical activity, and social class, the health differential persists—African Americans still have a much higher incidence of hypertension than European Americans.

William Dressler suggests that stress is another possible cause of higher rates of hypertension. Despite increased economic mobility in recent years, African Americans are still subject to prejudice and may consequently have more stress even if they have higher income. Stress is related to higher blood pressure. In a color-conscious society, a very dark-skinned individual walking in a wealthy neighborhood at night may be thought not to live there and may be stopped by the police. If Dressler is correct, darker-skinned African Americans who have objective indicators of higher status should have much higher blood pressure than would be expected from their relative education, age, body mass, or social class alone. And that seems to be true. Racism may affect health.

Sources: Smedley et al. 2003, 3; Geiger 2003; Dressler 1993; Cooper et al. 1999, 56–63; Diamond 1991.

ancient Near Eastern population that spoke the Hebrew language. There are light-skinned Danish Jews and darker Jewish Arabs. One of the most orthodox Jewish groups in the United States is based in New York City and is composed entirely of African Americans.

The arbitrary and social basis of most racial classifications becomes apparent when you compare how they differ from one place to another. Consider, for example, what used to be thought about the "races" in South Africa. Under apartheid, which was a system of racial segregation and discrimination, someone with mixed "white" and "black" ancestry was considered "colored." However, when important people of African ancestry (from other countries) would visit South Africa, they were often considered "white." Chinese were considered "Asian"; but the Japanese, who were important economically to South Africa, were considered "white."[48] In some parts of the United States, laws against interracial marriage continued in force through the 1960s. You would be considered a "negro" if you had an eighth or more "negro" ancestry (if one or more of your eight grandparents were "negro").[49] In some states, an even smaller proportion made you "negro." Some refer to this concept as the "one-drop" rule—just a tiny bit of "negro" (now called "black") ancestry was sufficient to determine your "racial" classification.[50] So only a small amount of "negro" ancestry made a person "negro." But a small amount of "white" ancestry did not make a person "white." Biologically speaking, this makes no sense, but socially it was another story.[51]

In much of Latin America and the Caribbean, the reverse rule is the case. A small amount of European blood can make you "white." When people from Dominica, Haiti, or Cuba come to the United States, they often find that their "race" has changed. They might have been considered "white" at home, but they are considered "black" in the United States. In contrast to the United States with a two-part division of "white" and "black," concepts of race in Latin America are on more of a continuum from light to dark, with important middle positions (such as "mestizo"). Wealth makes a difference too—if you are dark-skinned, but wealthy, you will tend to be considered "whiter."[52]

If people of different "races" are viewed as inferior, they are more likely going to end up on the lower rungs of the social ladder in a socially stratified society. Discrimination will keep them out of the better-paying or higher-status jobs and in neighborhoods that are poorer. As the box "Unequal in Death" shows, people of different "races" also suffer from differential access to health care and have more health problems.

ETHNICITY AND INEQUALITY

If "race" is not a scientifically useful category because people cannot be clearly divided into different "racial" categories based on sets of physical traits, then racial classifications such as "black" and "white" in the United States might better be described as *ethnic* classifications. How else can we account for the following facts? Groups that are thought of as "white" now in the United States were earlier thought of as belonging to inferior "races." For example, in the latter half of the 19th century, newspapers would often talk about the new immigrants from Ireland as belonging to the Irish "race." Similarly, before World War II, Jews were thought of as a separate "racial" group, and only became "white" afterward.[53] It is hard to escape the idea that changes in "racial" classification occurred as the Irish, Jews, and other immigrant groups became more accepted by the majority in the United States.[54]

It is apparent that *ethnic groups* and *ethnic identities* emerge as part of a social and political process. The process of defining **ethnicity** usually involves a group of people emphasizing common origins and language,

Members of minority ethnic groups are more often at the bottom of the socioeconomic "ladder," but not always, as these pictures from the United States illustrate.

shared history, and selected cultural differences such as a difference in religion. Those doing the defining can be outside or inside the ethnic group. Outsiders and insiders often perceive ethnic groups differently. In a country with one large core majority group, often the majority group doesn't think of itself as an ethnic group. Rather, they consider only the minority groups to have ethnic identities. For example, in the United States, it is not common for the majority to call themselves European Americans, but other groups may be called African Americans, Asian Americans, or Native Americans. The minority groups, on the other hand, may also have different named identities.[55] Asian Americans may identify themselves more specifically as Japanese Americans, Korean Americans, Chinese Americans, or Hmong. The majority population often uses derogatory names to identify people who are different. The majority may also tend to lump people of diverse ethnicities together. Naming a group establishes a boundary between it and other ethnic groups.[56]

Ethnic differences can sometimes arise from class differences. Rwanda is a good case in point. By the end of the 19th century, Rwandans were part of a kingdom with significant class distinctions, but the distinctions between Hutu and Tutsi, so important in recent times, were not very important or clear.[57] Cattle were an important form of wealth and, although many people known as Tutsi were cattle herders and many known as Hutu were agriculturalists, many Tutsi and Hutu were both. If Hutu acquired wealth and intermarried with Tutsi, they could move up in rank. A Tutsi could lose cattle and turn to cultivation.[58] Colonialism did not create differentiation between Tutsi and Hutu, but it did accentuate it. For example, the Belgian administration tried to reinforce the power of the "natural rulers" (the Tutsi), and they issued identity cards in the 1930s to distinguish Tutsi, Hutu, and Twa (the Twa were discussed earlier in the caste section). During the colonial period, the idea developed that the three groups were biologically different from each other. It was commonly thought that the taller Tutsi were different people who originally conquered the others.[59]

When the Hutu united to demand more of the rewards of their labor in 1959, the king and many of the Tutsi ruling elite were driven out of the country. The Hutu then established a republican form of government and declared independence from Belgium in 1962. In 1990, Tutsi rebels invaded from Uganda, and attempts were made to negotiate a multiparty government. However, civil war continued, and in 1994 alone, over a million people, mostly Tutsi, were killed. Almost 2 million refugees, mostly Hutu, fled to Zaire as the Tutsi-led rebels established a new government.[60] In the intervening years, the Rwandan government has made progress in bringing home the refugees, bringing those who committed genocide to trial, and integrating different groups into the government.[61]

Ethnic identity may be manipulated, by insiders and by outsiders, in different situations. A particularly repressive regime that emphasizes nationalism and loyalty to the state may not only suppress the assertiveness of ethnic claims; it may also act to minimize communication among people who might otherwise embrace the same ethnic identity.[62] More democratic regimes may allow more expression of difference and celebrate ethnic difference. However, manipulation of ethnicity does not come just from the top. It may be to the advantage of minority groups to lobby for more equal treatment as a larger entity, such as Asian American, rather than as Japanese, Chinese, Hmong, Filipino, or Korean American. Similarly, even though there are hundreds of Native American groups, originally speaking different languages, there may be political advantages for all if they are treated as Native Americans.

In many multiethnic societies, ethnicity and diversity are things to be proud of and celebrated. Shared ethnic identity often makes people feel comfortable with similar people and gives them a strong sense of belonging. Still, ethnic differences in multiethnic societies are usually associated with inequities in wealth, power, and prestige. In other words, ethnicity is part of the system of *stratification*.

Although some people believe that inequities are deserved, the origins of ethnic stereotypes, prejudice, and discrimination usually follow from historical and political events that give some groups dominance over others. For example, even though there were many early stories of help given by native peoples to the English settlers in the 17th century in the land now known as North America, the English were the invaders, and negative stereotypes about native peoples developed to justify taking their land and their lives. Referring to the negative stereotypes of Native Americans that developed, J. Milton Yinger said, "One would almost think that it had been the Indian who had invaded Europe, driven back the inhabitants, cut their population to one-third of its original size, unilaterally changed treaties, and brought the dubious glories of firewater and firearms."[63]

Similarly, as we noted in the section on slavery, African slaves were initially acquired as cheap labor, but inhumane treatment of slaves was justified by beliefs about their inferiority. Unfortunately, stereotypes can become self-fulfilling prophesies, especially if those discriminated against come to believe the stereotypes. It is easy to see how this can happen. If there is a widespread belief that a group is inferior, and that group is given inferior schools and little chance for improvement or little chance for a good job, the members of that group may acquire few skills and not try hard. The result is often a vicious cycle.[64]

And yet, the picture is not all bleak. Change has occurred. The ethnic identity a minority group forges can help promote political activism, such as the nonviolent civil rights movement in the United States in the 1960s. That activism, helped by some people in the more advantaged groups, helped break down many of the legal barriers and segregationist practices that reinforced inequality.

The traditional barriers in the United States have mostly been lifted in recent years, but the "color line" has not disappeared. African Americans are found in all social classes, but they remain underrepresented in the wealthiest group and overrepresented at the bottom. Discrimination may be lessened, but it is still not gone. In research done with matched pairs of "whites" and "blacks" applying for jobs or for housing, discrimination is still evident.[65] Thus, African Americans may have to be better than others to get promoted, or it may be assumed that they got ahead just because they were African American and were hired because of affirmative action programs. European Americans often expect African Americans to be "ambassadors," to be called on mainly for knowledge about how to handle situations involving other African Americans. African Americans may work with others, but they usually go home to African American neighborhoods. Or they may live in mixed neighborhoods and experience considerable isolation. Few African Americans can completely avoid the anguish of racism.[66]

THE EMERGENCE OF STRATIFICATION

Anthropologists are not certain why social stratification developed. Nevertheless, they are reasonably sure that higher levels of stratification emerged relatively recently in human history. Archaeological sites dating before about 8,000 years ago do not show extensive evidence of inequality. Houses do not appear to vary much in size or content, and different communities of the same culture are similar in size and otherwise. Signs of inequality appear first in the Near East, about 2,000 years after agriculture emerged in that region. Inequality in burial suggests inequality in life. Particularly telling are unequal child burials. It is unlikely that children could achieve high status by their own achievements. So, when archaeologists find statues and ornaments only in some children's tombs, as at the 7,500-year-old site of Tell es-Sawwan in Iraq,[67] the grave goods suggest that those children belonged to a higher-ranking family or a higher class.

Another indication that stratification is a relatively recent development in human history is the fact that certain cultural features associated with stratification also developed relatively recently. For example, most societies that depend primarily on agriculture or herding have social classes.[68] Agriculture and herding developed within the past 10,000 years, so we may assume that most food collectors in the distant past lacked social classes. Other recently developed cultural features associated with class stratification include fixed settlements, political integration beyond the community level, the use of money as a medium of exchange, and the presence of at least some full-time specialization.[69]

In 1966, the comparative sociologist Gerhard Lenski suggested that the trend toward increasing inequality since 8,000 years ago was reversing. He argued that inequalities of power and privilege in industrial societies—measured in terms of the concentration of political power and the distribution of income—are less pronounced than inequalities in complex preindustrial societies. Technology in industrialized societies is so complex, he suggested, that those in power are compelled to delegate some authority to subordinates if the system is to work. In addition, a decline in the birth rate in industrialized societies, coupled with the need for skilled labor, has pushed the average wage of workers far above the subsistence level, resulting in greater equality in the distribution of income. Finally, Lenski also suggested that the spread of the democratic ideology, and particularly its acceptance by elites, has significantly broadened the political power of the lower classes.[70] A few studies have tested and supported Lenski's hypothesis that inequality has decreased with industrialization. In general, nations that are highly industrialized exhibit a lower level of inequality than nations that are only somewhat industrialized.[71] But, as we have seen, even the most industrialized societies may still have an enormous degree of inequality.

Why did social stratification develop in the first place? On the basis of his study of Polynesian societies, Marshall Sahlins suggested that an increase in agricultural productivity results in social stratification.[72] According to Sahlins, the degree of stratification is directly related to the production of a surplus, which is made possible by greater technological efficiency. The higher the level of productivity and the larger the agricultural surplus, the greater the scope and complexity of the distribution system. The status of the chief, who serves as redistributing agent, is enhanced. Sahlins argued that the differentiation between distributor and producer inevitably gives rise to differentiation in other aspects of life:

> First, there would be a tendency for the regulator of distribution to exert some authority over production itself—especially over productive activities which necessitate subsidization, such as communal labor or specialist labor. A degree of control of production implies a degree of control over the utilization of resources, or, in other words, some preeminent property rights. In turn, regulation of these economic processes necessitates the exercise of authority in interpersonal affairs; differences in social power emerge.[73]

Sahlins later rejected the idea that a surplus leads to chiefships, postulating instead that the relationship may be the other way around—that is, leaders encourage the development of a surplus so as to enhance their prestige through feasts, potlatches, and other redistributive events.[74] Of course, both trajectories are possible—surpluses may generate stratification, and stratification may generate surpluses; they are not mutually exclusive.

Lenski's theory of the causes of stratification is similar to Sahlins's original idea. Lenski, too, argued that production of a surplus is the stimulus in the development of stratification, but he focused primarily on the conflict that arises over control of that surplus. Lenski concluded that the distribution of the surplus will be determined on the basis of power. Thus, inequalities in power promote unequal access to economic resources and simultaneously give rise to inequalities in privilege and prestige.[75]

The "surplus" theories of Sahlins and Lenski do not really address the question of why the redistributors or leaders will want, or be able, to acquire greater control over resources. After all, the redistributors or leaders in many rank societies do not have greater wealth than others, and custom seems to keep things that way. One suggestion is that, as long as followers have mobility, they can vote with their feet by moving away from leaders they do not like. But when people start to make more permanent "investments" in land or technology (e.g., irrigation systems or weirs for fishing), they are more likely to put up with a leader's aggrandizement in exchange for protection.[76] Another suggestion is that access to economic resources becomes unequal only when there is population pressure on resources in rank or chiefdom societies.[77] Such pressure may be what induces redistributors to try to keep more land and other resources for themselves and their families.

C. K. Meek offered an example of how population pressure in northern Nigeria may have led to economic stratification. At one time, a tribal member could obtain the right to use land by asking permission of the chief and presenting him with a token gift in recognition of his higher status. But, by 1921, the reduction in the amount of available land had led to a system under which applicants offered the chief large payments for scarce land. As a result of these payments, farms came to be regarded as private property, and differential access to such property became institutionalized.[78]

Future research by archaeologists, sociologists, historians, and anthropologists should provide more understanding of the emergence of social stratification in human societies and how and why it may vary in degree.

SUMMARY ● ○ ○

1. Without exception, recent and modern industrial and postindustrial societies such as our own are socially stratified—that is, they contain social groups such as families, classes, or ethnic groups that have unequal access to important advantages, such as economic resources, power, and prestige. Anthropologists, based on firsthand observations, would say that such inequality has not always existed among the societies they have studied. Although even the simplest societies (in the technological sense) have some differences in advantages based on age, ability, or gender—adults have higher status than children, the skilled more than the unskilled, men more than women (we discuss gender stratification in the chapter on sex, gender, and culture)—anthropologists would argue that egalitarian societies exist where social groups (e.g., families) have more or less the same access to rights or advantages.

2. The presence or absence of customs or rules that give certain groups unequal access to economic resources, power, and prestige can be used to distinguish three types of societies. In egalitarian societies, social groups do not have unequal access to economic resources, power, or prestige; they are unstratified. In rank societies, social groups do not have very unequal access to economic resources or power, but they do have unequal access to prestige. Rank societies, then, are partially stratified. In class societies, social groups have unequal access to economic resources, power, and prestige. They are more completely stratified than are rank societies.

3. Stratified societies range from somewhat open class systems to caste systems, which are extremely rigid, because caste membership is fixed permanently at birth.

4. Slaves are people who do not own their own labor; as such, they represent a class and sometimes even a caste. Slavery has existed in various forms in many times and places, regardless of "race" and culture. Sometimes slavery is a rigid and closed, or caste, system; sometimes it is a relatively open class system.

5. Within a society composed of people from widely divergent backgrounds and different physical features, such as skin color, racism is almost invariably associated with social stratification. Those "races" considered inferior make up a larger proportion of the lower social classes or castes. In the opinion of many biological anthropologists, "race" is not a scientifically useful device for classifying humans. "Racial" classifications should be recognized for what they mostly are—social categories to which individuals are assigned, by themselves and others, on the basis of supposedly shared biological traits.

6. In multiethnic societies, ethnic differences are usually associated with inequities in wealth, power, and prestige. In other words, ethnicity is part of the system of stratification.

7. Social stratification appears to have emerged relatively recently in human history, about 8,000 years ago. This conclusion is based on archaeological evidence and on the fact that certain cultural features associated with stratification developed relatively recently.

8. One theory suggests that social stratification developed as productivity increased and surpluses were produced. Another suggestion is that stratification can develop only when people have "investments" in land or technology and therefore cannot move away from leaders they do not like. A third theory suggests that stratification emerges only when there is population pressure on resources in rank societies.

GLOSSARY TERMS ○ ● ○

caste   **141**
class   **139**
class societies   **136**
economic resources   **136**
egalitarian societies   **136**
ethnicity   **147**
manumission   **144**
power   **136**
prestige   **136**
racism   **145**
rank societies   **136**
slaves   **143**

CRITICAL QUESTIONS ○ ○ ●

1. What might be some of the social consequences of large differences in wealth? Explain your reasoning.

2. Is an industrial or a developed economy incompatible with a more egalitarian distribution of resources? Why or why not?

3. In a multiethnic society, does ethnic identity help or hinder social equality? Explain your answer.

4. Why do you suppose the degree of inequality has decreased in some countries in recent years?

Read "Haitians: From Political Repression to Chaos" by Robert Lawless on MyAnthroLab. Answer the questions below.

1. In what ways does Lawless suggest that the elite in Haiti maintain their power?

2. Why does Lawless say that "Voodoo" is an egalitarian religion?

3. Explain what role slavery played in Haitian history.

chapter 9

Culture
and the Individual

nthropology, with its focus on culture, may seem to ignore the individual. To be sure, individuals provide information about culture, but their psychological characteristics, a central concern of psychology, are often considered irrelevant. However, there are anthropologists who think that understanding individuals and psychological processes is vital to anthropological understanding. Take culture change as an example. As we discussed in the chapter on the concept of culture and culture change, *individuals* are ultimately the source of culture change. They discover and invent, they adopt new behaviors or ideas from others, or they resist or accommodate to changes other societies try to impose. Culture changes only when enough individuals alter their ideas or their patterns of behavior. Individuals are the *agents* of change.

Anthropologists who are interested in the relationships between culture and the individual and the importance of understanding psychological processes call themselves *psychological anthropologists*. Psychologists who study people in two or more societies call themselves *cross-cultural psychologists*. Four main questions seem to characterize psychological anthropology: (1) To what extent do all human beings develop psychologically in the same ways? (2) If there are differences, what are they and what may account for them? (3) How do people in different societies conceive of individuals and their psychological development? and (4) How can understanding individuals or psychological processes help us understand culture and culture change? This chapter discusses some of the attempts of researchers to answer some of these questions.

● ○ ●

THE UNIVERSALITY OF
PSYCHOLOGICAL DEVELOPMENT

Anthropologists became interested in psychology in the early years of the 20th century partly because they did not believe that human nature was completely revealed in Western societies, as psychologists then generally assumed. Only recently have many psychologists joined anthropologists in questioning the assumption that humans are exactly the same psychologically in all societies. Psychologist Otto Klineberg, for example, scolded his psychologist colleagues in 1974: "My contact with anthropology affected me somewhat like a religious conversion. How could psychologists speak of *human* attributes and *human* behavior when they knew only one kind of human being?"[1]

How can we know what is universal about human behavior and what is variable until we study all kinds of humans? Because humans the world over are the same species and share a very large proportion of their genes, we might assume that there is a good deal of similarity across societies in the way people develop psychologically from birth to maturity or in the ways they think, feel, and behave. We have already discussed many universals—culture, language, marriage, the incest taboo—but here we discuss some that are related more to psychology. Donald Brown compiled a list of probable human universals in the psychological

realm.[2] They include the ability to create taxonomies, make binary contrasts, order phenomena, use logical operators (e.g., *and, not, equals*), plan for the future, and have an understanding of the world and what it is about.

With regard to ideas about people, it seems universal to have a concept of the self or person, to recognize individual faces, to try to discern other peoples' intentions from observable clues in their faces, utterances, and actions, and to imagine what others are thinking. With regard to emotions, people seem universally to be able to empathize with the feelings of others; facially communicate and recognize, as well as hide or mimic, the emotions of happiness, sadness, anger, fear, surprise, disgust, and contempt (see the box "Do Masks Show Emotion in Universal Ways?" in the chapter on the arts); smile when friendly; cry when in pain or unhappy; play for fun; show and feel affection for others; feel sexual attraction, envy, and jealousy; and have similar childhood fears (e.g., fear of strangers). Indeed, it seems that people in different cultures even conceive of love in much the same ways, despite love's reputation as something mysterious and culturally variable.[3]

What about psychological development? We saw in the chapter on communication and language that certain aspects of language acquisition appear to be universal across cultures. In what respects is psychological development the same the world over? In what respects is it different?

Early Research on Emotional Development

When Margaret Mead went to American Samoa in the mid-1920s, psychologists believed that adolescence was universally a period of "storm and stress" because of the physiological changes that occur at puberty. Mead's observations of, and interviews with, Samoan adolescent girls led her to doubt the idea that adolescence was necessarily a time of turmoil. Samoan girls apparently showed little evidence of emotional upheaval and rebelliousness, and therefore it was questionable whether psychological development in adolescence was the same in all societies.[4]

Bronislaw Malinowski, another early anthropologist, questioned the universality of an assumption about emotional development, in this case Freud's assumption that young boys universally see themselves, unconsciously, as sexual rivals of their fathers for possession of their mothers. Freud called these feelings the *Oedipus complex,* after the character in Greek mythology who killed his father and married his mother without knowing that they were his parents. Freud thought that all boys before the age of 7 or so would show hostility toward their fathers, but Malinowski disagreed on the basis of his fieldwork in the Trobriand Islands.[5]

Malinowski suggested that young boys in male-oriented societies may feel hostility toward the father not as a sexual rival but as the disciplinarian. Malinowski proposed this theory because he thought that the Oedipus complex works differently in societies organized around the female line, such as the matrilineal Trobriands. In matrilineal

societies, the mother's brother is the main authority figure in the matrilineal kin group—than toward their father.

Derek Freeman criticized Mead's conclusions about Samoa,[6] and Melford Spiro challenged Malinowski's conclusions about the Trobriand Islanders.[7] Mead and Malinowski may or may not have been correct about the societies they studied, but the issues they raised remain crucial to the question of whether psychological development is similar across societies. To find out, we need research in many societies, not just a few. Only on the basis of extensive cross-cultural research will we be able to decide whether stages of emotional development can be affected by cultural differences.

For example, only recently has adolescence been systematically studied cross-culturally. Alice Schlegel and Herbert Barry reported that adolescence is generally not a period of overt rebelliousness. The reason, they suggested, is related to the fact that most people in most societies live with or near (and depend on) close kin before and after they grow up. Only in societies like our own, where children leave home when they grow up, might adolescents be rebellious, possibly to prepare emotionally for going out on their own.[8] (See the box "Neolocality and Adolescent Rebellion: Are They Related?" in the chapter on marital residence and kinship.)

Adolescence in many societies is a time for developing work skills. An Asmat boy in Indonesian New Guinea is learning to carve, and an adult is supervising.

Research on Cognitive Development

One day the Embers went out for pizza. The pizza maker was laughing hilariously, and we asked what was so funny. He told us: "I just asked the guy ahead of you, 'How many slices do you want me to cut the pizza into, six or eight?' 'Six,' he said, 'I'm not very hungry.'" According to a theory of cognitive (intellectual) development suggested by Jean Piaget, the renowned Swiss psychologist, the "not very hungry" guy may not have acquired the concept of *conservation*, which characterizes a stage of thinking normally acquired by children between the ages of 7 and 11 in Western societies.[9] The pizza customer ahead of us, like many very young children, seemed not to understand that certain properties of an object, such as quantity, weight, and volume, remain constant even if the object is divided into small pieces or removed to a container of a different shape. They have not acquired the mental image of *reversibility*, the ability to imagine that if you put the pizza back together again it would be the same size whether you had cut it into eight or six slices. To the child or adult who has not acquired the ability to reverse actions mentally, eight slices may seem like more pizza than six slices, because eight is more than six.

Piaget's theory says that the development of thinking in humans involves a series of stages, each of which is characterized by different mental skills. To get to a higher stage of thinking, one has to pass through a lower stage. So Piaget's theory would predict that the pizza customer would not be able to think systematically about the possible outcomes of hypothetical situations, a defining feature of Piaget's *formal-operational* stage, because he had not acquired the notion of conservation and the other mental skills that characterize the previous, *concrete-operational* stage of cognitive development.

What does the evidence suggest about the universality of Piaget's supposed stages? And do people the world over get to each stage at the same age? The first stage of development, *sensorimotor*, has not been investigated in many societies, but the results of studies conducted so far are remarkably consistent. They support Piaget's notion that there is a predictable order in the sequence of stages.[10] And, on the basis of their reactions to the same conditions, babies in different places seem to think similarly. For example, a comparison of French babies and Baoulé babies in the Ivory Coast showed that the Baoulé babies, who had never seen objects such as red plastic tubes and paper clips, nevertheless tried to pass the clips through the tubes in the same way the French babies did. The two sets of babies even made the same kinds of errors.[11] And even though they had few toys, the Baoulé babies showed advances over French babies on such tasks as using instruments to increase the reach of the arm. But Baoulé babies are allowed to touch all kinds of objects, even things that Europeans consider dangerous.[12]

Most of the cross-cultural studies of Piaget's stages have focused on the transition between the second, *preoperational*, and third, *concrete-operational*, stages, particularly the attainment of the concept of conservation. The results of many of these studies are somewhat puzzling. Although older children are generally more likely to show conservation than younger children, it is not clear what to make of the apparent finding that the attainment of conservation is much delayed in many non-Western populations. Indeed, in some places, most of the adults tested do not appear to understand one or more of the conservation properties.

Can this be true? Do people in different cultures differ that much in intellectual functioning, or is there some problem with the way conservation is measured? Is it possible that an adult who just brought water from the river in a large jug and poured it into five smaller containers does not know that the quantity of water is still the same? We may also be skeptical about the findings on the formal-operational stage. Most of the studies of formal-operational thinking have found little evidence of such thinking in non-Western populations. But people in nonliterate societies surely have formal-operational thinking if they can navigate using the stars, remember how to return to camp after a 15-mile trek, or identify how people are related to each other three and more generations back.

One reason to be skeptical about the apparent findings regarding delay of conservation and formal-operational thinking is that most of the cross-cultural psychologists have taken tests developed in our own and other Western countries to measure cognitive development elsewhere.[13] This procedure puts non-Westerners at a considerable disadvantage, because they are not as familiar as Westerners with the test materials and the whole testing situation. In tests of conservation, for example, researchers have often used strange-looking glass cylinders and beakers. Some researchers who have used natively familiar materials, however, have gotten different results. Douglass Price-Williams found no difference between Tiv, in West Africa, and European children in understanding the conservation of earth, nuts, and number.[14] Also, some researchers have retested children after brief training sessions and found that they improved substantially. It would seem, then, that children anywhere can acquire the concept of conservation if they have had preparatory life experiences or appropriate training.[15]

The results of tests elsewhere on formal-operational thinking may also be questionable. Such tests ask questions dealing with content that is taught in science and mathematics classes. It should not be surprising, then, that schooled individuals usually do better than the unschooled on tests of formal-operational thinking. Where compulsory schooling is lacking, we should not expect people to do well on tests of such thinking.[16]

In trying to find out what may be universal in emotional and cognitive development, researchers have discovered some apparent differences between societies. These differences, to which we now turn, need to be explored and explained.

THE ANTHROPOLOGY OF CHILDHOOD

One thing is common in all human societies—a long period in which the young are dependent on parents and other caretakers. This is one of the most notable human characteristics that differentiates us from our closest biological relatives. Also unusual is the parental role fathers play and the long stage of life following reproduction.[17] In many animals, life ends shortly after reproduction ends. Human females typically stop being able to reproduce much earlier than males, but this gives them a long period of time to be grandmothers and help their children with their reproduction. Exactly why the long period of dependency evolved is a matter of some debate,[18] but this period of time, which we are loosely calling childhood (including here infancy and adolescence), is critical for understanding what kind of people we become. It provides a long period of time to acquire much of the complexity of human social and cultural life. Childhood is also a time when learning from nonparental figures can lead to rapid changes in ideas and behavior. Consider the changes in technology in the world today. Children are much more comfortable, as well as much more adept, with technological innovations than their parents. Children often become the teachers of their parents, showing the parents how to use the new technology.

Anthropologists interested in childhood are increasingly looking at children as agents and actors, not just as recipients of socialization. Children not only have their own culture they can tell us about, but they also have opinions, anxieties, and fears that only they can express. But their voices are often ignored, just as women's voices were often ignored in the past.[19]

It is generally agreed that our personalities are the result of an interaction between genetic inheritance and life experiences. But a considerable portion of one's life experiences, as well as one's genes, is shared with others. Parents undoubtedly exert a major influence on the way we grow up. Because family members share similar life experiences and genes, they may be somewhat similar in personality. But we have to consider why a particular family raises children the way it does. Much of the way parents rear children is influenced by their culture—by typical

patterns of family life and by shared conceptions of the way to bring up children.

Socialization is a term both anthropologists and psychologists use to describe the development, through the influence of parents and other people, of patterns of behavior, and attitudes and values, in children that conform to cultural expectations. (The term **enculturation** has a similar meaning.) But, although these terms imply a mechanism to replicate culture (the "cookie-cutter" view of culture), we know that parents don't always follow societal dictates. Moreover, most parents consciously or unconsciously change with changing times, particularly as their family circumstances change. If a family no longer relies on agriculture because they now rely on wage labor, their expectations and their treatment of children will probably change.

It is not easy to determine the extent to which members of a society share conceptions about childrearing. As we look at families in our own society, we see differences in upbringing that reflect different ideas about the "right" way to raise children. Some parents seem to go along with "conventional" ideas about childrearing; others seem determined to bring up their children in ways that buck the conventional. Still, in a study of California families headed by single mothers, unmarried couples, or living in communes, researchers found that these so-called "unconventional parents" actually did not differ that much from "conventional" parents (married, living in nuclear families) compared with parents in other societies.[20] For example, even though unconventional California mothers breast-fed their children for a significantly longer period than conventional mothers did, both groups usually stopped breast-feeding after about a year, which is far below the worldwide average. In 70 percent of the world's societies, mothers typically breast-feed children for at least two years; last-born children may be weaned even later. In a few societies, such as the Chenchu of India, children typically were not weaned until they were 5 or 6 years old.[21] In the California study, no parent, conventional or unconventional, was observed to carry a baby more than 25 percent of the time, but it is common in many preindustrial societies for babies to be held more than half the day.[22] The point here is that, although some parents tried to be different, and indeed were different, they were in many respects not that different from each other when compared on a worldwide scale. But did the unconventional parents bring about culture change? The parental style of holding babies may not be that common in American culture, but it is much more common than it used to be. So although the new behaviors are not yet customary, cultural patterns have shifted.

Explaining Variation in Childhood and Beyond

When we discuss variation in how children are brought up in the following sections, there are two common types of explanation. The first has to do with general belief systems about children. Societies do not just have ideas about individual aspects of childrearing, such as how often to nurse

Children are adept at using new technology, as this young monk in Burma (Myanmar) demonstrates as he plays a video game.

and for how long, and where to put children to sleep, but societies also have their own theories about childhood. These theories suggest why societies do what they do. In heterogenous societies, different ethnic groups and different classes of people often have different theories. But what might explain these different belief systems? Some belief systems and consequently some childrearing systems may have consequences for survival. Adaptational explanations may suggest why different childrearing customs are adapted to different environments. Finally, there is the possibility that some aspects of personality have genetic or physiological explanations.

Parents' Belief Systems In most of the world, parents do not read books about how to bring up children. Indeed, they may not consciously think at all about their behavior toward children. But parents in all cultures do have ideas about what kinds of children they want to raise and how children should be treated. Many of these ideas are culturally patterned; they have been called "ethnotheories."[23] For example, Sara Harkness and Charles Super, who studied Dutch parents and infants, found that Dutch parents believe in what they term the "three Rs"—*rust* (rest), *regelmaat* (regularity), and *reinheid* (cleanliness). Parents follow a calm and regular routine for babies, try not to overstimulate their children by giving them too many things to look at, and surprisingly, for Americans, have babies who sleep a great deal more. (At six months of age, Dutch babies slept an average of 15 hours a day compared with 13 hours for American babies.) When an American mother will think a baby is bored and give her another toy, a Dutch mother will think the baby is tired and put her to sleep.[24]

Although it is important to understand parental ethnotheories, it is also important to evaluate whether parents behave in accordance with their theories, and whether parental behaviors produce the effects that parents want. Researchers need to observe parent-child behavior, not just understand what parents say they want to do, and they need to observe outcomes in children. Some behaviors by parents and other caretakers do not have the intended effects. American parents, particularly middle-class parents, stress independence and self-reliance, but behavior observations suggest that children frequently seek attention from parents and parents reward this kind of dependency. Even countercultural parents who reject many middle-class values behave in the same ways with their children.[25]

Adaptational Explanations Cultural anthropologists seek not only to establish connections between childrearing customs and personality traits but also to learn why those customs differ in the first place. Some anthropologists believe that childrearing practices are largely adaptive—that a society produces the kinds of personalities best suited to performance of the activities necessary for the survival of the society. As John Whiting and Irvin Child expressed it, "The economic, political and social organs of a society—the basic customs surrounding the nourishment, sheltering, and protection of its members . . . seem a likely source of influence on child training practices."[26]

The belief that childrearing practices are adaptive does not mean that societies always produce the kinds of people they need. Just as in the biological realm, where we see poor adaptations and extinctions of species and subspecies, so we may expect that societies sometimes produce personality traits that are maladapted to the requirements of living in that society. So we cannot assume that a trait must be adaptive just because it is present. We cannot come to that conclusion unless we carefully investigate whether the trait is beneficial or harmful.[27] But we do expect that most societies that have survived to be recorded have produced personality traits that are mostly adaptive.

The anthropology of childrearing involves comparison. Our own cultural conceptions begin to become apparent only when we examine other societies and their patterns of childrearing.

Possible Genetic and Physiological Influences
Some researchers have suggested that genetic or physiological differences between populations predispose them to have different personality characteristics. Daniel Freedman found differences in "temperament" in newborn babies of different ethnic groups; because he observed newborns, the differences between them were presumed to be genetic. Comparing Chinese and European American newborns with the families matched on income, number of previous children, and so on, Freedman found that European American babies cried more easily, were harder to console, and fought experimental procedures more. Chinese babies, on the other hand, seemed calmer and more adaptable. Navajo babies were similar to the Chinese, showing even more calmness.[28] Freedman also suggested that an infant's behavior can influence how the parents respond. A calm baby may encourage a calm parental response; a more active baby may encourage a more active response.[29] So, in Freedman's view, babies' genetically determined behavior can lead to ethnic differences in adult personality and caretaking styles. But we cannot rule out nongenetic explanations of babies' behavior. For example, the mother's diet or her blood pressure could affect the baby's behavior. And it may be that the baby can learn even in the womb. After all, babies in the womb apparently can hear and respond to sounds and other stimuli. Therefore, it is possible that in societies in which pregnant women are calm, their babies may have learned calmness even before they were born. Last, we still do not know if the initial differences observed in newborn babies persist to become personality differences in adulthood.

Just as the diet of the mother, including the intake of alcohol and drugs, may affect the developing fetus, the diet of infants and children may also affect their intellectual development and their behavior. Studies have shown that malnutrition is associated with lower levels of activity, less attentiveness, lack of initiative, and low tolerance of frustration. Behavior of children can change with short-term nutrition supplements. For example, Guatemalan children who were given nutritional supplements were observed to have less anxiety, more exploratoriness, and greater involvement in games than children who were not given supplements.[30] The problem of malnutrition is not just a matter

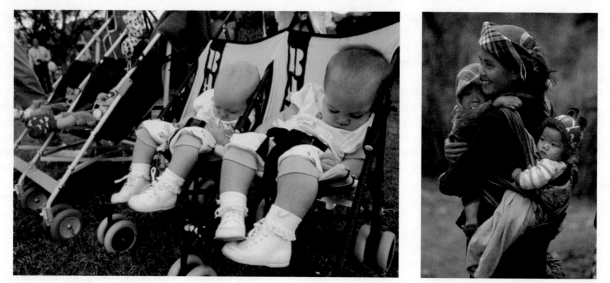

One major difference in childrearing between the West and other places is the degree to which caretakers hold infants during the day. In the United States and other Western countries, infants spend much of the day in a crib, playpen, or stroller. The Dao babies from Yunnan Province in China (on the right) spend a good deal of time in physical contact with their mother or other caretaker.

of nutrition. Other kinds of care may also be reduced. For example, caretakers of malnourished children may interact with them less than do caretakers of healthy children. As a malnourished child shows reduced activity, caretakers tend to respond to the child with lower frequency and less enthusiasm. Then the child withdraws from interaction, creating a potentially serious vicious cycle.[31] Another possible influence, which we discuss later, is how hypoglycemia may affect adult expressions of aggression.

CROSS-CULTURAL VARIATION IN CHILDREARING

In what follows, we examine some aspects of childhood that appear to vary cross-culturally.[32] When we can, we discuss possible explanations for these patterns.

Parental Responsiveness to Infants and Baby-Holding

Consider how societies vary in how quickly parents respond to an infant's needs, in other words, the degree of "indulgence." In many aspects of indulgence—amount of time holding, feeding on demand, responding to crying—industrialized societies such as the United States tend to indulge babies less than do preindustrialized societies. In contrast to those preindustrial societies in which babies are held more than half the day, sometimes almost all day, consider the United States, England, and the Netherlands, where babies may spend most of the day in devices such as playpens, rockers, swings, or cribs. It is estimated that babies are held or touched only 12 percent to 20 percent of their daytime hours in these countries and in Japan. The same pattern continues at nighttime. In most preindustrial societies, babies are much more apt to be close to another person, usually sleeping with the mother in the same bed or, if not in the same bed, in the same room. During the

day, babies are breast-fed in all preindustrial societies, usually on demand. In industrialized societies, bottle-feeding is common, and feeding is usually spaced out every few hours; in some preindustrial societies, babies are breast-fed 20 to 40 times a day. And in many preindustrial societies, people respond very quickly to an infant's crying. For example, among the Efe of the Ituri Forest in central Africa, a 3-month-old infant who cries gets a response within 10 seconds 75 percent of the time. In the United States, a caregiver deliberately *does not* respond at all about 45 percent of the time.[33]

The cross-cultural variation just described seems to reflect cultural attitudes toward childrearing. Parents in the United States say that they do not want their babies to be dependent and clingy; they want to produce independent and self-reliant children. Whether children become self-reliant because of our kind of childrearing is debatable,[34] but our attitudes about childrearing are certainly consistent with our practices.

We think of a quick response of parents to infants as "indulgence," but although many mothers respond quickly to the baby's physical needs, this does not mean that mothers interact with them when they respond, by looking at the baby in the eye, responding to babbling, or kissing and hugging them. Often the mother is doing something else while she nurses the baby.[35]

Ruth and Robert Munroe studied the effects of more versus less holding by the mother in infancy on Logoli children.[36] The Munroes had observational information on how often infants were held, and they were able to interview many of these individuals as children five years later. They were interested in seeing whether children who had been held more often by their mothers were more secure, trusting, and optimistic. So they designed a series of personality measures appropriate for young children. As a measure of optimism, they showed children smiling faces and non-smiling faces and asked which they preferred. As measures of trust, they looked to see how long a child was willing to stay in a room with a stranger or play with new toys.

The results of the study suggest that children who were often held or carried by their mothers as infants are significantly more trusting and optimistic at age 5 than are other children. Somewhat to their surprise, the Munroes found that, although time held by other caregivers did not predict more trust and optimism, the sheer number of different people who had held the infant did predict more trust and optimism. Holding by the mother was important, but trust was even greater if a large number of other people had held the baby. One possible explanation is that a highly trusting mother is likely to allow many others to hold the baby; by doing so, she conveys trust to the baby.

Robert LeVine suggested an adaptational explanation for the frequent holding and feeding of infants and quick response of caretakers in preindustrial societies.[37] Only 1 percent of infants die in industrial societies in the first year of life, but typically more than 20 percent die in preindustrial societies. What can parents do? Parents often do not have access to modern medical care, but they can respond to a baby's fussing immediately if the baby is with them. Also, babies may be safer off the ground if there are cooking fires, dangerous insects, and snakes in the vicinity. When survival is not so much at issue, LeVine suggests, parents can safely leave babies more on their own.

High mortality of infants may also explain why mothers in many of these same societies rarely interact with their infants in more emotional ways—it may help protect them emotionally in case of the infant's early death.

We really don't know much about the long-range effects of short or long response times on the infant. As long as a baby is fed fairly regularly and held some of the time, it might make little difference to the ultimate outcome. We can be more sure that, if a baby's needs are seriously ignored, there will be negative physical and social consequences.

Parent-Child Play

In Western societies, it is commonly thought that "good" parents should provide their children with toys and play with them frequently, starting from birth and continuing through adolescence. Parents who do not do this are viewed as deficient. Yet, cross-culturally. parent-child play is exceedingly rare except perhaps in foraging groups. It is not that play is rare. Children the world over play by themselves or with peers. Often, they make their own toys or pretend objects. Adults play too, usually games, but they don't play as often as children. And when children and adults play, they generally do so separately.[38]

Inuit mothers and babies are together for long periods in their houses when the weather is harsh. Under traditional conditions, there are often no playmates or other caretakers nearby, so perhaps it is not surprising that mothers play with their infants and young children, and make toys for them. Play with infants also occurs in many small foraging bands, but it is typically play with others beside their mothers.[39]

Lack of play with parents may be related to the same factor that probably explains high responsiveness to infant physical needs—high mortality of infants and the psychological need of parents to create emotional distance. But some societal ethnotheories suggest to parents that not playing may be better than play. The Yucatec Maya believe that "a quiet baby is a healthy baby" and, rather than stimulate babies, they are lulled to sleep whenever possible.[40] Babies are commonly thought to be "brainless" and so there is no point to interaction. On Ifaluk, in the Caroline Islands, parents say that "Infants younger than two years of age do not have any thoughts/feelings—*nunuwan*. Without nunuwan, . . . it's useless . . . talking to babies younger than two."[41]

We turn now to the period of time after infancy.

Parental Acceptance and Rejection of Children

What about the overall quality of parenting? Are there positive effects on personality when parents show love, warmth, and affection to their children and negative effects when parents are indifferent or hostile to their children?

Children the world over play, sometimes with toys they make themselves.

These questions are difficult to investigate cross-culturally because cultures vary in the ways feeling is expressed. If love and affection are not expressed in the same ways, outsiders may misinterpret parental behavior. Nevertheless, Ronald Rohner and his colleagues did extensive work on the effects of parental acceptance and rejection on children after infancy. In a cross-cultural comparison of 101 societies, using measures based on ethnographic materials, Rohner found that children tend to be hostile and aggressive when they are neglected and not treated affectionately by their parents. In societies in which children tend to be rejected, adults seem to view life and the world as unfriendly, uncertain, and hostile.[42] A large number of other studies have compared individuals in different cultures to see if the cross-cultural findings were supported. In general, they were. In addition to finding the world more unfriendly and hostile, individuals who think they were rejected are likely to be hostile and aggressive, emotionally unresponsive or unstable, and have negative evaluations of themselves.[43]

Under what conditions is parental rejection likely in childhood? The Rohner study suggests that rejection is likely where mothers get no relief from child care; when fathers and grandparents play a role in child care, rejection is less likely. Foraging societies (those dependent on wild food resources) tend to show warmth and affection to their children. More complex societies are less likely to be affectionate to their children.[44] It is not clear why this should be, but perhaps parental rejection is more likely where parents have less leisure time. Less leisure time may make parents more tired and irritable and therefore have less patience with their children. As we noted in the chapter on economic systems, leisure time probably decreases as cultural complexity increases. More complex societies, which rely on intensive agriculture, also tend to have more economic uncertainty, as we noted in the chapter on getting food. Not only do they tend to have more risk of famines and food shortages, but they also tend to have social inequality. In societies with social classes, many families may not have enough food and money to satisfy their needs, and this factor can also produce frustration in the parents. Whatever the reasons for parental rejection, it seems to perpetuate itself: Children who were rejected tend to reject their own children.

Compliance or Assertiveness

Herbert Barry, Irvin Child, and Margaret Bacon cross-culturally investigated the possibility that child-training practices are adapted to the economic requirements of a society. Such requirements, they theorized, might explain why some societies strive to develop "compliant" (responsible, obedient, nurturant) children, whereas others aim more for "assertiveness" (independence, self-reliance, and achievement).[45] The cross-cultural results indicated that agricultural and herding societies are likely to stress responsibility and obedience, whereas hunting and gathering societies tend to stress self-reliance and individual assertiveness. The investigators suggested that agricultural and herding societies cannot afford departures from established routine, because departures might jeopardize the food supply for long periods. Such societies, therefore,

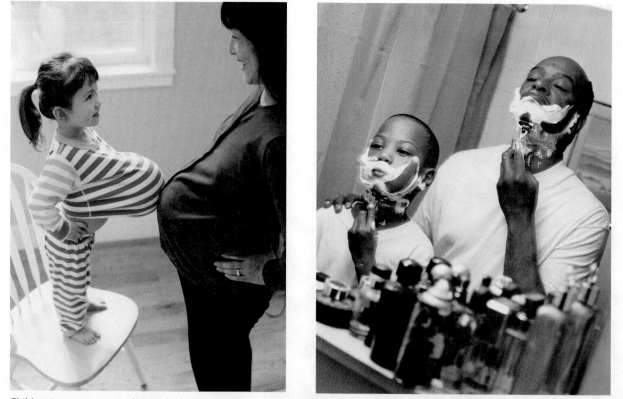

Children in many societies learn a lot by imitation as well as by instruction.

are likely to emphasize compliance with tradition. Departures from routine in a hunter-gatherer society cannot cause much damage to a food supply that has to be collected anew almost every day. So hunter-gatherers can afford to emphasize individual initiative.

Although our own society relies on food production and has large stores of accumulated food, we seem more like hunter-gatherers in emphasizing individual initiative. Are we, then, exceptions to the Barry et al. findings? Not really. Hardly any of us are farmers (in the United States, less than 2 percent of the total population is still on the farm), and most of us expect that we can "forage" in the supermarket or "store" just about anytime. Perhaps more important is the fact that our highly commercial economy, with most people dwelling in or near cities, requires us to compete to get jobs to make a living. In our kind of economy, then, individual initiative is important too. Consider the results of a cross-national comparison of eight countries in which the researchers asked parents what quality they most wanted their school-age children to have. Parents in the more rural countries (Indonesia, Philippines, and Thailand) seldom mentioned independence and self-reliance but those in the more urban countries (Korea, Singapore, and the United States) did.[46]

Attitudes Towards Aggression

Societies also differ considerably in their attitudes toward aggression in children. Some societies actively encourage children to be aggressive, not only to each other but even to the parents. Among the Xhosa of southern Africa, 2- or 3-year-old boys will be prodded to hit each other in the face and women look on laughing. Similar behavior is described for the Gapun of Papua New Guinea; even raising a knife to an older sibling is rewarded.[47] Yanomamö boys of the Venezuelan-Brazilian Amazon are encouraged to be aggressive and are rarely punished for hitting either their parents or the girls in the village. One father, for example, lets his son Ariwari

> beat him on the face and head to express his anger and temper, laughing and commenting on his ferocity. Although Ariwari is only about 4 years old, he has already learned that the appropriate response to a flash of anger is to strike someone with his hand or with an object, and it is not uncommon for him to give his father a healthy smack in the face whenever something displeases him. He is frequently goaded into hitting his father by teasing, being rewarded by gleeful cheers of assent from his mother and from the other adults in the household.[48]

In contrast, the Semai of central Malaya are famous for their timidity. Robert Dentan reports that they say that they do not get angry.[49] Whereas other societies clearly and actively encourage aggression, the Semai communicate nonviolence in more subtle ways. They say, in fact, that they do not teach children. The Semai expect children to be nonviolent and are shocked when they are not. When a child loses his or her temper, an adult will simply cart the child off. The Semai do not physically punish a child's

aggression, and this approach may be one of the most important teaching devices of all. With such teaching—by example—a child rarely sees an aggressive model and thus has no aggression to imitate.[50] In comparison, hardly any North American parents would encourage children to hit them in the face or encourage them to hit other children. Yet many probably use physical punishment sometimes, and many feel that boys especially should "stand up for themselves" if another child provokes a fight.

With regard to aggression, research has shown that children who are physically punished when they are aggressive (the parents trying to minimize aggression) actually exhibit more aggression than children who are not physically punished. Children who are hit may learn not to hit their parents and other caretakers, but the aggression caretakers exhibit seems to be a model for children's aggressive behavior. If children see a parent or other caretaker acting aggressively, they may conclude that it is okay for them to act aggressively.[51]

As we discuss later in the global problems chapter, a society's involvement in war cross-culturally predicts parental encouragement of aggression, particularly in boys. Socialization for aggression appears to decrease after a society is pacified or forced to stop fighting.[52]

Task Assignment

In our society, young children are not expected to help much with chores. If they do have chores, such as tidying up their rooms, they are not likely to affect the welfare of the family or its ability to survive. In contrast, in some societies known to anthropology, young children, even 3- and 4-year-olds, are expected to help prepare food, care for animals, and carry water and firewood, as well as clean. A child between 5 years and 8 years of age may even be given the responsibility of caring for an infant or toddler for much of the day while the mother works in the fields.[53] What are the effects of such task assignment on personality development?

We now have evidence from more than 10 cultures that children who regularly babysit are more nurturant—that is, offer more help and support to others—than are other children, even when the children who babysit are not babysitting. Some of this evidence comes from a project known as the Six Cultures study, in which different research teams observed children's behavior in Kenya (Nyansongo), Mexico, India, the Philippines, Okinawa, and the United States (New England).[54] Ruth and Robert Munroe collected data on children's behavior in four other cultures that show the same relationship between babysitting and nurturant behavior; the Munroes' data come from Kenya (Logoli), Nepal, Belize, and American Samoa.[55] Clearly, children who babysit infrequently are less attuned to others' needs than are children who babysit often.

Why might task assignment affect the behaviors of children? One possibility is that children learn certain behaviors during performance of the task, and these behaviors become habitual. For example, a responsible babysitter is supposed to offer help. Mothers might directly instruct the babysitter to make sure that happens. But there is probably also an intrinsic satisfaction in doing a job well. For example, it is pleasurable to see an infant smile and laugh, but it is unpleasant to hear a baby cry. We might therefore expect that a child who is assigned babysitting would learn that comforting a baby brings its own rewards.[56]

Children's Settings

Children who are assigned many tasks may spend their day in different kinds of settings, and these settings may indirectly influence behavior. For example, children who are asked to do many household chores are apt to be around both adults and younger children. Children who are assigned few or no tasks are freer to play with their age-mates. Beatrice Whiting suggests that one of the most powerful socializing influences on children is the type of setting they are placed in and the "cast of characters" there.[57] How does the setting influence a child's behavior? We have already noted that being around younger children may make older children more nurturant. Aggressive behaviors also appear to be influenced by who is in the child's setting. Results from the Six Cultures project suggest that children tend to be more aggressive the more they are in the company of other children of roughly the same age. In contrast, children tend to inhibit aggression when adults are on the scene.[58] In the next chapter on sex, gender, and culture, we note that boys usually exhibit more aggression than girls. Part of that difference may be due to the fact that girls are generally assigned more work in and around the home (where adults are), whereas boys are

more often free to play with their peers. Parents may not be deliberately trying to inculcate certain behaviors, but they may produce certain behaviors by arranging the settings in which children spend their time.

Schooling One of the most important settings for children in some societies is school. Most researchers focus on the parents when they investigate how children are brought up. But in our own and other societies, children may spend a substantial part of their time in school from the age of 3 or so. What influence does school have on children's social behavior and on how they think as measured by tests? To investigate the effect of schooling, researchers have compared children or adults who have not gone to school with those who have. All of this research has been done in societies that do not have compulsory schooling; otherwise, we could not compare the schooled with the unschooled. We know relatively little about the influence of school on social behavior. In contrast, we know more about how schooling influences performance on cognitive tests.

Schooling clearly predicts "superior" performance on many cognitive tests, and within the same society, schooled individuals will generally do better than the unschooled on those tests. So, for example, unschooled individuals in non-Western societies are not as likely as schooled individuals to perceive depth in two-dimensional pictures, do not perform as well on tests of memory, are not as likely to classify items in certain ways, and do not display evidence of formal-operational thinking.[59] But schooling does not

Attending school has become customary in many parts of the world, as among the Baoulé of the Ivory Coast. Schooling seems to affect cognitive development, but we do not know exactly why or how.

In many societies, children work. Kurdish boys in Iraq herd the family's sheep.

always produce superior performance on tests of inferential reasoning.[60]

Why does schooling have these effects? Although it is possible that something about schooling creates higher levels of cognitive thinking in some respects, there are other possible explanations. The observed differences may be due to the advantages that schoolchildren have because of their experiences in school, advantages that have nothing to do with general cognitive ability. For example, consider research that asks people to classify or group drawings of geometric shapes that belong together. Suppose a person is shown three cards—a red circle, a red triangle, and a white circle—and is asked which two are most alike. A person could choose to classify in terms of color or in terms of shape. In the United States, young children usually classify by color, and they classify more often by shape as they get older. Many psychologists assume that classification by color is more "concrete" and classification by shape or function is more "abstract." Unschooled adults in many parts of Africa sort by color, not by shape. Does this mean that they are classifying less abstractly? Not necessarily. It may just be that unschooled Africans classify differently because they are likely to be unfamiliar with the test materials (drawings on paper, geometric shapes).

How can people classify "abstractly" (e.g., by shape) if they have never had the experience of handling or seeing shapes that are drawn in two dimensions? Is it likely that they would classify things as triangles if they had never seen a three-pointed figure with straight sides? In contrast, consider how much time teachers in the United States spend drilling children on various geometric shapes. People who are familiar with certain materials may for that reason alone do better on cognitive tests that use those materials.[61]

A comparative study of Liberian rice farmers in West Africa and U.S. undergraduates also illustrates the point that choice of materials may influence research results. The comparison involved a set of materials familiar to the rice farmers—bowls of rice—and a set of materials familiar to the undergraduates—geometric cards. Rice farmers appeared to classify more "abstractly" than undergraduates when they were asked to classify rice, and undergraduates seemed to classify more "abstractly" than rice farmers when they classified geometric cards.[62]

Schooled individuals may also enjoy an advantage on many cognitive tests just because they are familiar with tests and the way tests ask them to think of new situations. For example, consider the reaction of an unschooled person in central Asia who was asked the following question by a Russian psychologist interested in measuring logical thinking: "In the Far North where there is snow, all bears are white. Novaya Zemlya is in the Far North and there is always snow there. What color are the bears there?" The reply was, "We don't talk about what we haven't seen." Such a reply was typical of unschooled individuals; they did not even try to answer the question because it was not part of their experience.[63] Clearly, we cannot judge whether people think logically if they do not want to play a cognitive game.

Much research needs to be done on exactly how and why schooling affects cognition. Is it important which specific things are taught? Is it important to be asked to attend to questions that are out of context? Is being literate a factor? This last question was the subject of research among the Vai of Liberia, who had a somewhat unusual situation in that schooling and literacy were not completely confounded. The Vai had an indigenous script learned outside of school. Thus, researchers Sylvia Scribner and Michael Cole were able to see how Vai individuals who were literate but not formally schooled compared with others who were formally schooled (and literate) and those who were unschooled (and illiterate). They found some, but relatively minor, effects of literacy itself; the number of years of schooling affected cognitive test performance much more. Similar results come from a study of the Cree of northern Ontario who have their own syllabic script learned outside of school.[64] These comparisons suggest that some other aspects of schooling are more important than literacy as determinants of cognitive performance.

By studying other societies where schooling is not universal, we may be better able to understand just what role schooling plays in cognitive and other development. That schooling makes for so much difference in cognitive

applied anthropology

Schools: Values and Expectations

Most people think of schools as teaching skills such as reading and writing and subjects such as history, math, biology, or social science. But schools also convey much more about the society and individuals' places in it. They do not just teach content. We focus here on cultural values and expectations.

Joseph Tobin, David Wu, and Dana Davidson videotaped preschool classroom scenes in Japan, China, and the United States. In each country, they asked children, teachers, parents, and school administrators to comment on the scenes in all three countries. We can get a feel for how different values are implicitly taught in each country by reviewing the comments.

When individuals in the United States viewed the Japanese tape, two things generally bothered them. One was the fact that children in Japan often did the same things simultaneously as a group. For example, the teacher showed what to fold first and subsequently to make an origami bird figure, and the children followed along. Parents and teachers in the United States said that children should have more choice in what to do and how to do it. The second

thing that bothered people in the United States, as well as in China, was that the teacher in Japan appeared to ignore what we might consider "unruly" behavior by the children. For example, when children got restless during a group workbook activity, they would leave their seats, joke with friends, or go to the bathroom. In the tape, a particularly troublesome boy talked loudly, sometimes purposely hurt other children, and threw things around, but the teacher seemed to ignore these behaviors. People in the United States and China thought that the teacher should try to do something in such situations. In Japan, however, most of the teachers preferred not to call attention to, or single out, a troublesome child. Japanese teachers expect such a child eventually to behave more appropriately, and they encourage the other children to exert social pressure in that direction. In Lois Peak's words: "Learning to go to school in Japan is primarily defined as training in group life."

Most of the activities in the Chinese preschool were highly structured. For example, the first task of the day was building with blocks, but in contrast to the style at the

Japanese preschool, the children in China were expected to complete the task on their own and to do so in silence. If they spoke, the teacher reprimanded them. They used a picture as a guide for what to do. When they were done, the teachers checked their work. If they got it right, they took it apart and rebuilt it; if they got it wrong, they were asked to correct it. An arithmetic lesson followed. Children then ate the lunch that was brought for them into the classroom. Teachers monitored the lunch to make sure that the children ate all their food and ate in silence. After an afternoon nap, the children listened to a patriotic story and then had relay races, which were followed by 15 minutes of free play. Supper was served at 5:00 P.M. and parents came at 6:00. In seeing the videotapes, Americans and Japanese were bothered by the rigidity and "over-control" of the children and by the lack of privacy in their communal bathroom.

In the U.S. preschool, in Honolulu, as in Japan, parents brought their children at different times, but some parents stayed with the child for as long as a half hour. Compared with the other preschools, the U.S.

performance raises the serious issue of how much of what we observe about child development in our society and in other Western societies is simply a function of what children are taught in school. After all, children who grow up in this society not only get older each year, they also go one year further in school. Schools are not just places to learn a particular curriculum. Children learn to interact with one another and with adults who are not parents and family. Therefore, we might expect that schools not only shape cognition but also convey important cultural attitudes, values, and appropriate ways of behaving toward others (see the box "Schools: Values and Expectations").

Schooling does seem to predict having a personality trait we call "patience." The more schooling you have, the more patience you have. In a study conducted among the Tsimane, a horticultural people living in the Bolivian Amazon, patience or a tolerance for delayed gratification is associated with a wide range of advantages, including higher income, more wealth, and better health. These positive

outcomes may be partly the result of respect for authority, obedience, and conformity, which schooling may instill.[65]

PSYCHOLOGICAL VARIATION IN ADULTHOOD

So far, we have focused on the anthropology of childhood. But there are characteristics of adults (as well as children) that appear to vary as well. Some of these concepts, such as ideas about the self, may shape childrearing as well.

Concepts of the Self   Anthropologists have begun to study different cultural ideas of personhood or concept of the "self." Many have concluded that the concept of self in many non-Western societies is quite different from the Western conception. Clifford Geertz described the Western conception of the person as "bounded, unique, . . . a dynamic center of awareness, emotion, judgment, and action organized into a distinctive whole."[66] He claimed, preschool emphasized individual participation and individualized activity. For example, "show and tell" was voluntary; sometimes only three kids decided to get up and talk. In an activity involving a felt board, each child was asked to add something to the board. Much of the rest of the day was spent in "learning centers"; the teachers helped the children decide which center they would like to go to. Children started at one activity but could change if they wished. Even lunch was more individual. All children took their lunch boxes to a big table where they all ate and talked animatedly. The U.S. teacher, in contrast to the Japanese teacher, intervened when a child misbehaved, such as when one boy grabbed a block from another. Without raising her voice, the teacher asked the two children to talk to each other about the disagreement. She resorted to a "time-out" (a period of isolation) when the dispute was not settled by talking.

Even though they do not teach values explicitly, these preschools clearly convey values. The value of the individual appears to be stressed most in the U.S. preschool, where most of the daily activities allowed individual choice of some kind. In both Japan and China, group activities predominated, although the Japanese preschool allowed flexible arrival times, more free play, and more freedom to talk or move about than the Chinese preschool. Second

is the source of control. The Japanese teachers relied informally on the group to control the children's behavior. For example, after nine months, the unruly boy sat by himself at lunch; the other children did not want to sit with him. In contrast, the Chinese teachers saw to it that the children behaved like others in the group by exerting strong control over the children's behavior. The U.S. teachers also intervened in response to unruly behavior.

Cultural values are not unchanging. For example, although many Japanese educational administrators thought that the Japanese preschool was quite "Japanese" in style, and therefore satisfactory, a considerable number of Japanese parents and teachers were critical of the school and said there were "better" schools in Japan that were more like the U.S. preschool. And some Japanese thought that more attention should be paid to the individual needs of troubled children. When some Chinese saw the tapes of the Chinese school, they complained that it was too "old-fashioned."

Recent research also shows how much cultural expectations shape school performance. Most of this research has focused on minority students. Most of them are not often expected to do well by their teachers and others because of cultural stereotypes. Indeed, in most tests in school, these students do less well. The important

question is whether stereotyped expectations hamper performance, or whether performance has to do with factors having nothing to do with school. Many experiments have confirmed that, even after controlling for factors like family wealth, even subtle reminders of cultural stereotypes cause performance to suffer. The cues can be as simple as saying that the test measures intelligence (in contrast to the control group told that they will not be evaluated on their performance) or asking the person for their "race" (in contrast to not asking) as one of a number of background questions.

What can be done to improve performance? Some suggestions are to tell students that human abilities and skills are changeable, not fixed; another is to give them challenging work that conveys that they are capable. One of the most fascinating studies was a comparison of African American and European American students before and after Barack Obama was elected President of the United States. Before the election, the African Americans, even though matched on ability, did worse than the European Americans. After the election, the differences practically disappeared. This study strongly suggests that conditions in the larger society affect performance.

Sources: Tobin et al. 1989; Peak 1991; Lock 2009; Aronson 2002; Nisbett 2009.

on the basis of his fieldwork in Java, Bali, and Morocco, that those societies have very different conceptions of a person, not only different from each other but quite different from the Western conception. For example, Geertz said that the Balinese describe a person as having many different roles, like an actor who plays different characters. The unique characteristics of a person are not emphasized; what is emphasized are the "masks" people wear and the "parts" they play.

Geertz focused on the variation and uniquenesses in different cultures' conceptions of the self. But other scholars think that there are recognizable and predictable patterns in this variation. One of the most talked-about patterns is the Western emphasis on the self as an autonomous individual and the non-Western emphasis on the relations a person has with others.[67] Labels used to describe such Western and non-Western cultural differences are "individualism" versus "holism" or "collectivism," "egocentric" versus "sociocentric," and the like.[68] For example,

the Japanese concept of self is often described as "relational" or "situational"; people exist in networks of relationships and the ideal person has the ability to shift easily from one social situation to another.[69]

There are two major objections to the idea that the Western sense of self should be contrasted with the non-Western. The first is that studies of other cultures have suggested other dimensions of variation besides "individualism" versus "collectivism." For example, the traditional Inuit concept *inummarik*, "a genuine person," seems to include a lifelong process of ecological involvement— interacting with animals and the environment as well as people.[70] A culture's concept of self, then, may include other dimensions besides individual versus collective. A second objection to the Western/non-Western contrast is that it may not be based on adequate evidence. As Melford Spiro pointed out, it is necessary to find out how a sample of individuals in a society actually view themselves. The ideal in the culture might be different from the actual.[71]

For example, individuals even in the United States do not just describe themselves as autonomous. When Jane Wellenkamp and Douglas Hollan interviewed Americans about their feelings about the death of someone close, they got statements about autonomy (such as "I can stand on my own" and "At least you have yourself"), but they also got statements reflecting interdependence ("You realize that they're gone and that a part of you has gone with them").[72] This is not to say that the autonomy of the individual isn't important in the United States. It is. But individuals also realize that they are interdependent. How we actually think of ourselves may not be so different from how people in other societies think of themselves.

If a cultural theme such as individualism is important, societies may express or convey this theme in many ways. It may start right after birth, as when a baby is put in a crib or bassinet to sleep alone rather than with someone in the family. Young children may be given their "own" toys. They may go to preschool or day care, where they are encouraged to make their own choices (see the Box "Schools: Values and Expectations"). And schools for older children may require individual, not group, achievement. Does the theme of individualism have to be taught explicitly? Probably not, because it can be conveyed in so many different ways.

Perceptual Style: Field Independence or Dependence

Might the environment influence the way people in different societies think and perceive (interpret sensory information)? John Berry suggested that different perceptual and cognitive processes may be selected and trained for in societies that differ in their adaptational requirements.[73] Berry's particular focus was on what psychologists call *field independence* and *field dependence*.[74] Field independence means being able to isolate a part of a situation from the whole. The opposite perceptual style, field dependence, means that parts are not perceived separately; rather, the whole situation is focused on.

The contrast between field independence and field dependence may become clear if we look at some of the ways they are measured. In the rod-and-frame test, a person seated in a darkened room is asked to adjust a tilted luminous rod so that it is upright within a luminous frame. Individuals are considered field dependent if they adjust the rod to line up with the frame when the frame is tilted. Individuals are considered field independent if they adjust the rod to a truly upright position even though the frame is tilted. Field independence is also measured by the ability to see a simply drawn figure when it is included but somewhat hidden in a more complex picture.

Why should some societies produce people who are more field independent or dependent? Berry suggested that people who rely a lot on hunting must be field independent to be successful, because hunting requires the visual isolation of animals from their backgrounds. Hunters must also learn to visualize themselves in precise relationship to their surroundings so that they can find

animals and get back home. In a comparative study of communities in four societies, Berry found that degree of reliance on hunting predicted field independence. The more a community relied on hunting, the more the individuals showed field independence on tests. Those communities more reliant on agriculture tested out to be more field dependent. How might hunters develop field independence as a cognitive style? Different child training might be involved. In the United States and a few other societies, it has been found that children whose parents are very strict are less likely to develop field independence than are children whose parents are lenient.[75] It seems that emotional independence from parents is necessary for the perceptual style of field independence to develop. No matter what the precise mechanism is, we know from the Barry et al. (1959) study that hunter-gatherers are more likely to train children to be individualistic and assertive, and that agriculturalists and herders are more likely to train their children to be compliant. So hunter-gatherers may cause their children to develop field independence by stressing emotional independence in childhood.

Investigations have shown that there are gender differences in the United States and other (but not all) cultures in degree of field dependence versus independence.[76] Perhaps these differences reflect the fact that girls are encouraged to be obedient and responsible and boys to be independent and self-reliant. And perhaps, too, gender differences in field dependence versus independence may be related to the fact that girls work more in and around the home, close to others. If so, we might expect that girls more field dependent are also likely to have a morality that stresses interpersonal concerns (see the box "Do Women Have a Different Morality?").

Expression of Aggression

Leaving aside behavior during warfare, which we discuss further in the chapter on political life, societies vary markedly in the degree to which adults express anger and act aggressively toward others. Not surprisingly, many of the societies that encourage children to be more aggressive also appear to have more aggressive adults. The Semai and the Yanomamö are good examples. The Semai are famous for their timidity and have never been described as hostile.[77] The Yanomamö, on the other hand, frequently show aggression within a village. Shouting and threatening to obtain demands are frequent, as are wife-beatings and bloody fights with clubs.[78] Cross-culturally, all kinds of aggression tend to co-occur, so much so that many researchers discuss a "culture of violence."[79] What drives this pattern is debatable, but as we discussed earlier, there is some evidence that when war ceases, socialization for aggression ceases. So, adults who grow up in more peaceful times may exhibit less aggression of all types.

Whether adults express aggression freely may also be related to a group's economy. In a comparative study of personality differences between pastoralists and farmers in four societies in East Africa, Robert Edgerton found

new perspectives on gender

Do Women Have a Different Morality?

There is widespread agreement that as children mature they develop a sense of self that distinguishes themselves from others. But what kind of sense of self do they develop? Some researchers suggest that different cultures have different conceptions of the self. In particular, the West seems to emphasize the separateness of each person; other cultures emphasize the connection of the self to others.

Several psychologists, including Carol Gilligan, proposed that women, in contrast to men, are more likely to develop a sense of themselves that involves social interaction and connectedness. Gilligan proposed that women also tend to have a different sense of morality, one that is more apt to consider the feelings of others and the preservation of relationships. Men, she suggested, are more likely to emphasize rules or principles that are applied equally and impartially to individuals. Is there any substantial evidence for her claims about gender differences in morality?

Some studies have interviewed females and males and explicitly compared their statements about themselves and about solutions to moral dilemmas. The responses are coded for the degree to which the self is described as "autonomous" or as "connected" and the degree to which responses to moral dilemmas are couched in "justice" or "care" terms. "Well, you have to think about whether it is right . . . or whether it is wrong" is an example of a statement couched in "justice" terms. "I wanted them to get along. . . . I didn't want anybody getting in fights or anything" is an example of a statement couched in "care" terms.

So far the research, conducted mostly in the United States among well-educated populations, suggests that, although women more often than men do tend to describe themselves as "connected" and more often display a "caring" morality, there is no absolute separation between the genders. Most people, regardless of gender, give "connected" and "autonomous" statements about themselves, and most people express "justice" and "care" concerns with regard to moral dilemmas. If there is a difference between the genders in a culture, it is only in tendency, not in a completely different approach to morality.

Although moral development in childhood has been studied in several cultures, there is relatively little research that directly addresses the issues raised by Gilligan. To be sure, research by David Stimpson and his colleagues compared educated university students in Korea, China, Thailand, and the United States and found support for the idea that women were more concerned with affection, compassion, and sensitivity to the needs of others, as compared with men. But that study did not specifically ask for responses to moral dilemmas. Some other researchers suggest that the picture may be more complicated, because concepts of morality may vary quite a bit from the two types described by Gilligan. For example, Joan Miller found that middle-class Hindu Indians generally had a very strong sense of interpersonal morality compared with people in the United States. But the Hindu Indian morality was not based on individual concern for others; rather, their responses to moral dilemmas were strongly influenced by considerations of social duty. And Miller found no gender differences in responses.

All we can conclude so far is that the genders may have somewhat different moralities in some cultures. We need more research on how morality may vary by gender as well as by culture.

Sources: Gilligan 1982; Lyons 1988; Gilligan and Attanucci 1988; Stimpson et al. 1992; J. G. Miller 1994.

---

that pastoralists were more willing than farmers to express aggression openly. As a matter of fact, pastoralists seemed freer to express all kinds of emotion, including sadness and depression. Although farmers displayed reluctance to express overt aggression themselves, they were quite willing to talk about witchcraft and sorcery practiced by others. How can we explain these personality differences? Edgerton proposed that the lifestyle of farmers, who must spend their lives cooperating with a fixed set of neighbors, requires them to contain their feelings, particularly hostile feelings. (But these feelings may not go away, and so the farmers might "see them" in others.) Pastoralists, on the other hand, can more readily move away in conflict situations because they are not as dependent on a fixed set of individuals. Not only might they be able to express aggression more openly, but such aggression may even be adaptive. The pastoralists studied by Edgerton engaged frequently in raids and counterraids involving cattle stealing, and the most aggressive individuals may have had the best chance of surviving the skirmishes.[80]

Physiological (not necessarily genetic) differences between populations may also be responsible for some personality differences in adulthood. Such differences could also have an effect in childhood. Research by Ralph Bolton suggests that a physiological condition known as hypoglycemia may be responsible for the high levels of aggression recorded among the Qolla of Peru.[81] (People with hypoglycemia experience a big drop in their blood sugar level after they ingest food.) Bolton found that about 55 percent of the males he tested in a Qolla village had hypoglycemia. Moreover, those men with the most aggressive life histories tended to be hypoglycemic. Whether hypoglycemia is induced by genetic or environmental factors or both, the condition can be alleviated by a change in diet.

PSYCHOLOGICAL EXPLANATIONS OF CULTURAL VARIATION

Psychological anthropologists, as well as other social scientists, have also investigated the possible *consequences* of psychological variation, particularly how psychological characteristics may help us understand certain aspects of cultural variation. For example, David McClelland's research suggests that societies that develop high levels of achievement motivation (a personality trait) in individuals will be likely to experience high rates of economic growth. Economic decline, McClelland suggested, will follow a decline in achievement motivation.[82] Differences in achievement motivation may even have political consequences. For example, Robert LeVine, who studied achievement motivation in three Nigerian ethnic groups, noted that the traditionally more influential groups may have resented the entry of one of them, the Ibo, into higher education and into many emerging professions.[83] Soon after LeVine's book was published, the friction between the rival groups escalated into rebellion by the Ibo and the defeat of a separatist Ibo state named Biafra.

Psychological factors may also help us explain why some aspects of culture are statistically associated with others. Abram Kardiner originally suggested that cultural patterns influence personality development through child training and that the resulting personality characteristics in turn influence the culture. He believed that **primary institutions**, such as family organization and subsistence techniques, give rise to certain personality characteristics. Once the personality is formed, though, it can have its own impact on culture. In Kardiner's view, the **secondary institutions** of society, such as religion and art, are shaped by common—he called them *basic*—personality characteristics. Presumably, these secondary institutions have little relation to the adaptive requirements of the society. But they may reflect and express the motives, conflicts, and anxieties of typical members of the society.[84] Thus, if we can understand why certain typical personality characteristics develop, we might, for example, be able to understand why certain kinds of art are associated with certain kinds of social systems (see the chapter on the arts).

Whiting and Child used the phrase **personality integration of culture** to refer to the possibility that an understanding of personality might help us explain connections between primary and secondary institutions.[85] As examples of how personality may integrate culture, we turn to some suggested explanations for cultural preferences in games and for the custom of male initiation ceremonies.

In a cross-cultural study conducted by John Roberts and Brian Sutton-Smith, cultural preferences for particular types of games were found to be related to certain aspects of childrearing. The researchers suggested that these associations are a consequence of conflict generated in many people in a society by particular types of childrearing pressures. Games of strategy, for example, are associated with child training that emphasizes obedience. Roberts and Sutton-Smith proposed that severe obedience training can create a conflict between the need to obey and the desire not to obey, a conflict that arouses anxiety. Such anxiety may or may not manifest itself against the person who instigates the anxiety. But the conflict and the aggression itself can be played out on the miniature battlefields of games of strategy such as chess or the Japanese game of *go*.[86] Politically complex and socially stratified societies are particularly likely to emphasize obedience, so it is not surprising that such societies are most likely to have games of strategy.[87] Similarly, games of chance may represent defiance of societal expectations of docility and responsibility. The general interpretation suggested by Roberts and Sutton-Smith is that

Children in Ghana playing *mancala*, a game of strategy that is now also played in North America.

players—and societies—initially become curious about games, learn them, and ultimately develop high involvement in them because of the particular kinds of psychological conflicts that are handled or expressed, but not necessarily resolved, by the games.

The possible role of psychological processes in connecting different aspects of culture is also illustrated in cross-cultural work on initiation ceremonies for boys at adolescence. In the ceremonies, boys are subjected to painful tests of manhood, usually including genital operations, which indicate the boys' transition to adulthood. Roger Burton and John Whiting found that initiation ceremonies tend to occur in male-oriented societies in which infant boys initially sleep exclusively with their mothers. They suggest that initiation rites in such societies are intended to break a conflict in sex identity. The conflict is believed to exist because boys in these societies would initially identify with their mothers, who exercise almost complete control over them in infancy. Later, when the boys discover that men dominate the society, they will identify secondarily with their fathers. This sex-role conflict is assumed to be resolved by the initiation ceremony, which demonstrates a boy's manhood, thus strengthening the secondary identification.[88]

In later chapters, we discuss cultural variation in religion and the arts. In doing so, we refer to some psychological explanations. Some researchers feel that such explanations may help us understand why gods in some societies are viewed as mean, why artists in some societies prefer repetitive designs, and why strangers in some societies tend to be the "bad ones" in folktales. Psychological anthropologists often assume that conceptions of gods and artistic creations are not constrained by any objective realities, so people are free to create them as they wish. In other words, people may tend to project their personalities—their feelings, their conflicts, their concerns—into these areas. This idea of projection underlies what psychologists call **projective tests**. In such tests, which presumably reveal personality characteristics, subjects are given stimuli that are purposely ambiguous. So, for example, in the Thematic Apperception Test (TAT), subjects are shown vague drawings and are asked what they think is going on in them, what happened before, and how they think things will turn out. Because the test materials give few instructions about what to say, it is assumed that subjects will interpret the materials by projecting their own personalities. As we will see in subsequent chapters, some aspects of religion and the arts may be similar to TAT stories and may express or reflect the common personality characteristics of a society.

INDIVIDUALS AS AGENTS OF CULTURAL CHANGE

Many of the processes we have been talking about involve culture change. For instance, in the section on expression of aggression, we referred to research by Edgerton, suggesting that pastoralists may be freer than farmers to express their aggressiveness as well as other emotions because they can move away in conflict situations. Farmers have to live their whole lives in close proximity to neighbors. The research suggests that, if pastoralists settle down and start farming, they may learn that it is important for them to repress some of their emotions. But even if individuals don't change when they settle down, change may occur in the next generation because the less aggressive may be imitated if they are perceived to be more successful. Either of these possibilities points to the importance of the individual in bringing about change. Ethnographers are focusing more explicitly now on how individual *agency* may bring about change.

Let us look at a few examples of how women are helping to bring about change in strongly patriarchal societies.

Large-scale changes in China have been pushed by the government since 1949, including the introduction of new marriage laws, the attack on patrilineal ideology, and the introduction of public ownership. But Yunxiang Yan, who studied women in rural north China, points out that the efforts of young women themselves, particularly those transitioning from teenager to young daughter-in-law, have contributed substantially to change. Young women traditionally had little to say about whom they married, the negotiations that took place before marriage, or when their husband would split from his extended family and form a new household. Because they were going to move into their husband's household after marriage, young women traditionally had little status in the household in which they grew up. In their husband's household, they became the in-marrying stranger. Yan observes that she began to notice from the complaints of women about their daughters and daughters-in-laws, and men's complaints about women, that young women were bringing about change. The ability of a woman to veto a marriage proposal was recognized in law in the early 1950s, but it was young women that used their veto power, sometimes repeatedly, that brought about change. Now women may select a husband. Young women have become more expressive emotionally and expect a more passionate and intimate relationship with their potential spouses and later with their husbands. Premarital sex has now become common. Young women have also pushed transformation of the custom of bridewealth (the gift of goods from the groom's family to the bride's family). They began to go with the groom to pick out items, they demanded that gifts be converted into cash to be given to the bride, and they started to engage in the negotiations between the families. Finally, young women have pushed for an early division of the extended family, so that less and less time is spent in the husband's family's household.[89] But why some women push more for change than other women is a question still to be investigated.

The world over, higher education is almost always associated with lower fertility. Jennifer Johnson-Hanks wanted to understand at the individual level why this may come about. Her research took place among the Beti in southern Cameroon. As in China, social organization was oriented around males. The Beti value the development of each individual child's potential, and in recent times with the introduction of schools, they value education for their children. School is not free, so parents have to sacrifice to send their children to school. Schoolgirls stress that schooling gives them more options, not only to get better paying jobs in the future, but also to have more freedom and less dependency on a husband. Schoolgirls emphasize that schooling allows them to be honorable. Honor brings privilege and prestige, but the concept also involves becoming more rational and controlling choices, including being more choosy about men with whom to be involved, and controlling the conditions under which they become mothers. It is not that young women believe in abstaining from sex—sex is viewed as natural and important, but young women employ strategies to delay motherhood. These include periodic abstinence, aborting pregnancies, and giving up children to fosterage if they are not ready to be mothers. Rationality also entails knowing that you cannot have a lot of children if there are not enough resources.[90]

In Senegal, after independence, development programs favored men by promoting plow agriculture and distributing seed to heads of households. But judging by the Wolof peanut farmers that Donna Perry studied, men's advantages were short-lived. In the mid-1980s, agricultural cooperatives were dissolved and economic supports were eliminated. Cash-cropping by small farm households has diminished, and men appear to be suffering a crisis of masculinity as their wives trade more in the weekly markets (*loumas*). Men express their frustration: "You wake up in the morning now and don't even know who the head of the household is!"[91] It is hard to know in advance where this anxiety will lead. It could be that, as males' authority diminishes, they will become more conservative in an attempt to recapture the old ways. Or, males and females could move toward more shared authority. Conflict may play out at the individual level, which may lead to culture change.

SUMMARY ● ○ ○

1. Anthropologists who are interested in the relationships between culture and the individual and the importance of understanding psychological processes call themselves psychological anthropologists. Four main questions characterize psychological anthropology: (1) To what extent do all human beings develop psychologically in the same ways? (2) If there are differences, what are they and what may account for them? (3) How do people in different societies conceive of individuals and their psychological development? and (4) How can understanding individuals or psychological processes help us understand culture and culture change?

2. Early research in psychological anthropology was concerned mainly with how cultural differences seem to affect supposedly universal stages of emotional development. Some doubt has been cast on the idea that

adolescence is necessarily a time of "storm and stress" and that the Oedipus complex, at least in the form stated by Freud, is universal. But there appear to be some universals in the psychological realm, including creating taxonomies, plans for the future, a concept of the self or person, trying to discern the intention of others, the ability to recognize emotions and to play, and to feel affection, sexual attraction, envy, and jealousy.

3. Recent research on universals in psychological development has been concerned more with cognitive, or intellectual, development. In looking for universals, many researchers have discovered some apparent differences. Most of the tests used in research may favor people in Western cultures and those who attend formal schools.

4. To understand cross-cultural variation in psychological characteristics, many researchers have tried to discover if variation in childrearing customs can account for the observed psychological differences.

5. Humans have a long period in which the young are dependent on caretakers. *Socialization* is a term anthropologists and psychologists use to describe the development, through the influence of parents and others, of patterns of behavior in children that conform to cultural expectations. But children are also agents and actors, not just recipients of socialization. They can learn from others, such as peers, in ways that may lead to rapid changes in behavior.

6. Many of the ideas parents have about childrearing come from societal belief systems or "ethnotheories" about children and how they should be treated. Some anthropologists believe societies produce the kinds of personality best suited to performance of the activities necessary for the survival of the society.

7. Societies vary considerably in how quickly they respond to an infant's needs, how much infants are held, how much parents play with infants and young children, how much warmth and affection they show children, how much they expect children to comply with adults or assert themselves, and how aggressive they want children to be. There is also considerable variation in how much children are assigned chores and responsibilities and go to school.

8. One of the most profound effects on cognitive thinking appears to be how much schooling a person has.

9. Some adult differences in psychological traits have been documented in different societies. These include a difference in perceptual style known as field independence versus field dependence (that may be related to economic differences) and difference in display of aggression (that may be also related to economic differences as well as to involvement in war).

10. Psychological anthropologists are interested not only in the possible causes of psychological differences between societies but also in the possible consequences of psychological variation, particularly how psychological

characteristics may help us understand statistical associations between various aspects of culture.

11. Recently, anthropologists have explored how individuals can be agents of culture change.

GLOSSARY TERMS ○ ● ○

enculturation   **156**
personality integration
   of culture   **168**
primary institutions   **168**

projective tests   **169**
secondary
   institutions   **168**
socialization   **156**

CRITICAL QUESTIONS ○ ○ ●

1. Do you think indulging children makes them more or less self-reliant as adults? Why do you think so?
2. What may explain adolescent rebelliousness?

3. Agriculturalists and foragers seem to have somewhat different personalities, so the method of food-getting may be related to personality. Do you think there is a similar relationship between occupation and personality? If so, why?

PEARSON
myanthrolab

Read the chapter by Susan Schaefer Davis titled "Morocco: Adolescents in a Small Town" on MyAnthroLab, and answer the following questions:

1. Why do many (but not all) cultures have a stage of life called "adolescence"?
2. Do you think that rebelliousness is inevitable in adolescence?
3. Describe some of the aspects of adolescence that are different in Morocco from your own culture.

chapter 10

Sex, Gender, and Culture

umans come in two major varieties or sexes—female and male. Each has different reproductive organs. The contrast between them is one of the facts of life shared with most animal species. But having different organs of reproduction does not explain why males and females may also differ in other physical ways. There are some animal species—such as pigeons, gulls, and laboratory rats—in which the two sexes differ little in appearance.[1] The fact that we are a species with two sexes does not explain why human females and males typically look different, nor why human males and females should differ in behavior or be treated differently by society. Yet, no society we know of treats females and males in exactly the same way; indeed, females usually have fewer advantages than males. That is why in the last chapter we were careful to say that egalitarian societies have no *social groups* with unequal access to resources, power, and prestige. But within social groups (e.g., families), even egalitarian societies usually allow males greater access to economic resources, power, and prestige.

Because many of the differences between females and males may reflect cultural expectations and experiences, many researchers now prefer to speak of those as **gender differences,** reserving the term **sex differences** for purely biological differences.[2] Unfortunately, biological and cultural influences are not always clearly separable, so it is sometimes hard to know which term to use. As long as societies treat males and females differently, we may not be able to separate the effects of biology from the effects of culture, and both may be present. As we discuss differences and similarities between females and males, keep in mind that not all cultures conceive of gender as including just two categories. Sometimes "maleness" and "femaleness" are thought of as opposite ends of a continuum, or there might be three or more categories of gender, such as "female," "male," and "other."[3]

In this chapter, we discuss what we know cross-culturally about how and why females and males may differ physically, in gender roles, and in personality. We also discuss how and why sexual behavior and attitudes about sex vary from culture to culture. First, we focus on how concepts about gender vary cross-culturally.

● ○ ●

GENDER CONCEPTS

In the United States and many Western societies, there are only two genders—female or male. Your gender is assigned at birth based on external biological attributes. However, not all individuals feel comfortable with their gender assignment. The term *transgender* is now used to describe people who don't feel that their assigned gender fits them well.

The division into just two genders—male/female—is very common cross-culturally. But a strict dichotomy is far from universal. Some societies, like the Cheyenne Native Americans of the Great Plains, recognized male, female, and a third gender, referred to by the Cheyennes as "two-spirits." "Two-spirit" people were usually biological males. The gender status of "two-spirit" was often recognized after a boy finished his vision quest, usually in his preadolescent years. A two-spirit person would wear women's dress and take on many of the activities of women. A two-spirit might even be taken as a second wife by a man, but whether the man and the two-spirit person engaged in sex is unknown. The role of a "two-spirit" person was not equivalent to becoming a woman, because two-spirits played special roles at weddings and childbirth. Europeans referred to a two-spirit individual as a *berdache*.[4] Accounts of "two-spirit" biological females who take on the role of men are relatively rare, but they do occur in a number of native North American societies, such as the Kaska of Yukon Territory, the Klamath of southern Oregon, and the Mohave of the Colorado River area in the southwestern United States. These biological female "two-spirits" could marry women, and such relationships were known to be lesbian relationships [5]

In Oman, there is a third gender role called *xanith*. Anatomically male, *xaniths* speak of themselves as "women." However, *xaniths* have their own distinctive dress—they wear clothes that are neither male nor female. In fact, their clothes and dress seem in-between. Men wear white clothes, women bright patterns, and *xaniths* wear unpatterned pastels. Men have short hair, women long, and *xaniths* are medium-length. Women are generally secluded in their houses and can only go out with permission from their husbands, but the *xanith* is free to come and go and works as a servant and/or a homosexual prostitute. But the *xanith* gender role is not necessarily forever. A *xanith* may decide to marry, and if he is able to have intercourse with his bride, he becomes a "man." An older *xanith* who is no longer attractive may decide to become an "old man."[6]

PHYSIQUE AND PHYSIOLOGY

As we noted earlier, males and females cannot readily be distinguished in some animal species. Although they differ in chromosome makeup and in their external and internal organs of reproduction, they do not differ otherwise. In contrast, humans are **sexually dimorphic**—that is, the two sexes of our species are generally different in size and appearance. Females have proportionately wider pelvises. Males typically are taller and have heavier skeletons. Females have a larger proportion of their body weight in fat; males have a larger proportion of body weight in muscle. Males typically have greater grip strength, proportionately larger hearts and lungs, and greater aerobic capacity (greater intake of oxygen during strenuous activity).

North American culture tends to view "taller" and "more muscled" as better, which may reflect a bias toward males. But how did these differences come about? Natural selection may have favored these traits in males but selected against them in females. Because females bear children, selection may have favored earlier cessation of growth, and therefore less ultimate height so that the nutritional needs of a fetus would not compete with a growing mother's needs.[7] (Females achieve their ultimate height shortly after puberty, but boys continue to grow for years after puberty.) Similarly, there is some evidence that females are less affected than males by nutritional shortages, presumably because they tend to be shorter and have proportionately more fat.[8] Natural selection may have favored more proportionate "fatness" in females because that resulted in greater reproductive success.

Athletes can build up their muscle strength and increase their aerobic work capacity through training. Given that fact, cultural factors, such as how much a society expects and allows males and females to engage in muscular activity, could influence the degree to which females and males differ muscularly and in aerobic capacity. Similar training may account for the recent trend toward decreasing differences between females and males in certain athletic events, such as marathons and swim meets. Even

Hmong women carry large loads of firewood to market.

when it comes to female and male physique and physiology, then, what we see may be the result of both culture and genes.[9]

GENDER ROLES

Productive and Domestic Activities

In the chapter on economic systems, we noted that all societies assign or divide labor somewhat differently between females and males. Because role assignments have a clear cultural component, we speak of them as **gender roles**. What is of particular interest here about the gender division of labor is not so much that every society has different work for males and females but rather that so many societies divide up work in similar ways. The question, then, is: Why are there universal or near-universal patterns in such assignments?

Table 10–1 summarizes the worldwide patterns indicating which activities are performed by which gender in all or almost all societies, which activities are usually performed by one gender, and which activities are commonly assigned to either gender or both. If every culture assigned work arbitrarily to the genders, there wouldn't be any patterns in the table. Although many tasks are assigned to both genders (the middle column), clearly some patterns are worldwide. One of the most striking is in primary subsistence activities; males almost always hunt and trap animals and females usually gather wild plants. Does this and the other distributions of activities in the table suggest

why females and males generally do different things? Scholars have suggested four explanations or theories that we label: *strength theory, compatibility-with-child-care theory, economy-of-effort theory,* and *expendability theory.*

The *strength theory* focuses on the generally greater strength of males and their superior capacity to mobilize their strength in quick bursts of energy (because of greater aerobic work capacity). Certainly, males may generally best perform activities that require lifting heavy objects (hunting large animals, butchering, clearing land, or working with stone, metal, or lumber), throwing weapons, and running with great speed (as in hunting). And none of the activities females usually perform, with the possible exception of collecting firewood, seem to require the same degree of physical strength or quick bursts of energy. But the strength theory is not completely convincing, if only because it cannot readily explain all the observed patterns. For example, it is not clear that the male activities of trapping small animals, collecting wild honey, or making musical instruments require much physical strength. Moreover, as we will see shortly, women do hunt in some societies, suggesting that differences in strength cannot play a very important role.

The *compatibility-with-child-care theory* emphasizes that women's tasks need to be compatible with child care. Although males can take care of infants, most traditional societies rely on breast-feeding of infants, which men cannot do. (In most societies, women breast-feed their children for two years on the average.) Women's tasks may be those that do not take them far from home for long

TABLE 10–1	Worldwide Patterns in the Division of Labor by Gender				
Type of Activity	Males Almost Always	Males Usually	Either Gender or Both	Females Usually	Females Almost Always
Primary subsistence activities	Hunt and trap animals, large and small	Fish Herd large animals Collect wild honey Clear land and prepare soil for planting	Collect shellfish Care for small animals Plant crops Tend crops Harvest crops Milk animals	Gather wild plants	
Secondary subsistence and household activities		Butcher animals	Preserve meat and fish	Care for children Cook Prepare vegetable foods, drinks, and dairy products Launder Fetch water Collect fuel	Care for infants
Other	Lumber Mine and quarry Make boats, musical instruments, and bone, horn, and shell objects Engage in combat	Build houses Make nets and rope Exercise political leadership	Prepare skins Make leather products, baskets, mats, clothing, and pottery	Spin yarn	

Source: Mostly adapted from Murdock and Provost 1973, 203–25. The information on political leadership and warfare comes from Whyte 1978a, 217. The information on child care comes from Weisner and Gallimore 1977, 169–80.

periods, do not place children in potential danger if they are taken along, and that can be stopped and resumed if an infant needs care. [10]

The compatibility theory may explain why *no* activities other than infant care are listed in the right-hand column of Table 10–1. That is, it may be that there are practically no universal or near-universal women-only activities because until recently most women have had to devote much of their time to nursing and caring for infants, as well as caring for other children. This theory may also explain why men usually perform tasks such as hunting, trapping, fishing, collecting honey, lumbering, and mining. Those tasks are dangerous for infants to be around, and in any case, would be difficult to coordinate with infant care. [11]

Finally, the compatibility theory may also explain why men seem to take over certain crafts in societies with full-time specialization. Although the distinction is not shown in Table 10–1, crafts such as making baskets, mats, and pottery are women's activities in noncommercial societies but tend to be men's activities in societies with full-time craft specialists. [12] Similarly, weaving tends to be a female activity unless it is produced for trade. [13] Full-time specialization and production for trade may increase incompatibility with child care. Cooking is a good example in our own society. Many women are excellent cooks and traditionally did most of the cooking at home, but chefs and bakers tend to be men. Women might be more likely to work as chefs if they could leave their babies and young children in safe places to be cared for by other people or if the hours chefs and bakers work were not so long.

But the compatibility theory does not explain why men usually prepare soil for planting, make objects out of wood, or work bone, horn, and shell. All of those tasks could probably be stopped to tend to a child, and none of them is any more dangerous to children nearby than is cooking. Why, then, do males tend to do them? The *economy-of-effort theory* may help explain patterns that cannot readily be explained by the strength and compatibility theories. For example, it may be advantageous for men to make wooden musical instruments because men generally lumber. [14] Lumbering may give men more knowledge about the physical properties of various woods and make it more likely that they know how to work with different woods. The economy-of-effort interpretation also suggests that it would be advantageous for one gender to perform tasks that are physically located near each other. If women have to be near home to take care of nursing and young children, it would be economical for them to perform other chores in or near the home.

Expendability theory suggests that men, rather than women, will tend to do the dangerous work in a society because the loss of men is less disadvantageous reproductively than the loss of women. If some men lose their lives in hunting, deep-water fishing, mining, quarrying, lumbering, and the like, reproduction need not suffer as long as most fertile women have sexual access to men—for example, if the society permits two or more women to be married to the same man. [15] If something is dangerous, why would anybody, male or female, be willing to do it?

In many farming societies, women can do some agriculture and take care of their young children at the same time, as this mother in Zambia demonstrates.

Perhaps only when society glorifies those roles and endows them with high prestige and other rewards.

Although the various theories, singly or in combination, seem to explain much of the division of labor by gender, there are some unresolved problems. Critics of the strength theory have pointed out that women in some societies do engage in very heavy labor. [16] If women in some societies can develop the strength to do such work, perhaps strength is more a function of training than traditionally has been believed.

The compatibility theory also has some problems. It suggests that labor is divided to conform to the requirements of child care. But sometimes it seems the other way around. For example, women who spend a good deal of time in agricultural work outside the home often ask others to watch and feed their infants while they are unavailable to nurse. [17] Consider, too, the mountain areas of Nepal, where agricultural work is incompatible with child care; heavy loads must be carried up and down steep slopes, fields are far apart, and labor takes up most of the day. Yet women do this work anyway and leave their infants with others for long stretches of time. [18]

Furthermore, in some societies, women hunt—one of the activities most incompatible with child care and generally not done by women. Many Agta women of the Philippines regularly hunt wild pig and deer; women alone or in groups kill almost 30 percent of the large game. [19] The women's hunting does not seem to be incompatible with child care. Women take nursing babies on hunting trips, and the women who hunt do not have lower reproductive rates than the women who choose not to hunt. Agta women may find it possible to hunt because the hunting grounds are only about a half hour from camp, the dogs that accompany the women assist in the hunting and protect the women and babies, and the women generally hunt in groups, so others can help carry babies as well as carcasses. Hunting by women is also fairly common among the Aka, forest foragers in the Central African Republic. Aka women participate in and sometimes lead in organizing cooperative net-hunting, in which an area is circled and animals are flushed out and caught in nets. Women spend approximately 18 percent of their time net-hunting, which is more than men do.[20] In the Canadian subarctic, teams of Chipewyan women would hunt small animals such as muskrats or rabbits, and would commonly join their husbands to hunt large animals such as moose. However, women noted that they would avoid hunting moose after their fourth or fifth month of pregnancy, so they mainly were part of the team when they were newly married and later when they were older. Women did not participate in long-distance hunts,[21] which also suggests that compatibility with child care was a consideration.

As the cases just described suggest, we need to know a lot more about labor requirements. More precisely, we need to know exactly how much strength is required in particular tasks, how dangerous those tasks are, and whether a person could stop working at a task to care for a child. So far, we have mostly guesses. When there is more systematically collected evidence on aspects of particular tasks, we will be in a better position to evaluate the various theories. In any case, none of the available theories implies that the worldwide patterns of division of labor shown in Table 10–1 will persist. As we know from our own and other industrial societies, a strict gender division of labor begins to disappear when machines replace human strength, when women have fewer children, and when women can assign child care to others.

RELATIVE CONTRIBUTIONS TO WORK

In the United States, there is a tendency to equate "work" with a job earning income. Until relatively recently, being a "homemaker" was not counted as an occupation. Anthropologists also tended to ignore household work; indeed, most of the research on division of labor by gender focuses on **primary subsistence activities**—gathering, hunting, fishing, herding, and farming—and relatively less attention is paid to gender contributions to **secondary subsistence activities,** those that involve the processing and preparation of food for eating or storing. With a few exceptions, food almost never can be consumed without preparation of some kind. For example, hunting cannot contribute much to the diet unless the meat is brought back home (cut up or carried whole) and butchered. If the animal is large, the meat often has to be prepared for distribution and/or storage. And as skins and other parts are

often used for clothing or tools, someone has to prepare those. As Hetty Jo Brumbach and Robert Jarvenpa point out, the Western model of hunting focuses on the "kill" (perhaps derived from the notion of sport-hunting) and ignores the complexity of processes associated with it. This view may hide women's role in "hunting" and emphasizes the male role as the "hunter."[22]

Overall Work

We can also ask whether males or females generally do more work. We do not yet have that many studies of how females and males spend their time, but studies of horticultural and intensive agricultural societies so far suggest that, if we count all the kinds of economic activities shown in Table 10–1, women typically work more total hours per day than men.[23] We do not know if this is a truly cross-cultural universal. However, we do know that, in many societies where women earn wages, they are still responsible for the bulk of the household work as well as the child care at home.

Subsistence Work

If we focus on contribution to primary subsistence activities, which are generally located further from the home, female and male contributions are more variable cross-culturally. Estimates of time actually working are not generally available, so most comparisons estimate how much each gender contributes to the diet in terms of caloric intake from primary subsistence activities.

In some societies, women have traditionally contributed more to the economy than men by any measure. For example, among the Tchambuli of New Guinea in the 1930s, the women did all the fishing—going out early in the morning by canoe to their fish traps and returning when the sun was hot. Some of the catch was traded for sago (a starch) and sugarcane, and it was the women who went on the long canoe trips to do the trading.[24]

In contrast, men did almost all of the primary subsistence work among the Toda of India. As they were described early in the 20th century, they depended for subsistence almost entirely on the dairy products of their water buffalo, either by using the products directly or by selling them for grain. Women were not allowed to have anything to do with dairy work; only men tended the buffalo and prepared the dairy products. Women's work was largely household work. Women prepared the purchased grain for cooking, cleaned house, and decorated clothing.[25]

A survey of a wide variety of societies has revealed that these extremes are not common. Usually both women and men contribute a good deal to primary food-getting activities, but men usually contribute more in most societies.[26] Because women are almost always occupied with infant and child care responsibilities, it is not surprising that men usually do most of the primary subsistence work, which generally has to be done away from the home.

Why do women in some societies do as much or more than men in primary subsistence work? Some of the variation is explained by the type of food-getting activities in the society. In societies that depend on hunting, fishing, and herding for most of their calories—generally male activities—men usually contribute more than women.[27] For example, among the Inuit who traditionally depended mostly on hunting and fishing, as well as among the Toda who depended mostly on herding, men did most of the primary subsistence work. In societies that depend on gathering, primarily women's work, women tend to do most of the food-getting.[28] The !Kung are an example. But the predominant type of food-getting is not always predictive. For example, among the Tchambuli who depended mostly on fishing, women did most of the work. Most societies depend upon some form of food production, rather than foraging. With the exception of clearing land, preparing the soil, and herding large animals, which are usually men's tasks, men, women, or both do the work of planting, crop tending (weeding, irrigating), and harvesting (see Table 10–1). So we need some explanation of why women do most of the farming work in some societies but men do it in others. Different patterns predominate in different areas of the world. In Africa, south of the Sahara, women generally do most of the farming. In much of Asia and Europe and the areas around the Mediterranean, men do more.[29]

The type of agriculture may help explain some of the variation. Many have pointed out that men's contribution to primary subsistence tends to be much higher than women's in intensive agricultural societies, particularly with plow agriculture. In contrast, women's contribution is relatively high compared with men's and sometimes higher in horticultural societies. According to Ester Boserup, when population increases and there is pressure to make more intensive use of the land, cultivators begin to use the plow and irrigation, and males start to do more.[30] But it is not clear why.

Why should women not contribute a lot to farming just because plows are used? In trying to answer this question, most researchers shift to considering how much time males and females spend in various farming tasks, rather than estimating the total caloric contribution of females versus males. The reason for this shift is that gender contribution to farming varies substantially over the various phases of the production sequence, as well as from one crop to another. Thus, the total amount of time females versus males work at farming tasks is easier to estimate than how much each gender contributes to the diet in terms of calories. How would caloric contribution be judged, for example, if men do the clearing and plowing, women do the planting and weeding, and both do the harvesting?

Perhaps plow agriculture increases male contribution to subsistence because plowing takes longer and minimizes weeding time. Cross-culturally, men usually clear land. (This doesn't mean that women are not able to plow because there are examples of women plowing when necessary.[31]) It has been estimated that, in one district in Nigeria, 100 days of work are required to clear one acre of virgin land for plowing by tractor; only 20 days are required to prepare the land for shifting cultivation. Weeding is a task that probably can be combined with child

Grinding corn is very time-consuming hard work. A woman in the highlands of Guatemala is grinding corn for tortillas.

care, and perhaps women may have mostly performed it previously for that reason.[32] But the fact that men do the plowing, which may take a lot of time, does not explain why women do relatively fewer farming tasks, including weeding, in societies that have the plow.[33]

Another explanation is that household chores increase substantially with intensive agriculture and limit the time women can spend in the fields. Intensive agriculturalists rely heavily on grain crops (such as corn, wheat, oats) that are usually dried before storing. To make these dried foods edible, they either have to be cooked in water for a long time or they have to be processed first to make cooking faster. Cooking usually requires collecting water and firewood, neither usually close by, and both tasks are usually done by women. The longer the cooking time, the more time is needed and the more water and firewood is needed. In addition, there is more cleaning of pots and utensils. Soaking, grinding, or pounding can reduce cooking time for hard grains, but the process that speeds up cooking the most—grinding—is itself very time-consuming unless done by machine.[34] Then there is also child care and the additional housework that children entail. Household work may increase substantially with intensive agriculture because women in such societies have *more* children than women in horticultural societies.[35] If household work increases in these ways, it is easy to understand why women cannot contribute more time than men, or as much time as men, to intensive agriculture. But women's contribution, although less than men's, is nonetheless substantial; they seem to work outside the home four and a half hours a day, seven days a week, on the average.[36]

We still have not explained why women contribute so much to horticulture in the first place. They may not have as much household work as intensive agricultural women, but neither do the men. Why, then, don't men do relatively more in horticulture also? Men in horticultural societies are often drawn away from cultivation into other types of activities. One of the most common is warfare, in which all able-bodied men are expected to participate. There is evidence that, if males are engaged in warfare when primary subsistence work has to be done, the women must do that subsistence work.[37] Men may also be withdrawn from primary subsistence work if they have to work in distant towns and cities for wages or if they periodically go on long-distance trading trips.[38]

When women contribute a lot to primary food-getting activities, we might expect effects on their childrearing. Several cross-cultural studies suggest that this expectation is correct. In societies with a high female contribution to primary subsistence (in terms of contributing calories), infants are fed solid foods earlier (so that other people besides mothers can feed them) than in societies with a low female contribution.[39] Girls are likely to be trained to be industrious (probably to help their mothers), and girl babies are more valued.[40]

POLITICAL LEADERSHIP AND WARFARE

In almost every known society, men rather than women are generally the leaders in the political arena. One cross-cultural survey found that, in about 88 percent of the surveyed societies, only men were leaders. In 10 percent of societies in which some women occupied leadership positions, the women were either outnumbered by or less powerful than the male leaders.[41] In the remaining 2 percent, leadership was fairly evenly distributed between men and women. If we look at countries, not cultures, women on the average make up only around 10 percent of the representatives in national parliaments or legislative bodies.[42] Whether or not we consider warfare to be part of the political sphere of life, we find an almost universal dominance of males in that arena. In 87 percent of the world's societies, women never participate actively in war.[43] (See the box "Why Do Some Societies Allow Women to Participate in Combat?" for a discussion of women in combat in the remaining 13 percent of societies.)

Even in *matrilineal* societies, which seem to be oriented around women (see the chapter on marital residence and kinship), men usually occupy formal political positions. Among the Iroquois of what is now New York State, women had control over resources, but men, not women, held political office. The highest political body among the League of the Iroquois, which comprised five tribal groups, was a council of 50 male chiefs. Nonetheless, women had considerable informal influence on political affairs. Women could nominate, elect, and impeach their male representatives. Women also could decide between life and death for prisoners of war, forbid the men of their households to go to war, and intervene to bring about peace.[44]

Why have men (at least so far) almost always dominated the political sphere of life? Some scholars have suggested that men's role in warfare gives them the edge in all kinds of political leadership, particularly because they control weapons, an important resource.[45] But evidence suggests that force is rarely used to obtain leadership positions;[46] superior strength is not the deciding factor. Still, warfare may be related to political leadership for another reason. Warfare clearly affects survival, and it occurs regularly in most societies. Therefore, decision making about war may be among the most important kinds of politics in most societies. If so, then the people who know the most about warfare should be making the decisions about it.

To explain why males and not females usually engage in fighting, let us refer to three of the possible explanations of the worldwide patterns in the gender division of labor. Warfare, like hunting, probably requires strength (for throwing weapons) and quick bursts of energy (for running). And certainly combat is one of the most dangerous and uninterruptible activities imaginable, hardly compatible with child care. Also, even if they do not at the time have children, women may generally be kept out of combat because their potential fertility is more important to a population's reproduction and survival than their potential usefulness as warriors.[47] So the strength theory, the compatibility theory, and the expendability theory might all explain the predominance of men in warfare.

Two other factors may be involved in male predominance in politics. One is the generally greater height of men. Why height should be a factor in leadership is unclear, but studies suggest that taller people are more likely to be leaders.[48] Finally, there is the possibility that men

Women in some societies engage in combat, as this Israeli helicopter gunner does.

new perspectives on gender

Why Do Some Societies Allow Women to Participate in Combat?

U.S. women can serve in the military but are not in units directly engaged in combat. Some women feel that such exclusion is unfair and decreases their chances of promotion in the military. Other people, including some women, insist that female participation in combat would be detrimental to military performance or is inappropriate for women. Women in the U.S. military have been attacked in the course of their duties in Iraq and some have died. Some countries currently allow women to engage in combat. And in the 18th and 19th centuries, women made up one wing of the standing army in the West African Kingdom of Dahomey and at one point constituted one-third of the armed forces. Most societies, however, have excluded women from combat, and some have excluded women from any involvement in military activities or planning.

Why, then, do some societies allow women to be warriors? Psychologist David Adams compared about 70 societies studied by anthropologists to try to answer that question. Although most societies exclude women from war, Adams found that women are active warriors, at least occasionally, in 13 percent of the sample societies. In native North America, such societies included the Comanche, Crow, Delaware, Fox, Gros Ventre, and Navajo. In the Pacific, there were active warrior women among the Maori of New Zealand, on Majuro Atoll in the Marshall Islands, and among the Orokaiva of New Guinea. In none of

these societies were the warriors usually women, but women were allowed to engage in combat if they wanted to.

How are the societies with women warriors different from those that exclude women from combat? They differ in one of two ways. Either they conduct war only against people in other societies (this is called "purely external" war) or they marry within their own community. Adams argues that these two conditions, which are not particularly common, preclude the possibility of conflicts of interest between wives and husbands, and therefore women can be permitted to engage in combat because their interests are the same as those of their husbands. Because marriages in most cases involve individuals from the same society, husbands and wives will have the same loyalties if the society has purely external war. And even if war occurs between communities and larger groups in the same society (what we call "internal" war), there will be no conflict of interest between husband and wife if they both grew up in the same community. In contrast, there is internal war at least occasionally in most societies, and wives usually marry in from other communities. In this situation, there may often be a conflict of interest between husband and wife; if women were to engage in combat, they might have to fight against their fathers, paternal uncles, and brothers. And wouldn't we expect the wives to try to warn kin in their home communities if the

husbands planned to attack them? Indeed, the men's likely fear of their wives' disloyalty would explain why women in these societies are forbidden to make or handle weapons or go near meetings in which war plans are discussed.

Many countries today engage in purely external war, so other things being equal, we would not expect conflicts of interest to impede women's participation in combat. Therefore, extrapolating from Adams's findings, we might expect that the barriers against female participation in combat will disappear completely. But other conditions may have to be present before women and men participate equally in combat. In Adams's study, not all societies with purely external war or intracommunity marriage had women warriors. So we may also have to consider the degree to which the society seeks to maximize reproduction (and therefore protect women from danger) and the degree to which the society depends on women for subsistence during wartime.

There are other related questions to explore: Does military participation by women increase women's participation in politics? Does the presence of war in a society decrease or increase women's political participation? Does women's participation in politics or in the military change the nature of war?

Source: From D. B. Adams 1983; J. S. Goldstein 2001; 2004.

dominate politics because they get around more in the outside world than do women. Men's activities typically take them farther from home; women tend to work more around the home. If societies choose leaders at least in part because of what they know about the larger world, then men will generally have some advantage. In support of this reasoning, Patricia Draper found that, in settled !Kung groups, women no longer engaged in long-distance gathering, and they seemed to have lost much of their former influence in decision making.[49] Involvement in child care may also detract from influence in decision making. In a study of village leadership among the Kayapo

of Brazil, Dennis Werner found that women with heavy child care burdens were less influential than women not as involved in child care; he suggests that they had fewer friends and missed many details of what was going on in the village.[50]

These various explanations suggest why men generally dominate politics, but we still need to explain why women participate in politics more in some societies than in others. Marc Ross investigated this question in a cross-cultural survey of 90 societies.[51] In that sample, the degree of female participation in politics varied considerably. For example, among the Mende of Sierra Leone, women regularly held high office, but among the Azande of Zaire, women took no part in public life. One factor that predicts the exclusion of women from politics is the organization of communities around male kin. As we will see later, when they marry, women usually have to leave their communities and move to their husband's place. If women are "strangers" in a community with many related males, then the males will have political advantages because of their knowledge of community members and past events.

THE RELATIVE STATUS OF WOMEN

There are probably as many definitions of status as there are researchers interested in the topic. To some, the relative status of the sexes means how much importance society confers on females versus males. To others, it means how much power and authority men and women have relative to each other. And to still others, it means what kinds of rights women and men possess to do what they want to do. In any case, many social scientists ask why the status of women appears to vary from one society to another. Why do women have few rights and little influence in some societies and more of each in other societies? In other words, why is there variation in degree of **gender stratification**?

In the small Iraqi town of Daghara, women and men live very separate lives.[52] In many respects, women appear to have very little status. Like women in some other parts of the Islamic world, women in Daghara live their lives mostly in seclusion, staying in their houses and interior courtyards. If women must go out, which they can do only with male approval, they must shroud their faces and bodies in long black cloaks. These cloaks must be worn in mixed company, even at home. Women are essentially excluded from political activities. Legally, they are considered to be under the authority of their fathers and husbands. Even the sexuality of women is controlled. There is strict emphasis on virginity before marriage. Because women are not permitted even casual conversations with strange men, the possibilities for extramarital or even premarital relationships are very slight. In contrast, hardly any sexual restrictions are imposed on men.

But some societies such as the Mbuti seem to approach equal status for males and females. Like most food collectors, the Mbuti have no formal political organization to make decisions or to settle disputes. Public disputes occur, and both women and men take part in the uproar that is part of such disputes. Not only do women make their positions known, but their opinions are often heeded. Even in domestic quarrels involving physical violence between husband and wife, others usually intervene to stop them, regardless of who hit whom first.[53] Women control the use of dwellings; they usually have equal say over the disposal of resources they or the men collect, over the upbringing of their children, and about whom their children should marry. One of the few signs of inequality is that women are somewhat more restricted than men with respect to extramarital sex.[54]

There are many theories about why women have relatively high or low status. One of the most common is that women's status will be high when they contribute substantially to primary subsistence activities. This theory would predict that women should have very little status when food-getting depends largely on hunting, herding, or intensive agriculture. A second theory suggests that men will be more valued and esteemed than women where warfare is particularly important. A third theory suggests that men will have higher status where there are centralized political hierarchies. The reasoning in this theory is essentially the same as the reasoning in the warfare theory: Men usually play the dominant role in political behavior, so men's status should be higher wherever political behavior is more important or frequent. Finally, there is the theory that women will have higher status where kin groups and couples' places of residence after marriage are organized around women.

One of the problems in evaluating these theories is that decisions have to be made about the meaning of *status*. Does it mean value? Rights? Influence? And do all these aspects of status vary together? Cross-cultural research by Martin Whyte suggests that they do not. For each sample society in his study, Whyte rated 52 items that might be used to define the relative status of the sexes. These items included such things as which sex can inherit property, who has final authority over disciplining unmarried children, and whether the gods in the society are male, female, or both. The results of the study indicate that very few of these items are related. Therefore, Whyte concluded, we cannot talk about status as a single concept. Rather, it seems more appropriate to talk about the relative status of women in different spheres of life.[55]

Even though Whyte found no necessary connection between one aspect of status and another, he decided to ask whether some of the theories correctly predict why some societies have many, as opposed to few, areas in which the status of women is high. Let us turn first to the ideas *not* supported by the available cross-cultural evidence. Contrary to popular belief, the idea that generally high status stems from a greater caloric contribution to primary subsistence activities is not supported.[56] For example, women seem to have higher status the more a society depends upon hunting, but women do little of the primary subsistence work in hunting societies. And it is commonly thought that warfare should bolster male status, but there is no consistent evidence that a high frequency of warfare generally lowers women's status in different spheres of life.[57]

What does predict higher status for women in many areas of life? Although the results are not strong, there is some support in Whyte's study for the theory that women have somewhat higher status where kin groups and marital residence are organized around women. (We discuss these features of society more fully in the chapter on marital residence and kinship.) The Iroquois are a good example. Even though Iroquois women could not hold formal political office, they had considerable authority within and beyond the household. Related women lived together in longhouses with husbands who belonged to other kin groups. In the

new perspectives on gender

Women's Electoral Success on the Northwest Coast

Political life has changed dramatically since first contact with Europeans for most Native American groups, including the Coast Salish of western Washington State and British Columbia. With impetus from the U.S. and Canadian governments, each of the recognized Coast Salish communities now has an elected council. But who is getting elected? Even though women did not have much of a role in traditional politics, now the Coast Salish groups are electing a lot of women. From the 1960s to the 1980s, women held over 40 percent of the council seats in the 12 Washington State groups, and in the 1990s, women held 28 percent of the seats in the 50 British Columbian groups. The proportion of women on the councils varies from 6 percent among the Tulalip to 62 percent among the Stillaguamish. What accounts for the women's electoral success? And why does that success vary from one group to another, even though the groups are closely related culturally?

According to Bruce Miller, who did a comparative study of women's electoral success in Coast Salish communities, women generally have more of a political role now perhaps because new economic opportunities in the service and technical sectors allow women to contribute more to the household economy. But why do women win proportionately more council seats in some communities than in others? Miller found that women win proportionately more seats in communities with less income, the least income derived from fishing, and the smallest populations. Why should lower household income predict more electoral success for women? Miller suggests that it is not so much the amount of income but rather the degree to which women (compared with men) contribute to household income. In groups with economic difficulties, the jobs women are able to get play a vital role in the household. Federally funded programs such as the War on Poverty helped women to acquire technical skills and jobs. Simultaneously many men in some communities lost their jobs in logging and agriculture.

But a high dependence on fishing income seems to favor men politically. Families that operate vessels with a large drawstring net to catch fish at sea can make hundreds of thousands of dollars a year. Men predominantly do such fishing, and where there is such lucrative fishing, the successful men dominate the councils. Even though women may have jobs too, their income is not as great as the successful fisherman's.

Why should women be more successful politically in smaller communities? Miller suggests that women have a better chance to be known personally when the community is small, even though working outside the home in technical or service jobs cuts down on the time women can devote to tribal ceremonials and other public events.

Does female income relative to male and community size help explain the relative political success of women elsewhere? We do not know yet, but subsequent research may help us find out.

Source: B. G. Miller 1992.

Women as well as men serve on political councils in many Coast Salish communities. Here, we see a swearing-in ceremony for the Special Chiefs' Council in Sardis, British Columbia.

applied anthropology

Economic Development and Women's Status

Based on the writings of Ester Boserup and subsequent scholarship on women in development, the prevailing opinion was that development usually made things worse for women. Development agents commonly targeted men for learning new technology and how to produce crops for sale. Today, women in developing countries are still largely left out and women still face difficulties, but recent research has documented how women often find creative solutions to participating in commercial enterprises. In many cases, involvement in commercial activity leads to improvement in women's lives, at least as judged from material and status benefits they receive. Producing for a market might range in scale from raising a few extra pigs for sale in southwestern China, to more complex involvement such as contract farming for crop exports in Kenya, or market trading in Ghana.

Some of the creative strategies women use in Kenya to get around their structural disadvantages include buying or renting land with their proceeds, "pooling" small pieces of land to meet minimum requirements for commercial growers, joining women's rotating credit associations, and looking to the private sector for training and materials for contract agriculture.

Almost everywhere, women in developing countries use money from their commercial enterprise to purchase things for their households. At first the money might go to food purchases, household goods, and education for their children. If their incomes or savings grow, women may pay for large appliances, furniture, and farm machinery and vehicles. Women, in contrast to men, tend to plow all their earnings into household expenditures.

Most of these recent studies suggest that bringing money into the household generally translates into lasting changes, including increased educational opportunities, greater say in household decisions, and higher social status in the community.

Some opportunities for women open up when men move into other domains. For example, among the Asante of Ghana, many men moved out of market trading to take advantage of more lucrative cocoa production. Women had long been traders along with men, but with the departure of men, women took over many of men's former market niches and began to engage in longer-distance trade. And, in Kenya, male migration has increased the number of women who manage the farm and head households.

The places we have discussed so far are largely agricultural. Women's work is primarily in or near the household. Commercial involvement gets women more into the public sector. But what about industrial societies, where only a small proportion of people engage in farming? According to a survey of 61 countries, gender equality is more favored in industrializing countries than in agricultural societies. With industrialization, infant and child mortality decline, lessening the pressure on women to reproduce. Perhaps this frees them to pursue education and work outside the home. Postindustrial countries, with even lower fertility rates, are even more accepting of gender equality. As women learn more and get out in the world more, gender inequality appears to decline.

Sources: Anita Spring 2000a; 2000b; 2000c; Bossen 2000; G. Clark 2000; Doyle 2005.

---

longhouse, the women's authority was clear, and they could ask objectionable men to leave. The women controlled the allocation of the food they produced. Allocation could influence the timing of war parties, because men could not undertake a raid without provisions. Women were involved in the selection of religious leaders, half of whom were women. Even in politics, although women could not speak or serve on the council, they largely controlled the selection of councilmen and could institute impeachment proceedings against those to whom they objected.[58]

In preindustrial societies, women have generally lower status in societies with more political hierarchy.[59] Lower status for women is also associated with other indicators of cultural complexity—social stratification, plow and irrigation agriculture, large settlements, private property, and craft specialization. Only one type of influence for women increases with cultural complexity—informal influence. But, informal influence may simply reflect a lack of *real* influence.[60] Why cultural complexity in preindustrial societies is associated with women having less authority in the home, less control over property, and more restricted sexual lives is not yet understood. However, the relationship between cultural complexity and gender equality appears to be reversed in industrial and postindustrial societies. Judging by a comparative study of gender attitudes in 61 countries, it seems that countries relying on agriculture such as Nigeria and Peru have the least favorable attitudes toward gender equality, industrial societies such as Russia and Taiwan have moderately favorable attitudes, and postindustrial societies such as Sweden and the United States have the most favorable attitudes toward gender equality.[61] One of the critical differences explaining this reversal may be the role that formal education plays in industrial and postindustrial societies. Education almost always increases status, and the more girls and young women are educated, the greater the likelihood that their status will increase. Furthermore, although the mechanisms are not well understood, education usually results in lowered fertility, which perhaps frees women to pursue other interests. As we discussed earlier, one study among the Kayapo found that women with more children are considered less influential.[62]

Western colonialism appears to have been generally detrimental to women's status. Although the relative status of men and women may not have been equal before the Europeans arrived, colonial influences seem generally to have undermined the position of women. There are plenty of examples of Europeans restructuring landownership around men and teaching men modern farming techniques, even in places where women were usually the farmers. In addition, men more often than women could earn cash through wage labor or through sales of goods (such as furs) to Europeans.[63] We are beginning to understand some of the conditions that may enhance or decrease certain aspects of women's status. If we can understand which of these conditions are most important, society may be able to reduce gender inequality if it wants to.[64]

PERSONALITY DIFFERENCES

Much of the research on gender differences in personality has taken place in the United States and other Western countries where psychology is a major field of study. Although such studies are informative, they do not tell us whether the observed differences hold true in cultures very different from our own. Fortunately, we now have systematic observational studies for various non-Western societies. These studies recorded the minute details of behavior of substantial numbers of males and females. Any conclusions about female-male differences in aggressiveness, for example, are based on actual counts of the number of times a particular individual tried to hurt or injure another person during a given amount of observation time. Almost all of these differences are subtle and a matter of degree, not a matter of a behavior being present or absent in females or males.

Which differences in personality are suggested by these systematic studies? Most of them have observed children in different cultural settings. The most consistent difference is in the area of aggression; boys try to hurt others more frequently than girls do. In an extensive comparative study of children's behavior, the Six Cultures project, this difference showed up as early as 3 years to 6 years of age.[65] In the Six Cultures project, six different research teams observed children's behavior in Kenya (among the Gusii),

Mexico, India, the Philippines, Okinawa, and the United States. A more recent cross-cultural comparison of four other cultures (the Logoli of Kenya, Nepal, Belize, and American Samoa) supports the sex difference in aggression.[66] Studies in the United States are consistent with the cross-cultural findings: In a large number of observation and experimental studies, boys exhibited more aggression than girls.[67]

Other female-male differences have turned up with considerable consistency, but we have to be cautious in accepting them, either because they have not been documented as well or because there are more exceptions. There seems to be a tendency for girls to exhibit more responsible behavior, including nurturance (trying to help others). Girls seem more likely to conform to adult wishes and commands. Boys try more often to exert dominance over others to get their own way. In play, boys and girls show a preference for their own gender. Boys seem to play in large groups, girls in small ones. And boys seem to maintain more distance between each other than girls do.[68]

If we assume that these differences are consistent across cultures, how can we explain them? Many writers and researchers believe that because certain female-male differences are so consistent, they are probably rooted in the biological differences between the two sexes. Aggression is one of the traits talked about most often in this connection, particularly because this male-female difference appears so early in life.[69] But an alternative argument is that societies bring up boys and girls differently because they almost universally require adult males and females to perform different types of roles. If most societies expect adult males to be warriors or to be prepared to be warriors, shouldn't we expect most societies to encourage or idealize aggression in males? And if females are almost always the caretakers of infants, shouldn't we also expect societies generally to encourage nurturant behaviors in females?

Researchers tend to adopt either the biological or the socialization view, but it is possible that both kinds of causes are important in the development of gender differences. For example, parents might turn a slight genetic difference into a large gender difference by maximizing that difference in the way they socialize boys versus girls.

Cross-culturally, girls more often play in small, intimate groups, boys in larger groups.

It is difficult for researchers to distinguish the influence of genes and other biological conditions from the influence of socialization. We have research indicating that parents treat boy and girl infants differently as early as birth.[70] In spite of the fact that objective observers can see no major "personality" differences between girl and boy infants, parents often claim to.[71] But parents may unconsciously want to see differences and may therefore produce them in socialization. So even early differences could be learned rather than genetic. Remember, too, that researchers cannot do experiments with people; for example, parents' behavior cannot be manipulated to find out what would happen if boys and girls were treated in exactly the same ways.

However, there is considerable experimental research on aggression in nonhuman animals. These experiments suggest that the hormone androgen is partly responsible for higher levels of aggression. For example, in some experiments, females injected with androgen at about the time the sexual organs develop (before or shortly after birth) behave more aggressively when they are older than do females without the hormone. These results may or may not apply to humans of course, but some researchers have investigated human females who were "androgenized" in the womb because of drugs given to their mothers to prevent miscarriage. By and large, the results of these studies are similar to the experimental studies—androgenized human females show similar patterns of higher aggression.[72] Some scholars take these results to indicate that biological differences between males and females are responsible for the male-female difference in aggression;[73] others suggest that even these results are not conclusive, because females who get more androgen show generally disturbed metabolic systems, and general metabolic disturbance may itself increase aggressiveness. Furthermore, androgen-injected females may look more like males because they develop male-like genitals; therefore, they may be treated like males.[74]

Is there any evidence that socialization differences may account for differences in aggression? Although a cross-cultural survey of ethnographers' reports on 101 societies does show that more societies encourage aggression in boys than in girls, most societies show no difference in aggression training.[75] The few societies that do show differences in aggression training can hardly account for the widespread sex differences in actual aggressiveness. But the survey does not necessarily mean that there are no consistent differences in aggression training for boys and girls. All it shows is that there are no *obvious* differences. For all we know, the learning of aggression and other "masculine" traits by boys could be produced by subtle types of socialization.

One possible type of subtle socialization that could create gender differences in behavior is the chores children are assigned. It is possible that little boys and girls learn to behave differently because their parents ask them to do different kinds of work. Beatrice and John Whiting reported from the Six Cultures project that, in societies where children were asked to do a great deal of work, they generally showed more responsible and nurturant behavior. Because girls are almost always asked to do more work than boys, they may be more responsible and nurturant for this reason alone.[76] If this reasoning is correct, we should find that, if boys are asked to do girls' work, they will learn to behave more like girls.

A study of Luo children in Kenya by Carol Ember supports this view.[77] Girls were usually asked to babysit, cook, clean house, and fetch water and firewood. Boys were usually asked to do very little because boys' traditional work was herding cattle, and most families in the community studied had few cattle. But for some reason, more boys than girls had been born, and many mothers without girls at home asked their sons to do girls' chores. Systematic behavior observations showed that much of the behavior of the boys who did girls' work was intermediary between the behavior of other boys and the behavior of girls. The boys who did girls' work were more like girls in that they were less aggressive, less domineering, and more responsible than other boys, even when they weren't working. So it is possible that task assignment has an important influence on how boys and girls learn to behave. These and other subtle forms of socialization need to be investigated more thoroughly.

Misconceptions About Differences in Behavior

Before we leave the subject of behavior differences, we should note some widespread beliefs about them that research does not support. Some of these mistaken beliefs are that girls are more dependent than boys, that girls are more sociable, and that girls are more passive. The results obtained by the Six Cultures project cast doubt on all these notions.[78] First, if we think of dependency as seeking help and emotional support from others, girls are generally no more likely to behave this way than boys. To be sure, the results do indicate that boys and girls have somewhat different styles of dependency. Girls more often seek help and contact; boys more often seek attention and approval. As for sociability, which means seeking and offering friendship, the Six Cultures results showed no reliable differences between the sexes. Of course, boys and girls may be sociable in different ways because boys generally play in larger groups than girls. As for the supposed passivity of girls, the evidence is also not particularly convincing. Girls in the Six Cultures project did not consistently withdraw from aggressive attacks or comply with unreasonable demands. The only thing that emerged as a female-male difference was that older girls were less likely than boys to respond to aggression with aggression. But this finding may not reflect passivity as much as the fact that girls are less aggressive than boys, which we already knew.

So some of our common ideas about female-male differences are unfounded. Others, such as those dealing with aggression and responsibility, cannot be readily dismissed and should be investigated further.

As we noted, an observed difference in aggression does not mean that males are aggressive and females are not. Perhaps because males are generally more aggressive, aggression in females has been studied less often. For that reason, Victoria Burbank focused on female aggression in an Australian aborigine community she calls Mangrove. During the 18 months that she was there, Burbank observed some act of aggression almost every other day. Consistent with the cross-cultural evidence, men initiated aggression more often than women, but women were initiators about 43 percent of the time. The women of Mangrove engaged in almost all the same kinds of aggression as men did, including fighting, except that it tended not to be as lethal as male violence. Men most often used lethal weapons; when women fought with weapons, they mostly used sticks, not spears, guns, or knives. Burbank points out that, in contrast to Western cultures, female aggression is not viewed as unnatural or deviant but rather as a natural expression of anger.[79]

SEXUALITY

In view of the way the human species reproduces, it is not surprising that sexuality is part of our nature. But no society we know of leaves sexuality to nature; all have at least some rules governing "proper" conduct. There is much variation from one society to another in the degree of sexual activity permitted or encouraged before marriage, outside marriage, and even within marriage. And societies vary markedly in their tolerance of nonheterosexual sexuality.

Cultural Regulations of Sexuality: Permissiveness Versus Restrictiveness

All societies seek to regulate sexual activity to some degree, and there is a lot of variation cross-culturally. Some societies allow premarital sex; others forbid it. The same is true for extramarital sex. In addition, a society's degree of restrictiveness is not always consistent throughout the life span or for all aspects of sex. For example, a number of societies ease sexual restrictions somewhat for adolescents, and many become more restrictive for adults.[80] Then, too, societies change over time. The United States has traditionally been restrictive, but until recently—before the emergence of the AIDS epidemic—more permissive attitudes were gaining acceptance.

Premarital Sex   The degree to which sex before marriage is approved or disapproved of varies greatly from society to society. The Trobriand Islanders, for example, approved of and encouraged premarital sex, seeing it as an important preparation for later marriage roles. Both girls and boys were given complete instruction in all forms of sexual expression at the onset of puberty and were allowed plenty of opportunity for intimacy. Some societies not only allow premarital sex on a casual basis but specifically encourage trial marriages between adolescents. Among the Ila-speaking peoples of central Africa, at harvest time, girls were given houses of their own where they could play at being wife with the boys of their choice.[81]

On the other hand, premarital sex was discouraged in many societies. For example, among the Tepoztlan Indians of Mexico, a girl's life became "crabbed, cribbed, confined"

from the time of her first menstruation. She was not to speak to or encourage boys in the least way. To do so would be to court disgrace, to show herself to be crazy. The responsibility of guarding the chastity and reputation of one or more daughters of marriageable age was often a burden for the mother. One mother said she wished her 15-year-old daughter would marry soon because it was inconvenient to "spy" on her all the time.[82] In many Muslim societies, a girl's premarital chastity was tested after her marriage. After the wedding night, blood-stained sheets were displayed as proof of the bride's virginity.

Cultures do not remain the same; attitudes and practices can change markedly over time, as in the United States. In the past, sex was generally delayed until after marriage; in the 1990s, most Americans accepted or approved of premarital sex.[83]

Sex in Marriage   Not surprisingly, there are many common features in the sexual relations in married couples, but there is considerable cross-cultural variation in many respects. In most societies, some form of face-to-face sexual intercourse or coitus is the usual pattern, most preferring the woman on her back and the man on top. Couples in most cultures prefer privacy. This is easier in societies with single-family dwellings or separate rooms, but privacy is difficult to attain in the house in societies with unpartitioned dwellings and multiple families living there. For example, the Siriono of Bolivia had as many as 50 hammocks 10 feet apart in their houses. Not surprisingly, couples in such societies prefer to have sex outdoors in a secluded location.[84]

Night is often preferred for sex, but some cultures specifically opted for day. For example, the Chenchu of India believed that a child conceived at night might be born blind. In some societies, couples engage in sex quickly with little or no foreplay; in others, foreplay may take hours.[85] Attitudes toward marital sex and the frequency of it vary widely from culture to culture. In one cross-cultural survey, frequent marital sex is generally viewed as a good thing, but frequent sex is viewed as undesirable, causing weakness, illness, and sometimes death in 9 percent of the societies.[86] People in most societies abstain from intercourse during menstruation, during at least part of pregnancy, and for a period after childbirth. Some societies prohibit sexual relations before various activities, such as hunting, fighting, planting, brewing, and iron smelting. Our own society is among the most lenient regarding restrictions on intercourse within marriage, imposing only rather loose restraints during mourning, menstruation, and pregnancy.[87]

Extramarital Sex   Extramarital sex is not uncommon in many societies. In about 69 percent of the world's societies, men have extramarital sex more than occasionally, and in about 57 percent of the societies women do so. The frequency of such sexual activity is higher than we might expect, given that only a slight majority of societies say they allow extramarital sex for men, and only a small number (11 percent) say they allow it for women.[88]

In quite a few societies, then, there is quite a difference between the restrictive code and actual practice. The

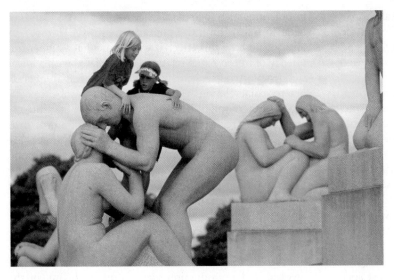

Some cultures are more relaxed about sexuality than others. Does public sculpture reflect that? A park in Oslo, Norway, is dedicated to sculptures by Gustav Vigeland.

Navajo of the 1940s were said to forbid adultery, but young married men under the age of 30 had about a quarter of their heterosexual contacts with women other than their wives.[89] And although people in the United States in the 1970s almost overwhelmingly rejected extramarital sex, 41 percent of married men and about 18 percent of married women had had extramarital sex. In the 1990s, proportionately more men and women reported that they had been faithful to their spouses.[90] Cross-culturally, most societies have a double standard with regard to men and women, with restrictions considerably greater for women.[91] A substantial number of societies openly accept extramarital relationships. The Chukchee of Siberia, who often traveled long distances, allowed a married man to engage in sex with his host's wife, with the understanding that he would offer the same hospitality when the host visited him.[92]

Although a society may allow extramarital sex, a recent cross-cultural study of individual reactions to extramarital sex finds that men and women try a variety of strategies to curtail such sex. Men are much more likely than women to resort to physical violence against their wives; women are more likely to distance themselves from their husbands. Gossip may be employed to shame the relationship and a higher authority may be asked to intervene in more complex societies. The researchers conclude that married women and men universally consider extramarital sex inappropriate, even in societies that permit it sometimes.[93]

Homosexuality When most anthropologists discuss homosexuality, they usually refer to sex between males or sex between females. But although the biological male-female dichotomy corresponds to the gender male-female dichotomy in the West, other societies do not have the same gender concepts, so that the meaning of homosexuality may be different in different societies. For example, the Navajo of the American Southwest traditionally recognized four genders. Only relationships between people of the same gender would be considered homosexual, and they considered such relationships inappropriate.[94] Biologically speaking, some of the cross-gender relationships

would be considered homosexual in the Western view. Most of the research to date has adopted the biological view that homosexuality is between people of the same biological sex.

The range in permissiveness or restrictiveness toward homosexual relations is as great as that for any other kind of sexual activity. Among the Lepcha of the Himalayas, a man was believed to become homosexual if he ate the flesh of an uncastrated pig. But the Lepcha said that homosexual behavior was practically unheard of, and they viewed it with disgust.[95] Perhaps because many societies deny that homosexuality exists, little is known about homosexual practices in the restrictive societies. Among the permissive ones, there is variation in the type and pervasiveness of homosexuality. In some societies, homosexuality is accepted but limited to certain times and certain individuals. For example, among the Papago of the southwestern United States, there were "nights of saturnalia" in which homosexual tendencies could be expressed. The Papago also had many male transvestites who wore women's clothing, did women's chores, and, if not married, could be visited by men.[96] A woman did not have the same freedom of expression. She could participate in the saturnalia feasts but only with her husband's permission, and female transvestites were nonexistent.

Homosexuality occurs even more widely in other societies. The Berber-speaking Siwans of North Africa expected all males to engage in homosexual relations. In fact, fathers made arrangements for their unmarried sons to be given to an older man in a homosexual arrangement. Siwan custom limited a man to one boy. Fear of the Egyptian government made this a secret matter, but before 1909, such arrangements were made openly. Almost all men were reported to have engaged in a homosexual relationship as boys; later, when they were between 16 and 20, they married girls.[97] Such prescribed homosexual relationships between people of different ages are a common form of homosexuality.[98] Among the most extremely pro-homosexual societies, the Etoro of New Guinea preferred homosexuality to heterosexuality. Heterosexuality was prohibited as many as 260 days a year and was forbidden in or near the house and gardens. Male homosexuality, on the other hand, was not prohibited at any time and was believed to make crops flourish and boys become strong.[99] Even among the Etoro, however, men were expected to marry women after a certain age.[100]

Only recently have researchers paid much attention to erotic relationships between females. Although early studies found relatively few societies with female-female sexual relationships, Evelyn Blackwood located reports of 95 societies with such practices, suggesting that it is more common than previously thought.[101] As with male homosexuality, some societies institutionalize same-sex sexual relationships—the Kaguru of Tanzania have female homosexual relationships between older and younger women as part of their initiation ceremonies, reminiscent of the male-male "mentor" relationships in ancient Greece.

Cross-culturally, it is extremely unusual to find "gays" or exclusive male or female homosexuals. In most societies, males and females are expected to marry, and homosexuality, if tolerated or approved, either occurs as a phase in one's life or occurs along with heterosexuality.[102]

Reasons for Restrictiveness

Before we deal with the question of why some societies are more restrictive than others, we must first ask whether all forms of restrictiveness go together. The research to date suggests that societies that are restrictive with regard to one aspect of heterosexual sex tend to be restrictive with regard to other aspects. Thus, societies that frown on sexual expression by young children also punish premarital and extramarital sex.[103] Furthermore, such societies tend to insist on modesty in clothing and are constrained in their talk about sex.[104] But societies that are generally restrictive about heterosexuality are not necessarily restrictive about homosexuality. Societies restrictive about premarital sex are neither more nor less likely to restrict homosexuality. In the case of extramarital sex, the situation is somewhat different. Societies that have a considerable amount of male homosexuality tend to disapprove of males having extramarital heterosexual relationships.[105] If we are going to explain restrictiveness, then, it appears we have to consider heterosexual and homosexual restrictiveness separately.

Let us consider homosexual restrictiveness first. Why do homosexual relationships occur more frequently in some societies, and why are some societies intolerant of such relationships? There are many psychological interpretations of why some people become interested in homosexual relationships, and many of these interpretations relate the phenomenon to early parent-child relationships. So far, the research has not yielded any clear-cut predictions, although several cross-cultural predictors about male homosexuality are intriguing.

One such finding is that societies that forbid abortion and infanticide for married women (most societies permit these practices for illegitimate births) are likely to be intolerant of male homosexuality.[106] This and other findings are consistent with the point of view that homosexuality is less tolerated in societies that would like to increase population. Such societies may be intolerant of all kinds of behaviors that minimize population growth. Homosexuality would have this effect, if we assume that a higher frequency of homosexual relations is associated with a lower frequency of heterosexual relations. The less frequently heterosexual relations occur, the lower the number of conceptions there might be. Another indication that intolerance may be related to a desire for population growth is that societies with famines and severe food shortages are more likely to allow homosexuality. Famines and food shortages suggest population pressure on resources; under these conditions, homosexuality and other practices that minimize population growth may be tolerated or even encouraged.[107]

The history of the Soviet Union may provide some other relevant evidence. In 1917, in the turmoil of revolution, laws prohibiting abortion and homosexuality were revoked and reproduction was discouraged. But, in the period between 1934 and 1936, the policy was reversed. Abortion and homosexuality were again declared illegal, and homosexuals were arrested. At the same time, awards were given to mothers who had more children.[108] Population pressure may also explain why our own society has become somewhat more tolerant of homosexuality recently. Of course, population pressure does not explain why certain individuals become homosexual or why most individuals in some societies engage in such behavior, but it might explain why some societies view such behavior more or less permissively.

Let us now turn to heterosexual behavior. What kinds of societies are more permissive than others? Although we do not yet understand the reasons, we do know that greater restrictiveness toward premarital sex tends to occur in more complex societies—societies that have hierarchies of political officials, part-time or full-time craft specialists, cities and towns, and class stratification.[109] It may be that, as social inequality increases and various groups come to have differential wealth, parents become more concerned with preventing their children from marrying "beneath them." Permissiveness toward premarital sexual relationships might lead a person to become attached to someone not considered a desirable marriage partner. Even worse, from the family's point of view, such "unsuitable" sexual liaisons might result in a pregnancy that could make it impossible for a girl to marry "well." Controlling mating, then, may be a way of trying to control property. Consistent with this view is the finding that virginity is emphasized in rank and stratified societies, in which families are likely to exchange goods and money in the course of arranging marriages.[110]

The biological fact that humans depend on sexual reproduction does not by itself help explain why females and males differ in so many ways across cultures, or why societies vary in the way they handle male and female roles. We are only beginning to investigate these questions. When we eventually understand more about how and why females and males are different or the same in roles, personality, and sexuality, we may be better able to decide how much we want the biology of sex to shape our lives.

SUMMARY ● ○ ○

1. That humans reproduce sexually does not explain why males and females tend to differ in appearance and behavior, and to be treated differently, in all societies.

2. All or nearly all societies assign certain activities to females and other activities to males. These worldwide gender patterns of division of labor may be explained by male-female differences in strength, by differences in compatibility of tasks with child care, or by economy-of-effort considerations and/or the expendability of men.

3. Perhaps because women almost always have infant and child care responsibilities, men in most societies contribute more to primary subsistence activities, in terms of calories. But women contribute substantially to primary subsistence activities in societies that depend heavily on gathering and horticulture and in which warfare occurs while primary subsistence work has to be done. When primary and secondary subsistence work is counted, women typically work more hours than men. In most societies, men are the leaders in the political arena, and warfare is almost exclusively a male activity.

4. The relative status of women compared with that of men seems to vary from one area of life to another. Whether women have relatively high status in one area does not necessarily indicate that they will have high status in another. Less complex societies, however, seem to approach more equal status for males and females in a variety of areas of life.

5. Recent field studies have suggested some consistent female-male differences in personality: Boys tend to be more aggressive than girls, and girls seem to be more responsible and helpful than boys.

6. Although all societies regulate sexual activity to some extent, societies vary considerably in the degree to which various kinds of sexuality are permitted. Some societies allow both masturbation and sex play among children, whereas others forbid such acts. Some societies allow premarital sex; others do not. Some allow extramarital sex in certain situations; others forbid it generally.

7. Societies that are restrictive toward one aspect of heterosexual sex tend to be restrictive with regard to other aspects. And more complex societies tend to be more restrictive toward premarital heterosexual sex than less complex societies.

8. Societal attitudes toward homosexuality are not completely consistent with attitudes toward sexual relationships between the sexes. Societal tolerance of homosexuality is associated with tolerance of abortion and infanticide and with famines and food shortages.

GLOSSARY TERMS ○ ● ○

gender differences	**172**	secondary subsistence
gender roles	**175**	activities **177**
gender stratification	**181**	sex differences **172**
primary subsistence		sexually dimorphic **174**
activities **177**		

CRITICAL QUESTIONS ○ ○ ●

1. Would you expect female-male differences in personality to disappear in a society with complete gender equality in the workplace?

2. Under what circumstances would you expect male-female differences in athletic performance to disappear?

3. What conditions may make the election of a female head of state most likely?

PEARSON
myanthrolab ⫻

Read "Andean Mestizos: Growing Up Female and Male" by Lauris McKee in MyAnthroLibrary and answer the following questions:

1. Which of the Andean Mestizos' ideas about conception, pregnancy, and birth are different from those of your own culture? (Identify your own culture in your answer).

2. According to McKee, what do the Mestizos say is the reason for the shorter breastfeeding of girls?

3. What are the consequences of the gender difference in breast-feeding? Are the parents aware of these consequences?

chapter 11

Marriage and the Family

early all societies known to anthropology have had the custom of marriage. Why marriage is customary in nearly every society we know of is a classic and perplexing question, and one we attempt to deal with in this chapter.

The near universality of marriage customs does not mean that everyone in a society gets married. In addition, when we say that marriage is nearly universal, we do not mean that marriage and family customs are the same in all societies. On the contrary, there is much variation from society to society in how one marries, whom one marries, and even how many people a person can be married to simultaneously. Indeed, although each marriage usually involves one pair at time, most societies in recent times have allowed a man to be married to more than one woman at a time.

Families are universal; all societies have parent-child groups, but the form and size of the family can vary from society to society. Some societies have large extended families with two or more related parent-child groups; others have smaller independent families. Today, marriage is not always the basis for family life. One-parent families are becoming increasingly common in our own and other societies. Marriage has not disappeared in these places—it is still customary to marry—but more individuals are choosing now to have children without being married.

● ○ ●

MARRIAGE

When anthropologists speak of marriage, they do not mean to imply that couples everywhere must get marriage certificates or have wedding ceremonies, as in our own society. **Marriage** merely means a socially approved sexual and economic union, usually between a woman and a man. It is presumed, by both the couple and others, to be more or less permanent, and it subsumes reciprocal rights and obligations between the two spouses and between spouses and their future children.[1] Marriage to more than one spouse at a time is quite common, as we shall see.

It is a socially approved sexual union in that a married couple does not have to hide the sexual nature of their relationship. A woman might say, "I want you to meet my husband," but she could not say, "I want you to meet my lover" without causing some embarrassment in most societies. Although the union may ultimately be dissolved by divorce, couples in all societies begin marriage with some idea of permanence in mind. Implicit too in marriage are reciprocal rights and obligations. These may be more or less specific and formalized regarding matters of property, finances, and childrearing.

Marriage entails both a sexual and an economic relationship, as George Peter Murdock noted: "Sexual relations can occur without economic cooperation, and there can be a division of labor between men and women without sex. But marriage unites the economic and the sexual."[2]

As we will see, the event that marks the commencement of marriage varies in different societies. A Winnebago bride, for example, knew no formal ritual such as a wedding ceremony. She went with her groom to his parents' house, took off her "wedding" clothes and finery, gave them to her mother-in-law, received plain clothes in exchange, and that was that.[3]

Bride, groom, and other guests at a wedding in the village at Yorilgan in Uzbekistan, Central Asia.

The Na Exception

The Na of Yunnan in southwest China, with a population of about 30,000, did not customarily marry or live with their sexual partners. People lived their whole lives in a residential group made up of maternal kin (grandmother, great-uncles, brothers, sisters, and their children). This group was the family, cooperating economically and raising the children together. Furtive sex was the norm.[4] Men would visit women, usually after midnight, and leave before anyone would notice them. There was no other tie between the lovers, nor any encouragement for the relationship to be long-standing. Only a few couples stayed together (the Na do not have words for marriage); but this usually occurred among aristocrats. On and off since 1959, the Chinese government has tried to impose monogamy and fines for illegitimate births, without much success. However, young people's attitudes are changing, largely because of education. At school, children are asked for their father's name, which embarrasses them because they usually don't know it. And the books often refer to married couples.

In the 19th century, the Nayar, a subcaste in India, also lacked the custom of marriage.[5] The Na and the Nayar may both have had frequently absent men. In the Nayar case, the men hired themselves out to fight for princes in various parts of India. In the Na case, between the 1920s and the 1950s, the Na raised horses and mules for caravans they organized to transport merchandise throughout the western part of Yunnan. Of course, the relative absence of men cannot be the only reason for the absence of marriage in these groups; long-distance travel by men occurs in some other ethnic groups along with marriage.

Rare Types of Marriage

In addition to the usual male-female marriages, some societies recognize marriages between people of the same biological sex. Such marriages are not typical in any known society. These same-sex marriages may be socially approved unions, modeled after regular marriages, and they often entail a considerable number of reciprocal rights and obligations. Sometimes the marriages involve an individual who is considered a

191

The bride's relatives arrive at the groom's home bearing gifts and Piki bread from the bride's family at a traditional Hopi engagement ceremony in Arizona.

"woman" or "man," even though "she" or "he" is not that sex biologically. As we noted in the previous chapter, the Cheyenne Indians allowed a married man to take as a second wife a biological man belonging to the third gender, "two-spirits."

Although it is not clear that the Cheyenne male-male marriages involved homosexual relationships, it is clear that temporary homosexual marriages did occur among the Azande of Africa. Before the British took control over what is now Sudan, Azande warriors who could not afford wives often married "boy-wives" to satisfy their sexual needs. As in normal marriages, gifts (although not as substantial) were given by the "husband" to the parents of his boy-wife. The husband performed services for the boy's parents and could sue any other lover of the boy in court for adultery. The boy-wives not only had sexual relations with their husbands but also performed many of the chores female wives traditionally performed for their husbands.[7]

Female-female marriages are reported to have occurred in many African societies, but there is no evidence of any sexual relationship between the partners. It seems, rather, that female-female marriages were a socially approved way for a woman to take on the legal and social roles of a father and husband.[8] For example, among the Nandi, a pastoral and agricultural society of Kenya, about 3 percent of the marriages are female-female marriages. Such marriages appear to be a Nandi solution to the problem of a regular marriage's failure to produce a male heir to property. The Nandi solution is to have the woman, even if her husband is still alive, become a "husband" to a younger female and "father" the younger woman's children. The female husband provides the marriage payments required for obtaining a wife, renounces female work, and takes on the obligations of the husband to that woman. Although no sexual relations are permitted between the female husband and the new wife (or between the female husband and her own husband), the female husband arranges a male consort so that the new wife can have children. Those children, however, consider the female husband to be their father because she (or more aptly the gender role "he") is the socially designated father. If asked who their

father is, a child of such a marriage will name the female who is the husband.[9]

WHY IS MARRIAGE NEARLY UNIVERSAL?

Because virtually all societies practice female-male marriage as we have defined it, we can assume that the custom is adaptive. But saying that does not specify exactly how it may be adaptive. Several interpretations have traditionally been offered to explain why all human societies have the custom of marriage. Each suggests that marriage solves problems found in all societies—how to share the products of a gender division of labor; how to care for infants, who are dependent for a long time; and how to minimize sexual competition. To evaluate the plausibility of these interpretations, we must ask whether marriage provides the best or the only reasonable solution to each problem. After all, we are trying to explain a custom that is virtually universal. The comparative study of other animals, some of which have something like marriage, may help us to evaluate these explanations.

Gender Division of Labor

We noted in the preceding chapter that every society known to anthropology has had a gender division of labor. Males and females in every society perform different economic activities. This gender division of labor has often been cited as a reason for marriage.[10] As long as there is a division of labor by gender, society has to have some mechanism by which women and men share the products of their labor. Marriage would be one way to solve that problem. But it seems unlikely that marriage is the only possible solution. The hunter-gatherer rule of sharing could be extended to include all the products brought in by both women and men. Or a small group of men and women, such as brothers and sisters, might be pledged to cooperate economically. Thus, although marriage may solve the problem of sharing the fruits of a division of labor, it clearly is not the only possible solution.

Prolonged Infant Dependency

Humans exhibit the longest period of infant dependency of any primate. The child's prolonged dependence places the greatest burden on the mother, who is the main child caregiver in most societies. The burden of prolonged child care by human females may limit the kinds of work they can do. They may need the help of a man to do certain types of work, such as hunting, that are incompatible with child care. Because of this prolonged dependency, it has been suggested, marriage is necessary.[11] But here the argument becomes essentially the same as the division-of-labor argument, and it has the same logical weakness. It is not clear why a group of women and men, such as a hunter-gatherer band, could not cooperate in providing for dependent children without marriage.

Sexual Competition

Unlike most other female primates, the human female may engage in intercourse at any time throughout the year. Some scholars have suggested that more or less continuous female sexuality may have created a serious problem—considerable sexual competition between males for females. It is argued that society had to prevent such competition to survive, that it had to develop some way of minimizing the rivalry among males for females to reduce the chance of lethal and destructive conflict.[12]

There are several problems with this argument. First, why should continuous female sexuality make for more sexual competition in the first place? One might argue the other way around. There might be more competition over the scarcer resources that would be available if females were less frequently interested in sex. Second, males of many animal species, even some that have relatively frequent female sexuality (as do many of our close primate relatives), do not show much aggression over females. Third, why couldn't sexual competition, even if it existed, be regulated by cultural rules other than marriage? For instance, society might have adopted a rule whereby men and women circulated among all the opposite-sex members

"I do love you. But, to be perfectly honest, I would have loved any other lovebird who happened to turn up."
(Rothco Cartoons)

of the group, each person staying a specified length of time with each partner. Such a system presumably would solve the problem of sexual competition. On the other hand, such a system might not work particularly well if individuals came to prefer certain other individuals. Jealousies attending those attachments might give rise to even more competition.

Other Mammals and Birds: Postpartum Requirements

None of the theories we have discussed explains convincingly why marriage is the only or the best solution to a particular problem. Also, we now have some comparative evidence on mammals and birds that casts doubt on those theories.[13] How can evidence from other animals help us evaluate theories about human marriage? If we look at the animals that, like humans, have some sort of stable female-male mating, as compared with those that are completely promiscuous, we can perhaps see what sorts of factors may predict male-female bonding in the warm-blooded animal species. Most species of birds, and some mammals such as wolves and beavers, have "marriage." Among 40 mammal and bird species, none of the three factors discussed previously—division of labor, prolonged infant dependency, and greater female sexuality—predicts or is correlated strongly with male-female bonding. With respect to division of labor by sex, most other animals have nothing comparable to a humanlike division of labor, but many have stable female-male matings anyway. The two other supposed factors—prolonged infant dependency and female sexuality—predict just the opposite of what we might expect. Mammal and bird species that have longer dependency periods or more female sexuality are less likely to have stable matings.

Does anything predict male-female bonding? One factor does among mammals and birds, and it may also help explain human marriage. Animal species in which females can simultaneously feed themselves and their babies after birth (*postpartum*) tend not to have stable matings; species in which postpartum mothers cannot feed themselves and their babies at the same time tend to have stable matings. Among the typical bird species, a mother would have difficulty feeding herself and her babies simultaneously. Because the young cannot fly for a while and must be protected in a nest, the mother risks losing them to other animals if she goes off to obtain food. But if she has a male bonded to her (as most bird species do), he can bring back food or take a turn watching the nest. Among animal species that have no postpartum feeding problem, babies are able to travel with the mother almost immediately after birth as she moves about to eat (as do grazers such as horses), or the mother can transport the babies as she moves about to eat (as do baboons and kangaroos). We think the human female has a postpartum feeding problem. When humans lost most of their body hair, babies could not readily travel with the mother by clinging to her fur. And when humans began to depend on certain kinds of food-getting that could be dangerous (such as hunting), mothers could not engage in such work with their infants along.[14]

Recent research on the Hadza foragers of Tanzania appears to support this view. Frank Marlowe found that the caloric contribution of mothers and fathers depends on whether or not they have a nursing infant. Women may generally contribute more calories than men to the diet, but married women who are nursing contribute substantially less than other married women. The lower contribution of nursing mothers appears to be made up by the father. Fathers with nursing children contribute significantly more food to the household than fathers with older children.[15]

Even if we assume that human mothers have a postpartum feeding problem, we still have to ask if marriage is the most likely solution to the problem. We think so, because other conceivable solutions probably would not work as well. For example, if a mother took turns babysitting with another mother, neither might be able to collect enough food for both mothers and the two sets of children dependent on them. But a mother and father share the same set of children, and therefore it would be easier for them to feed themselves and their children adequately. Another possible solution is no pair bonding at all, just a promiscuous group of males and females. But in that kind of arrangement, we think, a particular mother probably would not always be able to count on some male to watch her baby when she had to go out for food or to bring her food when she had to watch her baby. Thus, it seems to us that the problem of postpartum feeding by itself helps to explain why some animals, including humans, have relatively stable male-female bonds.[16] Of course, there is still the question of whether research on other animals can be applied to human beings. We think it can, but not everybody will agree.

HOW DOES ONE MARRY?

When we say that marriage is a socially approved sexual and economic union, we mean that all societies have some way of marking the onset of a marriage, but the ways of doing so vary considerably. For reasons that we don't fully understand, some cultures mark marriages by elaborate rites and celebrations; others mark marriages in much more informal ways. And most societies have economic transactions before, during, or even after the onset of the marriages.

Marking the Onset of Marriage

Many societies have ceremonies marking the beginning of marriage. But others, such as the Taramiut Inuit, the Trobriand Islanders of the South Pacific, and the Kwoma of New Guinea, use different social signals to indicate that a marriage has taken place. Among the Taramiut Inuit, the betrothal is considered extremely important and is arranged between the parents at or before the time their children reach puberty. Later, when the youth is ready, he moves in with his betrothed's family for a trial period. If all goes well—that is, if the girl gives birth to a baby within a year or so—the couple are considered married. At this time, the wife goes with her husband to his camp.[17]

In keeping with the general openness of their society's attitudes toward sexual matters, a Trobriand couple advertise their desire to marry "by sleeping together regularly, by showing themselves together in public, and by remaining with each other for long periods at a time."[18] When a girl accepts a small gift from a boy, she demonstrates that her parents favor the match. Before long, she moves to the boy's house, takes her meals there, and accompanies her husband all day. Then the word goes around that the two are married.[19]

The Kwoma of New Guinea practice a trial marriage followed by a ceremony that makes the couple husband and wife. The girl lives for a while in the boy's home. When the boy's mother is satisfied with the match and knows that her son is too, she waits for a day when he is away from the house. Until that time, the girl has been cooking only for herself, and the boy's food has been prepared by his womenfolk. Now the mother has the girl prepare his meal. The young man returns and begins to eat his soup. When the first bowl is nearly finished, his mother tells him that his betrothed cooked the meal, and his eating it means that he is now married. At this news, the boy customarily rushes out of the house, spits out the soup, and shouts, "Faugh! It tastes bad! It is cooked terribly!" A ceremony then makes the marriage official.[20]

Just in the last three decades, "living together" has become more of an option in the United States and other Western countries. For most, living together is a prelude to marriage or kind of a trial marriage. For some, living together has become an alternative to marriage. Statistics in the United States suggest that a third of married women under age 45 have lived together with a man for at least some time period.[21]

Among those societies that have ceremonies marking the onset of marriage, feasting is a common element. It expresses publicly the unification of the two families by marriage. The Reindeer Tungus of Siberia set a wedding date after protracted negotiations between the two families and their larger kin groups. Go-betweens assume most of the responsibility for the negotiating. The wedding day opens with the two kin groups, probably numbering as many as 150 people, pitching their lodges in separate areas and offering a great feast. After the groom's gifts have been presented, the bride's dowry is loaded onto reindeer and carried to the groom's lodge. There, the climax of the ceremony takes place. The bride takes the wife's place—that is, at the right side of the entrance of the lodge—and members of both families sit in a circle. The groom enters and follows the bride around the circle, greeting each guest, while the guests, in their turn, kiss the bride on the mouth and hands. Finally, the go-betweens spit three times on the bride's hands, and the couple are formally husband and wife. More feasting and revelry bring the day to a close.[22]

In many cultures, marriage includes ceremonial expressions of hostility. Mock fights are staged in many societies. On occasion, hostility can have genuinely aggressive overtones, as among the Gusii of Kenya:

Five young clansmen of the groom come to take the bride and two immediately find the girl and post

A young Iraqi couple in 2008 look at gold jewelry that will be part of her dowry. It is considered to be hers no matter what happens to the marriage.

themselves at her side to prevent her escape, while the others receive the final permission of her parents. When it has been granted the bride holds onto the house posts and must be dragged outside by the young men. Finally she goes along with them, crying and with her hands on her head.[23]

But the battle is not yet over. Mutual antagonism continues right onto the marriage bed, even up to and beyond coitus. The groom is determined to display his virility; the bride is equally determined to test it. "Brides," Robert and Barbara LeVine remarked, "are said to take pride in the length of time they can hold off their mates." Men can also win acclaim. If the bride is unable to walk the following day, the groom is considered a "real man."[24] Such expressions of hostility usually occur in societies in which the two sets of kin are actual or potential rivals or enemies. In many societies, it is common to marry women from "enemy" villages.

As this example suggests, marriage ceremonies often symbolize important elements of the culture. Whereas the Gusii ceremony may symbolize hostility between the two families, the ceremony may promote harmony between the families in other societies. For example, on the Polynesian island of Rotuma, a female clown is an important part of the ceremony. She is responsible for creating an enjoyable, joking atmosphere that facilitates interaction between the two sides.[25]

Economic Aspects of Marriage

"It's not man that marries maid, but field marries field, vineyard marries vineyard, cattle marry cattle." In its down-to-earth way, this German peasant saying indicates that, in many societies, marriage involves economic considerations. In our culture, economic considerations may or may not be explicit. However, in about 75 percent of the societies known to anthropology,[26] one or more explicit economic transactions take place before or after the marriage. The economic transaction may take several forms: bride price, bride service, exchange of females, gift exchange, dowry, or indirect dowry. The distribution of those forms among societies that have economic marriage transactions is shown in Figure 11–1.

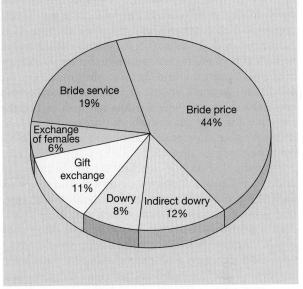

FIGURE 11–1 Distribution of Economic Marriage Transactions Among Societies That Have Them
Note that there are societies in the ethnographic record (25 percent) that lack any substantial economic transactions at marriage.

Source: Based on data from Schlegel and Eloul 1988, 291–309.

Bride Price **Bride price** or **bride wealth** is a gift of money or goods from the groom or his kin to the bride's kin. The gift usually grants the groom the right to marry the bride and the right to her children. Of all the forms of economic transaction involved in marriage, bride price is the most common. In one cross-cultural sample, 44 percent of the societies with economic transactions at marriage practiced bride price; in almost all of those societies, the bride price was substantial.[27] Bride price occurs all over the world but is especially common in Africa and Oceania. Payment can be made in different currencies; livestock and food are two of the more common. With the increased importance of commercial exchange, money has increasingly become part of the bride price payments. Among the Nandi, the bride price consists of about five to seven cattle, one or two sheep and goats, cowrie shells, and money equivalent to the value of one cow. Even in unusual female-female marriages, the female "husband" must pay a bride price to arrange the marriage and be considered the "father."[28]

The Subanun of the Philippines have an expensive bride price—several times the annual income of the groom plus three to five years of bride service (described in the next section).[29] Among the Manus of the Admiralty Islands off New Guinea, a groom requires an economic backer, usually an older brother or an uncle, if he is to marry, but it will be years before he can pay off his debts. Depending on the final bride price, payments may be concluded at the time of the marriage, or they may continue for years afterward.[30]

Despite the connotations that bride price may have for us, the practice does not reduce a woman to the position of slave—although it is associated, as we shall see, with relatively low status for women. The bride price may be important to the woman and her family. Indeed, the fee they receive can serve as a security. If the marriage fails through no fault of hers and the wife returns to her kin, the family might not return the bride price to the groom. On the other hand, the wife's kin may pressure her to remain with her husband, even though she does not wish to, because they do not want to return the bride price or are unable to do so. A larger bride price is associated with more difficulty in obtaining a divorce.[31]

What kinds of societies are likely to have the custom of bride price? Cross-culturally, societies with bride price are likely to practice horticulture and lack social stratification. Bride price is also likely where women contribute a great deal to primary subsistence activities[32] and where they contribute more than men to all kinds of economic activities.[33] Although these findings might suggest that women are highly valued in such societies, recall that the status of women relative to men is not higher in societies in which women contribute a lot to primary subsistence activities. Indeed, bride price is likely to occur in societies in which men make most of the decisions in the household,[34] and decision making by men is one indicator of lower status for women.

Bride Service **Bride service,** which is the next most common type of economic transaction at marriage—occurring in about 19 percent of the societies with economic transactions—requires the groom to work for the bride's family, sometimes before the marriage begins, sometimes after. Bride service varies in duration. In some societies, it lasts for only a few months; in others, as long as several years. Among the North Alaskan Eskimo, for example, the boy works for his in-laws after the marriage is arranged. To fulfill his obligation, he may simply catch a seal for them. The marriage may be consummated at any time while he is in service.[35] In some societies, bride service sometimes substitutes for bride price. An individual might give bride service to reduce the amount of bride price required. Native North and South American societies were likely to practice bride service, particularly if they were egalitarian food collectors.[36]

Exchange of Females Of the societies that have economic transactions at marriage, 6 percent have the custom whereby a sister or female relative of the groom is exchanged for the bride. Among these societies are the Tiv of West Africa and the Yanomamö of Venezuela and Brazil. These societies tend to be horticultural, egalitarian, and to have a relatively high contribution of women to primary subsistence.[37]

Gift Exchange Gift exchange, which involves the exchange of gifts of about equal value by the two kin groups about to be linked by marriage, occurs somewhat more often than the exchange of females (about 11 percent of those with economic transactions).[38] For example, among the Andaman Islanders, as soon as a boy and girl indicate their intention to marry, their respective sets of parents cease all communication and begin sending gifts of food and other objects to each other through a third party. This arrangement continues until the marriage is completed and the two kin groups are united.[39]

Dowry A **dowry** is usually a substantial transfer of goods or money from the bride's family to the bride, the groom, or the couple.[40] Unlike the types of transactions we have discussed so far, the dowry, which occurs in about 8 percent of the societies with economic transactions, is usually not a transaction between the kin of the bride and the kin of the groom. A family has to have wealth to give a dowry, but because the goods go to the new household, no wealth comes back to the family that gave the dowry. Payment of dowries was common in medieval and Renaissance Europe, where the size of the dowry often determined the desirability of the daughter. The custom is still practiced in parts of eastern Europe and in sections of southern Italy and France, where land is often the major item the bride's family provides. Parts of India also practice the dowry.

In contrast to societies with bride price, societies with dowry tend to be those in which women contribute relatively little to primary subsistence activities, there is a high degree of social stratification, and a man is not allowed to be married to more than one woman simultaneously.[41] Why does dowry tend to occur in these types of societies? One theory suggests that the dowry is intended to guarantee future support for a woman and her children, even though she will not do much primary subsistence work. Another theory is that the dowry is intended to attract the best bridegroom for a daughter in monogamous societies with a high degree of social inequality. The dowry strategy is presumed to increase the likelihood that the daughter and her children will do well reproductively. Both theories are supported by recent cross-cultural research, with the second predicting dowry better.[42] But many stratified societies in which women and men have only one spouse at a time (including our own) do not practice dowry. Why this is so still needs to be explained.

Indirect Dowry The dowry is provided by the bride's family to the bride, the groom, or the couple. But sometimes the payments to the bride originate from the groom's family. Because the goods are sometimes first given to the bride's father, who passes most if not all of them to her, this kind of transaction is called **indirect dowry**.[43] Indirect dowry occurs in about 12 percent of the societies in which marriage involves an economic transaction. For example, among the Basseri of southern Iran, the groom's father assumes the expense of setting up the couple's new household. He gives cash to the bride's father, who uses at least some of the money to buy his daughter household utensils, blankets, and rugs.[44]

RESTRICTIONS ON MARRIAGE: THE UNIVERSAL INCEST TABOO

Hollywood and its press agents notwithstanding, marriage is not always based solely on mutual love, independently discovered and expressed by the two life-partners-to-be. Nor is it based on sex or wealth alone. Even when love, sex, and economics are contributing factors, regulations specify whom one may or may not marry. Perhaps the most rigid regulation, found in *all* cultures, is the **incest taboo**, which prohibits sexual intercourse or marriage between some categories of kin.

The most universal aspect of the incest taboo is the prohibition of sexual intercourse or marriage between mother and son, father and daughter, and brother and sister. No society in recent times has permitted either sexual intercourse or marriage between those pairs. A few societies in the past, however, did permit incest, mostly within the royal and aristocratic families, though generally it was forbidden to the rest of the population. For example, the Incan and Hawaiian royal families allowed marriage within the family. Probably the best-known example of allowed incest involved Cleopatra of Egypt.

It seems clear that the Egyptian aristocracy and royalty indulged in father-daughter and brother-sister marriages. Cleopatra was married to two of her younger brothers at different times.[45] The reasons seem to have been partly religious—a member of the family of the pharaoh, who was considered a god, could not marry any "ordinary" human—and partly economic, for marriage within the family kept the royal property undivided. In Egypt, between 30 B.C. and A.D. 324, incest was allowed not just in the royal family; an estimated 8 percent of commoner marriages were brother-sister marriages.[46]

But, despite these exceptions, the fact remains that no culture we know of today permits or accepts incest within the nuclear family. Why is the familial incest taboo universal? Several explanations have been suggested.

Childhood-Familiarity Theory

The childhood-familiarity theory, suggested by Edward Westermarck, was given a wide hearing in the early 1920s. Westermarck argued that people who have been closely associated with each other since earliest childhood, such as siblings, are not sexually attracted to each other and therefore would avoid marriage with each other.[47] This theory was subsequently rejected because of evidence

Children eating in the Children's House's kitchen on an Israeli kibbutz.

that some children were sexually interested in their parents and siblings. Studies have suggested, however, that there might be something to Westermarck's theory.

Yonina Talmon investigated marriage patterns among the second generation of three well-established collective communities (*kibbutzim*) in Israel. In these collectives, children live with many members of their peer group in quarters separate from their families. They are in constant interaction with their peers, from birth to maturity. The study revealed that, among 125 couples, there was "not one instance in which both mates were reared from birth in the same peer group,"[48] despite parental encouragement of marriage within the peer group. Children reared in common not only avoided marriage, they also avoided any sexual relations among themselves.

Talmon stated that the people reared together firmly believed that overfamiliarity breeds sexual disinterest. As one of them told her, "We are like an open book to each other. We have read the story in the book over and over again and know all about it."[49] Talmon's evidence reveals not only the onset of disinterest and even sexual antipathy among children reared together, but a correspondingly heightened fascination with newcomers or outsiders, particularly for their "mystery."

Arthur Wolf's study of the Chinese in northern Taiwan also supports the idea that something about being reared together produces sexual disinterest. Wolf focused on a community still practicing the Chinese custom of *t'ung-yang-hsi*, or "daughter-in-law raised from childhood":

> When a girl is born in a poor family . . . she is often given away or sold when but a few weeks or months old, or one or two years old, to be the future wife of a son in the family of a friend or relative which has a little son not betrothed in marriage. . . . The girl

is called a "little bride" and taken home and brought up in the family together with her future husband.[50]

Wolf's evidence indicates that this arrangement is associated with sexual difficulties when the childhood "couple" later marry. Informants implied that familiarity results in disinterest and lack of stimulation. As an indication of their disinterest, these couples produce fewer offspring than spouses not raised together, they are more likely to seek extramarital sexual relationships, and they are more likely to get divorced.[51]

The Talmon and Wolf studies suggest, then, that children raised together are not likely to be sexually interested in each other when they grow up. Such disinterest is consistent with Westermarck's notion that the incest taboo may be more an avoidance of certain matings than a prohibition of them. There is one other piece of evidence consistent with this explanation of the incest taboo. Hilda and Seymour Parker compared two samples of fathers: those who had sexually abused their daughters and those who supposedly had not.[52] To maximize their similarities otherwise, the Parkers selected the two samples of fathers from the same prisons and psychiatric facilities. The Parkers found that the fathers who had committed incest with their daughters were much more likely than the other sample of fathers to have had little to do with bringing up their daughters, because they were not at home or hardly at home during the daughters' first three years of life. In other words, the fathers who avoided incest had been more closely associated with their daughters in childhood. That finding is consistent with Westermarck's suggestion that the incest taboo is a result of familiarity in childhood.

Although Westermarck was talking about the development of sexual aversion during early childhood, some researchers have asked how the childhood familiarity theory could explain the extension of incest taboos to first cousins. The familiarity argument implies that first-cousin marriage should be prohibited in societies in which first cousins grow up together in the same community. But that is not the case. Such societies are not more likely to prohibit first-cousin marriage.[53]

Even if there is something about familiarity in childhood that normally leads to sexual disinterest,[54] we still are left with the question of why societies have to prohibit marriages that would voluntarily be avoided because of disinterest. And why do many couples remain actively interested in each other sexually after years of marriage?

Freud's Psychoanalytic Theory

Sigmund Freud proposed that the incest taboo is a reaction against unconscious, unacceptable desires.[55] He suggested that the son is attracted to his mother (as the daughter is to her father) and as a result feels jealousy and hostility toward his father. But the son knows that these feelings cannot continue, for they might lead the father to retaliate against him; therefore, they must be renounced or repressed. Usually the feelings are repressed and retreat into the unconscious. But the desire to possess the mother continues to exist in the unconscious, and, according to Freud, the horror of incest is a reaction to, or a defense against, the forbidden unconscious impulse.

Although Freud's theory may account for the aversion felt toward incest, or at least the aversion toward parent-child incest, it does not explain why society needs an explicit taboo, particularly on brother-sister incest. Nor does it account for the findings of sexual disinterest we discussed in connection with the Westermarck hypothesis.

Family-Disruption Theory

The family-disruption theory, often associated with Bronislaw Malinowski,[56] can best be summed up as follows: Sexual competition among family members would create so much rivalry and tension that the family could not function as an effective unit. Because the family must function effectively for society to survive, society has to curtail competition within the family. The familial incest taboo is thus imposed to keep the family intact.

But there are inconsistencies in this approach. Society could have shaped other rules about the sexual access of one member of the family to another that would also eliminate potentially disruptive competition. Also, why would brother-sister incest be so disruptive? As we noted, such marriages did exist in ancient Egypt. Brother-sister incest would not disrupt the authority of the parents if the children were allowed to marry when mature. The family-disruption theory, then, does not explain the origin of the incest taboo.

Cooperation Theory

The cooperation theory was proposed by the early anthropologist Edward B. Tylor and was elaborated by Leslie A. White and Claude Lévi-Strauss. It emphasizes the value of the incest taboo in promoting cooperation among family groups and thus helping communities to survive. As Tylor saw it, certain operations necessary for the welfare of the community can be accomplished only by large numbers of people working together. To break down suspicion and hostility between family groups and make such cooperation possible, early humans developed the incest taboo to ensure that individuals would marry members of other families. The ties created by intermarriage would serve to hold the community together. Thus, Tylor explained the incest taboo as an answer to the choice "between marrying out and being killed out."[57]

The idea that marriage with other groups promotes cooperation sounds plausible, but is there evidence to support it? After all, there are societies such as the Gusii in which marriage is often between hostile groups. But is that society an exception? Does marriage promote cooperation? Because people in all recent societies marry outside the family, we cannot test the idea that such marriages promote cooperation more than marriages within the family. We can, however, ask whether other kinds of outmarriage, such as marriage with other communities, promote cooperation with those communities. The evidence on that question does not support the cooperation theory. There is no greater peacefulness between communities when marriages are forbidden within the community and always arranged with other communities than when they are not.[58]

But even if marriage outside the family promoted cooperation with other groups, why would it be necessary to prohibit all marriages within the family? Couldn't families have required some of their members to marry outside the family if they thought it necessary for survival but permitted incestuous marriages when such alliances were not needed? Although the incest taboo might enhance cooperation between families, the need for cooperation does not adequately explain the existence of the incest taboo in all societies; other customs might also promote alliances. Furthermore, the cooperation theory does not explain the sexual aspect of the incest taboo. Societies could conceivably allow incestuous sex and still insist that children marry outside the family.

Inbreeding Theory

One of the oldest explanations for the incest taboo is inbreeding theory. It focuses on the potentially damaging consequences of inbreeding or marrying within the family. People within the same family are likely to carry the same harmful recessive genes. Inbreeding, then, will tend to produce offspring who are more likely to die early of genetic disorders than are the offspring of unrelated spouses. Recent evidence also suggests that inbreeding tends to increase the likelihood of diseases that affect people later in life, such as heart disease and diabetes.[59] For many years, inbreeding theory was rejected because, on the basis of dog-breeding practices, it was thought that inbreeding need not be harmful. The inbreeding practiced to produce prize-winning dogs, however, is not a good guide to whether inbreeding is harmful; dog breeders don't count the runts they cull when they try to breed for success in dog shows. We now have a good deal of evidence, from humans as well as other animals, that the closer the degree of inbreeding, the more harmful the genetic effects.[60]

Genetic mutations occur frequently. Although many pose no harm to the individuals who carry a single recessive gene, matings between two people who carry the same gene often produce offspring with a harmful or lethal condition. Close blood relatives are much more likely than unrelated individuals to carry the same harmful recessive gene. So, if close relatives mate, their offspring have a higher probability than the offspring of nonrelatives of inheriting the harmful trait.

One study compared children produced by familial incest with children of the same mothers produced by non-incestuous unions. About 40 percent of the incestuously produced children had serious abnormalities, compared with about 5 percent of the other children.[61] Matings between other kinds of relatives not as closely related also show harmful, but not as harmful, effects of inbreeding. These results are consistent with inbreeding theory. The likelihood that a child will inherit a double dose of a harmful recessive gene is lower the more distantly the child's parents are related. Also consistent with inbreeding theory is the fact that rates of abnormality are consistently higher

in the offspring of uncle-niece marriages (which are allowed in some societies) than in the offspring of cousin marriages; for the offspring of uncle-niece marriages, the likelihood of inheriting a double dose of a harmful recessive is twice that for the offspring of first cousins.[62]

Although most scholars acknowledge the harmful effects of inbreeding, some question whether people in former days would have deliberately invented or borrowed the incest taboo because they knew that inbreeding was biologically harmful. William Durham's cross-cultural survey suggests that they did. Ethnographers do not always report the perceived consequences of incest, but in 50 percent of the reports Durham found, biological harm to the offspring was mentioned.[63] For example, Raymond Firth reported on the Tikopia, who live on an island in the South Pacific:

> The idea is firmly held that unions of close kin bear with them their own doom, their *mara*. . . . The idea [*mara*] essentially concerns barrenness. . . . The peculiar barrenness of an incestuous union consists not in the absence of children, but in their illness or death, or some other mishap. . . . The idea that the offspring of a marriage between near kin are weakly and likely to die young is stoutly held by these natives and examples are adduced to prove it.[64]

So, if the harm of inbreeding was widely recognized, people may have deliberately invented or borrowed the incest taboo.[65] But whether or not people actually recognized the harmfulness of inbreeding, the demographic consequences of the incest taboo would account for its universality, because reproductive and hence competitive advantages probably accrued to groups practicing the taboo. Thus, although cultural solutions other than the incest taboo might provide the desired effects assumed by the family-disruption theory and the cooperation theory, the incest taboo is the only possible solution to the problem of inbreeding.

As is discussed toward the end of the next section, a society may or may not extend the incest taboo to first cousins. That variation is also predictable from inbreeding theory, which provides additional support for the idea that the incest taboo was invented or borrowed to avoid the harmful consequences of inbreeding.

WHOM SHOULD ONE MARRY?

Probably every child in our society knows the story of Cinderella—the poor, downtrodden, but lovely girl who accidentally meets, falls in love with, and eventually marries a prince. It is a charming tale, but it is misleading as a guide to mate choice in our society. The majority of marriages simply do not occur in so free and coincidental a way in any society. In addition to the incest taboo, societies often have rules restricting marriage with other people, as well as preferences about which other people are the most desirable mates.

These young South Asian Hindus in Great Britain are "speed dating." They talk with potential spouses for three minutes each. Traditionally, parents arrange marriages.

Even in a modern, urbanized society such as ours, where theoretically mate choice is free, people tend to marry within their own class and geographic area. For example, studies in the United States consistently indicate that a person is likely to marry someone who lives close by.[66] Neighborhoods are frequently made up of people from similar class backgrounds, so it is unlikely that many of these alliances are Cinderella stories.

Arranged Marriages

In an appreciable number of societies, marriages are arranged; immediate families or go-betweens handle the negotiations. Sometimes betrothals are completed while the future partners are still children. This was formerly the custom in much of Hindu India, China, Japan, and eastern and southern Europe. Implicit in the arranged marriage is the conviction that the joining together of two kin groups to form new social and economic ties is too important to be left to free choice and romantic love.

An example of a marriage arranged for reasons of prestige comes from Clellan Ford's study of the Kwakiutl of British Columbia. Ford's informant described his marriage as follows:

> When I was old enough to get a wife—I was about 25—my brothers looked for a girl in the same position that I and my brothers had. Without my consent, they picked a wife for me—Lagius' daughter. The one I wanted was prettier than the one they chose for me, but she was in a lower position than me, so they wouldn't let me marry her.[67]

Arranged marriages are becoming less common in many places, and couples are beginning to have more say about their marriage partners. But in 1960, marriages were still arranged on the Pacific island of Rotuma, and sometimes the bride and groom did not meet until the wedding day. Today, weddings are much the same, but couples are allowed to "go out" and have a say about whom they wish to marry.[68] In a small Moroccan town, arranged marriages are still the norm, although a young man may ask his mother to make a marriage offer to a particular girl's parents, who may ask her whether she wants to accept the marriage offer. But dating is still not acceptable, so getting acquainted is hard to arrange.[69]

Exogamy and Endogamy

Marriage partners often must be chosen from outside one's own kin group or community; this is known as a rule of **exogamy.** Exogamy can take many forms. It may mean marrying outside a particular group of kin or outside a particular village or group of villages. Often, then, spouses come from a distance. For example, in Rani Khera, a village in India, 266 married women had come from about 200 different villages, averaging between 12 and 24 miles away; 220 local women had gone to 200 other villages to marry. As a result of these exogamous marriages, Rani Khera, a village of 150 households, was linked to 400 other nearby villages.[70] When there are rules of exogamy, violations are often believed to cause harm. On the islands of Yap in Micronesia, people who are related through women are referred to as "people of one belly." The elders say that, if two people from the same kinship group married, they would not have any female children and the group would die out.[71]

People in societies with very low population densities often have to travel considerable distances to meet mates. A study of foragers and horticulturalists found a clear relationship between population density and the distance between the communities of the husband and wife—the lower the density, the greater the marriage distance. Because foragers generally have lower densities than horticulturalists, they generally have further to go to find mates. Among the !Kung, for instance, the average husband and wife had lived 40 miles (65 kilometers) from each other before they were married.[72]

A rule of **endogamy** obliges a person to marry within some group. The caste groups of India traditionally have

migrants and immigrants

Arranging Marriages in the Diaspora

What happens when people move from a place with arranged marriage to a place where marriage is based on free choice and romantic love? Many people around the world or their parents are from places that reject love marriage because it could fizzle out. Love was not considered a sufficient basis for marriage. So parents and other kin, or hired go-betweens, would select your marriage partner, preferably someone from the same socioeconomic background. For example, in many parts of South Asia, one was supposed to marry someone from the same caste and class until recently. Many immigrant parents still insist that their children's marriages be arranged. But this is changing. Consider how some young South Asians in England are "arranging" their own marriages.

Go-betweens are replaced by Web sites, chat rooms, and personal advertisements on the Internet. A couple who "meet" first electronically might arrange a face-to-face meeting, in what's called "South Asian speed dating"; they agree to meet and talk—for just three minutes—at a restaurant or bar, and then they move on. The participants, who are in their 20s and middle class, consider themselves hip. They are quite comfortable blending behaviors from West and

East. But many marriages are still arranged by relatives or go-betweens. Is it because there is discrimination against South Asians and therefore it is difficult to meet and marry other kinds of people? Is the same true for South Asians in the United States?

The United States has had a long history of discrimination against people of color, and South Asians generally have darker skins. So they may also encounter social barriers. Most immigrant groups in the past and present have had restricted opportunities to meet and marry people from different ethnic and class backgrounds. Poor people didn't belong to country clubs. Certain ethnic groups were not admitted, or only admitted sparingly, to Ivy League colleges. To be sure, some people were able to "move up" economically, and this provided more opportunities to meet people from other backgrounds. But marriages were generally restricted to your own class, religion, and locality. And this is still true for the most part. We might expect then that immigrants who come from South Asia would continue to practice arranged marriage. And many do. Young people may say that they would prefer to have a love marriage. But they wouldn't dream of marrying someone who was not like

them. And so their parents hire a matchmaker to find them a spouse.

Rakhi is a lawyer in New York City. She is the daughter of Sikh immigrants from Punjab, India. (The Sikhs are a religious group.) As a young girl, Rakhi had built a shrine to an American movie star in her bedroom. But at the age of 27, she decided to marry someone like herself. But she was focused on her career and didn't have time to date. So her mother enlisted the help of a Sikh matchmaker who had been instructed by the mother of a man named Ranjeet to find a wife for him. Ranjeet also had thought he would marry for love. "But seeing how different cultures treated their families, I realized the importance of making the right match." When the matchmaker organized a party to which she invited Rakhi and Ranjeet (and their mothers), Rakhi's mother whispered: "I think he's the one." After the two young people dated secretly for two months, the matchmaker was once again summoned, this time to negotiate the marital arrangements. Some time later, Rakhi and Ranjeet were married in a Sikh temple in a New York suburb.

Sources: Alvarez 2003, Section 1, p. 3; Henderson 2002, Section 9, p. 2.

---

been endogamous. The higher castes believed that marriage with lower castes would "pollute" them, and such unions were forbidden. Caste endogamy is also found in some parts of Africa. In East Africa, a Masai warrior would never stoop to marry the daughter of an ironworker, nor would a former ruling caste Tutsi in Rwanda, in central Africa, think of marrying a person from the hunting caste Twa.

Cousin Marriages

Kinship terminology for most people in the United States does not differentiate between types of cousins. In some other societies, such distinctions may be important, particularly with regard to first cousins; the terms for the different kinds of first cousins may indicate which cousins are suitable marriage partners (sometimes even preferred mates) and which are not. Although most societies prohibit

marriage with all types of first cousins,[73] some societies allow and even prefer particular kinds of cousin marriage.

Cross-cousins are children of siblings of the opposite sex; that is, a person's cross-cousins are the father's sisters' children and the mother's brothers' children. **Parallel cousins** are children of siblings of the same sex; a person's parallel cousins, then, are the father's brothers' children and the mother's sisters' children. The Chippewa Indians used to practice cross-cousin marriage, as well as cross-cousin joking. With his female cross-cousins, a Chippewa man was expected to exchange broad, risqué jokes, but he would not do so with his parallel cousins, with whom severe propriety was the rule. In general, in any society in which cross-cousin marriage is allowed but parallel cousin is not, there is a joking relationship between a man and his female cross-cousins. This attitude contrasts with the formal and very respectful relationship the man maintains with female parallel cousins. Apparently, the joking relationship signifies the possibility of marriage, whereas the respectful relationship signifies the extension of the incest taboo to parallel cousins.

When first-cousin marriage is allowed or preferred, it is usually with some kind of cross-cousin. Parallel-cousin marriage is fairly rare, but Muslim societies usually prefer such marriages, allowing other cousin marriages as well. The Kurds, who are mostly Sunni Muslims, prefer a young man to marry his father's brother's daughter (for the young woman, this would be her father's brother's son). The father and his brother usually live near each other, so the woman will stay close to home in such a marriage. The bride and groom are also in the same kin group, so marriage in this case also entails kin group endogamy.[74]

What kinds of societies allow or prefer first-cousin marriage? There is evidence from cross-cultural research that cousin marriages are most apt to be permitted in relatively large and densely populated societies. Perhaps this is because the likelihood of such marriages, and therefore the risks of inbreeding, are minimal in those societies. Many small, sparsely populated societies, however, permit or even sometimes prefer cousin marriage. How can these cases be explained? They seem to cast doubt on the interpretation that cousin marriage should be prohibited in sparsely populated societies, in which marriages between close relatives are more likely just by chance and the risks of inbreeding should be greatest. It turns out that most of the small societies that permit cousin marriage have lost a lot of people to epidemics. Many peoples around the world, particularly in the Pacific and in North and South America, suffered severe depopulation in the first generation or two after contact with Europeans, who introduced diseases (such as measles, pneumonia, and smallpox) to which the native populations had little or no resistance. Such societies may have had to permit cousin marriage to provide enough mating possibilities among the reduced population of eligible mates.[75]

Levirate and Sororate

In many societies, cultural rules oblige individuals to marry the spouse of deceased relatives. **Levirate** is a custom whereby a man is obliged to marry his brother's widow. **Sororate** obliges a woman to marry her deceased sister's husband. Both customs are exceedingly common, being the obligatory form of second marriage in a majority of societies known to anthropology.[76]

Among the Chukchee of Siberia, levirate obliges the next oldest brother to become the successor husband. He cares for the widow and children, assumes the sexual privileges of the husband, and unites the deceased's reindeer herd with his own, keeping it in the name of his brother's children. If there are no brothers, the widow is married to a cousin of her first husband. The Chukchee regard the custom more as a duty than as a right. The nearest relative is obliged to care for a woman left with children and a herd.[77]

HOW MANY DOES ONE MARRY?

We are accustomed to thinking of marriage as involving just one man and one woman at a time—**monogamy**—but most societies known to anthropology have allowed a man to be married to more than one woman at the same time—**polygyny.** At any given time, however, the majority of men in societies permitting polygyny are married monogamously; few or no societies have enough women to permit most men to have at least two wives. Polygyny's mirror image—one woman being married to more than one man at the same time, called **polyandry**—is practiced in very few societies. Polygyny and polyandry are the two types of **polygamy,** or plural spouse marriage. **Group marriage,** in which more than one man is married to more than one woman at the same time, sometimes occurs but is not customary in any known society.

Polygyny

The Old Testament has many references to men with more than one wife simultaneously: King David and King Solomon are just two examples of men polygynously married. Just as in the society described in the Old Testament, polygyny in many societies is a mark of a man's great wealth or high status. In such societies, only the very wealthy can, and are expected to, support more than one wife. Some Muslim societies, especially Arabic-speaking ones, still view polygyny in this light. But a man does not always have to be wealthy to be polygynous; indeed, in some societies in which women are important contributors to the economy, it seems that men try to have more than one wife to become wealthier.

Among the Siwai, a society in the South Pacific, status is achieved through feast giving. Pork is the main dish at these feasts, so the Siwai associate pig raising with prestige. This great interest in pigs sparks an interest in wives, because in Siwai society, women raise the food needed to raise pigs. Thus, although having many wives does not in itself confer status among the Siwai, the increase in pig herds that may result from polygyny is a source of prestige for the owner.[78]

Polygynously married Siwai men do seem to have greater prestige, but they complain that a household with multiple wives is difficult. Sinu, a Siwai, described his plight:

> There is never peace for a long time in a polygynous family. If the husband sleeps in the house of one wife, the other one sulks all the next day. If the man is so stupid as to sleep two consecutive nights in the house of one wife, the other one will refuse to cook for him, saying, "So-and-so is your wife; go to her for food. Since I am not good enough for you to sleep with, then my food is not good enough for you to eat." Frequently the co-wives will quarrel and fight. My uncle formerly had five wives at one time and the youngest one was always raging and fighting the others. Once she knocked an older wife senseless and then ran away and had to be forcibly returned.[79]

Polygyny is practiced by some in this country, even though it is prohibited by law.

Co-wife conflict seems not to be present in some societies. For example, Margaret Mead reported that married life among the Arapesh of New Guinea, even in the polygynous marriages, was "so even and contented that there is nothing to relate of it at all."[80] Why might there be little or no obvious jealousy between co-wives in a society? One possible reason is that a man is married to two or more sisters—**sororal polygyny;** it seems that sisters, having grown up together, are more likely to get along and cooperate as co-wives than are co-wives who are not also sisters—**nonsororal polygyny.** Indeed, a recent cross-cultural study confirms that endemic conflict and persistent resentment were virtually ubiquitous in societies with nonsororal polygyny.[81] The most commonly reported reason for the conflict and resentment was insufficient access to the husband for sex and emotional support.

Perhaps because conflict is so common, polygynous societies have invented customs to try to lessen conflict and jealousy in co-wives:

1. Co-wives who are not sisters tend to have separate living quarters; sororal co-wives almost always live together. Among the Plateau Tonga in Africa, who practice nonsororal polygyny, the husband shares his personal goods and his favors among his wives, who live in separate dwellings, according to principles of strict equality. The Crow Indians practiced sororal polygyny, and co-wives usually shared a tepee.

2. Co-wives have clearly defined equal rights in matters of sex, economics, and personal possessions. For example, the Tanala of Madagascar require the husband to spend a day with each co-wife in succession. Failure to do so constitutes adultery and entitles the slighted wife to sue for divorce and alimony of up to one-third of the husband's property. Furthermore, the land is shared equally among all the women, who expect the husband to help with its cultivation when he visits them.

3. Senior wives often have special prestige. The Tonga of Polynesia, for example, grant to the first wife the status of "chief wife." Her house is to the right of her husband's and is called the "house of the father." The other wives are called "small wives," and their houses are to the left of the husband's. The chief wife has the right to be consulted before the small wives, and her husband is expected to sleep under her roof before and after a journey. Although this rule might seem to enhance the jealousy of the secondary wives, later wives are usually favored somewhat because they tend to be younger and more attractive. By this custom, then, the first wife may be compensated for her loss of physical attractiveness by increased prestige.[82]

We must remember that, although jealousy and conflict are commonly mentioned in polygynous marriages, they are not always present. People who practice polygyny may think it has considerable advantages. In a study conducted by Philip and Janet Kilbride in Kenya, female as well as male married people agreed that polygyny had economic and political advantages. Because they tend to be large, polygynous families provide plenty of farm labor and extra food that can be marketed. They also tend to be influential in their communities and are likely to produce individuals who become government officials.[83] And in South Africa, Connie Anderson found that women choose to be married to a man with other wives because the other wives could help with child care and household work, provide companionship, and allow more freedom to come and go. Some women said they chose polygynous marriages because there was a shortage of marriageable males.[84]

How can we account for the fact that polygyny is allowed and often preferred in most of the societies known to anthropology? Ralph Linton suggested that polygyny derives from a general male primate urge to collect females.[85] But if that were so, then why wouldn't all societies allow polygyny? Other explanations of polygyny have been suggested. We restrict our discussion here to those that statistically and strongly predict polygyny in worldwide samples of societies.

One theory is that polygyny will be permitted in societies that have a long **postpartum sex taboo.**[86] In these societies, a couple must abstain from intercourse until their child is at least a year old. John Whiting suggested that couples abstain from sexual intercourse for a long time after their child is born for health reasons. A Hausa woman reported:

> A mother should not go to her husband while she has a child she is suckling. If she does, the child gets thin; he dries up, he won't be strong, he won't be healthy. If she goes after two years it is nothing, he is already strong before that, it does not matter if she conceives again after two years.[87]

The symptoms the woman described seem to be those of *kwashiorkor*. Common in tropical areas, kwashiorkor is a protein-deficiency disease that occurs particularly in children suffering from intestinal parasites or diarrhea. By observing a long postpartum sex taboo, and thereby ensuring that her children are widely spaced, a woman can nurse each child longer. If a child gets protein from

current research and issues

The Husband-Wife Relationship: Variation in Love, Intimacy, and Sexual Jealousy

Americans believe that love should be a basis of marriage. Does this ideal characterize most societies? We know the answer to that question: No. In fact, in many places, romantic love is believed to be a poor basis for marriage and is strongly discouraged. However, even though romantic love may not be a basis for marriage everywhere, it does occur almost everywhere. A recent cross-cultural survey suggests that about 88 percent of the world's societies show signs of romantic love—accounts of personal longing, love songs or love depicted in folklore, elopement because of affection, and passionate love described by informants quoted in ethnographies. So if love is nearly universal, why is it often discouraged as a basis for marriage?

Three conditions appear to predict such discouragement. One is that the husband and wife live in an extended family. In this situation, the family seems more concerned with how the in-marrying person gets along with others, and less concerned with whether the husband and wife love each other. A second condition predicting the discouragement of romantic love as a basis for marriage is that one of the spouses does most of the primary subsistence work or earns most of the couple's income. Third, romantic love is unlikely when men have more sexual freedom than women. In general, then, romantic love is discouraged as a basis for marriage under conditions of inequality—if one of the spouses is highly dependent on the other or the other's kin or the woman has fewer sexual rights than the man.

Intimacy is different from romantic love. It refers to how close the mar-

The valentine, as in this 19th-century British card, symbolizes romantic love.

ried couple are to each other—eating together, sleeping in the same bed, spending their leisure time together, as well as having frequent sex. In some societies, couples are together a lot; in others, they spend very little time together. Foraging societies seem on average to have more marital intimacy than more complex herding and agricultural societies, but the reasons are not entirely clear. Also, a high involvement in war seems to detract from intimacy.

When it comes to sexual jealousy, men are far more likely to be violent than women. Incidentally, infidelity is the most frequently reported reason for a husband to divorce a wife. Anthropologists with a biological orientation point out that fathers always have some uncertainty about whether their children are theirs, so males are much more likely for that reason alone to try to guard against rival males. But how can we account for the considerable

variation in jealousy from one society to another? It does seem that the more a society emphasizes the importance of getting married, the more it limits sex to the marriage relationship, the more it emphasizes property, and the more its males appear to exhibit sexual jealousy.

How are these various aspects of marriage related to each other? Does romantic love as a basis for marriage increase or decrease sexual jealousy? Does romantic love predict intimacy, or is romantic love more likely with less frequent contact between the spouses? We are still far from understanding how these different aspects are related. All we know is that an emphasis on love and intimacy does not preclude marital violence or marital dissolution.

Sources: Hendrix 2009; Betzig 1989; Jankowiak and Fischer 1992; de Munck and Korotayev 1999.   ◢◢◢

---

mother's milk during its first few years, the likelihood of contracting kwashiorkor may be greatly reduced. Consistent with Whiting's interpretation is the fact that societies with low-protein staples (those whose principal foods are root and tree crops such as taro, sweet potatoes, bananas, and breadfruit) tend to have a long postpartum sex taboo. Societies with long postpartum sex taboos also tend to be

polygynous. Perhaps, then, a man's having more than one wife is a cultural adjustment to the taboo. As a Yoruba woman said,

> When we abstain from having sexual intercourse with our husband for the two years we nurse our babies, we know he will seek some other woman. We

would rather have her under our control as a co-wife so he is not spending money outside the family.[88]

Even if we agree that men will seek other sexual relationships during the period of a long postpartum sex taboo, it is not clear why polygyny is the only possible solution to the problem. After all, it is conceivable that all of a man's wives might be subject to the postpartum sex taboo at the same time. Furthermore, there may be sexual outlets outside marriage.

Another explanation of polygyny is that it is a response to an excess of women over men. Such an imbalanced sex ratio may occur because of the prevalence of warfare in a society. Because men and not women are generally the warriors, warfare almost always takes a greater toll of men's lives. Given that almost all adults in noncommercial societies are married, polygyny may be a way of providing spouses for surplus women. Indeed, there is evidence that societies with imbalanced sex ratios in favor of women tend to have both polygyny and high male mortality in warfare. Conversely, societies with balanced sex ratios tend to have both monogamy and low male mortality in warfare.[89]

A third explanation is that a society will allow polygyny when men marry at an older age than women. The argument is similar to the sex ratio interpretation. Delaying the age of marriage for men would produce an artificial, though not an actual, excess of marriageable women. Why marriage for men is delayed is not clear, but the delay does predict polygyny.[90]

Is one of these explanations better than the others, or are all three factors—long postpartum sex taboo, an imbalanced sex ratio in favor of women, and delayed age of marriage for men—important in explaining polygyny? One way of trying to decide among alternative explanations is to do what is called a *statistical-control analysis,* which allows us to see if a particular factor still predicts when the effects of other possible factors are removed. In this case, when the possible effect of sex ratio is removed, a long postpartum sex taboo no longer predicts polygyny and hence is probably not a cause of polygyny.[91] But both an actual excess of women and a late age of marriage for men seem to be strong predictors of polygyny. Added together, these two factors predict even more strongly.[92]

Behavioral ecologists have also suggested ecological reasons why both men and women might prefer polygynous marriages. If there are enough resources, men might prefer polygyny because they can have more children if they have more than one wife. If resources are highly variable and men control resources, women might find it advantageous to marry a man with many resources even if she is a second wife. A recent study of foragers suggests that foraging societies in which men control hunting or fishing territories are more likely to be polygynous. This finding is consistent with the theory, but the authors were surprised that control of gathering sites by men did not predict polygyny.[93] The main problem with the theory of variable resources and their marital consequences is that many societies, particularly in the "modern" world, have great variability in wealth, but

little polygyny. So behavioral ecologists have had to argue that polygyny is lacking because of socially imposed constraints. But why are those constraints imposed? The sex-ratio interpretation can explain the absence of polygyny in most commercialized modern societies. First, very complex societies have standing armies and male mortality in warfare is rarely as high *proportionately* as in simpler societies. Second, with commercialization, there are more possibilities for individuals to support themselves without being married. Degree of disease in the environment may also be a factor.

Bobbi Low has suggested that a high incidence of disease may reduce the prevalence of "healthy" men. In such cases, it may be to a woman's advantage to marry a "healthy" man even if he is already married, and it may be to a man's advantage to marry several unrelated women to maximize genetic variation (and disease resistance) among his children. Indeed, societies with many pathogens are more likely to have polygyny.[94] A recent cross-cultural study compared the degree of disease explanation of polygyny with the imbalanced sex-ratio explanation. Both were supported. The number of pathogens predicted particularly well in more densely populated complex societies, where pathogen load is presumably greater. The sex-ratio explanation predicted particularly well in sparser, nonstate societies.[95] Nigel Barber used data from modern nations to test these ideas. He found that sex-ratio and pathogen stress predicted polygyny in modern nations too.[96]

Polyandry

George Peter Murdock's "World Ethnographic Sample" included only four societies (less than 1 percent of the total) in which polyandry, or the marriage of several men to one woman, was practiced.[97] When the husbands are brothers we call it **fraternal polyandry;** if they are not brothers, it is **nonfraternal polyandry.** Some Tibetans, the Toda of India, and the Sinhalese of Sri Lanka have practiced fraternal polyandry. Among some Tibetans who practice fraternal polyandry, biological paternity seems to be of no particular concern; there is no attempt to link children biologically to a particular brother, and all children are treated the same.[98]

One possible explanation for the practice of polyandry is a shortage of women. The Toda practiced female infanticide;[99] the Sinhalese had a shortage of women but denied the practice of female infanticide.[100] A correlation between shortage of women and polyandry would account for why polyandry is so rare in the ethnographic record; an excess of men is rare cross-culturally.

Another possible explanation is that polyandry is an adaptive response to severely limited resources. Melvyn Goldstein studied Tibetans who live in the northwestern corner of Nepal, above 12,000 feet in elevation. Cultivable land is extremely scarce there, with most families having less than an acre. The people say they practice fraternal polyandry to prevent the division of a family's farm and animals. Instead of dividing up their land among them and each taking a wife, brothers preserve the family farm by sharing a wife. Although not recognized by the

Tibetans, their practice of polyandry minimizes population growth. There are as many women as men of marriageable age. But about 30 percent of the women do not marry, and, although these women do have some children, they have far fewer than married women. Thus, the practice of polyandry minimizes the number of mouths to feed and therefore maximizes the standard of living of the polyandrous family. In contrast, if the Tibetans practiced monogamy and almost all women married, the birth rate would be much higher and there would be more mouths to feed with the severely limited resources.[101]

Polyandry is still customary in some Tibetan communities although monogamous marriages actually outnumber polyandrous marriages. This is because a set of brothers may start off being married to one woman, younger brothers may later opt to marry separately and form their own households. Also, some households have only one son or daughter and polyandrous marriages are not possible. Wealth increases the likelihood of a young brother leaving, but mostly when the polyandrous household lacks agricultural fields, herds, and opportunities for trade.[102] Actually, in polygynous societies, monogamous marriages also outnumber polygynous marriages at any given time. But the reasons are different. Most polygynous societies practice nonsororal marriages and, when a man first marries, he is married monogamously. It usually requires significant resources to marry again (a bride price is common) and so subsequent marriages occur later in life.

THE FAMILY

Although family form varies from one society to another and even within societies, all societies have families. A **family** is a social and economic unit consisting minimally of one or more parents (or parent substitute) and their children. Members of a family always have certain reciprocal rights and obligations, particularly economic ones. Family members usually live in one household, but common residence is not a defining feature of families. In our society, children may live away while they go to college. Some members of a family may deliberately set up separate households to manage multiple business enterprises while maintaining economic unity.[103] In simpler societies, the family and the household tend to be indistinguishable; only in more complex societies, and in societies becoming dependent on commercial exchange, may some members of a family live elsewhere.[104]

Adoption

In many societies, the family does not have enough kin in the nuclear or extended family. They need to add new members to perform all of the necessary chores or to inherit access to family property. They may have a shortage because introduced diseases or natural disasters such as hurricanes have killed members (particularly young children) or because the adults don't get along and can't cooperate in the traditional ways. Many societies adopt children to deal with one or another of these problems. Or

they adopt one or more related children to relieve the pressure on resources in the family that adopts the child "out." This last one was the motive in the family Melvin Ember lived with at the beginning of his fieldwork in the Pacific islands of American Samoa.

The family already had six children. The oldest (Tavita), 11 at the time, was in school most of the day, as were three of the other children. Tavita was adopted informally. His natural mother, who lived in the same village, was a sister of Tavita's adoptive mother. By adopting Tavita "out," his natural family was relieved of the responsibility to feed and care for him; they already had nine children. The need to reduce the number of mouths to feed was a common motive for adoption in Samoan villages then, as it was elsewhere in the far Pacific islands because of depopulation and hurricanes.[105] In American Samoa, the availability of more jobs (teaching in the village, working for the central government and the canneries on the main island), and improved medical care (there was a medical dispensary in every village and a hospital on the main island) had generated unusual population growth. Many had already moved to Hawaii and the mainland United States to seek jobs. American Samoans can move to the United States without difficulty; all you need is the money to pay for an airline ticket. Remittances from living and working abroad constitute a major source of income for the family members still in American Samoa.[106]

Adoption does not just occur in developing societies. It occurs in industrial societies too. As of the 1990s (the latest figures available), there were more than 100,000 formal (legally recognized) adoptions in the United States per year. About 50 percent of the adoptions are of children who are relatives, usually close relatives; a large number of these adoptions may be solutions to resource problems for the natural mothers. Then more than 10,000 children from abroad who are not usually relatives are adopted each year. Most of the known adoptions, foreign and domestic, are arranged by middle-class or wealthier people. A sizeable amount of money may have to be spent, particularly with the foreign adoptions. Most of the adopted children, domestic and foreign, turn out as well as natural children.[107]

Variation in Family Form

The minimal family has one parent (or parent substitute). Single-parent families, usually headed by the mother, are common in some societies, but most societies typically have larger families. These larger family units usually include at least one **nuclear family** (a married couple and their children), but there is often polygamy, so there may be more than one spouse with more than one set of children. If a single-parent family, nuclear family, polygynous, or polyandrous family lives alone, each is an **independent family.** However, the **extended family** is the prevailing form of family in more than half the societies known to anthropology.[108] It may consist of two or more single-parent, monogamous, polygynous, or polyandrous families linked by a blood tie. Most commonly, the extended family consists of a

current research and issues

One-Parent Families: Why the Recent Increase?

Not only is the custom of marriage almost universal, but in most societies known to anthropology, most people marry. And they usually remarry if they divorce. This means that, except for the death of a spouse or temporarily during times of divorce or separation, one-parent families are relatively uncommon in most societies.

In many Western countries, however, there has been a dramatic increase recently in the percentage of one-parent families, most of which (about 90 percent) are female-headed families. For example, in the 1960s, about 9 percent of families in the United States were one-parent families, but in the mid-1980s, the figure jumped to about 24 percent. In 2004, the figure was 28 percent. Whereas Sweden once led the Western countries in percentage of one-parent families—about 13 percent in the 1970s—the United States now has the highest percentage.

Before we examine the reasons for the increase, we need to consider that there are a variety of ways to become a one-parent family. First, many one-parent families result from the divorce or separation of two-parent families. Second, many one-parent families result from births out of wedlock. In addition, some result from the death of a spouse, and others from the decision by a single person to have a child.

Many researchers suggest that the ease of divorce is largely responsible for the increase in one-parent families. On the face of it, this explanation seems plausible. But it is flawed. In many countries during the late 1960s and early 1970s, changes in the law made getting a divorce much easier, and the percentage of one-parent families did rise after that. But why did so many countries ease divorce restrictions at the same time? Did attitudes about marriage change first? A high divorce rate by itself will make for a higher percentage of one-parent households only if individuals do not remarry quickly. In the United States, for example, remarriage rates did decline sharply in the mid-1960s, particularly among younger, better-educated women, and so the

percentage of one-parent households may have risen for that reason. In many other countries, divorce rates stabilized in the 1980s, but the percentage of one-parent families still increased. Thus, easier divorce does not fully explain the increase in number of one-parent families.

Although some parents are clearly choosing to stay single, many might prefer to marry if they could find an appropriate spouse. In some countries, and among some ethnic groups within some countries, there are many fewer males than females, and sometimes a high proportion of the males have poor economic prospects. In the former Soviet Union, there are many more women than men because males are more likely to have died from war, alcoholism, and accidents. The United States does not have such a skewed sex ratio, but in some neighborhoods, particularly poor neighborhoods, there are very high mortality rates for young males. And many males in such neighborhoods do not have work. One study by Daniel Lichter and his colleagues estimated that for every 100 African American women between the ages of 21 and 28, there were fewer than 80 available African American men. If we count only men who are employed full- or part-time, the number of available men per 100 women drops below 50. And a recent comparison of 85 countries finds that single parenthood is much more likely when there is higher male unemployment as well as when there are fewer men than women of a comparable age. So there may be considerable merit to the argument that one-parent families (usually headed by women) will be likely when a spouse (particularly an employed one) is hard to find.

Another popular explanation for the rise in number of one-parent families is that, in contrast to the past, women can manage without husbands because of support from the state. This scenario seems to fit Sweden, where unmarried and divorced mothers receive many social supports and allowances for maternity

and educational leave. But Iceland has few social supports from the government and yet has the highest rate of out-of-wedlock births of all the Scandinavian countries. In the United States, the welfare argument fails to predict changes over time. The program called Aid to Families with Dependent Children provided aid largely to single mothers. If the theory about government help was correct, increases in such aid would generally predict increases in the percentage of mother-headed households. But, in fact, during the 1970s, the percentage of families receiving aid and the value of aid decreased, whereas the percentage of mother-headed households increased. In the 1980s, it was more difficult to go "on welfare," but the percentage of mother-headed households increased anyway.

Women might be more able to manage alone if they have high-paying employment, and therefore we might expect more one-parent families by choice, as more women enter the job market. But, although this may explain the choices of some women, recent research finds that employed women generally are *more* rather than less likely to marry.

In any case, there seems to be a general association between commercial economies and the possibility of one-parent families. Is there something about subsistence economies that promotes marriage and something about commercial economies that detracts from it? Although marriage is not universally based on love or companionship, it entails a great deal of economic and other kinds of interdependence, particularly in not-so-commercial economies. Market economies allow other possibilities; goods and services can be bought and sold, and governments may take over functions that kin and family normally handle. So the one-parent family is likely to remain an option—either a choice or a necessity—for some people.

Sources: Burns and Scott 1994; Lichter et al. 1992; Whitehead and Popenoe 2005; Barber 2003.

The traditional houses of an extended family on Satawal Island in the Carolines, Micronesia.

married couple and one or more of the married children, all living in the same house or household. The constituent nuclear families are normally linked through the parent-child tie. An extended family, however, is sometimes composed of families linked through a sibling tie. Such a family might consist of two married brothers, their wives, and their children. Extended families may be very large, containing many relatives and including three or four generations. A diagram of these different types of family can be found in Figure 11–2.

Extended-Family Households

In a society composed of extended-family households, marriage does not bring as pronounced a change in lifestyle as it does in our culture, where the couple typically moves to a new residence and forms a new, and basically independent, family unit. In extended families, the newlyweds are assimilated into an existing family unit. Margaret Mead described such a situation in Samoa:

> In most marriages there is no sense of setting up a new and separate establishment. The change is felt in the change of residence for either husband or wife and in the reciprocal relations which spring up between the two families. But the young couple live in the main household, simply receiving a bamboo pillow, a mosquito net and a pile of mats for their bed. . . . The wife works with all the women of the household and waits on all the men. The husband

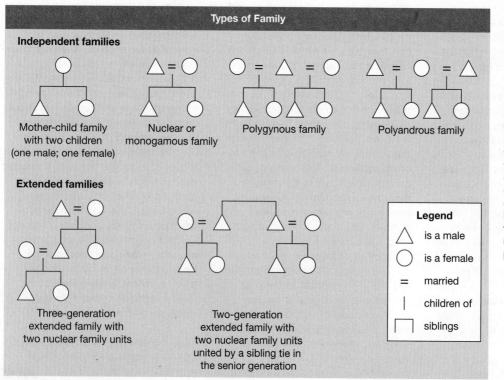

FIGURE 11–2 Anthropologists commonly use diagrams to represent family structures. At the top are four types of independent family assuming only two children (one male, one female) and only two spouses where multiple spouses are allowed. At the bottom are two types of extended family. These diagrams show only small extended families, but extended families can have many constituent family units if there are many children as well as plural marriages.

applied anthropology

Extended Families and Social Security: The Japanese Model in the 1950s and 1960s

For many years now, people in the United States (in and out of government) have warned that the Social Security system is in trouble, that it will be forced to reduce payments in the near future. There are two general ways to solve the problem, given the growing population to be served. The government could reduce payments, by extending the retirement age, for instance. Or it could increase funding for Social Security, by requiring taxpayers to pay more into the system while they are still working. But there is enormous resistance to changing the system. People don't want their Medicare and Medicaid payments to be reduced, and they are afraid of losing their medical insurance if they lose their jobs. In addition, many people don't want to wait to retire. So what else could be done? Have we explored all of the possible ways to repair the Social Security system?

One way is suggested by what the Japanese did in the 1950s and 1960s. Japan was industrializing. People were leaving the rural farming areas and moving to the cities to take jobs in industry. But there still were extended family households, particularly on the farm; many still lived with parents and children, sharing income and expenses. The extended families continued to exist because the economy was still lacking certain features common in the industrialized societies of

the West. (The boom in Japanese exports, in cameras, automobiles, etc., was yet to develop.) First, geographic mobility (moving to "chase the job") occurred less often than in Western industrial economies; workers and even professionals changed jobs only rarely. Second, the government had not taken over many of the health and welfare functions of the extended family; indeed, the government still enforced the obligation of relatives to care for the aged and infirm. And third, ascribed or inherited status was still an important basis for economic advancement, and perhaps as useful as marks of achievement (e.g., a university degree) in obtaining the first job. The key to understanding the persistence of the extended family in Japan may lie in the fact that the country had a surplus of employable labor throughout its industrial history. In the presence of the unemployment and competitiveness that characterize a tight labor market, the extended family may survive because no other agencies are available to provide economic and social security.

An industrial economy in severe recession may persuade some young adults to consider living with their parents. When the U.S. economy collapsed between 2008 and 2009, many young people lost their jobs and couldn't find new ones. They had to abandon their independence in favor of extended family living. If

you can't afford an apartment, even one you share with others, what can you do? You can move back home. At least that will limit your expenses. And it might also help relieve the pressure on the Social Security system, if the tax code were changed to provide additional deductions for older people who partially support children who have returned home. By moving back home, the younger generation could save money to buy an apartment or house later. And if the older people get a new tax deduction, there could be less need to revamp the Social Security system. Many young people have delayed marriage anyway. (More people are delaying marriage until their late 20s and early 30s.) The Congress could adjust the tax code to allow at least some people to choose to live in extended family households, which would allow the older people to receive lower Social Security payments. We might have to change the way we socialize our children—we may have to reduce the pressure to live independently. But it could be done. After all, necessity is the mother of invention. The tax code could favor the option of extended family living, and we might thereby relieve some of the financial pressure on the Social Security system.

Sources: M. Ember 1983; Long 2000.

---

shares the enterprises of the other men and boys. Neither in personal service given or received are the two marked off as a unit.[109]

A young couple in Samoa, as in other societies with extended families, generally has little decision-making power over the governing of the household. Often the responsibility of running the household rests with the senior male. Nor can the new family accumulate its own property and become independent; it is a part of the larger corporate structure:

So the young people bide their time. Eventually, when the old man dies or retires, they will own the

homestead, they will run things. When their son grows up and marries, he will create a new subsidiary family, to live with them, work for the greater glory of *their* extended family homestead, and wait for them to die.[110]

The extended family is more likely than the independent nuclear family to perpetuate itself as a social unit. In contrast with the independent nuclear family, which by definition disintegrates with the death of the senior members (the parents), the extended family is always adding junior families (monogamous, polygamous, or both), whose members eventually become the senior members when their elders die.

Possible Reasons for Extended-Family Households

Why do most societies known to anthropology commonly have extended-family households? Extended-family households are found most frequently in societies with sedentary agricultural economies, so economic factors may play a role in determining household type. M. F. Nimkoff and Russell Middleton suggested how agricultural life, as opposed to a hunter-gatherer life, may favor extended families. The extended family may be a social mechanism that prevents the economically ruinous division of family property in societies in which property such as cultivated land is important. Conversely, the need for mobility in hunter-gatherer societies may make it difficult to maintain extended-family households. During certain seasons, the hunter-gatherers may be obliged to divide into nuclear families that scatter into other areas.[111]

But agriculture is only a weak predictor of extended-family households. Many agriculturalists lack them, and many nonagricultural societies have them. A different theory is that extended-family households come to prevail in societies that have incompatible activity requirements—that is, requirements that cannot be met by a mother or a father in a one-family household. In other words, extended-family households are generally favored when the work a mother has to do outside the home (cultivating fields or gathering foods far away) makes it difficult for her to also care for her children and do other household tasks. Similarly, extended families may be favored when the required outside activities of a father (warfare, trading trips, or wage labor far away) make it difficult for him to do the subsistence work required of males. There is cross-cultural evidence that societies with such incompatible activity requirements are more likely to have extended-family households than societies with compatible activity requirements, regardless of whether or not the society is agricultural. Even though they have incompatible activity requirements, however, societies with commercial or monetary exchange may not have extended-family households. In commercial societies, a family may be able to obtain the necessary help by "buying" the required services.[112]

Of course, even in societies with money economies, not everyone can buy required services. Those who are poor may need to live in extended families, and extended-family living may become more common even in the middle class when the economy is depressed. As a popular magazine noted,

> Whatever happened to the all-American nuclear family—Mom, Pop, two kids and a cuddly dog, nestled under one cozy, mortgaged roof? What happened was an economic squeeze: layoffs, fewer jobs for young people, more working mothers, a shortage of affordable housing and a high cost of living. Those factors, along with a rising divorce rate, a trend toward later marriages and an increase in the over-65 population, all hitting at once, are forcing thousands

of Americans into living in multigenerational families.[113]

In many societies, there are kin groups even larger than extended families. The next chapter discusses the varieties of such groupings.

SUMMARY ● ○ ○

1. All societies known today have the custom of marriage. Marriage is a socially approved sexual and economic union usually between a man and a woman that is presumed to be more or less permanent and that subsumes reciprocal rights and obligations between the two spouses and between the spouses and their children.

2. The way marriage is socially recognized varies greatly; it may involve an elaborate ceremony or none at all. Variations include childhood betrothals, trial marriage periods, feasting, and the birth of a baby.

3. Marriage arrangements often include an economic element. The most common form is the bride price, in which the groom or his family gives an agreed-upon amount of money or goods to the bride's family. Bride service exists when the groom works for the bride's family for a specified period. In some societies, a female from the groom's family is exchanged for the bride; in others, gifts are exchanged between the two families. A dowry is a payment of goods or money by the bride's family, usually to the bride. Indirect dowry is provided by the groom's family to the bride, sometimes through the bride's father.

4. No society in recent times has allowed sex or marriage between brothers and sisters, mothers and sons, or fathers and daughters.

5. Every society tells people whom they cannot marry, whom they can marry, and sometimes even whom they should marry. In quite a few societies, marriages are arranged by the couple's kin groups. Implicit in arranged marriages is the conviction that the joining of two kin groups to form new social and economic ties is too important to be left to free choice and romantic love. Some societies have rules of exogamy, which require marriage outside one's own kin group or community; others have rules of endogamy, requiring marriage within one's group. Although most societies prohibit all first-cousin marriages, some permit or prefer marriage with cross-cousins (children of siblings of the opposite sex) and parallel cousins (children of siblings of the same sex). Many societies have customs providing for the remarriage of widowed people. Levirate is a custom whereby a man marries his brother's widow. Sororate is the practice whereby a woman marries her deceased sister's husband.

6. We think of marriage as involving just one man and one woman at a time (monogamy), but most societies allow a man to be married to more than one woman at a time (polygyny). Polyandry, the marriage of one woman to several husbands, is rare.

7. The prevailing form of family in most societies is the extended family. It consists of two or more single-parent, monogamous (nuclear), polygynous, or polyandrous families linked by blood ties.

GLOSSARY TERMS ○ ● ○

bride price (or bride
    wealth) **195**
bride service **196**
cross-cousins **201**
dowry **196**
endogamy **200**
exogamy **200**
extended family **206**
family **206**
fraternal polyandry **205**
group marriage **202**
incest taboo **197**
independent
    family **206**
indirect dowry **197**

levirate **202**
marriage **190**
monogamy **202**
nonfraternal
    polyandry **205**
nonsororal polygyny **203**
nuclear family **206**
parallel cousins **201**
polyandry **202**
polygamy **202**
polygyny **202**
postpartum sex
    taboo **203**
sororal polygyny **203**
sororate **202**

CRITICAL QUESTIONS ○ ○ ●

1. Will it remain customary in our society to marry? Why do you think it will or will not?
2. Do you think extended-family households will become more common in our society? Why?
3. Why is polyandry so much less common than polygyny?

PEARSON
myanthrolab

Read Alan Howard and Jan Rensel's "Rotuma: Interpreting a Wedding" on MyAnthroLab and answer the following questions:

1. Howard and Rensel suggest that weddings among the Rotuma express their core values. What core values are expressed in their weddings?
2. How has courtship and marriage changed?
3. Compare the essential features of weddings in your culture (make sure to mention the name of your culture) with those described for the Rotuma.

Marital Residence and Kinship

n the United States and Canada, as well as in many other industrial societies, a young man and woman usually establish a place of residence apart from their parents or other relatives when they marry, if they have not already moved away before that. Our society is so oriented toward this pattern of marital residence—*neolocal (new-place) residence*—that it seems to be the obvious and natural one to follow. Some upper-income families begin earlier than others to train their children to live away from home by sending them to boarding schools at age 13 or 14 or to sleep-away summer camps. Young adults of all income levels learn to live away from home most of the year if they join the army or attend an out-of-town college. In any case, when young people marry, they generally live apart from family.

So familiar is neolocal residence to us that we tend to assume that all societies must practice the same pattern. On the contrary, of the 565 societies in George Peter Murdock's "World Ethnographic Sample," only about 5 percent followed this practice.[1] About 95 percent of the world's societies have had some other pattern of residence whereby a new couple settles within, or very close to, the household of the parents or some other close relative of either the groom or the bride. When married couples live near kin, it stands to reason that kinship relationships will figure prominently in the social life of the society. Marital residence largely predicts the types of kin groups found in a society, as well as how people refer to and classify their various relatives.

As we will see, kin groups that include several or many families and hundreds or even thousands of people are found in many societies and structure many areas of social life. Kin groups may have important economic, social, political, and religious functions.

● ○ ●

PATTERNS OF MARITAL RESIDENCE

In societies in which newly married couples customarily live with or close to their kin, the pattern of residence varies. Children in all societies are required to marry outside the nuclear family because of the incest taboo, and with few exceptions, couples in almost all societies live together after they are married. Therefore, some children have to leave home when they marry. But which married children remain at home and which reside elsewhere? Societies vary in the way they deal with this question, but there are not many different patterns. The prevailing one could be one of the following (the percentages of each in the ethnographic record do not sum to 100 because of rounding):

1. **Patrilocal residence.** The son stays and the daughter leaves, so that the married couple lives with or near the husband's parents (67 percent of all societies).

2. **Matrilocal residence.** The daughter stays and the son leaves, so that the married couple lives with or near the wife's parents (15 percent of all societies).

An Iban family at mealtime in their longhouse apartment, Borneo, Malaysia.

3. **Bilocal residence.** Either the son or the daughter leaves, so that the married couple lives with or near either the wife's or the husband's parents (7 percent of all societies).

4. **Avunculocal residence.** Both son and daughter normally leave, but the son and his wife settle with or near his mother's brother (4 percent of all societies).[2]

In these definitions, we use the phrase "the married couple lives *with or near*" a particular set of in-laws. When couples live with or near the kin of a spouse, the couple may live in the same household with those kin, creating an *extended-family* household, or they may live separately in an *independent-family* household, but nearby. (Because matrilocal, patrilocal, and avunculocal residence specify just one pattern, they are often called nonoptional or **unilocal residence** patterns.)

A fifth pattern of residence is neolocal, in which the newly married couple does not live with or near kin.

5. **Neolocal residence.** Both son and daughter leave; married couples live apart from the relatives of both spouses (5 percent of all societies).

Figure 12–1 graphically shows the percentage of societies in the ethnographic record that practice each of the five marital residence patterns.

How does place of residence affect the social life of the couple? Because the pattern of residence governs with or near whom individuals live, it largely determines which people those individuals interact with and have to depend on. If the kin of the husband surrounds a married couple, for example, the chances are that those relatives will figure importantly in the couple's future. Whether the couple lives with or near the

213

In many societies known to anthropology, the bride goes to live with or near the husband's family. In a reenactment of a traditional Korean wedding ceremony, a bride is carried to the home of the groom.

husband's or the wife's kin can also be expected to have important consequences for the status of the husband or wife. If married couples live patrilocally, as occurs in most societies, the wife may be far from her own kin. In any case, she will be an outsider among a group of male relatives who have grown up together. The feeling of being an outsider is particularly strong when the wife has moved into a patrilocal extended-family household.

Among the Tiv of central Nigeria,[3] the patrilocal extended family consists of the "great father," who is the head of the household, and his younger brothers, his sons, and his younger brothers' sons. Also included are the in-marrying wives and all unmarried children. (The sisters and daughters of the household head who have married would have gone to live where their husbands lived.)

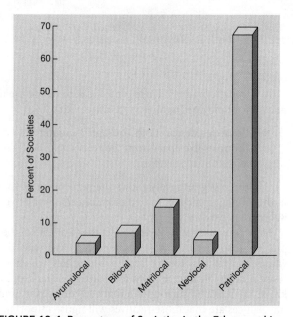

FIGURE 12–1 Percentage of Societies in the Ethnographic Record with Various Marital Residence Patterns

Source: Calculated from Allan D. Coult and Robert W. Habenstein 1965.

Authority is strongly vested in the male line, particularly the oldest of the household, who has authority over bride price, disputes, punishment, and plans for new buildings.

A somewhat different situation exists if the husband comes to live with or near his wife's parents. In this case, the wife and her kin take on somewhat greater importance, and the husband is the outsider. As we shall see, however, the matrilocal situation is not quite the mirror image of the patrilocal, because the husband's kin in matrilocal societies often are not far away. Moreover, even though residence is matrilocal, women often do not have as much to say in decision-making as their brothers do.

If the married couple does not live with or near the parents or close kin of either spouse, the situation is again quite different. It should not be surprising that relatives and kinship connections do not figure very largely in everyday life in neolocal residence situations.

Marital residence determines which kin will live, or not live, in the immediate vicinity of the married couple. Toward the end of this chapter, we consider the factors that may explain residential variation; these same factors may also help explain the types of kinship groups that develop.

THE STRUCTURE OF KINSHIP

In noncommercial societies, kinship connections structure many areas of social life—from the kind of access an individual has to productive resources to the kind of political alliances formed between communities and larger territorial groups. In some societies, in fact, kinship connections have an important bearing on matters of life and death.

Recall the social system described in Shakespeare's *Romeo and Juliet.* The Capulets and the Montagues were groups of kin engaged in lethal competition with each other, and the fatal outcome of Romeo and Juliet's romance was related to that competition. Although Romeo and Juliet's society had a commercial economy (but not, of course, an industrialized one), the political system of the city they lived in was a reflection of the way kinship was structured. Sets of kin of common descent lived together, and the various kin groups competed, and sometimes fought, for a prominent, or at least secure, place in the political hierarchy of the city-state.

If a preindustrial commercial society could be so structured by kinship, we can imagine how much more important kinship connections and kin groups are in many noncommercial societies that lack political mechanisms such as princes and councils of lords who try to keep the peace and initiate other activities on behalf of the community. It is no wonder that anthropologists often speak of the web of kinship as providing the main structure of social action in noncommercial societies.

If kinship is important, there is still the question of which set of kin a person affiliates with and depends on. After all, if every single relative were counted as equally important, there would be an unmanageably large number of people in each person's kinship network. Consequently, in most societies in which kinship connections are important, rules allocate each person to a particular and definable set of kin.

current research and issues

Neolocality and Adolescent Rebellion: Are They Related?

In our society, it is taken for granted that adolescence means turmoil and parent-child conflict. Teenagers, parents, and educators worry about how to reduce the conflict. But few in our society ask why the conflict occurs in the first place. Is it "natural" for adolescents to be rebellious? Are they rebellious in all cultures? If not, why do we have conflict in our society?

Margaret Mead first raised this issue. In her best-selling *Coming of Age in Samoa* (originally published in 1928), she said that conflict during adolescence was minimal in Samoa. Some researchers have recently criticized her analysis (see the discussion in the chapter on culture and the individual), but many field and comparative studies by anthropologists have since found that adolescence is not experienced in the same way in all societies. For example, in their systematic cross-cultural study of adolescence, Alice Schlegel and Herbert Barry concluded that relations between adolescents and their families were generally harmonious around the world. They suggested that, when family members need each other throughout their lives, independence, as expressed in adolescent rebelliousness, would be foolhardy. Indeed, Schlegel and Barry found that adolescents are likely to be rebellious only in societies, like our own, that have neolocal residence and considerable job and geographic mobility.

Why should this be? We might speculate that adolescent rebellion is an elaborate psychodrama that both parents and children play out to prepare themselves for separation. Children spend a considerable part of their lives being dependent on their parents. But they know they must move away, and that prospect may arouse anxiety. Children want to be independent, but independence is scary. Dependence is nice in some ways—at least it can make life easier (someone else cooks for you and so on)—but it is also less grown-up than independence. So what pushes a child to leave? Perhaps the conflict itself propels the departure. Teenagers ask for things they want, but they may know, at least unconsciously,

that their parents will say no. And parents often do say no, so the teenagers get angry and can't wait to be on their own. Parents are also ambivalent. They want their children to grow up, but they miss them when they leave. After a period of conflict, it may be a relief for all concerned when parents and children go their separate ways.

What if our social structure was different? What if parents and children knew that some of the children were going to spend the rest of their lives with or near the parents? And even those children who moved away, as some would have to in societies practicing matrilocal, patrilocal, avunculocal, or bilocal residence, would know they were going to spend the rest of their lives with or near their in-laws. Could teenagers in non-neolocal societies afford to have serious conflict with their parents? Could the parents afford to have serious conflict with the teenagers who will be staying put after their marriages? We think not. We suggest that adolescent conflict would be very disadvantageous in a non-neolocal society, and therefore we would expect its minimization or suppression when the residence pattern is other than neolocal.

There is another reason why rebelliousness might be associated with neolocality; it has to do with the fact that neolocality is predicted by commercial exchange. In the modern world, commercial societies are likely to have a great deal of occupational specialization and people with many different values. Thus, children are presented with a great many choices in a rapidly changing culture. Let us consider the effect of a rapidly changing technology. If children have to know and do things that the parents do not know about, how can we expect the children to want to follow in their parents' footsteps?

But a rapidly changing culture is not necessarily accompanied by parent-child conflict. Other conditions are probably also necessary to generate the conflict, if the situation in a Moroccan town is any guide. As part of a comparative research project on adolescence, Susan and Douglas Davis

interviewed young people in a small town in Morocco. The culture had changed a lot recently. Parents mostly worked at jobs in and related to agriculture; children aspired to white-collar jobs. Grandparents rarely saw a car; teenagers took trains to the capital. Only a few parents had gone to school; most teenagers did. Yet the Davises reported little serious parent-child conflict, despite the cultural changes. For example, 40 percent of the teenagers said that they had never disagreed with their mothers. Perhaps we need to consider other facets of the culture. For one thing, Morocco has an authoritarian political structure with a monarchy and a clear pyramid of offices; perhaps parent-child conflict is unlikely in such a political system because it emphasizes and requires obedience. A second possible consideration is that group life is more important than the individual. The family is the most important social group, and as such, cannot tolerate adolescent rebelliousness. A third possible consideration is that adults are supposed to avoid open conflict. The study by the Davises implies that adolescent rebelliousness is likely only in societies like the United States that emphasize individuality, personal autonomy, and individual achievement.

What we need is research that tries to untangle the various causal possibilities. To discover the possible effect of neolocality, rapid change, cultural emphasis on individual autonomy, or an authoritarian political system, we need to study samples of cultures that have different combinations of those traits. It is possible that they all are influential, or that some are more important than others, or that some cause the others. Whatever we discover in the future about the causality, we know now that adolescent rebelliousness is not inevitable or natural, that it is probably linked to some other aspects of cultural variation—as Margaret Mead suggested many years ago.

Sources: Mead 1961/1928; Schlegel and Barry 1991; M. Ember 1967; S. S. Davis 1993; 2009.

Totem poles often symbolize the history of a descent group. A totem pole in Ketchikan, Alaska.

Types of Affiliation with Kin

We distinguish three main types of affiliation with kin: *unilineal descent, ambilineal descent,* and *bilateral kinship.* The first two types (unilineal descent and ambilineal descent) are based on **rules of descent,** which are rules that connect individuals with particular sets of kin because of known or presumed common ancestry. By the particular rule of descent operating in their society, individuals can know more or less immediately which set of kin to turn to for support and help. As we shall see, bilateral kinship is not based on rules of descent or ancestry and does not create clear and unambigous groups.

Unilineal descent refers to the fact that a person is affiliated with a group of kin through descent links of one sex only—either males only or females only. Thus, unilineal descent can be either patrilineal or matrilineal.

1. **Patrilineal descent** affiliates individuals with kin of both sexes related to them *through men only.* As Figure 12–2 indicates, the children in patrilineal systems in each generation belong to the kin group of their father; their father, in turn, belongs to the group of his father; and so on. Although a man's sons and daughters are all members of the same descent group, affiliation with that group is transmitted only by the sons to their children. Just as patrilocal residence is much more common than matrilocal residence, patrilineal descent is more common than matrilineal descent.

2. **Matrilineal descent** affiliates individuals with kin of both sexes related to them *through women only.* In each generation, then, children belong to the kin

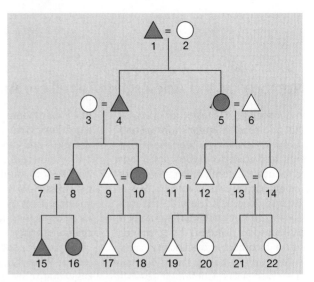

FIGURE 12–2 Patrilineal Descent
Individuals 4 and 5, who are the children of 1 and 2, affiliate with their father's patrilineal kin group, represented by the color red. In the next generation, the children of 3 and 4 also belong to the red kin group, because they take their descent from their father, who is a member of that group. However, the children of 5 and 6 do not belong to this patrilineal group, because they take their descent from their father, who is a member of a different group. That is, although the mother of 12 and 14 belongs to the red patrilineal group, she cannot pass on her descent affiliation to her children, and because her husband (6) does not belong to her patrilineage, her children (12 and 14) belong to their father's group. In the fourth generation, only 15 and 16 belong to the red patrilineal group, because their father is the only male member of the preceding generation who belongs to the red patrilineal group. In this diagram, then, 1, 4, 5, 8, 10, 15, and 16 are affiliated by the patrilineal descent; all the other individuals belong to other patrilineal groups.

group of their mother (see Figure 12–3). Although a woman's sons and daughters are all members of the same descent group, only her daughters can pass on their descent affiliation to their children.

Some have questioned the existence of unilineal descent and descent groups, suggesting that theorists have only imagined them. Reality could not possibly have been like that. But recent ethnohistorical analyses confirm that Native North American societies, like the Omaha, really did have patrilineal descent groups in the 19th century,[4] and the Chuuk (in the Pacific) still have functioning matrilineal groups, despite many years of Western contact.[5]

Unilineal rules of descent affiliate an individual with a line of kin extending back in time and into the future. By virtue of this line of descent, whether it extends through males or females, some very close relatives are excluded. For example, in a patrilineal system, your mother and your mother's parents do not belong to your patrilineal group, but your father and his father (and their sisters) do. In your own generation in a matrilineal or patrilineal system, some cousins are excluded, and in your children's generation, some of your nieces and nephews are excluded.

However, although unilineal rules of descent exclude certain relatives from membership in one's kin group, the excluded relatives are not necessarily ignored or forgotten, just as practical considerations restrict the effective size of

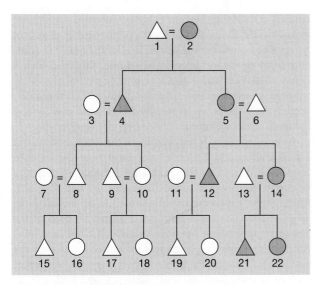

FIGURE 12–3 Matrilineal Descent
Individuals 4 and 5, who are the children of 1 and 2, affiliate with their mother's kin group, represented by the color green. In the next generation, the children of 5 and 6 also belong to the green kin group, because they take their descent from their mother, who is a member of that group. However, the children of 3 and 4 do not belong to this matrilineal group, because they take their descent from their mother, who is a member of a different group; their father, although a member of the green matrilineal group, cannot pass his affiliation on to them under the rule of matrilineal descent. In the fourth generation, only 21 and 22 belong to the green matrilineal group, because their mother is the only female member of the preceding generation who belongs. Thus, individuals 2, 4, 5, 12, 14, 21, and 22 belong to the same matrilineal group.

kinship networks in our own society. Indeed, in many unilineal societies, they may be entrusted with important responsibilities. For example, when a person dies in a patrilineal society, some members of the mother's patrilineal descent group may customarily be accorded the right to perform certain rituals at the funeral.

Unilineal rules of descent can form clear-cut, and hence unambiguous, groups of kin, which can act as separate units even after the death of individual members. Referring again to Figures 12–2 and 12–3, we can see that the individuals in the highlight color belong to the same patrilineal or matrilineal descent group without ambiguity; individuals in the fourth generation belong to the group just as much as those in the first generation. Say the patrilineal group has a name, the Hawks. Individuals know whether or not they are Hawks. If not, they belong to some other group, for each person belongs to only one line of descent. This fact is important if kin groups are to act as separate, nonoverlapping units. It is difficult for people to act together unless they know exactly who should get together. And it is easier for individuals to act together as a group if each one belongs to only one such group or line.

In contrast to unilineal descent, **ambilineal descent** affiliates individuals with kin related to them through men *or* women. In other words, some people in the society affiliate with a group of kin through their fathers; others affiliate through their mothers. Consequently, the descent groups show both female and male genealogical links, as illustrated in Figure 12–4.

These three rules of descent (patrilineal, matrilineal, and ambilineal) are usually, but not always, mutually exclusive. Most societies can be characterized as having only one rule of descent, but two principles are sometimes used to affiliate individuals with different sets of kin for different purposes. Some societies have, then, what is called **double descent or double unilineal descent,** whereby individuals affiliate for some purposes with a group of matrilineal kin and for other purposes with a group of patrilineal kin. Thus, two rules of descent, each traced through links of one sex only, are operative at the same time. For example, if there is a patrilineal system and a matrilineal one, individuals would belong to two groups at birth: the matrilineal group of the mother and the patrilineal group of the father. Imagine combining Figures 12–2 and 12–3. Individuals 4 and 5 would belong to both the patrilineal group (red in Figure 12–2) to which their father belongs and the matrilineal group (green in Figure 12–3) to which their mother belongs.

The way a society assigns names does not necessarily convey any information about a rule of descent. It is customary in North American society for children to have a last, or "family," name—usually their father's last name. All the people with the same last name do not conceive of themselves as descended from the same common ancestor; all Smiths do not consider themselves related. Nor do such people act together for any particular purpose. And many societies, even with rules of descent, do not give individuals the name of their kin group or of their father or mother. For example, among the patrilineal Luo of Kenya, babies were traditionally given names that described the circumstances of their birth (such as "born-in-the-morning"); their names did not include their father's or kin group's name. Only after the British established a colony in Kenya, and continuing after independence, did children get their father's personal name as a family name.

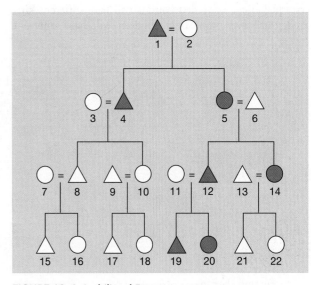

FIGURE 12–4 Ambilineal Descent
A hypothetical ambilineal group of kin is indicated by the color blue. Members 4 and 5 belong to this group because of a male link, their father (1); members 12 and 14 belong because of a female link, their mother (5); and members 19 and 20 belong because of a male link, their father (12). This is a hypothetical example because any combination of lineal links is possible in an ambilineal descent group.

Many societies, including our own, do not have lineal (matrilineal, patrilineal, or ambilineal) descent groups—sets of kin who believe they descend from a common ancestor. These are societies with **bilateral kinship.** *Bilateral* means "two-sided," and in this case, it refers to the fact that one's relatives on both the mother's and father's sides are equal in importance or, more usually, in unimportance. Kinship reckoning in bilateral societies does not refer to common descent but rather is horizontal, moving outward from close to more distant relatives rather than upward to common ancestors (see Figure 12–5).

The term **kindred** describes a person's bilateral set of relatives who may be called upon for some purpose. Most bilateral societies have kindreds that overlap in membership. In North America, we think of the kindred as including the people we might invite to weddings, funerals, or some other ceremonial occasion; a kindred, however, is not usually a definite group. As anyone who has been involved in creating a wedding invitation list knows, a great deal of time may be spent deciding which relatives ought to be invited and which ones can legitimately be excluded. Societies with bilateral kinship differ in precisely how distant relatives have to be before they are lost track of or before they are not included in ceremonial activities. In societies such as our own, in which kinship is relatively unimportant, fewer relatives are included in the kindred. In other bilateral societies, however, where kinship connections are somewhat more important, more would be included.

The distinctive feature of bilateral kinship is that, aside from brothers and sisters, no two people belong to exactly the same kin group. Your kindred contains close relatives spreading out on both your mother's and father's sides, but the members of your kindred are affiliated only by way of their connection to you (**ego,** or the focus). Thus, the kindred is an *ego-centered* group of kin. Because different people (except for brothers and sisters) have different mothers and fathers, your first cousins will have different kindreds, and even your own children will have different

kindred from yours. The ego-centered nature of the kindred makes it difficult for it to serve as a permanent or persistent group. The only thing the people in a kindred have in common is the ego or focal person who brings them together. A kindred usually has no name, no common purpose, and only temporary meetings centered around the ego.[6] Furthermore, because everyone belongs to many different and overlapping kindreds, the society is not divided into clear-cut groups.

Although kindreds may not form clear-cut groups as in a unilineal society, this does not mean that the kindred cannot be turned to for help. In a bilateral society, the kindred may provide social insurance against adversity. Among the Chipewyan of subarctic Canada, for example, people would borrow a fishing net from a kindred member, or ask a kindred member to provide child care for a young person whose parent was ill. But recently, with the national and provincial governments providing resources such as housing and medical assistance, and with the increase in opportunities for wage labor, the kindred has ceased to be the main source of help for people in need. Aid from the state is making kinship less useful.[7]

VARIATION IN UNILINEAL DESCENT SYSTEMS

In a society with unilineal descent, people usually refer to themselves as belonging to a particular unilineal group or set of groups because they believe they share common descent in either the male (patrilineal) or female (matrilineal) line. Anthropologists distinguish several types of unilineal descent groups: lineages, clans, phratries, and moieties.

Lineages A **lineage** is a set of kin whose members trace descent from a common ancestor through known links. There may be **patrilineages** or **matrilineages,** depending on whether the links are traced through males only or through females only. Lineages are often designated

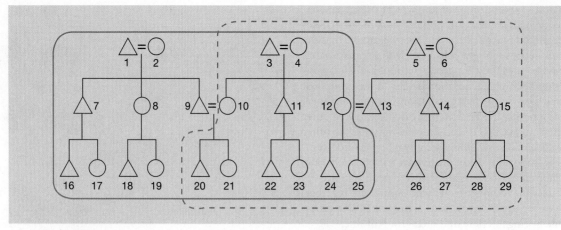

FIGURE 12–5 Bilateral Kinship

In a bilateral system, the kindred is ego-centered; hence, it varies with different points of reference (except for brothers and sisters). In any bilateral society, the kindred minimally includes parents, grandparents, aunts, uncles, and first cousins. So, if we look at the close kindred of the brother and sister 20 and 21 (enclosed by the solid line), it would include their parents (9 and 10), their aunts and uncles (7, 8, 11, 12), their grandparents (1, 2, 3, 4), and their first cousins (16–19, 22–25). But the kindred of the brother and sister 24 and 25 (shown by the dashed line) includes only some of the same people (3, 4, 10–12, 20–23); in addition, the kindred of 24 and 25 includes people not in the kindred of 20 and 21 (5, 6, 13–15, 26–29).

migrants and immigrants

Blood Is Thicker Than Water

With the spread of money economies, many societies no longer have kin groups like lineages, clans, phratries, and moieties—kin groups larger than families, sometimes much larger (possibly with hundreds and sometimes thousands of members). But if large kin groups are disappearing in the modern world, that doesn't mean they are completely gone. Lineages continue to be important for many Chinese, and for people in various parts of Africa and on islands in the Pacific. Lineages and clans in some places still "own" the cultivable land and other valuable property. Kinship may be particularly useful when it comes time to migrate to other countries. When that time comes, and it comes for millions of people every year, "blood is thicker than water," as the old saying goes. Migrants generally look to settle, at least at first, near or with relatives. The relatives may be genealogically close (siblings, uncles, aunts). Or they may be more distantly related, members of one's lineage or clan. Probably the most common reason migrants use kinship connections is that they need help, at least for a while, to make a living in the new country.

When looking for help from lineage mates or clansmen, you may not know exactly how you are related to them. All you might be able to say is that they belong to your lineage or clan. You know because they say they are "Li," "Park," or "Bear" like you. (Clans in some societies are believed to have animal ancestors.) It's like having an automatic friend in the new place, which can be very useful, particularly if you don't have close relatives there. Indeed, if you come from a region that has lineages, the first person you might look up (even before you leave home) might be a lineage mate.

This is often what happens when Chinese from the Hong Kong area go abroad to seek their fortune. Consider the lineage known as the "Man," one of the five major lineages that dominated political life until the 1960s in the Hong Kong New Territories. Anthropologist James L. Watson has studied this group for more than 35 years, in the area around Hong Kong and in other parts of the world to which they have migrated. He has particularly tracked people from the village of San Tin, located on what used to be one of the front lines of the Cold War, 400 yards south of the border between British-controlled Hong Kong and Communist-controlled China.

People involved in the San Tin diaspora began to move away in the late 1950s. They had little money or assets. By the mid-1970s, they had managed to establish a chain of Chinese restaurants in England and other parts of Europe. Today, most of the grandchildren of the original migrants are wealthy professionals, and some are multimillionaires. Many in the current generation cannot speak or read Cantonese, the Chinese language of their ancestors. They now speak English, Dutch, or German.

The people who consider themselves members of the Man lineage trace their descent from Man Sai-go, the ancestor who settled near San Tin in the 14th century. Today, about 4,000 people living in more than 20 countries claim descent from Man Sai-go. The exact number is known only to the lineage master (*zushang*) and elders who manage the ancestral estates (properties in land and other assets). For nearly 600 years, the Man survived on a kind of rice grown in the salty paddies along the Shenzhen River, which became the border between British Hong Kong and China in 1898. San Tin's farmers faced a crisis in the early 1950s. The markets for their rice were located on the Chinese side of the river, which was no longer regularly accessible. Unlike other lineages in the area, the Man could not convert to growing vegetables or white rice (which could not be grown in their salty paddies). They had two choices: go to Hong Kong to work in its booming factories or migrate to England to work in Chinese restaurants. Just before the British authorities banned migration to England in 1962, 85 percent to 90 percent of San Tin's able-bodied men left for Britain, lineage mates following lineage mates, to work in factories and hotels, as well as restaurants.

The village of San Tin became a remittance economy, with wives, children, and elders left behind, supported by the money sent home by the migrants who returned to San Tin for a visit every few years and then went back to Europe to work. Many of the migrants, when they retired, decided to join their children's families in the diaspora, and never again returned to San Tin.

The history of San Tin and its people illustrates how a supposedly premodern form of kinship, the Chinese lineage, is still very much alive in the modern world.

Sources: Brettell 1996, 793–97; McKeown 2005, 65–76; J. L. Watson 2004, 893–910.

---

by the name of the common male or female ancestor. In some societies, people belong to a hierarchy of lineages. That is, they first trace their descent back to the ancestor of a minor lineage, then to the ancestor of a larger and more inclusive major lineage, and so on.

Clans A **clan** (also sometimes called a **sib**) is a set of kin whose members believe themselves to be descended from a common ancestor, but the links back to that ancestor are not specified. In fact, the common ancestor may not even be known. Clans with patrilineal descent are called **patriclans**; clans with matrilineal descent are called **matriclans.** Clans often are designated by an animal name (Bear, Wolf), called a **totem,** which may have some special significance for the group and, at the very least, is a means of group identification. The word *totem* comes from the

Ojibwa Indian word *ototeman,* "a relative of mine." In some societies, people have to observe taboos relating to their clan totem animal. For example, clan members may be forbidden to kill or eat their totem.

Although it may seem strange that an animal or plant should be a symbol of a kin group, animals as symbols of groups are familiar in our own culture. Football and baseball teams, for example, are often named for animals (Detroit Tigers, Baltimore Ravens, Philadelphia Eagles, Chicago Bears). Voluntary associations, such as men's clubs, are sometimes called by the name of an animal (Elks, Moose, Lions). Entire nations may be represented by an animal; we speak, for instance, of the American eagle and the British lion.[8] Why humans so often choose animal names to represent groups is an intriguing question for which we have no tested answer as yet.

Phratries   A **phratry** is a unilineal descent group composed of supposedly related clans or sibs. As with clans, the descent links in phratries are unspecified.

Moieties   When a whole society is divided into two unilineal descent groups, we call each group a **moiety.** (The word *moiety* comes from a French word meaning "half.") The people in each moiety believe themselves to be descended from a common ancestor, although they cannot specify how. Societies with moiety systems usually have relatively small populations (fewer than 9,000 people). Societies with phratries and clans tend to be larger.[9]

Combinations   Although we have distinguished several different types of unilineal descent groups, we do not wish to imply that all unilineal societies have only one type of descent group. Many societies have two or more types in various combinations. For example, some societies have lineages and clans; others may have clans and phratries but no lineages; and still others may have clans and moieties but neither phratries nor lineages. Aside from the fact that a society that has phratries must also have clans (because phratries are combinations of clans), all combinations of descent groups are possible. Even if societies have more than one type of unilineal kin group—for example, lineages and clans—there is no ambiguity about membership. Small groups are simply subsets of larger units; the larger units include people who say they are unilineally related further back in time.

Patrilineal Organization

Patrilineal organization is the most frequent type of descent system. The Kapauku Papuans, a people living in the central highlands of western New Guinea, are an example of a patrilineal society with various types of descent groups.[10] The hierarchy of groups to which the Kapauku are affiliated by virtue of the patrilineal descent system plays an extremely important part in their lives. All Kapauku belong to a patrilineage, to a patriclan that includes their lineage, and to a patriphratry that includes their clan.

The male members of a patrilineage—all the living males who can trace their actual relationship through males to a common ancestor—constitute the male population of a single village or, more likely, a series of adjoining villages. In other words, the lineage is a *territorial unit.* The male members of the lineage live together by virtue of a patrilocal rule of residence and a fairly stable settlement pattern. A son stays near his parents and brings his wife to live in or near his father's house; the daughters leave home and go to live with their husbands. If the group lives in one place over a long period, the male descendants of one man will live in the same territory. If the lineage is large, it may be divided into sublineages composed of people who trace their descent from one of the sons of the lineage ancestor. The male members of a sublineage live in a contiguous block within the larger lineage territory.

The members of the same patrilineage address each other affectionately, and within this group, a headman maintains law and order. Killing within the lineage is considered a serious offense, and any fighting that takes place is done with sticks rather than lethal weapons such as spears. The sublineage headman tries to settle grievances within the sublineage as quickly and as peacefully as possible. If a sublineage mate commits a crime against outsiders, all members of the sublineage may be considered responsible and their property seized, or a member of the sublineage may be killed in revenge by the victim's kin.

The Kapauku also belong to larger and more inclusive patrilineal descent groups—clans and phratries. All the people of the same clan believe they are related to each other in the father's line, but they are unable to say how they are related. If a member of the patriclan eats the clan's plant or animal totem, it is believed that the person will become deaf. Kapauku are also forbidden to marry anyone from their clan. In other words, the clan is exogamous.

Unlike the members of the patrilineage, the male members of the patriclan do not all live together. Thus, the lineage is the largest group of patrilineal kinsmen that is localized. The lineage is also the largest group of kinsmen that acts together politically. Among clan members, there is no mechanism for resolving disputes, and members of the same patriclan (who belong to different lineages) may even go to war with one another.

The most inclusive patrilineal descent group among the Kapauku is the phratry, each of which is composed of two or more clans. The Kapauku believe that the phratry was originally one clan, but that, in a conflict between brothers of the founding family, the younger brother was expelled and he formed a new clan. The two resulting clans are viewed as patrilineally related, because their founders are said to have been brothers. The members of a phratry observe all the totemic taboos of the clans that belong to that phratry. Intermarriage of members of the same clan is forbidden, but members of the same phratry, if they belong to different clans, may marry.

The Kapauku, then, have lineages with demonstrated kinship links and two kinds of descent groups with unknown descent links (clans and phratries).

Matrilineal Organization

Although societies with matrilineal descent seem in many respects like mirror images of their patrilineal counterparts, they differ in one important way. That difference

new perspectives on gender

Variation in Residence and Kinship: What Difference Does It Make to Women?

When we say that residence and kinship have profound effects on people's lives, what exactly do we mean? We may imagine that it is hard for a woman in a patrilocal society to move at marriage into another village where her husband has plenty of relatives and she has few. But do we have evidence of that? Most ethnographies usually do not give details about people's feelings, but some do. For example, Leigh Minturn gives us the text of a letter that one new Rajput bride (who grew up in the village of Khalapur, India) sent to her mother shortly after she married into her husband's village. The letter was written when the bride had been gone six weeks, but she repeatedly asked if her mother, her father, and her aunts had forgotten her. She begged to be called home and said her bags were packed. She described herself as "a parrot in a cage" and complained about her in-laws. The bride's mother was not alarmed; she knew that such complaints were normal, reflections of her daughter's separation anxiety. Seven years later, when Minturn returned to India, the mother reported the daughter to be happy. Still, a few other brides did have more serious symptoms: ghost possession, 24- to 36-hour comas, serious depression, or suicide. What research has not told us is whether these serious symptoms are present more often in patrilocal, patrilineal societies than in other societies, particularly matrilocal, matrilineal societies. Conversely, do men have some symptoms in matrilocal, matrilineal societies that they do not have in patrilocal societies? We do not know.

What about the status of women? Some research suggests that matrilocality and matrilineality enhance some aspects of women's status, but perhaps not as much as we might think. Even in matrilineal societies, men are usually the political leaders. The main effect of matrilocality and matrilineality appears to be that women control property, but they also tend to have more domestic authority in the home, more equal sexual restrictions, and more value placed on their lives. Alice Schlegel pointed out that women's status is not always relatively high in matrilineal societies, because they can be dominated by the husband or by brothers (because brothers play important roles in their kin groups). Only when neither the husband nor the brother dominates may women have considerable control over their own lives. Certainly the combination of matrilocality and matrilineality is better for women's status than patrilocality and patrilineality. Matrilocality and matrilineality might not enhance women's status because of the dominance of male matrilineal kin, but patrilocality and patrilineality are very likely to detract from women's status. Norma Diamond stated that, even after the Chinese Communist revolution, which abolished the landholding estates of patrilineages and gave women access to education as well as jobs outside the home, male dominance continued. The mode of production and labor changed, but patrilocality did not. Women were still usually the in-marrying strangers, and members of the patrilineage became a work team on the collective farm. Diamond pointed out that those few women who became local leaders were likely to have atypical marriages that allowed them to live in the villages of their birth.

Residence and descent also predict societal attempts to control reproduction. According to Suzanne Frayser, patrilineal societies have several sexual and reproductive dilemmas. One dilemma is the contradiction between the importance of males in kinship and the women's role in reproduction. If patrilineal societies denigrate women too much, women may try to decrease their reproduction. If patrilineal societies exalt women too much, that exaltation may detract from the value of men. A second dilemma has to do with paternity, which is essential for patrilineal descent but harder than maternity to be certain of. Frayser argued that, because kin group links are traced through males in patrilineal societies, they will do more to ensure that the man a woman marries is the father. Frayser suggested that patrilineal societies therefore will be more restrictive about a woman's sexuality. Indeed, the results of her cross-cultural study indicate that patrilineal societies are more likely than other societies to prohibit premarital and extramarital sex for women, and they are more likely to make it very difficult for a woman to divorce her husband.

Of course, we have to remember that there is considerable variation within patrilocal/patrilineal societies and matrilocal/matrilineal societies. In the patrilineal society that Audrey Smedley studied—the Birom of the Jos Plateau in Nigeria—women were formally barred from owning property, from holding political offices, and from major decision making. Yet, her fieldwork revealed that they had considerable autonomy in their personal lives in everyday life, including the legal right to take on lovers. Indeed, they had considerable indirect influence on decision making and were strong supporters of the patrilineal system. Smedley speculates that women support patrilineality in some environmental circumstances because it serves their interests and those of their children too. For example, male crops are highly valued, but such crops are grown on the more dangerous plains where men risked death at the hands of raiders from other groups. Food was scarce, so it may have been adaptive for everyone, including women, to give special status to men for growing crops in dangerous places.

Sources: Minturn 1993, 54–71; M. K. Whyte 1978b, 132–34; Schlegel 2009; N. Diamond 1975; Smedley 2004; Frayser 1985, 338–47.

has to do with who exercises authority. In patrilineal systems, descent affiliation is transmitted through males, and it is also the males who exercise authority. Consequently, in the patrilineal system, lines of descent and of authority converge. In a matrilineal system, however, although the line of descent passes through females, females rarely exercise authority in their kin groups. Usually males do. Thus, the lines of authority and descent do not converge.[11] Anthropologists do not completely understand why this is so, but it is an ethnographic fact. In any case, because males exercise authority in the kin group, an individual's mother's brother becomes an important authority figure, because he is the individual's closest male matrilineal relative in the parental generation. The individual's father does not belong to the individual's own matrilineal kin group and thus has no say in kin group matters.

The divergence of authority and descent in a matrilineal system has some effect on community organization and marriage. Most matrilineal societies practice matrilocal residence. Daughters stay at home after marriage and bring their husbands to live with them; sons leave home to join their wives. But the sons who are required to leave will be the ones who eventually exercise authority in their kin groups. This situation presents a problem. The solution that seems to have been realized in most matrilineal societies is that, although the males move away to live with their wives, they usually do not move too far away; indeed, they often marry women who live in the same village. Thus, matrilineal societies tend not to be locally exogamous—that is, members often marry people from inside the village—whereas patrilineal societies are often locally exogamous.[12]

The matrilineal organization on Chuuk, a group of small islands in the Pacific, illustrates the general pattern of authority in matrilineal systems.[13] The Chuukese have both matrilineages and matriclans. The matrilineage is a property-owning group whose members trace descent from a known common ancestor in the female line. The female lineage members and their husbands occupy a cluster of houses on the matrilineage's land. The property of the lineage group is administered by the oldest brother of the group, who allocates the productive property of his matrilineage and directs the work of the members. He also represents the group in dealings with the district chief and all outsiders, and he must be consulted on any matter that affects the group. There is also a senior woman of the lineage who exercises some authority, but only insofar as the activities of the women are concerned. She may supervise the women's cooperative work (they usually work separately from the men) and manage the household.

Within the nuclear family, the father and mother have the primary responsibility for raising and disciplining their children. When a child reaches puberty, however, the father's right to discipline or exercise authority over the child ceases. The mother continues to exercise her right of discipline, but her brother may interfere. A woman's brother rarely interferes with his sister's child before puberty, but he may exercise some authority after puberty, especially because he is an elder in the child's own matrilineage. On Chuuk, men rarely move far from their birthplace. As Ward Goodenough pointed out, "Since matrilocal residence takes the men away from their home lineages, most of them marry women whose lineage houses are within a few minutes' walk of their own."[14]

Although there are some differences between patrilineal and matrilineal systems, there are many similarities. In both types of systems there may be lineages, clans, phratries, and moieties, alone or in any combination. These kin groups, in either matrilineal or patrilineal societies, may perform any number of functions. They may regulate marriage, they may come to each other's aid economically or politically, and they may perform rituals together.

FUNCTIONS OF UNILINEAL DESCENT GROUPS

Unilineal descent groups exist in societies at all levels of cultural complexity.[15] Apparently, however, they are most common in noncommercial food-producing, as opposed to food-collecting, societies.[16] Unilineal descent groups often have important functions in the social, economic, political, and religious realms of life.

Regulating Marriage

In unilineal societies, individuals are not usually permitted to marry within their own unilineal descent groups. In some, however, marriage may be permitted within more inclusive kin groups but prohibited within smaller kin groups. In a few societies, marriage within the kin group is actually preferred.

But, in general, the incest taboo in unilineal societies is extended to all presumed unilineal relatives. For example, on Chuuk, which has matriclans and matrilineages, people are forbidden to marry anyone from their matriclan by the rule of descent group exogamy. The matrilineage is included within the matriclan, so the rule of descent group exogamy also applies to the matrilineage. Among the Kapauku, who have patriphratries, patriclans, and patrilineages, the largest descent group that is exogamous is the patriclan. The phratry may once have been exogamous, but the exogamy rule no longer applies to it. Some anthropologists have suggested that rules of exogamy for descent groups may have developed because the alliances between descent groups generated by such rules may be selectively favored under the conditions of life most unilineal societies face.

Economic Functions

Members of a person's lineage or clan are often required to side with that person in any quarrel or lawsuit, to help him or her get established economically, to contribute to a bride price or fine, and to support the person in life crises. Mutual aid often extends to economic cooperation on a regular basis. The unilineal descent group may act as a corporate unit in landownership. For example, among the Chuukese and the Kapauku, a lineage owns house sites and farmland. Descent group members may also support one another in such enterprises as clearing virgin bush or forest for farmland and providing food and other items for feasts, potlatches, curing rites, and ceremonial occasions, such as births, initiations, marriages, and funerals.

The descent group sometimes views money earned—either by harvesting a cash crop or by leaving the community for a time to work for cash wages—as belonging to all. In recent times, however, young people in some places have shown an unwillingness to part with their money, viewing it as different from other kinds of economic assistance.

Political Functions

The word *political,* as used by members of an industrialized society, generally does not apply to the vague powers that may be entrusted to a headman or the elders of a lineage or clan. But these people may have the right to assign land for use by a lineage member or a clan member. Headmen or elders may also have the right to settle disputes between two members within a lineage, although they generally lack power to force a settlement. And they may act as intermediaries in disputes between a member of their own clan and a member of an opposing kin group.

Certainly one of the most important political functions of unilineal descent groups is their role in warfare—the attempt to resolve disputes within and outside the society by violent action. In societies without towns or cities, the organization of such fighting is often in the hands of descent groups. The Tiv of central Nigeria, for instance, know very well at any given moment which lineages they will fight against, which lineages they will join as allies in case of a fight, which they will fight against using only sticks, and which must be attacked using bows and arrows.

Religious Functions

A clan or lineage may have its own religious beliefs and practices, worshiping its own gods or goddesses and ancestral spirits. The Tallensi of West Africa revere and try to pacify their ancestors. They view life as we know it as only a part of human existence; for them, life existed before birth and will continue after death. The Tallensi believe that the ancestors of their descent groups have changed their form but have retained their interest in what goes on within their society. They can show their displeasure by bringing sudden disaster or minor mishap and their pleasure by bringing unexpected good fortune. But people can never tell what will please them; ancestral spirits are, above all, unpredictable. Thus, the Tallensi try to account for unexplainable happenings by attributing them to the ever-watchful ancestors. Belief in the presence of ancestors also provides security; if their ancestors have survived death, so will they. The Tallensi religion is thus a religion of that descent group. The Tallensi are not concerned with other people's ancestors; they believe only one's own ancestors can plague or protect one.[17]

In some cultures, people worship or give gifts to ancestral spirits, as is common in China.

AMBILINEAL SYSTEMS

Societies with ambilineal descent groups are far less numerous than unilineal or even bilateral societies. Ambilineal societies, however, resemble unilineal ones in many ways. For instance, the members of an ambilineal descent group believe that they are descended from a common ancestor, although frequently they cannot specify all the genealogical links. The descent group is commonly named and may have an identifying emblem or even a totem; the descent group may own land and other productive resources; and myths and religious practices are often associated with the group. Marriage is often regulated by group membership, just as in unilineal systems, although kin group exogamy is not nearly as common as in unilineal systems. Moreover, ambilineal societies resemble unilineal ones in having various levels or types of descent groups. They may have lineages and higher orders of descent groups, distinguished (as in unilineal systems) by whether or not all the genealogical links to the supposed common ancestors are specified.[18]

The Samoans of the South Pacific are an example of an ambilineal society.[19] Samoa has two types of ambilineal descent groups, corresponding to what would be called clans and subclans in a unilineal society. Both groups are exogamous. Associated with each ambilineal clan are one or more chiefs. A group takes its name from the senior chief; subclans, of which there are always at least two, may take their names from junior chiefs.

The distinctiveness of the Samoan ambilineal system, compared with unilineal systems, is that individuals could belong to a number of ambilineal groups because people may be affiliated with an ambilineal group through their father or mother (and the parents, in turn, could be affiliated with any of their parents' groups). Affiliation with a Samoan descent group is optional, and people may theoretically affiliate with any or all of the ambilineal groups to which they are related. In practice, however, people are primarily associated with one group—the ambilineal group whose land they actually live on and cultivate—although they may participate in the activities (e.g., house building) of several groups. Because a person may belong to more than one ambilineal group, the society is not divided into separate kin groups, in contrast with unilineal societies. Consequently, the core members of each ambilineal group cannot all live together, as they could in unilineal societies, because each person belongs to more than one group and cannot live in several places at once.

Not all ambilineal societies have the multiple descent group membership that occurs in Samoa. In some ambilineal societies, a person may belong to only one group at any one time. In such cases, the society can be divided into separate, nonoverlapping groups of kin.

EXPLAINING VARIATION IN RESIDENCE

Questions can be raised as to why different societies have different patterns of residence. If married couples in most societies live with or near kin, as in patrilocal, matrilocal, bilocal, and avunculocal patterns of residence, then why do couples in some societies, such as our own, typically live apart from kin? And, among the societies in which couples live with or near kin, why do most choose the husband's side (patrilocal residence), but some the wife's side (matrilocal residence)? Why do some non-neolocal societies allow a married couple to go to either the wife's or the husband's kin (bilocal residence), whereas most others do not allow a choice?

Neolocal Residence

Many anthropologists have suggested that neolocal residence is related to the presence of a money or commercial economy. They argue that, when people can sell their labor or their products for money, they can buy what they need to live, without having to depend on kin. Because money is not perishable, unlike crops and other foods in a world largely lacking refrigeration, it can be stored for exchange at a later time. Thus, a money-earning family can resort to its own savings during periods of unemployment or disability, or it might be able to rely on monetary aid from the government, as in our own society. This strategy is impossible in nonmonetary economies, where people must depend on relatives for food and other necessities if they cannot provide their own for some reason.

There is cross-cultural evidence to support this interpretation. Neolocal residence tends to occur in societies with monetary or commercial exchange, whereas societies without money tend to have patterns of residence that locate a couple near or with kin.[20] The presence of money, then, partially accounts for neolocal residence: Money seems to allow couples to live on their own. Still, this fact does not quite explain why they choose to do so.

One reason may be that couples in commercial societies do better on their own because the jobs available require physical or social mobility. Or perhaps couples prefer to live apart from kin because they want to avoid some of the interpersonal tensions and demands that may be generated by living with or near kin. But why couples, when given money, should *prefer* to live on their own is not completely understood.

Matrilocal versus Patrilocal Residence

It is traditionally assumed that, in societies in which married children live near or with kin, the pattern of residence will tend to be patrilocal if males contribute more to the economy and matrilocal if women contribute more. However plausible that assumption may seem, the cross-cultural evidence does not support it. Where men do most of the primary subsistence work, residence is patrilocal no more often than would be expected by chance. Conversely, where women do an equal amount or more of the subsistence work, residence is no more likely to be matrilocal than patrilocal.[21] And if we counted all work inside and outside the home, most societies should be matrilocal because women usually do more. But that is not true either; most societies are not matrilocal.

applied anthropology

From Cross-Cultural Research to Archaeology: Reconstructing Marital Residence in the Prehistoric U.S. Southwest

Applied anthropology uses anthropological knowledge to solve problems. Usually, the problem is a practical problem outside anthropology. For example, forensic anthropology applies biological anthropology to help solve murders and other crimes. But sometimes the application is from one subfield of anthropology to another.

Cross-cultural studies using ethnographic data indicate that sisters are very likely to live in the same household if marital residence is matrilocal. The family unit is likely to be larger therefore with matrilocal residence, and the living (nonstorage) floor area of the house is also likely to be larger. In contrast to patrilocal societies, where the average living floor area is less than 72 square yards (60 square meters), the living floor area in matrilocal societies tends to be larger than 120 square yards (100 square meters). Apparently, sisters have less trouble living together than nonsisters, perhaps because they have grown up together.

Most anthropologists would assume that a relationship derived from comparative ethnography on preindustrial societies would apply also to human behavior in the prehistoric past. If that's true, and there is no good reason to doubt it, archaeological sites with living floor areas totaling more than 120 square yards (100 square meters) are likely to have had matrilocal marital residence. This prediction has been applied to the transition from pit houses to great houses in the U.S. Southwest. The pit houses between A.D. 500 and A.D. 700 averaged 18 square yards (15 square meters) in floor area, in contrast to the multiroom households from A.D. 900 to A.D. 1100 (as in Pueblo Bonito in New Mexico's Chaco Canyon) that ranged in size from 84 square yards to more than 360 square yards (70 square meters to 300 square meters). The latter households were probably matrilocal. Archaeologists know that the households had multiple rooms because there are double walls between adjacent households.

Years ago, some archaeologists suggested that a descent line of matrilineally related women, who would have occupied a site over time if couples lived matrilocally, should exhibit distinctive pottery design elements when compared with the pottery from other sites. After all, mothers would have taught daughters who would have taught their daughters. Perhaps because their calculations and measures were not simple counts such as number of potsherds found, the work by these pioneering archaeologists was ignored if not rejected. The study of kinship in archaeology, following the findings of cross-cultural research, is still wide open, particularly to investigators who are trained in statistical methods.

Sources: Peregrine 2001; M. Ember 1973; Divale 1977; Hill 1970; Longacre 1970.

We can predict whether residence will be matrilocal or patrilocal, however, from the type of warfare practiced in the society. In most societies known to anthropology, neighboring communities or districts are enemies. The type of warfare that breaks out periodically between such groups is called *internal*, because the fighting occurs between groups that speak the same language. In other societies, the warfare is never within the same society but only with other language groups. This pattern of warfare is referred to as purely *external*. Cross-cultural evidence suggests that, in societies where warfare is at least sometimes internal, residence is almost always patrilocal rather than matrilocal. In contrast, residence is usually matrilocal when warfare is purely external.[22]

How can we explain this relationship between type of warfare and matrilocal versus patrilocal residence? One theory is that patrilocal residence tends to occur with internal warfare because there may be concern over keeping sons close to home to help with defense. Because women do not usually constitute the fighting force in any society, having sons reside at home after marriage might be favored as a means of maintaining a loyal and quickly mobilized fighting force in case of surprise attack from nearby. If warfare is purely external, however, people may not be so concerned about keeping their sons at home because families need not fear attack from neighboring communities or districts.

With purely external warfare, then, the pattern of residence may be determined by other considerations, especially economic ones. If the women do most of the primary subsistence work in societies with purely external warfare, families might want their daughters to remain at home after marriage, so the pattern of residence might become matrilocal. If warfare is purely external but men still do more of the primary subsistence work, residence should still be patrilocal. Thus, the need to keep sons at home after marriage when there is internal warfare may take precedence over any considerations based on division of labor. Perhaps only when internal warfare is nonexistent may a female-dominant division of labor give rise to matrilocal residence.[23]

The frequent absence of men because of long-distance trade or wage labor in distant places may also provide an impetus for matrilocal residence even after warfare ceases. For example, among the Miskito of eastern Central America, matrilocality allowed domestic and village life to continue without interruption when men were away from home for long periods of time, working as lumberers, miners,

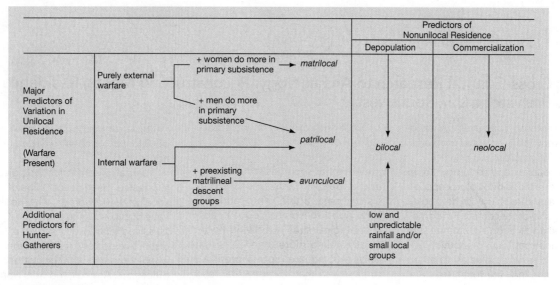

FIGURE 12–6 The Main Predictors of Marital Residence Patterns
An arrow indicates the suggested causal direction.

Source: Adapted from M. Ember and C. R. Ember 1983.

and river transporters. More recently, men have worked away from home as deep-sea divers for lobster, for which there is a lot of demand in the international economy. These jobs were not always available, but when they were, the men went away to work at them to earn money. Even though some men would always be away from home, the Miskito continued to get food in their traditional ways, from farming (done mostly by the women) and from hunting and fishing (which was mostly men's work).[24]

Bilocal Residence

In societies that practice bilocal residence, a married couple goes to live with or near either the husband's or the wife's parents. Although this pattern seems to involve a choice for the married couple, theory and research suggest that bilocal residence may occur out of necessity instead. Elman Service suggested that bilocal residence is likely to occur in societies that have recently suffered a severe and drastic loss of population because of the introduction of new infectious diseases.[25] Over the last 400 years, contact with Europeans in many parts of the world has resulted in severe population losses among non-European societies that lacked resistance to the Europeans' diseases. If couples need to live with some set of kin to make a living in non-commercial societies, it seems likely that couples in depopulated, noncommercial societies might have to live with whichever spouse's parents and other relatives are still alive. This interpretation is supported by the cross-cultural evidence. Recently depopulated societies tend to have bilocal residence or frequent departures from unilocality, whereas societies that are not recently depopulated tend to have one pattern or another of unilocal residence.[26]

In hunter-gatherer societies, a few other circumstances may also favor bilocal residence. Bilocality tends to be found among those hunter-gatherers who have very small bands or unpredictable and low rainfall. Residential

"choice" in these cases may be a question of adjusting marital residence to where the couple will have the best chance to survive or to find close relatives with whom to live and work.[27] Figure 12–6 illustrates the main predictors of the various marital residence patterns.

Avunculocal Residence

Now that we have learned about matrilineal systems, the avunculocal pattern of residence, whereby married couples live with or near the husband's mother's brother, may become clearer. Although avunculocal residence is relatively rare, just about all avunculocal societies are matrilineal. As we have seen, the mother's brother plays an important role in decision making in most matrilineal societies. Aside from his brothers, who is a boy's closest male matrilineal relative? His mother's brother. Going to live with the mother's brother, then, provides a way of

Trobriand Islanders have avunculocal residence and matrilineal descent groups.

localizing male *matrilineal* relatives. But why should some matrilineal societies practice that form of residence? The answer may involve the prevailing type of warfare.

Avunculocal societies, in contrast with matrilocal societies, fight internally. Just as patrilocality may be a response to keep patrilineally related men home after marriage, avunculocality may also be a way of keeping related—in this case, matrilineally related—men together after marriage to provide for quick mobilization in case of surprise attack from nearby. Societies that already have strong, functioning matrilineal descent groups may choose initially, when faced with the emergence of fighting close to home, to switch to avunculocality rather than patrilocality. This is assuming that the close warfare results in high male mortality, which might make it more difficult to trace descent patrilineally than matrilineally. So such a society might begin to practice avunculocality rather than switch to patrilocality. Avunculocal residence would keep a higher number of related men together after marriage, compared with patrilocality, because there would be more possible links through women than through men if many men were dying relatively young in warfare.[28]

THE EMERGENCE OF UNILINEAL SYSTEMS

Unilineal kin groups play very important roles in the organization of many societies. But not all societies have such groups. In societies that have complex systems of political organization, officials and agencies take over many of the functions that kin groups might perform, such as organizing work and warfare and allocating land. But not all societies that lack complex political organization have unilineal descent systems. Why, then, do some societies have unilineal descent systems, but others do not?

It is generally assumed that unilocal residence, patrilocal or matrilocal, is necessary for the development of unilineal descent. Patrilocal residence, if practiced for some time in a society, will generate a set of patrilineally related males who live in the same territory. Matrilocal residence over time will similarly generate a localized set of matrilineally related females. It is no wonder, then, that matrilocal and patrilocal residence are cross-culturally associated with matrilineal and patrilineal descent, respectively.[29]

But, although unilocal residence might be necessary for the formation of unilineal descent groups, it is apparently not the only condition required. For one thing, many societies with unilocal residence lack unilineal descent groups. For another, merely because related males or related females live together by virtue of a patrilocal or matrilocal rule of residence, it does not necessarily follow that the related people will actually view themselves as a descent group and function as such. Thus, it appears that other conditions are needed to supply the impetus for the formation of unilineal descent groups.

There is evidence that unilocal societies that engage in warfare are more apt to have unilineal descent groups than unilocal societies without warfare.[30] It may be, then, that the presence of fighting in societies lacking complex systems of political organization provides an impetus to the formation of unilineal descent groups. Unilineal descent groups provide individuals with unambiguous groups of people who can fight or form alliances as discrete units.[31] There is no ambiguity about an individual's membership. It is perfectly clear whether someone belongs to a particular clan, phratry, or moiety. This feature of unilineal descent groups enables them to act as separate and distinct units—mostly, perhaps, in warfare.

EXPLAINING AMBILINEAL AND BILATERAL SYSTEMS

Why do some societies have ambilineal descent groups? Although the evidence is not clear-cut, it may be that societies with unilineal descent groups are transformed into ambilineal ones under special conditions, particularly in the presence of depopulation. We have already noted that depopulation may transform a previously unilocal society into a bilocal society. If that previously unilocal society also had unilineal descent groups, the descent groups may become transformed into ambilineal groups. If a society used to be patrilocal and patrilineal, for example, but some couples began to live matrilocally, then their children would be associated through their mother with a previously patrilineal descent group on whose land they may be living. Once this situation happens regularly, the unilineal principle may become transformed into an ambilineal principle.[32] Thus, ambilineal descent systems may have developed recently as a result of depopulation caused by the introduction of European diseases.

The conditions that favor bilateral systems are in large part opposite to those favoring unilineal descent. As we discussed, unilineal descent seems to develop in a nonstate society with unilocal residence that has warfare. If one needs an unambigious set of allies, bilateral systems are unlikely to provide them. Recall that bilateral systems are ego-centered; and every person, other than siblings, has a slightly different set of kin to rely on. Consequently, in bilateral societies, it is often not clear to whom one can turn and which person has responsibility for aiding another. Such ambiguity, however, might not be a liability in societies without warfare. In complex political systems that organize fighting on behalf of large populations, a standing army usually provides the fighting force, and mobilization of kin is not so important. Perhaps because warfare is somewhat less likely in foraging societies,[33] bilateral systems may often develop in foraging societies, just like bilaterality is likely in more complex societies because they don't need to rely on descent groups for war. Neolocal residence, which becomes more common with commercialization and market exchange, also works against unilineal descent, and therefore also makes a bilateral system more likely.

KINSHIP TERMINOLOGY

Our society, like all others, refers to a number of different kin by the same **classificatory terms.** Most of us probably never stop to think about why we name relatives the way we do. For example, we call our mother's brother and father's brother (and often mother's sister's husband and father's sister's husband) by the same term—*uncle*. It is not that we are unable to distinguish between our mother's or father's brother or that we do not know the difference between **consanguineal kin** (blood kin) and **affinal kin** (kin by marriage, or what we call *in-laws*). Instead, it seems that we do not usually find it necessary to distinguish between various types of uncles in our society.

However natural our system of classification may seem to us, countless field studies by anthropologists have revealed that societies differ markedly in how they group or distinguish relatives. The kinship terminology used in a society may reflect its prevailing kind of family, its rule of residence, its rule of descent, and other aspects of its social organization. Kin terms may also give clues to prior features of the society's social system, if, as many anthropologists believe,[34] the kin terms of a society are very resistant to change. The major systems of kinship terminology are the Omaha system, the Crow system, the Iroquois system, the Sudanese system, the Hawaiian system, and the Inuit (Eskimo) system.

Because it is the most familiar to us, let us first consider the kinship terminology system employed in our own and many other commercial societies. But it is by no means confined to commercial societies. In fact, this system is found in many Inuit societies.

Inuit, or Eskimo, System

The distinguishing features of the Inuit, or Eskimo, system (see Figure 12–7) are that all cousins are lumped together under the same term but are distinguished from brothers and sisters; all aunts are lumped under the same term and distinguished from the mother; and all uncles are lumped under the same term and distinguished from the father. In Figure 12–7 and in subsequent figures, the kin types that are referred to by the same term are colored and marked in the same way; for example, in the Inuit system, kin types 2 (father's brother) and 6 (mother's brother) are referred to by the same term (*uncle* in English). Note that, in this system—in contrast to the others we will examine—no other relatives are generally referred to by the same terms used for members of the nuclear family—mother, father, brother, and sister.

The Inuit type of kinship terminology is not generally found where there are unilineal or ambilineal descent groups; the only kin group that appears to be present is the bilateral kindred.[35] Remember that the kindred in a bilateral kinship system is an ego-centered group. Although relatives on both my mother's and my father's sides are equally important, my most important relatives are generally those closest to me. This is particularly true in our society, where the nuclear family generally lives alone, separated from and not particularly involved with other relatives except on ceremonial occasions. Because the nuclear family is most important, we would expect to find that the terminology for kin types in the nuclear family is different from the terminology for all other relatives. And the mother's and father's sides are equally important (or unimportant), so it makes sense that we use the same terms (*aunt*, *uncle*, and *cousin*) for both sides of the family.

Omaha System

The Omaha system of kin terminology is named after the Omaha of North America, but the system is found in many societies around the world, usually those with patrilineal descent.[36] Referring to Figure 12–8, we can see immediately which types of kin are lumped together in an Omaha system. First, father and father's brother (numbers 2 and 3) are both referred to by the same term. This way of classifying relatives contrasts markedly with ours, in which no term that applies to a member of the nuclear family (father, mother, brother, sister) is applied to any other relative. What could account for the Omaha system of lumping? One interpretation is that father and father's brother are lumped in this system because most societies in which this system is found have patrilineal kin groups. Both father and father's brother are in the parental generation of my patrilineal kin group and may behave toward me similarly. My father's brother also probably lived near me as a child, because patrilineal societies usually have patrilocal residence. The term for father and father's brother, then, might be translated "male member of my patrilineal kin group in my father's generation."

A second lumping, which at first glance appears similar to the lumping of father and father's brother, is that of mother and mother's sister (4 and 5), both of whom are called by the same term. But more surprisingly, mother's brother's daughter (16) is also referred to by this term. Why? If we think of the term as meaning "female member of my mother's patrilineage of *any* generation," then the term makes sense. Consistent with this view, all the male members of my mother's patrilineage of any generation

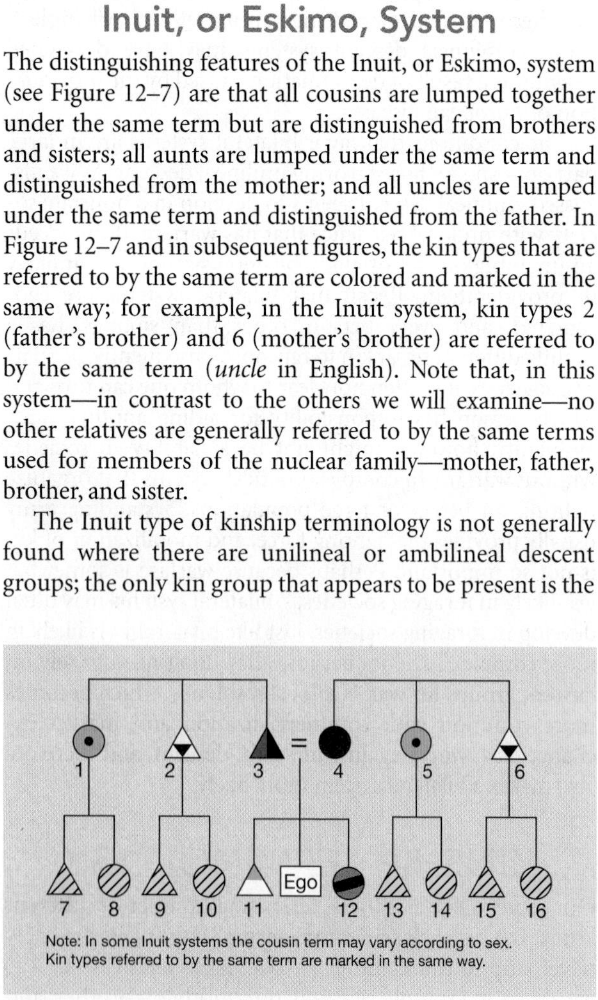

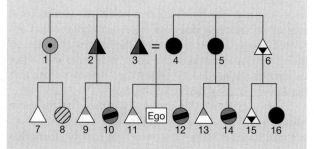

FIGURE 12–7 Inuit (Eskimo) Terminology System

Note: In some Inuit systems the cousin term may vary according to sex. Kin types referred to by the same term are marked in the same way.

FIGURE 12–8 Omaha Kinship Terminology System

(mother's brother, 6; mother's brother's son, 15) are also referred to by one term.

It is apparent, then, that relatives on the father's and the mother's sides are grouped differently in this system. For members of my mother's patrilineal kin group, I lump all male members together and all female members together regardless of their generation. Yet, for members of my father's patrilineal kin group, I have different terms for the male and female members of different generations. George Peter Murdock suggested that a society lumps kin types when there are more similarities than differences among them.[37]

Using this principle, and recognizing that societies with an Omaha system usually are patrilineal, I realize that my father's patrilineal kin group is the one to which I belong and in which I have a great many rights and obligations. Consequently, people of my father's generation are likely to behave quite differently toward me than are people of my own generation. Members of my patrilineal group in my father's generation are likely to exercise authority over me, and I am required to show them respect. Members of my patrilineal group in my own generation are those I am likely to play with as a child and to be friends with. Thus, in a patrilineal system, people on my father's side belonging to different generations are likely to be distinguished. On the other hand, my mother's patrilineage is relatively unimportant to me (because I take my descent from my father). And because my residence is probably patrilocal, my mother's relatives will probably not even live near me. Thus, inasmuch as my mother's patrilineal relatives are comparatively unimportant in such a system, they become similar enough to be lumped together.

Finally, in the Omaha system, I refer to my male parallel cousins (my father's brother's son, 9; and my mother's sister's son, 13) in the same way I refer to my brother (12). I refer to my female parallel cousins (my father's brother's daughter, 10; and my mother's sister's daughter, 14) in the same way I refer to my sister (12). Considering that my father's brother and mother's sister are referred to by the same terms I use for my father and mother, this lumping of parallel cousins with **siblings** (brothers and sisters) is not surprising. If I call my own mother's and father's children (other than myself) "brother" and "sister," then the children of anyone whom I also call "mother" and "father" ought to be called "brother" and "sister" as well.

Crow System

The Crow system, named after another North American culture, has been called the mirror image of the Omaha system. The same principles of lumping kin types are employed, except that the Crow system is associated with matrilineal descent,[38] so the individuals in my mother's matrilineal group (which is my own) are not lumped across generations, whereas the individuals in my father's matrilineal group are. Comparing Figure 12–9 with Figure 12–8, we find that the lumping and separating of kin types are much the same in both, except that the lumping across generations in the Crow system appears on the father's side rather than on the mother's side. In other words, I call both

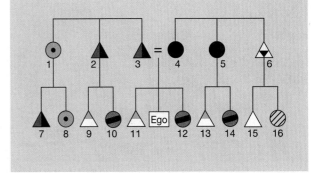

FIGURE 12–9 Crow Kinship Terminology System

my mother and my mother's sister by the same term (because both are female members of my matrilineal descent group in my mother's generation). I call my father, my father's brother, and my father's sister's son by the same term (all male members of my father's matrilineal group in any generation). I call my father's sister and my father's sister's daughter by the same term (both female members of my father's matrilineal group). And I refer to my parallel cousins in the same way I refer to my brother and sister.

Iroquois System

The Iroquois system, named after the Iroquois of North America, is similar to both the Omaha and Crow systems in the way in which I refer to relatives in my parents' generation (see Figure 12–10). That is, my father and my father's brother (2 and 3) are referred to by the same term, and my mother and my mother's sister (4 and 5) are referred to by the same term. However, the Iroquois system differs from the Omaha and Crow systems regarding my own generation. In the Omaha and Crow systems, one set of cross-cousins was lumped in the kinship terminology with the generation above. In the Iroquois system, both sets of cross-cousins (mother's brother's children, 15 and 16; and father's sister's children, 7 and 8) are referred to by the same terms, distinguished by sex. That is, mother's brother's daughter and father's sister's daughter are both referred to by the same term. Also, mother's brother's son and father's sister's son are referred to by the same term.

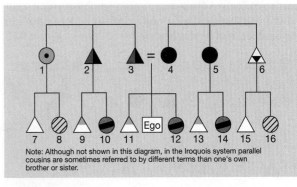

Note: Although not shown in this diagram, in the Iroquois system parallel cousins are sometimes referred to by different terms than one's own brother or sister.

FIGURE 12–10 Iroquois Terminology System

The Iroquois longhouses could house over 80 people. The female members of a matrilineage with their in-marrying husbands traditionally lived in one longhouse.

Parallel cousins always have terms different from those for cross-cousins and are sometimes, but not always, referred to by the same terms as one's brother and sister.

Like the Omaha and Crow systems, the Iroquois system has different terms for relatives on the father's and mother's sides. Such differentiation tends to be associated with unilineal descent, which is not surprising because unilineal descent involves affiliation with either mother's or father's kin. Why Iroquois, rather than Omaha or Crow, terminology occurs in a unilineal society requires explanation. One possible explanation is that Omaha or Crow is likely to occur in a developed, as opposed to a developing or decaying, unilineal system.[39] Another possibility is that Iroquois terminology emerges in societies that prefer marriage with both cross-cousins,[40] who are differentiated from other relatives in an Iroquois system.

Sudanese System

Unlike the Omaha, Crow, and Iroquois systems, the Sudanese system usually does not lump any relatives in the parents' and ego's generations. That is, the Sudanese system is usually a *descriptive system*, in which a different **descriptive term** is used for *each* of the relatives, as shown in Figure 12–11. What kinds of societies are likely to have such a system? Although societies with Sudanese terminology are likely to be patrilineal, they probably are different from most patrilineal societies that have Omaha or Iroquois terms. Sudanese terminology is associated with relatively great political complexity, class stratification, and occupational specialization. It has been suggested that, under such conditions, a kinship system may reflect the need to make fine distinctions among members of descent groups who have different opportunities and privileges in the occupational or class system.[41]

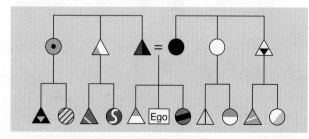

FIGURE 12–11 Sudanese Kinship Terminology System

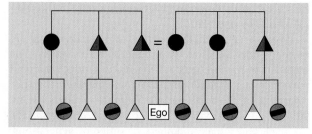

FIGURE 12–12 Hawaiian Kinship Terminology System

The Omaha, Crow, Iroquois, and Sudanese systems, although different from one another and associated with somewhat different predictors, share one important feature: The terms used for the mother's and father's side of the family are not the same. If you imagine folding the kinship terminology diagrams in half, the two sides would not be the same. As we have seen in the Inuit system, however, the terms on the mother's and father's side of the family are *exactly* the same. This feature suggests that the two sides of the family are equally important or equally unimportant. The Hawaiian system discussed next also has the same terms on both sides, but kinship outside the nuclear family is more important.

Hawaiian System

The Hawaiian system of kinship terminology is the least complex in that it uses the smallest number of terms. In this system, all relatives of the same sex in the same generation are referred to by the same term (see Figure 12–12). Thus, all my female cousins are referred to by the same term as my sister; all male cousins are referred to by the same term as my brother. Everyone known to be related to me in my parents' generation is referred to by one term if female (including my mother) and by another term if male (including my father).

The fact that societies with Hawaiian kin terminology tend not to have unilineal descent groups[42] helps explain why kinship terms are the same on both sides of the family. Why are the terms for mother, father, sister, and brother used for other relatives? Perhaps because societies with Hawaiian terminology are likely to have large extended families[43] to which every type of relative in Figure 12–12 may belong because of alternative (bilocal) residence patterns.[44] So, in contrast to our own society, many kin are very important, a fact that seems to be reflected in the practice of referring to other relatives with the same terms that are used for nuclear family members.

SUMMARY ● ○ ○

1. In our society, and in many other industrial societies, a newly married couple usually establishes a place of residence apart from parents or relatives (neolocal residence). But about 95 percent of the world's societies have some pattern of residence whereby the new couple settles within or very close to the household of the parents or some other close relative of the groom or bride.

2. The four major patterns in which married couples live with or near kinsmen are the following:
   a. Patrilocal residence: The couple lives with or near the husband's parents (67 percent of all societies).
   b. Matrilocal residence: The couple lives with or near the wife's parents (15 percent of all societies).
   c. Bilocal residence: The couple lives with or near either the husband's parents or the wife's parents (7 percent of all societies).
   d. Avunculocal residence: The son and his wife settle with or near his mother's brother (4 percent of all societies).

3. In most societies where kinship is important, rules of affiliation allocate each person to a particular and definable set of kin. The three main types of affiliation with kin are: *unilineal descent, ambilineal descent,* and *bilateral kinship.*

4. Unilineal descent and ambilineal descent are based on rules of descent, which are rules that connect individuals with particular sets of kin because of known or presumed common ancestry. Unilineal descent refers to the fact that a person is affiliated with a group of kin through descent links of one sex only—either males only or females only. Thus, unilineal descent can be either patrilineal or matrilineal.
   a. Patrilineal descent affiliates individuals with kin of both sexes related to them through men only. In each generation, then, children belong to the kin group of their father.
   b. Matrilineal descent affiliates individuals with kin related to them through women only. In each generation, then, children belong to the kin group of their mother.

5. Ambilineal descent affiliates individuals with kin related to them through either men or women. Consequently, the descent groups show both female and male genealogical links.

6. Societies without lineal descent rules are bilateral societies. Relatives on both the mother's and father's sides of the family are of equal importance or, more usually, unimportance. Kindreds are ego-centered sets of kin who may be called together temporarily for some purpose.

7. With unilineal descent, people usually refer to themselves as belonging to a particular unilineal group or set of groups because they believe they share common descent in either the male or the female line. These people form what is called a unilineal descent group. There are several types, and a society may have more than one type:
   a. Lineages are sets of kin whose members trace descent from a common ancestor through known links.
   b. Clans are sets of kin who believe they are descended from a common ancestor but cannot specify the genealogical links.
   c. Phratries are groups of supposedly related clans.
   d. Moieties are said to exist when the whole society is divided into two unilineal descent groups without specified links to the supposed common ancestor of each.

8. Unilineal descent groups are most common in societies in the middle range of cultural complexity—that is, in noncommercial food-producing, as opposed to food-collecting, societies. In such societies, unilineal descent groups often have important functions in the social, economic, political, and religious realms of life.

9. Societies differ markedly in how they group or distinguish relatives under the same or different kinship terms. The major systems of terminology are the Inuit (Eskimo), Omaha, Crow, Iroquois, Sudanese, and Hawaiian systems.

GLOSSARY TERMS ○ ● ○

affinal kin **228**
ambilineal descent **217**
avunculocal
   residence **213**
bilateral kinship **218**
bilocal residence **213**
clan or sib **219**
classificatory term **227**
consanguineal kin **228**
descriptive term **230**
double descent or double
   unilineal descent **217**
ego **218**
kindred **218**
lineage **218**
matriclans **219**

matrilineage **218**
matrilineal descent **216**
matrilocal residence **212**
moiety **220**
neolocal residence **213**
patriclans **219**
patrilineage **218**
patrilineal descent **216**
patrilocal residence **212**
phratry **220**
rules of descent **216**
siblings **229**
totem **219**
unilineal descent **216**
unilocal residence **213**

CRITICAL QUESTIONS ○ ○ ●

1. What other things about our society would change if we practiced other than neolocal residence?
2. Why does kinship provide the main structure of social action in noncommercial societies?
3. Why might it be important for unilineal descent groups to be nonoverlapping in membership?

PEARSON myanthrolab

Read William L. Anderson's "Cherokee: The European Impact on the Cherokee Culture" on MyAnthroLab. Answer the following questions.

1. Describe the patterns of marital residence and descent practiced by the Cherokee.
2. What functions did the kin groups have?
3. How did European contact affect patterns of residence and descent?

Associations and Interest Groups

amuel Johnson, the 18th-century English author, was once asked to describe James Boswell, his companion and biographer. "Boswell," he boomed, "is a very clubable man." Johnson did not mean that Boswell deserved to be attacked with bludgeons. He was referring to Boswell's fondness for all sorts of clubs and associations, a fondness he shared with many of his contemporaries. The tendency to form associations was not unique to 18th-century England.

The notion of clubs may make us think of something extracurricular and not very important, but associations play very important roles in the economy and political life of many societies. Indeed, the associations we call nongovernmental organizations (NGOs) have a lot of influence in our own and other modern societies (see the box on NGOs). In this chapter, we examine the various kinds of associations formed in different societies, how these groups function, and what general purposes they serve. When we speak of **associations,** we mean different kinds of groups that are not based on kinship, as discussed in the preceding chapter, or on territory, which we take up in the next chapter. Associations, then, are nonkin and nonterritorial groups; and, although they vary, they also have several common characteristics: (1) some kind of formal, institutionalized structure; (2) the exclusion of some people; (3) members with common interests or purposes; and (4) members with a discernible sense of pride and feeling of belonging. Contemporary American society has an abundance of *interest groups*—to use the terminology of the political scientist—that display these general characteristics of associations. Such groups vary considerably in size and social significance, ranging from national organizations such as the Democratic and Republican parties to more local organizations such as college sororities and fraternities.

But societies differ considerably in the degree to which they have such associations and, if they do have them, in what kind they have. To make our discussion somewhat easier, we focus on two dimensions of how associations vary from one society to another. One is whether or not recruitment into the association is voluntary. In U.S. society, with the exception of the government's right to draft men into the military, just about all associations are voluntary—that is, people can choose to join or not join. But in many societies, particularly the more egalitarian ones, membership is nonvoluntary: All people of a particular category must belong.

A second dimension of variation in associations is what qualifies a person for membership. There are two possible kinds of qualifications: those that are achieved and those that are ascribed. **Achieved qualities** are those people acquire during their lifetime, such as superior skills in a sport or the skills required to be an electrician. **Ascribed qualities** are those determined for people at birth, either because of genetic makeup (e.g., sex) or because of family background (ethnicity, place of birth, religion, social class). We speak of two kinds of ascribed qualities or characteristics: **universally ascribed qualities,**

applied anthropology

NGOs: Powerful National and International Interest Groups in the Modern World

The associations discussed so far in this chapter are mostly local organizations. Their activities and influence do not affect whole societies, and they have little or no effect on the economic and political state of the world. Even large modern voluntary organizations such as political parties, trade unions, and professional societies, powerful as they are in our own society, do not directly influence international relations and the fortunes of other societies. But there is a relatively new type of interest group that does—what we call nongovernmental organizations or "NGOs." Many anthropologists work for them, applying anthropological findings and understanding to the solution of practical problems. The World Bank and International Monetary Fund are two well-known examples that employ anthropologists and other social scientists to foster national and international economic development.

One of the main lessons of this chapter is that associations, nonkin and nonterritorial organizations, seem to develop to satisfy social needs that cannot be easily satisfied otherwise. So, for example, if you can't depend on kin to defend against a raid because the members of your kin group are dispersed, you can turn to members of your age-set, some of whom will always be nearby and could more quickly come to your defense. If you can't exert enough pressure on your employer to pay decent wages, you may join others in a trade union to negotiate with the employer. An association of nations (the UN, military alliances such as NATO) can try to organize international responses to threats to world peace. And it appears that NGOs operating in different countries make war less likely between those countries. The presence of the NGO seems to encourage peace between the countries as much as shared democratic institutions and economic interdependence.

NGOs are powerful interest groups in the modern world probably because the political states of the world cannot always agree on what should be done to resolve disputes and mitigate global problems. Or they cannot arrange for the necessary funding. But organizations that can raise money privately or from interested business organizations can work (often behind the scenes) to get things done. They can direct investments in new activities, as the World Bank does. Think of how the American colonies first organized to resist British rule. The Declaration of Independence marked the emergence of a large-scale association that was not a kin group, and not (at least to begin with) a territorial organization. The formation of a unified state, the "United States of America," was still to come.

During the 1990s, the number of NGOs rose from 6,000 to more than 25,000. Now there are thousands more. Some of the world's NGOs restrict their activities to their home countries. Others are international in scope. The attention they attract, and the influence they exert, means that they are doing some things that need to get done, and that could not get done otherwise. As much as they sometimes deserve criticism, the increasing number of NGOs may be a predictor of the growing unification of the world.

Sources: Fisher 1997; Russett and Oneal 2001.

---

those that are found in all societies, such as age and sex; and **variably ascribed qualities,** those that are found only in some societies, such as ethnic, religious, or social class differences.

Table 13–1 gives these two dimensions of variation in associations—voluntary versus nonvoluntary recruitment and criteria for membership— and some kinds of associations that fit neatly into our classification. Some associations do not fit so neatly—for example, the criteria that qualify someone for Girl Scout membership include an interest in joining, an achieved quality, as well as biological sex, an ascribed characteristic.

● ○ ●

TABLE 13–1 Some Examples of Associations		
Membership	**Criteria**	**Recruitment**
	Voluntary	**Nonvoluntary**
Universally Ascribed		Age-set Most unisex associations
Variably Ascribed	Ethnic associations Regional associations	Conscripted army
Achieved	Occupational associations Political parties Special interest groups	

NONVOLUNTARY ASSOCIATIONS

Although complex societies may have nonvoluntary associations, such associations are more characteristic of relatively unstratified or egalitarian societies. In relatively unstratified societies, associations tend to be based on the universally ascribed characteristics of age and sex. Such associations take two forms: age-sets and male or female (unisex) associations.

Age-Sets

All societies use a vocabulary of age terms, just as they use a vocabulary of kinship terms. For instance, as we distinguish among *brother, uncle,* and *cousin,* we also differentiate between *infant, adolescent,* and *adult. Age terms* refer to categories based on age, or age-grades. An **age-grade** is simply a category of people who happen to fall within a particular culturally distinguished age range. **Age-set,** on the other hand, is the term for a group of people of similar age and the same sex who move through some or all of life's stages together. For example, all the boys of a certain age range in a particular district might simultaneously become ceremonially initiated into "manhood." Later in life, the group as a whole might become "elders," and still later "retired elders." Entry into an age-set system is generally nonvoluntary and is based on the universally ascribed characteristics of sex and age.

Kinship forms the basis of the organization and administration of most noncommercial societies. In some noncommercial societies, however, age-sets crosscut kinship ties and form strong supplementary bonds. Two such societies are the Karimojong of East Africa and the Shavante of Brazil.

Karimojong Age-Sets The Karimojong number some 60,000 people. Predominantly cattle herders, they occupy about 4,000 acres of semiarid country in northeastern Uganda. Their society is especially interesting because of its organization into combinations of age-sets and generation-sets. These groupings provide "both the source of political authority and the main field within which it is exercised."[1]

A Karimojong age-set comprises all the men who have been initiated into manhood within a span of about five to six years. A generation-set consists of a combination of five such age-sets, covering 25 to 30 years. Each generation-set is seen as "begetting" the one that immediately follows it, and two generation-sets are in existence at any one time. The senior unit—whose members perform the administrative, judicial, and priestly functions—is closed; the junior unit, whose members serve as warriors and police, continues to recruit. When all five age-sets in the junior generation-set are established, that generation-set will be ready—actually impatient—to assume the status of its senior predecessor. Eventually, grumbling but realistic, the elders agree to a succession ceremony, moving those who were once in a position of obedience to a position of authority.

Once initiated, a boy has become a man, one with a clearly defined status and the ultimate certainty of exercising full authority together with his set partners. Indeed, a Karimojong is not expected to marry—and is certainly barred from starting a family—until he has been initiated.

The initiation ceremony itself illustrates the essential political and social characteristics of the age-set system. Without the authority of the elders, the ceremony cannot be held; throughout the proceedings, their authority is explicit. The father-son relationship of adjacent generation-sets is emphasized, for fathers are initiating their sons.

The Karimojong age system, then, comprises a cyclical succession of four generation-sets in a predetermined continuing relationship. The *retired generation-set* consists of elders who have passed on the mantle of authority, because most of the five age-sets within the retired generation-set are depleted, if not defunct. The *senior generation-set* contains the five age-sets that actively exercise authority. The *junior generation-set* is still recruiting members and, although obedient to elders, has some administrative powers. The noninitiates are starting a generation-set. Figure 13–1 illustrates the Karimojong age system.

Shavante Age-Sets The Shavante inhabit the Mato Grosso region of Brazil. Right into the middle of the 20th century, they were hostile to Brazilians of European ancestry who tried to move into their territory. Not until the 1950s was peaceful contact with the 2,000 or so Shavante achieved. Although the Shavante practice some agriculture, they rely primarily on food collection. Wild roots, nuts, and fruits are their staple foods, and hunting is their passion.[2] The Shavante have villages, but they rarely stay in them for more than a few weeks at a time. Instead, they make frequent community treks lasting 6 to 24 weeks to hunt or collect. They spend no more than four weeks a year at their gardens, which are located at least a day's journey from the villages.

Age-sets are an extremely important part of Shavante society, particularly for males. Boys emerge from the status of childhood when they are formally inducted into a named age-set and take up residence in the "bachelor hut." An induction ceremony takes place every five years, and boys from 7 to 12 years of age are inducted at the same time. The five-year period of residence in the bachelor hut

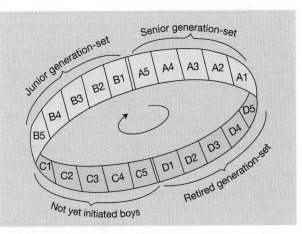

FIGURE 13–1   The Karimojong age system is composed of four distinct generation-sets (labeled A, B, C, and D in this diagram), which succeed each other cyclically. Each generation-set, in turn, is divided into five age-sets or potential age-sets. The senior generation-set (A) exercises authority. The junior age-set (B), the warriors and policemen, is still recruiting. Generation-set D consists of retired age-sets. Noninitiated and not-yet-born boys constitute the potential age-sets C1 through C5.

Some circumstances have changed, but the age-sets of the Nandi of Kenya still have importance. This young Nandi man (in a suit) is told by a traditional spiritual leader (in a skin cloak): "In the past, when our young warriors went out for the first time, we gave them spears and shields and told them to bring back wealth to the community. Today we give you a pen and paper and ask the same."

is relatively free of responsibility. The boys' families provide food for them, and they go out hunting and collecting when they feel like it. But during their residence, the boys are instructed in hunting, weapon making, and ceremonial skills. At the end of the five years, an elaborate series of initiation ceremonies marks the boys' entry into a different status—that of "young men." The day they emerge from the bachelor hut for the last time, during the final rites of initiation, the whole age-set is married, each to a young girl, usually not yet mature, chosen by the boys' parents. Marriages cannot be consummated at this time, because the young men must wait until their wives are more mature. When the ceremonies are over, the young men make war clubs, for now they are thought of as the warriors of the community, and they earn the privilege of sitting in the evening village council. But they have no authority at this stage and few responsibilities.

The next stage is that of the "mature men," and when an age-set is inducted into this stage, the members begin to experience some authority. In the mature men's council, important community decisions are made. This last status position actually consists of five consecutive age-sets, because new age-sets are formed every five years and each one continues in existence until the death of its members. Among the mature men, the oldest sets are considered senior to the younger ones. Members of the most junior mature men's age-set rarely talk in the council; they assert themselves more as they progress in the system.

In contrast to the Karimojong, who have age-sets just for males, the Shavante also have them for females. Shavante girls are inducted into an age-set when boys about their age enter the bachelor hut, but they belong to the age-set in name only. They do not participate in the bachelor hut, nor do they have their own equivalent; they are not initiated; and they cannot participate in the village council, which makes community decisions. About the only thing the age-set gives girls is occasional participation with males in a few ceremonies. For Shavante women, then, the age-set system does not function as an association.

Unisex Associations

Unisex, as used here, has quite a different meaning from its current connotation in contemporary North America,

where it signifies something that is suitable for both sexes. We use **unisex association** to describe a type of association that restricts its membership to one sex, usually male. Sex as a qualification is directly related to the purpose of the unisex association. In many male unisex associations, this purpose is to strengthen the concept of male superiority and to offer men a refuge from females. In noncommercial societies, men's associations are similar to age-sets, except that there are only two sets, or stages—mature males, who are association members, and immature males, who are nonmembers. Like societies with age-sets, societies with male unisex associations are very likely to have traumatic and dramatic male ceremonies initiating males into the group of "mature" men. We discuss these ceremonies further in the chapter on culture and the individual.

In most noncommercial societies, women have few associations, perhaps because the men in such societies are dominant in the kinship, property, and political spheres of life. (There is also the possibility that ethnographers, most of whom were men, have given women's associations less attention than men's associations.) In some partly commercialized economies, such as in West Africa, women's associations are more common.[3] Unisex associations or clubs are also a feature of very industrialized societies. The Boy Scouts and the Kiwanis, the Girl Scouts and the League of Women Voters, are cases in point. Joining these clubs, however, is voluntary; in noncommercial and less complex societies, membership is more often nonvoluntary.

Mae Enga Bachelor Associations The Mae Enga are a subgroup of 30,000 sedentary horticulturalists living in the New Guinea highlands. Anthropologists have paid a great deal of attention to their society because of its practice of sexual segregation—indeed, the strain of active hostility toward women that runs through its culture.[4] It is the custom for Mae men to live in a separate, communal house. Up to the age of 5, a young boy is permitted to live in his mother's house, although he is unconsciously aware of the "distance" between his father and mother. As he grows older, this awareness is made explicit by his father and elder clansmen. It is undesirable, he is told, to be so much in the company of women; it is better that he join the menfolk in their house and in their activities. As the

Many societies have male unisex organizations. Shown here is a decorated men's house among the Abelam of New Guinea.

Source: Photo Courtesy of Anthony Forge, 1962. From George A. Corgin, "Native Arts of North America, Africa and the South Pacific: An Introduction". New York. Harper & Row, Publishers, Inc., 1988.

boy grows up, the need to avoid contact with women is made abundantly clear to him. He is told that contact with menstrual blood or menstruating women, if not countered by magic rites, can "pollute" a man. It can "corrupt his vital juices so that his skin darkens and wrinkles and his flesh wastes, permanently dull his wits, and eventually lead to a slow decline and death."[5]

Because Mae culture regards a woman as potentially unclean, to say the least, it enforces strict codes of male-female behavior. These codes are designed to safeguard male integrity, strength, and possession of crops and other property. So strict are these regulations that many young men are reluctant to marry. But the elders do try to impress upon the young men their duty to marry and reproduce. The men's association attempts to regulate the males' sexual relationships. The association is said to have several purposes: to cleanse and strengthen its members; to promote their growth; to make them attractive to women; and, most important, to supervise contact between the sexes so that ultimately the "right" wives are procured for the men and the "right" children are born into the clan.

By the time males are 15 or 16 years old, Mae youths have joined the village bachelors' association. They agree to take scrupulous care neither to copulate with a woman nor to accept food from a woman's hands. As club members, they will participate in the *sanggai* rituals. Bachelors, under the supervision of senior club members, go into seclusion, in a clubhouse deep in the forest, to undergo "purification." During four days of "exercises," which are similar in purpose to those of a religious retreat, each youth observes additional prohibitions to protect himself from all forms of sexuality and impurity. For instance, they are denied pork (women have cared for the pigs), and they may not look at the ground during excursions into

the forest, lest they see feminine footprints or pig feces. Their bodies will be scrubbed, and their dreams discussed and interpreted. Finally, together with the club, now restored to purity and reprotected at least for a while against contamination, they will participate in organized dances and feasting with their chosen female partner.

The *sanggai* festivals afford the entire clan an opportunity to display its size, solidarity, and magnificence to its enemies, whom on other occasions it fights. Hostility toward women may not be surprising in view of the fact that a man's wife and mother come from neighboring clans (the Mae clan villages are exogamous) perpetually in conflict with his own. Male-female hostility, then, seems to reflect the broader, interclan hostility. The Mae have a succinct way of describing the situation: "We marry the people we fight."[6]

Men's houses, and occasionally women's, are found among many peoples, especially in Melanesia, Polynesia, Africa, and South America. Men's associations generally involve bachelors, although older married men will often come by to instruct the youngsters and pass on the benefits of their experience. In more militant days, men's houses acted as fortresses and arsenals, even as sanctuaries for fugitives. By and large, they serve to strengthen, certainly to symbolize, male power and solidarity. As do age-sets, men's clubs often provide ties that cut across and supplement kinship bonds. Hence, they permit a given group of men in a given society to act together toward the realization of mutually agreed-upon objectives, irrespective of kin relationships.

Poro and Sande   All associations usually have some secrecy, as in social life in general. In the examples we have discussed, many of the details of male initiation ceremonies usually are kept secret. But more secrecy seems to be required in the *Poro* and *Sande* associations of West Africa. The Poro and Sande associations exist in several cultural groups that speak Mande languages and are located in what is now Liberia, Sierra Leone, Ivory Coast, and Guinea. In Guinea, the Poro and the Sande have been declared illegal, but in the other countries, they are not only legal, they are an integral part of local political structure. Membership in them is public and nonvoluntary; all men in the community must belong to the Poro, and all women must belong to the Sande.[7]

Where the Poro and the Sande associations are legal, the community has two political structures—the "secular" and the "sacred." The secular structure consists of the town chief, neighborhood and kin group headmen, and elders. The sacred structure, or *Zo,* consists of the hierarchies of "priests" in the Poro and Sande associations. Among the Kpelle of Liberia, for example, the Poro and Sande *Zo* take turns in assuming responsibility for dealing with in-town fighting, murder, rape, incest, and disputes over land.

So, in what sense are the Poro and Sande secret? If all adults belong to them, their membership and what they do can hardly be described as secret. Furthermore, anthropologists have not only written about these associations; some have even joined them. Beryl Bellman, who joined the Poro of the Kpelle,[8] suggested that what is "secret" about these associations is the necessity for members to learn to keep secrets, particularly about how people are initiated into membership. Only when people learn to

new perspectives on gender

Do Separate Women's Associations Increase Women's Status and Power?

Some women's associations, like those of the Ijaw of southern Nigeria, are reported to have considerable power. Do women generally have more power where women create and join their own associations? We might assume that the existence of such organizations would increase the status of women overall, or at least lead to more equality with men. But it could also be argued the other way around, that "separate" does not generally lead to more equality; it may just increase separateness. As far as we know, researchers have not yet tried to assess the cross-cultural effect of women's associations on female status in various domains of life, but there has been one cross-cultural attempt to see if the presence of women's associations predicts various aspects of women's participation in the political process.

Marc Howard Ross looked at four aspects of women's political participation: (1) the degree of inequality between women's and men's participation in public or community decision making; (2) the degree to which women participate in politics privately; (3) the degree to which women have access to positions of authority; and (4) the degree to which women have separate associations that are under their exclusive control. This last domain concerns us here. Does the presence of separate women's associations increase women's participation in public decision making and their access to positions of authority? Ross's cross-cultural data indicate that the answer is no. The presence of separate women's organizations *does not* generally increase the participation of women in public decision making, their access to positions of authority, or even their private participation in politics. This is not to say that women in organizations do not have influence. They do, but probably only or mainly within their organizations. The influence of women in their organizations, however, does not carry over into other political arenas.

Of course, we might need to consider other possible factors in future research. Perhaps women's participation in political arenas is more likely if female organizations control important economic resources. Such resources may give women more leverage politically. Also, some types of female organizations may have more power than others; for example, stand-alone organizations may have more power than those that are connected to male organizations. But it is also possible that these additional conditions would not change the basic finding: Separate female organizations—perhaps because they *are* separate—do not have any impact on women's participation in other political arenas.

Recently, people in the United States have started to discuss a related issue, the possible effects of female "separateness" on women's success. For example, do separate math and science classes for women lead to more equality between women and men in academic performance, in obtaining advanced degrees in math and science, and in access to high-paying positions in those areas? It is well known that women are very underrepresented in the math and physical science professions in the United States. Even though the percentages have been increasing, in 2006, women obtained only 20 percent of the doctorates in engineering, 28 percent in physical science, and 25 percent in mathematics and computer science; in contrast, women obtained 57 percent of the doctorates received in anthropology and 71 percent in psychology that year.

These differences could be mostly a result of social conditions that discourage females in various subjects and professions. Researchers have found that teachers of math and science pay more attention to boys. When boys give wrong answers, teachers are apt to challenge them; when girls give wrong answers, teachers tend to express sympathy. Boys are more likely to operate scientific equipment; girls are more likely to take notes. In the seventh grade, girls perform similarly to boys in math and

science, but girls display less confidence in their abilities. By the time they graduate from high school, women have taken fewer math and science courses, so they are at a disadvantage for continuing in those fields.

If the dampening effects on women are social, or mostly social, what can be done? Because current research suggests that girls do best in learning science and math without boys, some researchers have advocated separate math and science activities (classes and clubs). So, for example, voluntary girls' clubs (Operation SMART) have been set up in 240 locations to interest elementary and junior high school girls in science. A majority of the girls from those schools voluntarily attend. Moreover, many of them now say they want to go into science. Whether they stay in science, or how well they do if they stay, is not yet clear. But if these programs work, we would have to conclude that "separate" is more equal than "together."

The two situations we have described here do not seem to be parallel in their effects on women's status. Separate women's associations by themselves do not make for equality between the genders in political participation. But separate training for girls in math and science may make for more equality. What is different about the two situations? At least one thing is different. Separate women's associations are usually nonvoluntary; women more or less have to join because that's how the society structures what women can do. Separate training for females in math and science is usually voluntary; girls may opt for the separateness to acquire the skills and the confidence they need to move into arenas open to both genders. In other words, when achievement and not gender defines how far you can go, temporary separateness for women might increase the likelihood of gender equality in professions that do not have it now.

Sources: Ross 1986; "Women in Science" 1993; S. T. Hill 2000; National Science Foundation 2006.

keep secrets are they considered trustworthy for participation in political life.

The Poro leadership establishes the place where the initiates will undergo scarification and live in seclusion for about a year (formerly it was three or four years). The boys are taken out of town, where they engage in a mock battle with a *ngamu* (a member of the Poro masquerading as a forest devil), who incises marks on their necks, chests, and backs. These marks symbolize being killed and eaten by the devil; but then the initiates are "reborn." In the initiation "village" outside of town, the boys learn crafts, hunting, and the use of basic medicines. The children of the *Zo* are given special instruction so that they can take over the rituals from their fathers. Some are trained to perform as "devils." At the end of the year, the initiates are given Poro names, by which they will be known from then on. Secrecy is attached to events surrounding the initiates; everyone knows that the boys are not killed and eaten by the devil, but only some can speak of it. For example, women must say that the boys are in the devil's stomach; if they say otherwise, they might be killed in punishment.[9]

The initiation of females into the Sande (every seven years or so) also involves taking the initiates into the forest for a year (formerly three years). The girls not only undergo scarification; they also undergo a clitoridectomy, that is, the removal of the clitoris. Like the boys, the girls receive training in adult activities. In the years just before and during the Sande initiation, the women are responsible for the moral behavior of the community. People who commit crimes are first brought before the women. If a man is the accused, he is tried by the Poro *Zo,* but a portion of any fine is given to the women.[10]

The Poro and Sande *Zo* are held in great respect, and the devils are viewed with fear and awe for the powers they possess. Some authors suggest that fear of the Poro and the Sande strengthens the hands of secular political authority, because chiefs and landowners occupy the most powerful positions in the associations.[11]

Secret associations are common in many areas of the world—the Pacific, North and South America, as well as various parts of Africa—although they may be voluntary organizations in some places. In Africa, according to a recent cross-cultural study, secret associations are usually involved in political activities, as are the Poro and Sande. These activities punish people who, according to the secret society, have committed some wrongs. The fact that the punished people almost never seem to be members of the native elite or foreign rulers supports the observation about the Poro and Sande that they typically strengthen the hand of existing political authority.[12]

Ijaw Women's Associations Among the Ijaw of southern Nigeria, only women in the northern part of this society are organized into associations. In one northern Ijaw village, there are seven women's associations.[13] Once a married woman shows herself capable of supporting a household independent of her mother-in-law, which she does by engaging in marketing and trading, she has to belong to the women's association linked to her husband's patrilineage. Membership in such an association is

An N'jembe women's group in Gabon initiates young women into the group.

nonvoluntary; all eligible women must join, and members are fined if they do not come to meetings or arrive late.

The women's associations act as mediators in disputes and impose punishments even in cases that have gone to court. For example, an association may impose fines for "crimes" such as defaming a woman's character or adultery. An association may also adopt rules for proper behavior. Judgments and rules are arrived at by consensus of all the women members. If a punished member does not accept a judgment, the other members might get together and taunt the woman or take some important item from her house and refuse to have anything to do with her.

Some of the larger associations also act as lending institutions, using their cash reserves from fines to lend to members or nonmembers at an interest rate of 50 percent or more. Even a male in debt to the association might be held captive in his own house until he pays his debt. It is no wonder, then, that few resist an association's judgment for long. Although it is not clear why women's associations such as the Ijaw's are common in West Africa, one of the factors that may have been important is the women's participation in marketing and trade, which allows them to be financially independent of men. We shall see in the next section that women are increasingly forming voluntary self-help groups to improve themselves economically.

VOLUNTARY ASSOCIATIONS

Voluntary associations, such as the military associations of the Cheyenne of North America, may be found in some relatively simple societies. But voluntary associations tend to be more common in stratified and complex societies, presumably because stratified societies are composed of people with many different, and often competing, interests. We deal here with some examples of voluntary associations that are not familiar in North American experience.

Military Associations

Military associations in noncommercial societies may be compared to our own American Legion or Veterans of Foreign War posts. They all seem to exist to unite members

current research and issues

Why Do Street Gangs Develop, and Why Are They Often Violent?

The street gangs of young people that we read and hear about so often are voluntary associations. They are a little like age-sets in that the members are all about the same age, but they are unlike age-sets in being voluntary and they do not "graduate" through life stages together. Nobody has to join, although there may be strong social pressure to join the neighborhood gang. Gangs have a clear set of values, goals, roles, group functions, symbols, and initiations. Street gangs are also often like military associations in their commitment to violence in the defense of gang interests.

Violent street gangs are found in many U.S. cities, particularly in poor neighborhoods. But poverty alone does not appear sufficient to explain the existence of gangs. For example, there is plenty of poverty in Mexico, but gangs did not develop there. In Mexico, there was a *palomilla* (age-cohort) tradition; age-mates hung out together and continued their friendship well into adulthood, but there were no gangs as we know them. Mexican American gangs did develop in the *barrios* of cities such as Los Angeles. When we realize that *most* youths in poor neighborhoods do not join gangs, it is clear that poor neighborhoods cannot explain gangs. It is estimated that only 3 percent to 10 percent of Mexican American young people join gangs.

But why do some young people join and not others? If we look at who joins a gang, it seems to be those children who are subject to the most domestic stress. The gang "joiners" are likely to come from poor families, have several siblings, and have no father in the household. They seem to have had difficulty in school and have gotten into trouble early. What about gangs appeals to them? Most adolescents in this country have a difficult time deciding who they are and what kind of person they want to be, but young people who join gangs seem to have more identity problems. One 18-year-old said he "joined the gang for my ego to go higher," reflecting a low self-esteem. Those who are raised in female-centered households seem to be looking for a way to show how "masculine" they are. They look up to the tough male street gang members and want to act like them. But getting into a gang requires initiation. Most gangs have their own stylized rituals; for example, Mexican American gangs physically beat the initiate, who must show bravery and courage. As happens in most initiation ceremonies, the gang initiate identifies even more strongly with the group afterward. So, belonging to a gang may make some youths feel as if they belong to something important. This is a kind of psychological adjustment, but is it adaptive? Does being in a gang help such youths survive in a neighborhood where young men are often killed? Or are gang members *less* likely to survive? We really don't know the answers to those questions.

Why did gangs develop in the United States and not in Mexico? Were there some things different about life for Mexican Americans in the cities of the United States? Life in the United States was more difficult in several respects. First, many Mexican immigrants had to settle for very low pay and housing in marginal areas of the city. Second, they were subject to a lot of social and job discrimination. Third, they were immersed in a new culture that differed in many ways from their own. The young people who were least able to cope with these stresses were probably most likely to join gangs. But what explains the culture of violence of these gangs? Some scholars have suggested that the need to show exaggerated "masculine" behavior is a response to the absence of male models in the household. The association of many young men who have this same need may explain the violence of gangs. If aggressiveness is part of the male role (e.g., until recently only males were allowed to engage in military combat), then a young man who wants to exhibit his masculinity may be extremely aggressive.

We need much more research to uncover why gangs develop more often in some societies than in others and why they often are violent. Are there places where aggressiveness is not so much part of the male role, and are they therefore less likely to have violent gangs?

Sources: Vigil 1988, 2009; C. R. Ember and Ember 1994.

through their common experiences as warriors, to glorify the activities of war, and to perform certain services for the community. Membership in such associations is usually voluntary and based on the achieved criterion of participation in war. Among the North American Plains Indians, military societies were common. The Cheyenne, for example, had military associations that were not ranked by age but were open to any boy or man ready to go to war.[14]

In the beginning of the 19th century, the Cheyenne had five military associations: the Fox, Dog, Shield, Elk (or Hoof Rattle), and Bowstring (or Contrary). The last-named association was annihilated by the Pawnee in the middle of the 19th century. Later, two new associations were established, the Wolf and Northern Crazy Dogs. Although the various associations may have had different costumes, songs, and dances, they were alike in their internal organization, each being headed by four leaders who were among the most important war chiefs.

When various Plains groups were confined to reservations, the military associations lost many of their old functions, but they did not entirely disappear. For example, among the Lakota, warrior societies continue to be an important part of social life because many men and women have engaged in military activity on behalf of the United States in

World Wars I and II, in Korea and Vietnam, and in the wars in the Persian Gulf. Returning soldiers continue to be welcomed with traditional songs of honor and victory dances.[15]

Regional Associations

Regional associations bring together migrants from a common geographic background. Thus, they are often found in urban centers, which traditionally have attracted settlers from rural areas. In the United States, for example, migrants from rural Appalachia have formed associations in Chicago and Detroit. Many of these organizations have become vocal political forces in municipal government. Regional associations often form even when migrants have come from a considerable distance. For example, in the Chinatowns of the United States and Canada, there are many associations based on district of origin in China as well as on surname. The regional and family organizations are in turn incorporated into more inclusive ethnic associations, as we shall see later in this chapter.[16]

William Mangin described the role of regional associations in helping rural migrants adapt to urban life in Lima, Peru.[17] During the 1950s, Mangin studied a group of migrants from the rural mountains, the *serranos* from Ancash. Typically these *serranos,* about 120,000 in number, lived in a slumlike urban settlement called a *barriada.* The *barriada* was not officially recognized by either the national government or the city authorities. Accordingly, it lacked all usual city services, such as water supply, garbage removal, and police protection. Its inhabitants had left their rural birthplaces for reasons typical of such population movements, wherever they occur. These reasons were social and economic; most were related to population and land pressure, but the higher expectations associated with the big city—better education, social mobility, wage labor—were also compelling considerations.

Typically, also, the *serranos* from Ancash formed a regional association. Club membership was open to both sexes. Men generally controlled the executive positions, and club leaders were often men who had achieved political power in their hometowns. Women, who had relatively less economic and social freedom, nevertheless played an important part in club activities.

The *serrano* regional association performed three main services for its members. First, it lobbied the central government on matters of community importance—for example, the supplying of sewers, clinics, and similar public services. A club member had to follow a piece of legislation through the channels of government to make certain it was not forgotten or abandoned. Second, the *serrano* association assisted in acculturating newly arrived *serranos* to the urban life in Lima. The most noticeable rural traits—coca chewing, hairstyle, and clothing peculiarities—were the first to disappear, with the men generally able to adapt faster than the women. The association also provided opportunities for fuller contact with the national culture. And finally, the group organized social activities such as fiestas, acted as the clearinghouse for information transmitted to and from the home area, and supplied a range of other services to help migrants adapt to their new environment while retaining ties to their birthplace.

The functions of regional associations may change over time as social conditions change. For example, during the plantation period in Hawaii, many Filipino migrants joined hometown associations that served as mutual aid societies. As more Filipinos went to Hawaii, however, more people had kin to whom they could turn. The hometown associations continue to have some economic functions, such as assistance in times of emergency, serious illness, or death, and some scholarship aid, but meetings are infrequent and most members do not attend. Those members who are active seem to want the recognition and prestige that can be attained through leadership positions in the hometown association, which is much more than they can achieve in the wider Hawaiian arena.[18]

Although regional clubs may help to integrate their members into a more complex urban or changing environment, the presence of many such groups may increase divisiveness and rivalry among groups. In some areas, the smaller groups have banded together and become quite powerful. For example, within each Chinatown of a major U.S. or Canadian city, the various regional and family associations formed a larger Chinese Benevolent Association.[19] Thus, by banding together, the regional and family associations formed ethnic associations (see the box on Chinatowns).

Ethnic Associations

Various types of ethnic associations or interest groups are found in cities all over the world. Membership in these associations is based largely on ethnicity. Ethnic associations are particularly widespread in urban centers of West Africa. There, accelerated cultural change, reflected in altered economic arrangements, in technological advances, and in new urban living conditions, has weakened kinship relations and other traditional sources of support and solidarity.[20] Sometimes it is difficult to say whether a particular association is ethnic or regional in origin; it may be both.

Tribal unions are frequently found in Nigeria and Ghana. These are typical of most such associations in that they are extraterritorial—that is, they recruit members

An ethnic association (Hop Sing Tong) in San Francisco was established in 1870.

migrants and immigrants

Ethnic Associations in "Chinatowns"

When immigrants come to a new country, they often first live in urban neighborhoods that mostly contain people like themselves, people from the same regions and even from the same towns and villages. These neighborhoods are called "Chinatowns," "Korea Towns," and the like. These ethnic neighborhoods often have associations, nonkin and nonterritorial groups that protect their members in a variety of ways, which is probably why people wanted to live in the neighborhood in the first place. R. H. Thompson pointed out that, according to the constitution of the Chinese Benevolent Association in Victoria, British Columbia (a ferry ride from Vancouver), that association was established "to undertake social welfare, to settle disputes, to aid the poor and the sick, to eliminate evils within the community, and to defend the community against external threat."

Many Chinatowns grew up in the United States and Canada since the middle of the 19th century. After perhaps working first on the railroads, for which they were recruited to come to North America, the Chinese immigrants would settle in San Francisco or Vancouver. Often they joined an association of people with the same surname. This set of people considered themselves vaguely related (after all, they did have the same surname), but they usually couldn't trace how or even if they were related. Or the neighborhood contained people from the same district in China, with the same dialect. Some people migrated eastward, to the urban centers of New York, Boston, Philadelphia, Montreal, and Toronto. Most if not all of the "Chinatowns" continue to exist, even if subsequent generations have moved away from them. Suburban Chinese Americans often come to Chinatown on the weekend to visit with relatives and to shop for traditional foods. They are not different from other immigrants in this respect; most immigrants retain their food preferences for generations.

The earliest Chinese immigrants established themselves in various kinds of small business—hand laundries, restaurants, groceries. Such businesses were cheap to start up, and workers who were family members did not have to be paid much to keep them. Hand laundries were the first to disappear as the immigrants and their descendants prospered, and as many people in the general population started to do their laundry in machines at home or in a nearby "laundromat." Now, instead of working in the old family businesses, the descendants of people who used to live in Chinatown often go to college and become doctors and other professionals. Their jobs could be anyplace. Upward mobility often means geographic mobility: people often have to chase the job rather than stay close to home, if they want to maximize their income. This is true for many immigrant groups, not just the people from "Chinatown." When people move away from the old neighborhood, the ethnic association loses its attraction and value. In a generation or two, it may be gone. Just as you may have less opportunity to see cousins and other relatives when you move away, you are also unlikely to participate in your ancestral ethnic association when your job requires you to live in a new place. Mobility has costs as well as benefits.

Sources: R. H. Thompson 1996; 2009; Brettell and Kemper 2002.

who have left their tribal locations; also, they have a formal constitution, and they have been formed to meet certain needs arising out of conditions of urban life. One such need is to keep members in touch with their traditional culture. The Ibo State Union, for example, in addition to providing mutual aid and financial support in case of unemployment, sickness, or death, performs the service of "fostering and keeping alive an interest in tribal song, history, language and moral beliefs and thus maintaining a person's attachment to his native town or village."[21] Some tribal unions collect money to improve conditions in their ancestral homes. Education, for example, is an area of particular concern. Others publish newsletters that report members' activities. Most unions have a young membership that exercises a powerful democratizing influence in tribal councils, and the organizations provide a springboard for those with national political aspirations.

West African occupational clubs also fall into the ethnic category. African versions of trade unions are organized along tribal as well as craft lines, and their principal concern is the status and remuneration of their members as workers. The Motor Drivers' Union of Keta, in Ghana, was formed to fund insurance and legal costs, to contribute to

The Kafaina women's savings and loan associations in New Guinea often encourage relatives to start "daughter" organizations. At a ceremony for the new organization, a "daughter" doll is displayed.

medical care in case of accident or illness, and to help pay for funeral expenses.

Friendly societies differ from tribal unions in that their objectives are confined for the most part to mutual aid. Such a club was formed by the wives of Kru migrants in Freetown, Sierra Leone. Kru men normally go to sea, still a hazardous occupation. The club is classified into three grades. An admission fee permits entry into the lowest grade. Elevation to higher grades depends on further donations. At the death of a member or her husband, the family receives a lump sum commensurate with her status in the club.[22]

Rotating Credit Associations

A common type of mutual aid society is the *rotating credit association*. The basic principle is that each member of the group agrees to make a regular contribution, in money or in kind, to a fund, which is then handed over to each member in rotation.[23] The regular contributions promote savings by each member, but the lump sum distribution enables the recipient to do something significant with the money. These associations are found in many areas of East, South, and Southeast Asia, Africa (particularly West Africa), and the West Indies.[24] They usually include a small number of people, perhaps between 10 or 30, so that rotations do not take that long. The associations are usually informal and may last only as long as one rotation.

How do these systems work? What prevents someone from quitting after getting a lump sum? Ethnographic evidence indicates that defaulting on regular contributions is so rare that participants consider it unthinkable. Once a person joins a rotating credit association, there is strong social pressure to continue paying regularly. A person who joins does not have to fill out paperwork, as in a bank. All that is needed is a reputation for trustworthiness. There is often a social component to the association. Some have regular meetings with socializing and entertainment.[25] A rotating credit association may have one of three types of distribution. In some, a leader may decide the order of rotation, usually making the judgment on perceived need. In others, distribution is based on a random drawing or the roll of dice. The third method is based on who is willing to pay the highest interest.[26]

The principle of a rotating credit association often has roots in traditional sharing systems. For example, among the Kikuyu, related women would work together to weed or harvest each other's fields in turn. When a person had special expenses, such as a funeral, there would be a contribution party and everyone who came would make a contribution. Nici Nelson describes a very successful rotating credit association that developed in a squatter area of Nairobi. The founding woman organized a group of women of similar economic status who came from the Kiambu district of Kenya. Early in 1971, the group had about 20 members, but expanded to about 30. In a few years, the founder also started a land-buying cooperative. Although the rotating credit association remained embedded in the cooperative, eventually it lost its usefulness as members became wealthy enough to have bank accounts of their own. It disbanded in the 1990s. At one point, men tried to join, but the women refused to allow it. One woman said: "They will take over and not let us speak in our own cooperative."[27]

In Ghana, despite 30 years of national banking institutions, most saving methods are still informal. In 1991, an estimated 55 percent of the money in the country was saved informally. Rotating credit associations flourish. Women are more likely to join rotating credit associations than men, and the associations or clubs tend to be sex-segregated. The club names often reflect their emphasis on mutual aid. One club in the Accra Makola Market has a name that translates as "Our Well-Being Depends on Others."[28] Most of the savings are used to provide capital for trading activities.

In societies that depend on sharing, saving money is difficult. Others may ask you for money, and there may be an obligation to give it to them. However, if there is a rotating credit association, you can say that you are obliged to save for your contribution and people will understand. Rotating credit associations also appear to work well when people find it hard to delay gratification. The social pressure of the group appears sufficient to push people to save enough for their regular contribution and the windfall you get when your turn comes is gratifying.[29]

When people move far outside their homelands, they may make even more use of such associations. For example, rotating credit associations in Korea go back to 1633. In the Los Angeles area, Koreans are even more likely to use rotating credit associations, mostly to accumulate sums for business.[30]

Multiethnic Associations

Although many voluntary associations draw on people from the same regional or ethnic background, voluntary groups in the modern world increasingly draw members from many different backgrounds. For example, the Kafaina, or Wok Meri ("women's work"), associations in Papua New Guinea are savings and loan associations that link thousands of women from different tribal areas.[31] Originally, smaller groups started as savings associations in particular localities, but links between groups developed as women who married out of a village encouraged a relative back home or in another village to start a "daughter" group. "Mother-daughter" visits between groups can last for three days, as one group hosts another and the groups exchange money. All money received from another group is placed in a net bag that is hidden and cannot be touched, so the savings grow over time. When a group accumulates a certain amount, a building the size of a men's house is built for the association and a very large ceremony is held.

Does the development of these women's associations translate into new power for women in their traditionally male-dominated societies? That has yet to happen (see the box "Do Separate Women's Associations Increase Women's Status and Power?"). Apparently frustrated by their exclusion from local politics, the women are increasingly participating in the Kafaina movement. They may have intergroup exchanges and they may now engage in public speaking, but so far their arena is still separate from the men's arena.

Just as the Kafaina women's associations seem to be a response to perceived deprivation, the formation of associations with multiethnic or regional membership is not

unusual where colonialism or other political domination is recognized as a common problem. For example, in Alaska in the 1960s, Native Americans felt threatened by proposals for economic development that they thought would threaten their subsistence resources. Many regional and ethnic associations formed during this crisis, but perhaps more significant from the point of view of achieving substantial compensation and titles to land was the formation of a pan-Alaska association called the Alaska Federation of Natives. What made the amalgamation possible? Like the leaders of multiethnic movements in many places, the leaders at the highest levels seem to have had a lot of things in common. They were educated, urban dwellers who worked at professional occupations. Perhaps most important, many of them had attended the same schools.[32]

Multiethnic and multiregional associations have often been involved in independence movements all over the world. Often, revolutionary political parties develop out of such associations and lead the efforts to gain independence. Why independence movements develop in some places but not in others is not yet understood.

Other Interest Groups

Societies such as the United States consist of people from many different ethnic backgrounds. Often there are voluntary ethnic and regional associations. But the majority of the voluntary associations in our own and other complex societies have members who belong because of common, achieved interests. These common interests include occupation (so we have trade unions and professional associations), political affiliation (as in national political parties and political action groups), recreation (sports and game clubs, fan clubs, music and theater groups), charities, and social clubs. The larger and more diversified the society, the more different kinds of associations there are. They bring together people with common interests, aspirations, or qualifications, and they provide opportunities to work for social causes, for self-improvement, or to satisfy a need for new and stimulating experiences. We join clubs and other interest groups because we want to achieve particular goals. Not the least of such goals is identification with a "corporate" group and, through it, the acquisition of status and influence.

Joining clubs is much more important in some societies than in others. Norway is an example of a society with a rich organizational life. Even in areas with small communities, there are many different clubs. For example, Douglas Caulkins found that in the municipality of Volda, a town of about 7,000, there were 197 organizations. People were expected to be active in at least a couple of organizations, and these groups met regularly. In fact, there were so many meetings that organizations were expected to coordinate their calendars so that the meetings would not interfere with one another.[33] Why some societies, like Norway, have so much involvement with voluntary associations is not well understood. Nor do we understand what the consequences of such involvement may be. Norway happens to have a particularly low crime rate and it scores high on other indicators of social and economic health.[34] Does the complexity of its organizational life and its many

overlapping involvements play a role in its social health? We don't know, because cross-cultural studies to test that possibility have not been done.

EXPLAINING VARIATION IN ASSOCIATIONS

Anthropologists are not content to provide descriptions of the structure and operation of human associations. They also seek to understand why different types of associations develop. For example, what may account for the development of age-set systems? S. N. Eisenstadt's comparative study of African age-sets led him to the hypothesis that, when kinship groups fail to carry out functions important to the integration of society—such as political, educational, and economic functions—age-set systems arise to fill the void. Age-set systems may provide a workable solution to a society's need for functional divisions among its members, because age is a criterion that can be applied to all members of society in the allocation of roles.[35] But it is not at all clear why age-set systems arise to fill the void left by lack of kinship organization. Many societies have kin structures that are limited in scope, yet the majority of them have not adopted an age-set system.

B. Bernardi, in his critical evaluation of Nilo-Hamitic age-set systems, also suggested that age-set systems arise to make up for a deficiency in social organization.[36] But, in contrast with Eisenstadt, Bernardi specifically suggested why more social organization is necessary and what particular deficiencies in the previous form of organization should favor development of age-sets. He hypothesized that age-set systems arise in societies that have a history of territorial rivalry, lack central authority, and have only dispersed kin groups. When all three factors are present, he argued, the need for a mechanism of territorial integration is supplied by an age-set system.

One cross-cultural study suggests that territorial rivalry, as indicated by warfare, may favor the development of age-set systems, but this study found no evidence to support Bernardi's hypothesis that age-sets develop in societies that lack central authority and have only dispersed kin groups.[37] So it does not seem that age-set societies are deficient in political or kinship organization. An alternative explanation, which is consistent with the cross-cultural evidence, is that age-set systems arise in societies that have both frequent warfare and local groups that change in size and composition throughout the year. In such situations, men may not always be able to rely on their kinsmen for cooperation in warfare because the kinsmen are not always nearby. Age-sets, however, can provide allies *wherever* one happens to be.[38] This interpretation suggests that age-set systems arise *in addition to,* rather than as alternatives to, kin-based and politically based forms of integration.[39]

As for voluntary associations whose membership is variably ascribed—that is, determined at birth but not found in all people of a given age-sex category—it is difficult to say exactly what causes them to arise. As already noted, there are suggestions that voluntary associations of all types become more numerous, and more important, as the society harboring them advances in technology, complexity, and scale. No definitive evidence is yet available to support this explanation, but the following trends seem to be sufficiently established to merit consideration.

First, there is urbanization. Developing societies are becoming urban, and as their cities grow, so does the number of people separated from their traditional kinship ties and local customs. It is not surprising, then, that the early voluntary associations should be mutual aid societies, established first to take over kin obligations in case of death and later broadening their benefits in other directions. In this respect, the recent associations of the developing African societies closely resemble the early English laboring-class associations. Those clubs also served to maintain the city migrants' contacts with former traditions and culture. The regional associations in Latin America resemble the regional associations of European immigrants in the United States. Such associations also seem to arise in response to the migrants' or immigrants' needs in the new home.

Second, there is an economic factor. Migrants and immigrants try to adapt to new economic conditions, and group interests in the new situations have to be organized, promoted, and protected.

Why, then, do variably ascribed associations tend to be replaced by clubs of the achieved category in highly industrialized societies? Perhaps the strong focus on specialization in industrialized societies is reflected in the formation of specialized groups. Possibly the emphasis on achievement in industrialized societies is another contributing factor. Perhaps, too, the trend toward uniformity, encouraged by mass marketing and the mass media, is progressively weakening the importance of regional and ethnic distinctions. The result seems to be that the more broadly based organizations are being replaced by more narrowly based associations that are more responsive to particular needs not being met by the institutions of mass society.

SUMMARY ●○○

1. Associations or interest groups have the following characteristics in common: (a) some kind of formal, institutional structure exists; (b) some people are excluded from membership; (c) membership is based on commonly shared interests or purposes; and (d) there is a clearly discernible sense of mutual pride and belonging. Membership varies according to whether or not it is voluntary and whether the qualities of members are universally ascribed, variably ascribed, or achieved.

2. Age-sets are nonvoluntary associations whose members belong because of universally ascribed characteristics—that is, groups of people of similar age and sex who move through life's stages together. Entry into the system is usually by an initiation ceremony. Transitions to new stages are usually marked by succession rituals. Unisex associations restrict membership to one sex. In noncommercial societies, membership in such associations (usually male) is generally nonvoluntary.

3. Regional and ethnic organizations are voluntary associations whose members belong because of variably ascribed characteristics. Both usually occur in societies where technological advance is accelerating, bringing with it economic and social complexity. Despite a variety of types, regional and ethnic associations have in common an emphasis on (a) helping members adapt to new conditions; (b) keeping members in touch with home area traditions; and (c) promoting improved living conditions for members who have recently migrated to urban areas.

4. Associations whose members belong because of variably ascribed characteristics tend to be replaced in highly industrialized societies by associations whose membership is based on achieved qualities.

GLOSSARY TERMS ○●○

achieved qualities **232**	unisex association **236**
age-grade **235**	universally ascribed
age-set **235**	qualities **232**
ascribed qualities **232**	variably ascribed
associations **232**	qualities **234**

CRITICAL QUESTIONS ○○●

1. How could young people who might join gangs be encouraged not to?

2. What associations do you belong to, and why?

3. Many formerly unisex associations have opened their membership to the opposite sex. What might be the results of this change?

PEARSON
myanthrolab

Read Richard H. Thompson's "Chinatowns: Immigrant Communities in Transition" on MyAnthroLab. Answer the following questions.

1. Describe the role that associations played in the earliest Chinatowns.

2. According to Thompson, the traditional associations were more important to certain classes of Chinese Americans. Explain.

3. Describe some of the tensions between the generations.

chapter 14

Political Life: Social Order and Disorder

or people in the United States, the phrase *political life* has many connotations. It may call to mind the various branches of government: the executive branch, from the president on the national level to governors on the state level to mayors on the local level; legislative institutions, from Congress to state legislatures to city councils; and administrative bureaus, from federal government departments to local agencies.

Political life may also evoke thoughts of political parties, interest groups, lobbying, campaigning, and voting. In other words, when people living in the United States think of political life, they may think first of "politics," the activities (not always apparent) that influence who is elected or appointed to political office, what public policies are established, how they get established, and who benefits from those policies.

But in the United States and in many other countries, *political life* involves even more than government and politics. Political life also involves ways of preventing or resolving troubles and disputes both within and outside the society. Internally, a complex society such as ours may employ mediation or arbitration to resolve industrial disputes, a police force to prevent crimes or track down criminals, and courts and a penal system to deal with lawbreakers as well as with social conflict in general. Externally, such a society may establish embassies in other nations and develop and utilize its armed forces both to maintain security and to support domestic and foreign interests.

By means of all these informal and formal political mechanisms, complex societies establish social order and minimize, or at least deal with, social disorder.

Formal governments have become more widespread around the world over the last 100 years, as powerful colonizing countries have imposed political systems upon others or as people less formally organized realized that they needed governmental mechanisms to deal with the larger world. But many societies known to anthropology did not have political officials, political parties, courts, or armies. Indeed, the band or village was the largest autonomous political unit in 50 percent of the societies in the ethnographic record, as of the times they were first described. And those units were only informally organized; that is, they did not have individuals or agencies formally authorized to make and implement policy or resolve disputes. Does this mean they did not have political life? If we mean political life as we know it in our own society, then the answer has to be that they did not. But if we look beyond our formal institutions and mechanisms—if we ask what functions these institutions and mechanisms perform—we find that all societies have had political activities and beliefs to create and maintain social order and cope with social disorder.

Many of the kinds of groups we discussed in the three previous chapters, on families, descent groups, and associations, have political functions. But

when anthropologists talk about *political organization* or *political life*, they are particularly focusing on activities and beliefs pertaining to *territorial groups.* Territorial groups, on whose behalf political activities may be organized, range from small communities, such as bands and villages, to large communities, such as towns and cities, to multilocal groups, such as districts or regions, entire nations, or even groups of nations.

As we shall see, the different types of political organization, as well as how people participate in politics and how they cope with conflict, are often strongly linked to variation in food-getting, economy, and social stratification.

● ○ ●

VARIATION IN TYPES OF POLITICAL ORGANIZATION

Societies in the ethnographic record vary in *level of political integration*—that is, the largest territorial group on whose behalf political activities are organized—and in the degree to which political authority is centralized or concentrated in the integrated group. When we describe the political integration of particular societies, we focus on their traditional political systems. In many societies known to anthropology, the small community (band or village) was traditionally the largest territorial group on whose behalf political activities were organized. The authority structure in such societies did not involve any centralization; there was no political authority whose jurisdiction included more than one community. In other societies, political activities were traditionally organized sometimes on behalf of a multilocal group, but there was no permanent authority at the top. And in still other societies, political activities were often traditionally organized on behalf of multilocal territorial groups, and there was a centralized or supreme political authority at the top. In the modern world, however, every society has been incorporated into some larger, centralized political system.

Elman Service suggested that most societies can be classified into four principal types of political organization: bands, tribes, chiefdoms, and states.[1] Although Service's classification does not fit all societies, it is a useful way to show how societies vary in trying to create and maintain social order. We often use the present tense in our discussion, because that is the convention in ethnographic writing, but readers should remember that most societies that used to be organized at the band, tribe, or chiefdom level are now incorporated into larger political entities. With a handful of exceptions, there are no politically autonomous bands or tribes or chiefdoms in the world anymore.

Band Organization

Some societies were composed of fairly small and usually nomadic groups of people. Each of these groups is conventionally called a **band** and is politically autonomous. That is, in **band organization,** the local group or community is the largest group that acts as a political unit. Because most recent foragers had band organization, some anthropologists contend that this type of political organization characterized nearly all societies before the development of agriculture, or until about 10,000 years ago. But we have to remember that almost all of the described food-collecting societies are or were located in marginal environments; and almost all were affected by more dominant societies nearby.[2] So it is possible that what we call "band organization" may not have been typical of foragers in the distant or prehistoric past.

Bands are typically small, with less than 100 people usually, often considerably less. Each small band occupies a large territory, so population density is low. Band size often varies by season, with the band breaking up or recombining according to the food resources available at a given time and place. Inuit bands, for example, are smaller in the winter, when food is hard to find, and larger in the summer, when there is sufficient food to feed a larger group.

Political decision making within the band is generally informal. The "modest informal authority"[3] that does exist can be seen in the way decisions affecting the group are made. Because the formal, permanent office of leader typically does not exist, decisions such as when camp has to be moved or how a hunt is to be arranged are either agreed upon by the community as a whole or made by the best qualified member. Leadership, when an individual exercises it, is not the consequence of bossing or throwing one's weight about. Each band may have its informal **headman,** or its most proficient hunter, or a person most accomplished in rituals. There may be one person with all these qualities, or several people, but such a person or people will have gained status through the community's recognition of skill, good sense, and humility. Leadership, in other words, stems not from power but from influence, not from office but from admired personal qualities.

In Inuit bands, each settlement may have its headman, who acquires his influence because the other members of the community recognize his good judgment and superior skills. The headman's advice concerning the movement of the band and other community matters is generally heeded, but he possesses no permanent authority and has no power to impose sanctions of any kind. Inuit leaders are male, but men often consult their wives in private, and women who hunt seem to have more influence than those who do not.[4] In any case, leadership exists only in a very restricted sense, as among the Iglulik Inuit, for example:

> Within each settlement . . . there is as a rule an older man who enjoys the respect of the others and who decides when a move is to be made to another

TABLE 14–1 Suggested Trends in Political Organization and Other Social Characteristics

Type of Organization	Highest Level of Political Integration	Specialization of Political Officials	Predominant Mode of Subsistence	Community Size and Population Density	Social Differentiation	Major Form of Distribution
Band	Local group or band	Little or none; informal leadership	Foraging or food collecting	Very small communities; very low density	Egalitarian	Mostly reciprocity
Tribe	Sometimes multilocal group	Little or none; informal leadership	Extensive (shifting) agriculture and/or herding	Small communities; low density	Egalitarian	Mostly reciprocity
Chiefdom	Multilocal group	Some	Extensive or intensive agriculture and/or herding	Large communities; medium density	Rank	Reciprocity and redistribution
State	Multilocal group; often entire language group	Much	Intensive agriculture and herding	Cities and towns; high density	Class and caste	Mostly market exchange

hunting center, when a hunt is to be started, how the spoils are to be divided, when the dogs are to be fed. . . . He is called *isumaitoq*, "he who thinks." It is not always the oldest man, but as a rule an elderly man who is a clever hunter or, as head of a large family, exercises great authority. He cannot be called a chief; there is no obligation to follow his counsel; but they do so in most cases, partly because they rely on his experience, partly because it pays to be on good terms with this man.[5]

A summary of the general features of band organization can be found in Table 14–1. Note, however, that there are exceptions to these generalizations. For example, not all known foragers are organized at the band level or have all the features of a band type of society. Classic exceptions are the Native American societies of the Northwest Pacific coast, who had enormous resources of salmon and other fish, relatively large and permanent villages, and political organization beyond the level of the typical band societies in the ethnographic record.

Tribal Organization

When local communities mostly act autonomously but there are kinship groups (such as clans or lineages) or associations (such as age-sets) that can potentially integrate several local groups into a larger unit (**tribe**), we say that the society has **tribal organization.** Unfortunately, the term *tribe* is sometimes used to refer to an entire society; that is, an entire language group may be called a tribe. But a tribal type of political system does not usually permit the entire society to act as a unit; all the communities in a tribal society may be linked only occasionally for some political (usually military) purpose. Thus, what distinguishes tribal from band political organization is the presence in the former of

some multilocal, but not usually societywide, integration. The multilocal integration, however, is *not permanent,* and it is *informal* in the sense that political officials do not head it. Frequently, the integration is called into play only when an outside threat arises; when the threat disappears, the local groups revert to self-sufficiency.[6] Tribal organization may seem fragile—and, of course, it usually is—but the fact that there are social ways to integrate local groups into larger political entities means that societies with tribal organization are militarily a good deal more formidable than societies with band organization.

In tribal societies, as among the Kayapo of Brazil, leadership tends not to be hereditary, but based on leadership qualities. There are no permanent chiefs of more than one community. Shown here is a Kayapo leader smoking a pipe.

Societies with tribal political organization are similar to band societies in their tendency to be egalitarian (see Table 14–1). At the local level, informal leadership is also characteristic. In those tribal societies where kinship provides the basic framework of social organization, the elders of the local kin groups tend to have considerable influence; where age-sets are important, a particular age-set is looked to for leadership. But, in contrast to band societies, societies with tribal organization generally are food producers. And because cultivation and animal husbandry are generally more productive than hunting and gathering, the population density of tribal societies is generally higher, local groups are larger, and the way of life is more sedentary than in hunter-gatherer bands.

Kinship Bonds Frequently communities are linked to each other by virtue of belonging to the same kin group, usually a unilineal group such as a lineage or clan. A **segmentary lineage system** is one type of tribal integration based on kinship. A society with such a system is composed of segments, or parts, each similar to the others in structure and function. Every local segment belongs to a hierarchy of lineages stretching farther and farther back genealogically. The hierarchy of lineages, then, unites the segments into larger and larger genealogical groups. The closer two groups are genealogically, the greater their general closeness. In the event of a dispute between members of different segments, people related more closely to one contestant than to another take the side of their nearest kinsman.

The Tiv of northern Nigeria offer a classic example of a segmentary lineage system, one that happens to link all the Tiv into a single genealogical structure or tribe. The Tiv are a large society, numbering more than 800,000. Figure 14–1 is a representation of the Tiv lineage structure as described by Paul Bohannan. In the figure, there are four levels of lineages. Each of the smallest lineages, symbolized by *a* through *h*, is in turn embedded in more inclusive lineages. So minimal lineages *a* and *b* are together in lineage *1*. Lineages *1* and *2* are embedded in lineage *A*. Territorial organization follows lineage hierarchy. As shown in the bottom of the figure, the most closely related lineages have territories near each other. Minimal lineages *a* and *b* live next to each other; their combined territory is the territory of their higher-order lineage, *1*. Lineage *A* in turn has a territory that is differentiated from lineage *B*. All of Tivland is said to descend from one ancestor, represented by *I*.[7]

Tiv lineage organization is the foundation of Tiv political organization. A look at Figure 14–1 helps to explain how. A dispute between lineages (and territories) *a* and *b* remains minor, because no more than "brother" segments are involved. But a dispute between *a* and *c* involves lineages *1* and *2* as well, with the requirement that *b* assist *a* and *d* support *c*. This process of mutual support, called **complementary opposition,** means that segments will unite only in a confrontation with some other group. Groups that will fight with each other in a minor dispute might coalesce at some later time against a larger group.

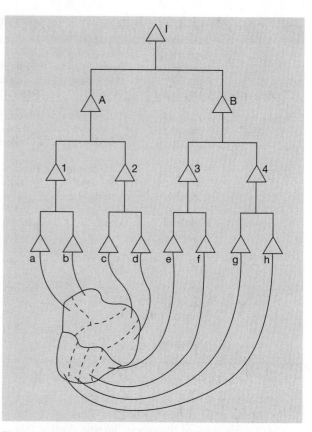

Figure 14–1 Tiv Lineage Segments and Their Territories

Source: Adapted from P. Bohannan 1954.

The segmentary lineage system was presumably very effective in allowing the Tiv to intrude into new territory and take land from other tribal societies with smaller descent groups. Individual Tiv lineage segments could call on support from related lineages when faced with border troubles. Conflicts within the society—that is, between segments—especially in border areas, were often turned outward, "releasing internal pressure in an explosive blast against other peoples."[8]

Segmentary lineage systems may have military advantages even when they do not unite the entire society. A classic example is the Nuer of the Upper Nile region, who had tribal, but not societywide, organization because of their segmentary lineages. In the early 1800s, the Nuer had a territory of about 8,700 square miles, and the neighboring Dinka had ten times that much. But by 1890, the Nuer had cut a 100-mile swath through Dinka territory, increasing Nuer territory to 35,000 square miles. Even though the Nuer and Dinka were culturally very similar, the segmentary lineage organization of the Nuer seems to have given them a significant military advantage in their incursions into Dinka territory.[9]

A segmentary lineage system may generate a formidable military force, but the combinations of manpower it produces are temporary, forming and dissolving as the occasion demands.[10] Tribal political organization does not make for a political system that more or less permanently integrates a number of communities.

Age-Set Systems In the previous chapter, we described age-set systems in general. Here we discuss how age-sets can function as the basis of a tribal type of political organization, as among the Karimojong of northeastern Uganda.[11]

The Karimojong age-set system has an important bearing on day-to-day tribal life. As herders, Karimojong adults are often separated from their usual settlements. Herders will meet, mingle for a while, then go their separate ways, but each may call upon other members of his age-set wherever he goes. The age-set system is important among the Karimojong because it immediately allocates to each individual a place in the system and thereby establishes for him an appropriate pattern of response. A quarrel in camp will be settled by the representatives of the senior age-set who are present, regardless of which section of the tribe they may belong to.

Among the Karimojong, political leaders are not elected from among the elders of a particular age-set, nor are they appointed; they acquire their positions informally. Usually a man's background, and the ability he has demonstrated in public debates over a period of time, will result in his being considered by the men of his neighborhood to be their spokesman. His function is to announce what course of action seems required in a particular situation, to initiate that action, and then to coordinate it after it has begun.

Most political leaders exercise their authority within the local sphere because the pastoral nature of the Karimojong economy, with its dispersed groups and movement from one feeding ground to another, offers no alternative. From time to time, an elder may acquire the status of a prophet and be awarded respect and obedience on a tribal scale. He will be called upon to lead sacrifices (to avert misfortune), to undertake rainmaking (to bring prosperity), and so on. Yet even a prophet's prestige and authority do not warrant him a position of overlord or chief.[12]

Chiefdom Organization

Whereas a tribe has some informal mechanism that can integrate more than one community, a **chiefdom** has some *formal* structure that integrates more than one community into a political unit. The formal structure could consist of a council with or without a chief, but most commonly there is a person—the **chief**—who has higher rank or authority than others. Most societies at the chiefdom level of organization contain more than one multicommunity political unit or chiefdom, each headed by a district chief or a council. There may also be more than one level of chief beyond the community, such as district chiefs and higher-level chiefs. Compared with tribal societies, societies with chiefdoms are more densely populated and their communities more permanent, partly as a consequence of their generally greater economic productivity (see Table 14–1).

The position of chief, which is sometimes hereditary and generally permanent, bestows high status on its holder. Most chiefdoms have social ranking and accord the chief and his family greater access to prestige. The chief may redistribute goods, plan and direct the use of public labor, supervise religious ceremonies, and direct military activities on behalf of the chiefdom. In South Pacific chiefdoms, the chiefs carried out most of these duties. In Fijian chiefdoms, for example, the chief was responsible for the redistribution of goods and the coordination of labor:

> [The chief] could summon the community's labor on his own behalf, or on behalf of someone else who requested it, or for general purposes. . . . Besides his right to summon labor he accumulated the greater proportion of the first fruits of the yam crop . . . and he benefited from other forms of food presentation, or by the acquisition of special shares in ordinary village distribution. . . . Thus, the paramount [chief] would collect a significant part of the surplus production of the community and redistribute it in the general welfare.[13]

In contrast to leaders in tribal societies, who generally have to earn their privileges by their personal qualities, hereditary chiefs are said to have those qualities in their "blood." A high-ranking chief in Polynesia, a huge triangular area of islands in the South Pacific, inherited special religious power called *mana*. *Mana* sanctified his rule and protected him.[14] Chiefs in Polynesia had so much religious power that missionaries could convert people to Christianity only after their chiefs had been converted.[15]

Samoan chiefs gather at an open meeting house for a *saofa'i*, or entitlement ceremony, during which a new chief gains his position.

In most chiefdoms, the chiefs did not have the power to compel people to obey them; people would act in accordance with the chief's wishes because the chief was respected and often had religious authority. But in the most complex paramount chiefdoms, such as those of Hawaii and Tahiti, the chiefs seemed to have more compelling sanctions than the "power" of respect or *mana*. Substantial amounts of goods and services collected by the chiefs were used to support subordinates, including specialists such as high priests, political envoys, and warriors who could be sent to quell rebellious factions.[16] When redistributions do not go to everybody—when chiefs are allowed to keep items for their own purposes—and when a chief begins to use armed force, the political system is on the way to becoming what we call a state.

State Organization

A **state**, according to one more or less standard definition, is "an autonomous political unit, encompassing many communities within its territory and having a centralized government with the power to collect taxes, draft men for work or war, and decree and enforce laws."[17] States, then, have a complex, centralized political structure that includes a wide range of permanent institutions with legislative, executive, and judicial functions and a large bureaucracy. Central to this definition is the concept of legitimate force used to implement policies both internally and externally. In states, the government tries to maintain a monopoly on the use of physical force.[18] This monopoly can be seen in the development of formal and specialized instruments of social control: a police force, a militia, or a standing army.

Just as a particular society may contain more than one band, tribe, or chiefdom, so may it contain more than one state. The contiguously distributed population speaking a single language may or may not be politically unified in a single state. Ancient Greece was composed of many city-states; so, too, was Italy until the 1870s. German speakers are also not politically unified; Austria and Germany are separate states, and Germany itself was not politically unified until the 1870s. We say that a society has **state organization** when it is composed of one or more political units that are states.

A state may include more than one society. Multisociety states are often the result of conquest or colonial control when the dominant political authority, itself a state, imposes a centralized government over a territory with many different societies and cultures, as the British did in Nigeria and Kenya.

Colonialism is a common feature of state societies. But not all colonialisms are alike. Archaeology and history tell us about various kinds of colonialism. The expanding state society may send people to build a new imperial settlement in some other place to trade or protect trade routes, like the British, Spanish, and others did. Or the colonial power may displace and move parts of the original population, as the Inka empire did.[19] Most of the expanding state societies we know about are usually called

empires. They incorporated other societies and states. The extension of U.S. power in modern times, for example, by persuading other countries to let the U.S. build military bases, has led some commentators to refer to an American empire, even though the United States did not always establish colonies where they had economic and political control.[20]

Nearly all of the multisociety states that emerged after World War II were the results of successful independence movements against colonial powers.[21] Most have retained their political unity despite the fact that they still contain many different societies. For example, Nigeria remains unified despite a civil war; the eastern section called Biafra (mostly populated by people of Ibo culture) tried unsuccessfully 30 years ago to secede, and subsequently there has been serious conflict among some of the constituent societies.

Multisociety or multiethnic states may also form voluntarily, in reaction to external threat. Switzerland comprises cantons, each of which speaks mainly French, German, Italian, or Romansch; the various cantons confederated originally to shake off control by the Holy Roman Empire. But some states have lost their unity recently, including the former Union of Soviet Socialist Republics (USSR) and much of Yugoslavia.

In addition to their strictly political features, intensive agriculture generally supports state-organized societies. The high productivity of the agriculture allows for the emergence of cities, a high degree of economic and other kinds of specialization, and market or commercial exchange. In addition, state societies usually have class stratification (see Table 14–1). Cities have grown tremendously in the last 100 years, largely as a result of migration and immigration. (See the Migrants and Immigrants box on the growth of cities.)

When states come into existence, people's access to scarce resources is radically altered. So, too, is their ability not to listen to leaders: You usually cannot refuse to pay taxes or avoid labor or military conscription and go unpunished. Of course, the rulers of a state do not maintain the social order by force alone. The people must believe, at least to some extent, that those in power have a legitimate right to govern. If the people think otherwise, history suggests that those in power may eventually lose their ability to control. Witness the recent downfall of Communist parties throughout most of eastern Europe and the former Soviet Union.

So force and the threat of force are not enough to explain the legitimacy of power, and the inequities that occur commonly, in state societies. But then what does? There are various theories. The rulers of early states often claimed divine descent to buttress their legitimacy, but this claim is rare nowadays. Another theory is that, if parents teach their children to accept all authority, such lessons may generalize to the acceptance of political authority. Some analysts think that people accept state authority for no good reason; the rulers are just able to fool them. Finally, some theorists think that states must provide people with real or rational advantages; otherwise,

migrants and immigrants

The Growth of Cities

Humans are a social bunch. They generally live in groups or communities. These groups range in size from bands to villages to town and cities. Each may function as a political entity; headmen, mayors, councils, and other political "officials" and groups organize activities on their behalf. Nearly half of the world's human population now lives in cities, which are usually defined as communities where few are directly involved in food getting. An even larger proportion of humanity will be urban dwellers 30 years from now.

The explosive growth of cities over the past century or so is not due to more births than deaths in the cities. Rather, cities have grown mostly because of migration from rural areas of the country, and from rural areas in other countries. Recall the exodus of the Irish to Britain and the United States because of the "potato famine," the massive migrations from the villages of Germany, Italy, and Greece in the 19th and 20th centuries, and the huge migrations particularly in the last 50 years from rural Mexico and China. It is probably safe to say that many millions of people in many parts of the world would move to the United States, Canada, and Western Europe tomorrow, if they could. Poverty is one "push" factor. Flight from persecution is another. Many parts of the world are not safe, particularly for poor people. Or other places look more promising. Think of the state of California in the United States. The vast majority of its inhabitants were born elsewhere. True, in the modern world, it is possible for some people to go "home" for a visit, even halfway around the world. But,

for many migrants now and in the recent past, the move was one way. Because you may have run away from poverty, persecution, and war, you couldn't (or wouldn't) go home again.

An increasing number of anthropologists call themselves "urban anthropologists." They study why people move, and how they adjust to new places. They do so because so many people are moving now. There are villages in rural Spain and France that are mostly empty during the week. The owners live and work in Barcelona or Paris, and they hardly ever go "home." Indeed, their village houses may not even be available to them much, because they are usually rented to tourists—from across the Atlantic, no less.

Cities everywhere have problems, even in the most developed countries. Providing water, power, sanitation, and other services to perhaps millions of city dwellers is difficult and expensive. Yet in every country, people are leaving rural areas and going to cities for a variety of reasons. Some are political refugees, like the Hmong from Laos who now live in St. Paul, Minnesota. Then there are the people from Congo and Sudan, from Kosovo and Northern Ireland, who have fled civil wars. There are other reasons to leave too. Technological improvements may have reduced the need for rural labor, which happened in the U.S. South after the 1930s. Or the rural opportunities cannot support the increased number of mouths to be fed. Where do they go? Usually not to other rural areas but rather to cities, often in other countries, where jobs are available. In the more urban-

ized countries, the cities have acquired "suburbs," where many of the people in a metropolitan area may actually live. But hardly anyone is left on the farm—only just a few percent of the population in the more developed countries.

In the last half of the 20th century, with the building of suburbs, there seems to have been a turning away from cities in many countries. Cities lost population as people moved to the suburbs to have more living space, a garden, "better" schools for their children, or to escape from the threat of violence. But recently, the flow has started to reverse in North America and elsewhere. The suburbanites are coming back to the cities, perhaps because people are getting tired of commuting longer distances to jobs and recreation. This is particularly so with wealthier people whose children have grown up and moved away, and with more people living until older ages, many want to move closer to the places where they mostly spend their time. Despite the social inequality and violence, cities have always been the places to go for jobs and other activities. Concerts, theaters, restaurants, museums, amusement parks, hospitals, and professional sports stadiums have always been located in cities or nearby.

The "push" out of the rural areas and the "pull" of the cities are hard to resist, despite the enormous political problems of urban living. As the old song laments, "Howya goin' keep 'em down on the farm after they've seen Paree?"

Source: M. Ember and Ember 2002.

---

people would not think that the rulers deserve to exercise authority. Legitimacy is not an all-or-none phenomenon; it varies in degree.[22]

A state society can retain its legitimacy, or at least its power, for a long time. For example, the Roman Empire was a complex state society that dominated the Mediterranean and Near East for hundreds of years. It began as

a city-state that waged war to acquire additional territory. At its height, the Roman Empire embraced more than 55 million people;[23] the capital city of Rome had a population of well over a million.[24] The empire included parts of what are now Great Britain, France, Spain, Portugal, Germany, Rumania, Turkey, Greece, Armenia, Egypt, Israel, and Syria.

Popular will can change governments. Massive protest in the Ukraine led a newly elected president to resign.

Another example of a state society was the kingdom of Nupe in West Africa, now part of the nation-state of Nigeria. Nupe society was rigidly stratified. At the top of the social system was the king, or *etsu*. Beneath the king, members of the royal family formed the highest aristocratic class. Next in order were two other classes of nobility, the local chiefs and the military leaders. At the bottom were the commoners, who had neither prestige nor power and no share in political authority.

The Nupe king possessed ultimate authority in many judicial matters. Local village councils handled minor disputes and civil cases, but serious criminal cases were the prerogative of the king. Such cases, referred to as "crimes for the king," were brought before the royal court by the king's local representatives. The king and his counselors judged the cases and determined suitable punishments.

The most powerful influence of the state over the Nupe people was in the area of taxation. The king was given the power to impose taxes and collect them from every household. Payment was made either in money (cowrie shells originally and, later, British currency) or certain gifts, such as cloth, mats, and slaves. The king kept much of the revenue collected, and his local representatives and lords shared the remainder. In return for the taxes they paid, the people received security—protection against invasion and domestic disorder.[25]

Although all state societies employ coercion or the threat of it, some states are more autocratic than others. This is not just today, or in the recent past, but also in the distant past. The less autocratic states are characterized by more "collective action." They produce more public goods, such as transportation systems and redistribution systems, in times of need. The rulers do not aggrandize themselves as much or live that luxuriously. And, the rulers must rule within limits and must respond to grievances. They are accountable. The Lozi state of central southern Africa had more collective action than the Nupe state described. The Lozi built an extensive system of drainage canals that also facilitated transportation. In hungry times, royal herds and the "state" gardens were used to feed distressed villages. And rulers were not that much more elevated in standard of living. In contrast, the Nupe state financed very little in the way of public works, had little redistribution, and the rulers lived in elaborate palaces.[26] Collective action is a continuum; states at the higher end of that continuum have not been limited to a few world regions or particular time periods. Collection action theorists suggest that, when the state relies more heavily on resources from taxpayers, the rulers must give the public more in return or else face noncompliance and rebellion. Richard Blanton and Lane Fargher's comparative study of premodern states supports collection action theory.[27]

Factors Associated with Variation in Political Organization

The kinds of political organization we call band, tribal, chiefdom, and state are points on a continuum of levels of political integration or unification, from small-scale local autonomy to large-scale regional unification. There also is variation in political authority, from a few temporary and informal political leaders to large numbers of permanent, specialized political officials, from the absence of coercive political power to the monopoly of public force by a central authority. These aspects of variation in political organization are generally associated with shifts from foraging to more intensive food production, from small to large communities, from low to high population densities, from an emphasis on reciprocity to redistribution to market exchange, and from egalitarian to rank to fully stratified class societies.

The associations just outlined, which seem to be confirmed by the available cross-cultural evidence, are summarized in Table 14–1. With regard to the relation between level of subsistence technology and political complexity, one cross-cultural study employing a small random sample of societies found that the greater the importance of agriculture in a society, the larger the population that is politically unified and the greater the number and types of political officials.[28] A massive cross-cultural survey reported a similar trend: The more intensive the agriculture, the greater the likelihood of state organization; conversely, societies with no more than local political institutions are likely to depend on hunting, gathering, and fishing.[29]

With regard to community size, the first of these studies also suggested that the larger the leading community, the wider the range of political officials in the society.[30] Robert Textor presented a similar finding: Societies with state organization tend to have cities and towns, whereas those with only local political organization are more likely to have communities with an average population of fewer than 200 people.[31] Cross-cultural research also tends to confirm that societies with higher levels of political integration are more likely to exhibit social differentiation, especially in the form of class distinctions.[32]

Does this evidence provide us with an explanation for why political organization varies? Clearly, the data indicate that several factors are associated with political development, but exactly why changes in organization occur is not yet understood. Although economic development may be a necessary condition for political development,[33] that relation does not fully explain why political organization should become more complex just because the economy can support it. Some theorists have suggested that competition between groups may be a more important reason for political consolidation. For example, Elman Service suggested competition as a reason why a society might change from a band level of political organization to a tribal level. Band societies are generally hunter-gatherers. With a changeover to agriculture, population density and competition between groups may increase. Service believed that such competition would foster the development of some informal organization beyond the community—namely, tribal organization—for offense and defense.[34] Indeed, as we saw in the chapters on marital residence and kinship, and associations, both unilineal kinship groups and age-set systems seem to be associated with warfare.

Among agriculturalists, defensive needs might also be the main reason for switching from informal multivillage political organization to more formal chiefdom organization. Formally organized districts are probably more likely to defeat autonomous villages or even segmentary lineage systems.[35] In addition, there may be economic reasons for political development. With regard to chiefdoms, Service suggested that chiefdoms will emerge when redistribution between communities becomes important or when large-scale coordinated work groups are required. The more important these activities are, the more important—and hence more "chiefly"—the organizer and his family presumably become.[36] But redistribution is far from a universal activity of chiefs.[37]

Theory and research on the anthropology of political development have focused mostly on the high end of the scale of political complexity, and particularly on the origins of the first state societies. Those earliest states apparently rose independently of one another, after about 3500 B.C., in what are now southern Iraq, Egypt, northwestern India, northern China, and central Mexico. Several theories have been proposed to explain the rise of the earliest states, but no one theory seems to fit all the known archaeological sequences culminating in early state formation. The reason may be that different conditions in different places favored the emergence of centralized government. The state, by definition, implies the power to organize large populations for collective purposes. In some areas, the impetus may have been the need to organize necessary local or long-distance trade or both. In other areas, the state may have emerged as a way to control defeated populations that could not flee. In still other instances, other factors or a combination of factors may have fostered the development of states. It is still not clear what the specific conditions were that led to the emergence of the state in each of the early centers.[38]

THE SPREAD OF STATE SOCIETIES

The state level of political development has come to dominate the world. Societies with states have larger communities and higher population densities than do band, tribal, and chiefdom societies. They also have armies that are ready to fight at almost any time. State systems that have waged war against chiefdoms and tribes have almost always won, and the result has usually been the political incorporation of the losers. For example, the British and, later, the U.S. colonization of much of North America led to the defeat and incorporation of many Native American societies.

A meeting of European Union heads of state and government in Rome. The EU is an organization encompassing many nation-states.

The defeat and incorporation of the Native Americans was at least partly due to the catastrophic depopulations they suffered because of epidemic diseases, such as smallpox and measles, that European colonists introduced. Catastrophic depopulation was commonly the outcome of the first contacts between European Americans and the natives of North and South America, as well as the natives of the far islands in the Pacific. People in the New World and the Pacific had not been exposed, and therefore were not resistant to the diseases the European Americans carried with them when they began to colonize the world. Before the expansion of Europeans, the people of the New World and the Pacific had been separated for a long time from the people and diseases on the geographically continuous landmass we separate into Europe, Africa, and Asia. Smallpox, measles, and the other former scourges of Europe had largely become childhood diseases that most individuals of European ancestry survived.[39]

Whether by depopulation, conquest, or intimidation, the number of independent political units in the world has decreased strikingly in the last 3,000 years, and especially in the last 200 years. Robert Carneiro estimated that in 1000 B.C., there may have been between 100,000 and 1 million separate political units in the world; today, there are fewer than 200.[40] In the ethnographic record, about 50 percent of the 2,000 or so societies described within the last 150 years had only local political integration. That is, the highest level of political integration in one out of two recent societies was the local community.[41] Thus, most of the decrease in the number of independent political units has occurred fairly recently.

But the recent secessions from the former Soviet Union and Yugoslavia and other separatist movements around the world suggest that ethnic rivalries may make for departures from the trend toward larger and larger political units. Ethnic groups that have been dominated by others in multinational states may opt for political autonomy, at least for a while. On the other hand, the separate nations of western Europe are becoming more unified every day, both politically and economically. So the trend toward larger political units may be continuing, even if there are departures from it now and then.

Extrapolating from past history, a number of investigators have suggested that the entire world will eventually come to be politically integrated, perhaps as soon as the 23rd century and no later than A.D. 4850.[42] Only the future will tell if this prediction will come true. And only the future will tell if further political integration in the world will occur peacefully—with all parties agreeing—or by force or the threat of force, as has happened so often in the past.

VARIATION IN POLITICAL PROCESS

Anthropologists are increasingly interested in the politics, or political processes, of the societies they study: who acquires influence or power, how they acquire it, and how political decisions are made. But even though we have descriptive accounts of politics in many societies, there is still little comparative or cross-cultural research on what may explain variation in politics.[43]

Getting to Be a Leader

In those societies that have hereditary leadership, which is common in rank societies and in state societies with monarchies, rules of succession usually establish how leadership is inherited. Such leaders are often identifiable in some obviously visible way; they may be permanently marked or tattooed, as in chiefdoms in Polynesia, or they may wear elaborate dress and insignia, as in class-stratified societies (see the discussion of body adornment in the chapter on the arts). But for societies whose leaders are *chosen,* either as informal leaders or as political officials, we need a lot more research to understand why some kinds of people are chosen over others.

A few studies have investigated the personal qualities of leaders in tribal societies. One study, conducted among the Mekranoti-Kayapo of central Brazil, found that leaders, in contrast to followers, tend to be rated by their peers as higher in intelligence, generosity, knowledgeability, ambitiousness, and aggressiveness. Leaders also tend to be older and taller. And despite the egalitarian nature of Mekranoti society (at least with respect to sharing resources), sons of leaders are more likely than others to become leaders.[44]

Research in another Brazilian society, the Kagwahiv of the Amazon region, suggests another personal quality of leaders: They seem to have positive feelings about their fathers and mothers.[45] In many respects, studies of leaders in the United States show them to be not that different from their counterparts in Brazil. But there is one major difference: Mekranoti and Kagwahiv leaders are not wealthier than others; in fact, they give their wealth away. U.S. leaders are generally wealthier than others.[46]

"Big Men" In some egalitarian tribal societies, the quest for leadership seems quite competitive. In parts of New Guinea and South America, "big men" compete with other ambitious men to attract followers. Men who want to compete must show that they have magical powers, success in gardening, and bravery in war. But, most important, they have to collect enough goods to throw big parties at which the goods are given away. Big men have to work very hard to attract and keep their followings, for dissatisfied followers can always join other aspiring men.[47] The wives of big men are often leaders too. Among the Kagwahiv, for example, a headman's wife is usually the leader of the women in the community; she is responsible for much of the planning for feasts and often distributes the meat at them.[48]

Although the phenomenon of big men leaders is common throughout New Guinea, researchers are beginning to see variation in the type and extent of "bigmanship" in different areas of New Guinea. For example, in the southern Highlands, groups of men (not just big men) may engage in large-scale giveaways, so big men are not so different from ordinary men. In the northwestern Highlands, on the other hand, big men stand out from other men in striking ways. They make policy for groups of people and organize collective events, they have substantial access to pigs or to valuables acquired in exchanges, and they have control over a substantial amount of labor (more than one wife and fellow kin).[49]

We know that some big men are "bigger" than others, but how does a man get to be a big man? Among the Kumdi-Engamoi, a central Highlands group, a man who wants to be considered a *wua nium* (literally, a "great-important-wealthy man") needs to have many wives and daughters, because the amount of land controlled by a man and how much can be produced on that land depend on the number of women in his family. The more wives he has, the more land he is given to cultivate. He must also be a good speaker. Everyone has the right to speak and give speeches, but to get to be known as a big man requires speaking well and forcefully and knowing when to sum up a consensus. It usually takes a man until his thirties or forties to acquire more than one wife and to make his name through exchanges. When a man wants to inaugurate an exchange, he needs to get shells and pigs from his family and relatives. Once he has achieved a reputation as a *wua nium*, he can keep it only if he continues to perform well—that is, if he continues to distribute fairly, make wise decisions, speak well, and conduct exchanges.[50]

In many egalitarian societies, leadership shifts informally from one person to another. In much of New Guinea, there is more competition for achieving "big" status. On Vanatinai, the women compete as well as the men, so there are "big women" as well as "big men." Here a "big woman" paints the face of her cousin's widow for a feast honoring the dead man.

"Big Women" In contrast to most of mainland New Guinea, the islands off the southeastern coast are characterized by matrilineal descent. But, like the rest of New Guinea, the islands also have a shifting system of leadership in which people compete for "big" status. Here, though, the people competing are women as well as men, and so there are "big women" as well as "big men." On the island of Vanatinai, for example, women and men compete with each other to exchange valuables. Women lead canoe expeditions to distant islands to visit male as well as female exchange partners, women mobilize relatives and exchange partners to mount large feasts, and the women get to keep the ceremonial valuables exchanged, at least for a while.[51]

The prominence of women on Vanatinai may be linked to the disappearance of warfare—the colonial powers imposed peace; we call this "pacification." Inter-island exchanges became frequent when war became rarer in the early 20th century, giving women and men more freedom to travel. For men, but not women, war provided a path to leadership; champion warriors would acquire great renown and influence. It is not that women did not participate in war; they did, which is unusual cross-culturally, but a woman could not become a war leader. Now, in the absence of war, women have an opportunity through exchanges to become leaders, or "big women."

In one respect, however, women have less of an opportunity to acquire influence now. There are local government councils now, but all the councillors are male. Why? Some women were nominated for the posts, but they withdrew in embarrassment because they could not speak English. Big men or big women do not automatically have a path to these new positions; mostly young males who know English become the councillors. But this situation may change. With the opening of a government primary school in 1984, both girls and boys are learning English, so women in the future may be more likely to achieve leadership by becoming councillors.

Researchers continue to explore other features that may enhance a person's ability to become leaders where leadership is not hereditary. One fascinating new finding is that in the United States, after controlling for age and perceived attractiveness, individuals who are judged prior to the election to be more "competent" from photographs of their faces are more likely to win in congressional elections.[52] What makes a face look more "competent"? It has fewer "babyish" features—it is less round, has a bigger chin, smaller eyes, and a smaller forehead.[53] Whether these facial features also predict leadership cross-culturally is not yet known.

Political Participation

Political scientist Marc Ross conducted cross-cultural research on variation in degree of political participation. Ross phrased the research question: "Why is it that in some polities there are relatively large numbers of persons involved in political life, while in others political action is the province of very few?"[54]

Political participation in preindustrial societies ranges from widespread to low or nonexistent. In 16 percent of the societies examined, there is widespread participation; decision-making forums are open to all adults. The forums may be formal (councils and other governing bodies) or informal. Next in degree of political participation are societies (37 percent) that have widespread participation by some but not all adults (men but not women, certain classes but not others). Next are societies (29 percent) that have some but not much input by the community. Finally, 18 percent of the societies have low or nonexistent participation, which means that leaders make most decisions, and involvement of the average person is very limited.

Degree of political participation seems to be high in small-scale societies, as well as in modern democratic nation-states, but not in between (feudal states and preindustrial empires). Why? In small-scale societies, leaders do not have the power to force people to act; thus, a high degree of political participation may be the only way to get people to go along with decisions. In modern democracies, which have many powerful groups outside the government—corporations, unions, and other associations are examples—the central authorities may only theoretically have the power to force people to go along; in reality, they rely mostly on voluntary compliance. For example, the U.S. government failed when it tried with force (Prohibition, 1920–1933) to stop the manufacture, transport, and sale of alcoholic beverages.

Another factor may be early family experiences. Some scholars recently have suggested that the type of family people are raised in predicts the degree of political participation in a society. A large extended family with multiple generations tends to be hierarchical, with the older generations having more authority. Children may learn that they have to obey and subordinate their wishes to their elders. Societies with polygyny also seem to have less political participation. The ways of interacting in the family may carry over to the political sphere.[55]

A high degree of political participation seems to have an important consequence. In the modern world, democratically governed states rarely go to war with each other.[56] So, for example, the United States invaded three countries—Grenada, Panama, and Iraq—between 1980 and 1993, but no democracies. Similarly, it appears that more participatory, that is, more "democratic," political units in the ethnographic record fight with each other significantly less often than do less participatory political units, just as seems to be the case among modern nation-states.[57] Does this mean that democracies are more peaceful in general? Here there is more controversy. Judging by the frequency of war, modern democratic states do not look very different from autocratic states in their tendency to go to war. However, if you look at the severity of war as measured by casualty rates, democratic societies do look less warlike.[58] Exactly why more participation or more democracy is likely to lead to peace remains to be established. But there are policy implications

of the relationship, which we explore in the chapter on global problems.

RESOLUTION OF CONFLICT

The resolution of conflict may be accomplished peacefully by avoidance, community action, mediation or the negotiation of compromises, apology, appeal to supernatural forces, or adjudication by a third party. As we shall see, the procedures used usually vary with degree of social complexity; decisions by third parties are more likely in hierarchical societies.[59] But peaceful solutions are not always possible, and disputes may erupt into violent conflict. When violence occurs within a political unit in which disputes are usually settled peacefully, we call such violence crime, particularly when committed by an individual. When the violence occurs between groups of people from separate political units—groups between which there is no procedure for settling disputes—we usually call such violence *warfare*. When violence occurs between subunits of a population that had been politically unified, we call it *civil war*.

Peaceful Resolution of Conflict

Most modern industrialized states have formal institutions and offices, such as police, district attorneys, courts, and penal systems, to deal with minor disputes and more serious conflicts that may arise in society. All these institutions generally operate according to **codified laws**—that is, a set of explicit, usually written rules stipulating what is permissible and what is not. Transgression of the law by individuals gives the state the right to take action against them. The state has a monopoly on the legitimate use of force in the society, for it alone has the right to coerce subjects into agreement with regulations, customs, political edicts, and procedures.

Many societies lack such specialized offices and institutions for dealing with conflict. Yet, because all societies have peaceful, regularized ways of handling at least certain disputes, some anthropologists speak of the *universality of law*. E. Adamson Hoebel, for example, stated the principle as follows:

> Each people has its system of social control. And all but a few of the poorest of them have as a part of the control system a complex of behavior patterns and institutional mechanisms that we may properly treat as law. For, "anthropologically considered, law is merely one aspect of our culture—the aspect which employs the force of organized society to regulate individual and group conduct and to prevent redress or punish deviations from prescribed social norms."[60]

Law, then, whether informal as in simpler societies, or formal as in more complex societies, provides a means of dealing peacefully with whatever conflicts develop. That does not mean that conflicts are always resolved peacefully. But that also does not mean that people cannot learn

applied anthropology

Democracy and Economic Development

The subsistence economies that anthropologists traditionally study are becoming more commercialized as people increasingly produce goods and services for a market. And the pace of economic development is quickening, particularly in places that lacked industrial wage labor until recently, as their economies are increasingly integrated into the world system. What effect, if any, does economic development have on political participation? Can we speculate about the future on the basis of comparative research?

Most of the comparative research on the relationship between economic development and political participation has been cross-national, comparing data on different countries. Some countries are more democratic than others, with characteristics such as contested elections, an elected head of state, an elected powerful legislature, and the protection of civil liberties. In capitalist countries, more democracy is generally associated with higher levels of economic development, as measured by indicators such as per capita output; in countries that are not very industrialized, there is little democracy at the national level. Why should more democracy be associated with more economic development? The prevailing opinion is that economic development increases the degree of social equality in the country; and the more equality among interest groups, the more they demand participation in the political process, and hence the more democracy. Or, to put this theory another

way, as the economy develops, the more what we might call the middle and working classes can demand rewards and power, and therefore the less power the elite can retain.

What about the societies usually studied by anthropologists, the ones in what we call the cross-cultural or ethnographic record? We know that some of the highest levels of political participation occur in the least complex societies, such as foraging societies. Many adults in such societies have a say in decisions, and leadership is informal; leaders can retain their roles only if people voluntarily go along with them. Concentrated power and less political participation are more likely in chiefdoms and states than in band and tribal societies. The more hierarchical chiefdoms and states usually depend on agriculture, particularly intensive agriculture, which can produce more goods and services per capita than foraging economies can. So the relationship between economic development and political participation in the ethnographic record is *opposite* to what we find cross-nationally. That is, the more economic development, the less political participation in the societies studied by anthropologists. Why should this be so? It seems that social equality *decreases* as economic development increases in the ethnographic record (which does not include many industrialized societies). In that record, an economically developed society is likely to have features such as plowing, fertilizers, and irrigation, which make permanent cultiva-

tion of the fields and permanent communities possible. Such intensive agricultural activity is more conducive to concentrated wealth than is hunter-gatherer subsistence or shifting cultivation (horticulture). Thus, in the ethnographic record, the more economically developed societies have more social inequality and therefore less democracy.

The two sets of findings, the cross-national and the cross-cultural, are not that hard to reconcile. Social and economic inequality appears to work against democracy and extensive political participation. Social inequality increases with the switch from foraging to agriculture. But social inequality decreases with the switch from preindustrial agriculture to high (industrial) levels of economic development. Political participation decreases with the first switch and increases with the second, because social inequality first increases and then decreases.

So what does comparative research suggest about the future? If the middle and working classes feel they are not getting a fair return on their labor, their demands should increase. The elite may be willing to satisfy those increased demands; if they do, their power will be reduced. In either case, unless the elite try to retain their power at any cost, there should be more political participation and more democracy, at least in the long run.

Sources: Bollen 1993; Muller 1997; M. Ember, Ember, and Russett 1997; Ross 2009b.

---

to resolve their conflicts peacefully. The fact that there are societies with little or no violent conflict means that it may be possible to learn from them; it may be possible to discover how to avoid violent outcomes of conflicts. How come South Africa could move relatively peacefully from a society dominated by people from Europe to one with government and civil rights shared by all groups? On the other hand, Bosnia had very violent conflict between

ethnic groups and needed intervention by outside parties to keep the warring sides apart.[61]

Avoidance Violence can often be avoided if the parties to a dispute voluntarily avoid each other or are separated until emotions cool down. Anthropologists have frequently remarked that foragers are particularly likely to make use of this technique. People may move to other bands or move their dwellings to opposite ends of camp. Shifting horticulturalists may also split up when conflicts get too intense. Avoidance is obviously easier in societies, such as band societies, that are nomadic or seminomadic and in which people have temporary dwellings. And avoidance is more feasible when people live independently and self-sufficiently (e.g., in cities and suburbs).[62] But even if conditions in such societies may make avoidance easier, we still need to know why some societies use avoidance more than confrontation as a way of resolving conflict.

Community Action   Societies have found various ways of resolving disputes peacefully. One such way involves action by a group or the community as a whole; collective action is common in simpler societies that lack powerful authoritarian leaders.[63] Many Inuit societies, for example, frequently resolve disputes through community action. An individual's failure to heed a taboo or to follow the suggestions of a shaman leads to expulsion from the group, because the community cannot accept a risk to its livelihood. People who fail to share goods voluntarily will find them confiscated and distributed to the community, and they may be executed in the process. A single case of murder, as an act of vengeance (usually because of the abduction of a wife or as part of a blood feud), does not concern the community, but repeated murders do. Franz Boas gave a typical example:

> There was a native of Padli by the name Padlu. He had induced the wife of a native of Cumberland Sound to desert her husband and follow him. The deserted husband, meditating revenge . . . visited his friends in Padli, but before he could accomplish his intention of killing Padlu, the latter shot him. . . . A brother of the murdered man went to Padli to avenge the death . . . but he also was killed by Padlu. A third native of Cumberland Sound, who wished to

avenge the death of his relatives, was also murdered by him.

> On account of these outrages the natives wanted to get rid of Padlu, but yet they did not dare to attack him. When the *pimain* (headman) of the Akudmurmuit learned of these events he started southward and *asked every man in Padli whether Padlu should be killed. All agreed;* so he went with the latter deer hunting . . . and . . . shot Padlu in the back.[64]

The killing of an individual is the most extreme action a community can take—we call it *capital punishment.* The community as a whole or a political official or a court may decide to administer such punishment, but capital punishment seems to exist in nearly all societies, from the simplest to the most complex.[65] It is often assumed that capital punishment deters crime. If it did, we would expect the abolition of capital punishment to be followed by an increase in homicide rates. But that does not seem to happen. A cross-national study indicates that the abolition of capital punishment tends to be followed by a decrease in homicide rates.[66]

Negotiation and Mediation   In many conflicts, the parties to a dispute may come to a settlement themselves by **negotiation.** There aren't necessarily any rules for how they will do so, but any solution is "good" if it restores peace.[67] Sometimes an outside or third party is used to help bring about a settlement between the disputants. We call it **mediation** when the outside party tries to help bring about a settlement, but that third party does not have the formal authority to force a settlement. Both negotiation and mediation are likely when the society is relatively egalitarian and it is important for people to get along.[68]

Among the Nuer of East Africa, a pastoral and horticultural people, disputes within the community can be settled with the help of an informal mediator called the "leopard-skin chief." His position is hereditary, and makes its holder responsible for the social well-being of the district. Matters such as cattle stealing rarely come to the attention of the leopard-skin chief. But if, for example, a murder has been committed, the culprit will go at once to the house of the leopard-skin chief. Immediately the chief cuts the culprit's arm so that blood flows; until the cut has been made, the murderer may not eat or drink. If the murderer is afraid of vengeance by the slain man's family, he will remain at the house of the leopard-skin chief, which is considered sanctuary. Then, within the next few months, the chief attempts to mediate between the parties to the crime. He tries to arrange compensation by the slayer's kin to avoid a feud, and he persuades the dead man's kin that they ought to accept the compensation, usually in the form of cattle. The chief then collects the cattle—40 to 50—and takes them

Although mediation is commonly used in relatively egalitarian societies, it is also used in societies with courts and other formal adjudication procedures for minor conflicts. A teacher in the United States tries to mediate a dispute between two boys.

to the dead man's home, where he performs various sacrifices of cleansing and atonement.[69] Throughout the process, the chief acts as a go-between. He has no authority to force either party to negotiate, and he has no power to enforce a solution once it has been arrived at. However, he is able to take advantage of the fact that both disputants are anxious to avoid a blood feud.

Ritual Reconciliation—Apology

The desire to restore a harmonious relationship may also explain ceremonial apologies. An apology is based on deference—the guilty party shows obeisance and asks for forgiveness. Such ceremonies tend to occur in recent chiefdoms.[70] For example, among the Fijians of the South Pacific, when a person offends someone of higher status, the offended person and other villagers begin to avoid, and gossip about, the offender. If offenders are sensitive to village opinion, they will perform a ceremony of apology called *i soro*. One of the meanings of *soro* is "surrender." In the ceremony, the offender bows the head and remains silent while an intermediary speaks, presents a token gift, and asks the offended person for forgiveness. The apology is rarely rejected.[71]

Oaths and Ordeals

Still another way of peacefully resolving disputes is through oaths and ordeals, both of which involve appeals to supernatural power. An **oath** is the act of calling upon a deity to bear witness to the truth of what one says. An **ordeal** is a means used to determine guilt or innocence by submitting the accused to dangerous or painful tests believed to be under supernatural control.[72]

A common kind of ordeal, found in almost every part of the world, is scalding. Among the Tanala of Madagascar, the accused person, having first had his hand carefully examined for protective covering, has to reach his hand into a cauldron of boiling water and grasp, from underneath, a rock suspended there. He then plunges his hand into cold water, has it bandaged, and is led off to spend the night under guard. In the morning, his hand is unbandaged and examined. If there are blisters, he is guilty.

Oaths and ordeals have also been practiced in Western societies. Both were common in medieval Europe. Even today, in our own society, vestiges of oaths can be found. Children can be heard to say, "Cross my heart and hope to die," and witnesses in courts of law are obliged to swear to tell the truth.

Why do some societies use oaths and ordeals? John Roberts suggested that their use tends to be found in fairly complex societies in which political officials lack sufficient power to make and enforce judicial decisions or would make themselves unnecessarily vulnerable were they to attempt to do so. So the officials may use oaths and ordeals to let the gods decide guilt or innocence.[73] In contrast, smaller and less complex societies probably have no need for elaborate mechanisms such as courts, oaths, and ordeals to ascertain guilt. In such societies, everyone is aware of what crimes have been committed and who the guilty parties probably are.

Adjudication, Courts, and Codified Law

We call it **adjudication** when a third party acting as judge makes a decision that the disputing parties have to accept. Judgment may be rendered by one person (a judge), a panel of judges, a jury, or a political agent or agency (a chief, a royal personage, a council). Judges and courts may rely on codified law and stipulated punishments, but codified law is not necessary for decisions to be made. Codified laws and courts are not limited to Western societies. From the late 17th century to the early 20th century, for example, the Ashanti of West Africa had a complex political system with elaborate legal arrangements. The Ashanti state was a military-based empire possessing legal codes that resembled those of many ancient civilizations.[74] Ashanti law was based on a concept of natural law, a belief that there is an order of the universe whose principles lawmakers should follow in the decisions they make and in the regulations they design. In Ashanti court procedure, elders examined and cross-examined witnesses as well as parties to the dispute. There were also quasi-professional advocates, and appeals against a verdict could be made directly to a chief. Particularly noteworthy was the emphasis on intent when assessing guilt. Drunkenness constituted a valid defense for all crimes except murder and cursing a chief, and a plea of insanity, if proved, was upheld for all offenses. Ashanti punishments could be severe. Physical mutilation, such as slicing off the nose or an ear—even castration in sexual offenses—was often employed. Fines were more frequent, however, and death sentences could often be commuted to banishment and confiscation of goods.

Why do some societies have codified systems and others do not? One explanation, advanced by E. Adamson Hoebel, A. R. Radcliffe-Brown, and others, is that there is little need for formal legal guidelines in small, closely knit communities because competing interests are minimal. Hence, simple societies need little codified law. There are relatively few matters to quarrel about, and the general will of the group is sufficiently well known and demonstrated frequently enough to deter transgressors.

This point of view is echoed in Richard Schwartz's study of two Israeli settlements. In one communal kibbutz, a young man aroused a good deal of community resentment because he had accepted an electric teakettle as a gift. The general opinion was that he had overstepped the code about not having personal possessions, and he was so informed. Accordingly, he gave the kettle to the communal infirmary. Schwartz observed that "no organized enforcement of the decision was threatened, but had he disregarded the expressed will of the community, his life . . . would have been made intolerable by the antagonism of public opinion."[75]

In this community, where people worked and ate together, not only did everyone know about transgressions, but a wrongdoer could not escape public censure. Thus, public opinion was an effective sanction. In another Israeli community, however, where individuals lived in widely separated houses and worked and ate separately, public opinion did not work as well. Not only were community members less aware of problems, but they had no quick way of making their feelings known. As a result, they established a judicial body to handle trouble cases.

Larger, more heterogeneous and stratified societies are likely to have more frequent disputes, which at the same time are less visible to the public. Individuals in stratified societies are generally not so dependent on community members for their well-being and hence are less likely to know of, or care about, others' opinions. In such societies, codified laws and formal authorities for resolving disputes develop—in order, perhaps, that disputes may be settled impersonally enough so that the parties can accept the decision and social order can be restored.

A good example of how more formal systems of law develop is the experience of towns in the American West during the gold rush period. These communities were literally swamped by total strangers. The townsfolk, having no control (authority) over these intruders because the strangers had no local ties, looked for ways to deal with the trouble cases that were continually flaring up. A first attempt at a solution was to hire gunslingers, who were also strangers, to act as peace officers or sheriffs, but this strategy usually failed. Eventually, towns succeeded in having federal authorities send in marshals backed by federal power.

Is there some evidence to support the theory that codified law is necessary only in larger, more complex societies? Data from a large, worldwide sample of societies suggest that codified law is associated with political integration beyond the local level. Murder cases, for example, are dealt with informally in societies that have only local political organization. In societies with multilocal political units, specialized political authorities tend to judge or adjudicate murder cases.[76] There is also some cross-cultural evidence that violence within a society tends to be less frequent when there are formal authorities (chiefs, courts) who have the power to punish murderers.[77] In general, adjudication or enforced decisions by outside authorities tend to occur in hierarchical societies with social classes and centralized power.[78]

Violent Resolution of Conflict

People often resort to violence when regular, effective alternative means of resolving a conflict are not available. Violence between individuals that is not considered legitimate is generally called **crime.** What is considered legitimate varies considerably from society to society. As we discuss further in the chapter on global problems, researchers who study crime usually focus on the observed behaviors such as assault and homicide. When violence occurs between territorial entities such as communities, districts, or nations, we call it **warfare.** The type of warfare varies in scope and complexity from society to society. Sometimes a

distinction is made among feuding, raiding, and large-scale confrontations.[79]

Some scholars talk about a cultural pattern of violence. More often than not, societies with one type of violence have others. Societies with more war tend to have warlike sports, malevolent magic, severe punishment for crimes, high murder rates, feuding, and family violence.[80]

There are more peaceful societies. These societies are not conflict-free, but they try more to resolve conflict nonviolently. And like the Semai, they discourage aggression in their children without providing an aggressive model. What explains these more peaceful cultural patterns? Cross-cultural evidence supports the view that frequent warfare is the key to understanding all kinds of violence. Not only is war correlated with other kinds of aggression, but societies that are forced to stop fighting by more powerful societies appear to encourage aggression in their children less. It seems that, if war is frequent, the society encourages boys to be aggressive, so that they will grow up to be effective warriors. But socializing for aggression can spill over into other areas of life; high rates of crime and other violence may be inadvertent or unintended consequences of the encouragement of aggressiveness.[81] And societies with a lot of war commonly bestow high status on their warriors. Warriors are generally proud of their accomplishments, considering it an honor to be a brave and fierce warrior.[82]

Individual Violence Although it may seem paradoxical at first, violent behavior itself is often used to try to control behavior. In some societies, it is considered necessary for parents to beat children who misbehave. They don't consider this criminal behavior or child abuse; they consider it punishment (see the discussion of family violence in the chapter on global problems). Similar views may attach to interpersonal behavior between adults. If a person trespasses on your property or hurts someone in your family, some societies consider it appropriate or justified to kill or maim the trespasser. Is this social control, or is it just lack of control?

Systems of individual self-help are characteristic of egalitarian societies.[83] How is this different from "community action," which earlier we classified under peaceful resolution of conflict? Because community action is explicitly based on obtaining a consensus, it is likely to lead to the ending of a particular dispute. Individual action, or self-help, particularly if it involves violence, is not.

Feuding Feuding is an example of how individual self-help may not lead to a peaceful resolution of conflict. **Feuding** is a state of recurring hostilities between families or groups of kin, usually motivated by a desire to avenge an offense—whether insult, injury, deprivation, or death—against a member of the group. The most common characteristic of the feud is that all members of the kin group carry the responsibility to avenge. The killing of any member of the offender's group is considered appropriate revenge, because the kin group as a whole is regarded as

new perspectives on gender

New Courts Allow Women to Address Grievances in Papua New Guinea

In most societies in New Guinea, women did not traditionally participate in the resolution of disputes. And they could not bring actions against men. But when village courts were introduced, women began to go to court to redress offenses against them.

In colonial times, the introduced Western-style courts followed Western law, primarily Australian and British common law, not native customary law. After Papua New Guinea became an independent country, those courts remained in place. The lowest of the courts, called local courts, were located in town centers, often far from villages, so villagers rarely brought cases to them. But, in 1973, a new kind of court was created. Called village courts, they were designed to settle local disputes in the villages, using a blend of customary law (relying on compromise) and Western law. In contrast to the local courts, magistrates in the village courts were not outsiders but were selected from the pool of traditional and local leaders who knew the local people.

When Richard Scaglion studied changes in village courts among the Abelam from 1977 to 1987, he noticed a shift toward the increased use of these courts by women. In 1977, most of the complainants were male, but most of them were female by 1987. In a wider study of court cases over many regions of Papua New Guinea, Scaglion and Rose Whittingham found that most of the cases in which women were the plaintiffs were attempts to redress sex-related offenses (sexual jealousy, rape, incest, domestic disputes) committed by males. Most disputes in New Guinea villages are settled informally by self-help or by appeal to a "big man"; the courts are appealed to only as a last resort. Serious sex-related cases are unlikely to be settled informally but, rather, in the village court. Apparently women do not believe that they can get satisfaction informally. So they go to the village court, where they win some sort of punishment for the defendant in about 60 percent of the cases, just about the same rate that men achieve when they bring a case seeking punishment.

Culture change introduced from the outside often works against native peoples. But Papuan New Guinea women have benefited from the new village court system, particularly in redressing grievances against males. The traditional system for resolving disputes was largely male-dominated (women could not be plaintiffs), and so the possibility of taking disputes to the new courts has given women some measure of legal equality with men.

Sources: Scaglion 1990; Scaglion and Whittingham 1985.

responsible. Nicholas Gubser told of a feud within a Nunamiut Inuit community, caused by a husband killing his wife's lover, that lasted for decades. The Nunamiut take feuds seriously, as do many societies, especially when murder has been committed. Closely related members of the murdered man recruit as many relatives as they can and try to kill the murderer or one of his close kin. Then the members of the murderer's kindred are brought into the feud. The two kindreds may snipe at each other for years.[84]

Feuds are by no means limited to small-scale societies; they occur as frequently in societies with high levels of political organization.[85]

Large-scale confrontations occur in societies with armies, but they also occur in nonstate societies. The Masai of Kenya (shown here) battled with Kalenjin (not shown) over a land dispute following the 2008 disputed election.

Raiding **Raiding** is a short-term use of force, planned and organized, to realize a limited objective. This objective is usually the acquisition of goods, animals, or other forms of wealth belonging to another, often neighboring community.

Raiding is especially prevalent in pastoral societies, in which cattle, horses, camels, or other animals are prized and an individual's own herd can be augmented by theft. Raids are often organized by temporary leaders or coordinators whose authority may not last beyond the planning and execution of the venture. Raiding may also be organized for the purpose of capturing people. Sometimes people are taken to marry—the capture of women to be wives or concubines is fairly common[86]—or to be slaves. Slavery has been practiced in about 33 percent of the world's known societies, and war has been one way of obtaining slaves either to keep or to trade for other goods.[87] Raiding, like feuding, is often self-perpetuating: The victim of a raid today becomes the raider tomorrow.[88]

Large-Scale Confrontations Individual episodes of feuds and raids usually involve relatively small numbers of people and almost always an element of surprise. Because they are generally attacked without warning, the victims are often unable to muster an immediate defense. Large-scale confrontations, in contrast, involve a large number of people and planning of strategies of attack and defense by both sides. Large-scale warfare is usually practiced among societies with intensive agriculture or industrialization. Only these societies possess a technology sufficiently advanced to support specialized armies, military leaders, strategists, and so on. But large-scale confrontations are not limited to state societies; they occur, for example, among the horticultural Dugum Dani of central New Guinea.

The military history of the Dani, with its shifting alliances and confederations, is reminiscent of that of Europe, although Dani battles involve far fewer fighters and less sophisticated weaponry. Among the Dani, long periods of ritual warfare are characterized by formal battles announced through a challenge sent by one side to the opposing side. If the challenge is accepted, the protagonists meet at the agreed-upon battle site to set up their lines. Fighting with spears, sticks, and bows and arrows begins at midmorning and continues either until nightfall or until rain intervenes. There may also be a rest period during the midday heat during which the two sides shout insults at each other or talk and rest among themselves.

The front line of battle is composed of about a dozen active warriors and a few leaders. Behind them is a second line, still within arrow range, composed of those who have just left the forward line or are preparing to join it. The third line, outside arrow range, is composed of noncombatants—males too old or too young to participate and those recovering from wounds. This third line merely watches the battle taking place on the grassy plain. On the hillsides far back from the front line, some of the old men help to direct ancestral ghosts to the battle by gouging a line in the ground that points in the direction of the battlefield.[89]

Yet, as total as large-scale confrontations may be, even such warfare has cultural rules. Among the Dani, for instance, no fighting occurs at night, and weapons are limited to simple spears and bows and arrows. Similarly, in state societies, governments will sign "self-denying" pacts restricting the use of poison gas, germ warfare, and so forth. Unofficially, private arrangements are common. One has only to glance through the memoirs of national leaders of the two world wars to become aware of locally arranged truces, visits to one another's front positions, exchanges of prisoners of war, and so on.

Explaining Warfare

Most societies in the anthropological record have had warfare between communities or larger territorial groups. The vast majority of the societies in a recent cross-cultural study had at least occasional wars when they were first described, unless they had been pacified or incorporated by more dominant societies.[90] Yet, relatively little research has been done on the possible causes of war and why it varies in type and frequency. For instance, why have some people fought a great deal, and others only infrequently? Why in some societies does warfare occur internally, within the society or language group?

We have answers, based on cross-cultural studies, to some of those questions. There is evidence that people in preindustrial societies go to war mostly out of fear, particularly a fear of expectable but unpredictable natural disasters that will destroy food resources (e.g., droughts, floods, locust infestations). People may think they can protect themselves against such disasters ahead of time by taking things from defeated enemies. In any case, preindustrial societies with higher frequencies of war are very likely to have had a history of expectable but unpredictable disasters. The fact that chronic (annually recurring and therefore predictable) food shortages do not predict higher frequencies of war suggests that people go to war in an attempt to cushion the impact of the disasters they expect to occur in the future but cannot predict. Consistent with this tentative conclusion is the fact that the victors in war almost always take land or other resources from the defeated. And this is true for simpler as well as more complex preindustrial societies.[91] Might similar motives affect decisions about war and peace in the modern world?

We know that complex or politically centralized societies are likely to have professional armies, hierarchies of military authority, and sophisticated weapons.[92] But surprisingly, the frequency of warfare seems to be not much greater in complex societies than in simple band or tribal societies.[93] We have some evidence that warfare is unlikely to occur internally (within a society or territory) if it is small in population (21,000 or fewer people); in a larger society, there is a high likelihood of warfare within the society, between communities or larger territorial divisions.[94] In fact, complex societies, even if they are politically unified, are not less likely than simpler societies to have internal warfare.[95]

Oil is a valuable resource in the world today. Iraq has more oil in the ground than most other countries.

What about the idea that men in band and tribal societies may mostly go to war over women?[96] If this were true, those band and tribal societies with the most frequent wars should have shortages of women, and those with little or no war—less often than once in 10 years—should have more equal numbers of women and men. But the cross-cultural evidence clearly contradicts this theory. Band and tribal societies with more wars do not have fewer women.[97]

What, if anything, do we know about recent warfare between nation-states? Although many people think that military alliances lessen the chance of war, it turns out that nations formally allied with other nations do not necessarily go to war less often than nations lacking formal alliances. Countries that are allies are, of course, less likely to go to war with each other; however, alliances can drag dependent allies into wars they don't want.[98] Countries that are economically interdependent, that trade with each other for necessities, are less likely to go to war with each other.[99] Finally, military equality between nations, particularly when preceded by a rapid military buildup, seems to increase rather than lessen the chance of war between those nations.[100]

Clearly, these findings contradict some traditional beliefs about how to prevent war. Military buildups do not make war less likely, but trade does. What else may? We have already noted that participatory ("democratic") political systems are less likely to go to war with each other than are authoritarian political systems. Later, in the chapter on global problems, we discuss how the results of cross-cultural and cross-national studies may translate into policies that could minimize the risk of war in the world. Although war may be common in the world, it is not inevitable. Societies change over time. The Vikings were extremely militaristic, but Norway today is now a peaceful society. A comparative study of Polynesian societies shows that, although all derive from a common cultural heritage, the size of the islands people settled on strongly influenced their patterns of interpersonal violence and warfare. The smallest islands had the lowest levels of violence and the least warfare. It appears that cooperation and harmony were more likely than violence in small "face-to face" societies.[101]

Political and Social Change

In addition to commercialization and religious change brought about by the expansion of Western and other countries, political changes have often occurred when a foreign system of government has been imposed. But, as recent events in the former Soviet Union and South Africa indicate, dramatic changes in a political system can also occur more or less voluntarily. Perhaps the most striking type of political change in recent years is the spread of participatory forms of government—"democracy."

To political scientists, democracy is usually defined in terms of voting by a substantial proportion of the citizenry, governments brought to power by periodic contested elections, a chief executive either popularly elected or responsible to an elected legislature, and often also civil liberties such as free speech. Depending on which criteria are used, only 12 to 15 countries qualified as democracies as of the beginning of the 20th century. The number decreased after World War I, as emerging dictatorships in Russia, Italy, Germany, central Europe, Japan, and elsewhere replaced democratic institutions. After World War II, despite all the rhetoric associated with the founding of the United Nations, the picture was not much different. Some members of the new North Atlantic Treaty Organization (NATO) were not democracies, and neither were many members of the wider Western alliance system, in Latin America, the Middle East, and Asia.

Not until the 1970s and 1980s did people, not just political scientists, start noticing that democracy was becoming more common in the world. By the early 1990s, President George H. W. Bush and then-candidate Bill Clinton were talking about the spread of the "democratic peace." As of 1992, about half of the countries in the world had more or less democratic governments, and others were in transition to democracy.[102] Social scientists do not yet understand why this change is happening. But it is possible that the global communication of ideas has a lot to do with it. Authoritarian governments can censor their own newspapers and prevent group meetings, and sophisticated technology can block Internet use and cell phone connections, but ultimately authoritarian governments really cannot stop the movement of ideas. The movement of ideas, of course, does not explain the acceptance of those ideas. Why democracy has recently diffused to more countries than ever before still requires explanation, as does why some countries do not find it appealing.

SUMMARY ● ○ ○

1. All societies have customs or procedures that, organized on behalf of territorial groups, result in decision making and the resolution of disputes. These ways of creating and maintaining social order and coping with social disorder vary from society to society.

2. Societies with a band type of political organization are composed of fairly small, usually nomadic groups. Each of these bands is politically autonomous, the band being the largest group that acts as a political unit. Authority within the band is usually informal. Societies with band organization generally are egalitarian hunter-gatherers. But band organization may not have been typical of foragers in the distant past.

3. Societies with tribal organization are similar to those with band organization in being egalitarian. But, in contrast with band societies, they generally are food producers, have a higher population density, and are more sedentary. Tribal organization is defined by the presence of groupings, such as clans and age-sets, that can integrate more than one local group into a larger whole.

4. The personal qualities of leaders in tribal societies seem to be similar to the qualities of leaders in the United States, with one major difference: U.S. leaders are generally wealthier than others in their society.

5. Chiefdom organization differs from tribal organization in having formal authority structures that integrate multicommunity political units. Compared with societies with tribal organization, societies with chiefdoms are more densely populated and their communities are more permanent. In contrast to "big men" in tribal societies, who generally have to earn their privileges by their personal qualities, chiefs generally hold their positions permanently. Most chiefdom societies have social ranking.

6. A state has been defined as a political unit composed of many communities and having a centralized government with the authority to make and enforce laws, collect taxes, and draft men for military service. In state societies, the government tries to maintain a monopoly on the use of physical force. In addition, states are generally characterized by class stratification, intensive agriculture (the high productivity of which presumably allows the emergence of cities), commercial exchange, a high degree of economic and other specialization, and extensive foreign trade. The rulers of a state cannot depend forever on the use or threat of force to maintain their power; the people must believe that the rulers are legitimate or have the right to govern.

7. Degree of political participation varies in the societies that anthropologists study, just as among modern nation-states. Degree of political participation seems to be high in small-scale societies, as well as in modern democratic nation-states, but not in those in between, such as feudal states and preindustrial empires.

8. Many societies lack specialized offices and institutions for dealing with conflict. Yet all societies have peaceful, regularized ways of handling at least certain disputes. Avoidance, community action, and negotiation and mediation are more common in simpler societies. Ritual apology occurs frequently in chiefdoms. Oaths and ordeals tend to occur in complex societies in which political officials lack power to enforce judicial decisions. Adjudication is more likely in stratified, more complex societies. Capital punishment seems to exist in nearly all societies, from the simplest to the most complex.

9. People are likely to resort to violence when regular, effective alternative means of resolving a conflict are not available. Violence can occur between individuals, within communities, and between communities. Violence that occurs between political entities such as communities, districts, or nations is generally referred to as warfare. The type of warfare varies in scope and complexity from society to society. Preindustrial societies with higher warfare frequencies are likely to have had a history of unpredictable disasters that destroyed food supplies. More often than not, societies with one type of violence have others.

10. One of the most striking types of political change in recent years is the spread of participatory forms of government—"democracy."

GLOSSARY TERMS ○ ● ○

CRITICAL QUESTIONS ○ ○ ●

1. When, if ever, do you think the world will be politically unified? Why do you think so?
2. Why don't informal methods of social control work well in societies like our own? Why don't formal methods work better than they do?
3. What does research on war and violence suggest about how to reduce their likelihood?

PEARSON
myanthrolab

Read the chapter by Thomas Abler, "Iroquois: The Tree of Peace and the War Kettle" on MyAnthroLab and answer the following questions:

1. What was the Iroquois Confederacy? What kind of political organization was it?
2. What role did men and women play in making war and making peace?
3. What kinds of impacts did the Europeans have on the Iroquois?

Religion and Magic

s far as we know, all societies have possessed beliefs that can be grouped under the term *religion*. These beliefs vary from culture to culture and from time to time. Yet, despite their variety, we shall define **religion** as any set of attitudes, beliefs, and practices pertaining to *supernatural power*, whether that power be forces, gods, spirits, ghosts, or demons.

In our society, we divide phenomena into the natural and the supernatural, but not all languages or cultures make such a neat distinction. Moreover, what is considered **supernatural**—powers believed to be not human or not subject to the laws of nature—varies from society to society. Some of the variation is determined by what a society regards as natural. For example, some illnesses commonly found in our society are believed to result from the natural action of bacteria and viruses. In other societies, and even among some people in our own society, illness is thought to result from supernatural forces, and thus it forms a part of religious belief.

Beliefs about what is, or is not, a supernatural occurrence also vary within a society at a given time or over time. In Judeo-Christian traditions, for example, floods, earthquakes, volcanic eruptions, comets, and epidemics were once considered evidence of supernatural powers intervening in human affairs. It is now generally agreed that they are simply natural occurrences—even though many still believe that supernatural forces may be involved. Thus, the line between the natural and the supernatural varies in a society according to what people believe about the causes of things and events in the observable world. Similarly, what is considered sacred in one society may not be so considered in another.

In many cultures, what we would consider religious is embedded in other aspects of everyday life. That is, it is often difficult to separate the religious, economic, or political from other aspects of the culture. Such cultures have little or no specialization of any kind; there are no full-time priests, no purely religious activities. So the various aspects of culture we distinguish (e.g., in the chapter titles of this book) are not separate and easily recognized in many societies, as they are in complex societies such as our own. However, it is sometimes difficult even for us to agree whether or not a particular custom of ours is religious. After all, the categorizing of beliefs as religious, political, or social is a relatively new custom. The ancient Greeks, for instance, did not have a word for religion, but they did have many concepts concerning the behavior of their gods and their own expected duties to the gods.

When people's duties to their gods are linked with duty to their princes, it is difficult to separate religious from political ideas. As an example of our own difficulty in labeling a particular class of actions or beliefs as religious or social, consider our attitudes about wearing clothes. Is our belief that it is necessary to wear clothing, at least in the company of nonlovers, a religious principle, or is it something else? Recall that, in Genesis, the wearing of clothes or fig leaves is distinctly associated with the loss of innocence: Adam and Eve, after eating the apple, covered their nakedness. Accordingly,

269

when Christian missionaries first visited islands in the Pacific in the 19th century, they forced the native women to wear more clothes, particularly to cover their sexual parts. Were the missionaries' ideas about sex religious or social, or perhaps both?

● ○ ●

THE UNIVERSALITY OF RELIGION

Religious beliefs and practices are found in all known contemporary societies, and archaeologists think they have found signs of religious belief associated with *Homo sapiens* who lived at least 60,000 years ago. People then deliberately buried their dead, and many graves contain the remains of food, tools, and other objects that were probably thought to be needed in an afterlife. Some of the artistic productions of modern humans after about 30,000 years ago may have been used for religious purposes. For example, sculptures of females with ample secondary sex characteristics may have been fertility charms. Cave paintings in which the predominant images are animals of the hunt may reflect a belief that the image had some power over events. Perhaps early humans thought that their hunting would be more successful if they drew images depicting good fortune in hunting. The details of religions practiced in the distant past cannot be recovered. Yet evidence of ritual treatment of the dead suggests that early people believed in the existence of supernatural spirits and tried to communicate with, and perhaps influence, them.

We may reasonably assume the existence of prehistoric religion and we have evidence of the universality of religion in historic times, so we can understand why the subject of religion has been the focus of much speculation, research, and theorizing. As long ago as the 5th century B.C., Herodotus made fairly objective comparisons among the religions of the 50 or so societies he traveled to from his home in Greece. He noted many similarities among their gods and pointed out evidence of diffusion of religious worship. Since Herodotus's time some 2,500 years ago, scholars, theologians, historians, and philosophers have speculated about religion. Some have claimed superiority for their own forms of religion; others have derided the naive simplicity of others' beliefs; and some have expressed skepticism concerning all beliefs.

Speculation about which religion is superior is not an anthropological concern. What is of interest to anthropologists is why religion is found in all societies and how and why it varies from society to society. Many social scientists—particularly anthropologists, sociologists, and psychologists—have offered theories to account for the universality of religion. Most think that religions are created by humans in response to certain universal needs or conditions. We consider four such needs or conditions here: (1) a need for intellectual understanding, (2) reversion to childhood feelings, (3) anxiety and uncertainty, and (4) a need for community.

The Need to Understand

One of the earliest social scientists to propose a major theory of the origin of religion was Edward Tylor. In Tylor's view, religion originated in people's speculation about dreams, trances, and death. The dead, the distant, those in the next house, animals—all seem real in dreams and trances. Tylor thought that the lifelike appearances of these imagined people and animals suggest a dual existence for all things—a physical, visible body and a psychic, invisible soul. In sleep, the soul can leave the body and appear to other people; at death, the soul permanently leaves the body. Because the dead appear in dreams, people come to believe that the souls of the dead are still around.

Tylor thought that the belief in souls was the earliest form of religion; **animism** is the term he used to refer to belief in souls.[1] But many scholars criticized Tylor's theory for being too intellectual and not dealing with the emotional component of religion. One of Tylor's students, R. R. Marett, felt that Tylor's animism was too sophisticated an idea to be the origin of religion. Marett suggested that **animatism**—a belief in impersonal supernatural forces (e.g., the power of a rabbit's foot)—preceded the creation of spirits.[2] A similar idea is that, when people believe in gods, they are *anthropomorphizing*—attributing human characteristics and motivations to nonhuman, particularly supernatural, events.[3] Anthropomorphizing may be an attempt to understand what is otherwise incomprehensible and disturbing.

Reversion to Childhood Feelings

Sigmund Freud believed that early humans lived in groups, each of which was dominated by a tyrannical man who kept all the women for himself.[4] Freud postulated that, on maturing, the sons were driven out of the group. Later, they joined together to kill and eat the hated father. But then the sons felt enormous guilt and remorse, which they expressed (projected) by prohibiting the killing of a totem animal (the father substitute). Subsequently, on ritual occasions, the cannibalistic scene was repeated in the form of a totem meal. Freud believed that these early practices gradually became transformed into the worship of deities or gods modeled after the father.

Most social scientists today do not accept Freud's interpretation of the origin of religion. But there is widespread agreement with his idea that events in infancy can have long-lasting and powerful effects on beliefs and practices in adult life. Helpless and dependent on parents for many years, infants and children inevitably and unconsciously view their parents as all-knowing and all-powerful. When adults feel out of control or in need, they may unconsciously revert to their infantile and childhood feelings. They may then look to gods or magic to do what they cannot do for themselves, just as they looked to their parents to take care of their needs. As we shall see, there is evidence that feelings about the supernatural world parallel feelings in everyday life.

Anxiety and Uncertainty

Freud thought that humans would turn to religion during times of uncertainty, but he did not view religion positively, believing that humans would eventually outgrow the need for religion. Others viewed religion more positively. Bronislaw Malinowski noted that people in all societies are faced with anxiety and uncertainty. They may have skills and knowledge to take care of many of their needs, but knowledge is not sufficient to prevent illness, accidents, and natural disasters. The most frightening prospect is death itself. Consequently, there is an intense desire for immortality. As Malinowski saw it, religion is born from the universal need to find comfort in inevitable times of stress. Through religious belief, people affirm their convictions that death is neither real nor final, that people are endowed with a personality that persists even after death. In religious ceremony, humans can commemorate and communicate with those who have died, and achieve some measure of comfort in these ways.[5]

Theorists such as William James, Carl Jung, Erich Fromm, and Abraham Maslow have viewed religion even more positively: Religion is not just a way of relieving anxiety; it is thought to be therapeutic. James suggested that religion provides a feeling of union with something larger than oneself,[6] and Jung suggested that it helps people resolve their inner conflicts and attain maturity.[7] Fromm proposed that religion gives people a framework of values,[8] and Maslow argued that it provides a transcendental understanding of the world.[9]

The idea that religion relieves anxiety in times of greater stress is supported by a comparative study of fishermen. John Poggie and Richard Pollnac interviewed

commercial fishermen from three New England ports about their ritual beliefs and practices. Most frequently mentioned were taboos such as "Don't turn a hatch cover upside down," "Don't whistle on a boat," and "Don't mention the word *pig* on board." When the fishermen were asked what these taboos meant, they talked about personal safety and preventing bad luck. Those fishermen who stay out for only a day at a time, fish closer to shore, or collect shellfish close to shore, report fewer taboos, consistent with the fact that they are less at risk from rough seas, storms, and inability to repair their boats if they break down.[10]

The Need for Community

All those theories of religion agree on one thing: Whatever the beliefs or rituals, religion may satisfy psychological needs common to all people. But some social scientists believe that religion springs from society and serves social, rather than psychological, needs. Émile Durkheim, a French sociologist, pointed out that living in society makes humans feel pushed and pulled by powerful forces. These forces direct their behavior, pushing them to resist what is considered wrong, pulling them to do what is considered right. These are the forces of public opinion, custom, and law. Because they are largely invisible and unexplained, people would feel them as mysterious forces and therefore come to believe in gods and spirits. Durkheim suggested that religion arises out of the experience of living in social groups; religious belief and practice affirm a person's place in society, enhance feelings of community, and give people confidence. He proposed that society is really the object of worship in religion.

Consider how Durkheim explained totemism, so often discussed by early religious theorists. He thought that nothing inherent in a lizard, rat, or frog—animal totems for some Australian aboriginal groups—would be sufficient to make them *sacred*. The totem animal therefore must be a symbol. But a symbol of what? Durkheim noted that the people are organized into clans, and each clan has its own totem animal; the totem distinguishes one clan

Fishermen working on a boat deck in choppy seas. The more danger involved in fishing, the more taboos fisherman seem to have.

from another. So the totem is the focus of the clan's religious rituals and symbolizes both the clan and the clan's spirits. It is the clan that is affirmed in ritual.[11]

Guy Swanson accepted Durkheim's belief that certain aspects or conditions of society generate the responses we call religious, but he thought that Durkheim was too vague about exactly what in society would generate the belief in spirits or gods. So what might? Swanson suggested that the belief in spirits derives from the existence of *sovereign groups* in a society. These are the groups that have independent jurisdiction (decision-making powers) over some sphere of life—the family, the clan, the village, the state. Such groups are not mortal; they persist beyond the lifetimes of their individual members. According to Swanson, then, the spirits or gods that people invent personify or represent the powerful decision-making groups in their society. Just like sovereign groups in a society, the spirits or gods are immortal and have purposes and goals that supersede those of individuals.[12]

VARIATION IN RELIGIOUS BELIEFS

There is no general agreement among scholars as to why people need religion, or how spirits, gods, and other supernatural beings and forces come into existence. (Any or all of the needs we have discussed, psychological or social, may give rise to religious belief and practice.) Yet there is general recognition of the enormous variation in the details of religious beliefs and practices. Societies differ in the kinds of supernatural beings or forces they believe in and the character of those beings. They also differ in the structure or hierarchy of those beings, in what the beings actually do, and in what happens to people after death. Variation exists also in the ways in which the supernatural is believed to interact with humans.

Types of Supernatural Forces and Beings

Supernatural Forces   Some supernatural forces have no personlike character. As we discussed earlier, Marett referred to such religious beliefs as animatism. For example, a supernatural, impersonal force called **mana,** after its Malayo-Polynesian name, is thought to inhabit some objects but not others, some people but not others. A farmer in Polynesia places stones around a field; the crops are bountiful; the stones have mana. During a subsequent year, the stones may lose their mana and the crops will be poor. People may also possess mana, as, for example, the chiefs in Polynesia were said to do. However, such power is not necessarily possessed permanently; chiefs who were unsuccessful in war or other activities were said to have lost their mana.

The word *mana* may be Malayo-Polynesian, but a similar concept is also found in our own society. We can compare mana to the power that golfers may attribute to some but, unhappily not all, of their clubs. A ballplayer might think a certain sweatshirt or pair of pants has supernatural

power or force, and that more runs or points will be scored when they are worn. A four-leaf clover has mana; a three-leaf clover does not.

Objects, people, or places can be considered **taboo.** Anthony Wallace distinguished mana from taboo by pointing out that things containing mana are to be touched, whereas taboo things are not to be touched, for their power can cause harm.[13] Thus, those who touch them may themselves become taboo. Taboos surround food not to be eaten, places not to be entered, animals not to be killed, people not to be touched sexually, people not to be touched at all, and so on. An Australian aborigine could not normally kill and eat the animal that was his totem; Hebrew tribesmen were forbidden to touch a woman during menstruation or for seven days afterward.

Supernatural Beings   Supernatural beings fall within two broad categories: those of nonhuman origin, such as gods and spirits, and those of human origin, such as ghosts and ancestral spirits. Chief among the beings of nonhuman origin, **gods** are named personalities. They are often *anthropomorphic*—that is, conceived in the image of a person—although they are sometimes given the shapes of other animals or of celestial bodies, such as the sun or moon. Essentially, the gods are believed to have created themselves, but some of them then created, or gave birth to, other gods. Although some are seen as creator gods, not all peoples include the creation of the world as one of the acts of gods.

After their efforts at creation, many creator gods retire. Having set the world in motion, they are not interested in its day-to-day operation. Other creator gods remain interested in the ordinary affairs of human beings, especially the affairs of one small, chosen segment of humanity. Whether or not a society has a creator god, the job of running the creation is often left to lesser gods. The Maori of New Zealand, for example, recognize three important gods: a god of the sea, a god of the forest, and a god of agriculture. They call upon each in turn for help and try to get all three to share their knowledge of how the universe runs. The gods of the ancient Romans, on the other hand, specialized to a high degree. There were three gods of the plow, one god to help with the sowing, one for weeding, one for reaping, one for storing grain, one for manuring, and so on.[14]

Beneath the gods in prestige, and often closer to people, are multitudes of unnamed **spirits.** Some may be guardian spirits for people. Some, who become known for particularly efficacious work, may be promoted to the rank of named gods. Some spirits who are known to the people but are never invoked by them are of the hobgoblin type. Hobgoblins delight in mischief and can be blamed for any number of small mishaps; still other spirits take pleasure in deliberately working evil on behalf of people.

Many Native American groups believed in guardian spirits that had to be sought out, usually in childhood. For example, among the Sanpoil of northeastern Washington, boys and sometimes girls would be sent out on overnight vigils to acquire their guardians. Most commonly the spirits were animals, but they could also be uniquely shaped

A Guatemalan Maya family visits a cemetery on the Day of the Dead. It is believed that the spirits of the dead return for a visit on that day.

rocks, lakes, mountains, whirlwinds, or clouds. The vigil was not always successful. When it was, the guardian spirit appeared in a vision or dream, and always at first in human form. Conversation with the spirit would reveal its true identity.[15]

Ghosts are supernatural beings who were once human, and **ancestor spirits** are ghosts of dead relatives. The belief that ghosts or their actions can be perceived by the living is almost universal.[16] The near-universality of the belief in ghosts may not be difficult to explain. There are many cues in everyday experience that are associated with a loved one, and even after the death, those cues might arouse the feeling that the dead person is still somehow present. The opening of a door or the smell of tobacco or cologne in a room may evoke the idea that the person is still present, if only for a moment. Then, too, loved ones live on in dreams. Small wonder, then, that most societies believe in ghosts. If the idea of ghosts is generated by these familiar associations, we might expect that ghosts in most societies would be close relatives and friends, not strangers—and they are.[17]

Although the belief in ghosts is nearly universal, the spirits of the dead do not play an active role in the life of the living in all societies. In his cross-cultural study of 50 societies, Swanson found that people are likely to believe in active ancestral spirits where descent groups are important decision-making units. The descent group is an entity that exists over time, back into the past as well as forward into the future, despite the deaths of individual members.[18] The dead feel concern for the fortunes, the prestige, and the continuity of their descent group as strongly as the living. As a Lugbara elder (in northern Uganda in Africa) put it, "Are our ancestors not people of our lineage? They are our fathers and we are their children whom they have begotten. Those that have died stay near us in our homes and we feed and respect them. Does not a man help his father when he is old?"[19]

The Character of Supernatural Beings

Whatever type they may be, the gods or spirits venerated in a given culture tend to have certain personality or character traits. They may be unpredictable or predictable, aloof from or interested in human affairs, helpful or punishing. Why do the gods and spirits in a particular culture exhibit certain character traits rather than others?

We have some evidence from cross-cultural studies that the character of supernatural beings may be related to the nature of child training. Melford Spiro and Roy D'Andrade suggested that the god-human relationship is a projection of the parent-child relationship, in which case child-training practices might well be relived in dealings with the supernatural.[20] For example, if a child was nurtured immediately by her parents when she cried or waved her arms about or kicked, she might grow up expecting to be nurtured by the gods when she attracted their attention by performing a ritual. On the other hand, if her parents often punished her, she would grow up expecting the gods to punish her if she disobeyed them. William Lambert, Leigh Minturn Triandis, and Margery Wolf, in another cross-cultural study, found that societies with hurtful or punitive child-training practices are likely to believe that their gods are aggressive and malevolent; societies with less punitive child training are more likely to believe that the gods are benevolent.[21] These results are consistent with the Freudian notion that the supernatural world should parallel the natural. It is worth noting in this context that some peoples refer to the god as their father and to themselves as his children.

Structure or Hierarchy of Supernatural Beings

The range of social structures in human societies from egalitarian to highly stratified has its counterpart in the supernatural world. Some societies have gods or spirits that are not ranked; one god has about as much power as another. Other societies have gods or spirits that are ranked in prestige and power. For example, on the Pacific islands of Palau, which was a rank society, gods were ranked as people were. Each clan worshiped a god and a goddess that had names or titles similar to clan titles. Although a clan god was generally important only to the members of that clan, the gods of the various clans in a village were believed to be ranked in the same order that the clans were. Thus, the god of the highest-ranking clan was respected by all the clans of the village. Its shrine was given the place of honor in the center of the village and was larger and more elaborately decorated than other shrines.[22]

Although the Palauans did not believe in a high god or supreme being who outranked all the other gods, some societies do. Consider Judaism, Christianity, and Islam, which we call **monotheistic** religions. Although *monotheism* means "one god," most monotheistic religions actually include more than one supernatural being (e.g., demons, angels, the Devil). But the supreme being or high god, as the creator of the universe or the director of events (or both), is believed to be ultimately responsible for all events.[23] A **polytheistic** religion recognizes many important gods, no one of which is supreme.

Why do some societies have a belief in a high god and others do not? Recall Swanson's suggestion that people invent gods who personify the important decision-making groups in their society. He therefore hypothesized that societies with hierarchical political systems should be more likely to believe in a high god. In his cross-cultural study of 50 societies (none of which practiced any of the major world religions), he found that belief in a high god is strongly associated with three or more levels of "sovereign" (decision-making) groups. Of the 20 sample societies that had a hierarchy of three or more sovereign groups—for instance, family, clan, and chiefdom—17 possessed the idea of a high god. Of the 19 societies that had fewer than three levels of decision-making groups, only two had a high god.[24] Consistent with Swanson's findings, societies dependent on food production are more likely to have a belief in a high god than are food-collecting societies.[25] These results strongly suggest, then, that the realm of the gods parallels and may reflect the everyday social and political worlds. In the past, many state societies had state religions in which the political officials were also the officials of the temples (e.g., the pharaohs in Egypt). In recent times, most state societies have separated church and state, as in the United States and Canada.

Intervention of the Gods in Human Affairs

According to Clifford Geertz, when people face ignorance, pain, and the unjustness of life, they explain the events by the intervention of the gods.[26] Thus, in Greek religion, the direct intervention of Poseidon as ruler of the seas prevented Odysseus from getting home for 10 years. In the Old Testament, the direct intervention of Yahweh caused the great flood that killed most of the people in the time of Noah. In other societies, people may search their memories for a violated taboo that has brought punishment through supernatural intervention.

In addition to unasked-for divine interference, there are numerous examples of requests for divine intervention, either for good for oneself and friends or for evil for others. Gods are asked to intervene in the weather and to make the crops grow, to send fish to the fisherman and game to the hunter, to find lost things, and to accompany travelers and prevent accidents. They are asked to stop the flow of lava down the side of a volcano, to stop a war, or to cure an illness.

The gods do not intervene in all societies. In some, they intervene in human affairs; in others, they are not the slightest bit interested; and in still others, they interfere only occasionally. We have little research on why gods are believed to interfere in some societies and not in others. We do, however, have some evidence suggesting when the gods will take an interest in the morality or immorality of human behavior. Swanson's study suggests that the gods are likely to punish people for immoral behavior when there are considerable differences in wealth in the society.[27] His interpretation is that supernatural support of moral behavior is particularly useful where inequalities tax the ability of the political system to maintain social order and minimize social disorder. Envy of others' privileges may motivate some people to behave immorally; the belief that the gods will punish such behavior might deter it. More generally, the concern of gods with moral behavior is more likely in large, complex societies (see the box "Religion: A Force for Harmony and Cooperation?").

Life after Death

In many societies, ideas about an afterlife are vague and seemingly unimportant, but many other peoples have very definite and elaborate ideas of what happens after death. The Lugbara of Uganda see the dead as joining the ancestors of the living and staying near the family homesite. They retain an interest in the behavior of the living, both rewarding and punishing them. The Zuni of the southwestern United States think the dead join the past dead, known as the *katcinas,* in a katcina village at the bottom of a nearby lake. There they lead a life of singing and dancing and bring rain to the living Zuni. Just as they are swift to punish the priest who fails in his duty, they also punish the people in masks who ineffectively impersonate the katcinas during the dance ceremonies.[28]

The Chamulas have merged the ancient Mayan worship of the sun and moon with the Spanish conquerors' Jesus and Mary. Their vision of life after death contains a blending of the two cultures. All souls go to the underworld, where they live a humanlike life except that they are incapable of sexual intercourse. After the sun travels over the world, it travels under the underworld, so that the dead have sunlight. Only murderers and suicides are punished, being burned by the Christ-sun on their journey.[29]

Many Christians believe that the dead are divided into two groups: The unsaved are sent to everlasting

applied anthropology

Religion: A Force for Cooperation and Harmony?

Most social science theories about religion suggest that religious beliefs and rituals promote social cohesion and cooperation within the group that shares them. Some religions, including the major religions in the modern world (Buddhism, Christianity, Islam, Hinduism, Judaism), are more explicit than others in their direct concern with moral behavior. Moralizing religions believe that the gods will reward moral behavior and punish immoral behavior, and are generally found in large and complex societies. Such societies are likely to have towns or cities and less reliance on kinship and reciprocity to encourage moral behavior. Neighbors may not know each other well and although there may be codified law and courts, these mechanisms may not be sufficient to promote social order. Complex societies are also likely to have a large amount of social inequality, which increases the likelihood of property-related crime. The cross-cultural evidence is consistent with the theory that morality-based religions and collective rituals minimize antisocial behavior in groups of unrelated individuals. Perhaps to promote solidarity among unrelated people, religions in complex societies often extend kin terms to members of the religious communities, calling each other "brothers" and "sisters" or sometimes "God's children." Experimental evidence suggests individuals are more generous toward strangers if their religious feelings have been aroused. Religious communes are also four times as likely to survive compared with secular communes.

These studies raise important questions about exactly why and when moralizing religions came into existence and whether the spread of these religions had to do with their adaptive consequences. But there are also questions raised about mechanisms. For example, religious communes, as compared with secular communes, usually impose more requirements from members, such as food taboos, fasts, constraints on sex and possessions, and so on. A comparative study of communes suggests that the religious elements are more important than the commitments themselves. However, in experimental research, there are some hints that nonreligious conditions could also make people more cooperative. Experimental reminders of secular morality had as much effect as reminders of God. Also, there are examples of modern societies, especially in northern Europe, that are very cooperative, but not very religious.

But, even if religious belief and ritual promote greater in-group trust and cooperation, there is a dark side to strongly held religious belief—the potential for greater out-group conflict. History is replete with examples of people hurting others in the name of religion. Christianity and Islam are the two largest religions, possibly because of their zeal to convert others. Some of the biggest conflicts have occurred where the two largest religions meet. The Christian Crusades of the 11th century through 13th century were attempts to "liberate" sites in the Holy Land controlled by Muslims. Osama bin Laden cited the establishment of U.S. bases in Saudi Arabia, which "defiled" sacred lands in his view, as justification for the September 11, 2001, attacks on the United States. Religions, or, more precisely, religious groups, do not necessarily promote violence. After all, some of the founders of various religions preached nonviolence and harmony. Exactly what persuades a religious group to commit violence is not well understood. There are five warning signs. One is when leaders act as if only they know the truth. A second is a call to blind obedience to a religious leader. A third is when the people believe it is possible to establish an "ideal world." A fourth is acting as if "the end justifies the means." Lastly, and perhaps the clearest, is a call for "a holy war."

In the globalized world today, there is more admixture of all types—heterogeneous cities full of people of different colors, dress, ethnicities, and religions. This situation has two potential outcomes—the potential for different groups to live together peacefully, or a greater potential for violence. Whether the major religions will adapt to create a new morality for the new global circumstances remains to be seen. Research has not told us enough yet about how to achieve more harmony across different religions or across different ethnicities. We can hope that simply learning more about other individuals and groups—their hopes, dreams, and expectations, how they have adapted to their environments—may enhance tolerance.

Sources: Winkelman and Baker 2010, 259–65; 314-318; Norenzayan and Shariff 2008; Sosis and Bressler 2003; Stark 2001; Roes and Raymond 2003.

punishment and the saved to everlasting reward. Accounts differ, but hell is often associated with torture by fire, heaven with mansions. Several societies see the dead as returning to earth to be reborn. The Hindus use this pattern of reincarnation to justify one's caste in this life and to promise eventual release from the pain of life through the attainment of *nirvana*, or inclusion into the One.

A recent cross-cultural study asks why some societies judge where you will go after death and others do not. Support was found for the idea that judgmental beliefs parallel the society's economic practices. Some societies have considerable delay between labor inputs and return of food. For example, intensive agriculturalists need considerable labor input to plow, fertilize, or create irrigation systems, and many months go by until crops can be

A ghost festival in Thailand. The belief in ghosts is practically a cross-cultural universal.

harvested. Not planning ahead has dire long-term consequences. In contrast, mistakes by hunter-gatherers are realized more quickly and can be corrected more quickly. Religions that foster the idea that actions in the present will be judged after death reinforce the need for long-term planning. Consistent with this idea, societies with intensive agriculture are the most likely to believe that their actions in life affect where their souls will go after death.[30] This finding is consistent with Swanson's conclusion discussed previously that the gods are generally likely to punish people for immoral behavior when there are considerable differences in wealth in the society. Intensive agricultural societies tend to have considerable differences in wealth.

In many respects, the afterworld in many religions may resemble the everyday world, but we still have only a few comparative studies that show exactly how.

VARIATION IN RELIGIOUS PRACTICES

Beliefs are not the only elements of religion that vary from society to society. Societies vary in the kinds of religious practitioners they have. There is also variation in how people interact with the supernatural. The manner of approach to the supernatural varies from supplication—requests, prayers, and so on—to manipulation. Many of these interactions are highly *ritualized*. **Rituals** are repetitive sets of behaviors that occur in essentially the same patterns every time they occur. Religious rituals involve the supernatural in some way. They are generally collective, follow customary patterns, and are thought to strengthen faith.[31]

Ways to Interact with the Supernatural

How to get in touch with the supernatural has proved to be a universal problem. Wallace identified a number of

ways people the world over use, though not necessarily all together, including, but not limited to, prayer (asking for supernatural help), physiological experience (doing things to the body and mind), simulation (manipulating imitations of things), feasts, and sacrifices.[32] Prayer can be spontaneous or memorized, private or public, silent or spoken. The Lugbara do not say the words of a prayer aloud, for doing so would be too powerful; they simply think about the things that are bothering them. The gods know all languages.

Doing things to the body or mind may involve drugs (hallucinogenics such as peyote or opiates) or alcohol; social isolation or sensory deprivation; dancing or running until exhausted; being deprived of food, water, and sleep; and listening to repetitive sounds such as drumming. Such behaviors may induce trances or altered states of consciousness.[33] Erika Bourguignon found that achieving these altered states, which she generally referred to as *trances*, is part of religious practice in 90 percent of the world's societies.[34] In some societies, trances are thought to involve the presence of a spirit or power inside a person that changes or displaces that person's personality or soul. These types are referred to as possession trances. Other types of trances may involve the journey of a person's soul, experiencing visions, or transmitting messages from spirits. Possession trances are especially likely in societies that depend on agriculture and have social stratification, slavery, and more complex political hierarchies. Nonpossession trances are most likely to occur in food-collecting societies. Societies with moderate levels of social complexity have both possession and nonpossession trances.[35]

One puzzle is why there is a preponderance of women thought to be possessed. Alice Kehoe and Dody Giletti suggested that women are more likely than men to suffer from nutritional deficiencies because of pregnancy, lactation, and men's priority in gaining access to food. Calcium deficiency in particular can cause muscular spasms, convulsive seizures, and disorientation, all of which may foster the belief that an individual is possessed.[36] Douglas

Raybeck and his colleagues suggest that women's physiology makes them more susceptible to calcium deficiency even with an equivalent diet. In addition, women are subject to more stress because they are usually less able to control their lives. Higher levels of stress, they suggest, lower the body's reserves of calcium.[37] Erika Bourguignon suggests a more psychological explanation of women's preponderance in possession trances. In many societies, women are brought up to be submissive. But when possessed, women are taken over by spirits and they are not responsible for what they do or say—therefore, they can unconsciously do what they are not able to do consciously.[38] Although intriguing, these suggestions need to be tested on individuals in field situations.

Voodoo employs simulation, or the imitation of things. Dolls are made in the likeness of an enemy and then are maltreated in hopes that the original enemy will experience pain and even death.

Divination seeks practical answers from the supernatural about anything that is troublesome—decisions to be made, interpersonal problems, or illness. (We discuss divination's role in curing illness in the chapter on medical anthropology.) Diviners use a variety of methods, including altered states of consciousness and simulation through the use of objects such as Ouija boards or tarot cards.[39]

Omar Moore suggested that, among the Naskapi hunters of Labrador, divination is an adaptive strategy for successful hunting. The Naskapi consult the diviner every three or four days when they have no luck in hunting. The diviner holds a caribou bone over the fire, as if the bone were a map, and the burns and cracks that appear in it indicate where the group should hunt. Moore, unlike the Naskapi, did not believe that the diviner really can find out where the animals will be; the cracks in the bones merely provide a way of randomly choosing where to hunt. Because humans are likely to develop customary patterns of action, they might be likely to look for game according to some plan. But game might learn to avoid hunters who operate according to a plan. Thus, any method of ensuring against patterning or predictable plans—any random strategy—may be advantageous. Divination by "reading" the bones would seem to be a random strategy. It also relieves any individual of the responsibility of deciding where to hunt, a decision that might arouse anger if the hunt failed.[40]

The eating of a sacred meal is found in many religions. For instance, Holy Communion is a simulation of the Last Supper. Australian aborigines, normally forbidden to eat their totem animal, have one totem feast a year at which they eat the totem. Feasts are often part of marriage and funeral ceremonies, as well as a fringe benefit of the sacrifice of food to the gods.

Some societies make sacrifices to a god in order to influence the god's action, either to divert anger or to attract goodwill. Characteristic of all sacrifices is that something of value is given up to the gods, whether it be food, drink, sex, household goods, or the life of an animal or person. Some societies feel that the god is obligated to act on their behalf if they make the appropriate sacrifice.

A woman with offerings at a Hindu temple in Bali.

Others use the sacrifice in an attempt to persuade the god, realizing there is no guarantee that the attempt will be successful.

Of all types of sacrifice, we probably think that the taking of human life is the ultimate. Nevertheless, human sacrifice is not rare in the ethnographic and historical records. Why have some societies practiced it? One cross-cultural study found that, among preindustrial societies, those with full-time craft specialists, slavery, and the corvée are most likely to practice human sacrifice. The suggested explanation is that the sacrifice mirrors what is socially important: Societies that depend mainly on human labor for energy (rather than animals or machines) may think of a human life as an appropriate offering to the gods when people want something very important.[41] Later studies found that societies with human sacrifice were at a mid-range level of political complexity, having alliances and confederacies with other polities, but only weak political integration. Such societies also seemed to be subject to population pressure and frequently carried out warfare for land and other resources. Human sacrifice, with humans from the outside groups, may have been an attempt to terrorize people from the other polities.[42]

Magic

All these modes of interacting with the supernatural can be categorized in various ways. One dimension of variation is how much people in society rely on pleading, asking, or trying to persuade the supernatural to act on their behalf, as opposed to whether they believe they can compel the supernatural to help by performing certain acts. For example, prayer is asking; performing voodoo is presumably compelling. When people believe their action can compel the supernatural to act in some particular and intended way, anthropologists often refer to the belief and related practice as **magic.**

Magic may involve manipulation of the supernatural for good or for evil. Many societies have magical rituals designed to ensure good crops, the replenishment of game, the fertility of domestic animals, and the avoidance and cure of illness in humans. We tend to associate the belief in magic with societies simpler than our own, but some people in complex societies take magic seriously and many follow some magical practices.

People who engage in risky activities may try to ensure their safety by carrying or wearing lucky charms. They believe the charms protect them by invoking the help of supernatural beings or forces. We might also believe we can protect ourselves by not doing some things. For example, baseball players on a hitting streak may choose not to change their socks or sweatshirt for the next game (to continue their luck). Why magic appeals to some individuals but not others in our own society may help us explain why magic is an important part of religious behavior in many societies.

As we will see, the witch doctor and the shaman often employ magic to effect a cure. But the use of magic to bring about harm has evoked perhaps the most interest.

Sorcery and Witchcraft   Sorcery and witchcraft are attempts to invoke the spirits to work harm against people. Although the words *sorcery* and *witchcraft* are often used interchangeably, they are also often distinguished. **Sorcery** may include the use of materials, objects, and medicines to invoke supernatural malevolence. **Witchcraft** may be said to accomplish the same ills by means of thought and emotion alone. Evidence of witchcraft can never be found. This lack of visible evidence makes an accusation of witchcraft both harder to prove and harder to disprove.

To the Azande of Zaire, in central Africa, witchcraft was part of everyday living. It was not used to explain events for which the cause was known, such as carelessness or violation of a taboo, but to explain the otherwise unexplainable. A man is gored by an elephant. He must have been bewitched, because he had not been gored on other elephant hunts. A man goes to his beer hut at night, lights some straw, and holds it aloft to look at his beer. The thatch catches fire and the hut burns down. The man has been bewitched, for huts did not catch fire on hundreds of other nights when he and others did the same thing. Some of the pots of a skilled potter break; some of the bowls of a skilled carver crack. Witchcraft. Other pots, other bowls treated exactly the same have not broken.[43]

The witch craze in Europe during the 16th and 17th centuries and the witch trials in 1692 in Salem, Massachusetts, remind us that the fear of others, which the belief in witchcraft presumably represents, can increase and decrease in a society within a relatively short period of time. Many scholars have tried to explain these witch hunts. One factor often suggested is political turmoil, which may give rise to widespread distrust and a search for scapegoats. In the case of Europe during the 16th and 17th cen-

turies, small regional political units were being incorporated into national states, and political allegiances were in flux. In addition, as Swanson noted, the commercial revolution and related changes were producing a new social class, the middle class, and "were promoting the growth of Protestantism and other heresies from Roman Catholicism."[44] In the case of Salem, the government of Massachusetts colony was unstable and there was much internal dissension. In 1692, the year of the witchcraft hysteria, Massachusetts was left without an English governor, and judicial practices broke down. These extraordinary conditions saw the accusation of a single person for witchcraft become the accusation of hundreds and the execution of 20 people. Swanson suggested that the undermining of legitimate political procedures may have generated the widespread fear of witches.[45]

It is also possible that epidemics of witchcraft accusation, like in Salem as well as other New England and European communities, may be the result of real epidemics—epidemics of disease. The disease implicated in Salem and elsewhere is the fungus disease called ergot, which can grow on rye plants. (The rye flour that went into the bread that the Salem people ate may have been contaminated by ergot.) It is now known that people who eat grain products contaminated by ergot suffer from convulsions, hallucinations, and other symptoms, such as crawling sensations in the skin. We also now know that ergot contains LSD, the drug that produces hallucinations and other delusions that resemble those occurring in severe mental disorders.

The presumed victims of bewitchment in Salem and other places had symptoms similar to victims of ergot poisoning today. They suffered from convulsions and the sensations of being pricked, pinched, or bitten. They had visions and felt as if they were flying through the air. We cannot know for sure that ergot poisoning occurred during those times when witchcraft accusations flourished. There is no direct evidence, of course, because the "bewitched" were not medically tested. But we do have some evidence that seems to be consistent with the ergot theory. Ergot is known to flourish on rye plants under certain climatic conditions—particularly a very cold winter followed by a cool, moist spring and summer. Tree-ring growth indicates that the early 1690s were particularly cold in eastern New England, and the outbreaks of witchcraft accusation in Europe seem to have peaked with colder winter temperatures.[46] Interestingly, too, when witchcraft hysteria was greatest in Europe, Europeans were using an ointment containing a skin-penetrating substance that we now know produces hallucinations and a vivid sensation of flying.[47] It may not be cause for wonder, then, that our popular image of witches is of people flying through the air on broomsticks.

But whether or not epidemics of witchcraft hysteria are due to epidemics of ergot poisoning or episodes of political turmoil or both, we still have to understand why so many societies in the ethnographic record believe in witchcraft and sorcery in the first place. Why do so many societies believe that there are ways to invoke the spirits to work harm against people? One possible explanation, suggested by Beatrice Whiting, is that sorcery or witchcraft will be found in societies that lack procedures or judicial authorities to deal with crime and other offenses. Her theory is that all societies need some form of social control—some way of deterring most would-be offenders and of dealing with actual offenders. In the absence of judicial officials who, if present, might deter and deal with antisocial behavior, sorcery may be a very effective mechanism for social control. If you misbehave, the person you mistreated might cause you to become ill or even die. The cross-cultural evidence seems to support this theory. Sorcery is more important in societies that lack judicial authorities than in those that have them.[48]

Types of Practitioners

Individuals may believe that they can directly contact the supernatural, but almost all societies also have part-time or full-time religious or magical practitioners. Research suggests there are four major types of practitioners: shamans, sorcerers or witches, mediums, and priests. As we shall see, the number of types of practitioners in a society seems to vary with degree of cultural complexity.[49]

The Shaman   The word *shaman* may come from a language that was spoken in eastern Siberia. The **shaman** is usually a part-time male specialist who has fairly high status in his community and is often involved in healing.[50] We discuss the role of the shaman as healer in the chapter on applied, practicing, and medical anthropology. More generally, the shaman deals with the spirit world to try to get their help or to keep them from causing harm.[51] Here we focus on the methods shamans use to help others.

The shaman enters into a trance, or some other altered state of consciousness, and then journeys to other worlds to get help from guardians or other spirits. Dreams may be used to provide insight or as a way for shamans to commune with spirits. People may seek help for practical matters, such as where to get food resources or whether to relocate, but solving a health problem is most often the goal of the shaman.[52] Shamans may also bring news from spirits, such as a warning about an impending disaster.[53]

Someone may receive a "call" to the role of shaman in recovering from an illness, through a vision quest, or in a dream. Shamans-in-training may enhance the vividness of their imagery by using hallucinogens, sleep or food deprivation, or engaging in extensive physical activity such as dancing. An important part of the process of being a shaman is learning to control the imagery and the spirit powers. Shamanistic training can take several years under the guidance of a master shaman.[54]

Sorcerers and Witches   In contrast with shamans, who have fairly high status, sorcerers and witches of both sexes tend to have very low social and economic status in their societies.[55] Suspected sorcerers and witches are usually feared because they are thought to know how to invoke the supernatural to cause illness, injury, and death. Because sorcerers use materials for their magic, evidence of sorcery can be found, and suspected sorcerers are often killed for their malevolent activities. Because witchcraft supposedly is accomplished by thought and emotion alone, it may be harder to prove that someone is a witch, but the difficulty of proving witchcraft has not prevented people from accusing and killing others for being witches.

Mediums   **Mediums** tend to be females. These part-time practitioners are asked to heal and divine while in possession trances—that is, when they are thought to be possessed by spirits. Mediums are described as having tremors, convulsions, seizures, and temporary amnesia.

Priests   **Priests** are generally full-time male specialists who officiate at public events. They have very high status

Shamans are usually male. Here, female shamans in Korea perform a healing ritual.

and are thought to be able to relate to superior or high gods who are beyond the ordinary person's control. In most societies with priests, the people who get to be priests obtain their offices through inheritance or political appointment.[56] Priests are sometimes distinguished from other people by special clothing or a different hairstyle. The training of a priest can be vigorous and long, including fasting, praying, and physical labor, as well as learning the dogma and the ritual of his religion. Priests in the United States complete four years of theological school and sometimes serve first as apprentices under established priests. Priests do not receive a fee for their services but are supported by donations from parishioners or followers. Priests often have some political power as a result of their office—the chief priest is sometimes also the head of state or is a close adviser to the chief of state—and their material well-being is a direct reflection of their position in the priestly hierarchy.

The dependence on memorized ritual both marks and protects the priest. If a shaman repeatedly fails to effect a cure, he will probably lose his following, for he has obviously lost the support of the spirits. But if a priest performs his ritual perfectly and the gods choose not to respond, the priest will usually retain his position and the ritual will preserve its assumed effectiveness. The nonresponse of the gods will be explained in terms of the people's unworthiness of supernatural favor.

Practitioners and Social Complexity   More complex societies tend to have more types of religious or magical practitioners. If a society has only one type of practitioner, it is almost always a shaman; such societies tend to be nomadic or seminomadic food collectors. Societies with two types of practitioners (usually shaman healers and priests) have agriculture. Those with three types of practitioners are agriculturalists or pastoralists with political integration beyond the community (the additional practitioner type tends to be either a sorcerer or witch or a medium). Finally, societies with all four types of practitioners have agriculture, political integration beyond the community, and social classes.[57]

RELIGION AND ADAPTATION

Following Malinowski, many anthropologists take the view that religions are adaptive because they reduce the anxieties and uncertainties that afflict all peoples. We do not really know that religion is the only means of reducing anxiety and uncertainty, or even that individuals or societies *have* to reduce their anxiety and uncertainty. Still, it seems likely that certain religious beliefs and practices have directly adaptive consequences. For example, the Hindu belief in the sacred cow has seemed to many to be the very opposite of a useful or adaptive custom. Their religion does not permit Hindus to slaughter cows. Why do the Hindus retain such a belief? Why do they allow all those cows to wander around freely, defecating all over the place, and not slaughter any of them? The contrast with our own use of cows could hardly be greater.

Marvin Harris suggested that the Hindu use of cows may have beneficial consequences that some other use of cows would not have. Harris pointed out that there may be a sound economic reason for not slaughtering cattle in India. The cows, and the males they produce, provide resources that could not easily be gotten otherwise. At the same time, their wandering around to forage is no strain on the food-producing economy.

The resources provided by the cows are varied. First, a team of oxen and a plow are essential for the many small farms in India. The Indians could produce oxen with fewer cows, but to do so, they would have to devote some of their food production to feeding those cows. In the present system, they do not feed the cows, and even though poor nutrition makes the cows relatively infertile, males, which are castrated to make oxen, are still produced at no cost to the economy. Second, cow dung is essential as a cooking fuel and fertilizer. The National Council of Applied Economic Research estimated that an amount of dung equivalent to 45 million tons of coal is burned annually. Moreover, it is delivered practically to the door each day at no cost. Alternative sources of fuel, such as wood, are scarce or costly. In addition, about 340 million tons of dung are used as manure—essential in a country obliged to derive three harvests a year from its intensively cultivated land. Third, although Hindus do not eat beef, cattle that die naturally or are butchered by non-Hindus are eaten by the lower castes, who, without the upper-caste taboo against eating beef, might not get this needed protein. Fourth, the hides and horns of the cattle that die are used in India's enormous leather industry. Therefore, because the cows do not themselves consume resources needed by people and it would be impossible to provide traction, fuel, and fertilizer as cheaply by other means, the taboo against slaughtering cattle may be very adaptive.[58]

RELIGIOUS CHANGE

In any society, religious beliefs and practices change over time, but some types of change are quite dramatic. Perhaps the most dramatic is religious conversion, particularly when large numbers of people switch to a completely new religion presented by missionaries or other proselytizers. Changing religion so drastically is perplexing to many scholars of religion who believe that religious beliefs are deeply connected to one's sense of identity, one's family, one's community, and ideas about the world.[59] Within the last few centuries, conversion has sometimes followed Western expansion and exploration. Contact with Westerners and other outsiders has also produced religious change in more indirect ways. In some native societies, contact has led to a breakdown of social structure and the growth of feelings of helplessness and spiritual demoralization. *Revitalization movements* have arisen as apparent attempts to restore such societies to their former confidence and prosperity. In recent times, religious *fundamentalist* movements have flourished. Some scholars have argued that such movements are also responses to the stress of rapid social change.

A Catholic mass under open skies conducted by missionaries among the Karamojong of Uganda.

As we will see, religious change, particularly of the dramatic kind, usually does not occur in a vacuum, but is often associated with other dramatic changes—economic, political, and demographic.

Religious Conversion

The two world religions with the greatest interest now in obtaining converts have been Christianity and Islam. Christian missionaries, supported by their churches back home, have been some of the earliest Western settlers in interior regions and out-of-the-way places. Traders have been the main proselytizers of Islam. Conversion to one of the world religions has often been associated with colonization and the expansion of state societies (see the box on colonialism and religious affiliation). The presence of people from other religions does not necessarily mean that people convert to the new religion. For example, missionaries have not met with equal success in all parts of the world. In some places, large portions of the native population have converted to the new religion with great zeal. In others, missionaries have been ignored, forced to flee, or even killed. We do not fully understand why missionaries have been successful in some societies and not in others.

We now examine the process of conversion on the island of Tikopia, as an example of religious change brought about by direct contact with missionaries.

Christianity on Tikopia   Tikopia was one of the few Polynesian societies to retain its traditional religious system into the first decades of the 20th century. An Anglican mission was first established on the island in 1911. With it came a deacon and the founding of two schools for about

200 pupils. By 1929, approximately half the population had converted, and in the early 1960s, almost all of Tikopia gave at least nominal allegiance to Christianity.[60]

Traditional Tikopian belief embraced a great number of gods and spirits of various ranks who inhabited the sky, the water, and the land. One god in particular—the original creator and shaper of the culture—was given a place of special importance, but he was in no way comparable to the all-powerful God of Christianity. Unlike Christianity, Tikopian religion made no claim to universality. The Tikopian gods did not rule over all creation, only over Tikopia. It was thought that if one left Tikopia, one left the gods behind.

The people of Tikopia interacted with their gods and spirits primarily through religious leaders who were also the heads of descent groups. Clan chiefs presided over rituals associated with the everyday aspects of island life, such as house construction, fishing, planting, and harvesting. The chief was expected to intercede with the gods on the people's behalf, to persuade them to bring happiness and prosperity to the group. Indeed, when conditions were good, it was assumed that the chief was doing his job well. When disaster struck, the prestige of the chief often fell in proportion. Why did the Tikopia convert to Christianity? Firth suggested several contributing factors.

First, the mission offered the people the prospect of acquiring new tools and consumer goods. Although conversion alone did not provide such benefits, attachment to the mission made them more attainable. Later, it became apparent that education, particularly in reading and writing English, was helpful in getting ahead in the outside world. Mission schooling became valued and provided a further incentive for adopting Christianity.

Second, conversion may have been facilitated by the ability of chiefs, as religious and political leaders, to bring over entire descent groups to Christianity. Should a chief decide to transfer his allegiance to Christianity, the members of his kin group usually followed him. In 1923, when Tafua, chief of the Faea district of Tikopia, converted to the new religion, he brought with him his entire group—nearly half the population of the island. The ability of the chiefs to influence their kin groups, however, was both an asset and a hindrance to missionary efforts, because some chiefs steadfastly resisted conversion.

A final blow to traditional Tikopian religion came in 1955, when a severe epidemic killed at least 200 people in a population of about 1,700. According to Firth, "the epidemic was largely interpreted as a sign of divine discrimination," because three of the outstanding non-Christian religious leaders died.[61] Subsequently, the remaining non-Christian chiefs voluntarily converted to Christianity, and so did their followers. By 1966, all Tikopia, with the exception of one old woman, had converted to the new faith.

Although many Tikopians feel their conversion to Christianity has been a unifying, revitalizing force, the changeover from one religion to another has not been without problems. Christian missionaries on Tikopia have succeeded in eliminating the traditional Tikopian population-control devices of abortion, infanticide, and male

migrants and immigrants

Colonialism and Religious Affiliation

Many of us might like to think that we belong to a particular religious group because we prefer its beliefs and practices. And that may be true for people who have chosen to switch their religious affiliation. But many religious people affiliate with the religion they grew up with, or one very much like it.

Clearly, religious affiliation is a complex issue. But one thing stands out. You are not likely to choose an affiliation you have never been exposed to. This goes for people who believe in religion and also for people who don't. Most North Americans say they are Christians. But how come?

Would so many in North America be Christians if Europeans (mostly Christian) hadn't established colonies here and elsewhere in the last 500 years? Would there be Muslims in Indonesia, the Philippines, and North Africa if Arab kingdoms hadn't established colonies in those places after the 7th century? Would there have been Hindus in Sumatra if South Asians hadn't migrated and established the Srivijayan kingdom in Sumatra before the time of Christ? Would there have been Jews in

Yemen (until their emigration to Israel 50 years ago) if King Solomon's state had not colonized in the land of the Queen of Sheba more than 2,000 years ago? An expanding state society can directly or indirectly force a change in people's religious affiliation. It is not coincidental that the new religious affiliation usually matches the dominant society's.

Religion in some form may be a cultural universal. People may worship the supernatural, pray to it for help and guidance, and even try to control it (with "lucky charms" and other magic). But religion is not the same everywhere, as is evident in this chapter. Why people convert to a major religion carried by an expanding state society is still not completely understood. Sometimes the people do not convert, or do not convert right away. Anthropologist Elizabeth Brusco has written that one primary motivation for conversion, long recognized by scholars, is the desire to maximize advantages. In recent times, missionaries have offered new beliefs and practices that may be appealing, but they have also offered what

Brusco calls "protection, access to food and other desirable goods, medical care, literacy, technology, status, and, at times, political power." Was the same true, at least somewhat, in the past? Was adopting the new religion the best way to survive colonialism and its consequences?

Even if people adopt a religion, they often change important parts of it. For example, the Lahu of southwest China became Buddhist but the Buddha became a male-female couple rather than just a male. The Lahu were a stateless society (prior to the expansion of the Han Chinese) with a strong emphasis on gender equality. By identifying Buddha with their indigenous god, Xeul Sha, the image of the Buddha was changed. According to Lahu origin myths, Xeul Sha is a male-female pair of twins. They marry and propagate humanity. The identification of Xeul Sha with Buddha means that Buddha is considered a pair of male-female gods by most Lahu Buddhist villagers.

Sources: Brusco 1996; Stevens 1996; Du 2003.

---

celibacy. It is very possible that the absence of these controls will continue to intensify population pressure. The island, with its limited capacity to support life, can ill afford this outcome. Firth summed up the situation Tikopian society faced:

> In the history of Tikopia complete conversion of the people to Christianity was formerly regarded as a solution to their problems; it is now coming to be realized that the adoption and practice of Christianity itself represents another set of problems. As the Tikopia themselves are beginning to see, to be Christian Polynesians in the modern technologically and industrially dominated world, even in the Solomon Islands, poses as many questions as it supplies answers.[62]

Unfortunately, not all native peoples have made the transition to Christianity as painlessly as the Tikopia. In fact, the record is dismal in most cases. All too frequently, missionary activity tends to destroy a society's culture

and self-respect. It offers nothing in return but an alien, repressive system of values ill suited to the people's real needs and aspirations. Phillip Mason, a critic of European evangelists in Africa, pointed out some of the psychological damage inflicted by missionary activity.[63] The missionaries repeatedly stressed sin and guilt; they used the color black to represent evil and the color white to signify good; and they showed hostility toward pagan culture. Most damaging of all was their promise that Africans, provided they adopted the European's ways, would gain access both to the European's heaven and to European society. But no matter how diligently Africans attempted to follow missionary precepts or climb the socioeconomic ladder, they were soon blocked from entry into European homes, clubs, and even churches and seminaries.

Explaining Conversion Anthropologists have just begun to try to understand religious conversion. As the box on colonialism and religious affiliation and the Tikopia case suggest, some of the motivation for switching to a new religion may have to do with economic and political advantages associated with converting to the new religion. With regard to the recent spread of Islam in Africa, Jean Ensminger suggests that Islam provided opportunities for those who wanted to engage in trade— "Islam brought a common language of trade (Arabic), a monetary system, an accounting system, and a legal code to adjudicate financial contracts and disputes."[64] These institutions were shared across ethnic groups, making it possible to engage in long-distance trade. But what increased the attractiveness of Islamic trade? Ensminger's study of the Orma, a pastoralist group in Kenya, is instructive, for despite the presence of Islam for 300 years, it did not appear to be of interest to them. The Orma chiefs did trade, but the Orma were mostly self-sufficient and the need for trade appeared to be relatively low. However, the Orma were in serious trouble after successful attacks by the Masai and Somali in the late 1800s, which almost decimated them and depleted their cattle. After 1920, as they began to recover their population somewhat and their cattle began to be replenished, there was rapid conversion to Islam, mostly led by the young, who perhaps were attracted by the economic opportunities.[65]

Loss of population and the demoralization that it brings may also have played a significant role in conversion. Daniel Reff, comparing widespread conversion to Christianity in the Roman Empire after A.D. 150 and in northern Mexico after A.D. 1593, notes the parallels in both. In both situations, there were ravaging epidemics along with the presence of Christian personnel ready to help heal the sick. In Europe, about 8 percent of the population died before smallpox epidemics subsided in A.D. 190, and population continued to decline into the Middle Ages, perhaps to half of what it was. Population losses might have been more extreme in Mexico. In northern Mexico, an estimated 75 percent of the native populations died from disease. In Europe, Christians provided charity, food, and shelter for the ill, without regard to their status. The Jesuit missions in Mexico did not have that many personnel, but they did what they could to provide food, water, and "medicine."[66] Do epidemics play a role in other places? An exploratory cross-cultural study suggests that rapid population loss, usually from introduced diseases, predicts religious conversion, particularly when people believe that their traditional gods could help them.[67] If gods could have helped but didn't and people are dying in unusual numbers, people may think that the "gods have failed." In such circumstances, it is not surprising that people would be receptive to a new religion, particularly if it is preached by missionaries who are not dying.

Revitalization

The long history of religion includes periods of strong resistance to change as well as periods of radical change. Anthropologists have been especially interested in the founding of new religions or sects. The appearance of new religions is one of the things that may happen when cultures are disrupted by contact with dominant societies. Various terms have been suggested for these religious movements— cargo cults, nativistic movements, messianic movements, millenarian cults. Wallace suggested that they are all examples of **revitalization movements,** efforts to save a culture by infusing it with a new purpose and new life.[68] We turn to examples of such movements from North America and Melanesia.

The Seneca and the Religion of Handsome Lake The Seneca reservation of the Iroquois on the Allegheny River in New York State was a place of "poverty and humiliation" by 1799.[69] Demoralized by whiskey and dispossessed from their traditional lands, unable to compete with the new technology because of illiteracy and lack of training, the Seneca were at an impasse. In this setting, Handsome Lake, the 50-year-old brother of a chief, had the first of a number of visions. In them, he met with emissaries of the Creator who showed him heaven and hell and commissioned him to revitalize Seneca religion and society. This he set out to do for the next decade and a half. As his principal text, he used the *Gaiwiio,* or "Good Word," a gospel that contains statements about the nature of religion and eternity and a code of conduct for the righteous. The *Gaiwiio* is interesting both for the influence of Quaker Christianity it clearly reveals,[70] and for the way the new material was merged with traditional Iroquois religious concepts.

The first part of the "Good Word" has three main themes, one of which is the concept of an apocalypse. Handsome Lake offered many signs by which the faithful could recognize impending, cosmic doom. Great drops of fire would rain from the skies and a veil would be cast over the earth. False prophets would appear, witch women would openly cast spells, and poisonous creatures from the underworld would seize and kill those who had rejected the *Gaiwiio.* Second, the *Gaiwiio* emphasized sin. The great sins were disbelief in the "good way," drunkenness, witchcraft, and abortion. Sins had to be confessed and repented. Finally, the *Gaiwiio* offered salvation. Salvation could be won by following a code of conduct, attending certain important traditional rites, and performing public confession.

The second part of the *Gaiwiio* sets out the code of conduct. This code seems to orient the Seneca toward advantageous European American practices without separating them from their culture. The code has five main sections:

1. **Temperance.** All Seneca leaders were fully aware of the social disorders arising out of abuse of liquor. Handsome Lake went to great lengths to illustrate and explain the harmfulness of alcohol.

2. **Peace and social unity.** Seneca leaders were to cease their futile bickering, and all were to be united in their approach to the larger society.

3. **Preservation of tribal lands.** Handsome Lake, fearing the piecemeal alienation of Seneca lands, was far ahead of his contemporaries in demanding a halt in land sales to non-Seneca.

A revitalization movement that became known as the Ghost Dance spread eastward from the Northwest from the 1870s to the 1890s. It was generally believed that, if people did the dance correctly, ghosts would come to life with sufficient resources to allow the people to return to their old ways, and, as a result of some cataclysm, the whites would disappear.

Source: Ogallala Sioux performing the Ghost Dance at the Pine Ridge Indian Agency, South Dakota. Illustration by Frederic Remington, 1890.

4. **Proacculturation (favoring external culture traits).** Though individual property and trading for profit were prohibited, the acquisition of literacy in English was encouraged so that people would be able to read and understand treaties and to avoid being cheated.

5. **Domestic morality.** Sons were to obey their fathers, mothers should avoid interfering with daughters' marriages, and husbands and wives should respect the sanctity of their marriage vows.

Handsome Lake's teaching seems to have led to a renaissance among the Seneca. Temperance was widely accepted, as were schooling and new farming methods. By 1801, corn yields had been increased tenfold, new crops (oats, potatoes, flax) had been introduced, and public health and hygiene had improved considerably. Handsome Lake himself acquired great power among his people. He spent the remainder of his life fulfilling administrative duties, acting as a representative of the Iroquois in Washington, and preaching his gospel to neighboring tribes. By the time of Handsome Lake's death in 1815, the Seneca clearly had undergone a dramatic rebirth, attributable at least in part to the new religion. Later in the

century, some of Handsome Lake's disciples founded a church in his name that, despite occasional setbacks and political disputes, survives to this day.

Although many scholars believe cultural stress gives rise to these new religious movements, it is still important to understand exactly what the stresses are and how strong they have to become before a new movement emerges. Do different kinds of stresses produce different kinds of movements? And does the nature of the movement depend on the cultural elements already present? Let us consider some theory and research on the causes of the millenarian cargo cults that began to appear in Melanesia from about 1885 on.

Cargo Cults The *cargo cults* can be thought of as religious movements "in which there is an expectation of, and preparation for, the coming of a period of supernatural bliss."[71] Thus, an explicit belief of the cargo cults was the notion that some liberating power would bring all the Western goods (cargo in pidgin English) the people might want. For example, around 1932, on Buka in the Solomon Islands, the leaders of a cult prophesied that a tidal wave would sweep away the villages and a ship would arrive

current research and issues

One Appeal of Religion May Be the Wish for a Better World

There are many religions in the United States today, and new sects, often derisively called cults, emerge regularly. Few of us realize that nearly all of the major churches or religions in the world began as minority sects or cults. Indeed, some of the most established and prestigious Protestant churches were considered radical social movements at first. For example, what we now know as the United Church of Christ, which includes the Congregational Church, was founded by radicals in England who wanted church governance to be in the hands of the local congregation. Many of these radicals became the people we call Pilgrims, who had to flee to the New World. But they were very fundamentalist in their beliefs; for example, as late as the 1820s, Congregationalist-dominated towns in Connecticut prohibited celebrations of Christmas outside of church because such celebrations were not mentioned in the Bible. Nowadays, Congregationalists are among the most liberal Protestants.

We should not be surprised to learn that most of the various Protestant churches today, including some considered very conservative, began as militant sects that set out to achieve a better world. After all, that's why we call them "Protestant." At first, the rebellion was against Rome and the Catholic Church. Later, sects developed in opposition to church and government hierarchies. And remember that Christianity itself began as a radical group in the hinterland of the Roman Empire. So new sects or cults were probably always political and social, as well as religious, movements. Recall that the word *millennium*, as used in discussions of religious movements, refers to a wished-for or expected future time when human life and society will be perfect and free of troubles; the world will then be prosperous, happy, and peaceful. Nowadays, the wish for a better world may or may not be religiously inspired. Some people who seek a more perfect world believe that humans alone must achieve it.

How should we categorize this wish for a better world? Should we call it "conservative" because the imagined world may have existed in the past? If the imagined world does not yet exist, is it "radical" to believe it can be achieved? Maybe the wish for a more perfect world is neither conservative nor radical. Maybe it is just that people who are not satisfied with the world as it is think that something can be done to improve things, with or without divine assistance. However it will come, the "millennium" will be different from now, and better.

Ideas about the millennium, and the origins of new cults and religions, might best be viewed then as human hopes: Which ones do people have? Do they vary from culture to culture, and why? Are some hopes universal? And how might they be achieved?

Sources: Stark 1985; Trompf 1990.

---

with iron, axes, food, tobacco, cars, and arms. Work in the gardens ceased, and wharves and docks were built for the expected cargo.[72]

What may explain such cults? Peter Worsley suggested that an important factor in the rise of cargo cults and millenarian movements in general is the existence of oppression—in the case of Melanesia, colonial oppression. He suggested that the reactions in Melanesia took religious rather than political forms because they were a way of pulling together people who previously had no political unity and who lived in small, isolated social groups.[73] Other scholars, such as David Aberle, suggested that *relative deprivation* is more important than oppression in explaining the origins of cults; when people feel that they could have more, and they have less than what they used to have or less than others, they may be attracted to new cults.[74] Consistent with Aberle's general interpretation, Bruce Knauft's comparative study of cargo cults found that such cults were more important in Melanesian societies that had had decreasing cultural contact with the West, and presumably *decreasing* contact with valued goods, within the year prior to the cult's emergence.[75]

Fundamentalism For some scholars, one of the main attributes of fundamentalism is the literal interpretation of a sacred scripture. But recent scholars have suggested that fundamentalist movements need to be understood more broadly as religious or political movements that appear in response to the rapidly changing environment of the modern world. In this broader view, fundamentalism occurs in many religions, including those of Christians, Jews, Islamics, Sikhs, Buddhists, and Hindus. Although each movement is different in content, Richard Antoun suggests that fundamentalist movements have the following elements in common: the selective use of scripture to inspire and assert proof of particular certainties; the quest for purity and traditional values in what is viewed as an impure world; active opposition to what is viewed as a permissive secular society and a nation-state that separates religion from the state; and an incorporation of selected modern elements such as television to promote the movements' aims.[76]

Fundamentalist religious movements do appear to be linked to the anxieties and uncertainties associated with culture change in general and globalization in particular. Many people in many countries are repelled by new behaviors and attitudes, and react in a way that celebrates the old. As Judith Nagata puts it, fundamentalism is a "quest for certainty in an uncertain world."[77] Protestant fundamentalism flourished at the end of the 19th century in the United States as immigrant groups came into the country in great numbers and the country became industrialized and increasingly urbanized. The fundamentalists denounced foreign influences, the decline of the Bible as a guide to moral behavior, the teaching of evolution, and they succeeded in getting the country to prohibit the sale of alcoholic beverages. Recent Islamic fundamentalist movements seem to be responses to a different kind of challenge to the social order—increasing Westernization. Westernization may have first arrived in conjunction with colonial rule. Later, it may have been promoted by Western-educated native elites.[78] Antoun suggests that fundamentalist movements deliberately push certain practices because the leaders know they will outrage the secular opposition. Examples in recent Islamic fundamentalist movements are the extreme punishment of cutting off a hand for theft and requiring women to be covered by veils or head-to-toe covering in public.[79] Unfortunately, in present-day discourse, fundamentalism tends to be equated by Westerners with Islam itself. But, in historical perspective, all major religions have had fundamentalist movements in times of rapid culture change.

If the recent as well as distant past is any guide, we can expect religious belief and practice to be revitalized periodically, particularly during times of stress. As we discussed in the chapter on culture change and globalization, change associated with globalization appears to be accompanied by the rise of fundamentalist religious movements. Paradoxically, globalization has increased the spread of world religions but it has also increased the worldwide interest in shamanism and other features of religion that are different from the dominant religions. Thus, we can expect the world to continue to have religious variation.

SUMMARY ● ○ ○

1. Religion is any set of attitudes, beliefs, and practices pertaining to supernatural power. Such beliefs may vary within a culture as well as among societies, and they may change over time.

2. Religious beliefs are evident in all known cultures and are inferred from artifacts associated with *Homo sapiens* since at least 60,000 years ago.

3. Theories to account for the universality of religion suggest that humans create religion in response to certain universal needs or conditions, including a need for understanding, reversion to childhood feelings, anxiety or uncertainty, and a need for community.

4. There are wide variations in religious beliefs. Societies vary in the number and kinds of supernatural entities in which they believe. There may be impersonal supernatural forces (e.g., mana and taboo), supernatural

beings of nonhuman origin (gods and spirits), and supernatural beings of human origin (ghosts and ancestor spirits). The religious belief system of a society may include any or all such entities.

5. Gods and spirits may be unpredictable or predictable, aloof from or interested in human affairs, helpful or punishing. In some societies, all gods are equal in rank; in others, there is a hierarchy of prestige and power among gods and spirits, just as among the humans in those societies.

6. A monotheistic religion is one in which there is one high god, as the creator of the universe or the director of events (or both); all other supernatural beings are either subordinate to, or function as alternative manifestations of, this god. A high god is generally found in societies with a high level of political development.

7. Faced with ignorance, pain, and injustice, people frequently explain events by claiming intervention by the gods. Such intervention has also been sought by people who hope it will help them achieve their own ends. The gods are likely to punish the immoral behavior of people in societies that have considerable differences in wealth.

8. Various methods have been used to attempt communication with the supernatural. Among them are prayer, taking drugs or otherwise affecting the body and mind, simulation, feasts, and sacrifices.

9. When people believe that their actions can compel the supernatural to act in a particular and intended way, anthropologists refer to the belief and related practice as magic. Sorcery and witchcraft are attempts to make the spirits work harm against people.

10. Almost all societies have part-time or full-time religious or magical practitioners. Recent cross-cultural research suggests that there are four major types of practitioners: shamans, sorcerers or witches, mediums, and priests. The number of types of practitioners seems to vary with degree of cultural complexity: The more complex the society, the more types of practitioners.

11. The history of religion includes periods of strong resistance to change and periods of radical change. Perhaps the most dramatic is religious conversion, particularly when large numbers of people switch to a completely new religion presented by missionaries or other proselytizers. In some native societies, contact has led to a breakdown of social structure and the growth of feelings of helplessness and spiritual demoralization. *Revitalization movements* have arisen as apparent attempts to restore such societies to their former confidence and prosperity. In recent times, religious *fundamentalist* movements have flourished. Religious change, particularly of the dramatic kind, usually does not occur in a vacuum, but is often associated with other dramatic changes—economic, political, and demographic.

GLOSSARY TERMS ○ ● ○

ancestor spirits 273

animatism 270

animism 270

divination 277

ghosts 273

gods 272

magic 278

mana 272

mediums 279

monotheistic 274

polytheistic 274

priests 279

religion 268

revitalization
  movements 283

rituals 276

shaman 279

sorcery 278

spirits 272

supernatural 268

taboo 272

witchcraft 278

CRITICAL QUESTIONS ○ ○ ●

1. How does your conception of God compare with beliefs about supernatural beings in other religious systems?

2. What do you think is the future of religion? Explain your answer.

3. Could any of the religious practices you know about be classified as magic? Are they associated with anxiety-arousing situations?

PEARSON myanthrolab

Read the chapter by Debra Picchi titled "Bakairí: The Death of an Indian" on MyAnthroLab, and answer the following questions:

1. How come the Bakairi did not ask whether Western medicine works, but Westerners asked whether shamanism works?

2. Why would a shaman be able to settle disputes?

The Arts

ost societies do not have a word for art.[1] Perhaps that is because art, particularly in societies with relatively little specialization, is often an integral part of religious, social, and political life. Indeed, most of the aspects of culture we have already discussed—economics, kinship, politics, religion—are not easily separated from the rest of social life.[2]

The oldest art found so far comes from caves in South Africa. Pieces of red ochre were engraved there more than 77,000 years ago. In Australia, people painted on walls of rock shelters and on cliff faces between 70,000 and 60,000 years ago. And in southern Africa, Spain, and France, people painted slabs of rock 28,000 years ago (see the box on rock art on page 291). Art is clearly an old feature of human cultures. We say that those earliest paintings are art, but what do we mean by "art"? A stone spear point and a bone fishhook obviously require skill and creativity to make. But we do not call them art. Why do we feel that some things are art and others are not?

Some definitions of art emphasize its evocative quality. From the viewpoint of the person who creates it, art expresses feelings and ideas; from the viewpoint of the observer or participant, it evokes feelings and ideas. The feelings and ideas on each side may or may not be exactly the same. And they may be expressed in a variety of ways—drawing, painting, carving, weaving, body decoration, music, dance, or story. An artistic work or performance is intended to excite the senses, to stir the emotions of the beholder or participant. It may produce feelings of pleasure, awe, repulsion, or fear, but usually not indifference.[3]

But emphasizing the evocative quality of art may make it difficult to compare the art of different cultures because what is evocative in one culture may not be evocative in another. For example, a humorous story in one culture may not be funny in another. Thus, most anthropologists agree that art is more than an attempt by an individual to express or communicate feelings and ideas. There is also some cultural patterning or meaning; societies vary in their characteristic kinds and styles of art.[4]

Artistic activities are always cultural in part, involving shared and learned patterns of behavior, belief, and feeling. What are some of the ideas about art in our own culture? We tend to think that anything useful is not art. If a basket has a design that is not necessary to its function, we may possibly consider it art, especially if we keep it on a shelf; but the basket with bread on the table would probably not be considered art. The fact that such a distinction is not made in other societies strongly suggests that our ideas about art are cultural. Among Native Americans in the Pacific Northwest, elaborately carved totem poles not only displayed the crests of the lineages of their occupants, they also supported the house.[5] The fact that artistic activities are partly cultural is evident when we compare how people in different societies treat the outsides of their houses. Most North Americans share the value of decorating the interiors of their homes with pictures—paintings, prints, or photographs hung on the walls.

But they do not share the value of painting pictures on the outside walls of their houses, as Native Americans did in the Pacific Northwest.

In our society, we also insist that a work must be unique to be considered art. This aspect is clearly consistent with our emphasis on the individual. However, even though we require that artists be unique and innovative, the art they produce must still fall within some range of acceptable variation. Artists must communicate to us in a way we can relate to, or at least learn to relate to. Often, they must follow certain current styles of expression that other artists or critics have set, if they hope to have the public accept their art. The idea that an artist should be original is a cultural idea; in some societies, the ability to replicate a traditional pattern is more valued than originality.

So, art seems to have several qualities: It expresses as well as communicates. It stimulates the senses, affects emotions, and evokes ideas. It is produced in culturally patterned ways and styles. It has cultural meaning. In addition, some people are thought to be better at it than others.[6] Art does not require some people to be full-time artistic specialists; many societies in the ethnographic record had no full-time specialists of any kind. But, although everyone in some societies may participate in some arts (dancing, singing, body decoration), it is usually thought that certain individuals have superior artistic skill.

To illustrate the cross-cultural variation that exists in artistic expression, we will consider first the art of body decoration and adornment.

● ○ ●

BODY DECORATION AND ADORNMENT

In all societies, people decorate or adorn their bodies. The decorations may be permanent—scars, tattoos, or changes in the shape of a body part. Or they may be temporary, in the form of paint or objects such as feathers, jewelry, skins, and clothing that are not strictly utilitarian. Much of this decoration seems to be motivated by aesthetic considerations, which, of course, vary from culture to culture. The actual form of the decoration depends on cultural traditions. Body ornamentation includes the pierced noses of some women in India, the elongated necks of the Mangebetu of central Africa, the tattooing of North American males and females, the body painting of the Caduveo of South America, and the variety of ornaments found in almost every culture.

However, in addition to satisfying aesthetic needs, body decoration or adornment may be used to delineate social position, rank, sex, occupation, local and ethnic identity, or religion within a society. Along with social stratification come visual means of declaring status. The symbolic halo (the crown) on the king's head, the scarlet hunting jacket of the English gentleman, the eagle feathers of the Native American chief's bonnet, the gold-embroidered jacket of the Indian rajah—each mark of high status is recognized in its own society. Jewelry in the shape of a cross or the Star of David indicates Christian or Jewish inclinations. Clothes may set apart the priest, nun, or member of a sect such as the Amish.

The erotic significance of some body decoration is also apparent. Women draw attention to erogenous zones of the body by painting, as on the lips, and by attaching some object—an earring, a flower behind the ear, a necklace, a bracelet, brooch, anklet, or belt. Men draw attention, too, by beards, tattoos, and penis sheaths (in some otherwise naked societies) that point upward. We have only to follow the fashion trends for women of Europe and North America during the past 300 years, with their history of pinched waists, ballooned hips, bustled rumps, exaggerated breasts, painted faces, and exposed bosoms, to realize the significance of body adornment for sexual provocation. Why some societies emphasize the erotic adornment of women and others emphasize it in men is not yet understood.

Type of body adornment may reflect politics. Polynesians decorate their bodies with tattoos, which are permanent. In Samoa, for example, tattoos distinguished the chiefly class from commoners. Bands and stripes were restricted to people of high status; low-status people could have tattoos only of solid black and only from waist to knees. Within the ruling class, the number of tattooed triangles down a man's leg indicated his relative rank. Because tattooing is permanent, it is a form of body decoration well suited to a society with inherited social stratification. On the other hand, in Melanesia, typically with "big men" type of leadership which is somewhat fluid, Melanesians paint their bodies, and the painting is ephemeral. It disappears within a short time, or after the first wash.[7]

A need to decorate the human body seems universal. We have noted some of the various methods people have used to adorn themselves in different societies. We are also aware of body-decoration practices that raise questions to which we have no ready answers. What explains adornment of the body by permanent marking such as scarification, bound feet, elongated ears and necks, shaped heads, pierced ears and septums, and filed teeth? Why do different societies

applied anthropology

Rock Art: Preserving a Window into the Past

If the art of an ancient or earlier culture reflects the preoccupations and ideas of the culture, and if we are interested in understanding what the creators of the art thought, the art of the past and its surroundings must be preserved as much as possible. One type of ancient art frequently found is what anthropologists call "rock art," drawings and paintings on cliff faces and the walls of caves. Some of the most famous are the cave paintings of Europe, dating from about 30,000 years ago, but a large number of other rock art sites are in danger and in need of preserving.

Unlike a painting or a decorated object, rock art is part of its environment, and the environmental area as well as the rock art needs to be preserved. Excavation of the area may provide information that not only allows us to date the drawings and paintings, it may also tell us what the people did to produce the art and why they produced it. For example, in one French cave, analysis of charcoal indicates that the artists made fires to produce the charcoal they would use in their drawings. In another cave in Montana, pollen found below the paintings came from a number of

plants. Many of the plants have known medicinal properties, and the pollens may indicate what shamans had in their medicine bags. Talking to the descendants of the creators of the rock art is also essential. Sometimes anthropologists learn things that surprise them. For instance, near Alice Springs, Australia, some branches were knocking against some rock art and the preservers considered cutting some of the branches. The aboriginal elders were horrified at the idea because the trees were believed to harbor the souls of the deceased, and it would have been a crime to cut them.

Although there are natural threats to rock art, the greatest threats come from humans. Religious change with European contact often lessened the interest of indigenous populations in their earlier sacred sites, making for less protest when development projects are proposed. Tours to previously isolated sites often lead to more destruction from graffiti or unauthorized attempts to reproduce or photograph the art. Ironically though, making the rock art the center of a park helps protect it.

Raising awareness of rock art is one of the most important ways of protecting it

in its environment. Although nothing beats seeing rock art in its natural setting, modern methods (holograms, laser recording, 3D imagery) and computer-assisted enhancement have made it possible to have life-size replicas, allowing the public to see more than they can in some mostly inaccessible caves. These replicas and images also give anthropologists and other scientists materials for appreciation and study. The greater the number of displays in public facilities (museums, parks) that expose tourists to rock art, the more valuable it may become. Anthropologists or not, we all seem to be fascinated by the ancient graphics. We try to imagine what motivated the original artists. If we could reconstruct those motives, they might suggest why we choose subjects and techniques in our own art, as well as in our "graffiti."

The archaeological context of rock art can help us understand the rock art. Teaching people how to preserve rock art is applied anthropology that will help to preserve a priceless heritage and a source of knowledge about humans in the past.

Source: Clottes 2008.

---

adorn, paint, or otherwise decorate different parts of the body for sexual or other reasons? And what leads some members of our society to transfer body decoration to their animals? Why the shaped hair of the poodle, the braided manes of some horses, and diamond collars, painted toenails, coats, hats, and even boots for some pets?

EXPLAINING VARIATION IN THE ARTS

In our society, we stress the freedom of the artist, so it may seem to us that art is completely free to vary. But our emphasis on uniqueness obscures the fact that different cultures not only use or emphasize different materials and have different ideas of beauty, but they also may have characteristic styles and themes. It is easy to see styles when we look at art that is different from our own; it is harder to see similarity when we look at the art of our own culture. If we look at dance styles, for example, we may think that the dance style of the 1940s is completely different from the dance style of today. It might take an outsider to notice that, in our culture, we still generally see couples dancing as a

pair rather than in a group line or circle, as in dances we call "folk dances." And, in our culture, females and males dance together rather than separately. Furthermore, our popular music still has a beat or combination of beats and is made by many of the same kinds of instruments as in the past.

But where do these similarities in form and style come from? Much of the recent research on variation in the arts supports the idea that form and style in visual art, music, dance, and folklore are very much influenced by other aspects of culture. Some psychological anthropologists, as we saw in the chapter on culture and the individual, would go even further, suggesting that art, like religion, expresses the typical feelings, anxieties, and experiences of people in a culture. And the typical feelings and anxieties in turn are influenced by basic institutions such as childrearing, economy, social organization, and politics.

Consider how the physical form of art a society prefers may reflect its way of life. For example, Richard Anderson pointed out that the art of traditionally nomadic people such as the !Kung, Inuit, and Australian aborigines is mostly carryable.[8] Song, dance, and oral literature are very important in those societies and are as portable as they can be. Those societies decorate useful objects that they carry with them—harpoons for the Inuit, boomerangs for the Australian aborigines, ostrich egg "canteens" for the !Kung. But they don't have bulky things such as sculpture or elaborate costumes. And what about the presence of artists or art critics? Although some people in small-scale societies are more artistic than others, specialized artists, as well as critics or theoreticians of art, tend to be found only in societies with a complex, specialized division of labor.

Visual Art

Perhaps the most obvious way artistic creations reflect how we live is by mirroring the environment—the materials and technologies available to a culture. Stone, wood, bones, tree bark, clay, sand, charcoal, berries for staining, and a few mineral-derived ochers are generally available materials. In addition, depending on the locality, other resources are accessible: shells, horns, tusks, gold, copper, and silver. The different uses to which societies put these materials are of interest to anthropologists, who may ask, for example, why a people chooses to use clay and not copper when both items are available. Although we have no conclusive answers as yet, such questions have important ramifications. The way in which a society views its environment is sometimes apparent in its choice and use of artistic materials. Certain metals, for example, may be reserved for ceremonial objects of special importance. Or the belief in the supernatural powers of a stone or tree may cause a sculptor to be sensitive to that particular material.[9]

The traditional political systems of Africa ranged from centralized kingdoms (on the complex end of the continuum) to village-based or segmentary lineage systems in which leadership was ephemeral or secret (tied to secret societies). Masks that conceal identity are often used in the uncentralized systems; crowns or other headdresses indicating high status are frequent in the kingdoms. Among the uncentralized Ibo of eastern Nigeria, masks are often worn by the young men of a village when they criticize the

behavior of the village elders. In the kingdom of Ngoyo, in western Zaire, the king's status is indicated by his special cap as well as by his special three-legged stool.

What is particularly meaningful to anthropologists is the realization that, although the materials available to a society may to some extent limit or influence what it can do artistically, the materials by no means determine what is done. Why does the artist in Japanese society rake sand into patterns, the artist in Navajo society paint sand, and the artist in Roman society melt sand to form glass? Moreover, even when the same material is used in the same way in different societies, the form or style of the work varies enormously from culture to culture.

A society may choose to represent objects or phenomena that are especially important to the people or elite. An examination of the art of the Middle Ages tells us something about the medieval preoccupation with theological doctrine. In addition to revealing the primary concerns of a society, the content of that society's art may also reflect the culture's social stratification. Authority figures may be represented in obvious ways. In the art of ancient Sumerian society, the sovereign was portrayed as being much larger than his followers, and the most prestigious gods were given oversized eyes. Also, differences in clothing and jewelry styles within a society usually reflect social stratification.

Art historians have always recognized certain possible relationships between the art of a society and other aspects of its culture. Much of this attention has been concentrated on the content of art, because European art has been representational for such a long time. But the style of the art may reflect other aspects of culture. John Fischer, for example, examined the stylistic features of art with the aim of discovering "some sort of regular connection between some artistic feature and some social situation."[10] He argued that the artist expresses a form of social fantasy. In other words, in a stable society, artists will respond to those conditions in the society that bring security or pleasure to them and the society.

The same materials may be used artistically in different ways. In Japan (on the left), sand is raked into patterns. In the Northern Territory of Australia (on the right), the Yuendumu paint the sand.

Assuming that "pictorial elements in design are, on one psychological level, abstract, mainly unconscious representations of persons in the society,"[11] Fischer reasoned that egalitarian societies would tend to have different stylistic elements in their art as compared with stratified societies. Egalitarian societies are generally composed of small, self-sufficient communities that are structurally similar and have little differentiation between people. Stratified societies, on the other hand, generally have larger and more interdependent, and dissimilar, communities and great differences among people in prestige, power, and access to economic resources. Fischer hypothesized, and found in a cross-cultural study, that certain elements of design were strongly related to the presence of social hierarchy. His findings are summarized in Table 16–1.

Repetition of a simple element, for example, tends to be found in the art of egalitarian societies, which have little political organization and few authority positions. If each element unconsciously represents individuals within the society, the relative sameness of people seems to be reflected in the repetitiveness of design elements. Conversely, the combinations of different design elements in complex patterns that tend to be found in the art of stratified societies seem to reflect the high degree of social differentiation that exists in such societies.[12]

According to Fischer, the egalitarian society's empty space in a design represents the society's relative isolation. Because egalitarian societies are usually small and self-sufficient, they tend to shy away from outsiders, preferring to find security within their own group. In contrast, the art of stratified societies is generally crowded. The hierarchical society does not seek to isolate individuals or communities within the group because they must be interdependent, each social level ideally furnishing services for those above it and help for those beneath it. As Fischer suggested, we can, in general, discern a lack of empty space in the designs of societies in which security is not sought by avoiding strangers, but rather "security is produced by incorporating strangers into the hierarchy, through dominance or submission as the relative power indicates."[13]

Symmetry, the third stylistic feature related to type of society, is similar to the first. Symmetry may suggest likeness or an egalitarian society; asymmetry suggests difference and perhaps stratification. The fourth feature of interest here, the presence or absence of enclosures or boundaries—"frames" in our art—may indicate the presence or absence of hierarchically imposed rules circumscribing individual behavior. An unenclosed design may reflect free access to most property; in egalitarian societies, the fencing off of a piece of property for the use of only one person is unknown. In the art of stratified societies, boundaries or enclosures may reflect the idea of private property. Or they may symbolically represent the real differences in dress, occupation, type of food allowed, and manners that separate the different classes of people.

Studies such as Fischer's offer anthropologists new tools with which to evaluate ancient societies that are known only by a few pieces of pottery or a

TABLE 16–1	Artistic Differences in Egalitarian and Stratified Societies	
Egalitarian Society	**Stratified Society**
Repetition of simple elements	Integration of unlike elements
Much empty or irrelevant space	Little empty space
Symmetrical design	Asymmetrical design
Unenclosed figures	Enclosed figures

Source: Based on Fischer 1961.

few tools or paintings. If art reflects certain aspects of a culture, then the study of whatever art of a people has been preserved may provide a means of testing the accuracy of the guesses we make about their culture on the basis of more ordinary archaeological materials. For example, even if we did not know from classical Greek writings that Athens became much more socially stratified between 750 B.C. and 600 B.C., we might guess that such a transformation had occurred because of the changes we can see over time in the way the Athenians decorated vases. Consistent with Fischer's cross-cultural findings, as Athens became more stratified, its vase painting became more complex, more crowded, and more enclosed.[14]

Music

When we hear the music of another culture, we often don't know what to make of it. We may say it does not "mean" anything to us, not realizing that the "meaning" of music has been programmed into us by our culture. In music as well as in art, our culture largely determines what we consider acceptable variation, what we say has "meaning" to us. Even a trained musicologist, listening for the first time to music of a different culture, will not be able to hear the subtleties of tone and rhythm that members of the culture hear with ease. This predicament is similar to that of the linguist who, exposed to a foreign language,

Changes in Greek vases show how increasing stratification is associated with integration of unlike elements as well as more crowded design. The one on the left dates from around 1000 B.C. when there was less stratification. The vase on the right dates from the time period between 750 B.C. and 600 B.C., when stratification was at its maximum.

cannot at first distinguish phonemes, morphemes, and other regular patterns of speech.

Not only do instruments vary, but music itself varies widely in style from society to society. For example, in some societies, people prefer music with a regularly recurring beat; in others, they prefer changes in rhythm. There are also variations in singing styles. In some places, it is customary to have different vocal lines for different people; in other places, people all sing together in the same way.

Is variation in music, as in the other arts, related to other aspects of culture? On the basis of a cross-cultural study of more than 3,500 folk songs from a sample of the world's societies, Alan Lomax and his co-researchers found that song style seems to vary with cultural complexity. As we will see, these findings about variation in song style are similar to Fischer's findings about variation in art.

Lomax and his co-researchers found some features of song style to be correlated with cultural complexity. (The societies classified as more complex tend to have higher levels of food-production technology, social stratification, and higher levels of political integration.) For example, wordiness and clearness of enunciation were found to be associated with cultural complexity. The association is a reasonable one: The more a society depends on verbal information, as in giving complex instructions for a job or explaining different points of law, the more strongly will clear enunciation in transmitting information be a mark of its culture. Thus, hunter-gatherer bands, in which people know their productive role and perform it without ever being given complex directions, are more likely than we are to base much of their singing on lines of nonwords, such as our refrain line "tra-la-la-la-la." Their songs are characterized by lack of explicit information, by sounds that give pleasure in themselves, by much repetition, and by relaxed, slurred enunciation.[15]

Examples of the progression from repetition or nonwords to wordy information are found within our society. The most obvious, and universal, example of a song made entirely of repetition is the relaxed lullaby of a mother repeating a comforting syllable to her baby while improvising her own tune. But this type of song is not characteristic of our society. Although our songs sometimes have single lines of nonwords, it is rare for an entire song to be made of them. Usually, the nonwords act as respites from information:

> Deck the halls with boughs of holly,
> Fa la la la la,
> La la la la.[16]

In associating variation in music with cultural complexity, Lomax found that elaboration of song parts also corresponds to the complexity of a society. Societies in which leadership is informal and temporary seem to symbolize their social equality by an *interlocked* style of singing. Each person sings independently but within the group, and no one singer is differentiated from the others. Rank societies, in which there is a leader with prestige but no real power, are characterized by a song style in which one "leader" may begin the song, but the others soon drown out his voice. In stratified societies, where leaders have the power of force, choral singing is generally marked by a clear-cut role for the leader and a secondary "answering" role for the others. Societies marked by elaborate stratification show singing parts that are differentiated and in which the soloist is deferred to by the other singers.

Lomax also found a relationship between **polyphony,** where two or more melodies are sung simultaneously, and a high degree of female participation in food-getting. In societies in which women's work is responsible for at least half of the food, songs are likely to contain more than one simultaneous melody, with the higher tunes usually sung by women. Moreover:

> Counterpoint was once believed to be the invention of European high culture. In our sample it turns out to be most frequent among simple producers, especially gatherers, where women supply the bulk of the food. Counterpoint and perhaps even polyphony may then be very old feminine inventions. . . . Subsistence complementarity is at its maximum among gatherers, early gardeners, and horticulturalists. It is in such societies that we find the highest occurrence of polyphonic singing.[17]

In societies in which women do not contribute much to food production, the songs are more likely to have a single melody and to be sung by males.[18]

In some societies, survival and social welfare are based on a unified group effort; in those cultures, singing tends to be marked by cohesiveness. That is, cohesive work parties, teams of gatherers or harvesters, and kin groups, who work voluntarily for the good of the family or community, seem to express their interconnectedness in song by blending both tone and rhythm.

Some variations in music may be explained as a consequence of variation in childrearing practices. For example, researchers are beginning to explore childrearing as a way to explain why some societies respond to, and produce, regular rhythm in their music, whereas others enjoy free rhythm that has no regular beat. One hypothesis is that a regular beat in music is a simulation of the regular beat of the heart. For nine months in the womb, the fetus feels the mother's regular 80 or so heartbeats a minute. Moreover, mothers generally employ rhythmic tactics in quieting crying infants—patting their backs or rocking them. But the fact that children respond positively to an even tempo does not mean that the regular heartbeat is completely responsible for their sensitivity to rhythm. In fact, if the months in the womb were sufficient to establish a preference for rhythm, then every child would be affected in exactly the same manner by a regular beat, and all societies would have the same rhythm in their music.

Barbara Ayres suggested that the importance of regular rhythm in the music of a culture is related to the rhythm's *acquired reward value*—that is, its associations with feelings of security or relaxation. In a cross-cultural study of this possibility, Ayres found a strong correlation between a society's method of carrying infants and the type of musical rhythm the society produced. In some societies, the mother or an older sister carries the child, sometimes for two or three years, in a sling, pouch, or shawl, so that the child is in bodily contact with her for much of the day and

current research and issues

Do Masks Show Emotion in Universal Ways?

Anthropologists have documented how forms and styles in art vary from culture to culture. But with all this variation, it seems that certain forms of art may show emotion in universally similar ways. For example, research on masks from different cultures supports the conclusion that masks, like faces, tend to represent certain emotions in the same ways. Face masks are commonly used in rituals and performances. They not only hide the real face of the mask wearer but they often evoke powerful emotions in the audience—anger, fear, sadness, joy. You might think, because so many things vary cross-culturally, that the ways in which emotion is displayed and recognized in the face vary too. But apparently they do not vary that much. We now have some evidence that the symbolism used in masks is often universal.

The research on masks builds on work done by Paul Ekman and Carroll Izard, who used photographs of individuals experiencing, or actors simulating, various emotions. Ekman and Izard showed photographs to members of different cultural groups and asked them to identify the emotions displayed in the photographs. A particular emotion was identified correctly by most viewers, whatever the viewer's native culture. The results for the viewers from less Westernized cultures paralleled the results for viewers from more Westernized cultures. Coding schemes were developed to enable researchers to compare the detailed facial positions of individual portions of the face (eyebrows, mouth, etc.) for different emotions. What exactly do we do when we

scowl? We contract the eyebrows and lower the corners of the mouth; in geometric terms, we make angles and diagonals on our faces. When we smile, we raise the corners of the mouth; we make it curved.

Psychologist Joel Aronoff and his colleagues compared two types of wooden face masks from many different societies—masks described as threatening (e.g., designed to frighten off evil spirits) versus masks associated with nonthreatening functions (a courtship dance). As suspected, the two sets of masks had significantly different proportions of certain facial elements. The threatening masks had eyebrows and eyes facing inward and downward and a downward-facing mouth. The threatening masks also were more likely to have pointed heads, chins, beards, and ears, as well as projections from the face such as horns. In more abstract or geometrical terms, threatening features generally tend to be angular or diagonal, and nonthreatening features tend to be curved or rounded. A face with a pointed beard is threatening; a baby's face is not. The theory—originally suggested by Charles Darwin, the evolutionist—is that humans express and recognize basic emotions in uniform ways because all human faces are quite similar, skeletally and muscularly.

But, is it the facial features themselves that convey threat or is it the design elements of angularity and diagonality that convey threat? To help answer this question, students in the United States were asked to associate adjectives with drawings of abstract pairs of design features

(e.g., a V shape and a U shape). Even with abstract shapes, the angular patterns were thought of as less "good," more "powerful," and "stronger" than the curved shapes. In subsequent studies, students recognized the V shape more quickly than other shapes, and this shape triggered more response in the brain in areas associated with threat.

We should not be surprised to discover that humans all over the world use their faces, and masks, to show emotions in the same ways. Aren't we all members of the same species? Our skin color may vary from dark to light. Our hair may be straight, wavy, or kinky—or skimpy. We vary in the percentages of a lot of characteristics. But those are the characteristics we see. We are not so likely to notice the things about us (by far, most of the things about us) that don't vary, such as how we show emotion in our faces. That's why a movie made in Hollywood or Beijing may evoke the same feelings wherever people see it. The universality of human emotion as expressed in the face becomes obvious only when we see faces (and masks) from elsewhere, showing emotions in ways that are unmistakable to us.

Thus, we become aware of universality (in masks as well as other cultural things) in the same way we become aware of variation—by exposure through reading and direct experience with the ways cultures do and do not vary.

Sources: Aronoff et al. 1988; Aronoff et al. 1992; Larson et al. 2007; Larson et al. 2009.

---

experiences the motion of her rhythmic walking. Ayres discovered that such societies tend to have a regularly recurring beat in their songs. Societies in which the child is put into a cradle or is strapped to a cradleboard tend to have music based either on irregular rhythm or on free rhythm.[19]

The question of why some societies have great tonal ranges in music whereas others do not was also studied by Ayres, who suggested that this difference might also be explained by certain childrearing practices. Ayres theorized that painful stimulation of infants before weaning might

result in bolder, more exploratory behavior in adulthood, which would be apparent in the musical patterns of the culture. This hypothesis was suggested to her by laboratory experiments with animals. Contrary to expectations, those animals given electric shocks or handled before weaning showed greater than usual physical growth and more exploratory behavior when placed in new situations as adults. Ayres equated the range of musical notes (from low to high) with the exploratory range of animals and forcefulness of accent in music with boldness in animals.

Masks with V shapes represent threat. There are many such shapes on the masked individual from Panama shown on the right—the placement of the horns, the green spikes on the outside of the mask, over the eyes, the ears, the pointed chin, and of course the many pointed teeth. The nonthreatening Iroquois mask on the left has more curved lines and generally lacks any angles.

The kinds of stress Ayres looked for in ethnographic reports were those that would be applied to all children or to all of one sex—for example, scarification; piercing of the nose, lips, or ears; binding, shaping, or stretching of feet, head, ears, or any limb; inoculation; circumcision; or cauterization. The results showed that, in societies in which infants are stressed before the age of 2, music is marked by a wider tonal range than in societies in which children are not stressed or are stressed only at a later age. Also, a firm accent or beat is characteristic of music more often in societies that subject children to stress than in societies that do not.[20]

Cultural emphasis on obedience or independence in children is another variable that may explain some aspects of musical performance. In societies in which children are generally trained for compliance, cohesive singing predominates; where children are encouraged to be assertive, singing is mostly individualized. Moreover, assertive training of children is associated with a raspy voice or harsh singing. A raspy voice seems to be an indication of assertiveness and is most often a male voice quality. Interestingly enough, in societies in which women's work predominates in subsistence production, the women sing with harsher voices.

Other voice characteristics may also be associated with elements of culture. For example, sexual restrictions in a society seem to be associated with voice restrictions, especially with a nasalized or narrow, squeezed tone. These voice qualities are associated with anxiety and are especially noticeable in sounds of pain, deprivation, or sorrow. Restrictive sexual practices may be a source of pain and anxiety, and the nasal tone in song may reflect such emotions.[21]

The cross-cultural results about music should be able to explain change over time as well as variation within a society. Future research in a variety of societies may help test the theories of Lomax and Ayres.[22]

Folklore

Folklore is a broad category comprising all the myths, legends, folktales, ballads, riddles, proverbs, and superstitions

of a cultural group.[23] In general, folklore is transmitted orally, but it may also be written. Games are also sometimes considered folklore, although they may be learned by imitation as well as transmitted orally. All societies have a repertoire of stories that they tell to entertain each other and teach children. Examples of our folklore include fairy tales and the legends we tell about our folk heroes, such as George Washington's confessing that he chopped down the cherry tree. Folklore is not always clearly separable from the other arts, particularly music and dance; stories often are conveyed in those contexts.

Although some folklore scholars emphasize the traditional aspects of folklore and the continuity between the present and the past, more recently attention has been paid to the innovative and emergent aspects of folklore. In this view, folklore is constantly created by any social group that has shared experiences. So, for example, computer programmers may have their jokes and their own proverbs (e.g., "Garbage in, garbage out!").[24] Jan Brunvand compiled a set of recently arisen *urban legends*. One such legend is "The Hook." The story, which has many versions, is basically about a young couple parked on Lover's Lane with the radio on. There is an announcement that a killer with an artificial hand is loose, so the girl suggests that they leave. The boy starts the car and drives her home. When he walks around the car to open her door, he finds a bloody hook attached to the door handle.[25] There are even legends on college campuses. What is the answer to the question of how long students should wait for a tardy professor? Students have an answer, ranging from 10 to 20 minutes. Is this a rule, or only a legend? Brunvand reported that he never found a regulation about how long to wait for the professor on any campus that tells this story![26]

Some folklore scholars are interested in universal or recurrent themes. Clyde Kluckhohn suggested that five themes occur in the myths and folktales of all societies: catastrophe, generally through flood; the slaying of monsters; incest; sibling rivalry, generally between brothers; and castration, sometimes actual but more commonly symbolic.[27]

Just as in art and song, dance style seems to reflect societal complexity. In less complex societies, everyone participates in dances in much the same way, as among the Huli of New Guinea. In more complex societies, there tend to be leading roles and minor roles, as in a Japanese Geisha show.

migrants and immigrants

The Spread of Popular Music

Music is a very visceral art. You feel it in your gut. Hearing a piece of music can make your belly vibrate and give you goosebumps. You don't forget that experience. The ideas expressed in a song can get to you, but you're mostly moved by the sound. You feel it. Music can lift you up or make you sad.

But we wouldn't know about lots of music if not for migration. Would there be "country music" radio stations in the United States if lots of people hadn't moved out of the South in the 20th century? Country music itself was an amalgam of Appalachian folk music heavily influenced by music from the British Isles and also by African music. The banjo, adapted by country musicians, was created by African Americans who modeled the banjo on the African stringed musical instrument called a banjar. Though the fiddle, an important instrument in country music, was European in origin, many of the fiddlers in the South were African American, and country music incorporated African rhythmic styles and improvisation. There were other influences also—the guitar came from Spain, and yodeling from the Swiss. African American music also influenced much of popular American music—ragtime, the blues, jazz, rhythm and blues, rock

and roll, disco and rap, to name just a few. African influences also came to the United States via the Caribbean and South America where people from different cultures created a creolized music. Would we like "salsa" dancing, a form of Afro-Cuban music, or reggae and hip-hop from Jamaica, if there were no immigration? The answer is probably not. If people didn't migrate, it is unlikely that we would know so many styles of music. To get to know music, you need personal contact with it through your own ears. Of course, it is possible that you learn to like music from concerts, on CDs, the radio, or now on the Internet, without hearing it from migrants or immigrants. But most people don't listen to everything; they need to know something about the music before they listen to it further.

Probably no place imports or accepts all kinds of music. The movement of popular music is not guaranteed. For example, although there are many immigrants and migrants of Chinese or South Asian descent in the United States and Canada, Chinese or South Asian music has not become popular. Of course, it might in the future. Why the music of some immigrants and migrants is adopted or incorporated whereas other music is not is not yet

understood. The spread of music is quite different from the spread of technology. The computer and the automobile, like many technologies, can and do spread widely, as people earn more and can afford to buy them. In the case of technologies, there is an easy test of usefulness; a steel ax is better than a stone ax (which is why we don't see people making stone axes anymore). Music is not something that is or is not useful—the ideas and feelings communicated answer our needs. Although young people, the most frequent consumers of popular music, are often looking for something "new," the latest style is probably not that different in some respects from the last style. Cultures have musical preferences, and musical styles that are very different are not readily accepted. And there are those who still like their "golden oldies."

With all the migration and immigration in the modern world, it is likely that the market demand for new popular music will continue to expand. In a few years, we may have Internet-based radio for every demographic niche. Wouldn't that be a blast!

Sources: Nicholls 1998; D. R. Hill 2005, 363–73.

Edward Tylor, who proposed that religion is born from the human need to explain dreams and death, suggested that hero myths follow a similar pattern the world over—the central character is exposed at birth, is subsequently saved by others (humans or animals), and grows up to become a hero.[28] Joseph Campbell argued that hero myths resemble initiations—the hero is separated from the ordinary world, ventures forth into a new world (in this case, the supernatural world) to triumph over powerful forces, and then returns to the ordinary world with special powers to help others.[29]

Myths may indeed have universal themes, but few scholars have looked at a representative sample of the world's societies, and therefore we cannot be sure that current conclusions about universality are correct. Indeed, most folklore researchers have not been interested in universal themes but in the particular folktales told in specific societies or regions. For example, some scholars have

focused on the "Star Husband Tale," a common Native American story. Stith Thompson presented 84 versions of this tale; his goal was to reconstruct the original version and pinpoint its place of origin. By identifying the most common elements, Thompson suggested that the basic story (and probably the original) is the following:

Two girls sleeping out of doors wish that stars would be their husbands. In their sleep the girls are taken to the sky where they find themselves married to stars, one of which is a young man and the other an old man. The women are warned not to dig, but they disregard the warning and accidentally open up a hole in the sky. Unaided they descend on a rope and arrive home safely.[30]

The tale, Thompson suggested, probably originated in the Plains and then spread to other regions of North America.

Alan Dundes has concentrated on the structure of folktales; he thinks that Native American folktales, including the "Star Husband Tale," have characteristic structures. One is a movement away from disequilibrium. Equilibrium is the desirable state; having too much or too little of anything is a condition that should be rectified as soon as possible. Disequilibrium, which Dundes calls *lack,* is indicated by the girls in the "Star Husband Tale" who do not have husbands. The lack is then corrected, in this case by marriage with the stars. This tale has another common Native American structure, says Dundes—a sequence of prohibition, interdiction, violation, and consequence. The women are warned not to dig, but they do—and as a consequence, they escape for home.[31] It should be noted that the consequences in folktales are not always good. Recall the Garden of Eden tale. The couple are warned not to eat the fruit of a tree; they eat the fruit; they are cast out of their paradise. Similarly, Icarus in the Greek tale is warned not to fly too high or low. He flies too high; the sun melts the wax that holds his feathered wings, and he falls and drowns.

As useful as it might be to identify where certain tales originated, or what their common structures might be, many questions remain. What do the tales mean? Why did they arise in the first place? Why are certain structures common in Native American tales? We are still a long way from answering many of these questions, and trying to answer them is difficult. How does one try to understand the meaning of a tale?

It is easy for people to read different meanings into the same myth. For example, consider the myth the Hebrews told of a paradise in which only a man was present until Eve, the first woman, arrived and ate the forbidden fruit of knowledge. One might conclude that men in that society had some grudge against women. If the interpreter were a psychoanalyst, he, or especially she, might assume that the myth reflected the male's deeply hidden fears of female sexuality. A historian might believe that the myth reflected actual historical events and that men were living in blissful ignorance until women invented agriculture—the effect of Eve's "knowledge" led to a life of digging rather than gathering.

It is clearly not enough to suggest an interpretation. Why should we believe it? We should give it serious consideration only if some systematic test seems to support it. For example, Michael Carroll suggested a Freudian interpretation of the "Star Husband Tale"—that the story represents repressed sentiments in the society. Specifically, he suggested that incestuous intercourse is the underlying concern of this myth, particularly the desire of a daughter to have intercourse with her father. He assumed that the stars symbolize fathers. Fathers, like stars, are high above, in children's eyes. Carroll predicted that, if the "Star Husband Tale" originated on the Plains, and if it symbolizes intercourse, then the Plains groups should be more likely than other societies to have intercourse imagery in their versions of the tale. That seems to be the case. Analyzing 84 versions of the tale, Carroll found that Plains societies are the Native American groups most likely to have imagery suggesting intercourse, including the lowering of a rope or ladder—symbolizing the penis—through a sky hole—symbolizing the vagina.[32]

Few studies have investigated why there is cross-cultural variation in the frequency of certain features in folktales. One feature of folktale variation that has been investigated cross-culturally is aggression. George Wright found that variation in childrearing patterns predicted some aspects of how aggression is exhibited in folktales. Where children are severely punished for aggression, more intense aggression appears in the folktales. And in such societies, strangers are more likely than the hero or friends of the hero to be the aggressors in the folktales. It seems that where children may be afraid to exhibit aggression toward their parents or those close to them because of fear of punishment, the hero or close friends in folktales are also not likely to be aggressive.[33]

Other kinds of fears may be reflected in folktales. A cross-cultural study by Alex Cohen found that unprovoked aggression is likely in folktales of societies that are subject to unpredictable food shortages. Why? One possibility is that the folktales reflect reality; after all, a serious drought may seem capricious, not possibly provoked by any human activity, brought on by the gods or nature "out of the blue." Curiously, however, societies with a history of unpredictable food shortages hardly mention natural disasters in their folktales, perhaps because disasters are too frightening. In any case, the capriciousness of unpredictable disasters seems to be transformed into the capricious aggression of characters in the folktales.[34]

Folklore, just like other aspects of art, may at least partly reflect the feelings, needs, and conflicts that people acquire as a result of growing up in their culture.

VIEWING THE ART OF OTHER CULTURES

Sally Price raised some critical questions about how Western museums and art critics look at the visual art of less complex cultures. Why is it that when artworks from Western or Oriental civilizations are displayed in a museum here, they carry the artist's name? In contrast, art from less complex cultures, often labeled "primitive art," tends to be displayed without the name of the artist; instead, it is often accompanied by a description of where it came from, how it was constructed, and what it may be used for. More words of explanation seem to accompany displays of unfamiliar art. Price suggested that the art pieces that we consider the most worthy require the least labeling, subtly conveying that the viewer needs no help to judge a real work of art.[35] In addition, art acquired from less complex cultures tends to be labeled by the name of the Westerner who acquired it. It is almost as if the fame of the collector, not the art itself, sets the value of such art.[36]

Just as the art from less complex cultures tends to be nameless, it also tends to be treated as timeless. We recognize that Western art and the art from classical civilizations change over time, which is why it must be dated, but the art from other places seems to be viewed as representing a timeless cultural tradition.[37] Do we know that the art of peoples with simpler technology changes less, or is this assumption a kind of ethnocentrism? Price, who has studied the art of the Saramakas of Suriname, points out that

Navajo rugs have changed over time. On the left are rugs from 1905; on the right, rugs from a modern trading post.

although Westerners think of Saramakan art as still representing its African ancestry, Saramakans themselves can identify shifts in their art styles over time. For example, they describe how calabashes used to be decorated on the outside, then the style changed to decorating the inside. They can also recognize the artist who made particular carved calabashes as well as identify those who were innovators of designs and techniques.[38]

When Westerners do notice changes over time in the art of less complex societies, it seems to be because they are concerned about whether the art represents traditional forms or is "tourist art." Tourist art is often evaluated negatively, perhaps because of its association with money. But famous Western artists often also worked for fees or were supported by elite patrons, and yet the fact that they were paid does not seem to interfere with our evaluation of their art.[39]

Although it seems that individual artists can usually be recognized in any community, some societies do appear to be more "communal" than others in their art style. For example, let us compare the Puebloan peoples of the Southwest with native peoples of the Great Plains. Traditionally, women Puebloan potters did not sign their pots, and they largely followed their pueblo's characteristic style. In contrast, each Plains warrior stressed his individual accomplishments by painting representations of those accomplishments on animal hides. Either the warrior would do it himself or he would ask someone else to do it for him. These hides were worn by the warrior or displayed outside his tipi.[40]

ARTISTIC CHANGE AND CULTURE CONTACT

It is unquestionably true that contact with the West did alter some aspects of the art of other cultures, but that does not imply that their art was changeless before. What kinds of things changed with contact? In some places, artists began to represent European contact itself. For example, in Australia, numerous rock paintings by aborigines portray sailing ships, men on horseback carrying pistols, and even cattle brands. With encouragement from Europeans,

indigenous artists also began drawing on tree bark, canvas, and fiberboard to sell to Europeans. Interestingly, the art for sale mostly emphasizes themes displayed before contact and does not include representations of ships and guns.[41] As aboriginal populations were decimated by European contact, a lot of their traditional art forms disappeared, particularly legends and rock paintings that were associated with the sacred sites of each clan. The legends described the creation of the sacred places, and art motifs with painted human or animal heroes marked the sites.[42]

In North America, contact between native groups produced changes in art even before the Europeans came. Copper, sharks' teeth, and marine shells were traded extensively in precontact times and were used in the artwork of people who did not have access to those materials locally. Ceremonies were borrowed among groups, and with the new ceremonies came changes in artistic traditions. Borrowing from other native groups continued after European contact. The Navajo, who are well known today for their rug weaving, were not weavers in the 17th century. They probably obtained their weaving technology from the Hopi and then began to weave wool and herd sheep. European contact also produced material changes in art; new materials, including beads, wool cloth, and silver, were introduced. Metal tools such as needles and scissors could now be used to make more tailored and more decorated skin clothing. In the Northwest, the greater availability of metal tools made it possible to make larger totem poles and house posts.[43]

After they were placed on reservations, virtually all Native Americans had to change their ways of making a living. Selling arts and crafts earned some of them supplementary income. Most of these crafts used traditional techniques and traditional designs, altered somewhat to suit European expectations. Outsiders played important roles in encouraging changes in arts and crafts. Some storekeepers became patrons to particular artists who were then able to devote themselves full time to their craft. Traders would often encourage changes, such as new objects—for example, ashtrays and cups made of pottery. Scholars have played a role too. Some have helped artisans learn about styles of the past that had disappeared. For example, with the encouragement of anthropologists and others in the Santa Fe area,

Maria and Julian Martinez of San Ildefonso Pueblo brought back a polished black-on-black pottery style originally produced by nearby ancient peoples.[44]

Some of the artistic changes that have occurred after contact with the West are partly predictable from the results of cross-cultural research on artistic variation. Remember that Fischer found that egalitarian societies typically had less complex designs and more symmetry than did stratified societies. With the loss of traditional ways of making a living and with the increase in wage labor and commercial enterprises, many Native American groups have become more socially stratified. Extrapolating from Fischer's results, we would predict that designs on visual art should become more complex and asymmetrical as social stratification increases. Indeed, if early reservation art (1870–1901) among the Shoshone-Bannock of southeastern Idaho is compared with their recent art (1973–1983), it is clear that the art has become more complex as social stratification has increased.[45] It could also be true that the art changed because the artists came to realize that more asymmetry and complexity would sell better to people who collect art.

SUMMARY ● ○ ○

1. Not all societies have a word for art, but art universally seems to have several qualities. It expresses as well as communicates. It stimulates the senses, affects emotions, and evokes ideas. It is produced in culturally patterned ways and styles. It has cultural meaning. And some people are thought to be better at it than others.

2. All societies decorate or adorn the body, temporarily or permanently. But there is enormous cultural variation in the parts decorated and how. Body decoration may be used to delineate social position, gender, or occupation. It may also have an erotic significance, as, for example, in drawing attention to erogenous zones of the body.

3. The materials used to produce visual art, the way those materials are used, and the natural objects the artist may choose to represent all vary from society to society and reveal much about a particular society's relation to its environment. Some studies indicate a correlation between artistic design and social stratification.

4. Like the visual arts, music is subject to a remarkable amount of variation from society to society. Some studies suggest correlations between musical styles and cultural complexity. Other research shows links between childrearing practices and a society's preference for certain rhythmical patterns, tonal ranges, and voice quality.

5. Folklore is a broad category including all the myths, legends, folktales, ballads, riddles, proverbs, and superstitions of a cultural group. In general, folklore is transmitted orally, but it may also be written. Some anthropologists have identified basic themes in myths—catastrophe, slaying of monsters, incest, sibling rivalry, and castration. Myths may reflect a society's deepest preoccupations.

6. Art is always changing, but recent culture contact has had some profound effects on art in various parts of the world. With the decimation of many indigenous populations, many areas have lost some of their artistic traditions. But the art also changed as individuals began to sell arts and crafts.

GLOSSARY TERMS ○ ● ○

folklore 296   polyphony 294

CRITICAL QUESTIONS ○ ○ ●

1. How innovative or original can a successful artist be? Explain your answer.

2. What kind of art do you prefer, and why?

3. Do you think art made for tourists is inferior? Whatever you think, why do you think so?

PEARSON
myanthrolab

Read the chapter by Donald Mitchell titled "Nimpkish: Complex Foragers on the Northwest Coast of North America" on MyAnthroLab, and answer the following questions:

1. The art form of dance was important to the Nimpkish. Why do you think?

2. In what season were the dances held, and why do you think they occurred then?

chapter 17

Applied, Practicing, and Medical Anthropology

nthropology is no longer a merely academic subject. A large number of anthropologists in the United States are applied and practicing anthropologists. Some estimates suggest that more than half of those with graduate degrees in anthropology are now employed outside of colleges and universities.[1] The fact that so many organizations hire anthropologists suggests an increasing realization that anthropology, what it has discovered and can discover about humans, is useful. Anthropologists who call themselves applied or practicing anthropologists work for a large variety of organizations, government agencies, international development agencies, private consulting firms, public health organizations, medical schools, public interest law firms, community development agencies, charitable foundations, and profit-seeking corporations (see the box on anthropology and business).

● ○ ○ ●

Applied or **practicing anthropology** as a profession is explicitly concerned with making anthropological knowledge useful. Applied or practicing anthropologists may be involved in one or more phases of a project: assembling relevant knowledge, developing plans and policies, assessing the likely social and environmental impacts, implementation, and evaluating the project and its effects.[2] Anthropologists are most often involved in gathering information, rather than constructing policy or initiating action.[3] The organizations that hire the applied anthropologists usually set policy and have staff to execute projects. However, anthropologists are increasingly finding themselves involved in policy making and action. The field of applied or practicing anthropology is very diverse. In this chapter, we first focus on general issues: ethics; evaluating the effects of planned change; and the difficulties of implementing change. In the course of this discussion, we cover a variety of projects, mostly development projects. We then turn to several other kinds of applications: *cultural resource management*, the "social impact" studies required in connection with many government or private programs, and *forensic anthropology*—the use of physical anthropology to help identify human remains and assist in solving crimes. The chapter concludes with an extensive discussion of the application of anthropological knowledge to the study of health and illness. In the chapter that follows, we describe how anthropology has been, or could be, used to solve global problems.

ETHICS OF APPLIED ANTHROPOLOGY

Anthropologists have usually studied people who are disadvantaged—by imperialism, colonialism, and other forms of exploitation—and so it is no wonder that we care about the people's lives we have shared. But caring is not enough to improve others' lives. We may need basic research that allows us to understand how a condition might be successfully treated. A particular proposed "improvement" might actually not be an improvement; well-meaning efforts have sometimes produced harmful consequences. And even if we know that a change would be an improvement, there is still the problem of how to make

As part of a study funded by USAID, a multidisciplinary team consisting of anthropologists, engineers, and agricultural experts from the United States met with villagers in Senegal to assess how the Manantali Dam might affect them.

that change happen. The people to be affected may not want to change. Is it ethical to try to persuade them? And, conversely, is it ethical *not* to try? Applied anthropologists must take all of these matters into consideration in determining whether and how to act in response to a perceived need.

Anthropology as a profession has adopted certain principles of responsibility. Above all, an anthropologist's first responsibility is to those who are being studied; everything should be done to ensure that their welfare and dignity will be protected. Anthropologists also have a responsibility to those who will read about their research; research findings should be reported openly and truthfully.[4] But because applied anthropology often deals with planning and implementing changes in some population, ethical responsibilities can become complicated. Perhaps the most important ethical question is: Will the change truly benefit the potentially affected population?

In May 1946, the Society for Applied Anthropology established a committee to draw up a specific code of ethics for professional applied anthropologists. After many meetings and revisions, a statement on ethical responsibilities was finally adopted in 1948, and in 1983, the statement was revised.[5] According to the code, the targeted community should be included as much as possible in the formulation of policy,

so that people in the community may know in advance how the program will affect them. Perhaps the most important aspect of the code is the pledge not to recommend or take any action that is harmful to the interests of the community. The National Association for the Practice of Anthropology goes further: If the work the employer expects of the employee violates the ethical principles of the profession, the practicing anthropologist has the obligation to try to change those practices or, if change cannot be brought about, to withdraw from the work.[6]

Ethical issues are often complicated. Thayer Scudder described the situation of Gwembe Tonga villagers who were relocated after a large dam was built in the Zambezi Valley of central Africa. Economic conditions improved during the 1960s and early 1970s, as the people increasingly produced goods and services for sale. But then conditions deteriorated. By 1980, the villagers were in a miserable state; rates of mortality, alcoholism, theft, assault, and murder were up. Why? One reason was that they had cut back on producing their own food in favor of producing for the world market. Such a strategy works well when world market prices are high; however, when prices fall, so does the standard of living.[7] The situation described by Scudder illustrates the ethical dilemma for many

303

applied anthropology

Anthropology and Business

Only relatively recently have business-people come to realize that anthropologists have useful knowledge to contribute, particularly with regard to the globalization of trade, the increase in international investments and joint ventures, and the spread of multinational corporations. What can anthropology offer? One of the most important contributions of anthropology is the understanding of how much culture can influence relationships between people of different cultures. For example, anthropologists know that communication is much more than the formal understanding of another language. People in some countries, such as the United States, expect explicit, straightforward verbal messages, but people in other countries are more indirect in their verbal messages. In Japan and China, for example, negative messages are less likely than messages expressing politeness and harmony. Many Eastern cultures have ways of saying no without saying the word.

It is also important to understand that different cultures may have different values. People in the United States place a high value on the individual, but as we discussed in the chapter on culture and the individual, the importance of relationships with others may take precedence over individual needs in other places. People in the United States emphasize the future, youth, informality, and competitiveness, but the emphases in other societies are often the opposite. In any business arrangement, perhaps no difference is as salient as the value a culture places on time. As we say, "Time is money." If a meeting is arranged and the other person is late, say, 45 minutes, people from the United States consider it rude; but such a delay is well within the range of acceptable behavior in many South American countries.

Anthropologists have helped businesses become aware of their own "cultures" (sometimes referred to as *organizational cultures*). The organizational culture of a business may interfere with the acceptance of new kinds of workers, or it may interfere with changing business needs. If parts of that culture need to be changed, it is necessary first to identify what the culture involves and to understand how and why it developed the way it did. Anthropologists know how to identify cultural patterns on the basis of systematic observation and interviewing individuals.

Anthropologist Jill Kleinberg studied six Japanese-owned firms in the United States to understand the impact of both the larger culture and the organizational culture of the workplace. All six firms employed both Japanese and Americans, although the Japanese dominated the managerial positions. The main goal of the study was to discover why there was considerable tension in the six firms. Kleinberg's first order of business was to interview people about their views of work and their jobs. She found clear differences between the Japanese and the American employees that seemed to reflect broader cultural differences. Americans wanted a clear definition of the job and its attached responsibilities, and they also wanted their job titles, authority, rights, and pay to match closely. The Japanese, on the other hand, emphasized the need to be flexible in their responsibilities as well as their tasks. They also felt that part of their responsibility was to help their co-workers. (See the box "Schools: Values and Expectations" in the chapter on culture and the individual, in which we discussed Japanese preschools and their emphasis on the good of the group.) Americans were uncomfortable because the Japanese managers did not indicate exactly what the workers were supposed to do; even if there was a job description, the manager did not appear to pay attention to it. Americans were given little information, were left out of decision making, and were frustrated by the lack of

opportunity to advance. The Japanese thought that the Americans were too hard to manage, too concerned with money and authority, and too concerned with their own interests.

Dissatisfaction is a problem in any business. Absenteeism, high turnover, and lack of incentive on the job all detract from job performance and business capability. Kleinberg recommended giving all employees more information about the company as well as conducting training sessions about cross-cultural differences in business cultures. She also recommended making the Japanese philosophy of management more explicit during the hiring process so that the company would be able to find Americans who were comfortable with that philosophy. But she also suggested that the managerial structure be somewhat "Americanized" so that American employees could feel at ease. Finally, she recommended that Americans be given more managerial positions and contact with their Japanese counterparts overseas. These suggestions might not eliminate all problems, but they would increase mutual understanding and trust.

In a way, then, as Andrew Miracle notes, the work of the practicing anthropologist is similar to the shaman's in traditional societies. The people who call on shamans for help believe in their abilities to help, and the shaman tries to find ways to empower the client to think positively. To be sure, there are profound differences between shamans and applied anthropologists. Perhaps the most important is that applied anthropologists use research, not trance or magic, to effect an organizational cure. Like shamans, however, applied anthropologists must make an understandable diagnosis and help clients see the way to health and restored power.

Sources: Ferraro 2002; Kleinberg 1994; Miracle 2009.

Businesses and consulting companies are doing more ethnographic research. Such research in the United States among families during the morning suggests that "breakfast" has become an intermittent series of snacks throughout the morning as families struggle with their time schedules and finding the right foods for their children.

applied anthropologists. As he said: "So how is it that I can still justify working for the agencies that fund such projects?" He points out that large-scale projects are almost impossible to stop. The anthropologist can choose to stand on the sidelines and complain or try to influence the project to benefit the affected population as much as possible.[8]

The problem described by Scudder comes about in part because the anthropologist is not often involved until after a decision is made to go ahead with a change program. This situation has begun to change as applied anthropologists are increasingly asked to participate in earlier stages of the planning process. Anthropologists are also increasingly asked to help in projects initiated by the affected party. Such requests may range from help in solving problems in corporate organizations to helping Native Americans with land claims. Because the project is consistent with the wishes of the affected population, the results are not likely to put the anthropologist into an ethical dilemma.

When physical anthropologists and archaeologists work with skeletal and even fossil materials, the ethical complications can become extremely complex. Consider the case of "Kennewick Man," a 9,200-year-old skeleton found in July 1996, along the Columbia River in Washington State. Before anthropologists could study the skeleton, the U.S. Army Corps of Engineers decided to turn the remains over to the Umatilla Indians, as the remains were found on Corps land within their reservation. The physical anthropologists and archaeologists who wanted to study this very old skeleton faced an ethical quandary: A group claiming to be related to the individual did not

want the study to be undertaken, but, without the study, the group's claim of relationship could not be firmly established.[9] The physical anthropologists and archaeologists filed a lawsuit under the Native American Graves Protection and Repatriation Act of 1900, which provides absolute protection to Native American graves on federal land, and which makes it a felony to collect, possess, or transfer human remains of known affinity to an existing Native American culture, except if approved by the members of that culture.[10]

At the core of the legal case was this question: To whom does this skeleton belong? If this is an individual who is related to contemporary Native Americans, then do the Umatilla get to speak for all Native American groups, even though 9,000 years separate them? Or should other Native American groups, who may also be descended from this individual or his group, also have a say in what happens? If this is an individual who appears not to be related to contemporary Native Americans, then should the U.S. government decide what happens to his remains? Underlying these questions was a deeper struggle between anthropologists and Native Americans over historic preservation and whose wishes and ideas carry the most weight. Archaeologists and physical anthropologists feel ethical responsibilities that can be in conflict when dealing with human remains. As part of the archaeological record, archaeologists and physical anthropologists have an ethical responsibility to protect and preserve human remains. As anthropologists, they have the ethical responsibility to consult with and follow the wishes of local groups with whom they are working. The "Kennewick Man" case highlights this ethical conflict, for which there seems no easy answer.

EVALUATING THE EFFECTS OF PLANNED CHANGE

The decision as to whether a proposed change would benefit the affected population is not always easy to make. In certain cases, as when improved medical care is involved, the benefits offered to the target group would seem to be unquestionable—we all feel sure that health is better than illness. However, what about the long-term effects? Consider a public health innovation such as inoculation against disease. Once the inoculation program was begun, the number of children surviving would probably increase. But will there be enough food for the additional population? Given the level of technology, capital, and land resources possessed by the population, there might not be enough resources to feed more people. Thus, the death rate, because of starvation, might rise to its previous level and perhaps even exceed it. Without additional changes to increase the food supply, the inoculation program in the long term might merely change the causes of death. This example shows that, even if a program of planned change has beneficial consequences in the short run, a great deal of thought and investigation has to be given to its long-term effects.

Debra Picchi raised questions about the long-term effects on the Bakairí Indians of a program by the Brazilian National Indian Foundation (FUNAI) to produce rice with machine technology.[11] The Bakairí of the Mato Grosso region largely practice slash-and-burn horticulture in gallery forests along rivers, with supplementary cattle raising, fishing, and hunting. In the early part of the 20th century, their population had declined to 150 people and they were given a relatively small reserve, much of it parched and infertile (*cerrado*). When the Bakairí population began to increase, FUNAI introduced a scheme to plant rice on formerly unused *cerrado* land, using machinery, insecticides, and fertilizer. FUNAI paid the costs for the first year and expected that the scheme would be self-supporting by the third year. The project did not go so well because FUNAI did not deliver all the equipment needed and did not provide adequate advice. Only half the expected rice was produced. Still, it was more food than the Bakairí had previously, so the program should have been beneficial to them.

But there were unanticipated negative side effects. Using *cerrado* land for agriculture reduced the area on which cattle could be grazed; cattle are an important source of high-quality protein. Mechanization also makes the Bakairí more dependent on cash for fuel, insecticides, fertilizer, and repairs. But cash is hard to come by. Only some individuals can be hired—usually men with outside experience who have the required knowledge of machinery. So the cash earned in the now-mechanized agriculture goes mainly to a relatively small number of people, creating new inequalities of income.

The benefits of programs or applied efforts are sometimes obvious. For example, Haiti has experienced serious deforestation. The process began in colonial times when the Spanish exported wood and the French cleared forests to grow sugarcane, coffee, and indigo. After Haiti's independence, foreign lumber companies continued to cut and sell hardwood. Wood is needed by the local population for fuel and for construction, but rapid population increases have increased the demand for fuel and wood, and the trees were rapidly diminishing. The loss of tree cover also speeds up erosion of topsoil. Forestry experts, environmentalists, and anthropologists all agree about the need to stop this trend. How to bring about the appropriate change is not so easy. The poorer people become, the more likely they are to cut down trees to sell.[12]

These failures were not the fault of anthropologists—indeed, most instances of planned change by governments and other agencies usually have begun without the input of anthropologists at all. Applied anthropologists have played an important role in pointing out the problems with programs like these that fail to evaluate long-term consequences. Such evaluations are an important part of convincing governments and other agencies to ask for anthropological help in the first place. Ironically, failure experiences are learning experiences: Applied anthropologists who study previous examples of planned change can often learn a great deal about what is likely or not likely to be beneficial in the long run.

DIFFICULTIES IN INSTITUTING PLANNED CHANGE

After numerous reforestation projects failed in Haiti, an anthropologist, Gerald Murray, was asked to help design a program that would work.[13] Understanding why previous projects failed was the first step in helping Murray design an effective project. One problem seems to have been that previous projects were run through the government's Ministry of Agriculture. The seedling trees that were given away were referred to as "the state's trees." So, when project workers told farmers not to cut the new trees down so as to protect the environment, farmers took this statement to mean that the land on which the trees were planted might be considered government land, which the farmers could not care less about. In the project proposed by Murray, private voluntary organizations rather than the Haitian government were used to distribute trees and the farmers were told that they were the tree owners. Ownership included the right to cut the trees and sell the wood, just as they could sell crops. In previous projects, farmers were given heavy, hard-to-transport seedlings that took a long time to mature. They were told to plant in a large communal woodlot, an idea inconsistent with the more individualistic Haitian land tenure arrangements. In the new plan, the tree seedlings given away were fast-growing species that matured in as little as four years. In addition, the new seedlings were very small and could be planted quickly. Perhaps most important of all, the new trees could be planted in borders or interspersed with other crops, interfering little with traditional crop patterns. To Murray's great surprise, by the end of two years, 2,500 Haitian households had planted 3 million seedlings. Over 20 years, the estimate is that over a 100 million trees were planted and over 350,000 farm families were involved in the project, more than 40 percent of rural households.[14] Also, farmers were not rushing to cut down trees. Because growing trees do not spoil, farmers were postponing their cutting and sales until they needed cash. So even though farmers were told that it was all right to cut down trees, a statement contrary to the message of previous reforestation projects, the landscape was filling up with trees.

People cut down trees in Haiti for firewood and to clear fields, resulting in severe deforestation. The need for reforestation is clear, but how to bring about change was not so clear.

Murray's lengthy participant observation and interviewing had helped him predict what might overcome the previous implementation difficulties and fit in with the Haitian farmers' needs. The idea that wood could be an important marketable cash crop was much more consistent with farmers' existing behavior—they already sold crops for cash when they needed it. The difference now was that, instead of cutting down naturally grown wood, they were raising wood just as they raised other crops.

Whether a program of planned change can be successfully implemented depends largely on whether the people want the proposed change and like the proposed program. Before an attempt can be made at cultural innovation, the innovators must determine whether the population is aware of the benefits of the proposed change. Lack of awareness can be a temporary barrier to solving the problem at hand. For example, health workers have often had difficulty convincing people that they were becoming ill because something was wrong with their water supply. Many people do not believe that disease can be transmitted by water. At other times, the population is perfectly aware of the problem. A case in point involved Taiwanese women who were introduced to family-planning methods beginning in the 1960s. The women knew they were having more children than they wanted or could easily afford, and they wanted to control their birth rate. They offered no resistance—they merely had to be given the proper devices and instructions, and the birth rate quickly fell to a more desirable, and more manageable, level.[15]

Overcoming Resistance

Many change projects experience resistance, and most of the time the change agents try to figure out how to overcome the resistance. But not all proposed change programs are beneficial to the recipients. Sometimes resistance is rational. Applied anthropologists have pointed to cases where the judgment of the affected population has been better than that of the agents of change. One such example occurred during a Venezuelan government–sponsored program to give infants powdered milk. The mothers rejected the milk, even though it was free, on the grounds that it implied that the mothers' milk was no good.[16] But who is to say that the resistance was not in fact intuitively smart, reflecting an awareness that such a milk program would not benefit the children? Medical research now indicates quite clearly that mothers' milk is far superior to powdered milk or formula. First, human milk best supplies the nutrients needed for human development. Second, it is now known that the mother, through her milk, is able to transmit antibodies (disease resistances) to the baby. And third, nursing delays ovulation and usually increases the spacing between births.[17]

The switchover to powdered milk and formula in many underdeveloped areas has been nothing short of a disaster, resulting in increased malnutrition and misery. For one thing, powdered milk must be mixed with water, but if the water and the bottles are not sterilized, more sickness is introduced. Then, too, if powdered milk has to be purchased, mothers without cash are forced to dilute the

milk to stretch it. And if a mother feeds her baby formula or powder for even a short time, the process is tragically irreversible, for her own milk dries up and she cannot return to breast-feeding even if she wants to.

As the Venezuelan example suggests, individuals may be able to resist proposed medical or health projects because acceptance is ultimately a personal matter. Large development projects planned by powerful governments or agencies rarely are stoppable, but even they can be resisted successfully. The Kayapo of the Xingu River region of Brazil were able to cancel a plan by the Brazilian government to build dams along the river for hydroelectric power. The Kayapo gained international attention when some of their leaders appeared on North American and European television and then successfully organized a protest in 1989, by members of several tribal groups. Their success seemed to come in part from their ability to present themselves to the international community as guardians of the rain forest—an image that resonated with international environmental organizations that supported their cause. Although to outsiders it might seem that the Kayapo want their way of life to remain as it was, the Kayapo are not opposed to all change. In fact, they want greater access to medical care, other government services, and manufactured goods from outside.[18]

Even if a project is beneficial to a population, it may still meet with resistance, as the tree reforestation project in Haiti illustrated. Factors that may hinder acceptance can be divided roughly into three, sometimes overlapping, categories: *cultural, social,* and *psychological* barriers.

Cultural barriers are shared behaviors, attitudes, and beliefs that tend to impede the acceptance of an innovation. For example, members of different societies may view gift giving in different ways. Particularly in commercialized societies, things received for nothing are often believed to be worthless. When the government of Colombia instituted a program of giving seedling orchard trees to

Medha Patkar leading a protest rally in New Delhi against Narmada dams.

farmers to increase fruit production, the farmers showed virtually no interest in the seedlings, many of which proceeded to die of neglect. When the government realized that the experiment had apparently failed, it began to charge each farmer a nominal fee for the seedlings. Soon the seedlings became immensely popular and fruit production increased.[19] Other examples of cultural resistance to change, which we discuss more when we discuss medical anthropology, are beliefs about sex that make it difficult for people to follow medical guidelines for safer sex.

It is very important for agents of change to understand what the shared beliefs and attitudes are. First, indigenous cultural concepts or knowledge can sometimes be used effectively to enhance educational programs. For instance, in a program in Haiti to prevent child mortality from diarrhea, change agents used the terminology for traditional native herbal tea remedies (*rafrechi*, or cool refreshment) to identify the new oral rehydration therapy, which is a very successful medical treatment. In native belief, diarrhea is a "hot" illness and appropriate remedies have to have cooling properties.[20] Second, even if indigenous beliefs are not helpful to the campaign, not paying attention to contrary beliefs can undermine the campaign. But uncovering contrary beliefs is not easy, particularly when they do not emerge in ordinary conversation.

The acceptance of planned change may also depend on social factors. Research suggests that acceptance is more likely if the change agent and the target or potential adopter are similar socially. But change agents may have higher social status and more education than the people they are trying to influence. So change agents may work more with higher-status individuals because they are more likely to accept new ideas. If lower-status individuals also have to be reached, change agents of lower status may have to be employed.[21]

Finally, acceptance may depend on psychological factors—that is, how the individuals perceive both the innovation and the agents of change. In the course of trying to encourage women in the southeastern United States to breast-feed rather than bottle-feed their infants, researchers discovered a number of reasons why women were reluctant to breast-feed their infants, even though they heard it was healthier. Many women did not have confidence that they would produce enough milk for their babies; they were embarrassed about breast-feeding in public; and their family and friends had negative attitudes.[22] In designing an educational program, change agents may have to address such psychological concerns directly.

Discovering and Utilizing Local Channels of Influence

In planning a project involving cultural change, the administrator of the project should find out what the normal channels of influence are in the population. In most communities, there are preestablished networks for communication, as well as people of high prestige or influence who are looked to for guidance and direction. An understanding of such channels of influence is extremely valuable when deciding how to introduce a program of change. In addition, it is useful to know at what times, and in what

sorts of situations, one channel is likely to be more effective in spreading information and approval than another.

An example of the effective use of local channels of influence occurred when an epidemic of smallpox broke out in the Kalahandi district of the state of Orissa in India. The efforts of health workers to vaccinate villagers against the disease were consistently resisted. The villagers, naturally suspicious and fearful of these strange men with their equally strange medical equipment, were unwilling to offer themselves, and particularly their babies, to the peculiar experiments the strangers wished to perform. Afraid of the epidemic, the villagers appealed for help to their local priest, whose opinions on such matters they trusted. The priest went into a trance, explaining that the illness was the result of the goddess Thalerani's anger with the people. She could be appeased, he continued, only by massive feasts, offerings, and other demonstrations of the villagers' worship of her. Realizing that the priest was the village's major opinion leader, at least in medical matters, the frustrated health workers tried to get the priest to convince his people to undergo vaccination. At first, the priest refused to cooperate with the strange men, but when his favorite nephew fell ill, he decided to try any means available to cure the boy. He thereupon went into another trance, telling the villagers that the goddess wished all her worshipers to be vaccinated. Fortunately, the people agreed, and the epidemic was largely controlled.[23]

If channels of influence are not stable, using influential people in a campaign can sometimes backfire. In the educational campaign in Haiti to promote the use of oral rehydration therapy to treat diarrhea in children, Madame Duvalier, the first lady of Haiti at the time, lent her name to the project. Because there were no serious social or cultural barriers to the treatment and mothers reported that children took to the solutions well, success was expected. But in the middle of the campaign, Haiti became embroiled in political turmoil and the first lady's husband was overthrown. Some of the public thought that the oral rehydration project was a plot by the Duvaliers to sterilize children, and this suspicion fueled resistance.[24] As the earlier discussion of Haiti deforestation shows, people in Haiti were suspicious of any government-sponsored program.

Applied anthropologists often advocate integrating indigenous healers into medical change programs. This idea may encounter considerable resistance by the medical profession and by government officials who view such healers negatively. But this strategy may be quite effective in more isolated areas where indigenous healers are the only sources of health care. If they are involved in medical change programs, indigenous healers are likely to refer patients to hospitals when they feel unable to cope with an illness, and the hospitals choose sometimes to refer patients to the healers.[25]

Need for More Collaborative Applied Anthropology

Most large-scale programs of planned change originate with governments, international aid organizations, or other agencies. Even if the programs are well intentioned and even if the appropriate evaluations are made to ensure that the population will not be harmed, the population targeted for the change is usually not involved in the decision making. Some anthropologists, like Wayne Warry, think that applied anthropology should be more collaborative. Warry explains that he was asked by a Native Canadian elder whether he (Warry) would tolerate his own methods and interpretations if he were the native.[26] This question prompted him to involve himself in a project with Native Canadian collaborators, directed by the Mamaweswen Tribal Council. The project assesses health care needs and develops plans to improve local community health care. Funding is provided by the Canadian government as part of a program to transfer health care to the First Nations. Native researchers are conducting the surveys and workshops to keep the community informed about the project. The tribal council also reviews any publications and shares in any profits resulting from those publications.

Applied anthropologists may be increasingly asked to work on behalf of indigenous grassroots organizations. As we saw in the chapter on associations, the developing world has seen a proliferation of such groups. In some cases, these small groups and networks of such groups are starting to hire their own technical assistance.[27] When such organizations do the hiring, they control the decision making. There is increasing evidence that grassroots organizations are the key to effective development. For example, Kenyan farmers who belong to grassroots organizations produce higher farm yields than those farmers who do not belong, even though the latter group is exposed to more agricultural extension agents.[28] Grassroots organizations can succeed where government or outside projects fail. We have plenty of instances of people effectively resisting projects. Their willingness to change, and their participation in crucial decision making, may be mostly responsible for the success of a change project.

There is another kind of collaboration that is becoming increasingly important. Many projects require team efforts, working with people from other disciplines. Anthropologists increasingly have to be conversant with the theory and methods in other fields to understand and negotiate with other members of their team. Earlier anthropologists might have been more likely to work alone. Now that is less likely.[29]

Commuters look at 4th century ruins uncovered as part of a large scale CRM project associated with construction of the Athens metro system.

CULTURAL RESOURCE MANAGEMENT

Large-scale programs of planned change like those discussed earlier in this chapter have an impact not only on living people. They can also have an impact on the archaeological record left by the ancestors of living people. Recovering and preserving the archaeological record before programs of planned change disturb or destroy it is called **cultural resource management (CRM).** CRM work is carried out by archaeologists who are often called "contract archaeologists" because they typically work under contract to a government agency, a private developer, or a native group.

What kinds of impact can programs of planned change have on the archaeological record? In the 1960s, a large number of hydroelectric dam projects were initiated to provide flood control and to bring a stable source of electrical power to developing nations. In Egypt, a dam was built on the Nile River at a site called Aswan. Archaeologists realized that once the dam was in place a huge lake would form behind it, submerging thousands of archaeological sites, including the massive temple of Rameses II. Something needed to be done; the archaeological record had to be salvaged or protected. In the language of CRM, there needed to be a *mitigation plan* put into action. And there was. As the Aswan dam was being built, archaeologists went to work excavating sites that would be flooded. Archaeologists and engineers designed a way to take apart the temple of Rameses II and rebuild it, piece by piece, on higher ground where it would not be flooded. By the time the dam was completed in 1965, hundreds of sites had been investigated and two entire temple complexes moved.

Large-scale development projects are not the only projects that involve CRM archaeologists. In many nations, including the United States and Canada, historic preservation laws require any project receiving federal funds to ensure that archaeological resources are protected or their damage mitigated. Highway construction projects in the United States are common places to find CRM archaeologists at work. Virtually all highway projects rely on federal funding, and before a highway can be built, a complete archaeological survey of the proposed right-of-way has to be made. If archaeological sites are found, potential damage to them must be mitigated. A CRM archaeologist will work with the construction company, the state archaeologist, and perhaps a federal archaeologist to decide on the best course of action. In some cases, the archaeological site will be excavated. In others, the right-of-way may be moved. In still others, the decision is to allow the archaeological site to be destroyed, because it would be too costly to excavate or the site may not be significant enough to warrant excavation. Regardless of the decision, the CRM archaeologist plays a crucial role in assessing and protecting the archaeological record.

CRM archaeologists do not work only for state or federal agencies. In many nations today, CRM archaeologists are also working with native peoples to protect, preserve, and manage archaeological materials for them. Indeed, archaeologist John Ravesloot recently stated that "the future of American archaeology is with Indian communities functioning as active, not passive, participants in the

A forensic anthropologist digs out a body, apparently a victim of state-sponsored violence in Argentina between 1976 and 1983.

interpretation, management, and preservation of their rich cultural heritage."[30] One example of such a working relationship is the Zuni Heritage and Historic Preservation Office. During the 1970s, the Pueblo of Zuni decided it needed to train tribal members in archaeology to ensure that Zuni cultural resources and properties were managed properly. It hired three professional archaeologists and, with additional assistance from the National Park Service and the Arizona State Museum, initiated a program to train and employ tribal members in cultural resource management. Working with these non-Zuni archaeologists, the Pueblo of Zuni were able to establish their own historic preservation office that today manages and coordinates all historic preservation on the Zuni reservation, a task that the federal government managed until 1992. The Pueblo also established the Zuni Cultural Resource Enterprise, a Zuni-owned CRM business that employs both Zuni and non-Zuni archaeologists and carries out contract archaeology projects both on and off the Zuni reservation.[31]

Cultural resource management accounts for the majority of archaeology jobs in the United States.[32] As development and construction projects continue to affect the archaeological record, the need for well-trained CRM archaeologists is likely to persist.

FORENSIC ANTHROPOLOGY

Many of us are fascinated by detective stories. We are interested in crimes and why they occur, and we like to read about them, fictional or not. **Forensic anthropology** is the specialty in anthropology that is devoted to helping solve crimes and identifying human remains, usually by applying knowledge of physical anthropology.[33] It is attracting increasing attention by the public, and an increasing number of practitioners. One forensic anthropologist says she is called "the bone lady" by law enforcement personnel.[34] Like others in her line of work, she is asked to dig up or

examine human bones to help solve crimes. Narrowing down identification is one of the first priorities, but it is not as simple as on television shows. Are these the bones of a man or woman? How old was the person? How well the forensic anthropologist can answer these seemingly simple questions depends upon whether the remains include most bones of the skeleton. Identification of an adult's sex from remains is easier if the pelvis is present, but establishing sex in nonadult remains is not reliable from skeletal remains.[35] With regard to estimating age, only a wide age range can be estimated for adults, but a much narrower range can be estimated for nonadult remains. Forensic anthropologists are often asked for "race" as well. As we discussed in earlier chapters, "race" is not a useful biological category when applied to humans, but it is a significant social category. Forensic anthropologists can estimate with fairly high accuracy whether a person's ancestors came from Asia, Europe, or Africa, but they cannot detect skin color.[36] The police files may suggest that an adult male with Asian ancestry disappeared five years ago. The forensic anthropologist could say with a high probability that the remains were of an Asian male adult. Dental, surgical, or hospital records from that individual might lead to unique features that could be matched for more precise identification. Sometimes the forensic anthropologist can suggest the cause of death when the law enforcement people are stumped.

Some cultural anthropologists have also done forensic work, often in connection with legal cases involving Native Americans. For example, in 1978, Barbara Joans was asked to advise the defense in a trial of six older Bannock-Shoshoni women from the Fort Hall reservation who were accused of fraud. They had received "supplemental security income (SSI)," which the social service agency claimed they had no right to receive because they had not reported receiving rent money on land that they owned. Joans presented evidence that the women, although they spoke some English, did not have enough proficiency to understand the nuances of what the SSI people told them. The judge agreed with the defense and ruled that the SSI would have to use a Bannock-Shoshoni interpreter in the future when they went to the reservation to describe the requirements of the program.[37]

In recent years, Clyde Snow and other forensic anthropologists have been called on to confirm horrendous abuses of human rights. Governments have been responsible for the systematic killing of their citizens, and forensic anthropologists have helped to bring the perpetrators to justice. For example, Snow and other forensic anthropologists helped to confirm that the military dictatorship in Argentina in the 1980s was responsible for the deaths of many Argentine civilians who had "disappeared." The forensic anthropologists were also able to determine the location of mass graves and the identity of victims of state-organized brutality in Guatemala. In addition to bringing the perpetrators to justice, confirming the massacres and identifying the victims help the families of the "disappeared" put their anguish behind them. A special session (called "Uncovering the 'Disappeared': Clyde Snow and Forensic Anthropologists Work for Justice"[38]) at the annual meeting of the American Anthropological Association in November 2000 honored Snow and other forensic anthropologists.

MEDICAL ANTHROPOLOGY

Illness and death are significant events for people everywhere. No one is spared. So it should not be surprising that how people understand the causes of illness and death, how they behave, and what resources they marshal to cope with these events are extremely important parts of culture. Some argue that we will never completely understand how to treat illness effectively until we understand the cultural behaviors, attitudes, values, and the larger social and political milieu in which people live. Others argue that society and culture have little to do with the outcome of illness—the reason that people die needlessly is that they do not get the appropriate medical treatment.

But anthropologists, particularly those in **medical anthropology,** who are actively engaged in studying health and illness, are increasingly realizing that biological *and* social factors need to be considered if we are to reduce human suffering. For instance, some populations have an appalling incidence of infant deaths due to diarrhea. The origin of this situation is mostly biological, in the sense that the deaths are caused by bacterial infection. But why are so many infants exposed to those bacteria? Usually, the main reason is social. The affected infants are likely to be poor. Because they are poor, they are likely to live with infected drinking water. Similarly, malnutrition may be the biological result of a diet poor in protein, but such a diet is usually also a cultural phenomenon, reflecting a society with classes of people with very unequal access to the necessities of life. In many ways, therefore, medical anthropology, and anthropology in general, are developing in the direction of a "biocultural synthesis."[39]

Medical anthropology is part of this developing synthesis. Indeed, the growth of jobs in medical anthropology is one of the more striking developments in contemporary anthropology. Medical anthropology has developed into a very popular specialty, and the Society for Medical Anthropology is now the second largest unit in the American Anthropological Association.[40]

The medical profession's ways of treating illness may be able to treat some conditions well, but by itself the medical profession cannot tell us why some groups are more affected than others, or why the effectiveness of treatment varies from group to group. This section discusses cultural variation in conceptions of health and illness, cultural universals and variables in how illness is treated, the political and social forces that affect health, and contributions of medical anthropology to the study and treatment of some diseases and health conditions.

CULTURAL UNDERSTANDINGS OF HEALTH AND ILLNESS

Medical researchers and medical practitioners in the United States and other Western societies do not exist in a social vacuum. Many of their ideas and practices are influenced by the culture in which they live. We may think of medicine as purely based on "fact," but it is clear on reflection that many ideas stem from the culture in which the researchers reside. Consider the recent shift in attitudes toward birth. Not so long ago in the United States, fathers were excluded from

In China and elsewhere, tai chi exercises are believed to bring harmony and balance.

the birth, hospitals whisked the baby away from the mother and only brought the baby to her infrequently, and visitors (but not attending nurses and doctors) had to wear masks when holding the baby. Rationalizations were given for those practices, but looking back at them, they do not appear to be based on scientific evidence. Many medical anthropologists now argue that the *biomedical paradigm* (the system in which physicians are trained) itself needs to be understood as part of the culture.

Discovering the health-related beliefs, knowledge, and practices of a cultural group—its **ethnomedicine**—is one of the goals of medical anthropology. How do cultures view health and illness? What are their theories about the causes of illness? Do those theories impact on how illnesses are treated? What is the therapeutic process? Are there specialized medical practitioners, and how do they heal? Are there special medicines, and how are they administered? These are just some of the questions asked by the anthropological study of ethnomedicine.

Concepts of Balance or Equilibrium

Many cultures have the view that the body should be kept in equilibrium or balance. The balance may be between hot and cold, or wet and dry, as in many cultures of Latin America and the Caribbean.[41] The notion of balance is not limited to opposites. For example, the ancient Greek system of medicine, stemming from Hippocrates, assumed that there were four "humors"—blood, phlegm, yellow bile, and black bile—that must be kept in balance. These humors have hot and cold as well as wet and dry properties. The Greek medical system was widely diffused in Europe and spread to parts of the Islamic world. In Europe, the humoral medical system was dominant until the germ theory replaced it in the 1900s.[42] In the Ayurvedic system, whose practice dates back 4,000 years in North India, Pakistan, Bangladesh, Sri Lanka, and in the Arab world, there are three humors (phlegm, bile, and flatulence), and a balance between hot and cold is also important.[43] The Chinese medical system, which dates back about 3,500 years, initially stressed the balance between the contrasting forces of *yin* and *yang* and later added the concept of humors, which were six in number in Chinese medicine.[44]

The concepts of hot and cold and *yin* and *yang* are illustrated in Emily Ahern's ethnographic description of the medical system of the Taiwanese Hokkien.[45] The body requires both hot and cold substances; when the body is out of balance, a lack of one substance can be restored by eating or drinking the missing substance. So, for example, when Ahern was faint with heat, she was told to drink some bamboo shoot soup because it was "cold." In the winter, you need more hot substances; in the summer, you want fewer. Some people can tolerate more imbalance than others; people who are older, for instance, can tolerate less imbalance than those who are young. A loss of blood means a loss of heat. So, for a month after childbirth, women eat mostly a soup made of chicken, wine, and sesame oil—all "hot" ingredients. Hot things to eat are generally oily, sticky, or come from animals; cold things tend to be soupy, watery, or made from plants.

The body also has *yin* and *yang* parts. The *yang* part is visible to the living. The *yin* part exists in the underworld in the shape of a house and tree. The roof of the house corresponds to a person's head, the walls to the skin, a woman's reproductive organs correspond to the flowers on the woman's tree, the roots of the tree to the legs, and so on. A shaman can enable villagers to go into a trance to look around in the underworld where the dead live. If a person has a health problem, a traveler may be sent to the underworld to see what is wrong with the person's *yin* house or tree. Fixing the *yin* house or tree should restore health to the *yang* part of the body. The *yin* world is also where ghosts reside; they sometimes may cause illness. In that case, people may ask for help from powerful gods who reside in the *yang* world.

Supernatural Forces

The Taiwanese Hokkien believe that most illnesses have natural or physiological causes, but around the world, it is more common to believe that illnesses are caused by supernatural forces. In fact, in a cross-cultural study of 139 societies, George P. Murdock found that only two societies did not have the belief that gods or spirits could cause illness, making such a belief a near universal. And 56 percent of those sample societies thought that gods or spirits were the major causes of illness.[46] As we discussed in the chapter on religion and magic, sorcery and witchcraft are common in the world's societies. Although humans practice both sorcery and witchcraft for good or evil, making people ill is one of their major uses. Illness can also be thought of as caused by the loss of one's soul, fate, retribution for violation of a taboo, or contact with a polluting or tabooed substance or object. Sorcery is believed to be a cause of illness by most societies on all continents; retribution because of violation of a taboo is also very frequent in all but one region of the world. The belief that soul loss can cause illness is absent in the area around the Mediterranean, uncommon in Africa, infrequent in the New World and the Pacific, and has its highest frequency in Eurasia.[47]

On Chuuk (Truk), an atoll in the central Pacific, serious illnesses and death are mainly believed to be the work of spirits. Occasionally, the spirits of relatives are to blame, although they usually do not cause serious damage. More often, illness is caused by the spirit of a particular locality or a ghost on a path at night.[48] Nowadays, one of two therapeutic options or their combination is often chosen—hospital medicine or Chuuk medicine. Chuuk medical treatment requires a careful evaluation of symptoms by the patient and the patient's relatives, because different spirits inflict different symptoms. If the symptom match is clear, the patient may choose an appropriate Chuuk medical formula to cure the illness. The patient may also ask whether he or she has done something wrong, and if so, what might point to the appropriate spirit and countervailing formula. For example, there is a taboo on having sexual relations before going to sea. If a person who violated this prohibition becomes ill, the reef spirits will be suspected. The Chuuk medical formula is supposed to cure illness quickly and dramatically. For this reason, Chuuk patients ask for a discharge from a hospital if their condition does not improve quickly. If treatment fails, the Chuukese believe that they need to reevaluate the diagnosis, sometimes with the aid of a diviner.[49] In contrasting their theories of illness to the American germ theory, the people of Chuuk point out that, although they have seen ghosts, they have never seen the germs that Americans talk about. Using both methods, some people recover and some do not, so the ultimate cause is a matter of faith.[50]

Among the Ojibwa, the most serious illnesses, the ones resistant to ordinary treatment, are thought to be due to retribution for doing wrong to another person, an animal, or a spirit. To cure such an illness, to yourself or to your children, you must reflect on your own conduct to see what you did wrong. Bad conduct cannot be withheld from the doctor or from the other people in the *wigwam*. On the contrary, only after confessing can medicine help.[51] The Hopi similarly believed that patients were responsible for their own illness, but the cause might be not just improper actions but also bad thoughts and anxiety. Witches could also cause illness, but the action of witches was most effective against people who were depressed or worried; so good thoughts ward off illness.[52]

The Biomedical Paradigm

In most societies, people simply think that their ideas about health and illness are true. Often people are not aware that there may be another way of viewing things until they confront another medical system. Western medical practice has spread widely. People with other medical systems have had to recognize that Western practitioners may consider their ideas about health and illness to be deficient, so they often need to decide which course (Western or non-Western) to follow in dealing with illness. Change, however, is not entirely one-way. For example, for a long time, the Western medical profession disparaged the Chinese practice of acupuncture, but now more medical practitioners are recognizing that acupuncture may provide effective treatment of certain conditions.

Most medical anthropologists use the term **biomedicine** to refer to the dominant medical paradigm in Western cultures today, with the *bio* part of the word emphasizing the biological emphasis of this medical system.

applied anthropology

Exploring Why an Applied Project Didn't Work

When applied projects do not succeed, it is important for researchers to try to figure out why. Part of the problem may be that the intended recipients' ideas about how things work may be very different from the researchers' ideas. Consider the following example.

In Guatemala, village health care workers were not only testing people for malaria but they were also offering free antimalarial drugs. Yet, surprisingly, a community survey found that only 20 percent of people with malaria symptoms took advantage of the free treatment. More surprisingly, most people with symptoms spent the equivalent of a day's wages to buy an injection that was not strong enough to be effective! Why? What was going on?

Finding the answer was not easy. First, researchers designed interviews to elicit folk concepts about illness. What kinds of illnesses are there? What are their causes? What are their symptoms, and how are different illnesses to be treated? They conducted interviews with a random sample of households to find out what illnesses people had and what they did about them. Then they asked people to consider different hypothetical scenarios (vignettes), with different types of people and different degrees of severity of illness, to find out what treatment they would choose. All of these methods were well thought out, but the answers still did not predict what people actually did when they thought they had malaria. Finally, the researchers devised precise comparisons of the kinds of pills the health care workers passed out and the pills and ampoules for

injections that the drugstore sold. They compared them two at a time, varying dosages and brands. People did think that more pills were more effective, as indeed they were. But they thought that the colorfully wrapped store-bought pill was more effective than the equivalent white unwrapped free pill, even though it was not. They also thought that one store-bought ampoule used for injections, for which they would pay a day's wages, was more effective than four pills of any kind! In fact, one ampoule was equivalent to only one pill.

Applied researchers often use such trial-and-error methods to find out how to get the information they need. Methods that work in one field setting don't always work in others. To get the information needed, researchers must sometimes let the subjects structure their own answers. At other times, as in this case, they may have to make very specific comparisons to get predictive answers. The people in the Guatemala study didn't believe that the free pills were strong enough to work, so they didn't use them. More research would be needed to uncover why they did not believe the free pills were effective. Was it because they were free? Was it because the store-bought drugs were attractively packaged? Or was there a belief that injections work better than pills? That's what the research process is like; it always leads to new questions, particularly more general questions requiring more extensive or more comparative research.

For example, the Guatemala project revealed why a particular program

was not successful in a particular area. But how widespread are the interfering beliefs? Are they found throughout Guatemala? Do they interfere with the introduction of other medicines? Are we dealing with problems that exist in other areas of Central and South America? Although we don't yet have answers to these more extensive questions, anthropologists have developed efficient methods for assessing variation in beliefs within and between cultures.

We now know that, if we ask one or two informants, we cannot assume that the answer is cultural. But that doesn't mean that we need to ask hundreds of people. If a belief is cultural and therefore commonly held, asking 10 to 20 individuals the same question is sufficient to provide the researcher with a high probability that an answer is correct. (The agreement among respondents is called *cultural consensus*.) So, for example, Guatemalan respondents mostly agreed about which illnesses were contagious. But they disagreed a lot about whether a particular disease should be treated with a "hot" or a "cold" remedy. Using cultural consensus methods, researchers can compare rural and urban residents, and they can also compare informants in different cultures. When we have more of these systematic comparisons, medical anthropologists and health practitioners may have a better understanding of how to implement medical care.

Sources: Weller 2009; Romney et al. 1986.

As Robert Hahn points out, biomedicine appears to focus on specific diseases and cures for those diseases. Health is not the focus, as it is thought to be the *absence* of disease. Diseases are considered to be purely natural, and there is relatively little interest in the person or the larger social and cultural systems. Doctors generally do not treat the whole body but tend to specialize, with the human body partitioned into zones that belong to different specialties. Death is seen as a failure, and biomedical practitioners do everything they can to prolong life, regardless of the circumstances under which the patient would live life.[53]

One of the most important discoveries that profoundly changed the course of Western medicine was Louis Pasteur's isolation of the organisms responsible for some major infectious diseases. Pasteur's discoveries stimulated the search for other disease-causing germs using scientific methods. But the *germ theory* of disease, although powerful, may have led researchers to pay less attention to the patient and the patient's social and cultural milieu.[54] For an example of how anthropologists try to redress the balance, see the box "Exploring Why an Applied Project Didn't Work."

TREATMENT OF ILLNESS

Anthropologists who study diseases in this and other cultures can be roughly classified into two camps. First, there are those (the more relativistic) who think that the culture so influences disease symptoms, incidence, and treatment that there are few if any cultural universals about any illness. If each culture is unique, we should expect its conception and treatment of an illness to be unique too, not like beliefs and practices in other cultures. Second, there are those (the more universalistic) who see cross-cultural similarities in the conception and treatment of illness, despite the unique qualities (particularly in the belief system) of each culture. For example, native remedies may contain chemicals that are the same as, or similar in effect to, chemicals used in remedies by Western biomedicine.[55] Readers should note that our classification here of medical anthropologists is a crude one; many medical anthropologists do not fall unambiguously into one or the other group. And the reality might be that a given culture is very much like other cultures in some respects but unique in other respects.

In their extensive research on Maya ethnomedicine, Elois Ann Berlin and Brent Berlin make a strong case that, although studies of the Maya have emphasized beliefs about illness that are based on supernatural causes, a good deal of Maya ethnomedicine is about natural conditions, their signs and symptoms, and the remedies used to deal with those conditions. In regard to gastrointestinal diseases, the Berlins found that the Maya have a wide-ranging and accurate understanding of anatomy, physiology, and symptoms. Furthermore, the remedies they use, including recommendations for food, drink, and herbal medicines, have properties that are not that different from those of the biomedical profession.[56]

Carole Browner also suggests that the emphasis on "hot-cold" theories of illness in Latin America has been overemphasized, to the neglect of other factors that influence choices about reproductive health and female health problems. In a study of the medical system in a highland Oaxacan community, Browner finds that certain plants are used to expel substances from the uterus—to facilitate labor at full term, to produce an abortion, or to induce menstrual flow. Other plants are used to retain things in the uterus—to prevent excess blood loss during menstruation, to help healing after delivery, and to prevent miscarriage. Most of these plant remedies appear to work.[57]

The biomedical establishment has become increasingly aware of the value of studying the "traditional" medicinal remedies discovered or invented by people around the world. In studying the indigenous medicines of the Hausa of Nigeria, Nina Etkin and Paul Ross asked individuals to describe the physical attributes of more than 600 plants and their possible medicinal uses, more than 800 diseases and symptoms, and more than 5,000 prepared medicines. Although many medicines were used for treating sorcery, spirit aggression, or witchcraft, most medicines were used for illnesses regarded by the Hausa as having natural causes. Malaria is a serious endemic medical problem in the Hausa region, as in many areas of Africa. The Hausa use approximately 72 plant remedies for conditions connected with malaria—among them anemia, intermittent fever, and jaundice. Experimental treatment of malaria in laboratory animals supports the efficacy of many of the Hausa remedies. But perhaps the most important part of the Etkin and Ross findings is the role of diet. Although most medical research does not consider the possible medical efficacy of the *foods* that people eat in combating illness, food is, of course, consumed in much larger quantities and more often than medicine. It is noteworthy, therefore, that the Hausa eat many plants with antimalarial properties; in fact, dietary consumption of these plants appears to be greatest during the time of year when the risk of malarial infection is at its highest. Recent research has also discovered that foods and spices like garlic, onions, cinnamon, ginger, and pepper have antiviral or antibacterial properties.[58]

Medical Practitioners

In our society, we may be so used to consulting a full-time medical specialist (if we do not feel better quickly) that we tend to assume that biomedical treatment is the only effective medical treatment. If we are given a medicine, we expect it to have the appropriate medical effect and make us feel better. So, many in the biomedical system, practitioners and patients alike, are perplexed by the seeming effectiveness of other medical systems that are based in part on symbolic or ritual healing. As we noted earlier, many native plants have been shown to be medically effective, but their use is often accompanied by singing, dancing, noise making, or rituals. Our difficulty in understanding the healing in such practices probably stems from the assumption in biomedicine that the mind is fundamentally different from the body. Yet, there is increasing evidence that the *form* of treatment may be just as important as the *content* of treatment.[59]

The practitioners who deal with more than the body are sometimes referred to as *personalistic* practitioners. In a personalistic view, illness may be viewed as being due to something in one's social life being out of order. The cause could be retribution for one's own bad behavior or thoughts, or the work of an angry individual practicing sorcery or witchcraft. Or a bad social situation or a bad

A Dayak woman in Malaysia collects herbal medicine.

relationship may be thought of as provoking physical symptoms because of anxiety or stress. In societies with occupational specialization, priests, who are formally trained full-time religious practitioners, may be asked to convey messages or requests for healing to higher powers.[60] Societies with beliefs in sorcery and witchcraft as causes of illness typically have practitioners who are believed to be able to use magic in reverse—that is, to undo the harm invoked by sorcerers and witches. Sometimes sorcerers or witches themselves may be asked to reverse illnesses caused by others. However, they may not be sought out because they are often feared and have relatively low status.[61] Shamans are perhaps the most important medical practitioners in societies lacking full-time occupational specialization.

The Shaman The *shaman,* usually a male part-time specialist, is often involved in healing.[62] Westerners often call shamans "witch doctors" because they don't believe that shamans can effectively cure people. Do shamans effectively cure people? Actually, Westerners are not the only skeptics. A Native American named Quesalid from the Kwakiutl of the Pacific Northwest didn't believe that shamanism was effective either. So he began to associate with the shamans to spy on them and was taken into their group. In his first lessons, he learned

A Navajo medicine man performs a healing ceremony involving a snake painted on the ground.

> a curious mixture of pantomime, prestidigitation, and empirical knowledge, including the art of simulating fainting and nervous fits, . . . sacred song, the technique for inducing vomiting, rather precise notions of auscultation or listening to sounds within the body to detect disorders and obstetrics, and the use of "dreamers," that is, spies who listen to private conversations and secretly convey to the shaman bits of information concerning the origins and symptoms of the ills suffered by different people. Above all, he learned the *ars magna.* . . . The shaman hides a little tuft of down in the corner of his mouth, and he throws it up, covered with blood at the proper moment—after having bitten his tongue or made his gums bleed—and solemnly presents it to his patient and the onlookers as the pathological foreign body extracted as a result of his sucking and manipulations.[63]

His suspicions were confirmed, but his first curing was a success. The patient had heard that Quesalid had joined the shamans and believed that only he could heal him. Quesalid remained with the shamans for the four-year apprenticeship, during which he could take no fee, and he became increasingly aware that his methods worked. He visited other villages, competed with other shamans in curing hopeless cases and won, and finally seemed convinced that his curing system was more valid than those of other shamans. Instead of denouncing the trickery of shamans, he continued to practice as a renowned shaman.[64]

After working with shamans in Africa, E. Fuller Torrey, a psychiatrist and anthropologist, concluded that they use the same mechanisms and techniques to cure patients as

psychiatrists and achieve about the same results. He isolated four categories used by healers the world over:

1. **The naming process.** If a disease has a name—"neurasthenia" or "phobia" or "possession by an ancestral spirit" will do—then it is curable; the patient realizes that the doctor understands his case.

2. **The personality of the doctor.** Those who demonstrate some empathy, nonpossessive warmth, and genuine interest in the patient get results.

3. **The patient's expectations.** One way of raising the patient's expectations of being cured is the trip to the doctor; the longer the trip—to the Mayo Clinic, Menninger Clinic, Delphi, or Lourdes—the easier the cure. An impressive setting (the medical center) and impressive paraphernalia (the stethoscope, the couch, attendants in uniform, the rattle, the whistle, the drum, the mask) also raise the patient's expectations. The healer's training is important. And high fees also help to raise a patient's expectations. (The Paiute doctors always collect their fees before starting a cure; if they don't, it is believed that they will fall ill.)

4. **Curing techniques.** Drugs, shock treatment, conditioning techniques, and so on have long been used in many different parts of the world.[65]

Biomedical research is not unaware of the effect of the mind on healing. In fact, considerable evidence has accumulated that psychological factors can be very important in illness. Patients who believe that medicine will help them often recover quickly even if the medicine is only a sugar pill or a medicine not particularly relevant to their condition. Such effects are called *placebo* effects.[66]

Placebos do not just have psychological effects. Although the mechanisms are not well understood, they may also alter body chemistry and bolster the immune system.[67]

Shamans may coexist with medical doctors. Don Antonio, a respected Otomi Indian shaman in central Mexico, has many patients, perhaps not as many as before modern medicine, but still plenty. In his view, when he was born, God gave him his powers to cure, but his powers are reserved for removing "evil" illnesses (those caused by sorcerers). "Good" illnesses can be cured by herbs and medicine, and he refers patients with those illnesses to medical doctors; he believes that doctors are more effective than he could be in those cases. The doctors, however, do not seem to refer any patients to Don Antonio or other shamans.[68]

Physicians   The most important full-time medical practitioner in the biomedical system is the physician, and the patient-physician relationship is central. In the ideal scheme of things, the physician is viewed as having the ability, with some limits, of being able to treat illness, alleviate suffering, and prolong the life of the patient, as well as offering promises of patient confidentiality and privacy. The patient relies on the physician's knowledge, skill, and ethics. Consistent with the biomedical paradigm, doctors tend to treat patients as having "conditions" rather than as complete people. Physicians presumably rely on science for authoritative knowledge, but they place a good deal of importance on the value of their own clinical experience. Often, physicians consider their own observations of the patient to be more valuable than the reports by the patient. Because patients commonly go to physicians to solve a particular condition or sickness, physicians tend to try to do something about it even in the face of uncertainty. Physicians tend to rely on technology for diagnoses and treatment and place relatively low value on talking with patients. In fact, physicians tend to give patients relatively little information, and they may not listen very well.[69]

Despite the importance of physicians in biomedicine, patients do not always seek physician care. In fact, one-third of the population of the United States regularly consults with alternative practitioners, such as acupuncturists or chiropractors, often unbeknownst to the physician. Somewhat surprisingly, individuals with more education are more likely to seek alternative care.[70]

POLITICAL AND ECONOMIC INFLUENCES ON HEALTH

People with more social, economic, and political power in a society are generally healthier.[71] Inequality in health in socially stratified societies is not surprising. The poor usually have more exposure to disease because they live in more crowded conditions. And the poor are more likely to lack the resources to get quality care. For many diseases, health problems, and death rates, incidence or relative frequency varies directly with social class. In the United Kingdom, for example, people in the higher social classes are less likely to have headaches, bronchitis, pneumonia, heart disease, arthritis, injuries, and mental disorders, to name just a few of the differences.[72] Ethnic differences also predict health

inequities. In South Africa under apartheid, the 14 percent minority population, referred to as "white," controlled most of the income of the country and most of the high-quality land. "Blacks" were restricted to areas with shortages of housing, inadequate housing, and little employment. To get a job, families often had to be disrupted; usually the husband would have to migrate to find work. "Blacks" lived, on average, about nine years less than "whites" in 1985, and "black" infants died at about seven times the rate of "white" infants. In the United States recently, the differences between African Americans and European Americans in health are not as stark as in South Africa, but those favoring European Americans are still substantial. As of 1987, the difference in life expectancy was seven years, and African American infant mortality was about twice the rate for European American infants. Robert Hahn has estimated that poverty accounts for about 19 percent of the overall mortality in the United States.[73]

Inequities, because of class and ethnicity, are not limited to within-society differences. Power and economic differentials *between* societies also have profound health consequences. Over the course of European exploration and expansion, indigenous peoples died in enormous numbers from introduced diseases, wars, and conquests; they had their lands expropriated and diminished in size and quality. When incorporated into colonial territories or into countries, indigenous people usually become minorities and they are almost always very poor. These conditions of life not only affect the incidence of disease, they also tend to lead to greater substance abuse, violence, depression, and other mental pathologies.[74]

HEALTH CONDITIONS AND DISEASES

Medical anthropologists have studied an enormous variety of conditions. What follows is only a small sampling.

AIDS

Epidemics of infectious disease have killed millions of people within short periods of time throughout recorded history. The Black Death—bubonic plague—killed between 25 percent and 50 percent of the population of Europe, perhaps 75 million people, during the 14th century; an epidemic during the 6th century killed an estimated 100 million people in the Middle East, Asia, and Europe. Less noted in our history books, but also devastating, was the enormous depopulation that accompanied the expansion of Europeans into the New World and the Pacific from the 1500s on. Not only were people killed directly by European conquerors, millions also died from introduced diseases to which the natives had little or no resistance, diseases such as smallpox and measles that the Europeans brought with them but were no longer dying from.

The current state of medical science and technology may lull us into thinking that epidemics are a thing of the past. But the recent and sudden emergence of the disease we call **AIDS (acquired immune deficiency syndrome)** reminds us that new diseases, or new varieties of

Millions of children in sub-Saharan Africa are orphaned because of AIDS. These orphaned children in Uganda look on during a visit by Britain's Queen Elizabeth to their center.

old diseases, can appear at any time. Like all other organisms, disease-causing organisms also evolve. The human immunodeficiency virus (HIV) that causes AIDS emerged only recently. Viruses and bacteria are always mutating, and new strains emerge that are initially a plague on our genetic resistance and on medical efforts to contain them.

Millions of people around the world already have the symptoms of AIDS, and millions more are infected with HIV but do not know they are infected. As of December 2007, 33 million adults and children in the world were living with HIV/AIDS.[75] There are a few signs of improvement since 2001. The percentage of people infected globally is now stable; some countries have improved with prevention efforts, and the number of new cases each year has gone down. However, AIDS is the major cause of death in sub-Saharan Africa and is still a leading cause of death worldwide.[76] There is still no cure. AIDS is a frightening epidemic not only because of its death toll. It is also frightening because it takes a long time (on average, four years) after exposure for symptoms to appear. This means that many people who have been infected by HIV but do not know they are infected may continue, unknowingly, to transmit the virus to others.[77]

Transmission occurs mostly via sexual encounters, through semen and blood. Drug users may also transmit HIV by way of contaminated needles. Transmission by blood transfusion has been virtually eliminated in this and other societies by medical screening of blood supplies. In many countries, however, there is still no routine screening of blood prior to transfusions. HIV may be passed from a pregnant woman to her offspring through the placenta and after birth through her breast milk. The rate of transmission between a mother and her baby is 20 percent to 40 percent. Children are also at great risk because they are likely to be orphaned by a parent's death from AIDS. At the turn of the 21st century, approximately 14 million children were parentless because of AIDS.[78]

Many people think of AIDS as only a medical problem that requires only a medical solution, without realizing

that behavioral, cultural, and political issues need to be addressed as well. It is true that developing a vaccine or a drug to prevent people from getting AIDS and finding a permanent cure for those who have it will finally solve the problem. But, for a variety of reasons, we can expect that the medical solution alone will not be sufficient, at least not for a while. First, to be effective worldwide, or even within a country, a vaccine has to be inexpensive and relatively easy to produce in large quantities; the same is true of any medical treatment. Second, governments around the world have to be willing and able to spend the money and hire the personnel necessary to manage an effective program.[79] Third, future vaccination and treatment will require the people at risk to be willing to get vaccinated and treated, which is not always the case. Witness the fact that the incidence of measles is on the rise in the United States because many people are not having their children vaccinated.

There are now expensive drug treatments that significantly reduce the degree of HIV infection, but we do not know if an effective and inexpensive vaccine or treatment will be developed soon. In the meantime, the risk of HIV infection can be reduced only by changes in social, particularly sexual, behavior. But to persuade people to change their sexual behavior, it is necessary to find out exactly what they do sexually, and why they do what they do.

Research so far suggests that different sexual patterns are responsible for HIV transmission in different parts of the world. In the United States, England, northern Europe, Australia, and Latin America, the recipients of anal intercourse, particularly men, are the most likely individuals to acquire HIV infection; vaginal intercourse can also transmit the infection, usually from the man to the woman. Needle sharing can transmit the infection, too. In Africa, the most common mode of transmission is vaginal intercourse, and so women get infected more commonly in Africa than elsewhere.[80] In fact, in Africa there are slightly more cases of HIV in women as compared with men.[81]

Some researchers are arguing that, although the immediate cause of HIV infection may be mostly related to sexual practice, larger political and social issues, such as poverty and gender inequality, increase the likelihood of such infection. For example, sexually transmitted diseases increase the risk of HIV infection three to five times, but those who are poor are less likely to get adequate treatment. And, in the developing world, rural and poorer areas are also more likely to get tainted blood transfusions. Gender inequality is likely to increase the likelihood that women have to submit to unsafe sex, and women are even less likely than men to have access to adequate medical care.[82]

As of now, there are only two known ways to reduce the likelihood of sexual HIV transmission. One way is to abstain from sexual intercourse; the other is to use condoms. Male circumcision now appears to decrease the risk of HIV infection, but studies have not yet evaluated long-term effects.[83] Educational programs that teach how AIDS spreads and what one can do about it may reduce the spread somewhat, but such programs may fail where people have incompatible beliefs and attitudes about sexuality. For example, people in some central African societies believe that deposits of semen after conception are necessary for a successful pregnancy and generally enhance a woman's health and ability to reproduce. It might be expected then that people who have these beliefs about semen would choose not to use condoms; after all, condoms in their view are a threat to public health.[84] Educational programs may also emphasize the wrong message. Promiscuity may increase the risk of HIV transmission, so hardly anyone would question the wisdom of advertising to reduce the number of sexual partners. And, at least in the homosexual community in the United States, individuals report fewer sexual partners than in the past. What was not anticipated, however, was that individuals in monogamous relationships, who may feel safe, are less likely to use condoms or to avoid the riskiest sexual practices. Needless to say, sex with a regular partner who is infected is not safe![85] In what may seem like something of a paradox, the United Nations observed that, for most women in the world today, the major risk factor for being infected with HIV is being married.[86] It is not marriage, *per se,* that heightens the risk of HIV infection; rather, the proximate cause may be the lower likelihood of condom use or less abstinence by a married couple.

The stigmas associated with AIDS also hinder efforts to reduce its spread. In some societies, there is the widespread belief that homosexual men are particularly likely to get infected.[87] In other societies, AIDS may be thought to be due to promiscuity. If a woman asks a man to use a condom, she may be assumed to be a prostitute. In addition, many people mistakenly fear even proximity to AIDS victims, as if any kind of contact could result in infection.

To solve the problem of AIDS, we may hope that medical science will develop an effective and inexpensive vaccination or treatment that all can afford. There is a vaccine that seems to reduce HIV infection in monkeys to hardly detectable levels.[88] Perhaps soon there will be a similar vaccine for humans. In the meantime, we can try to understand why people engage in certain risky sexual practices. Such understanding may allow us to design educational and other programs that would help inhibit the spread of AIDS.

Mental and Emotional Disorders

Diagnosing mental or emotional disorders in one culture is difficult enough; diagnosing them in others poses much greater difficulty. Many researchers start with Western categories of mental illness and try to apply them elsewhere, without first trying to understand native conceptions of mental disorder. In addition, "mental" and "physical" disorders are rarely separate. For example, a host of illnesses can produce a loss of energy that some may see as depression; and fear or anger can produce physical symptoms such as a heart attack.[89]

When Western anthropologists first started describing mental illness in non-Western societies, there seemed to be unique illnesses in different cultures. These are referred to as *culture-bound syndromes.* For example, a mental disorder called *pibloktoq* occurred among some Eskimo adults of Greenland, usually women, who became oblivious to their surroundings and acted in agitated, eccentric

Cultures vary in their ideals of beauty, and ideals change over time. In the United States in the 1950s, "somewhat plump" was idealized. Beginning in the 1960s, thinness became idealized.

ways. They might strip themselves naked and wander across the ice and over hills until they collapsed of exhaustion. Another disorder, *amok,* occurred in Malaya, Indonesia, and New Guinea, usually among males. John Honigmann characterized it as a "destructive maddened excitement . . . beginning with depression and followed by a period of brooding and withdrawal [culminating in] the final mobilization of tremendous energy during which the 'wild man' runs destructively berserk."[90] *Anorexia nervosa,* the disorder involving aversion to food, may be unique to the relatively few societies that idealize slimness.[91] (See the box "Eating Disorders, Biology, and the Cultural Construction of Beauty.")

Some scholars think that each society's views of personality and concepts of mental illness have to be understood in their own terms. Western understandings and concepts cannot be applied to other cultures. For example, Catherine Lutz suggested that the Western concept of depression cannot be applied to the Pacific island of Ifaluk. The people there have many words for thinking or feeling about "loss and helplessness," but all their words are related to a specific need for someone, such as when someone dies or leaves the island. Such thoughts and feelings of loss are considered perfectly normal, and there is no word in their language for general hopelessness or "depression."[92] Therefore, Lutz questioned the applicability of the Western concept of depression as well as other Western psychiatric categories.

Other researchers are not so quick to dismiss the possible universality of psychiatric categories. Some think they have found a considerable degree of cross-cultural uniformity in conceptions of mental illness. Jane Murphy studied descriptions by the Inuit and the Yoruba, in Nigeria, of severely disturbed people. She found that their

applied anthropology

Eating Disorders, Biology, and the Cultural Construction of Beauty

Cultures differ about what they consider beautiful, including people. In many cultures, fat people are considered more beautiful than thin people. Melvin Ember did fieldwork years ago on the islands of American Samoa. When he returned to the main island after three months on a distant island, he ran into a Samoan acquaintance, a prominent chief. The chief said: "You look good. You gained weight." In reality, he had lost 30 pounds! The chief may not have remembered how heavy the anthropologist had been, but he clearly thought that fat was better than thin. Among the Azawagh Arabs of Niger, fatness was not merely valued and considered beautiful; great care was taken to ensure that young girls became fat by insisting and sometimes forcing them to drink large quantities of milk-based porridge.

Around the world, fatness is generally considered more desirable than thinness, particularly for women. Fatness is widely valued in these cultures not only because it is considered more beautiful, but also because it is thought to be a marker of health, fertility, and higher status in societies with social stratification. This view is in strong contrast to the ideal in the United States and many other Western societies, where fatness is thought to be unattractive, and to reflect laziness, a lack of self-control, and poor health. Thinness, particularly in the upper classes, is considered beautiful. How can we explain these differences in what is considered beautiful?

Recent cross-cultural research suggests that the picture is more complicated. It appears that societies with unpredictable resources actually value thinness, particularly in societies that have no way of storing food. At first glance, this seems puzzling. Shouldn't an individual who stores calories on the body be better off than an individual who is thin when facing starvation, particularly if there is no food storage? Perhaps. But 10 thin individuals will generally consume less than 10 heavier people, so perhaps there is a group advantage to being thin. Indeed, many societies with frequent episodes of famine encourage fasting or eating very light meals, as among the Gurage of Ethiopia. The strongest cross-cultural predictor of valuing fatness in women is what is often referred to as "machismo" or "protest masculinity." Societies with a strong emphasis on male aggression, strength, and sexuality are the most likely to value fatness in women; those with little machismo value thinness. Why machismo is associated with valuing fatness in women is far from clear. One suggestion is that machismo actually reflects male insecurity and fear of women. Such men may not be looking for closeness or intimacy with their wives, but they may want to show how potent they are by having lots of children. If fatness suggests fertility, men may look for wives who are fatter. Consistent with this idea, the ideal of thinness in women became more common in North America with the rise of women's movements in the 1920s and late 1960s. Consider that Marilyn Monroe epitomized beauty in the 1950s; she was well-rounded, not thin. Thin became more popular only when women began to question early marriage and having many children.

Behaviors associated with machismo became less acceptable at those times.

Cultural beliefs about what is considered a beautiful body can impose enormous pressures on females to achieve the ideal body type—whether it be fat or thin. In the United States and other Western countries, the effort to be thin can be carried to an extreme, resulting in the eating disorders anorexia and bulimia. If you suffer from these often fatal illnesses, you may regularly eat little and you may regularly force yourself to throw up, thus depriving your body of nutrients in your quest to be thinner and thinner. The irony of "thinness" being idealized in the United States and other Western countries is that obesity is becoming more common in those societies. In 2001, the incidence of obesity increased in the United States to 31 percent, and medical researchers worried about the increase in heart disease and diabetes resulting from obesity. Whether or not obesity is a result of an eating disorder (in the psychological sense) is more debatable. Researchers are finding biological causes of obesity, such as resistance to the hormone leptin, which regulates appetite, suggesting that much of the obesity "epidemic" has biological causes. Still, fast food, increasing sedentariness, and extremely large portion sizes are probably contributing factors also.

Sources: P. J. Brown 1997, 100; Loustaunau and Sobo 1997, 85; N. Wolf 1991; R. Popenoe 2004; C. R. Ember et al. 2005: J. L. Anderson et al. 1992; J. M. Friedman 2003.

descriptions not only were similar to each other but also corresponded to North American descriptions of schizophrenia. The Inuit word for "crazy" is *nuthkavihak*. They use this word when something inside a person seems to be out of order. *Nuthkavihak* people are described as talking to themselves, believing themselves to be animals, making strange faces, becoming violent, and so on. The Yoruba have a word, *were*, for people who are "insane." People described as *were* sometimes hear voices, laugh when there is nothing to laugh at, and take up weapons and suddenly hit people.[93]

Robert Edgerton found similarities in conceptions of mental illness in four East African societies. He noted not only that the four groups essentially agreed on the symptoms of psychosis but also that the symptoms they described were the same ones that are considered psychotic here.[94] Edgerton believed that the lack of exact translation in different cultures, such as the one pointed out by Lutz regarding Ifaluk, does not make comparison impossible. If researchers can come to understand another culture's views of personality and if the researchers can manage to communicate these views to people of other cultures, we can compare the described cases and try to discover what may be universal and what may be found only in some cultures.[95]

Some mental illnesses, such as schizophrenia and depression, seem so widespread that many researchers think they are probably universal. Consistent with this idea is the fact that schizophrenic individuals in different cultures seem to share the same patterns of distinctive eye movements.[96] Still, cultural factors may influence the risk of developing such diseases, the specific symptoms that are expressed, and the effectiveness of different kinds of treatment.[97] There may be some truly culture-bound (nearly unique) syndromes, but others thought at one time to be unique may be culturally varying expressions of conditions that occur widely. *Pibloktoq*, for example, may be a kind of hysteria.[98]

Biological but not necessarily genetic factors may be very important in the etiology of some of the widespread disorders such as schizophrenia.[99] With regard to hysteria, Anthony Wallace theorized that nutritional factors such as calcium deficiency may cause hysteria and that dietary improvement may account for the decline of this illness in the Western world since the 19th century.[100] By the early 20th century, the discovery of the value of good nutrition, coupled with changes in social conditions, had led many people to drink milk, eat vitamin-rich foods, and spend time in the sun (although spending a lot of time in the sun is no longer recommended because of the risk of skin cancer). These changes in diet and activity increased the intake of vitamin D and helped people to maintain a proper calcium level. Consequently, the number of cases of hysteria declined.

Regarding *pibloktoq*, Wallace suggested that a complex set of related variables may cause the disease. The Inuit live in an environment that supplies only a minimum amount of calcium. A diet low in calcium could result in two different conditions. One condition, rickets, would produce physical deformities potentially fatal in the Inuit hunting economy. People whose genetic makeup made them prone to rickets would be eliminated from the population through natural selection. A low level of calcium in the blood could also cause muscular spasms known as tetany. Tetany, in turn, may cause emotional and mental disorientation similar to the symptoms of *pibloktoq*. Such attacks last for only a relatively short time and are not fatal, so people who developed *pibloktoq* would have a far greater chance of surviving in the Arctic environment with a calcium-deficient diet than would people who had rickets.

Although researchers disagree about the comparability of mental illnesses among cultures, most agree that effective treatment requires understanding a culture's ideas about a mental illness—why people think it occurs, what treatments are believed to be effective, and how families and others respond to those afflicted.[101]

Susto *Susto* is often described as a "folk illness" or a culture-bound syndrome because there doesn't seem to be any direct counterpart in biomedical terms. In many areas of Latin America, it is believed that a person suffers susto, or becomes *astudado,* when a nonmaterial essence from the body becomes detached during sleep, or after suffering a fright. This essence is either held captive by supernatural forces or wanders freely outside the body.[102] Susto patients are described as restless during sleep, and listless, depressed, debilitated, and indifferent to food and hygiene during the day. Some researchers have suggested that people labeled as suffering from susto may in fact be suffering from mental illness. Believing that such conclusions were incomplete or premature, Arthur Rubel, Carl O'Nell, and Rolando Collado-Ardón designed a three-culture comparative study to evaluate whether susto victims were suffering from social, psychological, or organic problems. They compared individuals suffering from susto to other individuals matched by culture, age, and sex who defined themselves as "sick" when they came to health clinics (but who did not claim susto as their illness). The three cultures were Chichimec, Zapotec, and a Spanish-speaking mestizo community.[103]

From previous study of susto victims, Rubel and his colleagues hypothesized that susto was likely to strike people in socially stressful situations where they may think they are inadequate in required roles. For example, two cases of susto occurred among women who desperately wanted more children, but each had had a number of miscarriages (one had seven, the other two). In addition to measuring social stress, the researchers also had physicians evaluate organic problems with reference to the World Health Organization's *International Classification of Diseases.* Degree of psychiatric impairment was judged in an interview based on questions other researchers had previously developed. And seven years after the study, the researchers found out which, if any, of the studied individuals had died.

The research results supported the social stress hypothesis: Susto victims were significantly more likely to feel inadequate about social roles. The researchers did not expect to find evidence that susto victims had more psychiatric impairment or more organic disease. However, to their surprise, susto victims were also more likely to have had serious physical health problems. In fact, susto victims were more likely to have died in the seven years after the study. It is hard to say whether the susto victims had more disease because they were debilitated by susto or they were more prone to susto because they were physically sicker. The researchers guess that, because many of the conditions that created social role impairment were of long duration (such as many miscarriages), it seemed likely that susto itself put its victims at risk for biological diseases.[104]

Depression Just as one kind of stress seems to be involved in the folk illness susto, researchers have considered the role of other kinds of stress in producing various other forms of mental illness. One of the most important stressors may be economic deprivation. Many studies have found that the lower classes in socially stratified societies have much higher proportions of all kinds of mental illness. Acute stressors like death of a loved one, divorce, loss of a job, or a natural disaster predict higher rates of mental illness for all social classes; however, these events take more of a toll in lower-class families.[105]

In a study designed to evaluate the effect of these and other stressors on the prevalence of depression in an African American community in a southern city, William Dressler combined fieldwork methods and hypothesis testing to try to better understand depression.[106] Although many studies rely on treatment or hospitalization rates, Dressler decided that such rates drastically underestimate the incidence of depression, inasmuch as many people do not seek treatment. He decided to rely on a symptom checklist, which asked such questions as how often in the last week a person felt like crying, felt lonely, or felt hopeless about the future. Although such checklists do not provide clear divisions for characterizing someone as mildly depressed or seriously depressed, they do allow researchers to compare people along a continuum.

Dressler measured a variety of different possible stressors, including life crises, economic worries, perceived racial inequality, and problems in social roles, and found that some of the objective stressors, like life crises and unemployment, predict depression in the expected direction only in the lower classes. That is, for lower-class African Americans, unemployment and other life crises predicted more depression, but that result was not found among middle- and upper-class individuals. These results are consistent with previous findings that many stressors take more of a toll among poorer individuals. On the other hand, more subjective economic stressors, such as feeling you are not making enough money, predict depression across all class lines. So does "social role" stress, such as thinking you are missing promotions because you are African American or thinking that your spouse expects too much.[107]

Undernutrition

What people eat is intrinsically connected to their survival and the ability of a population to reproduce itself, so we would expect that the ways people obtain, distribute, and consume food have been generally adaptive.[108] For example, the human body cannot synthesize eight amino acids. Meat can provide all of these amino acids, and combinations of particular plants can also provide them for a complete complement of protein. The combination of maize and beans in many traditional Native American diets, or *tortillas* and *frijoles* in Mexico, can provide all the needed amino acids. In places where wheat (often made into bread) is the staple, dairy products combined with wheat also provide complete protein.[109] Even the way that people have prepared for scarcity, such as breaking up into mobile bands, cultivating crops that can better withstand drought, and preserving food in case of famine, are probably adaptive practices in unpredictable environments. Geneticists have proposed that populations in famine-prone areas may have had genetic selection for "thrifty genes"—genes

A sisal plant in Bahia, Brazil. The switch to sisal production led to undernutrition in children.

that allow individuals to need a minimum of food and store the extra in fatty tissue to get them past serious scarcity.[110] Customary diets and genetic changes may have been selected over a long stretch of time, but many serious nutritional problems observed today are due to rapid culture change. For instance, although "thrifty genes" may be adaptive during famine, they may become maladaptive when food is readily available. The high prevalence of diabetes and obesity in many populations today may be linked to such genes.

Often the switch to commercial or cash crops has harmful effects in another direction—creating undernutrition. For example, when the farmer-herders of the arid region in northeastern Brazil started growing sisal, a drought-resistant plant used for making twine and rope, many of them abandoned subsistence agriculture. The small landholders used most of their land for sisal growing and, when the price of sisal fell, they had to work as laborers for others to try to make ends meet. Food then had to be mostly bought, but if a laborer or sisal grower didn't earn enough, there was not enough food for the whole family.

Analysis of allocation of food in some households by Daniel Gross and Barbara Underwood suggests that the laborer and his wife received adequate nutrition, but the children often received much less than required. Lack of adequate nutrition usually results in retarded weight and height in children. As is commonly the case when there is substantial social inequality, the children from lower-income groups weigh substantially less than those from higher-income groups. But even though there were some economic differences before sisal production, the effects on nutrition appeared negligible before, judging from the fact that there was little or no difference in weight among adults from higher and lower socioeconomic positions who grew up prior to sisal production. But more recently, 45 percent of the children from lower economic groups were undernourished as compared with 23 percent of those children from the higher economic groups.[111]

This is not to say that commercialization is always deleterious to adequate nutrition. For example, in the Highlands of New Guinea, there is evidence that the nutrition of children improved when families started growing coffee for sale. However, in this case, the families still had land to grow some crops for consumption. The extra money earned from coffee enabled them to buy canned fish and rice, which provided children with higher amounts of protein than the usual staple of sweet potatoes.[112]

Nutritional imbalances for females have a far-reaching impact on reproduction and the health of the infants they bear. In some cultures, the lower status of women has a direct bearing on their access to food. Although the custom of feeding males first is well known, it is less often realized that females end up with less nutrient-dense food such as meat. Deprivation of food sometimes starts in infancy where girl babies, as in India, are weaned earlier than boy babies.[113] Parents may be unaware that their differential weaning practice has the effect of reducing the amount of high-quality protein that girl infants receive. Indeed, in Ecuador, Lauris McKee found that parents thought that earlier weaning of girls was helpful to them. They believed that mothers' milk transmitted sexuality and aggression, both ideal male traits, to their infants and so it was important that girl babies be weaned early. Mothers weaned their girls at about 11 months and their boys at about 20 months, a 9-month difference. McKee found that girl infants had a significantly higher mortality than boy infants in their second year of life, suggesting that the earlier weaning time for girls and their probable undernutrition may have been responsible.[114]

Malnutrition and AIDS are biological and social problems. In the next chapter, we turn to other global social problems and how anthropology and other social sciences may contribute to their solution.

SUMMARY ●○○

1. Applied or practicing anthropology as a profession is explicitly concerned with making anthropological knowledge useful. Applied or practicing anthropologists may be involved in one or more phases of programs that are designed to change peoples' lives: assembling relevant knowledge, constructing alternative plans, assessing the likely social and environmental impact of particular plans, implementing the programs, and monitoring the programs and their effects.

2. Applied or practicing anthropologists work for a large variety of organizations, government agencies, international development agencies, private consulting firms, public health organizations, medical schools, public interest law firms, community development agencies, charitable foundations, and profit-seeking corporations.

3. The code of ethics for those who work professionally as applied anthropologists specifies that the target population should be included as much as possible in the formulation of policy, so that people in the community may know in advance how the program may affect them. But perhaps the most important aspect of the code is the pledge not to be involved in any plan whose effect will not be beneficial. It is often difficult to evaluate the effects of planned changes. Long-term consequences may be detrimental even if the changes are beneficial in the short run.

4. Even if a planned change will prove beneficial to the targeted population, the people may not accept it. And if the proposed innovation is not utilized by the intended population, the project cannot be considered a success. Affected populations may reject or resist a proposed innovation for cultural, social, or psychological reasons. It is important to understand what the reasons are. The population may also resist the proposed change because they unconsciously or consciously know it is not good for them.

5. To be effective, change agents may have to discover and use the traditional channels of influence in introducing their projects.

6. Cultural resource management usually takes the form of "contract archaeology" to record and/or conserve the archaeology of a building site.

7. Forensic anthropology is the specialty in anthropology that is devoted to helping solve crimes and identifying human remains, usually by applying knowledge of physical anthropology.

8. Medical anthropologists suggest that biological and social factors need to be considered if we are to understand how to treat illness effectively and reduce the suffering in human life.

9. Many of the ideas and practices of medical practitioners are influenced by the culture in which they reside. Understanding ethnomedicine—the medical beliefs and practices of a society or cultural group—is one of the goals of medical anthropology.

10. Many cultures have the view that the body should be kept in equilibrium or balance. The balance may be between hot and cold, or wet and dry, or there may be other properties that need to be balanced.

11. The belief that gods or spirits can cause illness is a near universal. The belief in sorcery or witchcraft as a cause of illness is also very common.

12. Some anthropologists think that there are few cultural universals about conceptions of illness or its treatment, but some researchers are finding evidence that many of the plant remedies that indigenous peoples use contain chemicals that are the same as, or similar in effect to, chemicals used in Western biomedicine remedies.

13. In the biomedical system, medical practitioners emphasize disease and cures, focusing on the body of the patient, not the mind or the social circumstances of the patient. In some societies, healers are more

"personalistic," and illness may be viewed as something out of order in one's social life. Shamans are perhaps the most important medical practitioners in societies lacking full-time specialization. Biomedical practitioners are becoming more aware of the psychological factors involved in healing.

14. People with more social, economic, and political power in a society are generally healthier. In socially stratified societies, the poor usually have increased exposure to disease because they are more likely to live in crowded and unsafe conditions and they are less likely to get access to quality care. Power and economic differentials between societies also have had profound health consequences.

15. The enormous death toll of AIDS, the leading cause of adult death in many countries today, will be reduced when medical science develops effective and inexpensive medicines to treat victims of HIV or AIDS and a vaccine to prevent individuals from getting HIV. In the meantime, if the death toll from AIDS is to be reduced, changes in attitudes, beliefs, and practices regarding sexual activity are needed.

16. Anthropologists debate the extent to which mental and emotional disorders are comparable across cultures. Some illnesses such as schizophrenia and depression seem so widespread as to be probably universal. Others, such as susto or anorexia nervosa, appear to be culture-bound syndromes.

17. The ways that people obtain, distribute, and consume food have been generally adaptive. Geneticists have proposed that populations in famine-prone areas may have had genetic selection for "thrifty genes." Now these populations with regular food supplies may be prone to diabetes and obesity. Many of the serious nutritional problems of today are due to rapid culture change, particularly those making for an increasing degree of social inequality.

GLOSSARY TERMS ○ ● ○

AIDS (acquired immune deficiency syndrome) **316**
applied or practicing anthropology **302**
biomedicine **312**
cultural resource management (CRM) **309**
ethnomedicine **311**
forensic anthropology **310**
medical anthropology **311**

CRITICAL QUESTIONS ○ ○ ●

1. What particular advantages do anthropologists have in trying to solve practical problems?
2. Is it ethical to try to influence people's lives when they have not asked for help? Explain your answer.
3. Why do native remedies often contain chemicals that are the same as, or similar in effect to, chemicals used in Western biomedicine remedies?
4. Why might people engage in sexual practices that increase their likelihood of contracting AIDS?

PEARSON
myanthrolab

Read the chapter by Andrew W. Miracle titled "A Shaman for Organizations" on MyAnthroLab. Answer the following questions:

1. Why does Miracle call himself a "shaman"?
2. According to Miracle, what skills are useful to an applied anthropologist? Why does he think so?

Read the chapter by Ruthbeth Finerman titled "Saraguro: Medical Choices, Medical Changes" on MyAnthroLab. Answer the following questions:

1. Why do the Saraguros continue mostly to rely on mothers to treat illness in the household?
2. How are Saraguro herbal treatments like your use of medicines? How are they unlike yours?

Global Problems

The news on television and in the newspapers makes us aware every day that terrible social problems threaten people around the world. War, crime, family violence, natural disasters, poverty, famine—all these and more are the lot of millions of people in many places. And now there is an increasing threat of terrorism. Can anthropological and other research help us solve these global social problems? Many anthropologists and other social scientists think so.

High-tech communications have increased our awareness of problems all over the world, and we seem to be increasingly more aware of, and bothered by, problems in our own society. For these two reasons, and perhaps also because we know much more than we used to about human behavior, we may be more motivated now to try to solve those problems. We call them "social problems" not just because a lot of people worry about them but also because they have social causes and consequences, and treating or solving them requires changes in social behavior. Even AIDS, which we discussed in the previous chapter, is partly a social problem. It may be caused by a virus, but it is mostly transmitted by social (sexual) contact with another person. And the main ways to avoid it—abstinence and "safe" sex—require changes in social behavior.

The idea that we can solve social problems, even the enormous ones such as war and family violence, is based on two assumptions. First, we have to assume that it is possible to discover the causes of a problem. And two, we have to assume that we may be able to do something about the causes, once they are discovered, and thereby eliminate or reduce the problem. Not everyone would agree with these assumptions. Some would say that our understanding of a social problem cannot ever be sufficient to suggest a solution guaranteed to work. To be sure, no understanding in science is perfect or certain; there is always some probability that even a well-supported explanation is wrong or incomplete. But the uncertainty of knowledge does not rule out the possibility of application. With regard to social problems, the possible payoff from even incomplete understanding could be a better and safer world. This possibility is what motivates many researchers who investigate social problems. After all, the history of the various sciences strongly supports the belief that scientific understanding can often allow humans to control nature, not just predict and explain it. Why should human behavior be any different?

So what do we know about some of the global social problems, and what policies or solutions are suggested by what we know?

● ○ ●

NATURAL DISASTERS AND FAMINE

Natural events such as floods, droughts, earthquakes, and insect infestations are usually but not always beyond human control, but their effects are not.[1] We call such events accidents or emergencies when only a few people are affected, but we call them disasters when large numbers of people or large areas are affected. The harm caused is not just a function of the

magnitude of the natural event. Between 1960 and 1980, 43 natural disasters in Japan killed an average of 63 people per disaster. During the same period, 17 natural disasters in Nicaragua killed an average of 6,235 people per disaster. In the United States, between 1960 and 1976, the average flood or other environmental disturbance killed just one person, injured a dozen, and destroyed fewer than five buildings. These comparative figures demonstrate that climatic and other events in the physical environment become disasters because of events or conditions in the social environment.

If people live in houses that are designed to withstand earthquakes—if governing bodies require such construction and the economy is developed enough so that people can afford such construction—the effects of an earthquake will be minimized. If poor people are forced to live in deforested floodplains to be able to find land to farm (as in coastal Bangladesh), if the poor are forced to live in shanties built on precarious hillsides (like those of Rio de Janeiro), the floods and landslides that follow severe hurricanes and rainstorms can kill thousands and even hundreds of thousands.

Thus, natural disasters can have greater or lesser effects on human life, depending on social conditions. And therefore disasters are also social problems, problems that have social causes and possible social solutions. Legislating safe construction of a house is a social solution. The 1976 earthquake in Tangsham, China, killed 250,000 people, mostly because they lived in top-heavy adobe houses that could not withstand severe shaking, whereas the 1989 Loma Prieta earthquake in California, which was of comparable intensity, killed 65 people.

Although earthquakes are not preventable, collapse of houses is mostly preventable by building houses to withstand earthquakes. In Bam, Iran, 20,000 people were killed during a 2003 earthquake and most of the houses collapsed. This woman sits amid the ruins of her house.

One might think that floods, of all disasters, are the least influenced by social factors. After all, without a huge runoff from heavy rains or snow melt, there cannot be a flood. But consider why so many people have died from Hwang River floods in China. (One such flood, in 1931, killed nearly 4 million people, making it the deadliest single disaster in history.) The floods in the Hwang River basin have occurred mostly because the clearing of nearby forests for fuel and farmland has allowed enormous quantities of silt to wash into the river, raising the riverbed and increasing the risk of floods that burst the dams that normally would contain them. The risk of disastrous flooding would be greatly reduced if different social conditions prevailed—if people were not so dependent on firewood for fuel, if they did not have to farm close to the river, or if the dams were higher and more numerous.

Famines, episodes of severe starvation and death, often appear to be triggered by physical events such as a severe drought or a hurricane that kills or knocks down food trees and plants. But famines do not inevitably follow such an event. Social conditions can prevent a famine or increase the likelihood of one. Consider what is likely to happen in Samoa after a hurricane.[2] Whole villages that have lost their coconut and breadfruit trees, as well as their taro patches, pick up and move for a period of time to other villages where they have relatives and friends. The visitors stay and are fed until some of their cultivated trees and plants start to bear food again, at which point they return home. This kind of intervillage reciprocity probably could occur only in a society that has relatively little inequality in wealth. Nowadays, the central government or international agencies may also help out by providing food and other supplies.

Researchers point out that famine rarely results from just one bad food production season. During one bad season, people can usually cope by getting help from relatives, friends, and neighbors or by switching to less desirable foods. The 1974 famine in the African Sahel occurred after eight years of bad weather; a combination of drought, floods, and a civil war in 1983 to 1984 contributed to the subsequent famine in the Sahel, Ethiopia, and Sudan.[3] Famine almost always has some social causes. Who has rights to the available food, and do those who have more food distribute it to those who have less? Cross-cultural research suggests that societies with individual property rights rather than shared rights are more likely to suffer famine.[4] Nonetheless, government assistance can lessen the risk of famine in societies with individual property.

Relief provided by government may not always get to those who need it the most. In India, for example, the central government provides help in time of drought to minimize the risk of famine. But the food and other supplies provided to a village may end up being unequally distributed, following the rules of social and gender stratification. Members of the local elite arrange to function as distributors and find ways to manipulate the relief efforts to their advantage. Lower-class and lower-caste families still suffer the most. Within the family, biases against females, particularly young girls and elderly women, translate into their getting less food. It is no wonder, then, that in times of food shortage and famine, the poor and other socially disadvantaged people are especially likely to die.[5]

Thus, the people of a society may not all be equally at risk in case of disaster. In socially stratified societies, the poor particularly suffer. They are likely to be forced to overcultivate, overgraze, and deforest their land, making it more susceptible to degradation. A society most helps those it values the most.

People in the past, and even recently in some places, viewed disasters as divine retribution for human immorality. For example, the great flood described in the Old Testament was understood to be God's doing. But scientific research increasingly allows us to understand the natural causes of disasters, and particularly the social conditions that magnify or minimize their effects. To reduce the impact of disasters, then, we need to reduce the social conditions that magnify the effects of disasters. If humans are responsible for those social conditions, humans can change them. If earthquakes destroy houses that are too flimsy, we can build stronger houses. If floods caused by overcultivation and overgrazing kill people directly (or indirectly by stripping their soils), we can grow new forest cover and provide new job opportunities to floodplain farmers. If prolonged natural disasters or wars threaten famine, social distribution systems can lessen the risk. In short, we may not be able to do much about the weather or other physical causes of disasters, but we can do a lot—if we want to—about the social factors that make disasters disastrous.

INADEQUATE HOUSING AND HOMELESSNESS

In most nations, those who are poor typically live in inadequate housing, in areas we call *slums*. In many of the developing nations, where cities are growing very rapidly, squatter settlements emerge as people build dwellings (often makeshift) that are typically declared illegal, either because the land is illegally occupied or because the dwellings violate building codes. Squatter settlements are often located in degraded environments that are subject to flooding and mudslides or have inadequate or polluted water. The magnitude of the problem is made clear in some statistics. As of the 1980s, 40 percent of the population in Nairobi, Kenya, lived in unauthorized housing, and 67 percent of the people in five of El Salvador's major cities lived in illegal dwellings.[6] In 2001, an estimated 32 percent of city-dwellers in the world lived in slums. The overall picture has not improved in the last ten years.[7]

But contrary to what some people have assumed, not all dwellers in illegal settlements are poor; all but the upper-income elite may be found in such settlements.[8] Moreover, although squatter settlements have problems, they are not chaotic and unorganized places that are full of crime. Most of the dwellers are employed, aspire to get ahead, live in intact nuclear families, and help each other.[9] People live in such settlements because they cannot find affordable housing and they house themselves as best they can. Many researchers think that such self-help tendencies should be assisted to improve housing, because governments in developing countries can seldom afford costly public housing projects. But they could invest somewhat in infrastructure—sewers, water supplies, roads—and provide construction materials to those who are willing to do the work required to improve their dwellings.[10]

Housing in slum areas or shantytowns does provide shelter, minimal though it may be. But many people in many areas of the world have no homes at all. Even in countries such as the United States, which are affluent by world standards, large numbers of people are homeless. They sleep in parks, over steam vents, in doorways, subways, and cardboard boxes. Homelessness is difficult to measure. In 1987, more than 1 million people were estimated to be homeless in the United States.[11] Homelessness has increased in the last few decades. About 3.5 million people experienced homelessness in 2000, almost 40 percent of them children.[12]

Who are the homeless, and how did they get to be homeless? We have relatively little research on these questions, but what we do have suggests differences in the causes of homelessness in different parts of the world. In the United States, unemployment and the shortage of decent low-cost housing appear to be at least partly responsible for the large number of homeless people.[13] But there is also another factor: the deliberate policy to reduce the number of people hospitalized for mental illness and other disabilities. For example, from the mid-1960s to the mid-1990s, New York State released thousands of patients from mental hospitals. Many of these ex-patients had to live in cheap hotels or poorly monitored facilities with virtually no support network. With very little income, they found it especially hard to cope with their circumstances. Ellen Baxter and Kim Hopper, who studied the homeless in New York City, suggest that one event is rarely sufficient to render a person homeless. Rather, poverty and disability

A homeless boy in Calcutta, India with his belongings.

current research and issues

Global Warming, Air Pollution, and Our Dependence on Oil

Scientists are increasingly sure that the world is heating up. And they are worried about the consequences. The more the temperature rises, the more the Greenland and Arctic ice will melt. The resulting higher sea level will flood many low-lying coastal areas, including many world cities. Storms, floods, and droughts will intensify. Places at high latitudes are likely to see increased rainfall and snow; places at low latitudes are likely to have less rainfall and more drought.

The world is warming probably for several reasons. One of them is our increasing use of fossil fuels, particularly oil. We burn those fuels to make electricity, to power our cars (with the gasoline made from oil), to heat our homes, and to cook food. The emissions from all that burning may contribute to a "greenhouse effect": The atmosphere reflects the warmth produced on earth, and temperatures rise. And the air gets dirtier, resulting in other harmful consequences such as a higher incidence of breathing disorders.

Can people do anything about global warming and air pollution? Surely the answer is yes. If at least some of the problem is of human making, we could change our behavior and at least partly solve the problem. One way would be to reduce our use of oil as fuel. But how could we do that?

In the year 2000, the first hybrid cars were sold in the United States. These cars are powered by an electric motor and a small gasoline engine. The combination reduces the amount of fuel needed, because the electric motor moves the car much of the time. The battery that powers the electric motor is recharged by braking and when the gasoline engine is on, which is not much of the time. (For example, at a stop light, the gasoline engine turns off.) So a hybrid car allows a gallon of gasoline to go a lot farther. If most cars were hybrid cars, we would need much less oil to make the gasoline needed.

It is estimated that hybrid cars could cut greenhouse emissions by up to half, which would help alleviate or even reverse global warming and air pollution. So, given this rosy scenario, what is discouraging the world from switching to hybrid cars?

The answer is probably economics and politics. There is money to be made from the dependence on oil, particularly when supplies are short. The shorter the supplies, the more the oil producers abroad and the refiners at home can charge their customers. And the more the oil comes from abroad, the more the U.S. and other governments may feel that they have to keep the foreign producers happy. But this obligation runs counter to a foreign policy that would encourage democracy in the world; many of the countries that produce our oil are dictatorships. So the oil companies are dependent on those regimes to keep their refineries going, and they lobby governments (ours included) to maintain friendly relations with many of those regimes. Can we expect the oil companies to want to escape their dependence on foreign suppliers, if they are making a lot of money from that dependence? Hardly.

Our market economy does offer a way out of this dilemma. If hybrid cars and other ways to reduce the need for fossil fuels become more economical, the marketplace will turn the tide. Ironically, the capitalist laws of supply and demand may reduce the influence of oil companies on politics and help us solve the problems of global warming and air pollution. Even if the automobile manufacturers wanted to continue doing business as usual, they will not be able to resist making more fuel-efficient cars. As the recent "cash for clunkers" program in the United States shows, consumers want to reduce their gasoline expenses. No car company will be able to ignore that kind of pressure from the marketplace. There is more interest in making and buying hybrid vehicles, and there is the possibility of transforming organic garbage into oil. Other solutions to our dependency on foreign oil are also being tested. So our consumption of oil may decrease significantly in the near future.

Sources: Oerlemans 2005; M. L. Wald 2000; Ambient Corporation 2000; Duane 2003; Baer and Singer 2009. ⋀⋀⋀

(mental or physical) seem to lead to one calamity after another and, finally, homelessness.[14]

Many people cannot understand why homeless individuals do not want to go to municipal shelters. But observations and interviews with the homeless suggest that violence pervades the municipal shelters, particularly the men's shelters. Many feel safer on the streets. Some private charities provide safe shelters and a caring environment. These shelters are filled, but the number of homeless they can accommodate is small.[15] Even single-room-occupancy hotels are hardly better. Many of them are infested with vermin, the common bathrooms are filthy, and they, like the shelters, are often dangerous.[16]

Some poor individuals may be socially isolated, with few or no friends and relatives and little or no social contact. But a society with many such individuals does not necessarily have much homelessness. Socially isolated individuals, even mentally ill individuals, could still have housing, or so the experience of Melbourne, Australia, suggests. Universal health insurance there pays for health care as well as medical practitioners' visits to isolated and ill individuals, wherever they live. Disabled individuals receive a pension or sickness benefits sufficient to allow them to live in a room or apartment. And there is still a considerable supply of cheap housing in Melbourne. Research in Melbourne suggests that a severe mental disorder often precedes living in marginal accommodations—city shelters, commercial shelters, and cheap single rooms. About 50 percent of the people living in such places were diagnosed as previously having some form of mental illness; this percentage is similar to what seems to be the case for homeless people and people living in marginal accommodations in the United States.

The contrast between the United States and Australia makes it clear that social and political policies cause homelessness. Individuals with similar characteristics live in both Australia and the United States, but a larger percentage of them are homeless in the United States.[17]

Because homelessness cannot occur if everybody can afford housing, some people would say that homelessness can happen only in a society with great extremes in income. Statistics on income distribution in the United States clearly show that, since the 1970s, the rich have gotten much richer and the poor have gotten much poorer.[18] The United States now has more income inequality than any country in western Europe and more than most high-income countries. In fact, the profile of inequality in the United States more closely resembles that of developing countries, such as Cambodia and Morocco[19] (see the discussion in the chapter on social stratification).

In the United States and many other countries, most homeless people are adults. Whereas adults are "allowed" to be homeless, public sensibilities in the United States appear to be outraged by the sight of children living in the streets; when authorities discover homeless children, they try to find shelters or foster homes for them. But many countries have "street children." In the late 1980s, 80 million of the world's children lived in the streets; 40 million in Latin America, 20 million in Asia, 10 million in Africa and the Middle East, and 10 million elsewhere.[20] In the 2000s, the estimated number grew to about 150 million worldwide.[21]

Lewis Aptekar, who studied street children in Cali, Colombia, reported some surprises.[22] Whereas many of the homeless in the United States and Australia are mentally disabled, the street children in Cali, ranging in age from 7 to 16, are mostly free of mental problems; by and large, they also test normally on intelligence tests. In addition, even though many street children come from abusive homes or never had homes, they usually seem happy and enjoy the support and friendship of other street children. They cleverly and creatively look for ways to get money, frequently through entertaining passersby.

Although observers might think that the street children must have been abandoned by their families, most of them in actuality have at least one parent they keep in touch with. Street life begins slowly, not abruptly; children usually do not stay on the streets full time until they are about 13 years old. Though street children in Cali seem to be in better physical and mental shape than their siblings who stay at home, they often are viewed as a "plague." The street children come from poor families and cope with their lives as best they can, so why are they not viewed with pity and compassion? Aptekar suggests that well-off families see the street children as a threat because a life independent of family may appeal to children, even those from well-off families, who wish to be free of parental constraint and authority.

Whether people become homeless, whether they have shantytowns, seems to depend on a society's willingness to share wealth and help those in need. The street children of Cali may remind us that children as well as adults need companionship and care. Addressing physical needs without responding to emotional needs may get people off the streets, but it won't get them a "home."

FAMILY VIOLENCE AND ABUSE

In U.S. society, we hear regularly about the abuse of spouses and children, which makes us think that such abuse is increasing—but is it? This seems to be a simple question, but it is not so simple to answer. We have to decide what we mean by *abuse*.

Is physical punishment of a child who does something wrong child abuse? Not so long ago, teachers in public schools in the United States were allowed to discipline children by hitting them with rulers or paddles, and many parents used switches or belts. Many would consider these practices to be child abuse, but were they abusive when they were generally accepted? Some would argue that abuse is going beyond what a culture considers appropriate behavior. Others would disagree and would focus on the violence and severity of parents' or teachers' behavior, not the cultural judgment of appropriateness. And abuse need not involve physical violence. It could be argued that verbal aggression and neglect may be just as harmful as physical aggression. Neglect presents its own problems of definition. People from other cultures might argue that we act abusively when we put an infant or child alone in a room to sleep.[23] Few would disagree about severe injuries that kill a child or spouse or require medical treatment, but other disciplinary behaviors are more difficult to judge.

To avoid having to decide what is or is not abuse, many researchers focus their studies on variation in the frequencies of specific behaviors. For example, one can ask which societies have physical punishment of children without calling physical punishment abusive.

According to four national interview surveys of married or cohabiting couples in the United States conducted from 1975 to 1995, physical violence against children appears to have decreased in frequency over time, as did serious assaults by husbands against wives. But serious assaults by wives on husbands did not decrease.[24] The decreasing rates of abuse may be mostly due to reporting differences: wife and child beating is less acceptable now. For example, men report dramatically fewer assaults on their wives, but wives report only slight declines.[25] However, the United States remains a society with a lot of physical violence in families. In 1992 alone, one out of 10 couples had a violent assault episode and one out of 10 children was severely assaulted by a parent.[26] A survey conducted in the mid-1990s found that about 75 percent of the violence against women comes from a male intimate partner, such as a husband. In contrast, most of the violence men experience comes from strangers and acquaintances. Just as women face more risk from those close to them, so do children. When a child is the target of violence, it usually comes from the birth mother.[27]

Cross-culturally, if one form of family violence occurs, others are also likely. So, for example, wife beating, husband beating, child punishment, and fighting among siblings are all significantly associated with each other. But the relationships between these types of family violence are not that strong, which means that they cannot be considered as different facets of the same phenomenon. Indeed, somewhat different factors seem to explain different forms of family violence.[28] We focus here on two forms of violence that are most prevalent cross-culturally: violence against children and violence against wives.

Violence Against Children

Cross-culturally, many societies practice and allow infanticide. Frequent reasons for infanticide include illegitimacy, deformity of the infant, twins, too many children, or that the infant is unwanted. Infanticide is usually performed by the mother, but this does not mean that she is uncaring; it may mean that she cannot adequately feed or care for the infant or that it has a poor chance to survive. The reasons for infanticide are similar to those given for abortion. Therefore, it seems that infanticide may be performed when abortion does not work or when unexpected qualities of the infant (e.g., deformity) force the mother to reevaluate her ability to raise the child.[29]

Physical punishment of children occurs at least sometimes in over 70 percent of the world's societies.[30] And physical punishment is frequent or typical in 40 percent of the world's societies. The finding that societies with class stratification and political hierarchy, either native or introduced (colonialism), are very likely to practice corporal punishment of children[31] suggests that parents are consciously or unconsciously preparing their children for a life of power inequality. Research in the United States is consistent with the cross-cultural finding: Those at the bottom of the socioeconomic hierarchy are more likely than those at the top to practice corporal punishment of children.[32] Unfortunately, parents probably do not realize that physical punishment may produce more violent behavior in their children, an outcome they probably do not want or intend (see box on corporal punishment of children).

Violence Against Wives

Cross-culturally, wife beating is the most common form of family violence; it occurs at least occasionally in about 85 percent of the world's societies. In about half the societies, wife beating is sometimes serious enough to cause permanent injury or death.[33] It is often assumed that wife beating is common in societies in which males control economic and political resources. In a cross-cultural test of this assumption, David Levinson found that not all indicators of male dominance predict wife beating, but many do. Specifically, wife beating is most common when men control the products of family labor, when men have the final say in decision making in the home, when divorce is difficult for women, when remarriage for a widow is

controlled by the husband's kin, and when women do not have any female work groups.[34] Similarly, in the United States, the more one spouse in the family makes the decisions and has the power, the more physical violence occurs in the family. Wife beating is even more likely when the husband controls the household and is out of work.[35]

Wife beating appears to be related to broader patterns of violence. Societies that have violent methods of conflict resolution within communities, physical punishment of criminals, high frequency of warfare, and cruelty toward enemies generally have more wife beating.[36] Corporal punishment of children may be related to wife beating. Research in the United States supports the idea that individuals (males and females) who were punished corporally as adolescents are more likely to approve of marital violence and are more likely to commit it.[37]

Reducing the Risk

What can be done to minimize family violence? First, we have to recognize that probably nothing can be done as long as people in a society do not acknowledge that a problem exists. If severe child punishment and wife beating are perfectly acceptable by almost everyone in a society, they are unlikely to be considered social problems that need solutions. In our own society, many programs are designed to take abused children or wives out of the family situation or to punish the abuser. (Of course, in these situations, the violence has already occurred and was serious enough to have been noticed.) Cross-culturally, at least with respect to wife beating, intervention by others seems to be successful only if the intervention occurs before violence gets serious. As one would expect, however, those societies most prone to a high rate of wife beating are the least likely to practice immediate intervention. More helpful perhaps, but admittedly harder to arrange, is the promotion of conditions of life that are associated with low family violence. Research so far suggests that promoting the equality of men and women and the sharing of child-rearing responsibilities may go a long way toward lessening incidents of family violence.[38] And reducing the risk of corporal punishment of children may reduce the risk of violence when they have families.

CRIME

What is a crime in one society is not necessarily a crime in another. Just as it is difficult to decide what constitutes abuse, it is difficult to define *crime*. In one society, it may be a crime to walk over someone's land without permission; in another, there might not be any concept of personal ownership, and therefore no concept of trespassing. In seeking to understand variation in crime, many researchers have not surprisingly preferred to compare those behaviors that are more or less universally considered crimes and that are reliably reported. For example, in a large-scale comparison of crime in 110 nations over a span of 70 years, Dane Archer and Rosemary Gartner concentrated on homicide rates. They argued that homicide is harder for the public to hide and for officials to ignore than are other crimes. A comparison of interviews about

applied anthropology

Corporal Punishment of Children: What Would Discourage It?

The old proverb warns: "Spare the rod and spoil the child." In 1995, one or four parents in the United States hit their children with objects, not just with their hands. Almost 95 percent hit 4- to 5-year-old children. In recent years, there has been some turning away from corporal or bodily punishment, and more people in this country and elsewhere would like parents to stop spanking their children. They point to evidence that spanking and other corporal punishment leads to wife beating and other violence by the children when they grow up. So if we want to reduce violence against household partners, one thing we could do is reduce the conditions that predict corporal punishment of children. The frequency of corporal punishment does not vary that much from one country to another, and most approve of the practice. There is more variation in the cross-cultural record, and we can use that record to predict the variation.

The main predictors of corporal punishment in the ethnographic or cross-cultural record are two conditions that are practically universal in the nation-states of the world, namely, a money economy and a stratified social system. If parents want children to do well when they grow up in a world with power in-

equality, might parents practice corporal punishment to convey that some people (particularly employers) are much more powerful than others? To a child, parents are clearly powerful. Not only are they taller and physically stronger, they also control and dispense important resources (food, love). So perhaps parents may consciously or unconsciously think that, if children fear those who are more powerful, they may be less likely to get into trouble and more likely to be able to get and keep a job. Donna Goldstein (1998, 411) poignantly describes the plight of a woman in a shantytown near Rio de Janeiro who supports more than 10 children in a one-room shack. Her discipline is harsh but she is trying, as Goldstein points out, to ensure that the kids "have the skills, as well as the attitudes of obedience, humility, and subservience, necessary for a poor black person to survive in urban Brazil."

Do these results suggest how corporal punishment of children could decrease? At one level, it is difficult to see how. Societies that use money and have social classes are not likely to become egalitarian. But societies could move in the direction of de-emphasizing economic and power inequality. When parents hit their

children, it is generally not because they want their children to be violent. They want them to behave properly. If they understood the connection between parental violence and child violence, they might begin to change their practices.

Some countries already have not-so-high rates of corporal punishment. These are the more democratic countries—with contested elections that allow people to replace leaders peacefully, and laws that protect civil rights such as the right to express dissent. (The agreement to disagree, and protecting civil rights, means that you don't have to worry so much about losing your job if you disagree with your employer's beliefs.) Sweden and the other Scandinavian countries have lower rates of approval of corporal punishment. Is this because Scandinavia is more democratic, allowing people (even workers in factories) to participate more in decision making in the workplace, and not just in elections? We think so. But only time will tell if increasing democracy, and less need for workers to act subservient, will translate into less violent ways of socializing children.

Sources: Straus 2001; 2009; C. R. Ember and Ember 2005; D. Goldstein 1998, 411.

---

crime with police records suggests that homicide is the most reliably reported crime in official records.[39]

Nations not only have very different crime rates when we compare them at a given point in time; the rates also vary over time within a nation. In the last 600 years, homicide rates have generally declined in Western societies. In England, where homicide rates have been well documented for centuries, the chance of murder during the 13th and 14th centuries was 10 times higher than in England today. But beginning in the 1960s, homicide and other crime rates have surged upward in many Western countries.[40] Around 1970, some of the lowest homicide rates were found in Iran, Dahomey, Puerto Rico, New Zealand, Norway, England, and France. Some of the highest homicide rates were in Iraq, Colombia, Burma, Thailand, Swaziland, and Uganda. Compared with other countries, the United States had a fairly high homicide

rate; approximately three-fourths of the countries surveyed had lower homicide rates than the United States.[41]

One of the clearest findings to emerge from comparative studies of crime is that war is associated with higher rates of homicide. Archer and Gartner compared changes in homicide rates of nations before and after major wars. Whether a nation is defeated or victorious, homicide rates tend to increase after a war. This result is consistent with the idea that a society or nation legitimizes violence during wartime. That is, during wartime, societies approve of killing the enemy; afterward, homicide rates may go up because inhibitions against killing have been relaxed.[42] Ted Gurr suggested that the long-term downtrend in crime in Western societies seems to be consistent with an increasing emphasis on humanistic values and nonviolent achievement of goals. But such goals may be temporarily suspended during wartime. In the United States, for

Theft tends to be more prevalent with social inequality and with higher unemployment. This man is stealing CDs from a music store in the United States.

example, surges in violent crime rates occurred during the 1860s and 1870s (during and after the Civil War), after World War I, after World War II, and during the Vietnam War.[43] But recently the homicide rate in the United States has declined.[44]

In the types of societies that anthropologists have typically studied, homicide statistics were not usually available; so cross-cultural studies of homicide usually measure homicide rates by comparing and rank-ordering ethnographers' statements about the frequency of homicide. For example, the statement that murder is "practically unheard of" is taken to mean that the murder rate is lower than where it is reported that "homicide is not uncommon." Despite the fact that the data on cultural homicide rates are not quantitative, the cross-cultural results are consistent with the cross-national results; more war is usually associated with more homicide and assault, as well as with socially approved aggressive behaviors (as in aggressive games) and severe physical punishment for wrongdoing.[45] A cross-cultural study suggests that the more war a society has, the more the society socializes or trains boys in aggression, and such socialization strongly predicts higher rates of homicide and assault.[46]

Capital punishment—execution of criminals—is severe physical punishment for wrongdoing. It is commonly thought that the prospect of capital punishment deters would-be murderers. Yet, cross-national research suggests otherwise. More countries show murder rates going down rather than up after capital punishment was abolished.[47] Capital punishment may legitimize violence rather than deter it.

Research conducted in the United States suggests that juvenile delinquents (usually boys) are likely to come from broken homes, with the father absent for much of the time the boy is growing up. The conclusion often drawn is that father absence somehow increases the likelihood of delinquency and adult forms of physical violence. But other conditions that may cause delinquency are also associated with broken homes, conditions such as the stigma of not having a "regular" family and the generally low standard of living of such families. It is therefore important to conduct research in other societies, in which father absence does not occur in concert with these other factors, to see if father absence by itself is related to physical violence.

For example, in many polygynous societies, children grow up in a mother-child household; the father lives separately and is seldom around the child. Does the father absence explanation of delinquency and violence fit such societies? The answer is apparently yes: Societies in which children are reared in mother-child households or the father spends little time caring for the child tend to have more physical violence by males than do societies in which fathers spend time with children.[48] The rate of violent crime is also more frequent in nations that have more women than men, which is consistent with the theory that father absence increases violence.[49]

More research is needed to discover exactly what accounts for these relationships. It is possible, as some suggest, that boys growing up without fathers are apt to act "supermasculine," to show how "male" they are. But it is also possible that mothers who rear children alone have more frustration and more anger, and therefore are likely to provide an aggressive role model for the child. In addition, high male mortality in war predicts polygyny, as we saw in the chapter on marriage and the family; therefore, boys in polygynous societies are likely to be exposed to a warrior tradition.[50]

Trying to act supermasculine, however, may be likely to involve violence only if aggression is an important component of the male gender role in society. If men were expected by society to be sensitive, caring, and nonviolent, boys who grew up without fathers might try to be supersensitive and supercaring. So society's expectations for males probably shape how growing up in a mother-child household affects behavior in adolescence and later.[51] The media may also influence the expectations for males. Numerous studies in the United States show that, even controlling for other factors like parental neglect, family income, and mental illness, more television watching in childhood and adolescence predicts more overt aggression later. Estimates show that an hour of prime-time television depicts 3 to 5 violent acts, and an hour of children's television depicts 20 to 25 violent acts.[52]

One widely held idea is that poor economic conditions increase the likelihood of crime, but the relationship does not appear to be strong. Also, the findings are somewhat different for different types of crime. For example, hundreds of studies in this and other countries do not show a clear relationship between changes in economic well-being as measured by unemployment rates and changes in violent crime as measured by homicide. The rate of homicide does not appear to increase in bad times. Property crimes, however, do increase with increases in unemployment. Violent crime does appear to be associated with one economic characteristic: Homicide is usually highest in nations or societies with high income inequality.[53] Why income inequality predicts homicide but downturns in the economy do not is something of a puzzle.[54]

The fact that property crime is linked to unemployment is consistent with the cross-cultural finding that theft (but not violent crime) tends to occur less often in egalitarian societies than in stratified ones. Societies with equal access to resources usually have distribution mechanisms that offset any differences in wealth. Hence, theft should be less of a temptation and therefore less likely in an egalitarian society. Theft rates are higher in socially stratified societies despite the fact that they are more likely than egalitarian societies to have police and courts to punish crime. Societies may try to deter property and other crimes when the rates of such are high, but we do not know that these efforts actually reduce the rates.

So what does the available research suggest about how we might be able to reduce crime? The results so far indicate that homicide rates are highest in societies that socialize their boys for aggression. Such socialization is linked to war and other forms of socially approved violence—capital punishment, television and movie violence by heroes, violence in sports. The statistical evidence suggests that war encourages socialization for aggression, which in turn results unintentionally in high rates of violence. The policy implication of these results is that, if we can reduce socialization for aggression by reducing the risk of war and therefore the necessity to produce effective warriors, and if we can reduce other forms of socially approved violence, we may thereby reduce the rates of violent crime. The reduction of inequalities in wealth may also help to reduce crime, particularly theft. And although it is not yet clear why, it appears that raising boys with a male role model around may reduce the likelihood of male violence in adulthood.

Evidence indicates that violence on TV encourages violence in real life.

WAR

War is an unfortunate fact of life in most societies known to anthropology, judging by the cross-cultural research we referred to in the chapter on political life. Almost every society had at least occasional wars when it was first described, unless it had been pacified (usually by Western colonial powers).[55] Since the Civil War, the United States has not had any wars on its territory, but it is unusual in that respect. Before pacification, most societies in the ethnographic record had frequent armed combat between communities or larger units that spoke the same language. That is, most warfare was internal to the society or language group. Even some wars in modern times involved speakers of the same language; recall the wars between Italian states before the unification of Italy and many of the "civil" wars of the last two centuries. Although people in some societies might fight against people in other societies, such "external" wars were usually not organized on behalf of the entire society or even a major section of it.[56] That is, warfare in the ethnographic record did not usually involve politically unified societies. The absolute numbers of people killed may have been small, but this does not mean that warfare in nonindustrial societies was a trivial matter. Indeed, it appears that nonindustrial warfare may have been even more lethal *proportionately* than modern warfare, judging by the fact that wars killed 25 percent to 30 percent of the males in some nonindustrial societies.[57]

Although warfare has occurred frequently in societies at all levels of complexity, changes over time tell us that war is not inevitable. For example, Norway is one of the world's most peaceful countries. The Viking age, as shown in this reenactment, was an era of militarism.

In the chapter on political life, we discussed the possibility that people in nonindustrial societies go to war mostly out of fear, particularly a fear of expectable but unpredictable natural disasters (droughts, floods, hurricanes, among others) that destroy food supplies.[58] People with more of a history of such disasters have more war. It seems as if people go to war to protect themselves ahead of time from disasters, inasmuch as the victors in war almost always take resources (land, animals, other things) from the defeated, even when the victors have no current resource problems. Another factor apparently making for more war is teaching children to mistrust others. People who grow up to be mistrustful of others may be more likely to go to war than to negotiate or seek conciliation with "enemies." Mistrust or fear of others seems to be partly caused by threat or fear of disasters.[59]

Is warfare in and between modern state societies explainable in much the same way that nonindustrial warfare seems to be explainable? If the answer to that question turns out to be yes, it will certainly be a modified yes, because the realities of industrialized societies require an expanded conception of disasters. In the modern world, with its complex economic and political dependencies among nations, we may not be worried only about weather or pest disasters that could curtail food supplies. Possible curtailments of other resources, particularly oil, may also scare us into going to war. According to some commentators, the decision in 1991 to go to war against Iraq after it invaded Kuwait fits this theory of war.

But even if the "threat-to-resources" theory is true, we may be coming to realize (since the end of the Cold War) that war is not the only way to ensure access to resources. There may be a better way in the modern world, a way that is more cost-effective as well as more preserving of human life. If it is true that war is most likely when people fear unpredictable disasters of any kind, the risk of war should lessen when people realize that the harmful effects of disasters could be reduced or prevented by international cooperation. Just as we have the assurance of disaster relief within our country, we could have the assurance of disaster relief worldwide. That is, the fear of unpredictable disasters and the fear of others, and the consequent risk of war, could be reduced by the assurance ahead of time that the world would help those in need in case of disaster. Instead of going to war out of fear, we could go to peace by agreeing to share. The certainty of international cooperation could compensate for the uncertainty of resources.

Consider how Germany and Japan have fared in the years since their "unconditional surrender" in World War II. They were forbidden to participate in the international arms race and could rely on others, particularly the United States, to protect them. Without a huge burden of armaments, Germany and Japan thrived. But countries that competed militarily, particularly the United States and the Soviet Union at the height of the Cold War, experienced economic difficulties. Doesn't that scenario at least suggest the wisdom of international cooperation, particularly the need for international agreements to ensure worldwide disaster relief? Compared with going to war and its enormous costs, going to peace would be a bargain!

Recent research in political science and anthropology suggests an additional way to reduce the risk of war. Among the societies known to anthropology, studies indicate that people in more participatory—that is, more "democratic"—political systems rarely go to war with each other.[60] Thus, if authoritarian governments were to disappear from the world because the powerful nations of the world stopped supporting them militarily and otherwise, the world could be more peaceful for this reason too.

Although democratically governed states rarely go to war with each other, it used to be thought that they are not necessarily more peaceful in general, that they are as likely to go to war as are other kinds of political systems, but not so much with each other. For example, the United States has gone to war with Grenada, Panama, and Iraq—all authoritarian states—but not with democratic Canada, with which the United States has also had disputes. But now a consensus is emerging among political scientists that democracies are not only unlikely to go to war with each other, they are also less warlike in general.[61] The theory suggested by the cross-national and cross-cultural results is that democratic conflict resolution within a political system generalizes to democratic conflict resolution between

▶current research and issues

Ethnic Conflicts: Ancient Hatreds or Not?

Ethnic conflicts appear to be on the rise. In recent years, violent conflicts have erupted between ethnic groups in the former Yugoslavia, Russia, and Spain (in Europe), in Rwanda and Sierra Leone (in Africa), and in Sri Lanka and Indonesia (in Asia)—to name just a few of the many instances. Such conflicts are often thought to be intractable and inevitable because they are supposedly based on ancient hatreds. But is that true?

Social scientists are a long way from understanding the conditions that predict ethnic conflicts, but they do know that ethnic conflicts are not necessarily ancient or inevitable. For example, anthropologists who did fieldwork in the former Yugoslavia in the 1980s described villages where different ethnic groups had lived side by side for a long time without apparent difficulty. The differences between them were hardly emphasized. Mary Kay Gilliland worked in a midsize town (Slavonski Brod) in the Slavonian region of Croatia, which was part of Yugoslavia. The people in the town identified themselves as from Slavonia, rather than as Croats, Serbs, Hungarians, Czechs, Muslims (from Bosnia or from Albania), or Roma (Gypsies). Mixed marriages were not uncommon and people discussed differences in background without anger. But in 1991, when Gilliland returned to Croatia, people complained about Serb domination of the Yugoslav government and there was talk of Croatia seceding. Symbols of Croat national-

ism had appeared—new place names, a new flag—and Croats were now said to speak Croatian, rather than the language they shared with the Serbs (Serbo-Croatian or Croato-Serbian). Later in 1991, violence broke out between Serbs and Croats, and atrocities were committed on both sides. Ethnicity became a matter of life or death, and Croatia seceded from Yugoslavia. At the same time, Tone Bringa, a Norwegian anthropologist who worked in Bosnia (which was then still a region of Yugoslavia), reported that the people there also paid little attention to ethnicity. A few years later, however, ethnic violence erupted among Bosnian Serbs, Muslims, and Croats, and only the intervention of the United Nations established a precarious peace.

Ethnic conflict is frequently associated with secessionist movements. That is, secession often occurs after the eruption of ethnic conflict. Remember the American Revolution? The region that became the United States of America seceded from Great Britain and declared independence. To be sure, the ethnic differences between the Americans and the British were not great. After all, not too many years had passed since the first British colonizers had come to America. But there still was a secessionist movement, and there was violence. Ethnic differences do not always lead to violence. Sometimes, probably even most of the time, people of different ethnic backgrounds live in peace with each other. So the

basic question is why do some places with ethnic differences erupt in violence, but not all? Why do different ethnic groups get along in some places?

We need research to answer this question. With all of the forced and voluntary immigration in the world, many countries are becoming more multiethnic or multicultural. The possibility of ethnic violence has become a global social problem. Gilliland suggests, among other things, that discontent over economic and political power (inequitable access to resources and opportunities) drove the Croatians to violence and secession. Other scholars have suggested other possible answers to the question of why ethnic relations do not always become ethnic conflict and violence. Violence may erupt in the absence of strong unifying interests (cross-cutting ties) between the parties. Another suggested factor is the absence of constitutional ways to resolve conflict. What we need now is cross-cultural, cross-national, and cross-historical studies to measure each of the possible explaining factors, so that we can compare how well (or poorly) they predict ethnic conflict throughout the world, controlling for the effects of the other factors. If we knew which factors generally give rise to ethnic violence, we might be able to think of ways to reduce or eliminate the causal conditions.

Sources: Gilliland 1995; Bringa 1995; M. H. Ross 2009a.

political systems, particularly if the systems are both democratic. If our participatory institutions and perceptions allow us to resolve our disputes peacefully, internally and externally, we may think that similarly governed people would also be disposed to settle things peacefully. Therefore, disputes between participatory political systems should be unlikely to result in war.

The understanding that participatory systems rarely fight each other, and knowing why they do not, would

have important consequences for policy in the contemporary world. The kinds of military preparations believed necessary and the costs people would be willing to pay for them might be affected. On the one hand, understanding the relationship between democracy and peace might encourage war making against authoritarian regimes to overturn them—with enormous costs in human life and otherwise. On the other hand, understanding the consequences of democracy might encourage us to assist the emergence and consolidation of more participatory systems of government in the countries of eastern Europe, the former Soviet Union, and elsewhere. In any case, the relationship between democracy and peace strongly suggests that it is counterproductive to support any undemocratic regimes, even if they happen to be enemies of our enemies, if we want to minimize the risk of war in the world. The latest cross-national evidence suggests that extending democracy around the world would minimize the risk of war. Encouraging nations to be more interdependent economically, and encouraging the spread of international nongovernmental organizations (like professional societies and trade associations) to provide informal ways to resolve conflicts, would also minimize the risk of war, judging by results of recent research by political scientists.[62]

TERRORISM

Ever since September 11, 2001, when terrorists crashed airliners into the World Trade Center towers in New York City and into the Pentagon in Arlington, Virginia, people all over the world realize that terrorism has become a social problem globally. It is now painfully clear that organized groups of terrorists can train their people to kill themselves and thousands of others half a world away, not only by hijacking airliners and flying them into skyscrapers, but also by using easily transported explosives and biological weapons. Social scientists are now actively trying to understand terrorism, in the hope that research may lead to ways to minimize the likelihood of future attacks. But there are lots of questions to answer. What is terrorism and how shall it be defined?

How long has terrorist activity been around? What are the causes of terrorism? What kind of people are likely to become terrorists? And what are the consequences of terrorism?

Answering these questions is not so simple. Most people can point to instances that hardly anyone would have trouble calling terrorism—spraying nerve gas in a Japanese subway, Palestinian suicide bombers targeting Israeli civilians, Ku Klux Klan members lynching African Americans.[63] It is harder to identify the boundaries between terrorism, crime, political repression, and warfare.[64] Most researchers agree that terrorism involves the threat or use of violence against civilians. Terrorism is usually also politically or socially organized, in contrast to most crimes, which are usually perpetrated by individuals acting on their own. (To be sure, crime can be socially organized too, as, for example, in what we call "organized crime.") One marker of the difference between most crime and terrorism is that criminals rarely take public credit for their activities, because they want to avoid being caught. In terrorism, the perpetrators usually proclaim their responsibility. In terrorism also, the violence is directed mostly at unarmed people, including women and children. It is intended to frighten the "enemy," to *terrorize* them, to scare them into doing something that the terrorists want to see happen. Generally, then, **terrorism** may be defined as the use or threat of violence to create terror in others, usually for political purposes.[65] Some define terrorism as perpetrated by groups that are not formal political entities. However, this criterion presents some difficulty. What are we to call it when governments support death squads and genocide against their own civilians? Some scholars call this "state terror."[66] And what are

A candlelight vigil after the terrorist attack in 2008 on the Taj Mahal Hotel in Mumbai, India.

migrants and immigrants

Refugees Are a Global Social Problem

The continuing turmoil in many countries throughout the world has created a flow of refugees that is much larger than ever before in world history. Refugees have become a worldwide social problem; their numbers are so high. In the past, thousands of people might have had to flee persecution and war. Now the refugees number in the millions. They flee to other parts of the country, to neighboring countries, and to countries on the other side of the world. As many as an estimated 140 million people became refugees in the 20th century. For example, the refugees from the civil wars in Somalia are not unusual; 10 percent of the Somali population is now living outside of Somalia, perhaps a million people altogether.

Conceivably, the problem could be handled with less suffering if countries were willing to accept any and all refugees. Shouldn't governments accept them for humanitarian reasons, just because the refugees could die otherwise? Or does there have to be an acknowledged or felt need in the accepting country for cheap labor? There is a fine line between people who want to migrate to have a better or safer life, and people who have to migrate because they would be killed if they don't flee. Refugees are a problem not just because they are suffering, and the world should do something. They are also a problem because countries may refuse to accept them, because their numbers are so large. Governments and charitable agencies have to provide support until the refugees acquire the skills for making a living on their own.

Compare how we think of refugees from different places. Some are accepted (however grudgingly), whereas others are not. The United States only half-heartedly tries to prevent poor Mexicans from entering the country. But people from Africa who are threatened with genocide are rejected much more. Why? Is it because Mexicans and others from Latin America have skills that we need, and they are willing to take jobs that no one else wants because the pay is low and the benefits nil? Who benefits from this state of affairs? Too many! Think of the employers who would otherwise have to pay their workers more or invest in labor-saving machinery. Think of the Chinese "coolies" who were brought in 150 years ago to build the railroads that linked the eastern and western United States. And, of course, think of the refugee laborers. If they didn't "cross the border" looking for work, their children left at home would suffer or even die from malnutrition and other consequences of poverty.

So, what are countries to do? Should they throw open their doors to everyone who wants to come in? Humanitarians might say yes. But this too would make for problems. Some would say that we should not accept and support refugees when we already have lots of poor people. Don't we owe them more than we owe poor people from somewhere else? Shouldn't our tax money go to improve the lives of people already here? What are taxes for, anyway?

How to help refugees is clearly a complex issue. But if we don't do anything to help them, is that ethical? Refugees are the consequences of social inequality and persecution. They are a global social problem that won't go away, as long as the world contains governments that persecute their own citizens, or allow some groups to persecute others. If the solution is not to rely on those governments because they are not likely to change what they are doing, it would seem that we will have to rely for the near future on international organizations (like the United Nations and charitable foundations) if we want to reduce or eliminate the worldwide problem of refugees.

Sources: Harrell-Bond 1996; Van Hear 2004.

---

we to call the activities of some governments that support secret operations against other countries (often referred to as "state-sponsored terrorism")? Finally, although some nations conducting war explicitly try to avoid civilian casualties and focus primarily on combatants (armed soldiers), their weapons, and resources or "assets" such as factories, air strips, and fuel depots, many attacks in wartime throughout history have purposefully targeted civilians (e.g., the United States dropped atomic bombs on Hiroshima and Nagasaki to persuade the Japanese to end World War II).

One thing is certain about terrorism: It is not a new development. Some of the words we use for terrorists—for example, "zealots" and "assassins"—derive from terrorist movements in the past. The Zealots, Jewish nationalists who revolted against the Romans occupying Judea in the first century, would hide in crowds and stab officials and priests as well as soldiers. In the 11th and 12th centuries in southwest Asia, the Fedayeen (a group of Muslim Isma'ili Shi'ites) undertook to assassinate Sunni rulers despite the almost certainty of their own capture or death. The rulers said that the Fedayeen were under the influence of hashish and called them "Hashshashin," which is the root of the later term *assassin*.[67] In the late 18th and early 19th centuries, the "reign of terror" occurred during and after the French Revolution. In the early and middle 20th century, the dictator Joseph Stalin ordered the execution of many millions of people who were considered enemies of the Soviet state. Six million Jews and millions of other innocents were exterminated by the German Third Reich in the 1930s and 1940s.[68] And many Latin American regimes, such as that in Argentina, terrorized and killed dissidents in the 1970s and 1980s.[69] Now there is a heightened fear of terrorists who may have access to weapons of mass destruction. In a world made smaller by global transportation, cell phones, and the Internet, terrorism is a greater threat than ever before.

We still lack systematic research that explains why terrorism occurs and why people are motivated to become terrorists. But there is a good deal of research about state terrorism. Political scientist R. J. Rummel estimates that governments have killed nearly 262 million people in the 20th century (he calls this kind of terrorism "democide"). State terrorism has been responsible for four times more deaths than all the wars, civil and international, that occurred in the 20th century. Regimes in the Soviet Union (1917–1987), China (1923–1987), and Germany (1933–1945) were responsible for killing more than a total of 190 million civilians. Proportionately the Khmer Rouge regime in Cambodia topped them all, killing over 30 percent of its population from 1975 to 1978.[70] What predicts state terrorism against one's own people? Rummel finds one clear predictor—totalitarian governments. By far, they have the highest frequencies of domestic state terrorism, controlling for factors such as economic wealth, type of religion, and population size. As Rummel puts it, "power kills; absolute power kills absolutely."[71] Democratic countries are less likely to practice state terrorism, but when they do, it occurs during or after a rebellion or a war.[72]

We know relatively little so far about what predicts who will become a terrorist. We do know that terrorists often come from higher social statuses and generally have more education than the average person.[73] If state terrorism is more likely to occur in totalitarian regimes, terrorists and terrorist groups may be more likely to occur in such societies. If so, the spread of democracy may be our best hope of minimizing the risk of terrorism in the world, just as the spread of democracy seems to minimize the likelihood of war between countries.

MAKING THE WORLD BETTER

Many social problems afflict our world, not just the ones discussed in this chapter.[74] We don't have the space to discuss the international trade in drugs and how it plays out in violence, death, and corruption. We haven't talked about the negative effects of environmental degradations such as water pollution, ozone depletion, and destruction of forests and wetlands. We haven't said much, if anything, about overpopulation, the energy crisis, and a host of other problems we should care and do something about, if we hope to make this a safer world. But we have tried in this chapter to encourage positive thinking about global social problems; we have suggested how the results of past and future scientific research could be applied to solving some of those problems.

We may know enough now that we can do something about our problems, and we will discover more through future research. Social problems are mostly of human making and are therefore susceptible to human unmaking. There may be obstacles on the road to solutions, but we can overcome them if we want to. So let's go for it!

SUMMARY ● ○ ○

1. We may be more motivated now to try to solve social problems because worldwide communication has increased our awareness of them elsewhere, because we seem to be increasingly bothered by problems in our own society, and because we know more than we used to about various social problems that afflict our world.

2. The idea that we can solve global social problems is based on two assumptions. We have to assume that it is possible to discover the causes of a problem, and we have to assume that we will be able to do something about the causes once they are discovered and thereby eliminate or reduce the problem.

3. Disasters such as earthquakes, floods, and droughts can have greater or lesser effects on human life, depending on social conditions. Therefore, disasters are partly social problems, with partly social causes and solutions.

4. Whether people become homeless, whether they have shantytowns, seems to depend on a society's willingness to share wealth and to help those in need.

5. Promoting the equality of men and women and the sharing of childrearing responsibilities may reduce family violence.

6. We may be able to reduce rates of violent crime if we can reduce socialization and training for aggression. To do that, we would have to reduce the likelihood of war, the high likelihood of which predicts more socialization for aggression and other forms of socially approved aggression. The reduction of inequalities in wealth may also help to reduce crime, particularly theft. And raising boys with a male role model around may reduce the likelihood of male violence in adulthood.

7. People seem to be most likely to go to war when they fear unpredictable disasters that destroy food supplies or curtail the supplies of other necessities. Disputes between more participatory (more "democratic") political systems are unlikely to result in war. Therefore, the more democracy spreads in the world, and the more people all over the world are assured of internationally organized disaster relief, the more they might go to peace rather than to war to solve their problems.

8. Terrorism has occurred throughout history. State terrorism has killed more than all wars in the 20th century and seems to be predicted mostly by totalitarianism.

GLOSSARY TERM ○ ● ○

CRITICAL QUESTIONS ○ ○ ●

1. What particular advantages do anthropologists have in trying to solve practical problems?

2. Select one of the social problems discussed in this chapter and suggest what you think could be done to reduce or eliminate it.

3. Do global problems require solutions by global agencies? If so, which?

PEARSON
myanthrolab

Read the chapter by Paul C. Rosenblatt titled "Human Rights Violations" on MyAnthroLab. Answer the following questions:

1. Rosenblatt states that human rights may be enhanced by "promoting more respectful, peaceful, and non-exploitive relations among different groups within countries." Explain why he thinks so.

2. Why does he say that "saints can be sinners and sinners can be saints"?

3. Rosenblatt asks: "Is it moral for the United States and a handful of other powerful nations to impose their will on other nations?" What do you think, and why do you think so?

glossary

Accent Differences in pronunciation characteristic of a group.

Acculturation The process of extensive borrowing of aspects of culture in the context of superordinate–subordinate relations between societies; usually occurs as the result of external pressure.

Achieved qualities Those qualities people acquire during their lifetime.

Adaptive customs Cultural traits that enhance survival and reproductive success in a particular environment.

Adjudication The process by which a third party acting as judge makes a decision that the parties to a dispute have to accept.

Affinal kin One's relatives by marriage.

Age-grade A category of people who happen to fall within a particular, culturally distinguished age range.

Age-set A group of people of similar age and the same sex who move together through some or all of life's stages.

AIDS (acquired immune deficiency syndrome) A disease caused by the HIV virus.

Ambilineal descent The rule of descent that affiliates individuals with groups of kin related to them through men or women.

Ancestor spirits Supernatural beings who are the ghosts of dead relatives.

Animatism A belief in supernatural forces.

Animism A belief in a dual existence for all things—a physical, visible body and a psychic, invisible soul.

Anthropological linguistics The anthropological study of languages.

Anthropology A discipline that studies humans, focusing on the study of differences and similarities, both biological and cultural, in human populations. Anthropology is concerned with typical biological and cultural characteristics of human populations in all periods and in all parts of the world.

Applied anthropology The branch of anthropology that concerns itself with applying anthropological knowledge to achieve practical goals, usually in the service of an agency outside the traditional academic setting.

Archaeology The branch of anthropology that seeks to reconstruct the daily life and customs of peoples who lived in the past and to trace and explain cultural changes. Often lacking written records for study, archaeologists must try to reconstruct history from the material remains of human cultures. *See* **Historical archaeology.**

Ascribed qualities Those qualities that are determined for people at birth.

Association An organized group not based exclusively on kinship or territory.

Avunculocal residence A pattern of residence in which a married couple settles with or near the husband's mother's brother.

Balanced reciprocity Giving with the expectation of a straightforward immediate or limited-time trade.

Band A fairly small, usually nomadic local group that is politically autonomous.

Band organization The kind of political organization where the local group or band is the largest territorial group in the society that acts as a unit. The local group in band societies is politically autonomous.

Behavioral ecology Typically tries to understand contemporary human behavior using evolutionary principles. In addition to the principle of individual selection, behavioral ecologists point to the importance of analyzing economic tradeoffs because individuals have limited time and resources.

Bilateral kinship The type of kinship system in which individuals affiliate more or less equally with their mother's and father's relatives; descent groups are absent.

Bilocal residence A pattern of residence in which a married couple lives with or near either the husband's parents or the wife's parents.

Biological (physical) anthropology The study of humans as biological organisms, dealing with the emergence and evolution of humans and with contemporary biological variations among human populations.

Biomedicine The dominant medical paradigm in Western countries today.

Bride price A substantial gift of goods or money given to the bride's kin by the groom or his kin at or before the marriage. Also called *bride wealth.*

Bride service Work performed by the groom for his bride's family for a variable length of time either before or after the marriage.

Cash crop A cultivated commodity raised for sale rather than for personal consumption by the cultivator.

Caste A ranked group, often associated with a certain occupation, in which membership is determined at birth and marriage is restricted to members of one's own caste.

Chief A person who exercises authority, usually on behalf of a multicommunity political unit. This role is generally found in rank societies and is usually permanent and often hereditary.

Chiefdom A political unit, with a chief at its head, integrating more than one community but not necessarily the whole society or language group.

Clan A set of kin whose members believe themselves to be descended from a common ancestor or ancestress but cannot specify the links back to that founder; often designated by a totem. Also called a **sib.**

Class A category of people who have about the same opportunity to obtain economic resources, power, and prestige.

Class societies Societies containing social groups that have unequal access to economic resources, power, and prestige.

Classificatory terms Kinship terms that merge or equate relatives who are genealogically distinct from one another; the same term is used for a number of different kin.

Codeswitching Using more than one language in the course of conversing.

Codified laws Formal principles for resolving disputes in heterogeneous and stratified societies.

Cognates Words or morphs that belong to different languages but have similar sounds and meanings.

Commercial exchange *See* **Market (or commercial) exchange.**

Commercialization The increasing dependence on buying and selling, with money usually as the medium of exchange.

Complementary opposition The occasional uniting of various segments of a segmentary lineage system in opposition to similar segments.

Consanguineal kin One's biological relatives; relatives by birth.

Core vocabulary Nonspecialist vocabulary.

Corvée A system of required labor.

Crime Violence not considered legitimate that occurs within a political unit.

Cross-cousins Children of siblings of the opposite sex. One's cross-cousins are the father's sisters' children and mother's brothers' children.

Cross-cultural researcher An ethnologist who uses ethnographic data about many societies to test possible explanations of cultural variation to discover general patterns about cultural traits—what is universal, what is variable, why traits vary, and what the consequences of the variability might be.

Cultural anthropology The study of cultural variation and universals in the past and present.

Cultural ecology The analysis of the relationship between a culture and its environment.

Cultural relativism The attitude that a society's customs and ideas should be viewed within the context of that society's problems and opportunities.

Cultural resource management (CRM) The branch of applied anthropology that seeks to recover and preserve the archaeological record before programs of planned change disturb or destroy it.

Culture The set of learned behaviors and ideas (including beliefs, attitudes, values, and ideals) that are characteristic of a particular society or population.

Descriptive (structural) linguistics The study of how languages are constructed.

Descriptive term Kinship term used to refer to a genealogically distinct relative; a different term is used for each relative.

Dialect A variety of a language spoken in a particular area or by a particular social group.

Diffusion The borrowing by one society of a cultural trait belonging to another society as the result of contact between the two societies.

Divination Getting the supernatural to provide guidance.

Double descent or double unilineal descent A system that affiliates individuals with a group of matrilineal kin for some purposes and with a group of patrilineal kin for other purposes.

Dowry A substantial transfer of goods or money from the bride's family to the bride.

Dual-inheritance theory In contrast to other evolutionary ecological perspectives, this theory gives much more importance to culture as part of the evolutionary process. Dual inheritance refers to both genes and culture playing different, but nonetheless important and interactive roles in transmitting traits to future generations.

Economic resources Things that have value in a culture, including land, tools and other technology, goods, and money.

Egalitarian societies Societies in which all people of a given age-sex category have equal access to economic resources, power, and prestige.

Ego In the reckoning of kinship, the reference point or focal person.

Enculturation *See* **Socialization.**

Endogamy The rule specifying marriage to a person within one's own group (kin, caste, community).

Ethnicity The process of defining ethnicity usually involves a group of people emphasizing common origins and language, shared history, and selected aspects of cultural difference such as a difference in religion. Because different groups are doing the perceiving, ethnic identities often vary with whether one is inside or outside the group.

Ethnocentric Refers to judgment of other cultures solely in terms of one's own culture.

Ethnocentrism The attitude that other societies' customs and ideas can be judged in the context of one's own culture.

Ethnogenesis The process of the creation of a new culture.

Ethnographer A person who spends some time living with, interviewing, and observing a group of people to describe their customs.

Ethnography A description of a society's customary behaviors and ideas.

Ethnohistorian An ethnologist who uses historical documents to study how a particular culture has changed over time.

Ethnology The study of how and why recent cultures differ and are similar.

Ethnomedicine The health-related beliefs, knowledge, and practices of a cultural group.

Ethnoscience An approach that attempts to derive rules of thought from the logical analysis of ethnographic data.

Eugenics Selectively breeding humans with desirable characteristics and preventing those with undesirable ones from having offspring.

Evolutionary psychology A type of evolutionary ecological approach that is particularly interested in universal human psychology. It is argued that human psychology was primarily adapted to the environment that characterized most of human history—the hunting-gathering way of life.

Exogamy The rule specifying marriage to a person from outside one's own group (kin or community).

Explanation An answer to a *why* question. In science, researchers try to achieve two kinds of explanations: associations and theories.

Extended family A family consisting of two or more single-parent, monogamous, polygynous, or polyandrous families linked by a blood tie.

Extensive cultivation A type of horticulture in which the land is worked for short periods and then left to regenerate for some years before being used again. Also called **shifting cultivation.**

Falsification Showing that a theory seems to be wrong by finding that implications or predictions derivable from it are not consistent with objectively collected data.

Family A social and economic unit consisting minimally of a parent and a child.

Feuding A state of recurring hostility between families or groups of kin, usually motivated by a desire to avenge an offense against a member of the group.

Fieldwork Firsthand experience with the people being studied and the usual means by which anthropological information is obtained. Regardless of other methods that anthropologists may use (e.g., censuses, surveys), fieldwork usually involves participant-observation for an extended period of time, often a year or more. *See* **Participant-observation.**

Folklore Includes all the myths, legends, folktales, ballads, riddles, proverbs, and superstitions of a cultural group. Generally, folklore is transmitted orally, but it may also be written.

Food production The form of subsistence technology in which food-getting is dependent on the cultivation and domestication of plants and animals.

Foragers People who subsist on the collection of naturally occurring plants and animals. Also referred to as **hunter-gatherers** or *food collectors.*

Foraging May be generally defined as a food-getting strategy that obtains wild plant and animal resources through gathering, hunting, scavenging, or fishing; also known as *food collection.*

Forensic anthropology The application of anthropology, usually physical anthropology, to help identify human remains and assist in solving crimes.

Fossils The hardened remains or impressions of plants and animals that lived in the past.

Fraternal polyandry The marriage of a woman to two or more brothers at the same time.

Functionalism The theoretical orientation that looks for the part (function) that some aspect of culture or social life plays in maintaining a cultural system.

Gender differences Differences between females and males that reflect cultural expectations and experiences.

Gender roles Roles that are culturally assigned to genders.

Gender stratification The degree of unequal access by the different genders to prestige, authority, power, rights, and economic resources.

General evolution The notion that higher forms of culture arise from and generally supersede lower forms.

General-purpose money A universally accepted medium of exchange.

Generalized reciprocity Gift giving without any immediate or planned return.

Genus A group of related species; pl., *genera.*

Ghosts Supernatural beings who were once human; the souls of dead people.

Globalization The ongoing spread of goods, people, information, and capital around the world.

Gods Supernatural beings of nonhuman origin who are named personalities; often anthropomorphic.

Group marriage Marriage in which more than one man is married to more than one woman at the same time; not customary in any known human society.

Group selection Natural selection of group characteristics.

Headman A person who holds a powerless but symbolically unifying position in a community within an egalitarian society; may exercise influence but has no power to impose sanctions.

Hermeneutics The study of meaning.

Historical archaeology A specialty within archaeology that studies the material remains of recent peoples who left written records.

Historical linguistics The study of how languages change over time.

Holistic Refers to an approach that studies many aspects of a multifaceted system.

Homo sapiens All living people belong to one biological species, *Homo sapiens,* which means that all human populations on earth can successfully interbreed. The first *Homo sapiens* may have emerged 200,000 years ago.

Horticulture Plant cultivation carried out with relatively simple tools and methods; nature is allowed to replace nutrients in the soil, in the absence of permanently cultivated fields.

Human paleontology The study of the emergence of humans and their later physical evolution. Also called **paleoanthropology.**

Human variation The study of how and why contemporary human populations vary biologically.

Hunter-gatherers People who collect food from naturally occurring resources, that is, wild plants, animals, and fish. The term *hunter-gatherers* minimizes sometimes heavy dependence on fishing. Also referred to as **foragers** or *food collectors.*

Hypotheses Predictions, which may be derived from theories, about how variables are related.

Incest taboo Prohibition of sexual intercourse or marriage between mother and son, father and daughter, and brother and sister; often extends to other relatives.

Independent family A family unit consisting of one monogamous (nuclear) family, or one polygynous or one polyandrous family.

Indirect dowry Goods given by the groom's kin to the bride (or her father, who passes most of them to her) at or before her marriage.

Individual selection Natural selection of individual characteristics.

Intensive agriculture Food production characterized by the permanent cultivation of fields and made possible by the use of the plow, draft animals or machines, fertilizers, irrigation, water-storage techniques, and other complex agricultural techniques.

Kindred A bilateral set of close relatives.

Kinesics The study of communication by nonvocal means, including posture, mannerisms, body movement, facial expressions, and signs and gestures.

Laws (scientific) Associations or relationships that almost all scientists accept.

Levirate A custom whereby a man is obliged to marry his brother's widow.

Lexical content Vocabulary or lexicon.

Lexicon The words and morphs, and their meanings, of a language; approximated by a dictionary.

Lineage A set of kin whose members trace descent from a common ancestor through known links.

Magic The performance of certain rituals that are believed to compel the supernatural powers to act in particular ways.

Maladaptive customs Cultural traits that diminish the chances of survival and reproduction in a particular environment.

Mana A supernatural, impersonal force that inhabits certain objects or people and is believed to confer success and/or strength.

Manumission The granting of freedom to a slave.

Market (or commercial) exchange   Transactions in which the "prices" are subject to supply and demand, whether or not the transactions occur in a marketplace.

Marriage   A socially approved sexual and economic union, usually between a man and a woman, that is presumed by both the couple and others to be more or less permanent, and that subsumes reciprocal rights and obligations between the two spouses and between spouses and their future children.

Matriclan   A clan tracing descent through the female line.

Matrilineage   A kin group whose members trace descent through known links in the female line from a common female ancestor.

Matrilineal descent   The rule of descent that affiliates individuals with kin of both sexes related to them through women only.

Matrilocal residence   A pattern of residence in which a married couple lives with or near the wife's parents.

Measure   To describe how something compares with other things on some scale of variation.

Mediation   The process by which a third party tries to bring about a settlement in the absence of formal authority to force a settlement.

Mediums   Part-time religious practitioners who are asked to heal and divine while in a trance.

Moiety   A unilineal descent group in a society that is divided into two such maximal groups; there may be smaller unilineal descent groups as well.

Monogamy   Marriage between only one man and only one woman at a time.

Monotheistic   Believing that there is only one high god and that all other supernatural beings are subordinate to, or are alternative manifestations of, this supreme being.

Morph   The smallest unit of a language that has a meaning.

Morpheme   One or more morphs with the same meaning.

Morphology   The study of how sound sequences convey meaning.

Negotiation   The process by which the parties to a dispute try to resolve it themselves.

Neolocal residence   A pattern of residence whereby a married couple lives separately, and usually at some distance, from the kin of both spouses.

Nonfraternal polyandry   Marriage of a woman to two or more men who are not brothers.

Nonsororal polygyny   Marriage of a man to two or more women who are not sisters.

Nuclear family   A family consisting of a married couple and their young children.

Oath   The act of calling upon a deity to bear witness to the truth of what one says.

Operational definition   A description of the procedure that is followed in measuring a variable.

Optimal foraging theory   The theory that individuals seek to maximize the returns (in calories and nutrients) on their labor in deciding which animals and plants they will go after.

Ordeal   A means of determining guilt or innocence by submitting the accused to dangerous or painful tests believed to be under supernatural control.

Paleoanthropology   *See* **Human paleontology.**

Paralanguage   Refers to all the optional vocal features or silences apart from the language itself that communicate meaning.

Parallel cousins   Children of siblings of the same sex. One's parallel cousins are the father's brothers' children and the mother's sisters' children.

Participant-observation   Living among the people being studied—observing, questioning, and (when possible) taking part in the important events of the group. Writing or otherwise recording notes on observations, questions asked and answered, and things to check out later are parts of participant-observation.

Pastoralism   A form of subsistence technology in which food-getting is based directly or indirectly on the maintenance of domesticated animals.

Patriclan   A clan tracing descent through the male line.

Patrilineage   A kin group whose members trace descent through known links in the male line from a common male ancestor.

Patrilineal descent   The rule of descent that affiliates individuals with kin of both sexes related to them through men only.

Patrilocal residence   A pattern of residence in which a married couple lives with or near the husband's parents.

Peasants   Rural people who produce food for their own subsistence but who must also contribute or sell their surpluses to others (in towns and cities) who do not produce their own food.

Personality integration of culture   The theory that personality or psychological processes may account for connections between certain aspects of culture.

Phone   A speech sound in a language.

Phoneme   A sound or set of sounds that makes a difference in meaning to the speakers of the language.

Phonology   The study of the sounds in a language and how they are used.

Phratry   A unilineal descent group composed of a number of supposedly related clans (sibs).

Physical (biological) anthropology   *See* **Biological (physical) anthropology.**

Political economy   The study of how external forces, particularly powerful state societies, explain the way a society changes and adapts.

Polyandry   The marriage of one woman to more than one man at a time.

Polygamy   Plural marriage; one individual is married to more than one spouse simultaneously. **Polygyny** and **polyandry** are types of polygamy.

Polygyny   The marriage of one man to more than one woman at a time.

Polyphony   Two or more melodies sung simultaneously.

Polytheistic   Recognizing many gods, none of whom is believed to be superordinate.

Postpartum sex taboo   Prohibition of sexual intercourse between a couple for a period of time after the birth of their child.

Potlatch   A feast among Pacific Northwest Native Americans at which great quantities of food and goods are given to the guests in order to gain prestige for the host(s).

Power   Is the ability to make others do what they do not want to do or influence based on the threat of force.

Practicing anthropology   *See* **Applied anthropology.**

Prairie   Grassland with a high grass cover.

Prehistory   The time before written records.

Prestige   Being accorded particular respect or honor.

Priest Generally full-time specialists, with very high status, who are thought to be able to relate to superior or high gods beyond the ordinary person's access or control.

Primary institutions The sources of early experiences, such as family organization and subsistence techniques, that presumably help form the basic, or typical, personality found in a society.

Primary subsistence activities The food-getting activities: gathering, hunting, fishing, herding, and agriculture.

Primate A member of the mammalian order *Primates,* divided into the two suborders of prosimians and anthropoids.

Primatologists People who study primates.

Probability value (*p*-value) The likelihood that an observed result could have occurred by chance.

Projective tests Tests that utilize ambiguous stimuli; test subjects must project their own personality traits in order to structure the ambiguous stimuli.

Protolanguage A hypothesized ancestral language from which two or more languages seem to have derived.

Race In biology, race refers to a subpopulation or variety of a species that differs somewhat in gene frequencies from other varieties of the species. All members of a species can interbreed and produce viable offspring. Many anthropologists do not think that the concept of race is usefully applied to humans because humans do not fall into geographic populations that can be easily distinguished in terms of different sets of biological or physical traits. Thus, "race" in humans is largely a culturally assigned category.

Racism The belief, without scientific basis, that some "races" are inferior to others.

Raiding A short-term use of force, generally planned and organized, to realize a limited objective.

Rank societies Societies that do not have any unequal access to economic resources or power but with social groups that have unequal access to status positions and prestige.

Reciprocity Giving and taking (not politically arranged) without the use of money.

Redistribution The accumulation of goods (or labor) by a particular person or in a particular place and their subsequent distribution.

Religion Any set of attitudes, beliefs, and practices pertaining to supernatural power, whether that power rests in forces, gods, spirits, ghosts, or demons.

Revitalization movements Religious movements intended to save a culture by infusing it with a new purpose and life.

Revolution A usually violent replacement of a society's rulers.

Rituals Repetitive sets of behaviors that occur in essentially the same patterns every time they occur. Religious rituals involve the supernatural in some way.

Rules of descent Rules that connect individuals with particular sets of kin because of known or presumed common ancestry.

Sampling universe The list of cases to be sampled from.

Savanna Tropical grassland.

Secondary institutions Aspects of culture, such as religion, music, art, folklore, and games, which presumably reflect or are projections of the basic, or typical, personality in a society.

Secondary subsistence activities Activities that involve the preparation and processing of food either to make it edible or to store it.

Segmentary lineage system A hierarchy of more inclusive lineages; usually functions only in conflict situations.

Sex differences The typical differences between females and males that are most likely due to biological differences.

Sexually dimorphic A marked difference in size and appearance between males and females of a species.

Shaman A religious intermediary, usually part-time, whose primary function is to cure people through sacred songs, pantomime, and other means; sometimes called *witch doctor* by Westerners.

Shifting cultivation *See* **Extensive cultivation.**

Sib *See* **Clan.**

Siblings A person's brothers and sisters.

Slash-and-burn A form of shifting cultivation in which the natural vegetation is cut down and burned off. The cleared ground is used for a short time and then left to regenerate.

Slaves A class of people who do not own their own labor or the products thereof.

Socialization A term anthropologists and psychologists use to describe the development, through the direct and indirect influence of parents and others, of children's patterns of behavior (and attitudes and values) that conform to cultural expectations. Also called **enculturation.**

Society A group of people who occupy a particular territory and speak a common language not generally understood by neighboring peoples. By this definition, societies do not necessarily correspond to nations.

Sociobiology Systematic study of the biological causes of human behavior. Compare with **behavioral ecology, evolutionary psychology,** and **dual-inheritance theory.**

Sociolinguistics The study of cultural and subcultural patterns of speaking in different social contexts.

Sorcery The use of certain materials to invoke supernatural powers to harm people.

Sororal polygyny The marriage of a man to two or more sisters at the same time.

Sororate A custom whereby a woman is obliged to marry her deceased sister's husband.

Special-purpose money Objects of value for which only some goods and services can be exchanged.

Specific evolution The particular sequence of change and adaptation of a society in a given environment.

Spirits Unnamed supernatural beings of nonhuman origin who are beneath the gods in prestige and often closer to the people; may be helpful, mischievous, or evil.

State An autonomous political unit with centralized decision making over many communities with power to govern by force (e.g., to collect taxes, draft people for work and war, and make and enforce laws). Most states have cities with public buildings; full-time craft and religious specialists; an "official" art style; a hierarchical social structure topped by an elite class; and a governmental monopoly on the legitimate use of force to implement policies.

State organization A society is described as having state organization when it includes one or more states.

Statistical association A relationship or correlation between two or more variables that is unlikely to be due to chance.

Statistically significant Refers to a result that would occur very rarely by chance. The result (and stronger ones) would occur fewer than 5 times out of 100 by chance.

Steppe Grassland with a dry, low grass cover.

Structural linguistics *See* **Descriptive (structural) linguistics.**

Structuralism The theoretical orientation that human culture is a surface representation of the underlying structure of the human mind.

Subculture The shared customs of a subgroup within a society.

Subsistence economies Economies in which almost all able-bodied adults are largely engaged in getting food for themselves and their families.

Supernatural Believed to be not human or not subject to the laws of nature.

Symbolic communication An arbitrary (not obviously meaningful) gesture, call, word, or sentence that has meaning even when its *referent* is not present.

Syntax The ways in which words are arranged to form phrases and sentences.

Taboo A prohibition that, if violated, is believed to bring supernatural punishment.

Terrorism The use or threat of violence to create terror in others, usually for political purposes.

Theoretical construct Something that cannot be observed or verified directly.

Theoretical orientation A general attitude about how phenomena are to be explained.

Theories Explanations of associations or laws.

Totem A plant or animal associated with a clan (sib) as a means of group identification; may have other special significance for the group.

Tribal organization The kind of political organization in which local communities mostly act autonomously but there are kin groups (such as clans) or associations (such as age-sets) that can temporarily integrate a number of local groups into a larger unit.

Tribe A territorial population in which there are kin or nonkin groups with representatives in a number of local groups.

Unilineal descent Affiliation with a group of kin through descent links of one sex only.

Unilocal residence A pattern of residence (patrilocal, matrilocal, or avunculocal) that specifies just one set of relatives that the married couple lives with or near.

Unisex association An association that restricts its membership to one sex, usually male.

Universally ascribed qualities Those ascribed qualities (age, sex) that are found in all societies.

Variable A thing or quantity that varies.

Variably ascribed qualities Those ascribed qualities (such as ethnic, religious, or social class differences) that are found only in some societies.

Warfare Violence between political entities such as communities, districts, or nations.

Witchcraft The practice of attempting to harm people by supernatural means, but through emotions and thought alone, not through the use of tangible objects.

notes

Chapter 1

1. Harrison 1975; Durham 1991, 228–37.
2. Chimpanzee Sequencing and Analysis Consortium 2005.
3. Nolan 2003, 2.
4. Van Willigen 2002, 7.
5. Kedia and van Willigen 2005; Miracle 2009.
6. White 1968.
7. Hall 1966, 144–53.

Chapter 2

1. Linton 1945, 30.
2. Sapir 1938, cited by Pelto and Pelto 1975, 1.
3. Pelto and Pelto 1975, 14–15.
4. de Waal 2001, 269.
5. de Munck 2000, 22.
6. Ibid. 2000, 22.
7. Ibid. 2000, 8.
8. Durkheim 1938/1895, 3.
9. Asch 1956.
10. Bond and Smith 1996.
11. Berns et al. 2005.
12. M. F. Brown 2008, 372.
13. Hewlett 2004.
14. Miner 1956, 504–05, reproduced by permission of the American Anthropological Association. Although Miner is not a foreign visitor, he wrote this description in a way that shows how these behaviors might be seen from an outside perspective.
15. Lee 1972.
16. M. F. Brown 2008, 364.
17. Hatch 1997.
18. Zechenter 1997.
19. Rosenblatt 2004.
20. Hall 1966, 159–60.
21. Ibid., 120.
22. R. Brown 1965, 549–609.
23. Wagley 1974.
24. Chibnik 1981, 256–68.
25. Linton 1936, 306.
26. Ibid., 310–11.
27. Silver 1981.
28. Greenfield et al. 2000.
29. Rogers 1983, 263–69.
30. Cancian 1980.
31. Hewlett and Cavalli-Sforza 1986; Cavalli-Sforza and Feldman 1981.
32. Valente 1995, 21.
33. W. Cohen 1995.
34. Linton 1936, 326–27.
35. *Britannica Online* 1998; *Academic American Encyclopedia* 1980.
36. Linton 1936, 338–39.
37. G. M. Foster 1962, 26.
38. Bodley 1990, 7.
39. Pelto and Müller-Wille 1987, 207–43.
40. Aporta and Higgs 2005.
41. Bodley 1990, 38–41.
42. T. Kroeber 1967, 45–47.
43. Schrauf 1999.
44. Roth 2001.
45. Boyd and Richerson 1996/1985, 106.
46. Ibid., p. 135.
47. D. T. Campbell 1965. See also Boyd and Richerson 1996/1985 and Durham 1991.
48. The historical information we refer to comes from a book by Nevins 1927. For how radical the American Revolution was, see G. Wood 1992.
49. Brinton 1938.
50. Paige 1975.
51. Bestor 2001, 76.
52. Trouillot 2001, 128.
53. Durrenberger 2001a; see also Hannerz 1996.
54. McNeill 1967, 283–87; Guest and Jones 2005, 4.
55. Guest and Jones 2005, 4
56. Traphagan and Brown 2002.
57. Trouillot 2001, 128.
58. Bradsher 2002, 3.
59. Guest and Jones 2005.
60. Yergin 2002, A29.
61. G. Thompson 2002, A3.
62. Sengupta 2002, A3.
63. Conklin 2002.
64. J. D. Hill 1996, 1.
65. Bilby 1996, 127–28, referring to Hoogbergen 1990, 23–51.
66. Bilby 1996, 128–37.
67. Sattler 1996, 42.
68. Ibid., 50–51.
69. Ibid., 54.
70. Ibid., 58–59.
71. Kottak 1996, 136; 153.
72. Roosens 1989, 9.
73. Cashdan 2001.
74. C. R. Ember and Levinson 1991.

Chapter 3

1. Lovejoy 1964, 58–63.
2. Lovejoy 1964, 63.
3. Mayr 1982, 339–60.
4. Wallace 1858/1970.
5. Mayr 1982, 423.
6. Darwin had a still longer title. It continued, *Or the Preservation of the Favoured Races in the Struggle for Life.* Darwin's notion of "struggle for life" is often misinterpreted to refer to a war of all against all. Although animals may fight with each other at times over access to resources, Darwin was referring mainly to their metaphorical "struggle" with the environment, particularly to obtain food.
7. Darwin 1970/1859.
8. Futuyma 1982 provides an overview of this long controversy.
9. Huxley 1970.
10. Tylor 1971/1958.
11. Morgan 1877/1964.
12. Peregrine 2007.
13. Lewontin 1972.
14. Ceci and Williams 2009.
15. Harris 1968, 380–84; Langness 1974, 50–53.
16. Ibid.
17. Langness 1974, 53–58; Harris 1968, 304–77.

18. Langness 1974, 50.
19. Boas 1940, 270–80.
20. Langness 1974, 85–93; Bock 1980, 57–82.
21. Kardiner and Linton 1946/1939; Whiting and Child 1953; Whiting and Whiting 1975.
22. Bock 1996, 1044.
23. Bock 1996, 1042.
24. Malinowski 1939.
25. Radcliffe-Brown 1952.
26. Ibid.
27. White 1949, 368–69.
28. Steward 1955b.
29. Sahlins and Service 1960.
30. Lévi-Strauss 1969a, 75.
31. Lévi-Strauss 1966; Lévi-Strauss 1969b.
32. Ortner 1984.
33. Douglas 1975.
34. Colby 1996.
35. Ibid.
36. Steward 1955a, 30–42.
37. Vayda and Rappaport 1968. For a selection of recent studies in human ecology, see Bates and Lees 1996.
38. Vayda and Rappaport 1968, 493.
39. Rappaport 1967.
40. Kottak 1999.
41. Ortner 1984, 141–42.
42. Sanderson 1995.
43. Roseberry 1988, 163; see also Wolf 1956 and Mintz 1956.
44. Roseberry 1988, 164; see also Leacock 1954.
45. Roseberry 1988, 166; see also Frank (1967).
46. Roseberry 1988, 166–67; see also Wallerstein (1974).
47. Gray 1996.
48. Gray 1996; Boyd and Richerson 1996; Richerson and Boyd 2005.
49. Irons 1979, 10–12.
50. Low 2009.
51. Richerson and Boyd 2005, 9.
52. Gray 1996; Richerson and Boyd 2005, 9.
53. Boyd and Richerson 2005, 103–04.
54. Lamphere 2006, x; Stockett and Geller 2006, 17.
55. Weiner 1987.
56. Slocum 1975.
57. Behar and Gordon 1995.
58. Clifford 1986, 3.
59. Geertz 1973b, 3–30, 412–53; see also Marcus and Fischer 1986, 26–29.
60. Geertz 1973a.
61. Sperber 1985, 34.
62. Bishop 1996, 993.
63. Foucault 1970.
64. Rubel and Rosman 1996.
65. Bishop 1996; Rubel and Rosman 1996.

Chapter 4
1. Hempel 1965, 139.
2. J. Whiting 1964.
3. Nagel 1961, 88–89.
4. Ibid., 83–90.
5. Ibid., 85. See also McCain and Segal 1988, 75–79.
6. McCain and Segal 1988, 62–64.
7. Caws 1969, 1378.
8. McCain and Segal 1988, 114.
9. Ibid., 56–57, 131–32.

10. J. Whiting 1964, 519–20.
11. McCain and Segal 1988, 67–69.
12. Blalock 1972, 15–20; and Thomas 1986, 18–28. See also M. Ember 1970, 701–03.
13. For examples, see Murdock 1967 and Murdock and White 1969, 329–69.
14. Sets of the HRAF in paper or microfiche format, and now in electronic format, are found in almost 450 universities and research institutions around the world. See the HRAF Web site: http://www.yale.edu/hraf.
15. Ogburn 1922, 200–80.
16. Bernard 2001, 323.
17. Peacock 1986, 54.
18. Lawless et al. 1983, xi–xxi; Peacock 1986, 54–65.
19. Romney et al. 1986.
20. Bernard 2001, 190.
21. Mead 1961/1928.
22. Freeman 1983.
23. Shankman 2004.
24. Ember 1985.
25. Shankman 2004.
26. DeWalt and DeWalt 1998.
27. American Anthropological Association 1991.
28. Szklut and Reed 1991.
29. K. Hill and Hurtado 2004.
30. See Murdock and White 1969 for a description of the SCCS sample; the HRAF Collection of Ethnography is described at http://www.yale.edu/hraf; for a description of many different cross-cultural samples, see C. R. Ember and M. Ember 2001, 76–88.
31. Helms 2004.

Chapter 5
1. Keller 1974/1902, 34.
2. Wilden 1987, 124, referred to in Christensen et al. 2001.
3. Lambert 2001.
4. Ekman and Keltner 1997, 32.
5. Poyatos 2002, 103–5, 114–18.
6. von Frisch 1962.
7. King 1999a; Gibson and Jessee 1999, 189–90.
8. Seyfarth and Cheney 1982, 242, 246.
9. Hockett and Ascher 1964.
10. T. S. Eliot 1963.
11. Snowdon 1999, 81.
12. Pepperberg 1999.
13. Mukerjee 1996, 28.
14. Savage-Rumbaugh 1992, 138–41.
15. J. H. Hill 1978, 94; J. H. Hill 2009.
16. Ibid.
17. Senner 1989.
18. Chomsky 1975.
19. Southworth and Daswani 1974, 312. See also Boas 1911/1964, 121–23.
20. Akmajian et al. 2001, 296.
21. Ibid., 298.
22. Bickerton 1983.
23. Ibid., 122.
24. B. Berlin 1992; Hays 1994.
25. G. Miller 2004.
26. Gleitman and Wanner 1982; Blount 1981.
27. R. Brown 1980, 93–4.
28. de Villiers and de Villiers 1979, 48; see also Wanner and Gleitman 1982.

29. Bickerton 1983, 122.
30. E. Bates and Marchman 1988 as referred to by Snowdon 1999, 88–91.
31. Crystal 1971, 168.
32. Ibid., 100–1.
33. Barinaga 1992, 535.
34. Akmajian et al. 1984, 136.
35. R. L. Munroe et al. 1996; M. Ember and C. R. Ember 1999. The theory about the effect of baby-holding on consonant-vowel alternation is an extension of the theory that regular baby-holding encourages a preference for regular rhythm in music; see Ayres 1973.
36. Sapir and Swadesh 1964, 103.
37. Akmajian et al. 2001, 149–54.
38. Chaucer 1926, 8. Our modern English translation is based on the glossary in this book.
39. Katzner 2002, 10.
40. Akmajian et al. 2001, 334.
41. Baldi 1983, 3.
42. Ibid., 12.
43. Friedrich 1970, 168.
44. Ibid., 166.
45. Gimbutas 1974, 293–95. See Skomal and Polomé 1987.
46. Anthony et al. 1991.
47. Renfrew 1987.
48. Greenberg 1972; see also Phillipson 1976, 71.
49. Phillipson 1976, 79.
50. Holmes 2001, 194–95.
51. Trudgill 1983, 34.
52. Gumperz 1961, 976–88.
53. Trudgill 1983, 35.
54. Gumperz 1971, 45.
55. Weinreich 1968: 31.
56. But see Thomason and Kaufman 1988 for a discussion of how grammatical changes due to contact may be more important than was previously assumed.
57. Berlin and Kay 1969.
58. Ibid.
59. Ibid., 5–6.
60. Ibid., 104; Witkowski and Brown 1978.
61. Bornstein 1973, 41–101.
62. M. Ember 1978, 364–67.
63. Ibid.
64. C. H. Brown 1977.
65. C. H. Brown 1979.
66. Witkowski and Burris 1981.
67. Ibid.
68. C. H. Brown and Witkowski 1980, 379.
69. C. H. Brown 1984, 106.
70. Hoijer 1964, 146.
71. Webb 1977, 42–9; see also Rudmin 1988.
72. Sapir 1931, 578; see also J. B. Carroll 1956.
73. Wardhaugh 2002, 222.
74. Denny 1979, 97.
75. Friedrich 1986.
76. Guiora et al. 1982.
77. Lucy 1992, 46.
78. Ibid., 85–148.
79. Hymes 1974, 83–117.
80. Fischer 1958; Wardhaugh 2002, 160–88.
81. Chambers 2002, 352; citing research by Shuy.
82. Trudgill 1983, 41–2.
83. Geertz 1960, 248–60; see also Errington 1985.
84. R. Brown and Ford 1961.
85. Wardhaugh 2002, 315.
86. Shibamoto 1987, 28.
87. Holmes 2001, 153.
88. Chambers 2002, 352, citing research by Shuy.
89. Lakoff 1973; Lakoff 1990.
90. Wardhaugh 2002, 328; Holmes 2001, 158–59; Trudgill 1983, 87–88.
91. M. R. Haas 1944, 142–49.
92. Keenan 1989.
93. Holmes 2001, 289.
94. Tannen 1990, 49–83.
95. Wardhaugh 2002, 100.
96. Heller 1988, 1.
97. Pfaff 1979.
98. Wardhaugh 2002, 108.
99. Gal 1988, 249–55.
100. Collins and Blot 2003, 1–3.

Chapter 6

1. Hitchcock and Beisele 2000, 5.
2. C. R. Ember 1978b.
3. Kent 1996.
4. Schrire 1984a; Myers 1988.
5. Morrison and Junker 2002.
6. The discussion of the Australian aborigines is based on R. A. Gould 1969.
7. Burbank 1994, 23; Burbank 2009b.
8. Burch 2009; 1988.
9. Data from Textor 1967 and Service 1979.
10. Murdock and Provost 1973, 207.
11. R. B. Lee 1968; DeVore and Konner 1974.
12. C. R. Ember 1978b.
13. McCarthy and McArthur 1960.
14. R. B. Lee 1979, 256–58, 278–80.
15. Palsson 1988; Roscoe 2002.
16. Keeley 1991.
17. R. L. Kelly 1995, 293–315.
18. Mitchell 2009; Tollefson 2009.
19. C. Ember 1975.
20. D. Werner 1978.
21. Textor 1967.
22. This section is largely based on Hames 2009.
23. Chagnon 1987, 60.
24. This section is based mostly on Melvin Ember's fieldwork on the islands of American Samoa in 1955 to 1956.
25. Oliver 1974, 252–53.
26. S. S. King 1979.
27. Friedl 1962.
28. Hickey 1964, 135–65.
29. C. R. Ember 1983, 289.
30. Textor 1967; Dirks 2009; Messer 1996, 244.
31. Finnis 2006.
32. Barlett 1989, 253–91.
33. U.S. Census Bureau 1993.
34. Salzman 1996.
35. Lees and Bates 1974; A. L. Johnson 2002.
36. Barth 1965.
37. Whitaker 1955; Itkonen 1951.
38. Paine 1994.
39. Textor 1967.
40. Dirks 2009.
41. Data from Textor 1967.
42. L. R. Binford 1990; see also Low 1990a, 242–43.
43. The few foragers in cold areas relying primarily on hunting have animals (dogs, horses, reindeer) that can carry transportable housing; see L. R. Binford 1990.
44. Bailey et al. 1989.

45. Data from Textor 1967.
46. Janzen 1973. For an argument supporting the "weeding" explanation, see Carneiro 1968.
47. L. R. Binford 1971; Flannery 1971.
48. G. A. Wright 1971, 470.
49. Flannery 1986b, 10–11.
50. M. N. Cohen 1977b, 138–41; see also M. N. Cohen 1977a, 279.
51. Byrne 1987, 21–34, referred to in Blumler and Byrne 1991; D. O. Henry 1989; McCorriston and Hole 1991.
52. Henry 1989, 41.
53. McCorriston and Hole 1991.
54. Weiss and Bradley 2001.
55. Speth and Spielmann 1983.
56. Boserup 1993/1965.
57. R. C. Hunt 2000.
58. Janzen 1973.
59. Roosevelt 1992.

Chapter 7

1. Hoebel 1968/1954, 46–63.
2. Woodburn 1968.
3. Pryor 2005, 36.
4. Ibid.
5. Leacock and Lee 1982, 8; Pryor 2005, 36.
6. R. Dyson-Hudson and Smith 1978, 121–41; E. Andrews 1994.
7. R. Murphy 1960, 69, 142–43.
8. Salzman 1996.
9. Not all pastoralists have individual ownership. For example, the Tungus of northern Siberia have kin group ownership of reindeer. See Dowling 1975, 422.
10. Barth 1961, 124.
11. Dowling 1975.
12. Salzman 2002.
13. Creed 2009.
14. Fratkin 2008.
15. Ibid., 86–9.
16. Bodley 1990, 77–93; Wilmsen 1989, 1–14.
17. Bodley 2008, 95–98.
18. Ibid., 106–08.
19. Salzman 1996, 904–05.
20. Fratkin 2008.
21. Service 1979, 10.
22. E. M. Thomas 1959, 22.
23. Gröger 1981.
24. Plattner 1989b, 379–96.
25. Hage and Powers 1992.
26. Carneiro 1968, cited in Sahlins 1972, 68.
27. M. Harris 1975, 127–28.
28. Sahlins (1972, 87) introduced North American anthropology to Alexander Chayanov and coined the phrase *Chayanov's rule*. See discussion in Durrenberger and Tannenbaum 2002.
29. Chayanov 1966, 78; for a discussion of Chayanov's analysis, see Durrenberger 1980.
30. Durrenberger and Tannenbaum 2002.
31. Chibnik 1987.
32. Durrenberger and Tannenbaum 2002.
33. Sahlins 1972, 101–48.
34. McClelland 1961.
35. Steward and Faron 1959, 122–25.
36. Bowie 2006, 251.
37. B. B. Whiting and Edwards 1988, 164.
38. Nag et al. 1978, 295–96.
39. B. B. Whiting and Edwards 1988, 97–107.
40. Draper and Cashdan 1988, 348.
41. N. B. Jones et al. 1996, 166–69.
42. Nag et al. 1978, 293; see also Bradley 1984–1985, 160–64.
43. C. R. Ember 1983, 291–97.
44. Udy 1970: 35–37.
45. Sahlins 1962, 50–52.
46. Pospisil 1963, 43.
47. Udy 1970, 35–39.
48. E. A. Smith 1983, 626.
49. K. Hill et al. 1987, 17–18.
50. Sih and Milton 1985.
51. Sosis 2002.
52. Gladwin 1980, 45–85.
53. Chibnik 1980.
54. Polanyi 1957.
55. Sahlins 1972, 188–96.
56. L. Marshall 1961, 239–41.
57. The "//" sign in the name for the G//ana people symbolizes a click sound not unlike the sound we make when we want a horse to move faster.
58. Cashdan 1980, 116–20.
59. H. Kaplan and Hill 1985; H. Kaplan et al. 1990; Gurven et al. 2002, 114.
60. Hames 1990.
61. Gurven et al. 2002, 114.
62. H. Kaplan et al. 1990.
63. Winterhalder 1990.
64. Mooney 1978.
65. Balikci 1970 quoted in Mooney 1978, 392.
66. Mooney 1978, 392.
67. Fehr and Fischbacher 2003; Ensminger 2002; Henrich et al. 2004, as cited by Ensminger 2002.
68. Angier 2002, F1, F8.
69. Marshall 1961, 242.
70. Abler 2009.
71. N. Peacock and Bailey 2004.
72. Gibbs 1965, 223.
73. Humphrey and Hugh-Jones 1992.
74. Blanton 2009; Gregory 1982.
75. Uberoi 1962.
76. Malinowski 1920; Uberoi 1962.
77. J. Leach 1983, 12, 16.
78. Weiner 1976, 77–117.
79. Sahlins 1972, 196–204.
80. Pryor 1977, 204, 276.
81. Vayda et al. 1962.
82. Drucker 1967.
83. M. Harris 1975, 120.
84. Tollefson 2009.
85. Beattie 1960.
86. Thurnwald 1934, 125.
87. Pryor 1977, 284–86.
88. Service 1962, 145–46.
89. M. Harris 1975, 118–21.
90. Plattner 1985, viii.
91. Pryor 1977, 31–33.
92. Thurnwald 1934, 122.
93. Plattner 1985, xii.
94. Pryor 1977, 153–83; Stodder (1995, 205) finds that monetary trade is more likely with capital-intensive agriculture.
95. Pryor 1977, 109–11.
96. B. Foster 1974.
97. Pryor 1977, 125–48.
98. E. Wolf 1955, 452–71; Carrasco 1961.
99. W. R. Smith 1977; M. Harris 1964.

100. Ibid.
101. See, e.g., Gross et al. 1979.
102. Pollier 2000.
103. Vohs et al. 2006.
104. The description of Tikopia is based on Firth 1959, Chapters 5, 6, 7, and 9, passim.
105. Monsutti 2004.
106. Monsutti 2004; Eversole 2005.
107. Eversole 2005.
108. Most of this discussion is based on R. F. Murphy and Steward 1956.
109. Burkhalter and Murphy 1989.
110. E. Wolf 1966, 3–4.
111. Hobsbawm 1970.
112. Gross and Underwood 1971.

Chapter 8

1. In an analysis of many native societies in the New World, Gary Feinman and Jill Neitzel argue that egalitarian and rank societies ("tribes" and "chiefdoms," respectively) are not systematically distinguishable. See Feinman and Neitzel (1984, 57).
2. Fried 1967, 33.
3. Boehm 1993, 230–31; Boehm 1999.
4. M. G. Smith 1966, 152.
5. Salzman 1999.
6. D. Mitchell 2009.
7. Drucker 1965, 56–64.
8. Service 1978, 249.
9. Sahlins 1958, 80–81.
10. Betzig 1988.
11. W. L. Warner and Lunt 1941.
12. Lynd and Lynd 1929; and Lynd and Lynd 1937.
13. Brittain 1978.
14. Higley 1995, 1–47.
15. Argyle 1994.
16. S. R. Barrett 1994, 17–19, 34–35.
17. Ibid., 155.
18. U.S. Census Bureau 2002.
19. Treiman and Ganzeboom 1990, 117; Featherman and Hauser 1978, 4, 481.
20. Solon 2002; Behrman et al. 2001.
21. S. R. Barrett 1994, 17, 41.
22. K. Phillips 1990; U.S. Census Bureau 1993; *New York Times* 1997, A26; Johnston 1999, 16.
23. Leonhardt and Fabrikant 2009.
24. Durrenberger 2001b, who refers to Goldschmidt 1999 and Newman 1988; 1993.
25. Scott and Leonhardt 2005.
26. Klass 2009.
27. Ruskin 1963, 296–314.
28. O. Lewis 1958.
29. Ibid.
30. Kristof 1995, A18.
31. For more information about caste in Japan, see Berreman 1973 and 1972, 403–14.
32. Takezawa 2006.
33. Kristof 1995; Kristof 1997.
34. Tamari 1991; 2005.
35. Taylor 2005.
36. Berreman 1960, 120–27.
37. O. Patterson 1982, vii–xiii, 105.
38. Pryor 1977, 219.
39. Euripides 1937, 52.
40. Nadel 1942.

41. Harper 2003.
42. Lassiter et al. 2004, 49–50.
43. Ibid., 59–67.
44. Pryor 1977, 217–47.
45. Brooks et al. 1993; Tishkoff et al. 2009.
46. M. D. Williams 2004.
47. S. S. Friedman 1980, 206.
48. M. H. Ross 2004a.
49. Marks 1994, 32.
50. Fluehr-Lobban 2006, 12.
51. Marks 1994, 32.
52. Fluehr-Lobban 2006, 12.
53. Armelagos and Goodman 1998, 365.
54. O. Patterson 2000.
55. M. Nash 1989, 2.
56. Ibid., 10.
57. Newbury 1998.
58. C. Taylor 2005.
59. Newbury 1998.
60. *Britannica Online* 1995.
61. See Rwanda in later Books of the Year from Britannica Online http://search.eb.com/search?query=rwanda&x=0& y= 0&ct=.
62. Barth 1994, 27.
63. Yinger 1994, 169.
64. Ibid., 169–71.
65. Ibid., 216–17.
66. Benjamin 1991; see also M. D. Williams 2004.
67. Flannery 1972.
68. Data from Textor 1967.
69. Ibid.
70. Lenski 1984/1966, 308–18.
71. Treiman and Ganzeboom 1990, 117; Cutright 1967, 564.
72. Sahlins 1958.
73. Ibid., 4.
74. Sahlins 1972.
75. Lenski 1984/1966.
76. Gilman 1990.
77. Fried 1967, 201ff; and Harner 1975.
78. Meek 1940, 149–50.

Chapter 9

1. Quoted in Klineberg, "Foreword," in Segall 1979, v.
2. D. E. Brown 1991.
3. C. C. Moore 1997, 8–9; see also C. C. Moore et al. 1999.
4. M. Mead 1961.
5. Malinowski 1927.
6. D. Freeman 1983. For reasons to be skeptical about Freeman's criticism, see M. Ember 1985, 906–909.
7. Spiro 1982.
8. Schlegel and Barry 1991, 44.
9. Piaget 1970, 703–32.
10. Berry et al. 1992, 40.
11. Ibid., 40–41.
12. Dasen and Heron 1981, 305–06.
13. C. R. Ember 1977; and Rogoff 1981.
14. Price-Williams 1961.
15. Segall et al. 1990, 149.
16. Rogoff 1981, 264–67.
17. Kaplan et al. 2000, 156.
18. Lancy 2008, 4–7.
19. A. James 2007.
20. Weisner et al. 1983.
21. J. W. M. Whiting and Child 1953, 69–71.
22. Weisner et al. 1983, 291; Hewlett 2004.

23. For a review of the concept of ethnotheories about parenting, see Super and Harkness 1997.
24. Harkness and Super 1997, in Small 1997, 45.
25. Weisner 2004.
26. J. W. M. Whiting and Child 1953, 310.
27. Edgerton 1992, 206.
28. D. G. Freedman 1979.
29. Ibid., 40–41. For a discussion of possible genetic influences on the social environment, see Scarr and McCartney 1983.
30. See Dasen et al. 1988 for references to research, particularly by Barrett 1984.
31. Dasen et al. 1988, 117–18, 126–28.
32. See R. A. LeVine 2007, for an overview of ethnographic studies of childhood.
33. See the research cited in Hewlett 2004; see also Small 1997.
34. Ibid.
35. Lancy 2008, 113–14.
36. R. H. Munroe and Munroe 1980b.
37. R. A. LeVine 1988, 4–6; see also discussion in Hewlett 2004.
38. Lancy 2007.
39. Ibid., 274.
40. Ibid., 275 referring to Howrigan 1988, 41.
41. Lancy 2007, 275, quoting Le 2000, 216, 218.
42. Rohner 1975, 97–105.
43. See research reported in Rohner and Britner 2002, 16–47.
44. Rohner 1975, 112–16.
45. Barry et al. 1959. For a somewhat different analysis of the Barry et al. data, see Hendrix 1985.
46. Hoffman 1988, 101–03.
47. Lancy 2008, 180–81, reporting on Mayer and Mayer 1970, 165, and Kulick 1992, 119.
48. Chagnon 1983, 115.
49. Dentan 1968, 55-56.
50. Ibid., 61.
51. Straus 2001.
52. C. R. Ember and Ember 1994.
53. B. B. Whiting and Whiting 1975, 94; see also R. H. Munroe et al. 1984.
54. B. B. Whiting and Edwards 1988, 265.
55. R. H. Munroe et al. 1984, 374–76; see also C. R. Ember 1973.
56. B. B. Whiting and Whiting 1975, 179.
57. B. B. Whiting and Edwards 1988, 35.
58. Ibid., 152–63; and C. R. Ember 1981, 560.
59. C. R. Ember 1977; Rogoff 1981.
60. Rogoff 1981, 285.
61. For how school experiences may improve particular cognitive skills, rather than higher levels of cognitive development in general, see Rogoff 1990, 46–49.
62. Irwin et al. 1974.
63. Luria 1976, 108; quoted in Rogoff 1981, 254.
64. Scribner and Cole 1981; Berry and Bennett 1989, 429–50, as reported in Berry et al. 1992, 123–24.
65. Godoy et al. 2004; Bowles et al. 2001.
66. Geertz 1984, 123–36.
67. Although Melford Spiro (1993) does not believe that this Western/non-Western pattern exists, readers are referred to his article for the many references to the works of those who do.
68. For a review of the literature on "individualism" versus "collectivism," which is mostly based on studies of educated individuals from industrialized cultures, see Triandis 1995. Using data collected by anthropologists on mostly preindustrial cultures, Carpenter (2000, 38–56), finds support for the idea that the concept of self differs in individualist as compared with collectivist cultures.
69. Bachnik 1992.

70. Stairs 1992.
71. Spiro 1993.
72. Research reported in Hollan 1992, 289–90.
73. Berry 1976.
74. Witkin 1967, 233–50.
75. Dawson 1967, 115–28, 171–85; and Berry 1971, 324–36.
76. C. R. Ember 2009; Halpern 2000, 110–12.
77. Dentan 1968, 55–56.
78. Chagnon 1983.
79. C. R. Ember and M. Ember 1994.
80. Edgerton 1971.
81. Bolton 1973.
82. McClelland 1961.
83. LeVine 1966, 2.
84. Kardiner 1946/1939, 471.
85. J. W. M. Whiting and Child 1953, 32–38.
86. J. M. Roberts and Sutton-Smith 1962, 178.
87. J. M. Roberts et al. (1959, 597–605) first established the relationship between games of strategy and social stratification and political complexity. Chick (1998) has replicated those findings.
88. R. V. Burton and Whiting 1961. See also R. L. Munroe, Munroe, and Whiting 1981. For a review of cross-cultural research on initiation, see Burbank 2009a.
89. Yan 2006.
90. Johnson-Hanks 2006.
91. Perry 2005, 217.

Chapter 10

1. Leibowitz 1978, 43–44.
2. Schlegel 1989, 266; Epstein 1988, 5–6; Chafetz 1990, 28.
3. Jacobs and Roberts 1989.
4. Segal 2004; Segal also cites the work of W. Williams 1992.
5. Lang 1999, 93–94; Blackwood 1984b.
6. Wikan 1982, 168–86.
7. Stini 1971.
8. Frayer and Wolpoff 1985, 431–32.
9. For reviews of theories and research on sexual dimorphism and possible genetic and cultural determinants of variation in degree of dimorphism over time and place, see Frayer and Wolpoff 1985 and Gray 1985, 201–09, 217–25.
10. J. K. Brown 1970b, 1074.
11. Among the Aché hunter-gatherers of Paraguay, women collect the type of honey produced by stingless bees (men collect other honey); this division of labor is consistent with the compatibility theory. See Hurtado et al. 1985, 23.
12. Murdock and Provost 1973, 213; Byrne 1994.
13. R. O'Brian 1999.
14. D. R. White et al. 1977, 1–24.
15. Mukhopadhyay and Higgins 1988, 473.
16. J. K. Brown 1970b, 1073–78; and D. R. White et al. 1977.
17. Nerlove 1974.
18. N. E. Levine 1988.
19. M. J. Goodman et al. 1985.
20. Noss and Hewlett 2001.
21. Brumbach and Jarvenpa 2006a; Jarvenpa and Brumbach 2006.
22. Brumbach and Jarvenpa 2006b.
23. C. R. Ember 1983, 288–89.
24. Mead 1950 [originally published 1935], 180–84.
25. Rivers 1967 [originally published 1906], 567.
26. M. Ember and Ember 1971, 573, table 1.
27. Schlegel and Barry 1986.
28. Wood and Eagly 2002, 706, drawing on data from H. Kaplan et al. 2000.

29. Boserup 1970, 22–25; see also Schlegel and Barry 1986, 144–45.
30. Boserup 1970, 22–25.
31. Bossen 2000.
32. Ibid., 31–34.
33. C. R. Ember 1983, 286–87; data from Murdock and Provost 1973, 212; Bradley 1995.
34. C. R. Ember 1983.
35. Ibid.
36. Ibid., 287–93.
37. M. Ember and Ember 1971, 579–80.
38. Ibid., 581; see also Sanday 1973, 1684.
39. Nerlove 1974.
40. Schlegel and Barry 1986.
41. Whyte 1978a, 217.
42. Nussbaum 1995, 2, based on data from Human Development Report 1993.
43. Whyte 1978a; D. B. Adams 1983.
44. J. K. Brown 1970a.
45. Sanday 1974; and Divale and Harris 1976.
46. Quinn 1977, 189–90.
47. Graham 1979.
48. D. Werner 1982; and Stogdill 1974, cited in ibid.; see also Handwerker and Crosbie 1982.
49. Draper 1975, 103.
50. D. Werner 1984.
51. M. H. Ross 1986.
52. This description is based on the fieldwork of Elizabeth and Robert Fearnea (1956–1958), as reported in M. K. Martin and Voorhies 1975, 304–31.
53. Begler 1978.
54. Ibid. See also Whyte 1978a, 229–32.
55. Whyte 1978b, 95–120; see also Quinn 1977.
56. Whyte 1978b, 124–29, 145; see also Sanday 1973.
57. Whyte 1978b, 129–30.
58. J. K. Brown 1970a.
59. Whyte 1978b, 135–36.
60. Ibid., 135.
61. Doyle 2005.
62. D. Werner 1984.
63. Quinn 1977, 85; see also Etienne and Leacock 1980, 19–20.
64. Chafetz 1990, 11–19.
65. B. B. Whiting and Edwards 1973.
66. R. L. Munroe et al. 2000, 8–9.
67. Maccoby and Jacklin 1974.
68. For a more extensive discussion of behavior differences and possible explanations of them, see C. R. Ember 1981.
69. B. B. Whiting and Edwards 1973.
70. For references to this research, see C. R. Ember 1981, 559.
71. Rubin et al. 1974.
72. For a discussion of this evidence, see Ellis 1986, 525–27; C. R. Ember 1981.
73. For example, Ellis (1986) considers the evidence for the biological view of aggression "beyond reasonable dispute."
74. For a discussion of other possibilities, see C. R. Ember 1981.
75. Rohner 1976.
76. B. B. Whiting and Whiting 1975; see also B. B. Whiting and Edwards 1988, 273.
77. C. R. Ember 1973, 424–39.
78. B. B. Whiting and Edwards 1973, 175–79; see also Maccoby and Jacklin 1974.
79. Burbank 1994.
80. Heise 1967.
81. C. S. Ford and Beach 1951, 191.
82. O. Lewis 1951, 397.
83. Farley 1996, 60.
84. C. S. Ford and Beach 1951, 23–25, 68–71.
85. Ibid., 40–41, 73.
86. Broude 2009.
87. C. S. Ford and Beach 1951, 82–83.
88. Broude and Greene 1976.
89. Kluckhohn 1948, 101.
90. M. Hunt 1974, 254–57; Lewin 1994.
91. Broude 1980, 184.
92. C. S. Ford and Beach 1951, 114.
93. Jankowiak et al. 2002.
94. Lang 1999, 97, citing Thomas 1993.
95. J. Morris 1938, 191.
96. Underhill 1938, 117, 186.
97. 'Abd Allah 1917, 7, 20.
98. Cardoso and Werner 2004.
99. R. C. Kelly 1974.
100. Cardoso and Werner 2004.
101. Blackwood and Wieringa 1999, 49; Blackwood 1984a.
102. Cardoso and Werner 2004, 207.
103. Data from Textor 1967.
104. W. N. Stephens 1972, 1–28.
105. Broude 1976, 243.
106. D. Werner 1979; D. Werner 1975.
107. D. Werner 1979, 345–62; see also D. Werner 1975, 36.
108. D. Werner 1979, 358.
109. Data from Textor 1967.
110. Schlegel 1991.

Chapter 11

1. W. N. Stephens 1963, 5.
2. Murdock 1949, 8.
3. Stephens 1963, 170–71.
4. Hua 2001.
5. Gough 1959; Unnithan 2009.
6. Hoebel 1960, 77.
7. Evans-Pritchard 1970, 1428–34.
8. D. O'Brien 1977; Oboler 1980.
9. Oboler 2009.
10. Murdock 1949, 7–8.
11. Ibid., 9–10.
12. See, for example, Linton 1936, 135–36.
13. M. Ember and C. R. Ember 1979.
14. Ibid.
15. Marlowe 2003, 221–223.
16. M. Ember and C. R. Ember 1979.
17. Graburn 1969, 188–200.
18. Malinowski 1932, 77.
19. Ibid., 88.
20. J. W. M. Whiting 1941, 125.
21. Doyle 2004.
22. Service 1978.
23. LeVine and LeVine 1963, 65.
24. Ibid.
25. For an extensive discussion of the symbolism of Rotuman weddings, see A. Howard and Rensel 2009.
26. Schlegel and Eloul 1987, 119.
27. Schlegel and Eloul 1988, 295, Table 1. We used the data to calculate the frequency of various types of economic transaction in a worldwide sample of 186 societies.
28. Oboler 2009.
29. Frake 1960.
30. Mead 1931, 206–208.
31. Borgerhoff Mulder et al. 2001.

32. Schlegel and Eloul 1988, 298–99.
33. Pryor 1977, 363–64.
34. Ibid.
35. Spencer 1968, 136.
36. Schlegel and Eloul 1988, 296–97.
37. Ibid.
38. Ibid.
39. Radcliffe-Brown 1922, 73.
40. Murdock 1967; Goody 1973, 17–21.
41. Pryor 1977, 363–65; Schlegel and Eloul 1988, 296–99.
42. Research is reported in Gaulin and Boster 1990, 994–1005. The first theory discussed herein is associated with Boserup 1970. The second is put forward by Gaulin and Boster.
43. Schlegel and Eloul 1988, following Goody 1973, 20.
44. Barth 1965, 18–19; as reported in (and coded as indirect dowry by) Schlegel and Eloul 1987, 131.
45. Middleton 1962, 606.
46. Durham 1991, 293–94, citing research by Hopkins 1980.
47. Westermarck 1894.
48. Talmon 1964, 492.
49. Ibid., 504.
50. A. Wolf 1968, 864.
51. A. Wolf and Chieh-shan Huang 1980, 159, 170, 185.
52. H. Parker and S. Parker 1986.
53. M. Ember 1975; Durham 1991, 341–57.
54. For a discussion of mechanisms that might lead to sexual aversion, see S. Parker 1976; 1984.
55. Freud 1943.
56. Malinowski 1927.
57. Quoted in L. A. White 1949, 313.
58. Kang 1979, 85–99.
59. Rudan and Campbell 2004.
60. Stern 1973, 494–95, as cited in M. Ember 1975, 256. For a review of the theory and evidence, see Durham 1991.
61. Seemanova 1971, 108–28, as cited in Durham 1991, 305–09.
62. Durham 1991, 305–09.
63. Ibid., 346–52.
64. Firth 1957, 287–88, cited (somewhat differently) in Durham 1991, 349–50.
65. A mathematical model of early mating systems suggests that people may have noticed the harmful effects of inbreeding once populations began to expand as a result of agriculture; people therefore may have deliberately adopted the incest taboo to solve the problem of inbreeding. See M. Ember 1975. For a similar subsequent suggestion, see Durham 1991, 331–39.
66. Goode 1982, 61–62.
67. C. S. Ford 1941, 149.
68. A. Howard and Rensel 2004.
69. S. S. Davis 2009.
70. Goode 1970, 210.
71. Lingenfelter 2009.
72. MacDonald and Hewlett 1999, 504–06.
73. M. Ember 1975, 262, Table 3.
74. Busby 2009.
75. M. Ember 1975, 260–69; see also Durham 1991, 341–57.
76. Murdock 1949, 29.
77. Bogoras 1909, cited in W. Stephens 1963, 195.
78. Oliver 1955, 352–53.
79. Ibid., 223–24, quoted in W. Stephens 1963, 58.
80. Mead 1950, 101.
81. Jankowiak et al. 2005.
82. The discussion of these customs is based on W. Stephens 1963, 63–67.
83. Kilbride and Kilbride 1990, 202–06.

84. C. Anderson 2000, 102–03.
85. Linton 1936, 183.
86. J. W. M. Whiting 1964.
87. Ibid., 518.
88. Ibid., 516–17.
89. M. Ember 1974b.
90. M. Ember 1984–1985. The statistical relationship between late age of marriage for men and polygyny was first reported by Witkowski 1975.
91. M. Ember 1974b, 202–205.
92. M. Ember 1984–1985. For other predictors of polygyny, see D. R. White and Burton 1988.
93. Sellen and Hruschka 2004.
94. Low 1990b.
95. M. Ember et al. 2007.
96. Barber 2008.
97. Coult and Habenstein 1965; Murdock 1957.
98. M. C. Goldstein 1987, 39.
99. Stephens 1963, 45.
100. Hiatt 1980.
101. M. Goldstein 1987. Formerly, in feudal Tibet, a class of serfs who owned small parcels of land also practiced polyandry. Goldstein suggests that a shortage of land would explain their polyandry too. See M. C. Goldstein 1971.
102. Haddix 2001.
103. For example, see M. L. Cohen 1976.
104. Pasternak 1976, 96.
105. Silk 1980; Damas 1983.
106. Melvin Ember, pers. comm.
107. K. Gibson 2009.
108. Coult and Habenstein 1965.
109. Mead 1961/1928, quoted in Stephens 1963, 134–35.
110. Ibid., 135.
111. Nimkoff and Middleton 1960.
112. Pasternak et al. 1976, 109–23.
113. Block 1983.

Chapter 12

1. Coult and Habenstein 1965; Murdock 1957.
2. Percentages calculated from Coult and Habenstein 1965.
3. L. Bohannan and P. Bohannan 1953.
4. J. H. Moore and Campbell 2002; Ensor 2003.
5. Lowe 2002.
6. J. D. Freeman 1961.
7. Jarvenpa 2004.
8. Murdock 1949, 49–50.
9. C. R. Ember et al. 1974, 84–89.
10. Pospisil 1963.
11. Schneider 1961a.
12. M. Ember and Ember 1971, 581.
13. Schneider 1961b.
14. Goodenough 1951, 145.
15. Coult and Habenstein 1965.
16. Data from Textor 1967.
17. Fortes 1949.
18. Davenport 1959.
19. The description of the Samoan descent system is based on M. Ember's 1955 to 1956 fieldwork. See also M. Ember 1959, 573–77; and Davenport 1959.
20. M. Ember 1967.
21. M. Ember and C. R. Ember 1971. See also Divale 1974.
22. M. Ember and Ember 1971, 583–85; Divale 1974.
23. M. Ember and Ember 1971. For a different theory—that matrilocal residence precedes, rather than follows, the development of purely external warfare—see Divale 1974.

24. Helms 2009; Herlihy 2007; see also M. Ember and Ember 1971.
25. Service 1962, 137.
26. C. R. Ember and M. Ember 1972.
27. C. R. Ember 1975.
28. M. Ember 1974a.
29. Data from Textor 1967.
30. C. R. Ember et al. 1974.
31. The importance of warfare and competition as factors in the formation of unilineal descent groups is also suggested by Service 1962 and Sahlins 1961, 332–45.
32. C. R. Ember and Ember 1972.
33. C. R. Ember and Ember 1997.
34. See, for example, Murdock 1949, 199–222.
35. Reported in Textor 1967.
36. Ibid.
37. Murdock 1949, 125.
38. Textor 1967.
39. L. A. White 1939.
40. Goody 1970.
41. Pasternak 1976, 142.
42. Textor 1967.
43. Ibid.
44. This conjecture is based on unpublished cross-cultural research by the Embers.

Chapter 13

1. This section is based on N. Dyson-Hudson 1966, 155.
2. This section is based on Maybury-Lewis 1967.
3. Leis 1974.
4. Meggitt 1964.
5. Ibid., 207. For why men in some societies may fear sex with women, see C. R. Ember 1978a.
6. Meggitt 1964, 218.
7. Bellman 1984, 8, 25–28, 33.
8. Ibid., 8.
9. Ibid., 8, 80–88.
10. Ibid., 33, 80; also Bledsoe 1980, 67.
11. K. Little 1965/1966; Bledsoe 1980, 68–70.
12. Ericksen 1989.
13. Leis 1974.
14. Hoebel 1960.
15. W. K. Powers and Powers 2004.
16. R. H. Thompson 2009.
17. Mangin 1965, 311–23.
18. Okamura 1983.
19. R. H. Thompson 2009.
20. K. Little 1965; and Meillassoux 1968.
21. K. Little 1957, 582.
22. Ibid., 583.
23. Ardener 1995b/1964, 1.
24. Ardener 1995a/1964, Appendix.
25. See the many chapters in Ardener and Burman 1995/1964 for examples.
26. Fessler 2002.
27. N. Nelson 1995/1964, 58.
28. Bortei-Doku and Aryeetey 1995/1964, 77–94.
29. Fessler 2002.
30. Light and Deng 1995/1964, 217–40.
31. Warry 1986.
32. Ervin 1987.
33. Caulkins 2009.
34. Naroll 1983, 74–75.
35. Eisenstadt 1954, 102.
36. Bernardi 1952.
37. Ritter 1980.

38. Ibid.
39. For an explanation of age-sets among North American Plains Indians, see Hanson 1988.

Chapter 14

1. Service 1962.
2. Schrire 1984b; see also Leacock and Lee 1982, 8.
3. Service 1962, 109.
4. Briggs 1974.
5. Mathiassen 1928, 213.
6. Service 1962, 114–15.
7. Bohannan 1954, 3.
8. Sahlins 1961, 342.
9. R. C. Kelly 1985, 1.
10. Sahlins 1961, 345.
11. N. Dyson-Hudson 1966, Chapters 5 and 6.
12. Ibid.
13. Sahlins 1962, 293–94.
14. Sahlins 1963, 295.
15. Sahlins 1983, 519.
16. Sahlins 1963, 297.
17. Carneiro 1970, 733.
18. Weber 1947, 154.
19. Lightfoot 2005.
20. Ferguson 2004.
21. Wiberg 1983.
22. For an extensive review of the various theories about legitimacy, see R. Cohen 1988, 1–3.
23. Finley 1983.
24. Carcopino 1940, 18–20.
25. Our discussion of Nupe is based on S. F. Nadel 1935, 257–303.
26. Blanton and Fargher 2008.
27. Ibid.
28. M. Ember 1963.
29. Textor 1967.
30. M. Ember 1963.
31. Textor 1967.
32. Naroll 1961. See also Ross 1981.
33. M. Ember 1963, 244–46.
34. Service 1962; see also Braun and Plog 1982; Haas 1990.
35. A. Johnson and Earle 1987, 158; Carneiro 1990.
36. Service 1962, 112, 145.
37. Feinman and Nietzel 1984.
38. For a more detailed description and evaluation of the available theories, see Chapter 13 in C. Ember et al. 2011.
39. McNeill 1976.
40. Carneiro 1978, 215.
41. Textor 1967.
42. Carneiro 1978; Hart 1948; Naroll 1967; Marano 1973, 35–40 (cf. Peregrine, Ember, and Ember 2004 and other articles in Graber 2004).
43. For a review of the descriptive literature until the late 1970s, see Vincent 1978.
44. D. Werner 1982.
45. Kracke 1979, 232.
46. D. Werner 1982.
47. Sahlins 1963.
48. Kracke 1979, 41.
49. Lederman 1990.
50. Brandewie 1991.
51. Lepowsky 1990.
52. Todorov et al. 2005.
53. Zebrowitz and Montepare 2005.
54. Ross 1988, 73. The discussion in this section draws mostly from Zebrowitz and Montepare 2005, 73–89, and from Ross 2009b.

55. Bondarenko and Korotayev 2000; Korotayev and Bondarenko 2000.
56. For studies of international relations that support these conclusions, see footnotes 2 and 3 in C. R. Ember, Ember, and Russett 1992; see also Chapter 3 in Russett and Oneal 2001.
57. C. R. Ember, Ember, and Russett 1992.
58. Rummel 2002b.
59. Scaglion 2009b.
60. Hoebel 1968/1954, 4, quoting S. P. Simpson and Field 1946, 858.
61. Fry and Björkqvist 1997.
62. D. Black 1993, 79–83.
63. Ross 1988.
64. Boas 1888, 668.
65. Otterbein 1986, 107.
66. Archer and Gartner 1984, 118–39.
67. Scaglion 2004b; D. Black 1993, 83–86.
68. Ibid.
69. Evans-Pritchard 1940, 291. The discussion of the Nuer follows this source.
70. Hickson 1986.
71. Ibid.; and Koch et al. 1977, 279.
72. J. M. Roberts 1967, 169.
73. Ibid., 192.
74. Hoebel 1968/1954, Chapter 9.
75. Schwartz 1954, 475.
76. Textor 1967.
77. Masumura 1977, 388–99.
78. Scaglion 2009b; Black 1993; Newman 1983, 131.
79. Otterbein and Otterbein 1965 and Fry 2006, 88 do not consider feuding to be warfare.
80. See summaries of the evidence in C. R. Ember and Ember 1994; see also Fry 2006.
81. C. R. Ember and Ember 1994.
82. Chacon and Mendoza 2007.
83. Newman 1983, 131; Ericksen and Horton 1992.
84. Gubser 1965, 151.
85. Otterbein and Otterbein 1965, 1476.
86. D. R. White 1988.
87. Patterson 1982, 345–52.
88. Gat 1999, 373, as referred to in Wadley 2003.
89. Heider 1970, 105–11; Heider 1979, 88–99.
90. M. Ember and Ember 1992, 188–89.
91. C. R. Ember and Ember 1992; M. Ember 1982. For a discussion of how Dani warfare seems to be motivated mainly by economic considerations, see Shankman 1991. B. W. Kang (2000, 878–79) finds a strong correlation between environmental stress and warfare frequency in Korean history.
92. Otterbein 1970.
93. C. R. Ember and Ember 1992; see also Otterbein 1970 and Loftin 1971.
94. C. R. Ember 1974.
95. Otterbein 1968, 283; Ross 1985.
96. Divale and Harris 1976, 521–38; see also Gibbons 1993.
97. C. R. Ember and Ember 1992, 251–52.
98. Singer 1980.
99. Russett and Oneal 2001, 89.
100. Ibid., 145–48.
101. Younger 2008.
102. Russett 1993, 10–11, 14, 138.

Chapter 15

1. Tylor 1979.
2. Marett 1909.
3. Guthrie 1993.
4. Freud 1967/1939; Badcock 1988, 126–27, 133–36.
5. Malinowski 1939, 959; Malinowski 1954, 50–51.
6. W. James 1902.
7. Jung 1938.
8. Fromm 1950.
9. Maslow 1964.
10. Poggie et al. 1976; Poggie and Pollnac 1988.
11. Durkheim 1961/1912.
12. Swanson 1969, 1–31.
13. A. Wallace 1966, 60–61.
14. Malefijt 1968, 153.
15. Ray 1954, 172–89.
16. Rosenblatt et al. 1976, 51.
17. Ibid., 55.
18. Swanson 1969, 97–108; see also Sheils 1975.
19. Middleton 1971, 488.
20. Spiro and D'Andrade 1958.
21. Lambert et al. 1959; Rohner 1975, 108.
22. H. G. Barnett 1960, 79–85.
23. Swanson 1969, 56.
24. Ibid., 55–81; see also W. D. Davis 1971. Peregrine (1996, 84–112) replicated Swanson's finding for North American societies.
25. Textor 1967; R. Underhill 1975.
26. Geertz 1966.
27. Swanson 1969, 153–74.
28. Bunzel 1971.
29. Gossen 1979.
30. Dickson et al. 2005.
31. Stark and Finke 2000, 107–08.
32. A. Wallace 1966, 52–67.
33. Winkelman 1986b, 178–83.
34. Bourguignon 1973.
35. Bourguignon and Evascu 1977; Winkelman 1986b, 196–98.
36. Kehoe and Giletti 1981.
37. Raybeck 1998, referring to Raybeck et al. 1989.
38. Bourguignon 2004, 572.
39. Winkleman and Peck 2004.
40. O. K. Moore 1957.
41. Sheils 1980.
42. Winkelman and Baker 2010, 293–96 and references therein.
43. Evans-Pritchard 1979, 362–66.
44. Swanson 1969, 150; see also H. R. Trevor-Roper 1971, 444–49.
45. Swanson 1969, 150–51.
46. Caporael 1976; Matossian 1982; and Matossian 1989, 70–80. For possible reasons to dismiss the ergot theory, see Spanos 1983.
47. Harner 1972.
48. B. B. Whiting 1950, 36–37; see also Swanson 1969, 137–52, 240–41.
49. Winkelman 1986a.
50. Ibid., 28–29.
51. Knecht 2003, 11.
52. Harner and Doore 1987, 3, 8–9; Noll 1987, 49; Krippner 1987, 128.
53. De Laguna 1972, 701C.
54. See Krippner 1987, 126-27; Noll 1987, 49–50.
55. Winkelman 1986a, 27–28.
56. Ibid., 27.
57. Ibid., 35–37.
58. M. Harris 1966.
59. Buckser and Glazier 2003; Rambo 2003.
60. Discussion is based on Firth 1970.
61. Ibid., 387.

62. Ibid., 418.
63. Mason 1962.
64. Ensminger 1997, 7.
65. Ibid.
66. Reff 2005; see also McNeill 1998 and Stark 1996.
67. C. R. Ember 1982.
68. A. Wallace 1966, 30.
69. A. Wallace 1970, 239.
70. The Quakers, long-time neighbors and trusted advisers of the Seneca, took pains not to interfere with Seneca religion, principles, and attitudes.
71. Worsley 1957, 12.
72. Ibid., 11, 115.
73. Ibid., 122.
74. Aberle 1971.
75. Knauft 1978.
76. Antoun 2001.
77. Nagata 2001.
78. Antoun 2001, 17–18.
79. Ibid., 45.

Chapter 16

1. Maquet 1986, 9.
2. R. L. Anderson 1989, 21.
3. R. P. Armstrong 1981, 11.
4. R. L. Anderson 1990, 278; R. L. Anderson 1992.
5. Malin 1986, 27.
6. R. L. Anderson 1989, 11.
7. Steiner 1990.
8. R. L. Anderson 1990, 225–26.
9. Sweeney 1952, 335.
10. Fischer 1961, 80.
11. Ibid., 81.
12. Peregrine 2007b also finds that the ceramics of complex societies tend toward nonrepetition and complex designs.
13. Ibid., 83.
14. Dressler and Robbins 1975, 427–34.
15. Lomax 1968, 117–28.
16. Words from "Deck the Halls", printed in the *Franklin Square Song Collection*, 1881.
17. Lomax 1968, 166–67.
18. Ibid., 167–69.
19. Ayres 1973.
20. Ayres 1968.
21. E. Erickson 1968.
22. For a study of variation in music within India that does not support some of Lomax's findings, see E. O. Henry 1976.
23. Dundes 1989.
24. Bauman 1992.
25. Brunvand 1993, 14.
26. Ibid., 296.
27. Kluckhohn 1965.
28. As discussed in Robert A. Segal 1987, 1–2.
29. J. Campbell 1949, 30, as quoted in Segal 1987, 4.
30. S. Thompson 1965, 449.
31. Dundes 1965a, reported in F. W. Young 1970.
32. Carroll 1979.
33. G. O. Wright 1954.
34. A. Cohen 1990.
35. S. Price 1989, 82–85.
36. Ibid., 102–103.
37. Ibid., 56–67.
38. Ibid., 112.
39. S. Price 1989, 77–81.

40. J. A. Warner 1986, 172–75.
41. Layton 1992, 93–94.
42. Ibid., 31, 109.
43. J. C. H. King 1986.
44. J. A. Warner 1986, 178–86.
45. Merrill 1987.

Chapter 17

1. Nolan 2003, 2.
2. Kushner 1991.
3. Van Willigen 2002, 10.
4. "Appendix C: Statements on Ethics . . ." 2002; and "Appendix I: Revised Principles . . ." 2002.
5. Appendix A: Report of the Committee on Ethics . . . 2002; and Appendix F: Professional and Ethical Responsibilities . . . 2002.
6. Appendix H: National Association of Practicing Anthropologists' Ethical Guidelines . . . 2002.
7. Scudder 1978.
8. Ibid., 204ff.
9. A good summary of this extraordinary case was put together by Slayman 1997.
10. Public Law 101–601 (25 U.S.C. 3001–3013).
11. Picchi 1991, 26–38; for a more general description of the Bakairí, see Picchi 2009.
12. Murray 1997, 131.
13. Wulff and Fiste 1987; Murray and Bannister 2004.
14. Ibid.
15. Niehoff 1966, 255–67.
16. G. M. Foster 1969, 8–9.
17. Jelliffe and Jelliffe 1975.
18. W. H. Fisher 1994.
19. G. M. Foster 1969, 122–23.
20. Coreil 1989, 149–50.
21. Rogers 1983, 321–31.
22. Bryant and Bailey 1990.
23. Niehoff 1966, 219–24.
24. Coreil 1989, 155.
25. Warren 1989.
26. Warry 1990, 61–62; see also Lassiter 2008.
27. J. Fisher 1996, 57.
28. Ibid., 91; data from Kenya referred to in Oxby 1983.
29. Kedia 2008.
30. Ravesloot 1997, 174.
31. Anyon and Ferguson 1995.
32. Society for American Archaeology 2009.
33. Komar and Buikstra 2008, 11–12.
34. Manhein 1999.
35. Komar and Buikstra 2008, 126–145.
36. Brace 1995.
37. Joans 1997.
38. "Association Business: Clyde Snow . . ." 2000.
39. A. H. Goodman and Leatherman 1998; Kleinman et al. 1997.
40. Baer et al. 1997, viii.
41. Rubel and Haas 1996, 120; Loustaunau and Sobo 1997, 80–81.
42. Loustaunau and Sobo 1997, 82–83, referring to Magner 1992, 93.
43. Loustaunau and Sobo 1997, referring to Gesler 1991, 16.
44. Loustaunau and Sobo 1997, referring to C. Leslie 1976, 4; and G. Foster 1994, 11.
45. Ahern 1975, 92–97, as appearing in eHRAF World Cultures, 2000.
46. Murdock 1980, 20.

47. C. C. Moore 1988.
48. T. Gladwin and Sarason 1953, 64–66.
49. Mahony 1971, 34–38, as seen in eHRAF World Cultures, 2000.
50. Gladwin and Sarason 1953, 65.
51. Hallowell 1976.
52. J. E. Levy 1994, 318.
53. Hahn 1995, 133–39.
54. Loustaunau and Sobo 1997, 115.
55. For an exhaustively documented presentation of the more universalistic approach, see E. A. Berlin and Berlin 1996; see also Browner 1985, 13–32; and Rubel et al. 1984.
56. E. A. Berlin 1996.
57. Browner 1985; Ortiz de Montellano and Browner 1985.
58. Etkin and Ross 1997.
59. Moerman 1997, 240–41.
60. Loustaunau and Sobo 1997, 98–101.
61. Winkelman 1986a.
62. Ibid., 28–29.
63. Levi-Strauss 1963a, 169.
64. Boas 1930, 1–41, reported in Lévi-Strauss 1963b, 169–73.
65. Torrey 1972.
66. Loustaunau and Sobo 1997, 101–102; and Moerman 1997.
67. Loustaunau and Sobo 1997, 102.
68. Dow 1986, 6–9, 125.
69. Hahn 1995, 131–72.
70. Ibid., 165.
71. For a discussion of some of the relevant research, see Hahn 1995, 80–82.
72. Mascie-Taylor 1990, 118–21.
73. See references in Hahn 1995, 82–87.
74. A. Cohen 1999.
75. UNAIDS 2007, 1.
76. Ibid., 4–6.
77. Bolton 1989.
78. Reported in Carey et al. 2004, 462.
79. Bolton 1989.
80. Carrier and Bolton 1991; Schoepf 1988, 625, cited in Carrier and Bolton 1991.
81. Simmons et al. 1996, 64.
82. Ibid., 39–57.
83. L. K. Altman 2008.
84. Schoepf 1988, 637–38.
85. Bolton 1992.
86. Farmer 1997, 414. Married men in Thailand are gradually turning away from commercial sex and having affairs with married women who are believed to be safe; see Lyttleton 2000, 299.
87. Feldman and Johnson 1986, 2.
88. Shen and Siliciano 2000.
89. A. Cohen 2004.
90. Honigmann 1967, 406.
91. Kleinman 1988, 3.
92. Lutz 1985, 63–100.
93. J. Murphy 1981, 813.
94. Edgerton 1966.
95. Edgerton 1992, 16–45.
96. J. S. Allen et al. 1996.
97. Kleinman 1988, 34–52; Berry et al. 1992, 357–64.
98. Honigmann 1967, 401.
99. Kleinman 1988, 19.
100. A. Wallace 1972.
101. Kleinman 1988, 167–85.
102. Rubel et al. 1984, 8–9.
103. Ibid., 15–29, 49–69.

104. Ibid., 71–111.
105. Dressler 1991, 11–16.
106. Ibid., 66–94.
107. Ibid., 165–208.
108. Quandt 1996, 272–89.
109. McElroy and Townsend 2002.
110. See discussion in Leslie Lieberman 2004.
111. Gross and Underwood 1971.
112. McElroy and Townsend 2002, 187, referring to Harvey and Heywood 1983, 27–35.
113. Quandt 1996, 277.
114. McKee 1984, 96.

Chapter 18

1. The discussion in this section draws extensively from Aptekar 1994.
2. Information collected during Melvin Ember's fieldwork in American Samoa, 1955–1956.
3. Mellor and Gavian 1987.
4. Dirks 1993.
5. Torry 1986.
6. Hardoy and Satterthwaite 1987.
7. United Nations Human Settlements Programme 2003, 16.
8. Rodwin and Sanyal 1987.
9. Mangin 1967.
10. Rodwin and Sanyal 1987; for a critique of self-help programs, see Ward 1982.
11. A. Cohen and Koegel 2009.
12. National Coalition for the Homeless 2008.
13. A. Cohen and Koegel 2009.
14. Baxter and Hopper 1981, 30–33, 50–74.
15. Ibid.
16. A. Cohen and Koegel 2009.
17. Herrman 1990.
18. Barak 1991, 63–65.
19. World Bank 2004.
20. Aptekar 1991, 326.
21. UN Works n.d.
22. Aptekar 1991, 326–49; Aptekar 1988.
23. Korbin 1981, 4.
24. Straus 2001, 195–96.
25. Straus and Kantor 1994.
26. Straus 1995, 30–33; Straus and Kantor 1995.
27. U.S. Department of Justice 2000; U.S. Department of Justice 1994; U.S. Department of Justice 1998; and Straus 1991.
28. Levinson 1989, 11–12, 44.
29. Minturn and Stashak 1982. Using a sociobiological orientation, a study by Daly and Wilson (1988, 43–59) also suggests that infanticide is largely due to the difficulty of raising the infant successfully.
30. Levinson 1989, 26–28.
31. C. R. Ember and Ember 2005; see also Petersen et al. 1982, as cited in Levinson 1989, 63.
32. Lareau 2003, 230.
33. Levinson 1989, 31.
34. Ibid., 71.
35. Gelles and Straus 1988, 78–88.
36. Erchak 2009; Levinson 1989, 44–45.
37. Straus and Yodanis 1996.
38. Levinson 1989, 104–107.
39. Archer and Gartner 1984, 35.
40. Gurr 1989b, 11–12.
41. The comparison described here is based on data the Embers retrieved from the extensive appendix in Archer and Gartner 1984.

42. Archer and Gartner 1984, 63–97.
43. Gurr 1989a, 47–48.
44. U.S. Department of Justice n.d.
45. Russell 1972; Eckhardt 1975; Sipes 1973.
46. C. R. Ember and Ember 1994.
47. Archer and Gartner 1984, 118–39.
48. Bacon et al. 1963; B. B. Whiting 1965; Barry 2007.
49. Barber 2000.
50. C. R. Ember and Ember 1994, 625.
51. C. R. Ember and Ember 1993, 227.
52. C. A. Anderson and Bushman 2002, 2377; J. G. Johnson et al. 2002.
53. In preindustrial societies, homicide and assault are similarly predicted by the presence of indigenous money, almost always associated with wealth concentration—see Barry 2007.
54. Loftin et al. 1989; Krahn et al. 1986, as referred to in Daly and Wilson 1988, 287–88; Gartner 2009.
55. C. R. Ember and Ember 1997.
56. Most of the discussion in this section comes from M. Ember and Ember 1992, 204–06.
57. Meggitt 1977, 201; Gat 1999, 563–83.
58. Data from Korea is consistent with this explanation of war: More environmental stress strongly predicts higher frequencies of warfare in Korea between the 1st century B.C. and the 8th century A.D. See B. W. Kang 2000, 878.
59. For the cross-cultural results suggesting the theory of war described here, see C. R. Ember and M. Ember 1992.
60. For the results on political participation and peace in the ethnographic record, see C. R. Ember, Ember, and Russett 1992. For the results on political participation and peace in the modern world, see the references in that essay.
61. Russett and Oneal 2001, 49.
62. Ibid., 125ff.
63. Some of these examples are from Henderson 2001.
64. See the discussions in Ibid., 3–9, and S. K. Anderson and Sloan 2002, 1–5.
65. S. K. Anderson and Sloan 2002, 465.
66. This definition is adapted from Chomsky, who is quoted in Henderson 2001, 5.
67. S. K. Anderson and Sloan 2002, 6–7.
68. Ibid., 6–8.
69. Suárez-Orozco 1992.
70. R. J. Rummel 2002a.
71. R. J. Rummel 2002c.
72. R. J. Rummel 2002d.
73. S. K. Anderson and Sloan 2002, 422.
74. Crossroads for Planet Earth 2005.

bibliography

'Abd Allah, Mahmud M. 1917. Siwan customs. *Harvard African Studies* 1:1–28.

Aberle, David. 1971. A note on relative deprivation theory as applied to millenarian and other cult movements. In *Reader in comparative religion.* 3rd ed., eds. W. A. Lessa and E. Z. Vogt, 528–31. New York: Harper & Row.

Abler, Thomas S. 2009. Iroquois: The tree of peace and the war kettle. In MyAnthroLibrary, eds. C. R. Ember, M. Ember, and P. N. Peregrine. MyAnthroLibrary.com. Pearson.

Academic American Encyclopedia . 1980. Paper. Encyclopedia. Princeton, NJ: Areté.

Acheson, James M. 2006. Lobster and groundfish management in the Gulf of Maine: A rational choice perspective. *Human Organization* 65:240–52.

Adams, David B. 1983. Why there are so few women warriors. *Behavior Science Research* 18:196–212.

Ahern, Emily M. 1975. Sacred and secular medicine in a Taiwan village: A study of cosmological disorders. In *Medicine in Chinese cultures: Comparative studies of health care in Chinese and other societies,* eds. A. Kleinman et al. Washington, DC: U.S. Department of Health, Education, and Welfare, National Institutes of Health, as seen in the eHRAF Collection of Ethnography on the Web.

Akmajian, Adrian, Richard A. Demers, Ann K. Farmer, and Robert M. Harnish. 2001. *Linguistics: An introduction to language and communication.* 5th ed. Cambridge, MA: The MIT Press.

Akmajian, Adrian, Richard A. Demers, and Robert M. Harnish. 1984. *Linguistics: An introduction to language and communication.* 2nd ed. Cambridge, MA: MIT Press.

Alexander, Richard D. 1975. The search for a general theory of behavior. *Behavioral Science* 20:77–100.

Allen, John S., A. J. Lambert, F. Y. Attah Johnson, K. Schmidt, and K. L. Nero. 1996. Antisaccadic eye movements and attentional asymmetry in schizophrenia in three Pacific populations. *Acta Psychiatrica Scandinavia* 94:258–65.

Altman, Lawrence K. 2008. Protective effects of circumcision are shown to continue after trials' end. *New York Times,* August 12. http://www.nytimes.com.

Alvarez, Lizette. 2003. Arranged marriages get a little rearranging. *The New York Times,* June 22, p. 1.3.

Ambient Corporation. 2000. Energy: Investing for a new century. *New York Times,* October 30, EN1–EN8. A special advertisement produced by energy companies.

American Anthropological Association. 1991. Revised principles of professional responsibility, 1990. In *Ethics and the profession of anthropology: Dialogue for a new era,* ed. C. Fluehr-Lobban, 274–79. Philadelphia: University of Pennsylvania Press.

Anderson, Connie M. 2000. The persistence of polygyny as an adaptive response to poverty and oppression in apartheid South Africa. *Cross-Cultural Research* 34:99–112.

Anderson, Craig A., and Brad J. Bushman. 2002. The effects of media violence on society. *Science* 295 (March 29):2377–79.

Anderson, J. L., C. B. Crawford, J. Nadeau, and T. Lindberg. 1992. Was the Duchess of Windsor right? A cross-cultural review of the socioecology of ideal female body shape. *Ethnology and Sociobiology* 13:197–227.

Anderson, Richard L. 1989. *Art in small-scale societies.* 2nd ed. Upper Saddle River, NJ: Prentice Hall.

Anderson, Richard L. 1990. *Calliope's sisters: A comparative study of philosophies of art.* Upper Saddle River, NJ: Prentice Hall.

Anderson, Richard L. 1992. Do other cultures have "art"? *American Anthropologist* 94:926–29.

Anderson, Sean K., and Stephen Sloan. 2002. *Historical dictionary of terrorism.* 2nd ed. Lanham, MD: Scarecrow Press.

Andrews, Elizabeth. 1994. Territoriality and land use among the Akulmiut of western Alaska. In *Key issues in hunter-gatherer research,* eds. E. S. Burch, Jr. and L. J. Ellanna, 65–92. Oxford: Berg.

Angier, Natalie. 2002. Why we're so nice: We're wired to cooperate. *New York Times,* Science Times, July 23, pp. F1, F8.

Anthony, David, Dimitri Y. Telegin, and Dorcas Brown. 1991. The origin of horseback riding. *Scientific American* (December): 94–100.

Antoun, Richard T. 2001. *Understanding fundamentalism: Christian, Islamic, and Jewish movements.* Walnut Creek, CA: AltaMira Press.

Anyon, Roger, and T. J. Ferguson. 1995 Cultural resources management at the Pueblo of Zuni, New Mexico, USA. *Antiquity* 69:913–30.

Aporta, Claudio, and Eric Higgs. 2005. Satellite culture: Global positioning systems, Inuit wayfinding, and the need for a new account of technology. *Current Anthropology* 46: 729–46.

Appendix A: Report of the Committee on Ethics, Society for Applied Anthropology. 2002. In *Ethics and the profession of anthropology,* ed. C. Fluehr-Lobban. Philadelphia: University of Pennsylvania Press.

Appendix C: Statements on Ethics: Principles of Professional Responsibility, Adopted by the Council of the American Anthropological Association, May 1971. 1991. In *Ethics and the profession of anthropology,* ed. C. Fluehr-Lobban. Philadelphia: University of Pennsylvania Press.

Appendix F: Professional and Ethical Responsibilities, SfAA. 2002. In *Ethics and the profession of anthropology,* ed. C. Fluehr-Lobban. Philadelphia: University of Pennsylvania Press.

Appendix H: National Association of Practicing Anthropologists' Ethical Guidelines for Practitioners, 1988. 1991. In *Ethics and the profession of anthropology,* ed. C. Fluehr-Lobban. Philadelphia: University of Pennsylvania Press.

Appendix I: Revised Principles of Professional Responsibility, 1990. 1991. In *Ethics and the profession of anthropology,* ed. C. Fluehr-Lobban. Philadelphia: University of Pennsylvania Press.

Aptekar, Lewis. 1988. *Street children of Cali.* Durham, NC: Duke University Press.

Aptekar, Lewis. 1991. Are Colombian street children neglected? The contributions of ethnographic and ethnohistorical approaches to the study of children. *Anthropology and Education Quarterly* 22:326–49.

Aptekar, Lewis. 1994. *Environmental disasters in global perspective*. New York: G. K. Hall/Macmillan.

Archer, Dane, and Rosemary Gartner. 1984. *Violence and crime in cross-national perspective*. New Haven, CT: Yale University Press.

Ardener, Shirley. 1995a/1964. The comparative study of rotating credit associations. In S. Ardener and S. Burman, *Money-go-rounds*. Oxford: Berg.

Ardener, Shirley. 1995b/1964. Women making money go round: ROSCAs revisited. In S. Ardener and S. Burman, *Money-go-rounds*. Oxford: Berg.

Ardener, Shirley, and Sandra Burman. 1995/1964. *Money-go-rounds: The importance of rotating savings and credit associations for women*. Oxford: Berg.

Argyle, Michael. 1994. *The psychology of social class*. New York: Routledge.

Armelagos, George J., and Alan H. Goodman. 1998. Race, racism, and anthropology. In *Building a new biocultural synthesis: Political-economic perspectives on human biology*, eds. A. H. Goodman and T. L. Leatherman. Ann Arbor: University of Michigan Press.

Armstrong, Robert P. 1981. *The powers of presence*. Philadelphia: University of Pennsylvania Press.

Aronoff, Joel, Andrew M. Barclay, and Linda A. Stevenson. 1988. The recognition of threatening facial stimuli. *Journal of Personality and Social Psychology* 54:647–55.

Aronoff, Joel, Barbara A. Woike, and Lester M. Hyman. 1992. Which are the stimuli in facial displays of anger and happiness? Configurational bases of emotion recognition. *Journal of Personality and Social Psychology* 62:1050–66.

Aronson, Joshua. 2002. Stereotype threat: Contending and coping with unnerving expectations. In *Improving academic performance*, ed. Joshua Aronson, 279–96. San Francisco: Academic Press.

Asch, Solomon. 1956. Studies of independence and conformity: A minority of one against a unanimous majority. *Psychological Monographs* 70:1–70.

Association business: Clyde Snow, forensic anthropologist, works for justice. *Anthropology News* (October 2000):12.

Ayres, Barbara C. 1968. Effects of infantile stimulation on musical behavior. In *Folk song style and culture*, ed. A. Lomax, 211–21. Washington, DC.

Ayres, Barbara C. 1973. Effects of infant carrying practices on rhythm in music. *Ethos* 1:387–404.

Bachnik, Jane M. 1992. The two "faces" of self and society in Japan. *Ethos* 20:3–32.

Bacon, Margaret, Irvin L. Child, and Herbert Barry III. 1963. A cross-cultural study of correlates of crime. *Journal of Abnormal and Social Psychology* 66:291–300.

Badcock, Christopher. 1988. *Essential Freud*. Oxford: Blackwell.

Baer, Hans A., and Merrill Singer. 2009. *Global warming and the political ecology of health: Emerging crises and systemic solutions*. Walnut Creek, CA: Left Coast Press.

Baer, Hans A., Merrill Singer, and Ida Susser. 1977. *Medical anthropology and the world system: A critical perspective*. Westport, CT: Bergin & Garvey.

Bailey, Robert C., Genevieve Head, Mark Jenike, Bruce Owen, Robert Rectman, and Elzbieta Zechenter. 1989. Hunting and gathering in tropical rain forest: Is it possible? *American Anthropologist* 91:59–82.

Baldi, Philip. 1983. *An introduction to the Indo-European languages*. Carbondale: Southern Illinois University Press.

Balikci, Asen. 1970. *The Netsilik Eskimo*. Garden City, NY: Natural History Press.

Barak, Gregg. 1991. *Gimme shelter: A social history of homelessness in contemporary America*. New York: Praeger.

Barber, Nigel. 2000. The sex ratio as a predictor of cross-national variation in violent crime. *Cross-Cultural Research* 34:264–82.

Barber, Nigel. 2003. Paternal investment prospects and cross-national differences in single parenthood. *Cross-Cultural Research* 37:163–77.

Barber, Nigel. 2008. Explaining cross-national differences in polygyny intensity: Resource-defense, sex-ratio, and infectious diseases. *Cross-Cultural Research* 42:103–17.

Barinaga, Maria. 1992. Priming the brain's language pump. *Science* (January 31):535.

Barlett, Peggy F. 1989. Industrial agriculture. In *Economic Anthropology*, ed. S. Plattner. Stanford, CA: Stanford University Press.

Barnett, H. G. 1960. *Being a Palauan*. New York: Holt, Rinehart & Winston.

Barrett, D. E. 1984. Malnutrition and child behavior: Conceptualization, assessment and an empirical study of social-emotional functioning. In *Malnutrition and behavior: Critical assessment of key issues*, eds. J. Brozek and B. Schürch, 280–306. Lausanne, Switzerland: Nestlé Foundation.

Barrett, Stanley R. 1994. *Paradise: Class, commuters, and ethnicity in rural Ontario*. Toronto: University of Toronto Press.

Barry, Herbert III. 2007. Wealth concentration associated with frequent violent crime in diverse communities. *Social Evolution & History* 6:29–38.

Barry, Herbert III, Irvin L. Child, and Margaret K. Bacon. 1959. Relation of child training to subsistence economy. *American Anthropologist* 61:51–63.

Barth, Fredrik. 1961. *Nomads of South Persia*. Boston: Little, Brown.

Barth, Fredrik. 1965. *Nomads of South Persia*. New York: Humanities Press.

Barth, Fredrik. 1994. Enduring and emerging issues in the analysis of ethnicity. In *The anthropology of ethnicity*, eds. H. Vermeulen and C. Govers. Amsterdam: Het Spinhuis.

Bates, Daniel G., and Susan H. Lees, eds. 1996. *Case studies in human ecology*. New York: Plenum Press.

Bates, E., and V. A. Marchman. 1988. What is and is not universal in language acquisition. In *Language, communication, and the brain*, ed. F. Plum, 19–38. New York: Raven Press.

Bauman, Richard. 1992a. Folklore. In *Folklore, cultural performances, and popular entertainments*, ed. R. Bauman, 29–40. New York: Oxford University Press.

Baxter, Ellen, and Kim Hopper. 1981. *Private lives/public spaces: Homeless adults on the streets of New York City*. New York: Community Service Society of New York.

Beattie, John. 1960. *Bunyoro: An African kingdom*. New York: Holt, Rinehart & Winston.

Begler, Elsie B. 1978. Sex, status, and authority in egalitarian society. *American Anthropologist* 80:571–88.

Behar, Ruth, and Deborah Gordon, eds. 1995. *Women writing culture*. Berkeley: University of California Press.

Behrman, Jere R., Alejandro Gaviria, and Miguel Székely. 2001. Intergenerational mobility in Latin America. Inter-American Development Bank, Working Paper #45. http://www.iadb.org/res/publications/pubfiles/pubWP-452.pdf (accessed June 2009).

Bellman, Beryl L. 1984. *The language of secrecy: Symbols and metaphors in Poro ritual*. New Brunswick, NJ: Rutgers University Press.

Benjamin, Lois. 1991. *The black elite: Facing the color line in the twilight of the twentieth century*. Chicago: Nelson-Hall.

Berlin, Brent. 1992. *Ethnobiological classification: Principles of categorization of plants and animals in traditional societies*. Princeton, NJ: Princeton University Press.

Berlin, Brent, and Paul Kay. 1969. *Basic color terms: Their universality and evolution*. Berkeley: University of California Press.

Berlin, E. A. General overview of Maya ethnomedicine. 1996. In *Medical ethnobiology of the highland Maya of Chiapas, Mexico*, eds. E. A. Berlin and B. Berlin, 52–53. Princeton, NJ: Princeton University Press.

Berlin, Elois Ann, and Brent Berlin. 1996. *Medical ethnobiology of the highland Maya of Chiapas, Mexico: The gastrointestinal diseases*. Princeton, NJ: Princeton University Press.

Bernard, H. Russell. 2001. *Research methods in cultural anthropology: Qualitative and quantitative approaches*. 3rd ed. Walnut Creek, CA: Alta Mira Press.

Bernardi, B. 1952. The age-system of the Nilo-Hamitic peoples. *Africa* 22:316–32.

Berns, G., J. Chappelow, C. Zink, G. Pagnoni, M. Martin-Skurski, and J. Richards. 2005. Neurobiological correlates of social conformity and independence during mental rotation. *Biological Psychiatry* 58: 245–53.

Berreman, Gerald D. 1960. Caste in India and the United States. *American Journal of Sociology* 66:120–27.

Berreman, Gerald D. 1972. Race, caste and other invidious distinctions in social stratification. *Race* 13:403–14.

Berreman, Gerald D. 1973. *Caste in the modern world*. Morristown, NJ: General Learning Press.

Berry, John W. 1971. Ecological and cultural factors in spatial perceptual development. *Canadian Journal of Behavioural Science* 3:324–36.

Berry, John W. 1976. *Human ecology and cognitive style*. New York: Wiley.

Berry, John W., and J. Bennett. 1989. Syllabic literacy and cognitive performance among the Cree. *International Journal of Psychology*, 429–50.

Berry, John W., Ype H. Poortinga, Marshall H. Segall, and Pierre R. Dasen. 1992. *Cross-cultural psychology: Research and applications*. New York: Cambridge University Press.

Bestor, Theodore C. 2001. Supply-side sushi: Commodity, market, and the global city. *American Anthropologist* 103:76–95.

Betts, Richard A., Yadvinder Malhi, and J. Timmons Roberts. 2008. The future of the Amazon: New perspectives from climate, ecosystem, and social sciences. *Philosophical Transactions of the Royal Society* B, 363:1729–35.

Betzig, Laura. 1988. Redistribution: Equity or exploitation?" In *Human reproductive behavior,* eds. L. Betzig, M. B. Mulder, and P. Turke, 49–63. Cambridge: Cambridge University Press.

Betzig, Laura. 1989. Causes of conjugal dissolution: A cross-cultural study. *Current Anthropology* 30:654–76.

Bickerton, Derek. 1983. Creole languages. *Scientific American* (July):116–22.

Bilby, Kenneth. 1996. Ethnogenesis in the Guianas and Jamaica: Two Maroon cases. In *Ethnogenesis in the Americas,* ed. J. D. Hill, 119–41. Iowa City: University of Iowa Press.

Binford, Lewis R. 1971. Post-Pleistocene adaptations. In *Prehistoric agriculture,* ed. S. Struever. Garden City, NY: Natural History Press.

Binford, Lewis R. 1990. Mobility, housing, and environment: A comparative study. *Journal of Anthropological Research* 46:119–52.

Bishop, Ryan. 1996. Postmodernism. In *Encyclopedia of cultural anthropology* , vol 3., eds. David Levinson and Melvin Ember, 993–98. New York: Henry Holt.

Black, Donald. 1993. *The social structure of right and wrong.* San Diego, CA: Academic Press.

Blackwood, Evelyn. 1984a. *Cross-cultural dimensions of lesbian relations.* Master's thesis, San Francisco State University. As referred to in Blackwood and Wieringa 1999.

Blackwood, Evelyn. 1984b. Sexuality and gender in certain Native American tribes: The case of cross-gender females. *Signs* 10:27–42.

Blackwood, Evelyn, and Saskia E. Wieringa. 1999. Sapphic shadows: Challenging the silence in the study of sexuality. In *Female desires: Same-sex relations and transgender practices across cultures,* eds. E. Blackwood and S. E. Weiringa, 39–63. New York: Columbia University Press.

Blalock, Hubert M., Jr. 1972. *Social statistics.* 2nd ed. New York: McGraw-Hill.

Blanton, Richard E. 2009. Variation in economy. In MyAnthroLibrary, eds. C. R. Ember, M. Ember, and P. N. Peregrine. MyAnthroLibrary.com. Pearson.

Blanton, Richard E., and Lane Fargher. 2008. *Collective action in the formation of pre-modern states.* New York: Springer.

Bledsoe, Caroline H. 1980. *Women and marriage in Kpelle society.* Stanford, CA: Stanford University Press.

Block, Jean L. 1983. Help! They've all moved back home! *Woman's Day* (April 26):72–76.

Blount, Ben G. 1981. The development of language in children. In *Handbook of cross-cultural human development,* eds. R. H. Munroe, R. L. Munroe, and B. B. Whiting. New York: Garland.

Blumler, Mark A., and Roger Byrne. 1991. The ecological genetics of domestication and the origins of agriculture. *Current Anthropology* 32:23–35.

Boas, Franz. 1888. *Central Eskimos.* Bureau of American Ethnology Annual Report No. 6. Washington, DC.

Boas, Franz. 1930. *The religion of the Kwakiutl. Columbia University contributions to Anthropology,* vol. 10, pt. 2. New York: Columbia University.

Boas, Franz. 1940. *Race, language, and culture.* New York: Macmillan.

Boas, Franz. 1964/1911. On grammatical categories. In *Language in culture and society,* ed. D. Hymes. New York: Harper & Row.

Bock, Philip K. 1980. *Continuities in psychological anthropology: A historical introduction.* San Francisco: W. H. Freeman and Company.

Bock, Philip K. 1996. Psychological anthropology. In *Encyclopedia of cultural anthropology,* vol. 3, eds. David

Levinson and Melvin Ember, 1042–45. New York: Henry Holt.

Bodley, John H. 1990. *Victims of progress.* 3rd ed. Mountain View, CA: Mayfield.

John H. Bodley. 2008. *Victims of progress.* 5th ed. Lanham, MD: AltaMira Press.

Boehm, Christopher. 1993. Egalitarian behavior and reverse dominance hierarchy. *Current Anthropology* 34:230–31.

Boehm, Christopher. 1999. *Hierarchy in the forest: The evolution of egalitarian behavior.* Cambridge, MA: Harvard University Press.

Bogoras, Waldemar. 1909. The Chukchee. Part 3. *Memoirs of the American Museum of Natural History, 2.*

Bohannan, Laura, and Paul Bohannan. 1953. *The Tiv of central Nigeria.* London: International African Institute.

Bohannan, Paul. 1954. The migration and expansion of the Tiv. *Africa* 24:2–16.

Bollen, Kenneth A. 1993. Liberal democracy: Validity and method factors in cross-national measures. *American Journal of Political Science* 37:1207–30.

Bolton, Ralph. 1973. Aggression and hypoglycemia among the Qolla: A study in psychobiological anthropology. *Ethnology* 12:227–57.

Bolton, Ralph. 1989. Introduction: The AIDS pandemic, a global emergency. *Medical Anthropology* 10:93–104.

Bolton, Ralph. 1992. AIDS and promiscuity: Muddled in the models of HIV prevention. *Medical Anthropology* 14:145–223.

Bond, Rod, and Peter B. Smith. 1996. Culture and conformity: A meta-analysis of studies using Asch's (1952b, 1956) line judgment task. *Psychological Bulletin* 11: 111–37.

Bondarenko, Dmitri, and Andrey Korotayev. 2000. Family size and community organization: A cross-cultural comparison. *Cross-Cultural Research* 34:152–89.

Brittanica Online. Book of the year (1995): World affairs: Rwanda, and Book of the year (1995): Race and ethnic relations: Rwanda's complex ethnic history. *Brittanica Online,* December.

Borgerhoff Mulder, Monique, Margaret George-Cramer, Jason Eshleman, and Alessia Ortolani. 2001. A study of East African kinship and marriage using a phylogenetically based comparative method. *American Anthropologist* 103:1059–82.

Bornstein, Marc H. 1973. The psychophysiological component of cultural difference in color naming and illusion susceptibility. *Behavior Science Notes* 8:41–101.

Bortei-Doku, Ellen, and Ernest Aryeetey. 1995/1964. Mobilizing cash for business: Women in rotating Susu clubs in Ghana. In *Money-go-rounds,* eds. S. Ardener and S. Burman, 77–94. Oxford: Berg.

Boserup, Ester. 1970. *Woman's role in economic development.* New York: St. Martin's Press.

Boserup, Ester. 1993/1965. *The conditions of agricultural growth: The economics of agrarian change under population pressure.* Toronto: Earthscan Publishers.

Bossen, Laurel. 2000. Women farmers, small plots, and changing markets in China. In *Women farmers and commercial ventures: Increasing food security in developing countries,* ed. Anita Spring, 171–89. Boulder, CO: Lynne Rienner Press.

Bourguignon, Erika. 1973. Introduction: A framework for the comparative study of altered states of consciousness. In *Religion, altered states of consciousness, and social change,* ed. E. Bourguignon. Columbus: Ohio State University Press.

Bourguignon, Erika. 2004. Suffering and healing, subordination and power: Women and possession trance. *Ethos* 32:557–74.

Bourguignon, Erika, and Thomas L. Evascu. 1977. Altered states of consciousness within a general evolutionary perspective: A holocultural analysis. *Behavior Science Research* 12:197–216.

Bowie, Katherine A. 2006. Of corvée and slavery: Historical intricacies of the division of labor and state power in northern Thailand. In *Labor in cross-cultural perspective,* eds. E. Paul Durrenberger and Judith E. Martí, 245–64. Lanham: Roman & Littlefield.

Bowles, S., H. Gintis, and M. Osborne. 2001. The determinants of earnings: A behavioral approach. *Journal of Economic Literature* 39:1137–76, as referred to in Godoy et al. 2004.

Boyd, Robert, and Peter J. Richerson, 2005. *The origin and evolution of cultures.* New York: Oxford University Press.

Brace, C. L. 1995. Region does not mean 'race'—reality versus convention in forensic anthropology. *Journal of Forensic Sciences* 40:171–75.

Bradley, Candice. 1984–1985. The sexual division of labor and the value of children. *Behavior Science Research* 19:159–85.

Bradley, Candice. 1995. Keeping the soil in good heart: Weeding, women and ecofeminism. In *Ecofeminism,* ed. K. Warren. Bloomington: Indiana University Press.

Bradsher, Keith. 2002. Pakistanis fume as clothing sales to U.S. tumble. *The New York Times,* June 23, p. 3.

Brandewie, Ernest. 1991. The place of the big man in traditional Hagen society in the central highlands of New Guinea. In *Anthropological approaches to political behavior,* eds, F. McGlynn and A. Tuden, 62–82. Pittsburgh, PA: University of Pittsburgh Press.

Braun, David P., and Stephen Plog. 1982. Evolution of "tribal" social networks: Theory and prehistoric North American evidence. *American Antiquity* 47:504–25.

Brettell, Caroline B. 1996. Migration. In *Encyclopedia of cultural anthropology,* vol. 3, 4 vols., eds. D. Levinson and M. Ember, 793–97. New York: Henry Holt.

Brettell, Caroline and Robert V. Kemper. 2002. Migration and cities. In *Encyclopedia of urban cultures: Cities and cultures around the world,* vol. 1, 4 vols., eds. M. Ember and C. R. Ember, 30–38. Danbury, CT: Grolier/Scholastic.

Briggs, Jean L. 1974. Eskimo women: Makers of men. In C. J. Matthiasson, *Many sisters: Women in cross-cultural perspective,* 261–304. New York: Free Press.

Bringa, Tone. 1995. *Being Muslim the Bosnian way: Identity and community in a central Bosnian village.* Princeton, NJ: Princeton University Press, as examined in the eHRAF Collection of Ethnography on the Web.

Brinton, Crane. 1938. *The anatomy of revolution.* Upper Saddle River, NJ: Prentice Hall.

Brittain, John A. 1978. *Inheritance and the inequality of material wealth.* Washington, DC: Brookings Institution.

Brittanica Online. 1998 (February). Printing, typography, and photoengraving: History of prints: Origins in China: Transmission of paper to Europe (12th century).

Brodwin, Paul E. 1996. Disease and culture. In *Encyclopedia of cultural anthropology,* 4 vols., vol. 1, eds. David Levinson and Melvin Ember, 355–59. New York: Henry Holt.

Brooks, Alison S., Fatimah Linda Collier Jackson, and R. Richard Grinker. 1993. Race and ethnicity in America. *Anthro Notes* (National Museum of Natural History Bulletin for Teachers), 15, no. 3:1–3, 11–15.

Broude, Gwen J. 1976. Cross-cultural patterning of some sexual attitudes and practices. *Behavior Science Research* 11:227–62.

Broude, Gwen J. 1980. Extramarital sex norms in cross-cultural perspective. *Behavior Science Research* 15:181–218.

Broude, Gwen J. 2004a. Sexual attitudes and practices. In *Encyclopedia of sex and gender: Men and women in the world's cultures*, vol. 1, eds. C. R. Ember and M. Ember, 177–86. New York: Kluwer Academic/Plenum Publishers.

Broude, Gwen J. 2004b. Variations in sexual attitudes, norms, and practices. In MyAnthroLibrary, eds. C. R. Ember, M. Ember, and P. N. Peregrine. MyAnthroLibrary.com. Pearson.

Broude, Gwen J., and Sarah J. Greene. 1976. Cross-cultural codes on twenty sexual attitudes and practices. *Ethnology* 15:409–29.

Brown, Cecil H. 1977. Folk botanical life-forms: Their universality and growth. *American Anthropologist* 79:317–42.

Brown, Cecil H. 1979. Folk zoological life-forms: Their universality and growth. *American Anthropologist* 81:791–817.

Brown, Cecil H. 1984. World view and lexical uniformities. *Reviews in Anthropology* 11:99–112.

Brown, Cecil H., and Stanley R. Witkowski. 1980. Language universals. In *Toward explaining human culture*, eds. D. Levinson and M. J. Malone, Appendix B. New Haven, CT: HRAF Press.

Brown, Donald E. 1991. *Human universals*. Philadelphia: Temple University Press.

Brown, Judith K. 1970a. Economic organization and the position of women among the Iroquois. *Ethnohistory* 17: 151–67.

Brown, Judith K. 1970b. A note on the division of labor by sex. *American Anthropologist* 72:1073–78.

Brown, Michael F. 2008. Cultural relativism 2.0. *Current Anthropology* 49: 363–83.

Brown, Peter J. 1997. Culture and the evolution of obesity. In *Applying cultural anthropology: An introductory reader*, eds. A. Podolefsky and P. J. Brown. Mountain View, CA: Mayfield.

Brown, Roger. 1965. *Social psychology*. New York: Free Press.

Brown, Roger. 1980. The first sentence of child and chimpanzee. In *Speaking of apes*, eds. T. A. Sebeok and J. Umiker-Sebeok. New York: Plenum Press.

Brown, Roger, and Marguerite Ford. 1961. Address in American English. *Journal of Abnormal and Social Psychology* 62:375–85.

Browner, C. H. 1985. Criteria for selecting herbal remedies. *Ethnology* 24:13–32.

Brumbach, Hetty Jo, and Robert Jarvenpa. 2006a. Chipewyan society and gender relations. In *Circumpolar lives and livelihood : A comparative ethnoarchaeology of gender and subsistence*, eds. R. Jarvenpa and H. J. Brumbach, 24–53. Lincoln, Nebraska: University of Nebraska Press.

Brumbach, Hetty Jo, and Robert Jarvenpa. 2006b. Conclusion: Toward a comparative ethnoarchaeology of gender. In *Circumpolar lives and livelihood : A comparative ethnoarchaeology of gender and subsistence*, ed. R. Jarvenpa and H. J. Brumbach, 287–323. Lincoln, Nebraska: University of Nebraska Press.

Brumfiel, Elizabeth M. 2002. Origins of social inequality. In *Archaeology: Original readings in method and practice*, eds. P. N. Peregrine, C. R. Ember, and M. Ember. Upper Saddle River, NJ: Prentice Hall.

Brumfiel, Elizabeth M. 2009. Origins of social inequality. In MyAnthroLibrary, eds. C. R. Ember, M. Ember, and P. N. Peregrine. MyAnthroLibrary.com. Pearson.

Brunvand, Jan Harold. 1993. *The baby train: And other lusty urban legends.* New York: Norton.

Brusco, Elizabeth E. 1996. Religious conversion. In *Encyclopedia of cultural anthropology*, 4 vols., vol. 3, eds. D. Levinson and M. Ember, 1100–04. New York: Henry Holt.

Bryant, Carol A., and Doraine F. C. Bailey. 1990. The use of focus group research in program development. In *Soundings*, eds. J. van Willigen and T. L. Finan. NAPA Bulletin No. 10. Washington, DC: American Anthropological Association, pp. 24–39.

Buckser, Andrew, and Stephen D. Glazier, eds. 2003. Preface. In *The anthropology of religious conversion*, eds. Andrew Buckser and Stephen D. Glazier. Lanham, MD: Roman & Littlefield.

Bunzel, Ruth. 1971. The nature of katcinas. In *Reader in comparative religion*, 3rd ed., eds. W. A. Lessa and E. Z. Vogt. New York: Harper & Row.

Burbank, Victoria K. 1994. *Fighting Women: Anger and Aggression in Aboriginal Australia.* Berkeley: University of California Press.

Burbank, Victoria K. 2009a. Adolescent socialization and initiation ceremonies. In MyAnthroLibrary, eds. C. R. Ember, M. Ember, and P. N. Peregrine. MyAnthroLibrary.com. Pearson.

Burbank, Victoria K. 2009b. Australian Aborigines: An adolescent mother and her family. In MyAnthroLibrary, eds. C. R. Ember, M. Ember, and P. N. Peregrine. MyAnthroLibrary.com. Pearson.

Burch, Ernest S., Jr. 1988. *The Eskimos.* Norman: University of Oklahoma Press.

Burch, Ernest S., Jr. 2009. North Alaskan Eskimos: A changing way of life. In MyAnthroLibrary, eds. C. R. Ember, M. Ember, and P. N. Peregrine. MyAnthroLibrary.com. Pearson.

Burkhalter, S. Brian, and Robert F. Murphy. 1989. Tappers and sappers: Rubber, gold and money among the Mundurucú. *American Ethnologist* 16:100–16.

Burns, Alisa, and Cath Scott. 1994. *Mother-headed families and why they have increased.* Hillsdale, NJ: Lawrence Erlbaum Associates.

Burton, Roger V., and John W. M. Whiting. 1961. The absent father and cross-sex identity. *Merrill-Palmer Quarterly of Behavior and Development* 7(2):85–95.

Busby, Annette. 2009. Kurds: A culture straddling national borders. In MyAnthroLibrary, eds. C. R. Ember, M. Ember, and P. N. Peregrine. MyAnthroLibrary.com. Pearson.

Byrne, Bryan. 1994. Access to subsistence resources and the sexual division of labor among potters. *Cross-Cultural Research* 28:225–50.

Byrne, Roger. 1987. Climatic change and the origins of agriculture. In *Studies in the neolithic and urban revolutions*, ed. L. Manzanilla. British Archaeological Reports International Series 349. Oxford.

Campbell, Donald T. 1965. Variation and selective retention in socio-cultural evolution. In *Social change in developing areas,* eds. H. Barringer, G. Blankstein, and R. Mack, 19–49. Cambridge, MA: Schenkman.

Campbell, Joseph. 1949. *The hero with a thousand faces.* New York: Pantheon.

Cancian, Frank. 1980. Risk and uncertainty in agricultural decision making. In *Agricultural decision making,* ed. P. F. Barlett, 161–202. New York: Academic Press.

Caporael, Linnda R. 1976. Ergotism: The Satan loosed in Salem? *Science* (April 2):21–26.

Carcopino, Jerome. 1940. *Daily life in ancient Rome: The people and the city at the height of the empire.* Edited with bibliography and notes by Henry T. Rowell. Translated from the French by E. O. Lorimer. New Haven, CT: Yale University Press.

Cardoso, Fernando Luis, and Dennis Werner. 2004. Homosexuality. In *Encyclopedia of sex and gender: Men and women in the world's cultures,* vol. 1, eds. C. R. Ember and M. Ember, 204–15. New York: Kluwer Academic/Plenum.

Carey, James W., Erin Picone-DeCaro, Mary Spink Neumann, Devorah Schwartz, Delia Easton, and Daphne Cobb St. John. 2004. HIV/AIDS research and prevention. In *Encyclopedia of medical anthropology: Health and illness in the world's cultures,* 2 vols., vol. 1, eds. C. R. Ember and M. Ember, 462–79. New York: Kluwer Academic/Plenum.

Carneiro, Robert L. 1968. Slash-and-burn cultivation among the Kuikuru and its implications for settlement patterns. In *Man in adaptation,* ed. Y. Cohen. Chicago: Aldine.

Carneiro, Robert L. 1970. A theory of the origin of the state. *Science* (August 21):733–38.

Carneiro, Robert L. 1978. Political expansion as an expression of the principle of competitive exclusion. In *Origins of the state,* eds. R. Cohen and E. R. Service. Philadelphia: Institute for the Study of Human Issues.

Carneiro, Robert L. 1990. Chiefdom-level warfare as exemplified in Fiji and the Cauca Valley. In *The anthropology of war,* ed. J. Haas, 190–211. New York: Cambridge University Press.

Carpenter, Sandra. 2000. Effects of cultural tightness and collectivism on self-concept and causal attributions. *Cross-Cultural Research* 34:38–56.

Carrasco, Pedro. 1961. The civil-religious hierarchy in Mesoamerican communities: Pre-Spanish background and colonial development. *American Anthropologist* 63:483–97.

Carrier, Joseph, and Ralph Bolton. 1991. Anthropological perspectives on sexuality and HIV prevention. *Annual Review of Sex Research* 2:49–75.

Carroll, John B., ed. 1956. *Language, thought, and reality: Selected writings of Benjamin Lee Whorf.* New York: Wiley.

Carroll, Michael. 1979. A new look at Freud on myth. *Ethos* 7:189–205.

Cashdan, Elizabeth A. 1980. Egalitarianism among hunters and gatherers. *American Anthropologist* 82:116–20.

Cashdan, Elizabeth. 2001. Ethnic diversity and its environmental determinants: Effects of climate, pathogens, and habitat diversity. *American Anthropologist* 103:968–91.

Caulkins, D. Douglas. 1997. Welsh. In *American immigrant cultures: Builders of a nation,* 2 vols., eds. D. Levinson and M. Ember, 935–41. New York: Macmillan.

Caulkins, D. Douglas. 2009. Norwegians: Cooperative individualists. In *MyAnthroLibrary,* eds. C. R. Ember, M.

Ember, and P. N. Peregrine. MyAnthroLibrary.com. Pearson.

Cavalli-Sforza, L. L., and M. W. Feldman. 1981. *Cultural transmission and evolution: A quantitative approach.* Princeton, NJ: Princeton University Press.

Caws, Peter. 1969. The structure of discovery. *Science* (December 12): 1375–80.

Ceci, Stephen, and Wendy M. Williams. 2009. YES: The scientific truth must be pursued. *Nature* 457 (February 12): 788–89.

Cernea, Michael, M., ed. 1991. *Putting people first: Sociological variables in development.* 2nd ed. New York: Oxford University Press.

Chacon, Richard J., and Rubén G. Mendoza. 2007. Ethical considerations and conclusions regarding indigenous warfare and ritual violence in Latin America. In *Latin American indigenous warfare and ritual violence,* eds. Richard J. Chacon and Rubén G. Mendoza. Tucson: University of Arizona Press.

Chafetz, Janet Saltzman. 1990. *Gender equity: An integrated theory of stability and change.* Sage Library of Social Research No. 176. Newbury Park, CA: Sage.

Chagnon, Napoleon. 1983. *Yanomamö: The fierce people.* 3rd ed. New York: Holt, Rinehart & Winston.

Chambers, J. K. 2002. Patterns of variation including change. In The *handbook of language variation and change,* eds. J. K. Chambers, Peter Trudgill, and Natalie Schilling-Estes. Malden, MA: Blackwell Publishers.

Chatty, Dawn. 1996. *Mobile pastoralists: Development planning and social change in Oman.* New York: Columbia University Press.

Chaucer, Geoffrey. 1926. *The prologue to the Canterbury Tales, the Knights Tale, the Nonnes Prestes Tale,* ed. Mark H. Liddell. New York: Macmillan.

Chayanov, Alexander V. 1966. *The theory of peasant economy,* eds. Daniel Thorner, Basile Kerblay, and R. E. F. Smith. Homewood, IL: Richard D. Irwin.

Chibnik, Michael. 1980. The statistical behavior approach: The choice between wage labor and cash cropping in rural Belize. In *Agricultural decision making,* ed. P. F. Barlett, 87–114. New York: Academic Press.

Chibnik, Michael. 1981. The evolution of cultural rules. *Journal of Anthropological Research* 37:256–68.

Chibnik, Michael. 1987. The economic effects of household demography: A cross-cultural assessment of Chayanov's theory. In *Household economies and their transformations,* ed. M. D. MacLachlan. Monographs in Economic Anthropology, No. 3. Lanham, MD: University Press of America.

Chick, Garry. 1998. Games in culture revisited: A replication and extension of Roberts, Arth, and Bush [1959]. *Cross-Cultural Research* 32:185–206.

Chimpanzee Sequencing and Analysis Consortium. 2005. Initial Sequence of the chimpanzee genome and comparison with the human genome. *Nature* 437 (September 1): 69–87.

Chomsky, Noam. 1975. *Reflections on language.* New York: Pantheon.

Christensen, Pia, Jenny Hockey, and Allison James. 2001. Talk, silence and the material world: Patterns of indirect communication among agricultural farmers in northern England. In *An anthropology of indirect communication,* eds. J. Hendry and C. W. Watson, 68–82. London: Routledge.

Clark, Gracia. 2000. Small-scale traders' key role in stabilizing and diversifying Ghana's rural communities and livelihoods. In *Women farmers and commercial ventures: Increasing food security in developing countries*, ed. Anita Spring, 253–70. Boulder, CO: Lynne Rienner Publishers, Inc.

Clifford, James. 1986. Introduction: Partial truths. In *Writing culture: The poetics and politics of ethnography*, eds. J. Clifford and G. E. Marcus. Berkeley: University of California Press.

Clottes, Jean. 2008. Rock art: An endangered heritage worldwide. *Journal of Anthropological Research* 64:1–18.

Cohen, Alex. 1990. A cross-cultural study of the effects of environmental unpredictability on aggression in folktales. *American Anthropologist* 92:474–79.

Cohen, Alex. 1999. *The mental health of indigenous peoples: An international overview*. Geneva: Department of Mental Health, World Health Organization.

Cohen, Alex. 2004. Mental disorders. In *Encyclopedia of medical anthropology: Health and illness in the world's cultures*, 2 vols., vol. 1, eds. C. R. Ember and M. Ember, 486–93. New York: Kluwer Academic/Plenum.

Cohen, Alex, and Paul Koegel. 2009. Homelessness. In MyAnthroLibrary, eds. C. R. Ember, M. Ember, and P. N. Peregrine. MyAnthroLibrary.com. Pearson.

Cohen, Mark N. 1977a. *The food crisis in prehistory: Overpopulation and the origins of agriculture*. New Haven, CT: Yale University Press.

Cohen, Mark N. 1977b. Population pressure and the origins of agriculture. In *Origins of agriculture*, ed. C. A. Reed. The Hague: Mouton.

Cohen, Myron L. 1976. *House united, house divided: The Chinese family in Taiwan*. New York: Columbia University Press.

Cohen, Ronald. 1988. Introduction. In *State formation and political legitimacy*, vol. 6: *Political anthropology*, eds. R. Cohen and J. D. Toland. New Brunswick, NJ: Transaction Books.

Cohen, Ronald, and Elman R. Service, eds. 1978. *Origins of the state: The anthropology of political evolution*. Philadelphia: Institute for the Study of Human Issues.

Cohen, Wesley. 1995. Empirical studies of innovative activity. In *Handbook of the economics of innovation and technological change*, ed. P. Stoneman, 182–264. Oxford: Blackwell.

Colby, Benjamin N. 1996. Cognitive anthropology. In *Encyclopedia of cultural anthropology*, vol. 1, 4 vols., eds. D. Levinson and M. Ember, 209–15. New York: Henry Holt.

Collins, James, and Richard Blot. 2003. *Literacy and literacies*. Cambridge: Cambridge University Press.

Conklin, Beth A. 2002. Shamans versus pirates in the Amazonian treasure chest. *American Anthropologist* 104: 1050–61.

Cooper, Richard S., Charles N. Rotimi, and Ryk Ward. 1999. The puzzle of hypertension in African Americans. *Scientific American* (February):56–63.

Coreil, Jeannine. 1989. Lessons from a community study of oral rehydration therapy in Haiti. In *Making our research useful*, eds. J. van Willigen, B. Rylko-Bauer, and A. McElroy. Boulder, CO: Westview.

Coreil, Jeannine. 2004. Malaria and other major insect vector diseases. In *Encyclopedia of medical anthropology: Health and illness in the world's cultures*, 2 vols., vol. 1, eds. C. R. Ember and M. Ember, 479–85. New York: Kluwer Academic/Plenum.

Coult, Allan D., and Robert W. Habenstein. 1965. *Cross tabulations of Murdock's "World Ethnographic Sample."* Columbia: University of Missouri Press.

Creed, Gerald W. 2009. Bulgaria: Anthropological corrections to Cold War stereotypes. In MyAnthroLibrary, eds. C. R. Ember, M. Ember, and P. N. Peregrine. MyAnthroLibrary. com. Pearson.

Crystal, David. 1971. *Linguistics*. Middlesex, UK: Penguin.

Crystal, David. 2000. *Language death*. Cambridge: Cambridge University Press.

Cutright, Phillips. 1967. Inequality: A cross-national analysis. *American Sociological Review* 32:562–78.

Daly, Martin, and Margo Wilson. 1988. *Homicide*. New York: Aldine.

Damas, David. 1983. Demography and kinship as variables of adoption in the Carolines. *American Ethnologist* 10: 328–44.

Darwin, Charles. 1859/1970. The origin of species. In *Evolution of man*, ed. L. B. Young. New York: Oxford University Press.

Dasen, Pierre R., and Alastair Heron. 1981. Cross-cultural tests of Piaget's theory. In *Handbook of cross-cultural psychology*, vol. 4: *Developmental psychology*, eds. H. C. Triandis and A. Heron. Boston: Allyn & Bacon.

Dasen, Pierre R., John W. Berry, and N. Sartorius, eds. 1988. *Health and cross-cultural psychology: Toward applications*. Newbury Park, CA: Sage.

Davenport, William. 1959. Nonunilinear descent and descent groups. *American Anthropologist* 61:557–72.

Davis, Deborah, and Stevan Harrell, eds. 1993. *Chinese families in the post-Mao era*. Berkeley: University of California Press.

Davis, Susan Schaefer. 1993. Rebellious teens? A Moroccan instance. Paper presented at MESA, November.

Davis, Susan Schaefer. 2009. Morocco: Adolescents in a small town. In MyAnthroLibrary, eds. C. R. Ember, M. Ember, and P. N. Peregrine. MyAnthroLibrary.com. Pearson.

Davis, William D. 1971. Societal complexity and the nature of primitive man's conception of the supernatural. Ph.D. dissertation, University of North Carolina, Chapel Hill.

Dawson, J. L. M. 1967. Cultural and physiological influences upon spatial-perceptual processes in West Africa. *International Journal of Psychology* 2:115–28, 171–85.

DeLaguna, Frederica. 1972. *Under Mount Saint Elias: The history and culture of the Yakutat Tlingit*. Washington, DC: Smithsonian Institution Press; as seen in the eHRAF Collection of Ethnography on the Web.

de Munck, Victor. 2000. *Culture, self, and meaning*. Prospect Heights, IL: Waveland Press.

de Munck, Victor C., and Andrey Korotayev. 1999. Sexual equality and romantic love: A reanalysis of Rosenblatt's study on the function of romantic love. *Cross-Cultural Research* 33:265–73.

Denny, J. Peter. 1979. The "extendedness" variable in classifier semantics: Universal features and cultural variation. In *Ethnolinguistics*, ed. M. Mathiot. The Hague: Mouton.

Dentan, Robert K. 1968. *The Semai: A nonviolent people of Malaya.* New York: Holt, Rinehart & Winston.

De Villiers, Peter A., and Jill G. de Villiers. 1979. *Early language.* Cambridge, MA: Harvard University Press.

DeVore, Irven, and Melvin J. Konner. 1974. Infancy in hunter-gatherer life: An ethological perspective. In *Ethology and psychiatry,* ed. N. F. White. Toronto: Ontario Mental Health Foundation and University of Toronto Press.

de Waal, Frans. 2001. *The ape and the sushi master: Cultural reflections of a primatologist.* New York: Basic Books.

DeWalt, Kathleen M., Billie R. DeWalt with Coral B. Wayland. 1998. Participant observation. In *Handbook of methods in cultural anthropology,* ed. H. Russell Bernard, 259–99. Walnut Creek, CA: AltaMira Press.

Diament, Michelle. 2005. Diversifying their crops: Agriculture schools, focusing on job prospects, reach out to potential students from cities and suburbs. *The Chronicle of Higher Education,* May 6, pp. A32–34.

Diamond, Jared. 1991. The saltshaker's curse—Physiological adaptations that helped American Blacks survive slavery may now be predisposing their descendants to hypertension. *Natural History* (October).

Diamond, Norma. 1975. Collectivization, kinship, and the status of women in rural China. In R. R. Reiter, *Toward an anthropology of women.* New York: Monthly Review Press.

Dickson, D. Bruce, Jeffrey Olsen, P. Fred Dahm, and Mitchell S. Wachtel. 2005. Where do you go when you die? A cross-cultural test of the hypothesis that infrastructure predicts individual eschatology. *Journal of Anthropological Research* 1:53–79.

Dirks, Robert. 1993. Starvation and famine. *Cross-Cultural Research* 27:28–69.

Dirks, Robert. 2009. Hunger and famine. In MyAnthroLibrary, eds. C. R. Ember, M. Ember, and P. N. Peregrine. MyAnthroLibrary.com. Pearson.

Divale, William T. 1974. Migration, external warfare, and matrilocal residence. *Behavior Science Research* 9:75–133.

Divale, William T. 1977. Living floor area and marital residence: A replication. *Behavior Science Research* 2:109–15.

Divale, William T., and Marvin Harris. 1976. Population, warfare, and the male supremacist complex. *American Anthropologist* 78:521–38.

Douglas, Mary. 1975. *Implicit meanings: Essays in anthropology.* London: Routledge and Kegan Paul.

Dow, James. 1986. *The shaman's touch: Otomi Indian symbolic healing.* Salt Lake City: University of Utah Press.

Dowling, John H. 1975. Property relations and productive strategies in pastoral societies. *American Ethnologist* 2:419–26.

Doyle, Rodger. 2004. Living together: In the U.S. cohabitation is here to stay. *Scientific American* (January):28.

Doyle, Rodger. 2005. Leveling the playing field: Economic development helps women pull even with men. *Scientific American* (June):32.

Draper, Patricia. 1975. !Kung women: Contrasts in sexual egalitarianism in foraging and sedentary contexts. In *Toward an anthropology of women,* ed. R. R. Reiter. New York: Monthly Review Press.

Draper, Patricia, and Elizabeth Cashdan. 1988. Technological change and child behavior among the !Kung. *Ethnology* 27:339–65.

Dressler, William W. 1991. *Stress and adaptation in the context of culture.* Albany: State University of New York Press.

Dressler, William W. 1993. Health in the African American community: Accounting for health inequalities. *Medical Anthropology Quarterly* 7:325–45.

Dressler, William W., and Michael C. Robbins. 1975. Art styles, social stratification, and cognition: An analysis of Greek vase painting. *American Ethnologist* 2:427–34.

Drucker, Philip. 1965. *Cultures of the north Pacific Coast.* San Francisco: Chandler.

Drucker, Philip. 1967. The potlatch. In *Tribal and peasant economies,* ed. G. Dalton. Garden City, NY: Natural History Press.

Du, Shanshan. 2003. Is Buddha a couple: Gender-unitary perspectives from the Lahu of southwest China. *Ethnology* 42:253–71.

Duane, Daniel. 2003. Turning garbage into oil. *New York Times Magazine,* December 14, p. 100.

Dundes, Alan. 1965. Structural typology in North American Indian folktales. In *The study of folklore,* ed. A. Dundes, 206–15. Upper Saddle River, NJ: Prentice Hall.

Dundes, Alan. 1989. *Folklore matters.* Knoxville: University of Tennessee Press.

Durham, William H. 1991. *Coevolution: Genes, culture and human diversity.* Stanford, CA: Stanford University Press.

Durkheim, Émile. 1938/1895. *The rules of sociological method.* 8th ed. Trans. Sarah A. Soloway and John H. Mueller. Ed. George E. Catlin. New York: Free Press.

Durkheim, Émile. 1961/1912. *The elementary forms of the religious life.* Trans. Joseph W. Swain. New York: Collier Books.

Durrenberger, E. Paul. 1980. Chayanov's economic analysis in anthropology. *Journal of Anthropological Research* 36:133–48.

Durrenberger, E. Paul. 2001a. Anthropology and globalization. *American Anthropologist* 103:531–35.

Durrenberger, E. Paul. 2001b. Explorations of class and consciousness in the U.S. *Journal of Anthropological Research* 57:41–60.

Durrenberger, E. Paul, and Nicola Tannenbaum. 2002. Chayanov and theory in economic anthropology. In *Theory in economic anthropology,* ed. J. Ensminger, 137–53. Walnut Creek, CA: AltaMira Press.

Dyson-Hudson, Neville. 1966. *Karimojong politics.* Oxford: Clarendon Press.

Dyson-Hudson, Rada, and Eric Alden Smith. 1978. Human territoriality: An ecological reassessment. *American Anthropologist* 80:21–41.

Eckhardt, William. 1975. Primitive militarism. *Journal of Peace Research* 12:55–62.

Eddy, Elizabeth M., and William L. Partridge, eds. 1987. *Applied anthropology in America.* 2nd ed. New York: Columbia University Press.

Edgerton, Robert B. 1966. Conceptions of psychosis in four East African societies. *American Anthropologist* 68:408–25.

Edgerton, Robert B. 1971. *The individual in cultural adaptation: A study of four East African peoples.* Berkeley: University of California Press.

Edgerton, Robert B. 1992. *Sick societies: Challenging the myth of primitive harmony.* New York: Free Press.

Eisenstadt, S. N. 1954. African age groups. *Africa* 24:100–11.

Eiseley, Loren C. 1958. The dawn of evolutionary theory. In *Darwin's century: Evolution and the men who discovered it,* ed. L. C. Eiseley, Garden City, NY: Doubleday.

Ekman, Paul, and Dachner Keltner. 1997. Universal facial expressions of emotion: An old controversy and new findings. In *Nonverbal communication: Where nature meets culture,* eds. U. Segerstrale and P. Molnar. Mahwah, NJ: Lawrence Erlbaum.

Eliot, T. S. 1963. The love song of J. Alfred Prufrock. In *Collected poems, 1909–1962.* New York: Harcourt, Brace & World.

Ellis, Lee. 1986. Evidence of neuroandrogenic etiology of sex roles from a combined analysis of human, nonhuman primate and nonprimate mammalian studies. *Personality and Individual Differences* 7:519–52.

Ember, Carol R. 1973. Feminine task assignment and the social behavior of boys. *Ethos* 1:424–39.

Ember, Carol R. 1974. An evaluation of alternative theories of matrilocal versus patrilocal residence. *Behavior Science Research* 9:135–49.

Ember, Carol R. 1975. Residential variation among hunter-gatherers. *Behavior Science Research* 9:135–49.

Ember, Carol R. 1977. Cross-cultural cognitive studies. *Annual Review of Anthropology* 6:33–56.

Ember, Carol R. 1978a. Men's fear of sex with women: A cross-cultural study. *Sex Roles* 4:657–78.

Ember, Carol R. 1978b. Myths about hunter-gatherers. *Ethnology* 17:439–48.

Ember, Carol R. 1981. A cross-cultural perspective on sex differences. In *Handbook of cross-cultural human development,* eds. R. H. Munroe, R. L. Munroe, and B. B. Whiting, 531–80. New York: Garland.

Ember, Carol R. 1982. The conditions favoring religious conversion. Paper presented at the annual meeting of the Society for Cross-Cultural Research, February. Minneapolis, Minnesota.

Ember, Carol R. 1983. The relative decline in women's contribution to agriculture with intensification. *American Anthropologist* 85:285–304.

Ember, Carol R. 2009. Universal and variable patterns of gender difference. In MyAnthroLibrary, eds. C. R. Ember, M. Ember, and P. N. Peregrine. MyAnthroLibrary.com. Pearson.

Ember, Carol R., and Melvin Ember. 1972. The conditions favoring multilocal residence. *Southwestern Journal of Anthropology* 28:382–400.

Ember, Carol R., and Melvin Ember. 1992. Resource unpredictability, mistrust, and war: A cross-cultural study. *Journal of Conflict Resolution* 36:242–62.

Ember, Carol R., and Melvin Ember. 1993. Issues in cross-cultural studies of interpersonal violence. *Violence and Victims* 8:217–33.

Ember, Carol R., and Melvin Ember. 1994. War, socialization, and interpersonal violence: A cross-cultural study. *Journal of Conflict Resolution* 38:620–46.

Ember, Carol R., and Melvin Ember. 1997. Violence in the ethnographic record: Results of cross-cultural research on war and aggression. In *Troubled times,* eds. D. Frayer and D. Martin, 1–20. Langhorne, PA: Gordon and Breach.

Ember, Carol R., and Melvin Ember. 2005. Explaining corporal punishment of children: A cross-cultural study. *American Anthropologist* 107:609–19.

Ember, Carol R., and Melvin Ember. 2009. *Cross-cultural research methods.* 2nd ed. Lanham, CA: AltaMira Press.

Ember, Carol R., Melvin Ember, and Peter N. Peregrine. 2007. *Anthropology.* 12th ed. Upper Saddle River, NJ: Prentice Hall.

Ember, Carol R., Melvin Ember, Andrey Korotayev, and Victor de Munck. 2005. Valuing thinness or fatness in women: Reevaluating the effect of resource scarcity. *Evolution and Human Behavior* 26:257–70.

Ember, Carol R., Melvin Ember, and Burton Pasternak. 1974. On the development of unilineal descent. *Journal of Anthropological Research* 30:69–94.

Ember, Carol R., Melvin Ember, and Bruce Russett. 1992. Peace between participatory polities: A cross-cultural test of the "democracies rarely fight each other" hypothesis. *World Politics* 44:573–99.

Ember, Carol R., and David Levinson. 1991. The substantive contributions of worldwide cross-cultural studies using secondary data. *Behavior Science Research* (special issue, Cross-cultural and comparative research: Theory and method), 25:79–140.

Ember, Melvin. 1959. The nonunilinear descent groups of Samoa. *American Anthropologist* 61:573–77.

Ember, Melvin. 1963. The relationship between economic and political development in nonindustrialized societies. *Ethnology* 2:228–48.

Ember, Melvin. 1967. The emergence of neolocal residence. *Transactions of the New York Academy of Sciences* 30: 291–302.

Ember, Melvin. 1970. Taxonomy in comparative studies. In *A handbook of method in cultural anthropology,* eds. R. Naroll and R. Cohen. Garden City, NY: Natural History Press.

Ember, Melvin. 1973. An archaelogical indicator of matrilocal versus patrilocal residence. *American Antiquity* 38: 177–82.

Ember, Melvin. 1974a. The conditions that may favor avunculocal residence. *Behavior Science Research* 9:203–209.

Ember, Melvin. 1974b. Warfare, sex ratio, and polygyny. *Ethnology* 13:197–206.

Ember, Melvin. 1975. On the origin and extension of the incest taboo. *Behavior Science Research* 10:249–81.

Ember, Melvin. 1978. Size of color lexicon: Interaction of cultural and biological factors. *American Anthropologist* 80:364–67.

Ember, Melvin. 1982. Statistical evidence for an ecological explanation of warfare. *American Anthropologist* 84:645–49.

Ember, Melvin 1983. The emergence of neolocal residence. In *Marriage, family, and kinship: Comparative studies of social organization,* eds. M. Ember and C. R. Ember, 333–57. New Haven, CT: HRAF Press.

Ember, Melvin. 1984–1985. Alternative predictors of polygyny. *Behavior Science Research* 19:1–23.

Ember, Melvin. 1985. Evidence and science in ethnography: Reflections on the Freeman-Mead controversy. *American Anthropologist* 87:906–09.

Ember, Melvin, and Carol R. Ember. 1971. The conditions favoring matrilocal versus patrilocal residence. *American Anthropologist* 73:571–94.

Ember, Melvin, and Carol R. Ember. 1979. Male-female bonding: A cross-species study of mammals and birds. *Behavior Science Research* 14:37–56.

Ember, Melvin, and Carol R. Ember. 1983. *Marriage, family, and kinship: Comparative studies of social organization.* New Haven, CT: HRAF Press.

Ember, Melvin, and Carol R. Ember. 1992. Cross-cultural studies of war and peace: Recent achievements and future possibilities. In *Studying war,* eds. S. P. Reyna and R. E. Downs. New York: Gordon and Breach.

Ember, Melvin, and Carol R. Ember. 1999. Cross-language predictors of consonant-vowel syllables. *American Anthropologist* 101:730–42.

Ember, Melvin, and Carol R. Ember, eds. 2002. *Encyclopedia of urban cultures: Cities and cultures around the world,* 4 vols. Danbury, CT: Grolier/Scholastic.

Ember, Melvin, Carol R. Ember, and Ian Skoggard, eds. 2005. *Encyclopedia of diasporas: Immigrant and refugee cultures around the world,* 2 vols. New York: Kluwer Academic/Plenum.

Ember, Melvin, Carol R. Ember, and Bobbi S. Low. 2007. Comparing explanations of polygyny. *Cross-Cultural Research* 41:428–40.

Ember, Melvin, Carol R. Ember, and Bruce Russett. 1997. Inequality and democracy in the anthropological record. In *Inequality, democracy, and economic development,* ed. M. I. Midlarsky, 110–30. Cambridge: Cambridge University Press.

Ensminger, Jean. 1997. Transaction costs and Islam: Explaining conversion in Africa. *Journal of Institutional and Theoretical Economics* 153:4–29.

Ensminger, Jean. 2002. Experimental economics: A powerful new method for theory testing in anthropology. In *Theory in economic anthropology,* ed. J. Ensminger, 59–78. Walnut Creek, CA: AltaMira Press.

Ensor, Bradley E. 2003. Kinship and marriage among the Omaha, 1886–1902. *Ethnology* 42:1–14.

Epstein, Cynthia Fuchs. 1988. *Deceptive distinctions: Sex, gender, and the social order.* New York: Russell Sage Foundation.

Erchak, Gerald M. 2009. Family violence. In MyAnthroLibrary, eds. C. R. Ember, M. Ember, and P. N. Peregrine. MyAnthroLibrary.com. Pearson.

Ericksen, Karen Paige. 1989. Male and female age organizations and secret societies in Africa. *Behavior Science Research* 23:234–64.

Ericksen, Karen Paige, and Heather Horton. 1992. "Blood feuds": Cross-cultural variations in kin group vengeance. *Behavior Science Research* 26:57–85.

Erickson, Edwin. 1968. Self-assertion, sex role, and vocal rasp. In *Folk song style and culture,* ed. A. Lomax, 90–97. Washington, DC.

Errington, J. Joseph. 1985. On the nature of the sociolinguistic sign: Describing the Javanese speech levels. In *Semiotic mediation,* eds. E. Mertz and R. J. Parmentier, 287–310. Orlando, FL: Academic Press.

Ervin, Alexander M. 1987. Styles and strategies of leadership during the Alaskan Native land claims movement: 1959–71. *Anthropologica* 29:21–38.

Etienne, Mona, and Eleanor Leacock, eds. 1980. *Women and colonization: Anthropological perspectives.* New York: Praeger.

Etkin, Nina L., and Paul J. Ross. 1997. Malaria, medicine, and meals: A biobehavioral perspective. In *The anthropology of medicine,* eds. L. Romanucci-Ross, D. E. Moerman, and L. R. Tancredi, 169–209. Westport, CT: Bergin & Garvey.

Euripides. 1937. The Trojan women. In *Three Greek plays,* trans. E. Hamilton, 52. New York: Norton.

Evans-Pritchard, E. E. 1940. The Nuer of the Southern Sudan. In *African political systems,* eds. M. Fortes and E. E. Evans-Pritchard. New York: Oxford University Press.

Evans-Pritchard, E. E. 1970. Sexual inversion among the Azande. *American Anthropologist* 72:1428–34.

Evans-Pritchard, E. E. 1979. Witchcraft explains unfortunate events. In *Reader in comparative religion,* 4th ed., eds. W. A. Lessa and E. Z. Vogt. New York: Harper & Row.

Eversole, Robyn. 2005. "Direct to the poor": Revisited: Migrant remittances and development assistance. In *Migration and economy: Global and local dynamics,* ed. Lillian Trager, 289–322. Walnut Creek, CA: AltaMira Press.

Farley, Reynolds. 1996. *The new American reality: Who we are, how we got here, where we are going.* New York: Russell Sage Foundation.

Farmer, Paul. 1997. Ethnography, social analysis, and the prevention of sexually transmitted HIV infection among poor women in Haiti. In *The anthropology of infectious disease,* eds. M. C. Inhorn and P. J. Brown, pp. 413–38. Amsterdam: Gordon and Breach.

Fearnea, Elizabeth, and Robert Fearnea. 1975. As reported in M. Kay Martin and Barbara Voorhies, *Female of the Species.* New York: Columbia University Press.

Featherman, David L., and Robert M. Hauser. 1978. *Opportunity and change.* New York: Academic Press.

Fehr, Ernst, and Urs Fischbacher. 2003. The nature of human altruism. *Nature* 23:785–91.

Feinman, Gary, and Jill Neitzel. 1984. Too many types: An overview of sedentary prestate societies in the Americas. In *Advances in archaeological methods and theory,* ed. M. B. Schiffer, vol. 7, 39–102. Orlando, FL: Academic Press.

Feldman, Douglas A., and Thomas M. Johnson. 1986. Introduction. In *The social dimensions of AIDS,* eds. D. A. Feldman and T. M. Johnson. New York: Praeger.

Ferguson, Niall. 2004. *Colossus: The price of America's empire.* New York: Penguin Press.

Ferraro, Gary P. 2002. *The cultural dimension of international business.* 4th ed. Upper Saddle River, NJ: Prentice Hall.

Fessler, Daniel M. T. 2002. Windfall and socially distributed willpower: The psychocultural dynamics of rotating savings and credit associations in a Bengkulu village. *Ethos* 30:25–48.

Finley, M. I. 1983. *Politics in the ancient world.* Cambridge: Cambridge University Press.

Finnis, Elizabeth. 2006. Why grow cash crops? Subsistence farming and crop commercialization in the Kolli Hills, South India. *American Anthropologist* 108:363–69.

Firth, Raymond. 1957. *We, the Tikopia.* Boston: Beacon Press.

Firth, Raymond. 1959. *Social change in Tikopia.* New York: Macmillan.

Firth, Raymond. 1970. *Rank and religion in Tikopia.* Boston: Beacon Press.

Fischer, John L. 1958. Social influences on the choice of a linguistic variant. *Word* 14:47–56.

Fischer, John. 1961. Art styles as cultural cognitive maps. *American Anthropologist* 63:80–83.

Fisher, Julie. 1996. Grassroots organizations and grassroots support organizations: Patterns of interaction. In *Transforming societies, transforming anthropology,* ed. E. F. Moran. Ann Arbor: University of Michigan Press.

Fisher, William F. 1997. Doing good? The politics and antipolitics of NGO practices. *Annual Review of Anthropology* 26:439–64.

Fisher, William H. 1994. Megadevelopment, environmentalism, and resistance: The institutional context of Kayapo indigenous politics in central Brazil. *Human Organization* 53:220–32.

Flannery, Kent V. 1971. The origins and ecological effects of early domestication in Iran and the Near East. In *Prehistoric agriculture,* ed. S. Struever. Garden City, NY: Natural History Press.

Flannery, Kent V. 1972. The cultural evolution of civilizations. *Annual Review of Ecology and Systematics* 3:399–426.

Flannery, Kent V. 1986b. The research problem. In *Guila Naquitz,* ed. K. V. Flannery. Orlando, FL: Academic Press.

Fluehr-Lobban, Carolyn. 2006. *Race and racism: An introduction.* Lanham: AltaMira Press.

Ford, Clellan S. 1941. *Smoke from their fires.* New Haven, CT: Yale University Press.

Ford, Clellan S., and Frank A. Beach. 1951. *Patterns of sexual behavior.* New York: Harper.

Fortes, Meyer. 1949. *The web of kinship among the Tallensi.* New York: Oxford University Press.

Foster, Brian L. 1974. Ethnicity and commerce. *American Ethnologist* 1:437–47.

Foster, George M. 1962. *Traditional cultures and the impact of technological change.* New York: Harper & Row.

Foster, George M. 1969. *Applied anthropology.* Boston: Little, Brown.

Foster, George M. 1994. *Hippocrates' Latin American legacy: Humoral medicine in the New World.* Amsterdam: Gordon and Breach.

Foucault, Michel. 1970. *The order of things: An archaeology of the human sciences.* New York: Random House.

Frake, Charles O. 1960. The Eastern Subanun of Mindanao. In *Social structure in Southeast Asia,* ed. G. P. Murdock, 51–64. Chicago: Quadrangle.

Frank, André Gunder. 1967. *Capitalism and underdevelopment in Latin America: Historical studies of Chile and Brazil.* New York: Monthly Review Press.

Fratkin, Elliot. 2008. Pastures lost: The decline of mobile pastoralism among Maasai and Rendille in Kenya, East Africa. In *Economies and the transformation of landscape,* eds. Lisa Cliggett and Christopher A. Pool, 149–68. Lanham, AltaMira Press.

Frayer, David W., and Milford H. Wolpoff. 1985. Sexual dimorphism. *Annual Review of Anthropology* 14:429–73.

Frayser, Suzanne G. 1985. *Varieties of sexual experience.* New Haven, CT: HRAF Press.

Freedman, Daniel G. 1979. Ethnic differences in babies. *Human Nature* (January):36–43.

Freeman, Derek. 1983. *Margaret Mead and Samoa: The making and unmaking of an anthropological myth.* Cambridge, MA: Harvard University Press.

Freeman, J. D. 1961. On the concept of the kindred. *Journal of the Royal Anthropological Institute* 91:192–220.

Freud, Sigmund. 1943/1917. *A general introduction to psychoanalysis.* Garden City, NY: Garden City Publishing. [in German]

Freud, Sigmund. 1967/1939. *Moses and monotheism.* Katherine Jones, trans. New York: Vintage Books.

Fried, Morton H. 1967. *The evolution of political society: An essay in political anthropology.* New York: Random House.

Friedl, Ernestine. 1962. *Vasilika: A village in modern Greece.* New York: Holt, Rinehart & Winston.

Friedman, Jeffrey M. 2003. A war on obesity, not the obese. *Science* (February 7):856–58.

Friedman, Saul S. 1980. Holocaust. In *Academic American [now Grolier] Encyclopedia.* Vol. 10. Princeton, NJ: Aréte.

Friedrich, Paul. 1970. *Proto-Indo-European trees: The arboreal system of a prehistoric people.* Chicago: University of Chicago Press.

Friedrich, Paul. 1986. *The language parallax.* Austin: University of Texas Press.

Fromm, Erich. 1950. *Psychoanalysis and religion.* New Haven, CT: Yale University Press.

Fry, Douglas P. 2006. *The human potential for peace: An anthropological challenge to assumptions about war and violence.* New York: Oxford University Press.

Fry, Douglas P., and Kaj Björkqvist, eds. 1997. *Cultural variation in conflict resolution: Alternatives to violence.* Mahwah, NJ: Lawrence Erlbaum.

Futuyma, Douglas. 1982. *Science on trial.* New York: Pantheon.

Gal, Susan. 1988. The political economy of code choice. In *Codeswitching,* ed. M. Heller, 345–64. Berlin: Mouton de Gruyter.

Gartner, Rosemary. 2009. Crime variations across cultures and nations. In *MyAnthroLibrary,* eds. C. R. Ember, M. Ember, and P. N. Peregrine. MyAnthroLibrary.com. Pearson.

Gat, Azar. 1999. The pattern of fighting in simple, small-scale, prestate societies. *Journal of Anthropological Research* 55:563–83.

Gaulin, Steven J. C., and James S. Boster. 1990. Dowry as female competition. *American Anthropologist* 92:994–1005.

Geertz, Clifford. 1960. *The religion of Java.* New York: Free Press.

Geertz, Clifford. 1966. Religion as a cultural system. In *Anthropological approaches to the study of religion,* ed. M. Banton, 1–46. New York: Praeger.

Geertz, Clifford. 1973a. Deep play: Notes on the Balinese cockfight. In C. Geertz, *The interpretation of cultures,* 412–54. New York: Basic Books.

Geertz, Clifford. 1973b. Thick description: Toward an interpretative theory of culture. In *The interpretation of cultures,* ed. C. Geertz. New York: Basic Books.

Geertz, Clifford. 1984. "From the native's point of view": On the nature of anthropological understanding. In *Culture Theory,* eds. R. A. Shweder and R. A. LeVine. New York: Cambridge University Press.

Geiger, H. Jack. 2003. Racial and ethnic disparities in diagnosis and treatment: A review of the evidence and a consideration of causes. In *Unequal treatment: confronting racial and ethnic disparities in health care,* eds. B. D. Smedley, A. Y. Stith, and A. R. Nelson, 417–54. Washington, DC: National Academy Press.

Gelles, Richard J., and Murray A. Straus. 1988. *Intimate violence.* New York: Simon & Schuster.

Gesler, W. 1991. *The cultural geography of health care.* Pittsburgh, PA: University of Pittsburgh Press.

Gibbons, Ann. 1993. Warring over women. *Science* (August 20):987–88.

Gibbs, James L., Jr. 1965. The Kpelle of Liberia. In *Peoples of Africa,* ed. J. L. Gibbs, Jr. New York: Holt, Rinehart & Winston.

Gibson, Kathleen R., and Stephen Jessee. 1999. Language evolution and expansions of multiple neurological processing areas. In *The origins of language,* ed. B. J. King, 189–227. Santa Fe: School of American Research Press.

Gibson, Kyle. 2009. Differential parental investment in families with both adopted and genetic children. *Evolution and Human Behavior* 30:184–89.

Gilligan, Carol. 1982. *In a different voice: Psychological theory and women's development.* Cambridge, MA: Harvard University Press.

Gilligan, Carol, and Jane Attanucci. 1988. Two moral orientations. In *Mapping the moral domain,* eds. C. Gilligan, J. V. Ward, and J. M. Taylor, 73–86. Cambridge, MA: Harvard University Press.

Gilliland, Mary Kay. 1995. Nationalism and ethnogenesis in the former Yugoslavia. In *Ethnic identity: Creation, conflict, and accommodation,* 3rd ed., eds. L. Romanucci-Ross and G. A. De Vos, 197–221. Walnut Creek, CA: Altamira Press.

Gilman, Antonio. 1990. The development of social stratification in Bronze Age Europe. *Current Anthropology* 22:1–23.

Gimbutas, Marija. 1974. An archaeologist's view of PIE* in 1975. *Journal of Indo-European Studies* 2:289–307.

Gladwin, Christina H. 1980. A theory of real-life choice: Applications to agricultural decisions. In *Agricultural decision making,* ed. P. F. Barlett. New York: Academic Press.

Gladwin, Thomas, and Seymour B. Sarason. 1953. *Truk: Man in paradise.* New York: Wenner-Gren Foundation for Anthropological Research, 1953, as seen in eHRAF Collection of Ethnography on the Web, 2000.

Gleitman, Lila R., and Eric Wanner. 1982. Language acquisition: The state of the state of the art. In *Language acquisition,* eds. E. Wanner and L. R. Gleitman. Cambridge: Cambridge University Press.

Godoy, Ricardo, Elizabeth Byron, Victoria Reyes-Garcia, William R. Leonard, Karishma Patel, Lilian Apaza, Eddy Pérez, Vincent Vadez, and David Wilke. 2004. Patience in a foraging-horticultural society: A test of competing hypotheses. *Journal of Anthropological Research* 60:179–202.

Goldschmidt, Walter. 1999. Dynamics and status in America. *Anthropology Newsletter* 40(5):62, 64.

Goldstein, Donna. 1998. Nothing bad intended: Child discipline, punishment, and survival in a shantytown in Rio de Janeiro. In *Small wars: The cultural politics of childhood,* eds. Nancy Scheper-Hughes and Carolyn Sargeant, 389–415. Berkeley: University of California-Berkeley Press.

Goldstein, Joshua S. 2001. *War and gender: How gender shapes the war system and vice versa.* New York: Cambridge University Press.

Goldstein, Joshua S. 2004. War and gender. *Encyclopedia of sex and gender: Men and women in the world's cultures,* vol. 1, eds. C. R. Ember and M. Ember, 107–16. New York: Kluwer Academic/Plenum.

Goldstein, Melvyn C. 1971. Stratification, polyandry, and family structure in central Tibet. *Southwestern Journal of Anthropology* 27:65–74.

Goldstein, Melvyn C. 1987. When brothers share a wife. *Natural History* (March):39–48.

Goode, William J. 1970. *World revolution and family patterns.* New York: Free Press.

Goode, William J. 1982. *The family.* 2nd ed. Upper Saddle River, NJ: Prentice Hall.

Goodenough, Ward H. 1951. *Property, kin, and community on Truk.* New Haven, CT: Yale University Press.

Goodman, Alan H., and Thomas L. Leatherman, eds. 1998. *Building a new biocultural synthesis: Political-economic perspectives on human biology.* Ann Arbor: University of Michigan Press.

Goodman, Madeleine J., P. Bion Griffin, Agnes A. Estioko-Griffin, and John S. Grove. 1985. The compatibility of hunting and mothering among the Agta hunter-gatherers of the Philippines. *Sex Roles* 12:1199–209.

Goody, Jack. 1970. Cousin terms. *Southwestern Journal of Anthropology* 26:125–42.

Goody, Jack. 1973. Bridewealth and dowry in Africa and Eurasia. In *Bridewealth and dowry,* eds. J. Goody and S. H. Tambiah. Cambridge: Cambridge University Press.

Gossen, Gary H. 1979. Temporal and spatial equivalents in Chamula ritual symbolism. In *Reader in comparative religion,* 4th ed., eds. W. A. Lessa and E. Z. Vogt, 116–28. New York: Harper & Row.

Gough, Kathleen. 1959. The Nayars and the definition of marriage. *Journal of the Royal Anthropological Institute* 89:23–34.

Gould, Richard A. 1969. *Yiwara: Foragers of the Australian desert.* New York: Scribner's.

Graber, Robert, ed. 2004. Special issue. The future state of the world: An anthropological symposium. *Cross-Cultural Research* 38:95–207.

Graburn, Nelson H. 1969. *Eskimos without igloos.* Boston: Little, Brown.

Graham, Susan Brandt. 1979. Biology and human social behavior: A response to van den Berghe and Barash. *American Anthropologist* 81:357–60.

Gray, J. Patrick. 1985. *Primate sociobiology.* New Haven, CT: HRAF Press.

Gray, J. Patrick. 1996. Sociobiology. In *Encyclopedia of cultural anthropology,* vol 4., eds. D. Levinson and M. Ember, 1212–19. New York: Henry Holt.

Greenberg, Joseph H. 1972. Linguistic evidence regarding Bantu origins. *Journal of African History* 13:189–216.

Greenfield, Patricia M., Ashley E. Maynard, and Carla P. Childs. 2000. History, culture, learning, and development. *Cross-Cultural Research* 34:351–74.

Gregory, C. A. 1982. *Gifts and commodities.* New York: Academic Press.

Grenoble, Lenore A., and Lindsay J. Whaley. 2006. *Saving languages: An introduction to language revitalization* Cambridge: Cambridge University Press.

Gröger, B. Lisa. 1981. Of men and machines: Cooperation among French family farmers. *Ethnology* 20:163–75.

Gross, Daniel R., George Eiten, Nancy M. Flowers, Francisca M. Leoi, Madeline Lattman Ritter, and Dennis W. Werner. 1979. Ecology and acculturation among native peoples of central Brazil. *Science* (November 30):1043–50.

Gross, Daniel R., and Barbara A. Underwood. 1971. Technological change and caloric costs: Sisal agriculture in northeastern Brazil. *American Anthropologist* 73:725–40.

Gubser, Nicholas J. 1965. *The Nunamiut Eskimos: Hunters of caribou.* New Haven, CT: Yale University Press.

Guest, Greg, and Eric C. Jones. 2005. Globalization, health, and the environment: An introduction. In *Globalization, health, and the environment: An integrated perspective,* ed. Greg Guest, 3–26. Lanham, MD: Roman & Littlefield.

Guiora, Alexander Z., Benjamin Beit-Hallahmi, Risto Fried, and Cecelia Yoder. 1982. Language environment and gender identity attainment. *Language Learning* 32:289–304.

Gumperz, John J. 1961. Speech variation and the study of Indian civilization. *American Anthropologist* 63:976–88.

Gumperz, John J. 1971. Dialect differences and social stratification in a North Indian village. In *Language in social* groups: *Essays by John L. Gumperz*, selected and introduced by Anwar S. Dil. Stanford, CA: Stanford University Press.

Gurr, Ted Robert. 1989a. Historical trends in violent crime: Europe and the United States. In *Violence in America*, vol. 1: *The history of crime*, ed. T. R. Gurr. Newbury Park, CA: Sage.

Gurr, Ted Robert. 1989b. The history of violent crime in America: An overview. In *Violence in America*, vol. 1: *The history of crime*, ed. T. R. Gurr. Newbury Park, CA: Sage.

Gurven, Michael, Kim Hill, and Hillard Kaplan, 2002. From forest to reservation: Transitions in food-sharing behavior among the Ache of Paraguay. *Journal of Anthropological Research* 58:93–120.

Guthrie, Stewart Elliott. 1993. *Faces in the clouds: A new theory of religion.* New York: Oxford University Press.

Haas, Jonathan. 1990. Warfare and the evolution of tribal polities in the prehistoric Southwest. In *The anthropology of war*, ed. J. Haas, 171–89. New York: Cambridge University Press.

Haas, Mary R. 1944. Men's and women's speech in Koasati. *Language* 20:142–49.

Haddix, Kimber A. 2001. Leaving your wife and your brothers: When polyandrous marriages fall apart. *Evolution and Human Behavior* 22:47–60.

Hage, Jerald, and Charles H. Powers. 1992. *Post-industrial lives: Roles and relationships in the 21st century.* Newbury Park, CA: Sage.

Hahn, Robert A. 1995. *Sickness and healing: An anthropological perspective.* New Haven, CT: Yale University Press.

Hall, Edward T. 1966. *The hidden dimension.* Garden City, NY: Doubleday.

Hallowell, A. Irving. 1976. Ojibwa world view and disease. In *Contributions to anthropology: Selected papers of A. Irving Hallowell.* Chicago: University of Chicago Press, pp. 410–13.

Halpern, Diane F. 2000. *Sex differences in cognitive abilities.* 3rd ed. Mahwah, NJ: Lawrence Erlbaum Associates.

Hames, Raymond. 1990. Sharing among the Yanomamö. Part I, The effects of risk. In *Risk and uncertainty in tribal and peasant economies*, ed. E. Cashdan. Boulder, CO: Westview.

Hames, Raymond. 2009. Yanomamö: Varying adaptations of foraging horticulturalists. In MyAnthroLibrary, eds. C. R. Ember, M. Ember, and P. N. Peregrine. MyAnthroLibrary.com. Pearson.

Handwerker, W. Penn, and Paul V. Crosbie. 1982. Sex and dominance. *American Anthropologist* 84:97–104.

Hannerz, Ulf. 1996. *Transnational connections: Culture, people, places.* London: Routledge.

Hanson, Jeffery R. 1988. Age-set theory and Plains Indian age-grading: A critical review and revision. *American Ethnologist* 15:349–64.

Hardin, Garrett. 1968. The tragedy of the commons. *Science* 162:1243–48.

Hardoy, Jorge, and David Satterthwaite. 1987. The legal and the illegal city. In *Shelter, settlement, and development*, ed. L. Rodwin, 304–38. Boston: Allen & Unwin.

Harkness, Sara, and Charles M. Super. 1997. An infant's three Rs. A box in Small, Our babies, ourselves, *Natural History* (October):45.

Harner, Michael. 1972. The role of hallucinogenic plants in European witchcraft. In *Hallucinogens and shamanism*, ed. M. Harner, 127–50. New York: Oxford University Press.

Harner, Michael J. 1975. Scarcity, the factors of production, and social evolution. In *Population, ecology, and social evolution,* ed. S. Polgar, 123–38. The Hague: Mouton.

Harner, Michael, and Gary Doore. 1987. The ancient wisdom in shamanic cultures. In *Shamanism,* comp. S. Nicholson, 3–16. Wheaton, IL: Theosophical Publishing House.

Harper, Douglas. 2003. Slavery in the North. http://www.slavenorth.com/ (accessed June, 2009).

Harrell-Bond, Barbara. 1996. Refugees. In *Encyclopedia of cultural anthropology,* 4 vols., vol. 3, eds. D. Levinson and M. Ember, 1076–81. New York: Henry Holt.

Harris, Marvin. 1964. *Patterns of race in the Americas.* New York: Walker.

Harris, Marvin. 1966. The cultural ecology of India's sacred cattle. *Current Anthropology* 7:51–63.

Harris, Marvin. 1968. *The rise of anthropological theory: A history of theories of culture.* New York: Thomas Y. Crowell.

Harris, Marvin. 1975. *Cows, pigs, wars and witches: The riddles of culture.* New York: Random House, Vintage.

Harrison, Gail G. 1975. Primary adult lactase deficiency: A problem in anthropological genetics. *American Anthropologist* 77: 812–35.

Hart, Hornell. 1948. The logistic growth of political areas. *Social Forces* 26:396–408.

Harvey, Philip W., and Peter F. Heywood. 1983. Twenty-five years of dietary change in Simbu Province, Papua New Guinea. *Ecology of Food and Nutrition* 13:27–35.

Hatch, Elvin. 1997. The good side of relativism. *Journal of Anthropological Research* 53:371–81.

Hays, Terence E. 1994. Sound symbolism, onomatopoeia, and New Guinea frog names. *Journal of Linguistic Anthropology* 4:153–74.

Heider, Karl. 1970. *The Dugum Dani.* Chicago: Aldine.

Heider, Karl. 1979. *Grand Valley Dani: Peaceful warriors.* New York: Holt, Rinehart & Winston.

Heise, David R. 1967. Cultural patterning of sexual socialization. *American Sociological Review* 32:726–39.

Heller, Monica, ed. 1988. *Codeswitching: Anthropological and sociolinguistic perspectives.* Berlin: Mouton de Gruyter.

Helms, Mary W. 2009. Miskito: Adaptations to colonial empires, past and present. In MyAnthroLibrary, eds. C. R. Ember, M. Ember, and P. N. Peregrine. MyAnthroLibrary.com. Pearson.

Hempel, Carl G. 1965. *Aspects of Scientific explanation.* New York: Free Press.

Henderson, Harry. 2001. *Global terrorism: The complete reference guide.* New York: Checkmark Books.

Henderson, Stephen. 2002. Weddings: Vows; Rakhi Dhanoa and Ranjeet Purewal. *The New York Times,* August 18, p. 9.2.

Hendrix, Llewellyn. 1985. Economy and child training reexamined. *Ethos* 13:246–61.

Hendrix, Llewellyn. 2009. Varieties of marital relationships. In MyAnthroLibrary, eds. C. R. Ember, M. Ember, and P. N. Peregrine. MyAnthroLibrary.com. Pearson.

Henry, Donald O. 1989. *From foraging to agriculture: The Levant at the end of the ice age.* Philadelphia: University of Pennsylvania Press.

Henry, Edward O. 1976. The variety of music in a North Indian village: Reassessing cantometrics. *Ethnomusicology* 20:49–66.

Herlihy, Laura Hobson. 2007. Matrifocality and women's power on the Miskito Coast. *Ethnology* 46:133–49.

Herrman, Helen. 1990. A survey of homeless mentally ill people in Melbourne, Australia. *Hospital and Community Psychiatry* 41:1291–92.

Hewlett, Barry. 2009. Diverse contexts of human infancy. MyAnthroLibrary, eds. C. R. Ember, M. Ember, and P. N. Peregrine. MyAnthroLibrary.com. Pearson.

Hewlett, Barry S., and L. L. Cavalli-Sforza. 1986. Cultural transmission among Aka Pygmies. *American Anthropologist* 88:922–34.

Hiatt, L. R. 1980. Polyandry in Sri Lanka: A test case for parental investment theory. *Man* 15:583–98.

Hickey, Gerald Cannon. 1964. *Village in Vietnam.* New Haven, CT: Yale University Press.

Hickson, Letitia. 1986. The social contexts of apology in dispute settlement: A cross-cultural study. *Ethnology* 25: 283–94.

Higley, Stephen Richard. 1995. *Privilege, power, and place: The geography of the American upper class.* Lanham, MD: Roman & Littlefield.

Hill, Carole. Strategic issues for rebuilding a theory and practice synthesis. *NAPA Bulletin* 18 (2000):1–16.

Hill, Donald R. 2005. Music of the African diaspora in the Americas. In *Encyclopedia of diasporas: Immigrant and refugee cultures around the world,* 2 vols., eds. M. Ember, C. Ember, and I. Skoggard, 363–73. New York: Kluwer Academic/Plenum.

Hill, James N. 1970. Broken K Pueblo: Prehistoric social organization in the American Southwest. Anthropological papers of the University of Arizona, Number 18. Tucson: University of Arizona Press.

Hill, Jane H. 1978. Apes and language. *Annual Review of Anthropology* 7:89–112.

Hill, Jane H. 2009. Do apes have language? In MyAnthroLibrary, eds. C. R. Ember, M. Ember, and P. N. Peregrine. MyAnthroLibrary.com. Pearson.

Hill, Jonathan D. 1996. Introduction: Ethnogenesis in the Americas. 1492–1992. In *Ethnogenesis in the Americas,* ed. J. D. Hill, 1–19. Iowa City: University of Iowa Press.

Hill, Kim, and A. Magdalena Hurtado. 2004. The ethics of anthropological research with remote tribal populations. In *Lost paradises and the ethics of research and publication,* eds. F. M. Salzano and A. M. Hurtado, 193–210. Oxford: Oxford University Press.

Hill, Kim, Hillard Kaplan, Kristen Hawkes, and A. Magdalena Hurtado. 1987. Foraging decisions among Aché hunter-gatherers: New data and implications for optimal foraging models. *Ethology and Sociobiology* 8:1–36.

Hill, Susan T. 2001. *Science and engineering doctorate awards: 2000,* NSF 02-305. National Science Foundation, Division of Science Resources Statistics. VA: Arlington.

Hillel, Daniel. 2000. *Salinity management for sustainable irrigation: Integrating science, environment, and economics.* Washington, DC. The World Bank.

Himmelgreen, David A., and Deborah L. Crooks. 2005. Nutritional anthropology and its application to nutritional issues and problems. In *Applied anthropology: Domains of application,* eds. S. Kedia and J. van Willigen, 149–88. Westport, CT: Praeger.

Hitchcock, Robert K., and Megan Beisele. 2000. Introduction. In *Hunters and gatherers in the modern world: Conflict, resistance, and self-determinations,* eds. P. P. Schweitzer, M. Biesele, and R. K. Hitchcock, 1–27. New York: Berghahn Books.

Hobsbawm, E. J. 1970. *Age of revolution.* New York: Praeger.

Hockett, C. F., and R. Ascher. 1964. The human revolution. *Current Anthropology* 5:135–68.

Hoebel, E. Adamson. 1960. *The Cheyennes: Indians of the Great Plains.* New York: Holt, Rinehart & Winston.

Hoebel, E. Adamson. 1968/1954. *The law of primitive man.* New York: Atheneum.

Hoffman, Lois Wladis. 1988. Cross-cultural differences in child-rearing goals. In *Parental behavior in diverse societies,* eds. R. A. LeVine, P. M. Miller, and M. M. West. San Francisco: Jossey-Bass.

Hoijer, Harry. 1964. Cultural implications of some Navaho linguistic categories. In *Language in culture and society,* ed. D. Hymes. New York: Harper & Row.

Hollan, Douglas. 1992. Cross-cultural differences in the self. *Journal of Anthropological Research* 48:289–90.

Holloway, Marguerite. 1993. Sustaining the Amazon. *Scientific American* (July):91–99.

Holmes, Janet. 1992. *An introduction to sociolinguistics.* London: Longman.

Honigmann, John J. 1967. *Personality in culture.* New York: Harper & Row.

Hoogbergen, Wim. 1990. *The Boni Maroon wars in Suriname.* Leiden: E. J. Brill.

Hopkins, K. 1980. Brother-sister marriage in Roman Egypt. *Comparative Studies in Society and History* 22:303–54.

Howard, Alan, and Jan Rensel. 2009. Rotuma: Interpreting a wedding. In MyAnthroLibrary, eds. C. R. Ember, M. Ember, and P. N. Peregrine. MyAnthroLibrary.com. Pearson.

Howrigan, Gail A. 1988. Fertility, infant feeding, and change in Yucatan. *New Directions for Child Development* 40: 37–50.

Hua, Cai. 2001. *A society without fathers or husbands: The Na of China,* trans. Asti Hustvedt. New York: Zone Books.

Human Development Report 1993. 1993. Published for the United Nations Development Programme. New York: Oxford University Press, 9–25.

Humphrey, Caroline, and Stephen Hugh-Jones. 1992. Introduction: Barter, exchange and value. In *Barter, exchange and value,* eds. C. Humphrey and S. Hugh-Jones. New York: Cambridge University Press.

Hunt, Morton. 1974. *Sexual behavior in the 1970s.* Chicago: Playboy Press.

Hunt, Robert C. 2000. Labor productivity and agricultural development: Boserup revisited. *Human Ecology* 28:251–77.

Hurtado, Ana M., Kristen Hawkes, Kim Hill, and Hillard Kaplan. 1985. Female subsistence strategies among the Aché hunter-gatherers of eastern Paraguay. *Human Ecology* 13:1–28.

Huxley, Thomas H. 1970. Man's place in nature. In *Evolution of man,* ed. L. Young. New York: Oxford University Press.

Hymes, Dell. 1974. *Foundations in sociolinguistics: An ethnographic approach.* Philadelphia: University of Pennsylvania Press.

Irons, William. 1979. Natural selection, adaptation, and human social behavior. In *Evolutionary biology and human social behavior,* eds. N. Chagnon and W. Irons. North Scituate, MA: Duxbury.

Irwin, Marc H., Gary N. Schafer, and Cynthia P. Feiden. 1974. Emic and unfamiliar category sorting of mano farmers and U.S. undergraduates. *Journal of Cross-Cultural Psychology* 5:407–23.

Itkonen, T. I. 1951. The Lapps of Finland. *Southwestern Journal of Anthropology* 7:32–68.

Jacobs, Sue-Ellen, and Christine Roberts. 1989. Sex, sexuality, gender and gender variance. In *Gender and anthropology*, ed. S. Morgen, 438–62. Washington, DC: American Anthropological Association.

James, Allison. 2007. Giving voice to children's voices: Practices and problems, pitfalls and potentials. *American Anthropologist* 109:261–72.

James, William. 1902. *The varieties of religious experience: A study in human nature.* New York: Modern Library.

Jankowiak, William R. 2009. Urban Mongols: Ethnicity in Communist China. In MyAnthroLibrary, eds. C. R. Ember, M. Ember, and P. N. Peregrine. MyAnthroLibrary. com. Pearson.

Jankowiak, William R., and Edward F. Fischer. 1992. A cross-cultural perspective on romantic love. *Ethnology* 31: 149–55.

Jankowiak, William, M. Diane Nell, and Ann Buckmaster. 2002. Managing infidelity: A cross-cultural perspective. *Ethnology* 41:85–101.

Jankowiak, William, Monica Sudakov, and Benjamin C. Wilreker. 2005. Co-wife conflict and co-operation. *Ethnology* 44:81–98.

Janzen, Daniel H. 1973. Tropical agroecosystems. *Science* (December 21):1212–19.

Jarvenpa, Robert. 2004. *Silot'ine:* An insurance perspective on Northern Dene kinship networks in recent history. *Journal of Anthropological Research* 60:153–78.

Jarvenpa, Robert, and Hetty Jo Brumbach. 2006. Chipewyan hunters: A task differentiation analysis. In *Circumpolar lives and livelihood: A comparative ethnoarchaeology of gender and subsistence,* eds. R. Jarvenpa and H. J. Brumbach, 54–78. Lincoln, Nebraska: University of Nebraska Press.

Jelliffe, Derrick B., and E. F. Patrice Jelliffe. 1975. Human milk, nutrition, and the world resource crisis. *Science* 9 (may):557–61.

Joans, Barbara. 1997. Problems in Pocatello: A study in linguistic misunderstanding. In *Applying cultural anthropology: An introductory reader*, 3rd ed., eds. A. Podolefsky and P. J. Brown, 51–54. Mountain View, CA: Mayfield.

Johannes, R. E. 1981. *Words of the lagoon: Fishing and marine lore in the Palau District of Micronesia.* Berkeley: University of California Press.

Johnson, Allen, and Timothy Earle. 1987. *The evolution of human societies: From foraging group to agrarian state.* Stanford, CA: Stanford University Press.

Johnson, Amber Lynn. 2002. Cross-cultural analysis of pastoral adaptations and organizational states: A preliminary study. *Cross-Cultural Research* 36:151–80.

Johnson-Hanks, Jennifer. 2006. *Uncertain honor: Modern motherhood in an African crisis.* Chicago: University of Chicago Press.

Johnson, Jeffrey G., Patricia Cohen, Elizabeth M. Smailies, Stephanie Kasen, and Judith S. Brook. 2002. Television viewing and aggressive behavior during adolescence and adulthood. *Science* 295 (March 29):2468–70.

Johnston, David Cay. 1999. Gap between rich and poor found substantially wider. *New York Times,* September 5, p. 16.

Jones, Nicholas Blurton, Kristen Hawkes, and James F. O'Connell. 1996. The global process and local ecology: How should we explain differences between the Hadza and the !Kung? In *Cultural diversity among twentieth-century foragers,* ed. S. Kent. Cambridge: Cambridge University Press.

Jung, Carl G. 1938. *Psychology and religion.* New Haven, CT: Yale University Press.

Kang, Bong W. 2000. A reconsideration of population pressure and warfare: A protohistoric Korean case. *Current Anthropology* 4:873–81.

Kang, Gay Elizabeth. 1979. Exogamy and peace relations of social units: A cross-cultural test. *Ethnology* 18:85–99.

Kaplan, Hillard, and Kim Hill. 1985. Food sharing among Aché foragers: Tests of explanatory hypotheses. *Current Anthropology* 26:223–46.

Kaplan, Hillard, Kim Hill, Jane Lancaster, and A. Magdalena Hurtado. 2000. A theory of human life history evolution, diet, intelligence, and longevity. *Evolutionary Anthropology* 9:156–84.

Kaplan, Hillard, Kim Hill, and A. Magdalena Hurtado. 1990. Risk, foraging and food sharing among the Aché. In *Risk and uncertainty in tribal and peasant economies,* ed. E. Cashdan. Boulder, CO: Westview.

Kardiner, Abram, and Ralph Linton. 1946/1939. *The individual and his society.* New York: Golden Press.

Katzner, Kenneth. 2002. *Languages of the world.* Routledge.

Kedia, Satish. 2008. Recent changes and trends in the practice of anthropology. *NAPA Bulletin* 29:14–28.

Kedia, Satish, and John van Willigen, eds. 2005. *Applied anthropology: Domains of application.* Wesport, CT: Praeger.

Keeley, Lawrence H. 1991. Ethnographic models for late glacial hunter-gatherers. In *The late glacial in north-west Europe: Human adaptation and environmental change at the end of the Pleistocene,* eds. N. Barton, A. J. Roberts, and D. A. Roe. *CBA Research Report* 77:179–90. London: Council for British Archaeology.

Keenan, Elinor. 1989. Norm-makers, norm-breakers: Uses of speech by men and women in a Malagasy community. In *Explorations in the ethnography of speaking,* 2nd ed., eds. R. Bauman and J. Sherzer. New York: Cambridge University Press.

Kehoe, Alice B., and Dody H. Giletti. 1981. Women's preponderance in possession cults: The calcium-deficiency hypothesis extended. *American Anthropologist* 83:549–61.

Keller, Helen. 1974 [1902]. *The story of my life.* New York: Dell.

Kelly, Raymond C. 1974. Witchcraft and sexual relations: An exploration in the social and semantic implications of the structure of belief. Paper presented at the annual meeting of the American Anthropological Association, Mexico City.

Kelly, Raymond C. 1985. *The Nuer conquest: The structure and development of an expansionist system.* Ann Arbor: University of Michigan Press.

Kelly, Robert L. 1995. *The foraging spectrum: Diversity in hunter-gatherer lifeways.* Washington: Smithsonian Institution Press.

Kent, Susan, ed. 1996. *Cultural diversity among twentieth-century foragers: An African perspective.* Cambridge: Cambridge University Press.

Khosroshashi, Fatemeh. 1989. Penguins don't care, but women do: A social identity analysis of a Whorfian problem. *Language in Society* 18:505–25.

Kilbride, Philip L., and Janet C. Kilbride. 1990. Polygyny: A modern contradiction? In P. L. Kilbride and J. C. Kilbride,

Changing family life in East Africa: Women and children at risk. University Park: Pennsylvania State University Press.

King, Barbara J. 1999a. Introduction. In *The origins of language,* ed. B. J. King, 3–19. Santa Fe: School of American Research Press.

King, J. C. H. 1986. Tradition in Native American art. In *The arts of the North American Indian,* ed. E. L. Wade, 74–82. New York: Hudson Hills Press.

King, Seth S. 1979. Some farm machinery seems less than human. *New York Times,* April 8, p. E9.

Klass, Morton. 2009. Is there "caste" outside of India? In MyAnthroLibrary, eds. C. R. Ember, M. Ember, and P. N. Peregrine. MyAnthroLibrary.com. Pearson.

Kleinberg, Jill. 1994. Practical implications of organizational culture where Americans and Japanese work together. In *Practicing anthropology in corporate America,* ed. A. T. Jordan. Arlington, VA: American Anthropological Association.

Kleinman, Arthur. 1988. *Rethinking psychiatry: From cultural category to personal experience.* New York: Macmillan.

Kleinman, Arthur, Veena Das, and Margaret Lock, eds. 1997. *Social suffering.* Berkeley: University of California Press.

Klineberg, Otto. 1979. Foreword. In M. H. Segall, *Cross-cultural psychology.* Monterey, CA: Brooks/Cole.

Kluckhohn, Clyde. 1948. As an anthropologist views it. In *Sex habits of American men,* ed. A. Deutsch. Upper Saddle River, NJ: Prentice Hall.

Kluckhohn, Clyde. 1965. Recurrent themes in myths and mythmaking. In *The study of folklore,* ed. A. Dundes, 158–68. Upper Saddle River, NJ: Prentice Hall.

Knauft, Bruce M. 1978. Cargo cults and relational separation. *Behavior Science Research* 13:185–240.

Knecht, Peter. 2003. Aspects of shamanism: An introduction. In *Shamans in Asia,* eds. Clark Chilson and Peter Knecht, 1–30. London: RoutledgeCurzon.

Koch, Klaus-Friedrich, Soraya Altorki, Andrew Arno, and Letitia Hickson. 1977. Ritual reconciliation and the obviation of grievances: A comparative study in the ethnography of law. *Ethnology* 16:269–84.

Kolbert, Elizabeth. 2005. Last words. *The New Yorker* (June 6):46–59.

Komar, Debra A., and Jane E. Buikstra. 2008. *Forensic anthropology: Contemporary theory and practice.* New York: Oxford University Press.

Korbin, Jill E., ed. 1981. *Child abuse and neglect: Cross-cultural perspectives.* Berkeley: University of California Press.

Korotayev, Andrey, and Dmitri Bondarenko. 2000. Polygyny and democracy: A cross-cultural comparison. *Cross-Cultural Research* 34:190–208.

Kottak, Conrad P. 1999. The new ecological anthropology. *Current Anthropology* 101:23–35.

Kottak, Conrad Phillip. 1996. The media, development, and social change. In *Transforming societies, transforming anthropology,* ed. E. F. Moran. Ann Arbor: University of Michigan Press.

Kracke, Waud H. 1979. *Force and persuasion: Leadership in an Amazonian society.* Chicago: University of Chicago Press.

Krahn, H., T. F. Hartnagel, and J. W. Gartrell. 1986. Income inequality and homicide rates: Cross-national data and criminological theories. *Criminology* 24:269–95.

Krippner, Stanley. 1987. Dreams and shamanism. In *Shamanism,* comp. S. Nicholson, 125–32. Wheaton, IL: Theosophical Publishing House.

Kristof, Nicholas D. 1995. Japan's invisible minority: Better off than in past, but still outcasts. *New York Times,* International, November 30, A18.

Kristof, Nicholas D. 1997. Japan's invisible minority: Burakumin. *Brittanica Online,* December.

Kroeber, Theodora. 1967. *Ishi in two worlds.* Berkeley: University of California Press.

Kushner, Gilbert. 1991. Applied anthropology. In *Career explorations in human services,* eds. W. G. Emener and M. Darrow. Springfield, IL: Charles C. Thomas.

Kulick, Don. 1992. *Language shift and cultural reproduction.* Cambridge: Cambridge University Press.

Lakoff, Robin. 1973. Language and woman's place. *Language in Society* 2:45–80.

Lakoff, Robin. 1990. Why can't a woman be less like a man? In *Talking power,* ed. R. Lakoff. New York: Basic Books.

Lambert, Helen. 2001. Not talking about sex in India: Indirection and the communication of bodily intention. In *An anthropology of indirect communication,* eds. J. Hendry and C. W. Watson, 51–67. London: Routledge.

Lambert, Patricia M., Banks L. Leonard, Brian R. Billman, Richard A. Marlar, Margaret E. Newman, and Karl J. Reinhard. 2000 (April). Response to critique of the claim of cannibalism at Cowboy Wash. *American Antiquity* 65(2): 397–406.

Lambert, William W., Leigh Minturn Triandis, and Margery Wolf. 1959. Some correlates of beliefs in the malevolence and benevolence of supernatural beings: A cross-societal study. *Journal of Abnormal and Social Psychology* 58: 162–69.

Lamphere, Louise. 2006. Foreward: Taking stock—The transformation of feminist theorizing in anthropology. In *Feminist anthropology: Past, present, and future,* eds. Pamela L. Geller and Miranda K. Stockett, ix–xvi. Philadelphia: University of Pennsylvania Press.

Lancy, David F. 2007. Accounting for variability in mother-child play. *American Anthropologist* 109:273–84.

Lancy, David F. 2008. *The anthropology of childhood: Cherubs, chattel, changelings.* Cambridge: Cambridge University Press.

Lang, Sabine. 1999. Lesbians, men-women and two-spirits: Homosexuality and gender in Native American cultures. In *Female desires: Same-sex relations and transgender practices across cultures,* eds. E. Blackwood and S. E. Weiringa, 91–116. New York: Columbia University Press.

Langness, L. L. 1974. *The study of culture.* San Francisco: Lewis and Sharp.

Lareau, Annette. 2003. *Unequal childhoods: Class, race, and family life.* Berkeley, CA: University of California Press.

Larson, C. L., J. Aronoff, I. C. Sarinopoulos, and D. C. Zhu. 2009. Recognizing threat: A simple geometric shape activates neural circuitry for threat detection. *Journal of Cognitive Neuroscience* 21:1523–35.

Larson, C. L., J. Aronoff, and J. Stearns. 2007. The shape of threat: Simple geometric forms evoke rapid and sustained capture of attention. *Emotion* 7:526–34.

Lassiter, Luke. 2008. Moving past public anthropology and doing collaborative research. *NAPA Bulletin* 29:70–86.

Lassiter, Luke Eric, Hurley Goodall, Elizabeth Campbell, and Michelle Natasya Johnson, eds., 2004. *The other side of Middletown: Exploring Muncie's African American community.* Walnut Creek, CA: AltaMira Press.

Lawless, Robert, Vinson H. Sutlive, Jr., and Mario D. Zamora, eds. 1983. *Fieldwork: The human experience.* New York: Gordon and Breach.

Layton, Robert. 1992. *Australian rock art: A new synthesis.* Cambridge: Cambridge University Press.

Le, Huynh-Nhu. 2000. Never leave your little one alone: Raising an Ifaluk child. In *A world of babies: Imagined child care guides for seven societies,* eds. Judy DeLoache and Alma Gottlieb, 199–220. Cambridge: Cambridge University Press.

Leach, Jerry W. 1983. Introduction. In *The kula,* eds. J. W. Leach and E. Leach. Cambridge: Cambridge University Press.

Leacock, Eleanor, and Richard Lee. 1982. Introduction. In *Politics and history in band societies,* eds. E. Leacock and R. Lee. Cambridge: Cambridge University Press.

Lederman, Rena. 1990. Big men, large and small? Towards a comparative perspective. *Ethnology* 29:3–15.

Lee, Richard B. 1968. What hunters do for a living, or, how to make out on scarce resources. In *Man the hunter,* eds. R. B. Lee and I. DeVore. Chicago: Aldine.

Lee, Richard B. 1972. Population growth and the beginnings of sedentary life among the !Kung bushmen. In *Population growth,* ed. B. Spooner. Cambridge, MA: MIT Press.

Lee, Richard B. 1979. *The !Kung San: Men, women, and work in a foraging society.* Cambridge: Cambridge University Press.

Lees, Susan H., and Daniel G. Bates. 1974. The origins of specialized nomadic pastoralism: A systemic model. *American Antiquity* 39:187–93.

Leibowitz, Lila. 1978. *Females, males, families: A biosocial approach.* North Scituate, MA: Duxbury.

Leis, Nancy B. 1974. Women in groups: Ijaw women's associations. In *Woman, culture, and society,* eds. M. Z. Rosaldo and L. Lamphere. Stanford, CA: Stanford University Press.

Lenski, Gerhard. 1984/1966. *Power and privilege: A theory of social stratification.* Chapel Hill: University of North Carolina Press.

Leonhardt, David, and Geraldine Fabrikant. 2009. Rise of the super-rich hits a sobering wall. *New York Times,* August 20, p. A1 of the New York Edition.

Lepowsky, Maria. 1990. Big men, big women and cultural autonomy. *Ethnology* 29:35–50.

Leslie, C. 1976. Introduction. In *Asian medical systems: A comparative study,* ed. C. Leslie. Los Angeles: University of California Press.

Lett, James. 1996. Scientific anthropology. In *Encyclopedia of cultural anthropology,* eds. D. Levinson and M. Ember. New York: Henry Holt.

Levine, James A., Robert Weisell, Simon Chevassus, Claudio D. Martinez, and Barbara Burlingame. 2002. The distribution of work tasks for male and female children and adults separated by gender. In "Looking at Child Labor," *Science* (May 10):1025.

Levine, Nancy E. 1988. Women's work and infant feeding: A case from rural Nepal. *Ethnology* 27:231–51.

LeVine, Robert A. 1966. *Dreams and deeds: Achievement motivation in Nigeria.* Chicago: University of Chicago Press.

LeVine, Robert A. 1988. Human parental care: Universal goals, cultural strategies, individual behavior. In *Parental behavior in diverse societies,* eds. R. A. LeVine, P. M. Miller, and M. M. West. San Francisco: Jossey-Bass.

LeVine, Robert A. 2007. Ethnographic studies of childhood: A historical overview. *American Anthropologist* 109:247–60.

LeVine, Robert A., and Barbara B. Levine. 1963. Nyansongo: A Gusii community in Kenya. In *Six cultures,* ed. B. B. Whiting. New York: Wiley.

Levinson, David. 1989. *Family violence in cross-cultural perspective.* Newbury Park, CA: Sage.

Levinson, David, and Melvin Ember, eds. 1997. *American immigrant cultures: Builders of a nation,* 2 vols. New York: Macmillan Reference.

Lévi-Strauss, Claude. 1963a. The sorcerer and his magic. In C. Lévi-Strauss, *Structural anthropology.* New York: Basic Books.

Lévi-Strauss, Claude. 1963b. *Structural anthropology.* Trans. Claire Jacobson and Brooke Grundfest Schoepf. New York: Basic Books.

Lévi-Strauss, Claude. 1966. *The savage mind,* trans. George Weidenfeld and Nicolson, Ltd. Chicago: University of Chicago Press. [First published in French 1962.]

Lévi-Strauss, Claude. 1969a. *The elementary structures of kinship,* rev. ed., trans. James H. Bell and Ed. J. R. von Sturmer. Rodney Needham. Boston: Beacon Press. [First published in French 1949.]

Lévi-Strauss, Claude. 1969b. *The raw and the cooked,* trans. John Weightman and Doreen Weightman. New York: Harper & Row [First published in French 1964.]

Levy, Jerrold E. 1994. Hopi shamanism: A reappraisal. In *North American Indian anthropology: Essays on society and culture,* eds. Raymond J. DeMallie and Alfonzo Ortiz, 307–27. Norman: University of Oklahoma Press, as seen in eHRAF Collection of Ethnography on the Web.

Lewin, Tamar. 1994. Sex in America: Faithfulness in marriage is overwhelming. *New York Times,* National, October 7, A1, A18.

Lewis, Oscar. 1951. *Life in a Mexican village: Tepoztlan revisited.* Urbana: University of Illinois Press.

Lewis, Oscar (with the assistance of Victor Barnouw). 1958. *Village life in northern India.* Urbana: University of Illinois Press.

Lewontin, Richard. 1972. The apportionment of human diversity. *Evolutionary Biology* 6(1):381–98.

Lichter, Daniel T., Diane K. McLaughlin, George Kephart, and David J. Landry. 1992. Race and the retreat from marriage: A shortage of marriageable men? *American Sociological Review* 57:781–99.

Lieberman, Leslie Sue. 2004. Diabetes mellitus and medical anthropology. In *Encyclopedia of medical anthropology: Health and illness in the world's cultures,* vol. I, eds. C. R. Ember and M. Ember, 335–53. New York: Kluwer Academic Press/Plenum Publishers.

Light, Ivan, and Zhong Deng. 1995/1964. Gender differences in ROSCA participation within Korean business households in Los Angeles. In *Money-go-rounds: The importance of rotating savings and credit associations for women,* eds. S. Ardener and S. Burman, 217–40. Oxford: Berg.

Lightfoot, Kent G. 2005. The archaeology of colonialism: California in cross-cultural perspective. In *The archaeology of colonial encounters: Comparative perspectives,* ed. Gil J. Stein, 207–35. Santa Fe, NM: School of American Research.

Lingenfelter, Sherwood G. 2009. Yap: Changing roles of men and women. In MyAnthroLibrary, eds. C. R. Ember, M. Ember, and P. N. Peregrine. MyAnthroLibrary.com. Pearson.

Linton, Ralph. 1936. *The study of man.* New York: Appleton-Century-Crofts.

Linton, Ralph. 1945. *The cultural background of personality.* New York: Appleton-Century-Crofts.

Little, Kenneth. 1957. The role of voluntary associations in West African urbanization. *American Anthropologist* 59:582–93.

Little, Kenneth. 1965. *West African urbanization.* New York: Cambridge University Press.

Little, Kenneth. 1965/1966. The political function of the Poro. *Africa* 35:349–65; 36:62–71.

Lock, Margaret. 2009. Japan: Glimpses of everyday life. In MyAnthroLibrary, eds. C. R. Ember, M. Ember, and P. N. Peregrine. MyAnthroLibrary.com. Pearson.

Loftin, Colin K. 1971. Warfare and societal complexity: A cross-cultural study of organized fighting in preindustrial societies. Ph.D. dissertation, University of North Carolina at Chapel Hill.

Loftin, Colin, David McDowall, and James Boudouris. 1989. Economic change and homicide in Detroit, 1926–1979. In *Violence in America,* vol. 1: *The history of crime,* ed. T. R. Gurr, 163–77. Newbury Park, CA: Sage.

Lomax, Alan, ed. 1968. *Folk song style and culture.* American Association for the Advancement of Science Publication No. 88. Washington, DC.

Long, Susan Orpett. 2000. Introduction. In *Caring for the elderly in Japan and the U.S.,* ed. S. O. Long, 6–7. London: Routledge.

Longacre, William. 1970. Archaeology as anthropology: A case study. Anthropological papers of the University of Arizona, Number 17. Tucson: University of Arizona Press.

Los Angeles Times. 1994. Plundering earth is nothing new. News Service, as reported in the *New Haven Register,* June 12, pp. A18–A19.

Loustaunau, Martha O., and Elisa J. Sobo. 1997. *The cultural context of health, illness, and medicine.* Westport, CT: Bergin & Garvey.

Lovejoy, Arthur O. 1964. *The great chain of being: A study of the history of an idea.* Cambridge, MA: Harvard University Press.

Low, Bobbi. 1990a. Human responses to environmental extremeness and uncertainty. In *Risk and uncertainty in tribal and peasant economies,* ed. E. Cashdan. Boulder, CO: Westview.

Low, Bobbi. 1990b. Marriage systems and pathogen stress in human societies. *American Zoologist* 30:325–39.

Low, Bobbi S. 2009. Behavioral ecology, "sociobiology" and human behavior. In MyAnthroLibrary, eds. C. R. Ember, M. Ember, and P. N. Peregrine. MyAnthroLibrary.com. Pearson.

Lowe, Edward D. 2002. A widow, a child, and two lineages: Exploring kinship and attachment in Chuuk. *American Anthropologist* 104:123–37.

Lucy, John A. 1992. *Grammatical categories and cognition: A case study of the linguistic relativity hypothesis.* Cambridge: Cambridge University Press.

Luria, A. R. 1976. *Cognitive development: Its cultural and social foundations.* Cambridge, MA: Harvard University Press.

Lutz, Catherine. 1985. Depression and the translations of emotional worlds. In *Culture and depression,* eds. A. Kleinman and B. Good, 63–100. Berkeley: University of California Press.

Lynd, Robert S., and Helen Merrell Lynd. 1937. *Middletown in transition.* New York: Harcourt, Brace.

Lynd, Robert S., and Helen Merrell Lynd. 1929. *Middletown.* New York: Harcourt, Brace.

Lyons, Nona Plessner. 1988. Two perspectives: On self, relationships, and morality. In *Mapping the moral domain,* eds. C. Gilligan, J. V. Ward, and J. M. Taylor, 22–45. Cambridge, MA: Harvard University Press.

Lyttleton, Chris. 2000. *Endangered relations: Negotiating sex and AIDS in Thailand.* Bangkok: White Lotus Press.

Maccoby, Eleanor E., and Carol N. Jacklin. 1974. *The psychology of sex differences.* Stanford, CA: Stanford University Press.

MacDonald, Douglas H., and Barry S. Hewlett. 1999. Reproductive interests and forager mobility. *Current Anthropology* 40:501–23.

Magner, L. 1992. *A history of medicine.* New York: Marcel Dekker.

Mahony, Frank Joseph. 1971. *A Trukese theory of medicine.* Ann Arbor, MI: University Microfilms, 1070, as seen in the eHRAF Collection of Ethnography on the Web.

Malefijt, Annemarie De Waal. 1968. *Religion and culture: An introduction to anthropology of religion.* New York: Macmillan.

Malin, Edward. 1986. *Totem poles of the Pacific Northwest coast.* Portland, OR: Timber Press.

Malinowski, Bronislaw. 1920. Kula: The circulating exchange of valuables in the Archipelagoes of eastern New Guinea. *Man* 51(2):97–105.

Malinowski, Bronislaw. 1927. *Sex and repression in savage society.* London: Kegan Paul, Trench, Trubner.

Malinowski, Bronislaw. 1932. *The sexual life of savages in northwestern Melanesia.* New York: Halcyon House.

Malinowski, Bronislaw. 1939. The group and the individual in functional analysis. *American Journal of Sociology* 44:938–64.

Malinowski, Bronislaw. 1954a/1948. Magic, science, and religion. In B. Malinowski, *Magic, science, and religion and other essays.* Garden City, NY: Doubleday.

Mangin, William P. 1965. The role of regional associations in the adaptation of rural migrants to cities in Peru. In *Contemporary cultures and societies of Latin America,* eds. D. B. Heath and R. N. Adams, 311–23. New York: Random House.

Mangin, William. 1967. Latin American squatter settlements: A problem and a solution. *Latin American Research Review* 2:65–98.

Manhein, Mary H. 1999. *The bone lady: Life as a forensic anthropologist.* Baton Rouge: Louisiana State University Press.

Maquet, Jacques. 1986. *The aesthetic experience: An anthropologist looks at the visual arts.* New Haven, CT: Yale University Press.

Marano, Louis A. 1973 A macrohistoric trend toward world government. *Behavior Science Notes* 8:35–40.

Marcus, George E., and Michael M. J. Fischer. 1986. *Anthropology as cultural critique: An experimental moment in the human sciences.* Chicago: University of Chicago Press.

Marett, R. R. 1909. *The thresholds of religion.* London: Methuen.

Marks, Jonathan. 1994. Black, white, other: Racial categories are cultural constructs masquerading as biology. *Natural History* (December):32–35.

Marlowe, Frank W. 2003. A critical period for provisioning by Hadza men: Implications for pair bonding. *Evolution and Human Behavior* 24:217–29.

Marshall, Lorna. 1961. Sharing, talking and giving: Relief of social tensions among !Kung Bushmen. *Africa* 31:239–42.

Martin, M. Kay, and Barbara Voorhies. 1975. *Female of the species.* New York: Columbia University Press.

Mascie-Taylor, C. G. Nicholas. 1990. The biology of social class. In *Biosocial aspects of social class,* ed. C. G. N. Mascie-Taylor, 117–42. Oxford: Oxford University Press.

Maslow, Abraham H. 1964. *Religions, values, and peak-experiences.* Columbus: Ohio State University Press.

Mason, Philip. 1962. *Prospero's magic.* London: Oxford University Press.

Masumura, Wilfred T. 1977. Law and violence: A cross-cultural study. *Journal of Anthropological Research* 33:388–99.

Mathiassen, Therkel. 1928. *Material culture of Iglulik Eskimos.* Copenhagen: Glydendalske.

Matossian, Mary K. 1982. Ergot and the Salem witchcraft affair. *American Scientist* 70:355–57.

Matossian, Mary K. 1989. *Poisons of the past: Molds, epidemics, and history.* New Haven, CT: Yale University Press.

Maybury-Lewis, David. 1967. *Akwe-Shavante society.* Oxford: Clarendon Press.

Mayer, Philip, and Iona Mayer. 1970. Socialization by peers: The youth organization of the Red Xhosa. In *Socialization: The approach from social anthropology,* ed. Philip Mayer, 159–89. London: Tavistock.

Mayr, Ernst. 1982. *The growth of biological thought: Diversity, evolution, and inheritance.* Cambridge, MA: Belknap Press of Harvard University Press.

McCain, Garvin, and Erwin M. Segal. 1988. *The game of science.* 5th ed. Monterey, CA: Brooks/Cole.

McCarthy, Frederick D., and Margaret McArthur. 1960. The food quest and the time factor in Aboriginal economic life. In *Records of the Australian-American scientific expedition to Arnhem Land,* ed. C. P. Mountford, vol. 2: *Anthropology and Nutrition.* Melbourne: Melbourne University Press.

McClelland, David C. 1961. *The achieving society.* New York: Van Nostrand.

McCorriston, Joy, and Frank Hole. 1991. The ecology of seasonal stress and the origins of agriculture in the Near East. *American Anthropologist* 93:46–69.

McElreath, Richard, and Pontus Strimling. 2008. When natural selection favors imitation of parents. *Current Anthropology* 49:307–16.

McElroy, Ann, and Patricia Townsend, 2002. *Medical anthropology in ecological perspective.* 3rd ed. Boulder, CO: Westview.

McKee, Lauris A. 1984. Sex differentials in survivorship and the customary treatment of infants and children. *Medical Anthropology* 8:91–108.

McKeown, Adam. 2005. Chinese diaspora. In *Encyclopedia of diasporas: Immigrant and refugee cultures around the world,* vol. 1, 2 vols., eds. M. Ember, C. R. Ember, and I. Skoggard, 65–76. New York: Kluwer Academic/Plenum.

McNeill, William H. 1967. *A world history.* New York: Oxford University Press.

McNeill, William H. 1976. *Plagues and peoples.* Garden City, NY: Doubleday/Anchor.

McNeill, William H. 1998. *Plagues and peoples.* New York: Anchor Books/Doubleday.

Mead, Margaret. 1931. *Growing up in New Guinea.* London: Routledge & Kegan Paul.

Mead, Margaret. 1950/1935. *Sex and temperament in three primitive societies.* New York: Mentor.

Mead, Margaret. 1961/1928. *Coming of age in Samoa.* 3rd ed. New York: Morrow.

Meek, C. K. 1940. *Land law and custom in the colonies.* London: Oxford University Press.

Meggitt, Mervyn J. 1964. Male-female relationships in the highlands of Australian New Guinea. *American Anthropologist* 66:204–24.

Meggitt, Mervyn. 1977. *Blood is their argument: Warfare among the Mae Enga tribesmen of the New Guinea highlands.* Palo Alto, CA: Mayfield.

Meillassoux, Claude. 1968. *Urbanization of an African community.* Seattle: University of Washington Press.

Mellor, John W., and Sarah Gavian. 1987. Famine: Causes, prevention, and relief. *Science* (January 30):539–44.

Merrill, Elizabeth Bryant. 1987. Art styles as reflections of sociopolitical complexity. *Ethnology* 26:221–30.

Messer, Ellen. 1996. Hunger vulnerability from an anthropologist's food system perspective. In *Transforming societies, transforming anthropology,* ed. E. F. Moran. Ann Arbor: University of Michigan Press.

Middleton, John. 1971. The cult of the dead: Ancestors and ghosts. In *Reader in comparative religion,* 3rd ed., eds. W. A. Lessa and E. Z. Vogt. New York: Harper & Row.

Middleton, Russell. 1962. Brother-sister and father-daughter marriage in ancient Egypt. *American Sociological Review* 27:603–11.

Milanovic, Branko. 2005. *World's apart: Measuring international and global inequality* . Princeton: Princeton University Press.

Miller, Bruce G. 1992. Women and politics: Comparative evidence from the Northwest Coast. *Ethnology* 31:367–82.

Miller, Greg. 2004. Listen, baby. *Science* 12 (November).

Miller, Joan G. 1994. Cultural diversity in the morality of caring: Individually oriented versus duty-based interpersonal moral codes. *Cross-Cultural Research* 28:3–39.

Miner, Horace. 1956. Body rituals among the Nacirema. *American Anthropologist* 58:504–505.

Minturn, Leigh. 1993. *Sita's daughters: Coming out of Purdah: The Rajput women of Khalapur revisited.* New York: Oxford University Press.

Minturn, Leigh, and Jerry Stashak. 1982. Infanticide as a terminal abortion procedure. *Behavior Science Research* 17: 70–85.

Mintz, Sidney W. 1956. Canamelar: The subculture of a rural sugar plantation proletariat. In J. H. Steward et al., *The people of Puerto Rico.* Urbana: University of Illinois Press.

Miracle, Andrew W. 2009. A shaman to organizations. In MyAnthroLibrary, eds. C. R. Ember, M. Ember, and P. N. Peregrine. MyAnthroLibrary.com. Pearson.

Mitchell, Donald. 2009. Nimpkish: Complex foragers on the northwest coast of North America. In MyAnthroLibrary, eds. C. R. Ember, M. Ember, and P. N. Peregrine. MyAnthroLibrary.com. Pearson.

Moerman, Daniel E. 1997. Physiology and symbols: The anthropological implications of the placebo effect. In *The anthropology of medicine,* 3rd ed., eds. L. Romanucci-Ross, D. E. Moerman, and L. R. Tancredi, 240–53. Westport, CT: Bergin & Garvey.

Monot, Marc, et al. 2005. On the origin of leprosy. *Science* 308 (May 13):1040–42.

Monsutti, Alessandro. 2004. Cooperation, remittances, and kinship among the Hazaras. *Iranian Studies* 37:219–40.

Mooney, Kathleen A. 1978. The effects of rank and wealth on exchange among the coast Salish. *Ethnology* 17:391–406.

Moore, Carmella Caracci. 1988. An optimal scaling of Murdock's theories of illness data—An approach to the problem of interdependence. *Behavior Science Research* 22:161–79.

Moore, Carmella C. 1997. Is love always love? *Anthropology Newsletter* (November):8–9.

Moore, Carmella C., A. Kimball Romney, Ti-Lien Hsia, Craig D. Rusch. 1999. The universality of the semantic structure of emotion terms: Methods for the study of inter- and intra-cultural variability. *American Anthropologist* 101:529–546.

Moore, John H., and Janis E. Campbell. 2002. Confirming unilocal residence in Native North America. *Ethnology* 41:175–88.

Moore, Omar Khayyam. 1957. Divination: A new perspective. *American Anthropologist* 59:69–74.

Moran, Emilio F. 1993. *Through Amazon eyes: The human ecology of Amazonian populations.* Iowa City: University of Iowa Press.

Morgan, Lewis Henry. 1964/1877. *Ancient society.* Cambridge, MA: Harvard University Press.

Morris, John. 1938. *Living with Lepchas: A book about the Sikkim Himalayas.* London: Heinemann.

Morrison, Kathleen D., and Laura L. Junker. 2002. *Forager-traders in South and Southeast Asia: Long-term histories.* Cambridge: Cambridge University Press.

Mukerjee, Madhusree. 1996. Field notes: Interview with a parrot. *Scientific American* (April).

Mukhopadhyay, Carol C., and Patricia J. Higgins. 1988. Anthropological studies of women's status revisited: 1977–1987. *Annual Review of Anthropology* 17:461–95.

Muller, Edward N. 1997. Economic determinants of democracy. In *Inequality, democracy, and economic development,* ed. M. Midlarsky, 133–55. Cambridge: Cambridge University Press.

Munroe, Robert L., Robert Hulefeld, James M. Rodgers, Damon L. Tomeo, and Steven K. Yamazaki. 2000. Aggression among children in four cultures. *Cross-Cultural Research* 34:3–25.

Munroe, Robert L., and Ruth H. Munroe. 1969. A cross-cultural study of sex, gender, and social structure. *Ethnology* 8:206–11.

Munroe, Robert L., Ruth H. Munroe, and John W. M. Whiting. 1981. Male sex-role resolutions. In *Handbook of cross-cultural human development,* eds. R. H. Munroe, R. L. Munroe, and B. B. Whiting, 611–32. New York: Garland.

Munroe, Robert L., Ruth H. Munroe, and Stephen Winters. 1996. Cross-cultural correlates of the consonant-vowel (CV) syllable. *Cross-Cultural Research* 30:60–83.

Munroe, Ruth H., and Robert L. Munroe. 1980b. Infant experience and childhood affect among the Logoli: A longitudinal study. *Ethos* 8:295–315.

Munroe, Ruth H., Robert L. Munroe, and Harold S. Shimmin. 1984. Children's work in four cultures: Determinants and consequences. *American Anthropologist* 86:369–79.

Murdock, George P. 1949. *Social structure.* New York: Macmillan.

Murdock, George P. 1957. World ethnographic sample. *American Anthropologist* 59:664–87.

Murdock, George P. 1967. Ethnographic atlas: A summary. *Ethnology* 6: 109–236.

Murdock, George Peter. 1980. *Theories of illness: A world survey.* Pittsburgh PA: University of Pittsburgh Press.

Murdock, George P., and Caterina Provost. 1973. Factors in the division of labor by sex: A cross-cultural analysis. *Ethnology* 12:203–25.

Murdock, George P., and Douglas R. White. 1969. Standard cross-cultural sample. *Ethnology* 8: 329–69.

Murphy, Jane. 1981. Abnormal behavior in traditional societies: Labels, explanations, and social reactions. In *Handbook of cross-cultural human development,* eds. R. H. Munroe, R. L. Munroe, and B. B. Whiting. New York: Garland.

Murphy, Robert F. 1960. *Headhunter's heritage: Social and economic change among the Mundurucú.* Berkeley: University of California Press.

Murphy, Robert F., and Julian H. Steward. 1956. Tappers and trappers: Parallel process in acculturation. *Economic Development and Cultural Change* 4 (July):335–55.

Murray, Gerald F. 1997. The domestication of wood in Haiti: A case study in applied evolution. In *Applying cultural anthropology: An introductory reader,* eds. A. Podolefsky and P. J. Brown. Mountain View, CA: Mayfield.

Murray, G. F., and M. E. Bannister. 2004. Peasants, agroforesters, and anthropologists: A 20-year venture in income-generating trees and hedgerows in Haiti. *Agroforestry Systems* 61:383–97.

Myers, Fred R. 1988. Critical trends in the study of hunter-gatherers. *Annual Review of Anthropology* 17:261–82.

Nadel, S. F. 1935. Nupe state and community. *Africa* 8:257–303.

Nadel, S. F. 1942. *A black Byzantium: The kingdom of Nupe in Nigeria.* London: Oxford University Press.

Nag, Moni, Benjamin N. F. White, and R. Creighton Peet. 1978. An anthropological approach to the study of the economic value of children in Java and Nepal. *Current Anthropology* 19:293–301.

Nagata, Judith. 2001. Beyond theology: Toward an anthropology of "fundamentalism." *American Anthropologist* 103:481–98.

Nagel, Ernest. 1961. *The structure of science: Problems in the logic of scientific explanation.* New York: Harcourt, Brace & World.

Naroll, Raoul. 1961. Two solutions for Galton's problem. In *Readings in cross-cultural methodology,* ed. Frank Moore, 221–45. New Haven, CT: HRAF Press.

Naroll, Raoul. 1967. Imperial cycles and world order. *Peace Research Society: Papers* 7:83–101.

Naroll, Raoul. 1983. *The moral order: An introduction to the human situation.* Beverly Hills, CA: Sage.

Nash, Manning. 1989. *The cauldron of ethnicity in the modern world.* Chicago: University of Chicago Press.

National Coalition for the Homeless. 2008 (June). How many people experience homelessness? NCH Fact Sheet #2. http://www.nationalhomeless.org/factsheets/How_Many. html (accessed September 3, 2009).

National Science Foundation, Division of Science Resources Statistics. 2008. *Science and engineering doctorate awards: 2006.* Detailed Statistical Tables NSF 09-311. Arlington, VA. Available at http://www.nsf.gov/statistics/nsf09311/ (accessed August 14, 2009).

Nelson, Nici. 1995/1964. The Kiambu group: A successful women's ROSCA in Mathare Valley, Nairobi (1971 to 1990). In *Money-go-rounds: The importance of rotating savings and credit associations for women*, eds. S. Ardener and S. Burman, 49–69. Oxford: Berg.

Nepstead, Daniel C., Claudia M. Stickler, Britaldo Soares-Filho, and Frank Merry. 2008. Interactions among Amazon land use, forests, and climate: Prospects for a near-term forest tipping point. *Philosophical Transactions of the Royal Society* B, 363:1737–46.

Nerlove, Sara B. 1974. Women's workload and infant feeding practices: A relationship with demographic implications. *Ethnology* 13:207–14.

Nevins, Allan. 1927. *The American states during and after the revolution*. New York: Macmillan.

Newbury, Catherine. 1988. *The cohesion of oppression: Clientship and ethnicity in Rwanda, 1860–1960*. New York: Columbia University.

Newman, K. S. 1988. *Falling from grace: The experience of downward mobility in the American middle class*. New York: The Free Press.

Newman, K. S. 1993. *Declining fortunes: The withering of the American dream*. New York: Basic Books.

Newman, Katherine S. 1983. *Law and economic organization: A comparative study of preindustrial societies*. Cambridge, MA: Cambridge University Press.

Nicholls, David, ed. 1998. *The Cambridge history of American music*. Cambridge: Cambridge University Press.

Niehoff, Arthur H. 1966. *A casebook of social change*. Chicago: Aldine.

Nimkoff, M. F., and Russell Middleton. 1960. Types of family and types of economy. *American Journal of Sociology* 66: 215–25.

Nisbett, Richard E. 2009. Education is all in your mind. *New York Times*. Sunday Opinion, February 8, p. 12.

Nolan, Riall W. 2003. *Anthropology in practice: Building a career outside the academy*. Boulder: Lynne Rienner Publishers.

Noll, Richard. 1987. The presence of spirits in magic and madness. In *Shamanism*, comp. S. Nicholson, 47–61. Wheaton, IL: Theosophical Publishing House.

Norenzayan, Ara, and Azim F. Shariff. 2008. The origin and evolution of religious prosociality. *Science* 322 (October 3): 58–62.

Noss, Andrew J., and Barry S. Hewlett. 2001. The contexts of female hunting in central Africa. *American Anthropologist* 103:1024–40.

Nussbaum, Martha C. 1995. Introduction. In M. C. Nussbaum and J. Glover, *Women, culture, and development: A study of human capabilities*. Oxford: Clarendon Press.

Oboler, Regina Smith. 1980. Is the female husband a man: Woman/woman marriage among the Nandi of Kenya. *Ethnology* 19:69–88.

Oboler, Regina Smith. 2009. Nandi: From cattle-keepers to cash-crop farmers. In MyAnthroLibrary, eds. C. R. Ember, M. Ember, and P. N. Peregrine. MyAnthroLibrary.com. Pearson.

O'Brian, Robin. 1999. Who weaves and why? Weaving, loom complexity, and trade. *Cross-Cultural Research* 33:30–42.

O'Brien, Denise. 1977. Female husbands in southern Bantu societies. In *Sexual stratification*, ed. A. Schlegel, 109–26. New York: Columbia University Press.

Oerlemans, J. 2005. Extracting a climate signal from 169 glacial records. *Science* 38 (April 28):675–77.

Ogburn, William F. 1922. *Social change*. New York: Huebsch.

Okamura, Jonathan Y. 1983. Filipino hometown associations in Hawaii. *Ethnology* 22:341–53.

Oliver, Douglas L. 1955. *A Solomon Island society*. Cambridge, MA: Harvard University Press.

Oliver, Douglas L. 1974. *Ancient Tahitian society*, vol. 1: *Ethnography*. Honolulu: University of Hawaii Press.

Ortiz de Montellano, B. R., and C. H. Browner. 1985. Chemical bases for medicinal plant use in Oaxaca, Mexico. *Journal of Ethnopharmacology* 13:57–88.

Ortner, Sherry B. 1984. Theory in anthropology since the sixties. *Comparative Studies in Society and History* 26:126–66.

Otterbein, Keith. 1968. Internal war: A cross-cultural study. *American Anthropologist* 70:277–89.

Otterbein, Keith. 1970. *The evolution of war*. New Haven, CT: HRAF Press.

Otterbein, Keith. 1986. *The ultimate coercive sanction: A cross-cultural study of capital punishment*. New Haven, CT: HRAF Press.

Otterbein, Keith, and Charlotte Swanson Otterbein. 1965. An eye for an eye, a tooth for a tooth: A cross-cultural study of feuding. *American Anthropologist* 67:1470–82.

Oxby, Clare. 1983. Farmer groups in rural areas of the third world. *Community Development Journal* 18:50–59.

Paige, Jeffery M. 1975. *Agrarian revolution: Social movements and export agriculture in the underdeveloped world*. New York: Free Press.

Paine, Robert. 1994. *Herds of the tundra*. Washington, DC: Smithsonian Institution Press.

Palsson, Gisli. 1988. Hunters and gatherers of the sea. In *Hunters and gatherers. 1. History, evolution and social change*, eds. T. Ingold, D. Riches, and J. Woodburn. New York: St. Martin's Press.

Parker, Hilda, and Seymour Parker. 1986. Father-daughter sexual abuse: An emerging perspective. *American Journal of Orthopsychiatry* 56:531–49.

Parker, Seymour. 1976. The precultural basis of the incest taboo: Toward a biosocial theory. *American Anthropologist* 78:285–305.

Parker, Seymour. 1984. Cultural rules, rituals, and behavior regulation. *American Anthropologist* 86:584–600.

Pasternak, Burton. 1976. *Introduction to kinship and social organization*. Upper Saddle River, NJ: Prentice Hall.

Pasternak, Burton. 2009. Han: Pastoralists and farmers on a Chinese frontier. In MyAnthroLibrary, eds. C. R. Ember, M. Ember, and P. N. Peregrine. MyAnthroLibrary.com. Pearson.

Pasternak, Burton, Carol R. Ember, and Melvin Ember. 1976. On the conditions favoring extended family households. *Journal of Anthropological Research* 32:109–23.

Patterson, Orlando. 1982. *Slavery and social death: A comparative study*. Cambridge, MA: Harvard University Press.

Patterson, Orlando. 2000. Review of *One drop of blood: The American misadventure of race* by Scott L. Malcomson. *New York Times Book Review*, October 22, 2000, pp. 15–16.

Peacock, James L. 1986. *The anthropological lens: Harsh light, soft focus*. Cambridge: Cambridge University Press.

Peacock, Nadine, and Robert Bailey. 2009. Efe: investigating food and fertility in the Ituri rain forest. In MyAnthroLibrary, eds. C. R. Ember, M. Ember, and P. N. Peregrine. MyAnthroLibrary.com. Pearson.

Peak, Lois. 1991. *Learning to go to school in Japan: The transition from home to preschool*. Berkeley: University of California Press.

Pelto, Gretel H., Alan H. Goodman, and Darna L. Dufour. 2000. The biocultural perspective in nutritional anthropology. In *Nutritional anthropology: Biocultural perspectives on food and nutrition,* eds. Alan H. Goodman, Darna L. Dufour, and Gretel H. Pelto, 1–9. Mountain View, CA: Mayfield Publishing.

Pelto, Pertti J., and Ludger Müller-Wille. 1987. Snowmobiles: Technological revolution in the Arctic. In *Technology and social change,* 2nd ed., eds. H. R. Bernard and P. J. Pelto, 207–43. Prospect Heights, IL: Waveland Press.

Pelto, Pertti J., and Gretel H. Pelto. 1975. Intra-cultural diversity: Some theoretical issues. *American Ethnologist* 2:1–18.

Pepperberg, Irene Maxine. 1999. *The Alex studies: Cognitive and communicative abilities of grey parrots.* Cambridge, MA: Harvard University Press.

Peregrine, Peter. 1996. The birth of the gods revisited: A partial replication of Guy Swanson's (1960) cross-cultural study of religion. *Cross-Cultural Research* 30:84–112.

Peregrine, Peter N. 2001. Cross-cultural approaches in archaeology. *Annual Review of Anthropology* 30:1–18.

Peregrine, Peter N. 2007a. Racial hierarchy: I. Overview. In *Encyclopedia of race and racism,* ed. John H. Moore, 461–62. New York, Macmillian Reference.

Peregrine, Peter N. 2007b. Cultural correlates of ceramic styles. *Cross-Cultural Research* 41:223–35.

Peregrine, Peter N., Melvin Ember, and Carol R. Ember. 2004. Predicting the future state of the world using archaeological data: An exercise in archaeomancy. *Cross-Cultural Research* 38:133–46.

Perry, Donna L. 2005. Wolof women, economic liberalization, and the crisis of masculinity in rural Senegal. *Ethnology* 44:207–26.

Petersen, L. R., G. R. Lee, and G. J. Ellis. 1982. Social structure, socialization values, and disciplinary techniques: A cross-cultural analysis. *Journal of Marriage and the Family* 44: 131–42.

Pfaff, C. 1979. Constraints on language mixing. *Language* 55:291–318, as cited in *An introduction to sociolinguistics,* 2nd ed., ed. Wardhaugh. Oxford: Blackwell.

Phillips, Kevin. 1990. *The politics of rich and poor: Wealth and the American electorate in the Reagan aftermath.* New York: Random House.

Phillipson, D. W. 1976. Archaeology and Bantu linguistics. *World Archaeology* 8:65–82.

Piaget, Jean. 1970. Piaget's theory. In *Carmichael's manual of child psychology,* vol. 1, 3rd ed., ed. P. Mussen. New York: Wiley.

Picchi, Debra. 1991. The impact of an industrial agricultural project on the Bakairí Indians of central Brazil. *Human Organization* 50:26–38.

Picchi, Debra. 2009. Bakairí: The death of an Indian. In MyAnthroLibrary, eds. C. R. Ember, M. Ember, and P. N. Peregrine. MyAnthroLibrary.com. Pearson.

Plattner, Stuart, ed. 1985. *Markets and marketing.* Monographs in Economic Anthropology, No. 4. Lanham, MD: University Press of America.

Plattner, Stuart, ed. 1989a. *Economic Anthropology.* Stanford, CA: Stanford University Press.

Plattner, Stuart. 1989b. Marxism. In *Economic anthropology,* ed. S. Plattner. Stanford, CA: Stanford University Press.

Poggie, John J., Jr., Richard B. Pollnac, and Carl Gersuny. 1976. Risk as a basis for taboos among fishermen in southern New England. *Journal for the Scientific Study of Religion* 15:257–62.

Poggie, John J., Jr., and Richard B. Pollnac. 1988. Danger and rituals of avoidance among New England fishermen. *MAST: Maritime Anthropological Studies* 1:66–78.

Polanyi, Karl. 1957. The economy as instituted process. In *Trade and market in the early empires,* eds. K. Polanyi, C. M. Arensberg, and H. W. Pearson. New York: Free Press.

Pollier, Nicole. 2000. Commoditization, cash, and kinship in postcolonial Papua New Guinea. In *Commodities and globalization: Anthropological perspectives,* eds. Angelique Haugerud, M. Priscilla Stone, and Peter D. Little, 197–217. Lanham, MD: Rowman & Littlefield.

Popenoe, Rebecca. 2004. *Feeding desire: Fatness, beauty, and sexuality among a Saharan people.* London: Routledge.

Pospisil, Leopold. 1963. *The Kapauku Papuans of West New Guinea.* New York: Holt, Rinehart & Winston.

Powers, William K., and Marla N. Powers. 2009. Lakota: A study in cultural continuity. In MyAnthroLibrary, eds. C. R. Ember, M. Ember, and P. N. Peregrine. MyAnthroLibrary.com. Pearson.

Poyatos, Fernando. 2002. *Nonverbal communication across disciplines,* vol. 1. Philadelphia: John Benjamins.

Price, Sally. 1989. *Primitive art in civilized places.* Chicago: University of Chicago Press.

Price-Williams, Douglass. 1961. A study concerning concepts of conservation of quantities among primitive children. *Acta Psychologica* 18:297–305.

Pryor, Frederic L. 1977. *The origins of the economy: A comparative study of distribution in primitive and peasant economies.* New York: Academic Press.

Pryor, Frederic L. 2005. *Economic systems of foraging, agricultural, and industrial societies.* Cambridge: Cambridge University Press.

Public Law 101-601 (25 U.S.C. 3001–3013).

Quandt, Sara A. 1996. Nutrition in anthropology. In *Handbook of medical anthropology,* rev. ed., eds. C. F. Sargent and T. M. Johnson, 272–89. Westport, CT: Greenwood Press.

Quinn, Naomi. 1977. Anthropological studies on women's status. *Annual Review of Anthropology* 6:181–225.

Radcliffe-Brown, A. R. 1922. *The Andaman Islanders: A study in social anthropology.* Cambridge: Cambridge University Press.

Radcliffe-Brown, A. R. 1952. *Structure and function in primitive society.* London: Cohen & West.

Rambo, Lewis R. 2003. Anthropology and the study of conversion. In *The anthropology of religious conversion,* eds. Andrew Buckser and Stephen D. Glazier, 211–22. Lanham, MD: Roman & Littlefield.

Rappaport, Roy A. 1967. Ritual regulation of environmental relations among a New Guinea People. *Ethnology* 6:17–30.

Ravesloot, John. 1997. Changing Native American perceptions of archaeology and archaeologists. In *Native Americans and archaeologists,* eds. N. Swidler et al. Walnut Creek, CA: AltaMira Press.

Ray, Verne F. 1954. *The Sanpoil and Nespelem: Salishan peoples of northeastern Washington.* New Haven, CT: HRAF Press.

Raybeck, Douglas. 1998. Toward more holistic explanations: Cross-cultural research and cross-level analysis. *Cross-Cultural Research* 32:123–42.

Raybeck, Douglas, J. Shoobe, and J. Grauberger. 1989. Women, stress and participation in possession cults: A reexamination of the calcium deficiency hypothesis. *Medical Anthropology Quarterly* 3:139–61.

Reff, Daniel T. 2005. *Plagues, priests, and demons: Sacred narratives and the rise of Christianity in the Old World and the New.* Cambridge: Cambridge University Press.

Reisner, Marc. 1993. *Cadillac desert: The American West and its disappearing water.* Rev. ed. New York: Penguin.

Renfrew, Colin. 1987. *Archaeology and language: The puzzle of Indo-European origins.* London: Jonathan Cape.

Revkin, Andrew C. 2005. Tracking the imperiled bluefin from ocean to sushi platter. *The New York Times,* May 3, pp. F1, F4.

Rhoades, R. E. 2001. *Bridging human and ecological landscapes.* Dubuque, IA: Kendall/Hunt.

Rhoades, Robert E. 2005. Agricultural anthropology. In *Applied anthropology: Domains of application,* eds. Satish Kedia and John van Willigen, 61–85. Westport, CT: Praeger.

Richardson, Curtis J., Curtis J, Peter Reiss, Najah A. Hussain, Azzam J. Alwash, and Douglas J. Pool. 2005. The restoration potential of the Mesopotamian marshes of Iraq. *Science* 307 (February 25):1307–11.

Richerson, Peter J., and Robert Boyd. 2005. *Not by genes alone: How culture transformed human evolution.* Chicago: University of Chicago Press.

Ritter, Madeline Lattman. 1980. The conditions favoring age-set organization. *Journal of Anthropological Research* 36:87–104.

Rivers, W. H. R. 1967/1906. *The Todas.* Oosterhout, N.B., The Netherlands: Anthropological Publications.

Roberts, John M. 1967. Oaths, autonomic ordeals, and power. In *Cross-cultural approaches,* ed. C. S. Ford. New Haven, CT: HRAF Press.

Roberts, John M., Malcolm J. Arth, and Robert R. Bush. 1959. Games in culture. *American Anthropologist* 61:597–605.

Roberts, John M., and Brian Sutton-Smith. 1962. Child training and game involvement. *Ethnology* 1:166–85.

Rodwin, Lloyd, and Bishwapriya Sanyal. 1987. Shelter, settlement, and development: An overview. In *Shelter, settlement, and development,* ed. L. Rodwin, 3–31. Boston: Allen & Unwin.

Roes, Frans L., and Michel Raymond. 2003. Belief in moralizing gods. *Evolution and Human Behavior* 24:126–35.

Rogers, Everett M. 1983. *Diffusion of innovations.* 3rd ed. New York: Free Press.

Rogoff, Barbara. 1981. Schooling and the development of cognitive skills. In *Handbook of cross-cultural psychology,* vol. 4: *Developmental psychology,* eds. H. C. Triandis and A. Heron. Boston: Allyn & Bacon.

Rogoff, Barbara. 1990. *Apprenticeship in thinking: Cognitive development in social context.* New York: Oxford University Press.

Rohner, Ronald P. 1975. *They love me, they love me not: A worldwide study of the effects of parental acceptance and rejection.* New Haven, CT: HRAF Press.

Rohner, Ronald P. 1976. Sex differences in aggression: Phylogenetic and enculturation perspectives. *Ethos* 4:57–72.

Rohner, Ronald P., and Preston A. Britner. 2002. Worldwide mental health correlates of parental acceptance-rejection: Review of cross-cultural research and intracultural evidence. *Cross-Cultural Research* 36:16–47.

Romaine, Suzanne. 1994. *Language in society: An introduction to sociolinguistics.* Oxford: Oxford University Press.

Romney, A. Kimball, Susan C. Weller, and William H. Batchelder. 1986. Culture as consensus: A theory of culture and informant accuracy. *American Anthropologist* 88: 313–38.

Roosens, Eugeen E. 1989. *Creating ethnicity: The process of ethnogenesis.* Newbury Park, CA: Sage Publications.

Roosevelt, Anna Curtenius. 1992. Secrets of the forest. *The Sciences* (November/December):22–28.

Roscoe, Paul. 2002. The hunters and gatherers of New Guinea. *Current Anthropology* 43:153–162.

Roseberry, William. 1988. Political economy. *Annual Review of Anthropology* 17:161–259.

Rosenblatt, Paul C. 2009. Human rights violations. In MyAnthroLibrary, eds. C. R. Ember, M. Ember, and P. N. Peregrine. MyAnthroLibrary.com. Pearson.

Rosenblatt, Paul C., R. Patricia Walsh, and Douglas A. Jackson. 1976. *Grief and mourning in cross-cultural perspective.* New Haven, CT: HRAF Press.

Ross, Marc Howard. 1981. Socioeconomic complexity, socialization, and political differentiation: A cross-cultural study. *Ethos* 9:217–47.

Ross, Marc Howard. 1985. Internal and external conflict and violence. *Journal of Conflict Resolution* 29:547–79.

Ross, Marc Howard. 1986. Female political participation: A cross-cultural explanation. *American Anthropologist* 88: 843–58.

Ross, Marc Howard. 1988. Political organization and political participation: Exit, voice, and loyalty in preindustrial societies. *Comparative Politics* 21:73–89.

Ross, Marc Howard. 2009a. Ethnocentrism and ethnic conflict. In MyAnthroLibrary, eds. C. R. Ember, M. Ember, and P. N. Peregrine. MyAnthroLibrary.com. Pearson.

Ross, Marc Howard. 2009b. Political participation. In MyAnthroLibrary, eds. C. R. Ember, M. Ember, and P. N. Peregrine. MyAnthroLibrary.com. Pearson.

Roth, Eric Abella. 2001. Demise of the sepaade tradition: Cultural and biological explanations. *American Anthropologist* 103:1014–23.

Rubel, Arthur J., and Michael R. Hass. 1996. Ethnomedicine. In *Medical anthropology,* eds. T. M. Johnson and C. F. Sargent, 115–31. Westporft, CT: Praeger.

Rubel, Arthur J., Carl O'Nell, and Rolando Collado-Ardón (with the assistance of John Krejci and Jean Krejci). 1984. *Susto: A folk illness.* Berkeley: University of California Press.

Rubel, Paula, and Abraham Rosman. 1996. Structuralism and poststructuralism. In *Encyclopedia of cultural anthropology,* vol. 4., eds. David Levinson and Melvin Ember, 1263–72. New York: Henry Holt.

Rubin, J. Z., F. J. Provenzano, and R. F. Haskett. 1974. The eye of the beholder: Parents' views on the sex of new borns. *American Journal of Orthopsychiatry* 44:512–19.

Rudan, Igor, and Harry Campbell. 2004. Five reasons why inbreeding may have considerable effect on post-reproductive human health. *Collegium Antropologicum* 28:943–50.

Rudmin, Floyd Webster. 1988. Dominance, social control, and ownership: A history and a cross-cultural study of motivations for private property. *Behavior Science Research* 22:130–60.

Rummel, R. J. 2002a. "Death by Government." Chapter 1. Accessed at http://www.hawaii.edu/powerkills/DBG.CHAP1.HTM.

Rummel, R. J. 2002b. Democracies are less warlike than other regimes. Accessed at http://www.hawaii.edu/powerkills/DP95.htm.

Rummel, R. J. 2002c. Statistics of democide. Chapter 17. Accessed at http://www.hawaii.edu/powerkills/SOD.CHAP17.HTM.

Rummel, R. J. 2002d. Statistics of democide. Chapter 21. Accessed at http://www.hawaii.edu/powerkills/SOD.CHAP21.HTM.

Rummel, R. J. 2009. 20th century democide. http://www.hawaii.edu/powerkills/20th.htm (accessed September 5, 2009).

Ruskin, John. 1963. Of king's treasures. In *The genius of John Ruskin*, ed. J. D. Rosenberg. New York: Braziller.

Russell, Elbert W. 1972. Factors of human aggression. *Behavior Science Notes* 7:275–312.

Russett, Bruce (with the collaboration of William Antholis, Carol R. Ember, Melvin Ember, and Zeev Maoz). 1993. *Grasping the democratic peace: Principles for a post–cold war world*. Princeton, NJ: Princeton University Press.

Russett, Bruce, and John R. Oneal. 2001. *Triangulating peace: Democracy, interdependence, and international organizations*. New York: Norton.

Sahlins, Marshall D. 1958. *Social stratification in Polynesia*. Seattle: University of Washington Press.

Sahlins, Marshall D. 1961. The segmentary lineage: An organization of predatory expansion. *American Anthropologist* 63:332–45.

Sahlins, Marshall D. 1962. *Moala: Culture and nature on a Fijian island*. Ann Arbor: University of Michigan Press.

Sahlins, Marshall D. 1963. Poor man, rich man, big-man, chief: Political types in Melanesia and Polynesia. *Comparative Studies in Society and History* 5:285–303.

Sahlins, Marshall D. 1972. *Stone Age economics*. Chicago: Aldine.

Sahlins, Marshall. 1983. Other times, other customs: The anthropology of history. *American Anthropologist* 85:517–44.

Sahlins, Marshall, and Elman Service. 1960. *Evolution and culture*. Ann Arbor: University of Michigan Press.

Salzman, Philip Carl. 1996. Pastoralism. In *Encyclopedia of cultural anthropology*, vol. 3, eds D. Levinson and M. Ember, 899–905. New York: Henry Holt.

Salzman, Philip Carl. 1999. Is inequality universal? *Current Anthropology* 40:31–61.

Salzman, Philip Carl. 2002. Pastoral nomads: Some general observations based on research in Iran. *Journal of Anthropological Research* 58:245–64.

Sanday, Peggy R. 1973. Toward a theory of the status of women. *American Anthropologist* 75:1682–700.

Sanday, Peggy R. 1974. Female status in the public domain. In *Woman, culture, and society*, eds. M. Z. Rosaldo and L. Lamphere, 189–206. Stanford, CA: Stanford University Press.

Sanderson, Stephen K. 1995. Expanding world commercialization: The link between world-systems and civilizations. In *Civilizations and world systems: Studying world-historical change*, ed. S. K. Sanderson. Walnut Creek, CA: AltaMira Press.

Sapir, Edward. 1931. Conceptual categories in primitive languages. Paper presented at the autumn meeting of the National Academy of Sciences, New Haven, CT. Published in *Science* 74.

Sapir, Edward. 1938. Why cultural anthropology needs the psychiatrist. *Psychiatry* 1:7–12.

Sapir, Edward, and M. Swadesh. 1964. American Indian grammatical categories. In *Language in culture and society*, ed. D. Hymes. New York: Harper & Row.

Sattler, Richard A. 1996. Remnants, renegades, and runaways: Seminole ethnogenesis reconsidered. In *Ethnogenesis in the Americas*, J. D. Hill, 36–69. Iowa City: University of Iowa Press.

Savage-Rumbaugh, E. S. 1992. Language training of apes. In *The Cambridge encyclopedia of human evolution*, eds. S. Jones, R. Martin, and D. Pilbeam. New York: Cambridge University Press.

Scaglion, Richard. 1990. Legal adaptation in a Papua New Guinea village court. *Ethnology* 29:17–33.

Scaglion, Richard. 2009a. Abelam: Giant yams and cycles of sex, warfare and ritual. In MyAnthroLibrary, eds. C. R. Ember, M. Ember, and P. N. Peregrine. MyAnthroLibrary.com.Pearson.

Scaglion, Richard. 2009b. Law and society. In MyAnthroLibrary, eds. C. R. Ember, M. Ember, and P. N. Peregrine. MyAnthroLibrary.com. Pearson.

Scaglion, Richard, and Rose Whittingham. 1985. Female plaintiffs and sex-related disputes in rural Papua New Guinea. In *Domestic violence in Papua New Guinea*, ed. S. Toft. Port Moresby, Papua New Guinea: Law Reform Commission.

Scarr, Sandra, and Kathleen McCartney. 1983. How people make their own environments: A theory of genotype–environment effects. *Child Development* 54:424–35.

Schlegel, Alice. 1989. Gender issues and cross-cultural research. *Behavior Science Research* 23:265–80.

Schlegel, Alice. 1991. Status, property, and the value on virginity. *American Ethnologist* 18:719–34.

Schlegel, Alice. The status of women. 2009. In MyAnthroLibrary, eds. C. R. Ember, M. Ember, and P. N. Peregrine. MyAnthroLibrary.com. Pearson.

Schlegel, Alice, and Herbert Barry III. 1986. The cultural consequences of female contribution to subsistence. *American Anthropologist* 88:142–50.

Schlegel, Alice, and Herbert Barry III. 1991. *Adolescence: An anthropological inquiry*. New York: Free Press.

Schlegel, Alice, and Rohn Eloul. 1987. A new coding of marriage transactions. *Behavior Science Research* 21:118–40.

Schlegel, Alice, and Rohn Eloul. 1988. Marriage transactions: Labor, property, and status. *American Anthropologist* 90:291–309.

Schneider, David M. 1961a. The distinctive features of matrilineal descent groups. In *Matrilineal kinship*, eds. D. M. Schneider and K. Gough, 1–35. Berkeley: University of California Press.

Schneider, David M. 1961b. Truk. In *Matrilineal kinship*, eds. D. M. Schneider and K. Gough, 202–33. Berkeley: University of California Press.

Schoepf, B. 1988. Women, AIDS and economic crisis in central Africa. *Canadian Journal of African Studies* 22:625–44.

Schrauf, Robert W. 1999. Mother tongue maintenance among North American ethnic groups. *Cross-Cultural Research* 33:175–92.

Schrire, Carmel, ed. 1984a. *Past and present in hunter-gatherer studies*. Orlando, FL: Academic Press.

Schrire, Carmel. 1984b. Wild surmises on savage thoughts. In *Past and present in hunter-gatherer studies*, ed. C. Schrire, 1–25. Orlando, FL: Academic Press.

Schwartz, Richard D. 1954. Social factors in the development of legal control: A case study of two Israeli settlements. *Yale Law Journal* 63 (February):471–91.

Scientific American. 2005. Crossroads for Planet Earth. *Scientific American*. Special Issue, September.

Scott, Janny, and David Leonhardt. 2005. Class in America: Shadowy lines that still divide. *New York Times* National, May 15, pp. 1, 26.

Scribner, Sylvia, and Michael Cole. 1981. *The psychology of literacy.* Cambridge, MA: Harvard University Press.

Scudder, Thayer. 1978. Opportunities, issues and achievements in development anthropology since the mid-1960s: A personal view. In *Applied anthropology in America*, 2nd ed., eds. E. M. Eddy and W. L. Partridge. New York: Columbia University Press.

Seemanova, Eva. 1971. A study of children of incestuous matings. *Human Heredity* 21:108–28.

Segal, Edwin S. 2004. Cultural constructions of gender. In *Encyclopedia of sex and gender: Men and women in the world's cultures*, vol 1., eds. C. R. Ember and M. Ember, 3–10. New York: Kluwer Academic/Plenum.

Segal, Robert A. 1987. *Joseph Campbell: An introduction.* New York: Garland.

Segall, Marshall, Pierre R. Dasen, John W. Berry, and Ype H. Poortinga. 1990. *Human behavior in global perspective: An introduction to cross-cultural psychology.* New York: Pergamon.

Sellen, Daniel W., and Daniel J. Hruschka. 2004. Extracted-food resource-defense polygyny in Native western North American societies at contact. *Current Anthropology* 45:707–714.

Sengupta, Somini. 2002. Money from kin abroad helps Bengalis get by. *New York Times,* June 24, A3.

Senner, Wayne M. 1989b. Theories and myths on the origins of writing: A historical overview. In *The origins of writing*, ed. W. M. Senner. Lincoln: University of Nebraska Press.

Service, Elman R. 1962. *Primitive social organization: An evolutionary perspective.* New York: Random House.

Service, Elman R. 1978. *Profiles in ethnology.* 3rd ed. New York: Harper & Row.

Service, Elman R. 1979. *The hunters.* 2nd ed. Upper Saddle River, NJ: Prentice Hall.

Seyfarth, Robert M., and Dorothy L. Cheney. 1982. How monkeys see the world: A review of recent research on East African vervet monkeys. In *Primate communication,* eds. C. T. Snowdon, C. H. Brown, and M. R. Petersen. New York: Cambridge University Press.

Shankman, Paul. 1991. Culture contact, cultural ecology, and Dani warfare. *Man* 26:299–321.

Shankman, Paul. 2009. Sex, lies, and anthropologists: Margaret Mead, Derek Freeman, and Samoa. In MyAnthroLibrary, eds. C. R. Ember, M. Ember, and P. N. Peregrine. MyAnthroLibrary.com. Pearson.

Sheils, Dean. 1975. Toward a unified theory of ancestor worship: A cross-cultural study. *Social Forces* 54:427–40.

Sheils, Dean. 1980. A comparative study of human sacrifice. *Behavior Science Research* 15:245–62.

Shen, Xuefei, and Robert F. Siliciano. 2000. Preventing AIDS but not HIV-1 infection with a DNA vaccine. *Science* (October 20):463–65.

Shibamoto, Janet S. 1987. The womanly woman: Japanese female speech. In *Language, gender, and sex in comparative perspective,* eds. S. U. Philips, S. Steele, and C. Tanz. Cambridge: Cambridge University Press.

Shulman, Seth. 1993. Nurturing native tongues. *Technology Review* (May/June):16.

Shuy, Roger. 1960. Sociolinguistic research at the Center for Applied Linguistics: The correlation of language and sex. *Giornata internazionale di sociolinguistica.* Rome: Palazzo Baldassini.

Sih, Andrew, and Katharine A. Milton. 1985. Optimal diet theory: Should the !Kung eat mongongos? *American Anthropologist* 87:395–401.

Silk, Joan. 1980. Adoption and kinship in Oceania. *American Anthropologist* 82:799–820.

Silver, Harry R. 1981. Calculating risks: The socioeconomic foundations of aesthetic innovation in an Ashanti carving community. *Ethnology* 20:101–14.

Simmons, Janie, Paul Farmer, and Brooke G. Schoepf. 1996. A global perspective. In *Women, poverty, and AIDS: Sex, drugs, and structural violence,* eds. P. Farmer, M. Connors, and J. Simmons, 39–90. Monroe, ME: Common Courage Press.

Simpson, S. P., and Ruth Field. 1946. Law and the social sciences. *Virginia Law Review* 32:858.

Singer, J. David. 1980. Accounting for international war: The state of the discipline. *Annual Review of Sociology* 6:349–67.

Sipes, Richard G. 1973. War, sports, and aggression: An empirical test of two rival theories. *American Anthropologist* 75:64–86.

Skomal, Susan N., and Edgar C. Polomé, eds. 1987. *Proto-Indo-European: The archaeology of a linguistic problem.* Washington, DC: Washington Institute for the Study of Man.

Slayman, Andrew. 1997. A battle over old bones. *Archaeology* 50(1):16–23.

Slocum, Sally. 1975. Woman the gatherer: Male bias in anthropology. In *Toward an Anthropology of Women,* ed. R. Reiter. New York: Monthly Review Press.

Small, Meredith. 1997. Our babies, ourselves. *Natural History* (October):42–51.

Smedley, Audrey. 2004. *Women creating patrilyny.* Walnut Creek, CA: AltaMira.

Smedley, Brian D., Adrienne Y. Stith, and Alan R. Nelson, eds. 2003. *Unequal treatment: confronting racial and ethnic disparities in health care.* Washington, DC: National Academy Press.

Smith, Eric A. 1983. Anthropological applications of optimal foraging theory: A critical review. *Current Anthropology* 24:625–40.

Smith, Michael G. 1966. Preindustrial stratification systems. In *Social structure and mobility in economic development,* eds. N. J. Smelser and S. M. Lipset. Chicago: Aldine.

Smith, Waldemar R. 1977. *The fiesta system and economic change.* New York: Columbia University Press.

Snowdon, Charles T. 1999. An empiricist view of language evolution and development. In *The origins of language,* ed. B. J. King, 79–114. Santa Fe: School of American Research Press.

Society for American Archaeology. 2009. FAQs for students. http://www.saa.org/ForthePublic/FAQs/ForStudents/tabid/101/Default.aspx (accessed August 26, 2009).

Solon, Gary. 2002. Cross-country differences in intergenerational earnings mobility. *Journal of Economic Perspectives* 16:59–66.

Sosis, Richard. 2002. Patch choice decisions among Ifaluk fishers. *American Anthropologist* 104:583–98.

Sosis, Richard, and Eric R. Bressler. 2003. Cooperation and commune longevity: A test of the costly signaling theory of religion. *Cross-Cultural Research* 37:211–39.

Southworth, Franklin C., and Chandler J. Daswani. 1974. *Foundations of linguistics.* New York: Free Press.

Spanos, Nicholas P. 1983. Ergotism and the Salem witch panic: A critical analysis and an alternative conceptualization. *Journal of the History of the Behavioral Sciences* 19: 358–69.

Spencer, Robert F. 1968. Spouse-exchange among the North Alaskan Eskimo. In *Marriage, family and residence,* eds. P. Bohannan and J. Middleton. Garden City, NY: Natural History Press.

Sperber, Dan. 1985. *On anthropological knowledge: Three essays.* Cambridge: Cambridge University Press.

Speth, John D., and Katherine A. Spielmann. 1983. Energy source, protein metabolism, and hunter-gatherer subsistence strategies. *Journal of Anthropological Archaeology* 2: 1–31.

Spiro, Melford E. 1982. *Oedipus in the Trobriands.* Chicago: University of Chicago Press.

Spiro, Melford. 1993. Is the Western conception of the self "peculiar" within the context of the world cultures? *Ethos* 21:107–53.

Spiro, Melford E., and Roy G. D'Andrade. 1958. A cross-cultural study of some supernatural beliefs. *American Anthropologist* 60:456–66.

Spring, Anita. 2000a. Agricultural commercialization and women farmers in Kenya. In *Women farmers and commercial ventures: Increasing food security in developing countries,* ed. Anita Spring, 317–41. Boulder, CO: Lynne Rienner Publishers.

Spring, Anita. 2000b. Commercialization and women farmers: Old paradigms and new themes. In *Women farmers and commercial ventures: Increasing food security in developing countries,* ed. Anita Spring, 1–37. Boulder, CO: Lynne Rienner Publishers.

Spring, Anita, ed. 2000c. *Women farmers and commercial ventures: Increasing food security in developing countries.* Boulder, CO, Lynne Rienner Publishers.

Stairs, Arlene. 1992. Self-image, world-image: Speculations on identity from experiences with Inuit. *Ethos* 20:116–26.

Stark, Rodney. 1985. *The future of religion: Secularization, revival and cult formation.* Berkeley: University of California Press.

Stark, Rodney. 1996. *The rise of Christianity: A sociologist reconsiders history.* Princeton, NJ: Princeton University Press.

Stark, Rodney. 2001. Gods, rituals and the moral order. *Journal for the Scientific Study of Religion* 40:619–36.

Stark, Rodney, and Roger Finke. 2000. *Acts of faith: explaining the human side of religion.* Berkeley: University of California Press.

Steiner, Christopher B. 1990. Body personal and body politic: Adornment and leadership in cross-cultural perspective. *Anthropos* 85:431–45.

Stephens, William N. 1963. *The family in cross-cultural perspective.* New York: Holt, Rinehart & Winston.

Stephens, William N. 1972. A cross-cultural study of modesty. *Behavior Science Research* 7:1–28.

Stern, Curt. 1973. *Principles of human genetics.* 3rd ed. San Francisco: W. H. Freeman.

Stevens, Phillips, Jr. 1996. Religion. In *Encyclopedia of cultural anthropology,* 4 vols., vol. 3, eds. D. Levinson and M. Ember, 1088–100. New York: Henry Holt.

Steward, Julian H. 1955a. The concept and method of cultural ecology. In J. H. Steward, *Theory of culture change.* Urbana: University of Illinois Press.

Steward, Julian H. 1955b. *Theory of culture change.* Urbana: University of Illinois Press.

Steward, Julian H., and Louis C. Faron. 1959. *Native peoples of South America.* New York: McGraw-Hill.

Stimpson, David, Larry Jensen, and Wayne Neff. 1992. Cross-cultural gender differences in preference for a caring morality. *Journal of Social Psychology* 132:317–22.

Stini, William A. 1971. Evolutionary implications of changing nutritional patterns in human populations. *American Anthropologist* 73:1019–30.

Stockett, Miranda K., and Pamela L. Geller. 2006. Introduction: Feminist anthropology: Perspectives on our past, present, and future. In *Feminist anthropology: Past, present, and future,* eds. P. L. Geller and M. K. Stockett, 1–19. Philadelphia: University of Pennsylvania Press.

Stodder, James. 1995. The evolution of complexity in primitive exchange. *Journal of Comparative Economics* 20:205.

Stogdill, Ralph M. 1974. *Handbook of leadership: A survey of theory and research.* New York: Macmillan.

Stokstad, Erik. 2008. Privatization prevents collapse of fish stocks, global analysis shows. *Science* 321:1619.

Straus, Murray A. 1991. Physical violence in American families: Incidence rates, causes, and trends. In *Abused and battered,* eds. D. D. Knudsen and J. L. Miller, 17–34. New York: Aldine.

Straus, Murray A. 1995. Trends in cultural norms and rates of partner violence: An update to 1992. In *Understanding partner violence: Prevalence, causes, consequences, and solutions,* eds. S. M. Stith and M. A. Straus, 30–33. Minneapolis, MN: National Council on Family Relations. http:// pubpages.unh.edu/~mas2/v56.pdf/ (accessed August 2002).

Straus, Murray A. 2001. Physical aggression in the family: Prevalence rates, links to non-family violence, and implications for primary prevention of societal violence. In *Prevention and control of aggression and the impact on its victims,* ed. M. Martinez, 181–200. New York: Kluwer Academic/Plenum.

Straus, Murray A. 2009. Prevalence and social causes of corporal punishment by parents in world perspective. Paper presented at the annual meeting of the Society for Cross-Cultural Research, Las Vegas, Nevada, February 20, 2009.

Straus, Murray A., and Glenda Kaufman Kantor. 1994. Change in spouse assault rates from 1975 to 1992: A comparison of three national surveys in the United States. Paper presented at the 13th World Congress of Sociology, Bielefeld, Germany. http://pubpages.unh.edu/~mas2/v55.pdf/ (accessed August 2002).

Straus, Murray A., and Glenda Kaufman Kantor. 1995. Trends in physical abuse by parents from 1975 to 1992: A comparison of three national surveys. Paper presented at the annual meeting of the American Society of Criminology, Boston, November 18. http://pubpages.unh.edu/~mas2/V57.pdf/ (accessed August 2002).

Straus, Murray A., and Carrie L. Yodanis. 1996. Corporal punishment in adolescence and physical assaults on spouses in later life: What accounts for the link?" *Journal of Marriage and the Family* 58:825–41.

Suárez-Orozco, Marcelo. 1992. A grammar of terror: Psycho-cultural responses to state terrorism in dirty war and post-dirty war Argentina. In *The paths to domination, resistance, and terror,* eds. C. Nordstrom and J. Martin, 219–59. Berkeley, CA: University of California Press.

Super, Charles M., and Sara Harkness. 1997. The cultural structuring of child development. In *Handbook of cross-cultural psychology,* vol. 2, 2nd ed., eds. J. W. Berry, P. R. Dasen, and T. S. Saraswathi, 1–39. Boston: Allyn & Bacon.

Swanson, Guy E. 1969. *The birth of the gods: The origin of primitive beliefs.* Ann Arbor: University of Michigan Press.

Sweeney, James J. 1952. African negro culture. In *African folktales and sculpture,* ed. P. Radin. New York: Pantheon.

Szklut, Jay, and Robert Roy Reed. 1991. Community anonymity in anthropological research: A reassessment. In *Ethics and the profession of anthropology: Dialogue for a new era,* ed. C. Fluehr-Lobban, 97–116. Philadelphia: University of Pennsylvania Press.

Takezawa, Yasuko. 2006. Race should be discussed and understood across the globe. *Anthropology News* (February/March).

Talmon, Yonina. 1964. Mate selection in collective settlements. *American Sociological Review* 29:491–508.

Tamari, Tal. 1991. The development of caste systems in West Africa. *Journal of African History* 32:221–50.

Tamari, Tal. 2005. Kingship and caste in Africa: History, diffusion and evolution. In *The character of kingship,* ed. Declan Quigley, 141–70. Oxford: Berg Publishers.

Tannen, Deborah. 1990. *You just don't understand: Women and men in conversation.* New York: William Morrow.

Taylor, Christopher C. 2005. Mutton, mud, and runny noses: A hierarchy of distaste in early Rwanda. *Social Analysis* 49:213–30.

Textor, Robert B., comp. 1967. *A cross-cultural summary.* New Haven, CT: HRAF Press.

Thomas, David H. 1986. *Refiguring anthropology: First principles of probability and statistics.* Prospect Heights, IL: Waveland.

Thomas, Elizabeth Marshall. 1959. *The harmless people.* New York: Knopf.

Thomas, Wesley. 1993. A traditional Navajo's perspectives on the cultural construction of gender in the Navajo world. Paper presented at the University of Frankfurt, Germany. As referred to in Lang 1999.

Thomason, Sarah Grey, and Terrence Kaufman. 1988. *Language contact, Creolization, and genetic linguistics.* Berkeley: University of California Press.

Thompson, Ginger. 2002. Mexico is attracting a better class of factory in its south. *New York Times,* June 29, p. A3.

Thompson, Richard H. 1996. Assimilation. In *Encyclopedia of cultural anthropology,* vol. 1, 4 vols., eds. D. Levinson and M. Ember, 112–16. New York: Henry Holt.

Thompson, Richard H. 2009. Chinatowns: Immigrant communities in transition. In MyAnthroLibrary, eds. C. R. Ember, M. Ember, and P. N. Peregrine. MyAnthroLibrary.com. Pearson.

Thompson, Stith. 1965. Star Husband Tale. In *The study of folklore,* ed. A. Dundes. Upper Saddle River, NJ: Prentice Hall.

Thurnwald, R. C. 1934. Pigs and currency in Buin: Observations about primitive standards of value and economics. *Oceania* 5:119–41.

Timpane, John. 1991. Essay: The poetry of science. *Scientific American* (July): 128.

Tishkoff, Sarah A., et al. 2009. The genetic structure and history of Africans and African Americans. *Science Express* 22 (May 2009), 324(5930):1035–44.

Tobin, Joseph J., David Y. H. Wu, and Dana H. Davidson. 1989. *Preschool in three cultures: Japan, China, and the United States.* New Haven, CT: Yale University Press.

Todorov, Alexander, Anesu N. Mandisodza, Amir Goren, and Crystal C. Hall. 2005. Inference of competence from faces predict election outcomes. *Science* 308 (June 10):1623–26.

Tollefson, Kenneth D. 2009. Tlingit: Chiefs past and present. In MyAnthroLibrary, eds. C. R. Ember, M. Ember, and P. N. Peregrine. MyAnthroLibrary.com. Pearson.

Torrey, E. Fuller. 1972. *The mind game: Witchdoctors and psychiatrists.* New York: Emerson Hall.

Torry, William I. 1986. Morality and harm: Hindu peasant adjustments to famines. *Social Science Information* 25: 125–60.

Traphagan, John W., and L. Keith Brown. 2002. Fast food and intergenerational commensality in Japan: New styles and old patterns. *Ethnology* 41:119–34.

Treiman, Donald J., and Harry B. G. Ganzeboom. 1990. Cross-national comparative status-attainment research. *Research in Social Stratification and Mobility* 9:117.

Trevor-Roper, H. R. 1971. The European witch-craze of the sixteenth and seventeenth centuries. In *Reader in comparative religion,* 3rd ed., eds. W. A. Lessa and E. Z. Vogt. New York: Harper & Row.

Triandis, Harry C. 1995. *Individualism and collectivism.* Boulder, CO: Westview.

Trompf, G. W., ed. 1990. *Cargo cults and millenarian movements: Transoceanic comparisons of new religious movements.* Berlin: Mouton de Gruyter.

Trouillot, Michel-Rolph. 2001. The anthropology of the state in the age of globalization: Close encounters of the deceptive kind. *Current Anthropology* 42:125–38.

Trudgill, Peter. 1983. *Sociolinguistics: An introduction to language and society.* Rev. ed. New York: Penguin.

Tylor, Edward B. 1958/1971. *Primitive culture.* New York: Harper Torchbooks.

Tylor, Edward B. 1979. Animism. In *Reader in comparative religion,* 4th ed., eds. W. A. Lessa and E. Z. Vogt. New York: Harper & Row, pp. 9–18.

Uberoi, J. P. Singh. 1962. *The politics of the Kula Ring: An analysis of the findings of Bronislaw Malinowski.* Manchester, UK. University of Manchester Press.

Udy, Stanley H., Jr. 1970. *Work in traditional and modern society.* Upper Saddle River, NJ: Prentice Hall.

UNAIDS. 2007 (December). *AIDS epidemic update.* http://data.unaids.org/pub/EPISlides/2007/2007_epiupdate_en.pdf.

UN Works. n.d. Retrieved from http://www.un.org/works/goingon/mongolia/lessonplan_homelessness.html.

UN Works. n.d. Lesson plan: Street children. http://www.un.org/works/Lesson_Plans/WGO/WGO_LP_SC.pdf (accessed September 4, 2009).

Underhill, Ralph. 1975. Economic and political antecedents of monotheism: A cross-cultural study. *American Journal of Sociology* 80:841–61.

Underhill, Ruth M. 1938. *Social organization of the Papago Indians.* New York: Columbia University Press.

UN News Centre. 2005. Norway at top, Niger at bottom of UN's 2005 human development index. http://www.un.org/apps/news/story.asp?NewsID=15707&Cr=human&Cr1=development (accessed June, 20, 2009).

United Nation's Development Programme. 2007. *Human Development Report 2007/2008: Fighting climate change: Human solidarity in a divided world.* http://hdr.undp.org/en/media/HDR_20072008_EN_Complete.pdf (accessed June, 20, 2009).

United Nations Human Settlements Programme. 2003. The challenge of slums: global report on human settlements, 2003. Nairobi, Kenya.

Unnithan, N. Prabha. 2009. Nayars: Tradition and change in marriage and family. In MyAnthroLibrary, eds. C. R. Ember, M. Ember, and P. N. Peregrine. MyAnthroLibrary. com. Pearson.

U.S. Census Bureau. 1993. *Statistical abstract of the United States: 1993.* 113th ed. Washington, DC: U.S. Government Printing Office.

U.S. Census Bureau. 2002. The big payoff: Educational entertainment and synthetic estimates of work-life earnings. http://www.census.gov/prod/2002pubs/p23-210.pdf (accessed June 2009).

U.S. Department of Justice. 1994. Violent crime. NCJ-147486. Washington, DC.

U.S. Department of Justice. 1998 (November). *Prevalence, incidence, and consequences of violence against women: Findings from the National Violence against Women Survey.* Washington, DC: U.S. Department of Justice.

U.S. Department of Justice. 2000 (May). Children as victims. *Juvenile Justice Bulletin.* 1999 National Report Series. Washington, DC: U.S. Department of Justice.

U.S. Department of Justice. n.d. Bureau of Justice statistics homicide trends in the U.S: Long-term trends and patterns. http://www.ojp.gov/bjs/homicide/hmrt.htm (accessed Sept. 5, 2009).

U.S. Environmental Protection Agency. 2009. http://epa.gov/oecaagct/ag101/demographics.html (accessed October 15, 2009).

Vadez, Vincent, Victoria Reyes-Garcia, Tomás Huanca, William R. Leonard. 2008. Cash cropping, farm technologies, and deforestation: What are the connections? A model with empirical data from the Bolivian Amazon. *Human Organization* 67:384–96.

Valente, Thomas W. 1995. *Network models of the diffusion of innovations.* Cresskill, NJ: Hampton Press.

Van Hear, Nicholas. 2005. Refugee diasporas or refugees in diaspora. In *Encyclopedia of diasporas: Immigrant and refugee cultures around the world,* 2 vols., vol. 1, eds. M. Ember, C. R. Ember, and I. Skoggard, 580–89. New York: Kluwer Academic/Plenum.

Van Willigen, John. 2002. *Applied anthropology: An introduction.* 3rd ed. Westport, CT: Bergin and Garvey.

Vayda, Andrew P. 1967. Pomo trade feasts. In *Tribal and peasant economies,* ed. G. Dalton. Garden City, NY: Natural History Press.

Vayda, Andrew P., Anthony Leeds, and David B. Smith. 1962. The place of pigs in Melanesian subsistence. In *Symposium,* ed. V. E. Garfield. Seattle: University of Washington Press.

Vayda, Andrew P., and Roy A. Rappaport. 1968. Ecology: Cultural and noncultural. In *Introduction to cultural anthropology,* ed. J. H. Clifton, 477–97. Boston: Houghton Mifflin.

Vigil, James Diego. 1988. Group processes and street identity: Adolescent Chicano gang members. *Ethos* 16:421–45.

Vigil, James Diego. 2009. Mexican Americans: Growing up on the streets of Los Angeles. In MyAnthroLibrary, eds. C. R. Ember, M. Ember, and P. N. Peregrine. MyAnthroLibrary. com. Pearson.

Vincent, Joan. 1978. Political anthropology: Manipulative strategies. *Annual Review of Anthropology* 7:175–94.

Vohs, Kathleen D., Nicole L. Mead, and Miranda R. Goode. 2006. The psychological consequences of money. *Science* 314 (November 17):1154–56.

Von Frisch, Karl. 1962. Dialects in the language of the bees. *Scientific American* (August):78–87.

Wadley, Reed L. 2003. Lethal treachery and the imbalance of power in warfare and feuding. *Journal of Anthropological Research* 59:531–54.

Wagley, Charles. 1974. Cultural influences on population: A comparison of two Tupi tribes. In *Native South Americans,* ed. P. J. Lyon, 377–84. Boston: Little, Brown.

Wald, Matthew L. 2000. Hybrid cars show up in M.I.T.'s crystal ball. *New York Times,* November 3, p. F1.

Waldman, Amy. 2005. Sri Lankan maids' high price for foreign jobs. *The New York Times,* May 8, pp. 1, 20.

Wallace, Anthony. 1966. *Religion: An anthropological view.* New York: Random House.

Wallace, Anthony. 1970. *The death and rebirth of the Seneca.* New York: Knopf.

Wallace, Anthony. 1972. Mental illness, biology and culture. In *Psychological anthropology,* 2nd ed., ed. F. L. K. Hsu, 363–402. Cambridge, MA: Schenkman.

Wallerstein, Immanuel. 1974. *The modern world-system.* New York: Academic Press.

Wanner, Eric, and Lila R. Gleitman, eds. 1982. *Language acquisition: The state of the art.* Cambridge: Cambridge University Press.

Ward, Peter M. 1982. Introduction and purpose. In *Self-help housing,* ed. P. M. Ward. London: Mansell.

Wardhaugh, Ronald. 2002. *An introduction to sociolinguistics.* 4th ed. Oxford: Blackwell.

Warner, John Anson. 1986. The individual in Native American Art: A sociological view. In *The arts of the North American Indian,* ed. E. L. Wade. New York: Hudson Hills Press.

Warner, W. Lloyd and Paul S. Lunt. 1941. *The social life of a modern community.* New Haven, CT: Yale University Press.

Warren, Dennis M. 1989. Utilizing indigenous healers in national health delivery systems: The Ghanaian experiment. In *Making our research useful,* eds. J. van Willigen, B. Rylko-Bauer, and A. McElroy. Boulder, CO: Westview.

Warry, Wayne. 1986. Kafaina: Female wealth and power in Chuave, Papua New Guinea. *Oceania* 57:4–21.

Warry, Wayne. 1990. Doing unto others: Applied anthropology, collaborative research and native self-determination. *Culture* 10:61–62.

Watson, James L. 2004. Presidential address: Virtual kinship, real estate, and diaspora formation—the Man lineage revisited. *Journal of Asian Studies* 63:893–910.

Webb, Karen E. 1977. An evolutionary aspect of social structure and a verb "have." *American Anthropologist* 79:42–49.

Weber, Max. 1947. *The theory of social and economic organization.* Trans. A. M. Henderson and Talcott Parsons. New York: Oxford University Press.

Weiner, Annette B. 1976. *Women of value, men of renown: New perspectives in Trobriand exchange.* Austin: University of Texas Press.

Weiner, Annette. 1987. *The Trobrianders of Papua New Guinea.* New York: Holt, Rinehart, and Winston.

Weinreich, Uriel. 1968. *Languages in contact.* The Hague: Mouton.

Weisner, Thomas S. 2004. The American dependency conflict. *Ethos* 29:271–95.

Weisner, Thomas S., Mary Bausano, and Madeleine Kornfein. 1983. Putting family ideals into practice: Pronaturalism in conventional and nonconventional California families. *Ethos* 11:278–304.

Weisner, Thomas S., and Ronald Gallimore. 1977. My brother's keeper: Child and sibling caretaking. *Current Anthropology* 18:169–90.

Weiss, Harvey, and Raymond S. Bradley. 2001. What drives societal collapse? *Science* (January 26):609–10.

Weller, Susan C. 2009. The research process. In MyAnthroLibrary, eds. C. R. Ember, M. Ember, and P. N. Peregrine. MyAnthroLibrary.com. Pearson.

Werner, Dennis. 1975. On the societal acceptance or rejection of male homosexuality. Master's thesis, Hunter College of the City University of New York.

Werner, Dennis. 1978. Trekking in the Amazon forest. *Natural History* (November):42–54.

Werner, Dennis. 1979. A cross-cultural perspective on theory and research on male homosexuality. *Journal of Homosexuality* 4:345–62.

Werner, Dennis. 1982. Chiefs and presidents: A comparison of leadership traits in the United States and among the Mekranoti-Kayapo of Central Brazil. *Ethos,* 10:136–48.

Werner, Dennis. 1984. Child care and influence among the Mekranoti of Central Brazil. *Sex Roles* 10:395–404.

Westermarck, Edward. 1894. *The history of human marriage.* London: Macmillan.

Whitaker, Ian. 1955. *Social relations in a nomadic Lappish community.* Oslo: Utgitt av Norsk Folksmuseum.

White, Douglas R. 1988. Rethinking polygyny: Co-wives, codes, and cultural systems. *Current Anthropology* 29:529–88.

White, Douglas R., and Michael L. Burton. 1988. Causes of polygyny: Ecology, economy, kinship, and warfare. *American Anthropologist* 90:871–87.

White, Douglas R., Michael L. Burton, and Lilyan A. Brudner. 1977. Entailment theory and method: A cross-cultural analysis of the sexual division of labor. *Behavior Science Research* 12:1–24.

White, Leslie A. 1939. A problem in kinship terminology. *American Anthropologist* 41:569–70.

White, Leslie A. 1949. *The science of culture: A study of man and civilization.* New York: Farrar, Straus & Cudahy.

White, Leslie A. 1968. The expansion of the scope of science. In *Readings in anthropology,* vols. 1, 2nd ed., ed. M. H. Fried New York: Thomas Y. Crowell.

Whitehead, Barbara Defoe, and David Popenoe. 2005. *The state of our unions: Marriage and family: What does the Scandinavian experience tell us?* National Marriage Project: Rutgers University.

Whiting, Beatrice B. 1950. *Paiute sorcery.* Viking Fund Publications in Anthropology No. 15. New York: Wenner-Gren Foundation.

Whiting, Beatrice B. 1965. Sex identity conflict and physical violence. *American Anthropologist* 67:123–40.

Whiting, Beatrice B., and Carolyn Pope Edwards. 1973. A cross-cultural analysis of sex differences in the behavior of children aged three through eleven. *Journal of Social Psychology* 91:171–88.

Whiting, Beatrice B., and Carolyn Pope Edwards (in collaboration with Carol R. Ember, Gerald M. Erchak, Sara Harkness, Robert L. Munroe, Ruth H. Munroe, Sara B. Nerlove, Susan Seymour, Charles M. Super, Thomas S. Weisner, and Martha Wenger). 1988. *Children of different worlds: The formation of social behavior.* Cambridge, MA: Harvard University Press.

Whiting, Beatrice B., and John W. M. Whiting (in collaboration with Richard Longabaugh). 1975. *Children of six cultures: A psycho-cultural analysis.* Cambridge, MA: Harvard University Press.

Whiting, John W. M. 1941. *Becoming a Kwoma.* New Haven, CT: Yale University Press.

Whiting, John W. M. 1964. Effects of climate on certain cultural practices. In *Explorations in Cultural Anthropology,* ed. W. H. Goodenough, 511–44. New York: McGraw-Hill.

Whiting, John W. M., and Irvin L. Child. 1953. *Child training and personality: A cross-cultural study.* New Haven, CT: Yale University Press.

Whyte, Martin K. 1978a. Cross-cultural codes dealing with the relative status of women. *Ethnology* 17:211–37.

Whyte, Martin K. 1978b. *The status of women in preindustrial societies.* Princeton, NJ: Princeton University Press.

Wiberg, Hakan. 1983. Self-determination as an international issue. In *Nationalism and self-determination in the Horn of Africa,* ed. I. M. Lewis, 43–65. London: Ithaca Press.

Wikan, Unni. 1982. *Beyond the veil in Arabia.* Baltimore: Johns Hopkins University Press.

Wilden, Anthony. 1987. *The rules are no game: The strategy of communication.* London: Routledge and Kegan Paul.

Williams, Melvin D. 2009. Racism: The production, reproduction, and obsolescence of social inferiority. In MyAnthroLibrary, eds. C. R. Ember, M. Ember, and P. N. Peregrine. MyAnthroLibrary.com. Pearson.

Williams, Walter L. 1992. *The spirit and the flesh.* Boston: Beacon Press.

Wilmsen, Edwin N., ed. 1989. *We are here: Politics of aboriginal land tenure.* Berkeley: University of California Press.

Wilson, Monica. 1963/1951. *Good company: A study of Nyakyusa age villages.* Boston: Beacon Press.

Winkelman, Michael James. 1986a. Magico-religious practitioner types and socioeconomic conditions. *Behavior Science Research* 20:17–46.

Winkelman, Michael. 1986b. Trance states: A theoretical model and cross-cultural analysis. *Ethos* 14:174–203.

Winkelman, Michael, and John R. Baker. 2010. *Supernatural as natural: A biocultural approach to religion.* Upper Saddle River, NJ: Pearson Prentice Hall.

Winkleman, Michael, and Philip M. Peck, eds. 2004. *Divination and healing: Potent vision.* Tucson: University of Arizona Press.

Winterbottom, Robert. 1995. The Tropical Forestry Plan: Is it working? In *Global ecosystems: Creating options through anthropological perspectives,* ed. P. J. Puntenney. *NAPA Bulletin* 15, pp. 60–70.

Winterhalder, Bruce. 1990. Open field, common pot: Harvest variability and risk avoidance in agricultural and foraging societies. In *Risk and uncertainty in tribal and peasant economies,* ed. E. Cashdan. Boulder, CO: Westview.

Witkin, Herman A. 1967. A cognitive style approach to cross-cultural research. *International Journal of Psychology* 2:233–50.

Witkowski, Stanley R. 1975. *Polygyny, age of marriage, and female status.* Paper presented at the annual meeting of the American Anthropological Association, San Francisco.

Witkowski, Stanley R., and Cecil H. Brown. 1978. Lexical universals. *Annual Review of Anthropology* 7:427–51.

Witkowski, Stanley R., and Harold W. Burris. 1981. Societal complexity and lexical growth. *Behavior Science Research* 16:143–59.

Wolf, Arthur. 1968. Adopt a daughter-in-law, marry a sister: A Chinese solution to the problem of the incest taboo. *American Anthropologist* 70:864–74.

Wolf, Arthur P., and Chieh-shan Huang. 1980. *Marriage and adoption in China, 1845–1945.* Stanford, CA: Stanford University Press.

Wolf, Eric. 1955. Types of Latin American peasantry: A preliminary discussion. *American Anthropologist* 57:452–71.

Wolf, Eric R. 1956. San José: Subcultures of a 'traditional' coffee municipality. In J. H. Steward et al., *The people of Puerto Rico.* Urbana: University of Illinois Press.

Wolf, Eric. 1966. *Peasants.* Upper Saddle River, NJ: Prentice Hall.

Wolf, Naomi. 1991. *The beauty myth: How images of beauty are used against women.* New York: Morrow.

Women in science '93: Gender and the culture of science. 1993. *Science* (April 16):383–430.

Wood, Gordon S. 1992. *The radicalism of the American Revolution.* New York: Knopf.

Wood, Wendy, and Alice H. Eagly. 2002. A cross-cultural analysis of the behavior of women and men: Implications for the origins of sex differences. *Psychological Bulletin* 128:699–727.

Woodburn, James. 1968. An introduction to Hadza ecology. In *Man the hunter,* eds. R. B. Lee and I. DeVore, 49–55. Chicago: Aldine.

World Bank. 2004. *World development indicators 2004.* Washington, DC: World Bank Publications.

Worsley, Peter. 1957. *The trumpet shall sound: A study of "cargo" cults in Melanesia.* London: MacGibbon & Kee.

Wright, Gary A. 1971. Origins of food production in Southwestern Asia: A survey of ideas. *Current Anthropology* 12:447–78.

Wright, George O. 1954. Projection and displacement: A cross-cultural study of folktale aggression. *Journal of Abnormal and Social Psychology* 49:523–28.

Wulff, Robert, and Shirley Fiste. 1987. The domestication of wood in Haiti. In R. M. Wulff and S. J. Fiste, *Anthropological praxis.* Boulder, CO: Westview.

Yan, Yunxiang. 2006. Girl power: Young women and the waning of patriarchy in rural North China. *Ethnology* 45:105–23.

Yergin, Daniel. 2002. Giving aid to world trade. *New York Times,* June 27, p. A29.

Yinger, J. Milton. 1994. *Ethnicity: Source of strength? Source of conflict?* Albany: State University Press.

Young, Frank W. 1970. A fifth analysis of the Star Husband Tale. *Ethnology* 9:389–413.

Younger, Stephen M. 2008. Conditions and mechanisms for peace in precontact Polynesia. *Current Anthropology* 49:927–34.

Zebrowitz, Leslie A., and Joann M. Montepare. 2005. Appearance *does* matter. *Science* 308 (June 10):1565–66.

Zechenter, Elizabeth M. 1997. In the name of culture: Cultural relativism and the abuse of the individual. *Journal of Anthropological Research* 53: 319–47.

credits

Photos

Chapter 1. Page 3: Dave and Sigrun Tollerton/Alamy; Page 5: Spooner/Redmond-Callow/ZUMA Press—Gamma; Page 6: Robert Brenner/PhotoEdit Inc.; Page 7: The Granger Collection, New York; Page 8: Terence Hays; Page 11: © Christopher J. Morris/Corbis; Page 12: © Mark Peterson/SABA/CORBIS All Rights Reserved.

Chapter 2. Page 15: Greg Girard/Contact Press Images Inc.; Page 16: Kathy Sloane/Photo Researchers, Inc.; Page 18: N. Martin Haudrich/Photo Researchers, Inc.; Page 18: James L. Stanfield/National Geographic Image Collection; Page 21: Michael Newman/PhotoEdit Inc.; Page 21: © Doug Menuez/Photodisc/RF Getty Images, Inc.; Page 22: © Jeremy Horner/Bettmann/CORBIS All Rights Reserved; Page 22: © Jonathan Blair/Bettmann/CORBIS All Rights Reserved; Page 26: Dorling Kindersley © Jamie Marshall; Page 27: © Joseph Van Os/Image Bank/Getty Images, Inc.; Page 32: Currier & Ives, "Give Me Liberty or Give Me Death!," 1775. Lithograph, 1876. © The Granger Collection, New York; Page 34: John Chiasson; Page 37: © Hulton Archive/Getty Images Inc.

Chapter 3. Page 41: Private Collection/The Bridgeman Art Library; Page 42: Ben Mikaelsen/Peter Arnold, Inc.; Page 43: National History Museum, London, UK/Bridgeman Art Library; Page 44: CORBIS-NY; Page 45: Musée Nat. des Arts et Traditions Populaires, Paris, France/The Bridgeman Art Library; Page 47: © Neil Rabinowitz/CORBIS All Rights Reserved; Page 50: ©The British Library Board. All Rights Reserved Add. 15217, f.39v; Page 52: © Caroline Penn/CORBIS All Rights Reserved.

Chapter 4. Page 59: Richard Lord/PhotoEdit Inc.; Page 60: © Tetra Images RF/CORBIS All Rights Reserved; Page 62 (left): Victor Englebert/Photo Researchers, Inc.; Page 62 (right): Doc White/Nature Picture Library; Page 66: Peggy and YoramKahana/Peter Arnold, Inc.; Page 70: John White/Art Resource/The British Museum Great Court Ltd. Copyright The British Museum.

Chapter 5. Page 73: © Anthony Bannister/Gallo Images/CORBIS All Rights Reserved; Page 74: Susan Kuklin/Science Source/Photo Researchers, Inc.; Page 74: BlueMoon Stock/SuperStock; Page 79: Ellen Isaacs/age fotostock/Art Life Images; Page 80: © Roy Morsch/Bettmann/CORBIS All Rights Reserved; Page 83: Lebrecht Music & Arts 2/Lebrecht Music & Arts Photo Library; Page 85: Peter Wilson © Dorling Kindersley; Page 88: Rhoda Sidney; Page 88: Renate Hiller; Page 91: © Caroline Penn/CORBIS All Rights Reserved.

Chapter 6. Page 95: Yann Arthus-Bertrand/Altitude; Page 97: © Staffan Widstrand/CORBIS All Rights Reserved; Page 99: Victor Englebert/Photo Researchers, Inc.; Page 100: © Melvin Ember; Page 101: © KEREN SU/DanitaDelimont.com; Page 104: © Tiziana and Gianni Baldizzone/Bettmann/CORBIS All Rights Reserved; Page 106: Kaj R. Svensson/Photo Researchers, Inc.; Page 107: ALEX S. MACLEAN/Peter Arnold, Inc.

Chapter 7. Page 111: John D. Norman/CORBIS-NY; Page 113: GEORGE HOLTON/Photo Researchers, Inc.; Page 114: James P. Blair/National Geographic Image Collection; Page 115: Moises Castillo/AP Wide World Photos; Page 117: © Bernard Annebicque/Sygma/CORBIS All Rights Reserved; Page 118: © John Roberts/Stock Market/CORBIS All Rights Reserved; Page 119: Tony Savino/The Image Works; Page 121: H. Mark Weidman Photography/Alamy; Page 123: © Charles Lenars/CORBIS All Rights Reserved; Page 127: Dana Hyde/Photo Researchers, Inc.; Page 129: © Pete Saloutos/CORBIS All Rights Reserved; Page 130: Dorling Kindersley © Jamie Marshall.

Chapter 8. Page 135: © Catherine Karnow/CORBIS All Rights Reserved; Page 137: Wendy Stone/CORBIS-NY; Page 138: Charles Mahaux/age fotostock.; Page 139: © Philip Gould/CORBIS All Rights Reserved; Page

142: © sinopictures/Peter Arnold, Inc.; Page 145: Photograph provided courtesy of Syracuse University. All rights reserved; Page 147: © Kevin Fleming/CORBIS All Rights Reserved; Page 147: © Ghislain & Marie David de Lossy/Image Bank/Getty Images Inc.

Chapter 9. Page 153: Jamie Marshall © Dorling Kindersley; Page 154: BIOS (A. Compost)/Peter Arnold, Inc.; Page 156: © Keren Su/CORBIS All Rights Reserved; Page 158: © Annie Griffiths Belt/CORBIS All Rights Reserved; Page 158: © Tim; Page/CORBIS All Rights Reserved; Page 159: © Jon Hrusa/epa/CORBIS All Rights Reserved; Page 160: © Don Mason/Bettmann/CORBIS All Rights Reserved; Page 160: © George Simian/Bettmann/CORBIS All Rights Reserved; Page 162: Michael Dwyer/Alamy; Page 163: AP Wide World Photos; Page 168: © Margaret Courtney-Clarke/CORBIS All Rights Reserved.

Chapter 10. Page 173: © Marc Romanelli/Image Bank/Getty Images Inc.; Page 174: JORGEN SCHYTTE/Peter Arnold, Inc.; Page 176: JORGEN SHYTTE/Peter Arnold, Inc.; Page 178: © Laurence Fordyce, Eye Ubiquitous/CORBIS All Rights Reserved; Page 179: © Eldad Rafaeli/CORBIS All Rights Reserved; Page 182: Ann Mohs/Bruce Miller; Page 184: © Kevin Cozad/O'Brien Productions/CORBIS All Rights Reserved; Page 184: © Michael Newman/PhotoEdit, Inc.; Page 187: © Paul A. Souders/CORBIS All Rights Reserved.

Chapter 11. Page 191: David Beatty/Robert Harding World Imagery; Page 192: David McLain/Aurora Photos, Inc.; Page 193: © Punch/Rothco; Page 195: © Faleh Kheiber/CORBIS All Rights Reserved; Page 197: ASAP/Sarit Uzieli/Photo Researchers, Inc.; Page 200: Jonathan Player/Redux Pictures; Page 203: © Nik Wheeler/Bettmann/CORBIS All Rights Reserved; Page 204: Fine Art Photographic Library, London/Art Resource, NY; Page 208: © Anders Ryman/CORBIS All Rights Reserved.

Chapter 12. Page 213: Dean Conger/CORBIS-NY; Page 214: Porterfield/Chickering/Photo Researchers, Inc.; Page 216: © Harvey Lloyd/Taxi/Getty Images, Inc.; Page 223: Reed Kaestner/CORBIS-NY; Page 226: © Ludo Kuipers/CORBIS All Rights Reserved; Page 230: Stock Montage, Inc./Historical Pictures Collection.

Chapter 13. Page 233: © SW Productions/Photodisc/RF Getty Images, Inc.; Page 236: Leon Oboler/Regina Smith Oboler; Page 237: Photo Courtesy of Anthony Forge, 1962. From George A. Corgin, "Native Arts of North America, Africa and the South Pacific: An Introduction." New York: Harper & Row, Publishers, Inc., 1988; Page 239: Sylvain Grandadam/Photo Researchers, Inc.; Page 241: Bernard Wong; Page 242: Wayne Warry.

Chapter 14. Page 247: AP Wide World Photos; Page 249: © Arnold Newman/Peter Arnold Inc.; Page 251: © Anders Ryman/CORBIS All Rights Reserved; Page 254: © Peter Andrews/Reuters/CORBIS All Rights Reserved; Page 255: © Enrico Para/ANSA/epa/CORBIS All Rights Reserved; Page 257: Maria Lepowsky; Page 260: Bill Aron/PhotoEdit Inc.; Page 263: © Yasuyoshi Chiba/AFP/Getty Images, Inc.; Page 265: © Paul Assaker/Bettmann/CORBIS All Rights Reserved.

Chapter 15. Page 269: © Dallas and John Heaton/Free Agents Limited/CORBIS All Rights Reserved; Page 271: Tom Stewart/CORBIS-NY; Page 273: © Jorge Silva/Reuters/CORIS All Rights Reserved; Page 276: © Peter Arnold, Inc.; Page 277: © Reinhard Dirscherl/WaterFrame.de/Peter Arnold; Page 279: © Catherine Karnow/CORBIS All Rights Reserved; Page 281: © Joerg Boethling/Peter Arnold, Inc.; Page 284: Ogallala Sioux performing the Ghost Dance at the Pine Ridge Indian Agency, South Dakota. Illustration by Frederic Remington, 1890. The Granger Collection.

Chapter 16. Page 289: Art Wolfe/Photo Researchers, Inc.; Page 292: Jack Fields/Photo Researchers, Inc.; Page 292: © Charles & Josette Lenars/CORBIS All Rights Reserved; Page 293: © The Trustees of the British Museum, London, United Kingdom; Page 293: © Araldo de Luca/CORBIS All Rights Reserved; Page 296: Lynton Gardiner © Dorling Kindersley, Courtesy of The American Museum of Natural History; Page 296: © Peter Arnold, Inc.; Page 297: © Lightstone/CORBIS; Page 297: Susan McCartney/Photo Researchers, Inc.; Page 300: © Lake County Museum/Bettmann/CORBIS All Rights Reserved; Page 300: Demetrio

Carrasco © Dorling Kindersley, Courtesy of the Cameron Trading Post, Flagstaff, Arizona.

Chapter 17. Page 303: Michael Horowitz; Page 305: © Hallgerd/Shutterstock; Page 306: AFP/Getty Images; Page 307: © Joerg Boethling/Peter Arnold, Inc.; Page 309: © Yannis Kontos/Sygma/CORBIS All Rights Reserved; Page 310: © Horacio Villalobos/Corbis; Page 311: © Tibor Bognar/Alamy; Page 314: © Nigel Dickinson/Peter Arnold, Inc.; Page 315: Martha Cooper/Peter Arnold, Inc.; Page 317: © Jon Hursa/Pool/epa/CORBIS All Rights Reserved; Page 318: © Tony Anderson/CORBIS All Rights Reserved; Page 321: Michael J. Balick/Peter Arnold, Inc.

Chapter 18. Page 325: © David Greedy/News/Getty Images, Inc.; Page 326: © Shamil Zhumatov/Reuters/CORBIS All Rights Reserved; Page 327: © Sucheta Das/Reuters/CORBIS All Rights Reserved; Page 332: Lon C. Diehl/PhotoEdit Inc.; Page 333: © Edourd Berne/Stone/Getty Images, Inc.; Page 334: © Helen Harrison/E&E Image Library/H/age fotostock; Page 336: © epa/CORBIS All Rights Reserved.

Text

Chapter 3. Page 55: Ember, Melvin R; Ember, Carol R.; Levinson, David, *Portraits of Culture: Ethnographic Originals,* 1st, © 1994. Electronically reproduced by permission of Pearson Education, Inc., Upper Saddle River, New Jersey.

Chapter 4. Page 64: Based on John W. M. Whiting, "Effects of Climate on Certain Cultural Practices," in Ward H. Goodenough, ed., *Explorations in Cultural Anthropology* (New York: McGraw-Hill, 1964), p. 520.

Chapter 7. Page 119: From James A. Levine, Robert Weisell, Simon Chevassus, Claudio D. Martinez, and Barbara Burlingame. "The Distribution of Work Tasks for Male and Female Children and Adults Separated by Gender" in "Looking at Child Labor," *Science* 296 (10 May 2002): 1025.

Chapter 8: Page 141: These data are abstracted from Proportion of National Income Earned by the Richest 20 Percent of Households. From World Bank. 2004. World Development Indicators 2004. Washington, DC: World Bank Publications. ISBN/ISSN: 01635085.

Chapter 10: Page 182: Women's Electoral Success on the Northwest Coast SOURCE: B. G. Miller 1992. "Women and Politics: Comparative Evidence from the Northwest Coast,"Ethnology 32(4): 367–82. © 1992 by University of Pittsburgh.

Chapter 11. Page 195: Based on data from Alice Schlegel and Rohn Eloul, "Marriage Transactions: Labor, Property, and Status," *American Anthropologist* 90 (1988): 291–309.

Chapter 12. Page 226: Adapted from Melvin Ember and Carol R. Ember, *Marriage, Family, and Kinship: Comparative Studies of Social Organization* (New Haven, CT: HRAF Press, 1983).

Chapter 14. Page 250: Adapted from Paul Bohannan, "The Migration and Expansion of the Tiv," *Africa,* 24 (1954): 3; Page 253: Based on Ember and Ember 2002.

Chapter 16. Page 291: Clottes 2008—Jean Clottes, "Rock Art" An Endangered Heritage Worldwide." *Journal of Anthropological Research* 64 (2008): 1–18; Page 293: Based on Fischer 1961.

index

The following pages contain maps that have been adapted from the *DK Atlas of World History: Mapping the Human Journey* and *Atlas of Anthropology,* produced by Dorling Kindersley. Each map focuses on a topic that is discussed in more detail within the text itself and is intended to bring the richness of anthropology to life.

maps

 Prentice Hall would sincerely like to thank Dorling Kindersley for helping to put this feature together.

THE FIRST HOMINIDS

Members of the genus *Australopithecus* lived in eastern and southern Africa between about 4 and 1 million years ago. Fossilized footprints from Laetoli in Tanzania, dating from about 3.6 million years ago, show that the australopithecines had mastered bipedalism. At least six major australopithecine species, classified by variations in their skulls and teeth, have been identified. The earliest known fossils of the *Homo* genus date to about 2.3 million years ago. They are distinguished by larger brain size and more rounded skulls.

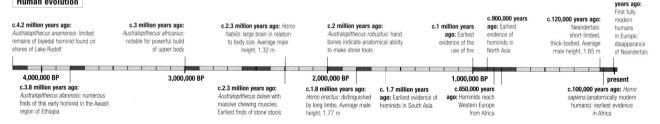

Human evolution

c.4.2 million years ago:
Australopithecus anamensis: limited remains of bipedal hominid found on shores of Lake Rudolf

c.3 million years ago:
Australopithecus africanus: notable for powerful build of upper body

c.2.3 million years ago: *Homo habilis:* large brain in relation to body size. Average male height, 1.32 m

c.2 million years ago:
Australopithecus robustus: hand bones indicate anatomical ability to make stone tools

c.1 million years ago: Earliest evidence of the use of fire

c.900,000 years ago: Earliest evidence of hominids in North Asia

c.120,000 years ago: Neandertals: short-limbed, thick-bodied. Average male height, 1.65 m

c.35,000 years ago: First fully modern humans in Europe; disappearance of Neandertals

4,000,000 BP   **3,000,000 BP**   **2,000,000 BP**   **1,000,000 BP**   **present**

c.3.8 million years ago:
Australopithecus afarensis: numerous finds of this early hominid in the Awash region of Ethiopia

c.2.3 million years ago:
Australopithecus boisei with massive chewing muscles. Earliest finds of stone stools

c.1.8 million years ago: *Homo erectus:* distinguished by long limbs. Average male height, 1.77 m

c. 1.7 million years ago: Earliest evidence of hominids in South Asia

c.850,000 years ago: Hominids reach Western Europe from Africa

c.100,000 years ago: *Homo sapiens* (anatomically modern humans): earliest evidence in Africa

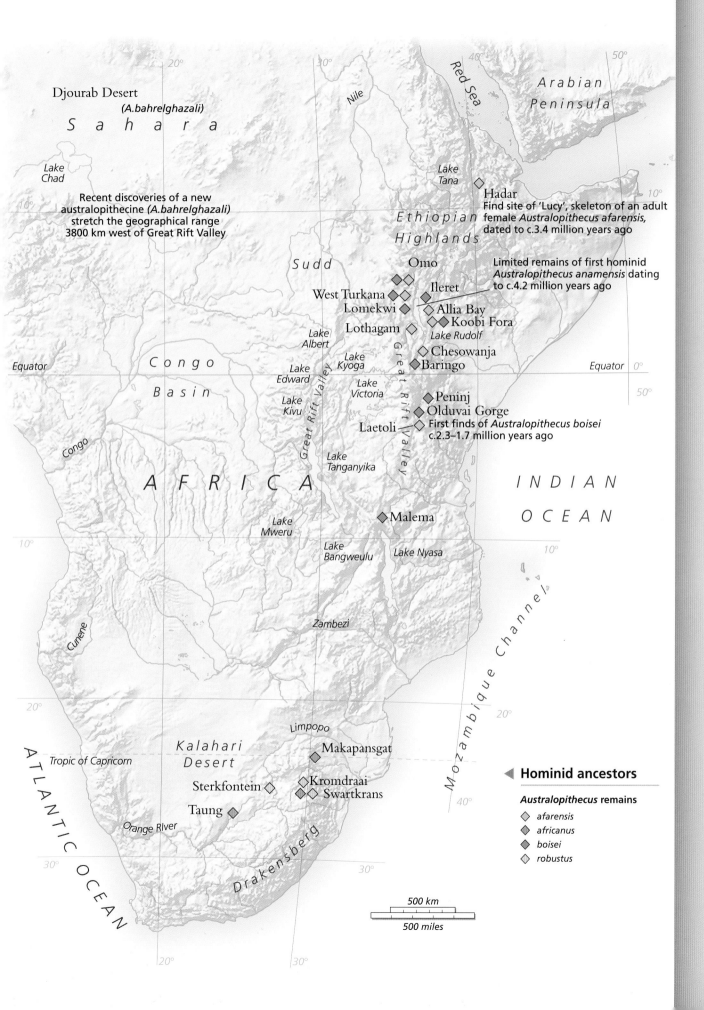

Djourab Desert
(A.bahrelghazali)

S a h a r a

*Lake
Chad*

Recent discoveries of a new
australopithecine *(A.bahrelghazali)*
stretch the geographical range
3800 km west of Great Rift Valley

Nile

Red Sea

*A r a b i a n
P e n i n s u l a*

*Lake
Tana*

Hadar
Find site of 'Lucy', skeleton of an adult
female *Australopithecus afarensis*,
dated to c.3.4 million years ago

E t h i o p i a n

H i g h l a n d s

Sudd

Omo

Limited remains of first hominid
Australopithecus anamensis dating
to c.4.2 million years ago

West Turkana

Ileret

Lomekwi

Allia Bay

Lothagam

Koobi Fora

*Lake
Albert*

*Lake
Kyoga*

Lake Rudolf

C o n g o

B a s i n

*Lake
Edward*

*Lake
Victoria*

Chesowanja

Baringo

Equator

*Lake
Kivu*

Great Rift Valley

Great Rift Valley

Equator   0°

50°

Congo

Peninj

Olduvai Gorge

First finds of *Australopithecus boisei*
c.2.3–1.7 million years ago

Laetoli

A F R I C A

*Lake
Tanganyika*

I N D I A N

O C E A N

*Lake
Mweru*

Malema

*Lake
Bangweulu*

Lake Nyasa

Zambezi

Limpopo

Mozambique Channel

Cunene

*K a l a h a r i
D e s e r t*

Makapansgat

Tropic of Capricorn

Sterkfontein

Kromdraai

Swartkrans

Taung

Orange River

A T L A N T I C   O C E A N

Drakensberg

500 km

500 miles

◄ **Hominid ancestors**

Australopithecus **remains**

◇ *afarensis*

◈ *africanus*

◆ *boisei*

◇ *robustus*

THE EMERGENCE OF MODERN HUMANS

The first representative of the *Homo* genus, *Homo habilis*, emerged about 2.3 million years ago and was presumably responsible for the earliest patterned stone tools. *Homo erectus*, which appeared about 1.8 million years ago, had a still larger brain capacity, and a tall long-legged physique. It adapted successfully to a wide range of environments, spreading from Africa to Asia and Europe over the next million years. The earliest fossil remains of fully modern humans, *Homo sapiens sapiens*, found in Africa, date to perhaps 100,000 years ago. Modern humans spread and/or colonized even more widely, even to the earth's most marginal regions, and became the sole surviving human species.

The emergence of modern humans ▶

◆ finds of *Homo habilis*
◇ finds of *Homo erectus*
◆ finds of *Homo heidelbergensis* and other transitional fossils
◇ finds of Neandertals
◇ finds of modern *Homo sapiens* (over 50,000 years old)

ARCTIC OCEAN

Barents Sea

Greenland

Scandinavia

Ob

Ural

Arctic Circle

EUROPE
It is thought that early humanoids arrived in Europe from Africa c.1 million years ago

Dnieper

Bilzingsleben
Evidence of big-game hunting and butchery at lakeside site

Pontnewydd
Swanscombe
Neandertal
Mauer
Steinheim
Biache
Boxgrove
Spy

Sipka
Külna Cave

Danube

Rhine

Neandertal bones show that they suffered from diseases including arthritis and blindness

La Chapelle-aux-Saints
St. Césaire
Montmaurin
Hortus
La Ferrassie
Arago
Lezetxiki
Atapuerca

Saccopastore
Circeo

ATLANTIC OCEAN

Cova Negra
Forbes Quarry
El Guettar
Taforalt
Mugharet el-'Aliya
Dar es-Soltan
Sidi Abderrahman
Thomas Quarry
Jebel Irhoud

Sa

Tropic of Cancer

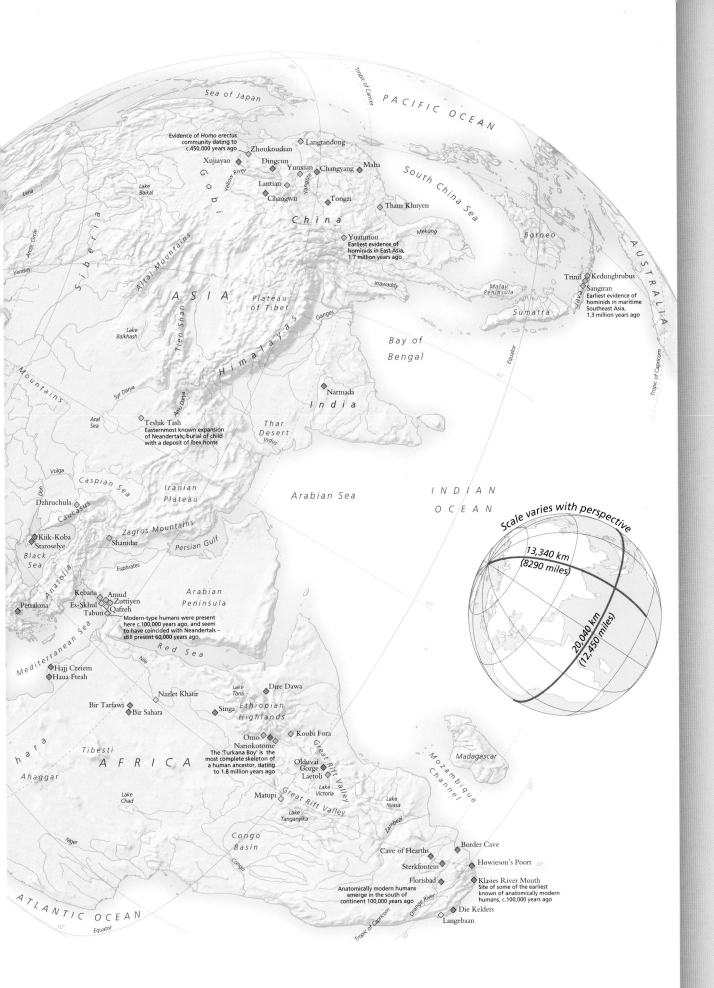

PACIFIC OCEAN

Sea of Japan

Evidence of *Homo erectus*
community dating to
c.450,000 years ago

Langtandong

Zhoukoudian

Xujiayao   Dingcun   Yunxian   Changyang   Maba

Lantian   Yangtze   Changwu   Tongzi

China   Tham Khuyen

South China Sea

Borneo

Yellow River

Gobi

Yuanmou
Earliest evidence
of hominids in East Asia,
1.7 million years ago

AUSTRALIA

Trinil   Kedungbrubus

Sangiran
Earliest evidence of
hominids in maritime
Southeast Asia,
1.3 million years ago

Malay
Peninsula

Sumatra

Java

Irrawaddy

Lena

Arctic Circle

Yenisey

Siberia

Altai Mountains

Lake
Baikal

ASIA

Plateau
of Tibet

Tien Shan

Lake
Balkhash

Himalayas

Ganges

Bay of
Bengal

Equator

Mountains

Syr Darya

Amu Darya

Aral
Sea

Teshik Tash
Easternmost known expansion
of Neandertals; burial of child
with a deposit of ibex horns

Thar
Desert

Indus

Narmada

India

Volga

Caspian Sea

Don

Dzhruchula

Caucasus

Iranian
Plateau

Arabian Sea

INDIAN

OCEAN

Scale varies with perspective

Kiik-Koba
Staroselye

Black
Sea

Zagros Mountains

Shanidar

Persian Gulf

13,340 km
(8290 miles)

Anatolia

Kebana   Amud
Es-Skhul   Zuttiyen
Tabun   Qafzeh

Petralona

Arabian
Peninsula

20,040 km
(12,450 miles)

Modern-type humans were present
here c.100,000 years ago, and seem
to have coincided with Neandertals –
still present 60,000 years ago.

Euphrates

Red Sea

Mediterranean Sea

Nile

Hajj Creiem
Haua Fteah

Nazlet Khatir

Lake
Tana

Dire Dawa

Bir Tarfawi

Bir Sahara

Singa

Ethiopian
Highlands

Madagascar

Mozambique
Channel

hara

Tibesti

AFRICA

Ahaggar

Koobi Fora

Omo
Nariokotome
The 'Turkana Boy' is the
most complete skeleton of
a human ancestor, dating
to 1.8 million years ago

Olduvai
Gorge
Laetoli

Great Rift Valley

Lake
Chad

Matupi

Great Rift Valley

Lake
Victoria

Lake
Nyasa

Niger

Congo
Basin

Lake
Tanganyika

Zambezi

Border Cave

Cave of Hearths

Sterkfontein

Howieson's Poort

Florisbad

Congo

Anatomically modern
humans emerge in the south of
continent 100,000 years ago

Orange River

Klasies River Mouth
Site of some of the earliest
known of anatomically modern
humans, c.100,000 years ago

Die Kelders

ATLANTIC OCEAN

Equator

Langebaan

Tropic of Capricorn

Tropic of Cancer

Mekong

THE SPREAD OF MODERN HUMANS

Fully modern humans evolved in Africa, probably between 200,000 and 100,000 years ago. By 30,000 years ago, they had colonized much of the globe. Rising temperatures at the end of the last Ice Age allowed plants and animals to become more abundant, and new areas were settled. By 8000 B.C., larger populations and intense hunting had contributed to the near extinction of large mammals, such as mastodons and

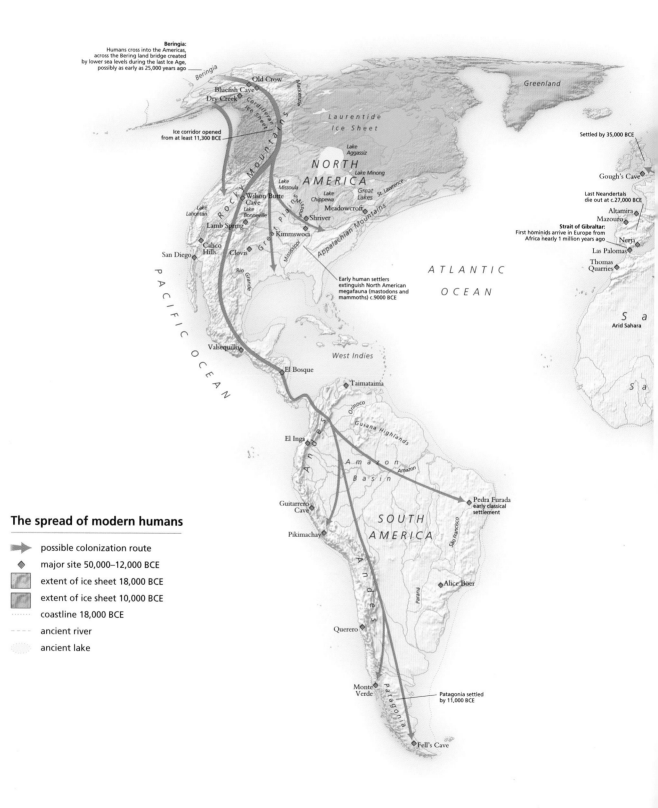

Beringia:
Humans cross into the Americas, across the Bering land bridge created by lower sea levels during the last Ice Age, possibly as early as 25,000 years ago

Beringia

Old Crow
Bluefish Cave
Dry Creek

Cordilleran Ice Sheet

Mackenzie

Ice corridor opened from at least 11,300 BCE

ROCKY Mountains

Laurentide Ice Sheet

Greenland

Lake Aggasiz

NORTH AMERICA

Lake Minong

Lake Missoula

Lake Chippewa

Great Lakes

St. Lawrence

Wilson Butte Cave
Lake Bonneville

Missouri

Meadowcroft

Appalachian Mountains

Lake Lahontan

Lamb Spring

Great Plains

Shriver

Kimmswoci

Calico Hills
Clovis

San Diego

Rio Grande

Mississippi

Early human settlers extinguish North American megafauna (mastodons and mammoths) c.9000 BCE

ATLANTIC

OCEAN

Settled by 35,000 BCE

Gough's Cave

Last Neandertals die out at c.27,000 BCE

Altamira
Mazouro

Strait of Gibraltar:
First hominids arrive in Europe from Africa nearly 1 million years ago

Nerja
Las Palomas
Thomas Quarries

S a

Arid Sahara

S a

Valsequillo

West Indies

El Bosque

Taimataima

PACIFIC OCEAN

Orinoco

Guiana Highlands

El Inga

Andes

Amazon Basin

Amazon

Guitarrero Cave

SOUTH AMERICA

São Francisco

Pedra Furada early classical settlement

Pikimachay

Andes

Alice Böer

Parana

Querero

Monte Verde

Patagonia

Patagonia settled by 11,000 BCE

Fell's Cave

The spread of modern humans

- ➤ possible colonization route
- ◆ major site 50,000–12,000 BCE
- extent of ice sheet 18,000 BCE
- extent of ice sheet 10,000 BCE
- ⋯⋯ coastline 18,000 BCE
- ‑ ‑ ‑ ancient river
- ancient lake

mammoths. In the Near East, groups of hunter gatherers were living in permanent settlements, harvesting wild cereals, and experimenting with the domestication of local animals. The transition to agriculture was under way.

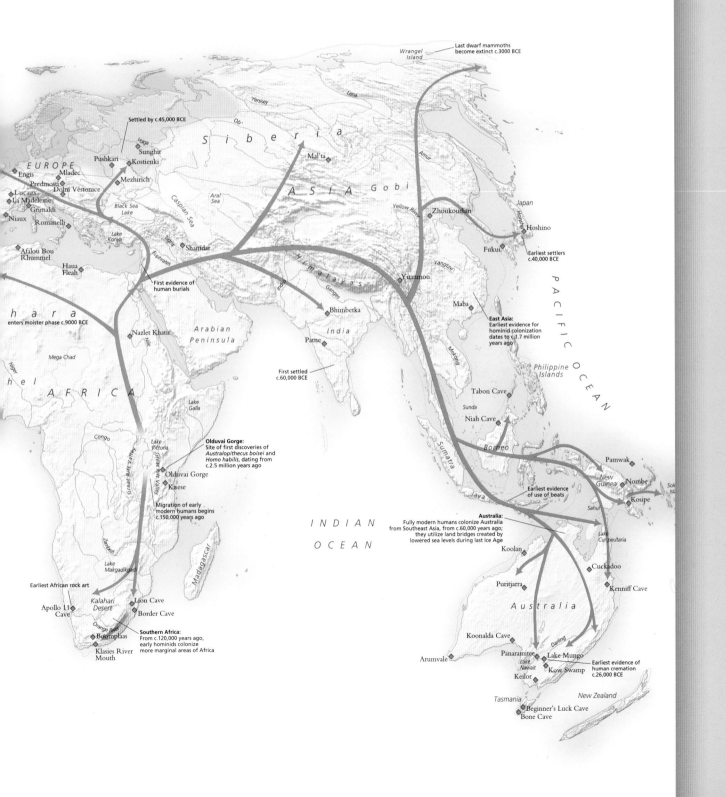

Last dwarf mammoths become extinct c.3000 BCE

Wrangel Island

Yenisey

Lena

Settled by c.45,000 BCE

Ob

S i b e r i a

Volga

Sunghir

Pushkari

Kostienki

Amur

A S I A   *Gobi*

Mal'ta

EUROPE

Engis   Mladec

Predmosti

Mezhirich

Dolni Věstonice

Japan

Lascaux

La Madeleine

Grimaldi

Black Sea Lake

Yellow River

Zhoukoudian

Honshu

Niaux

Romanelli

Lake Konya

Caspian Sea

Aral Sea

Hoshino

Fukui

Earliest settlers c.40,000 BCE

Afalou Bou Rhummel

Tigris

Shanidar

Euphrates

Yangtze

Haua Fleah

First evidence of human burials

H i m a l a y a s

Yuanmou

PACIFIC OCEAN

Maba

Indus

Ganges

Bhimbetka

East Asia: Earliest evidence for hominid colonization dates to c.1.7 million years ago

h a r a

enters moister phase c.9000 BCE

Nazlet Khatir

Arabian Peninsula

I n d i a

Patne

Nile

Mega Chad

Philippine Islands

Niger

First settled c.60,000 BCE

Tabon Cave

h e l   A F R I C A

Congo

Lake Victoria

Lake Galla

Sunda

Niah Cave

Olduvai Gorge: Site of first discoveries of *Australopithecus boisei* and *Homo habilis*, dating from c.2.5 million years ago

Great Rift Valley

Mekong

Borneo

Pamwak

Olduvai Gorge

Kisese

Sumatra

New Guinea

Nombe

Migration of early modern humans begins c.150,000 years ago

Java

Earliest evidence of use of boats

Kosipe

INDIAN

OCEAN

Sahul

Australia: Fully modern humans colonize Australia from Southeast Asia, from c.60,000 years ago; they utilize land bridges created by lowered sea levels during last Ice Age

Lake Carpeutaria

Zambezi

Madagascar

Lake Makgadikgadi

Koolan

Cuckadoo

Earliest African rock art

Kalahari Desert

Lion Cave

Puritjarra

Kenniff Cave

Apollo 11 Cave

Border Cave

A u s t r a l i a

Orange River

Boomplaas

Southern Africa: From c.120,000 years ago, early hominids colonize more marginal areas of Africa

Koonalda Cave

Klasies River Mouth

Arumvale

Panaramitee

Lake Mungo

Earliest evidence of human cremation c.26,000 BCE

Lake Nawait

Kow Swamp

Keilor

Tasmania

New Zealand

Beginner's Luck Cave

Bone Cave

THE SPREAD OF AGRICULTURE

The appearance of farming transformed the face of the earth. It was not merely a change in subsistence, it also transformed the way in which our ancestors lived. Agriculture, and the vastly greater crop yields it produced, enabled larger groups of people to live together, often in permanent villages. After agriculture emerged, craft, religious, and political specialization became more likely, and the first signs of social

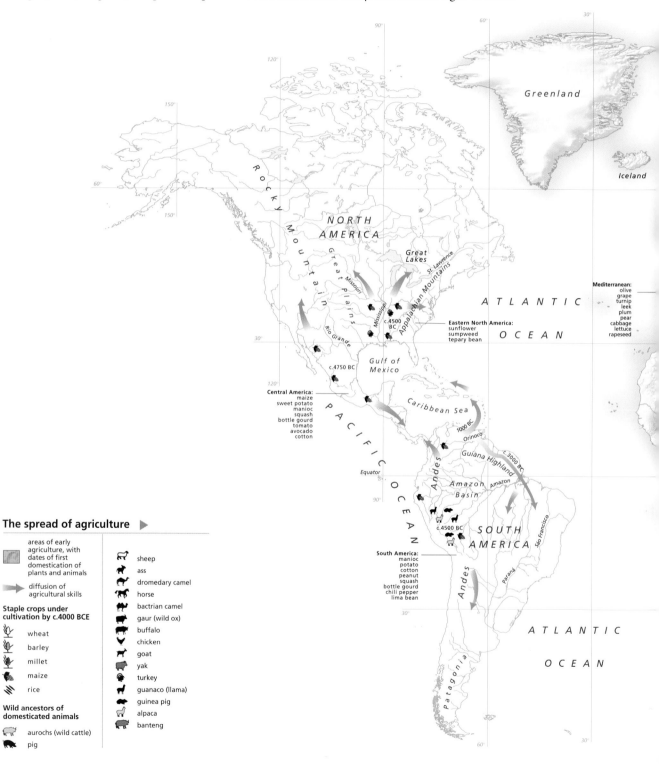

Greenland

Iceland

ROCKY Mountain

NORTH AMERICA

Great Plains

Missouri

Great Lakes

St. Lawrence

Appalachian Mountains

Rio Grande

Mississippi

c.4500 BC

c.4750 BC

Gulf of Mexico

Eastern North America:
sunflower
sumpweed
tepary bean

Mediterranean:
olive
grape
turnip
leek
plum
pear
cabbage
lettuce
rapeseed

ATLANTIC OCEAN

Central America:
maize
sweet potato
manioc
squash
bottle gourd
tomato
avocado
cotton

PACIFIC OCEAN

Caribbean Sea

1000 BC

Orinoco

Guiana Highland

c.3000 BC

Equator

Andes

Amazon Basin

Amazon

SOUTH AMERICA

São Francisco

c.4500 BC

South America:
manioc
potato
cotton
peanut
squash
bottle gourd
chili pepper
lima bean

Andes

Paraná

Patagonia

ATLANTIC OCEAN

The spread of agriculture ▶

- areas of early agriculture, with dates of first domestication of plants and animals
- diffusion of agricultural skills

Staple crops under cultivation by c.4000 BCE

- wheat
- barley
- millet
- maize
- rice

Wild ancestors of domesticated animals

- aurochs (wild cattle)
- pig

- sheep
- ass
- dromedary camel
- horse
- bactrian camel
- gaur (wild ox)
- buffalo
- chicken
- goat
- yak
- turkey
- guanaco (llama)
- guinea pig
- alpaca
- banteng

inequality appeared. In 5000 B.C., only a limited number of regions were fully dependent on agriculture. In many parts of the globe, small-scale farming began to supplement hunting and gathering, the first steps in the gradual transition to the sedentary agricultural way of life.

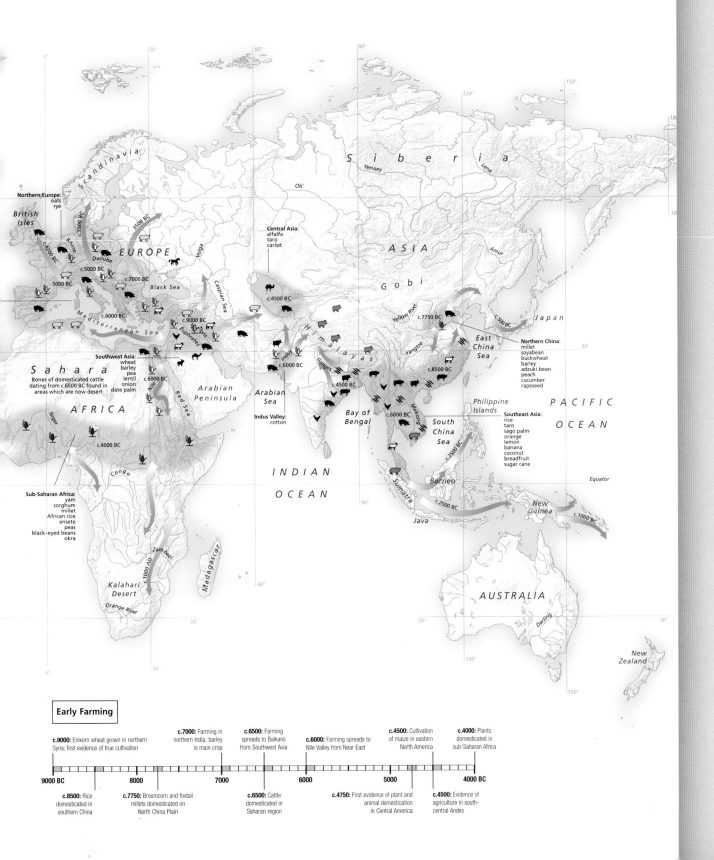

Early Farming

9000 BC   8000   7000   6000   5000   4000 BC

THE FIRST CIVILIZATIONS

The period between 5000 and 2500 B.C. saw the development of complex urban civilizations in the fertile river valleys of the Nile, Tigris, Euphrates, and Indus. Mesopotamian city states formed small kingdoms, which competed with one another. A literate elite ruled over each civilization, and their artisans experimented with new technologies such as bronze and copper metallurgy. Many village societies developed important ritual centers or buried their dead in communal sepulchers.

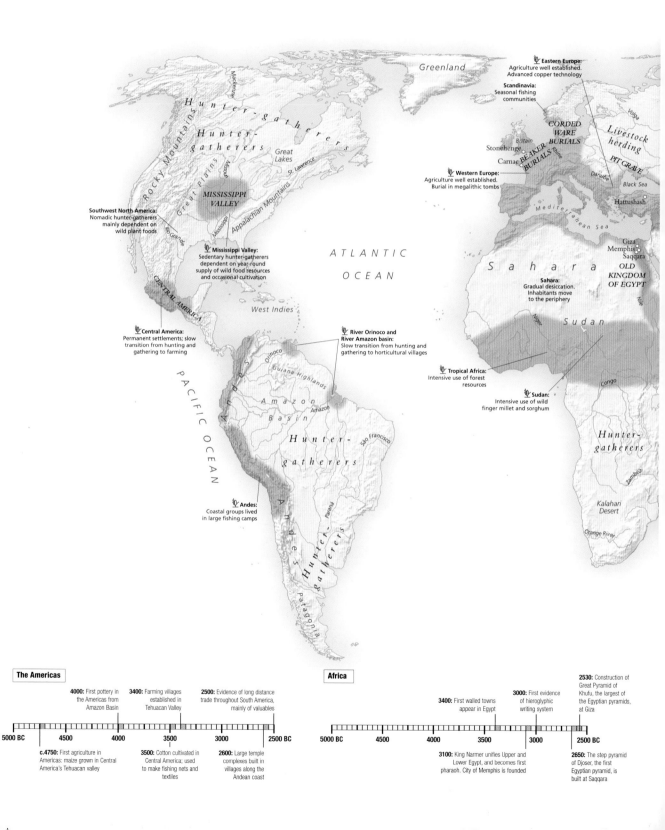

Greenland

Eastern Europe:
Agriculture well established.
Advanced copper technology

Scandinavia:
Seasonal fishing
communities

Hunter-gatherers

Hunter-gatherers

Mackenzie

Great
Lakes

St. Lawrence

Rocky Mountains

Missouri

*CORDED
WARE
BURIALS*

Britain
Stonehenge
Carnac *BEAKER
BURIALS*

Rhine

*Livestock
herding*

Volga

PIT GRAVE

Danube

Black Sea

Western Europe:
Agriculture well established.
Burial in megalithic tombs

Hattushash

*MISSISSIPPI
VALLEY*

Great Plains

Appalachian Mountains

Mississippi

Mediterranean Sea

Southwest North America:
Nomadic hunter-gatherers
mainly dependent on
wild plant foods

Rio Grande

Mississippi Valley:
Sedentary hunter-gatherers
dependent on year-round
supply of wild food resources
and occasional cultivation

*ATLANTIC
OCEAN*

Giza
Memphis
Saqqara

S a h a r a

*OLD
KINGDOM
OF EGYPT*

CENTRAL AMERICA

West Indies

Sahara:
Gradual desiccation.
Inhabitants move
to the periphery

Nile

Central America:
Permanent settlements; slow
transition from hunting and
gathering to farming

Niger

S u d a n

**River Orinoco and
River Amazon basin:**
Slow transition from hunting and
gathering to horticultural villages

PACIFIC OCEAN

Orinoco

Guiana Highlands

*A m a z o n
B a s i n*

Amazon

Tropical Africa:
Intensive use of forest
resources

Congo

Sudan:
Intensive use of wild
finger millet and sorghum

Andes

São Francisco

Hunter-gatherers

Hunter-gatherers

Zambezi

Andes:
Coastal groups lived
in large fishing camps

Andes

Paraná

Kalahari
Desert

Hunter-gatherers

Orange River

Patagonia

The Americas

4000: First pottery in the Americas from Amazon Basin

3400: Farming villages established in Tehuacan Valley

2500: Evidence of long distance trade throughout South America, mainly of valuables

5000 BC · 4500 · 4000 · 3500 · 3000 · 2500 BC

c.4750: First agriculture in Americas: maize grown in Central America's Tehuacan valley

3500: Cotton cultivated in Central America; used to make fishing nets and textiles

2600: Large temple complexes built in villages along the Andean coast

Africa

3400: First walled towns appear in Egypt

3000: First evidence of hieroglyphic writing system

2530: Construction of Great Pyramid of Khufu, the largest of the Egyptian pyramids, at Giza

5000 BC · 4500 · 4000 · 3500 · 3000 · 2500 BC

3100: King Narmer unifies Upper and Lower Egypt, and becomes first pharaoh. City of Memphis is founded

2650: The step pyramid of Djoser, the first Egyptian pyramid, is built at Saqqara

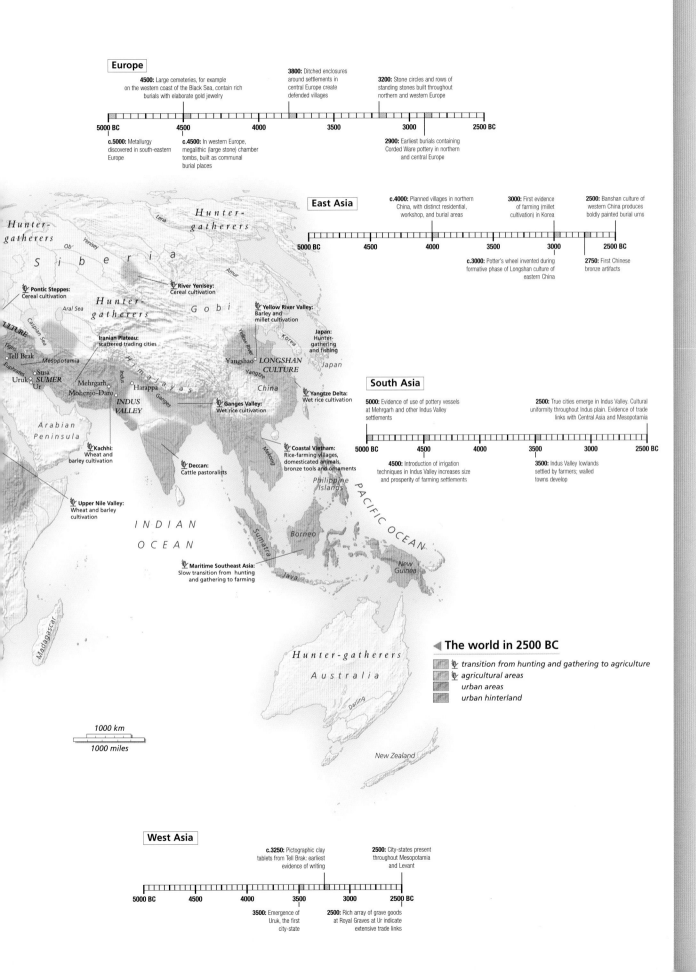

Europe

4500: Large cemeteries, for example on the western coast of the Black Sea, contain rich burials with elaborate gold jewelry

3800: Ditched enclosures around settlements in central Europe create defended villages

3200: Stone circles and rows of standing stones built throughout northern and western Europe

5000 BC — 4500 — 4000 — 3500 — 3000 — 2500 BC

c.5000: Metallurgy discovered in south-eastern Europe

c.4500: In western Europe, megalithic (large stone) chamber tombs, built as communal burial places

2900: Earliest burials containing Corded Ware pottery in northern and central Europe

East Asia

c.4000: Planned villages in northern China, with distinct residential, workshop, and burial areas

3000: First evidence of farming (millet cultivation) in Korea

2500: Banshan culture of western China produces boldly painted burial urns

5000 BC — 4500 — 4000 — 3500 — 3000 — 2500 BC

c.3000: Potter's wheel invented during formative phase of Longshan culture of eastern China

2750: First Chinese bronze artifacts

South Asia

5000: Evidence of use of pottery vessels at Mehrgarh and other Indus Valley settlements

2500: True cities emerge in Indus Valley. Cultural uniformity throughout Indus plain. Evidence of trade links with Central Asia and Mesopotamia

5000 BC — 4500 — 4000 — 3500 — 3000 — 2500 BC

4500: Introduction of irrigation techniques in Indus Valley increases size and prosperity of farming settlements

3500: Indus Valley lowlands settled by farmers; walled towns develop

Map labels

Hunter-gatherers

Siberia

Ob' · Yenisey · Lena · Amur

River Yenisey: Cereal cultivation

Pontic Steppes: Cereal cultivation

Hunter-gatherers

Gobi

Aral Sea · Caspian Sea

...CULTURE

Tigris · Euphrates

Tell Brak

Mesopotamia

Susa · **Uruk** · SUMER · Ur

Iranian Plateau: scattered trading cities

Mehrgarh · **Mohenjo-Daro** · **Harappa**

INDUS VALLEY

Himalayas

Indus · Ganges

Ganges Valley: Wet rice cultivation

Yellow River Valley: Barley and millet cultivation

Yellow River · Yangtze

Yangshao · *LONGSHAN CULTURE*

Korea · *Japan*

Japan: Hunter-gathering and fishing

China

Yangtze Delta: Wet rice cultivation

Coastal Vietnam: Rice-farming villages, domesticated animals, bronze tools and ornaments

Mekong

Arabian Peninsula

Kachhi: Wheat and barley cultivation

Deccan: Cattle pastoralists

Upper Nile Valley: Wheat and barley cultivation

INDIAN OCEAN

Philippine Islands

PACIFIC OCEAN

Sumatra · *Borneo* · *New Guinea*

Maritime Southeast Asia: Slow transition from hunting and gathering to farming

Java

Madagascar

Hunter-gatherers

Australia

Darling

1000 km

1000 miles

New Zealand

◀ The world in 2500 BC

- transition from hunting and gathering to agriculture
- agricultural areas
- urban areas
- urban hinterland

West Asia

c.3250: Pictographic clay tablets from Tell Brak: earliest evidence of writing

2500: City-states present throughout Mesopotamia and Levant

5000 BC — 4500 — 4000 — 3500 — 3000 — 2500 BC

3500: Emergence of Uruk, the first city-state

2500: Rich array of grave goods at Royal Graves at Ur indicate extensive trade links

TRADE, CROPS, AND THE SPREAD OF DISEASE, 500–1500 A.D.

Campaigns of imperial expansion, mass migration, cross-cultural trade, and long-distance travel all facilitated the spread of agricultural crops, domesticated animals, and diseases throughout much of the Old World. From 500 to 1500 A.D., an array of historical processes helped introduce biological species to new regions and peoples. Chinese rulers extended their authority south of the Yangtze River; Muslim armies pushed into India, Persia, and North Africa; Bantu-speaking peoples migrated throughout most of sub-Saharan Africa; Muslim merchants pursued commercial opportunities throughout the Indian Ocean basin and across the Sahara; and missionaries, pilgrims, diplomats, administrators, and other travelers ventured throughout Eurasia and North Africa. Biological exchanges resulting from these changes profoundly influenced the development of societies throughout the eastern hemisphere.

The spread of bubonic plague

Bubonic plague has long maintained an endemic presence in rodent communities in both Yunnan in southwest China and the Great Lakes region of East Africa. In the early 14th century, Mongol armies helped infected fleas spread from Yunnan to the rest of China. In 1331 an outbreak of plague reportedly carried away 90% of the population in parts of northeast China, and by the 1350s there were widely scattered epidemics throughout China. From China, bubonic plague spread rapidly west along the Silk Roads of Central Asia. By 1346 it had reached the Black Sea. Muslim merchants carried it south and west to southwest Asia, Egypt, and North Africa, while Italian merchants carried it west to Italy and then to northern and western Europe, where it became known as the Black Death. Up to one-third of Europe's population is thought to have died in this episode.

The diffusion of staple crops to c.1500

Original source areas (pre-700)
- 🍌 bananas
- ✹ sugarcane
- ✿ cotton
- ✾ sorghum

Spread of crops c.700–1500
- → spread of bananas
- → spread of sugarcane
- → spread of cotton
- → spread of sorghum

Areas to which crops had spread by 1500
- bananas
- sugarcane
- cotton
- sorghum

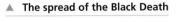

The spread of the Black Death

- Arab trade route
- Chinese trade route
- Genoese trade route
- main Hanseatic trade routes
- Silk Road } routes opened during the
- other route } "Mongol Peace" c.1250–1350
- Venetian trade route
- other trade route
- principal route of Hajj pilgrimage to Mecca
- ➤ progress of bubonic plague
- area of earliest outbreak of bubonic plague
- area of outbreak of bubonic plague
- ⊚ recorded outbreak of bubonic plague

The diffusion of staple crops

A massive diffusion of agricultural crops took place between about 700 and 1400 A.D. Most crops spread from tropical or subtropical lands in South and Southeast Asia to the more temperate regions of the eastern hemisphere. Many crops moved with the aid of Muslim merchants, administrators, diplomats, soldiers, missionaries, pilgrims, and other travelers who visited lands from Morocco and Spain to Java and southern China. Sugar cane, native to New Guinea, arrived in the Mediterranean basin as a result of this biological diffusion, along with hard wheat, eggplants, spinach, artichokes, lemons, and limes. Other crops that dispersed widely during this era included rice, sorghum, bananas, coconuts, watermelons, oranges, mangoes, cotton, indigo, and henna.

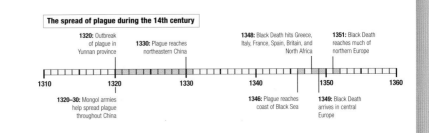

The spread of plague during the 14th century

1320: Outbreak of plague in Yunnan province

1330: Plague reaches northeastern China

1348: Black Death hits Greece, Italy, France, Spain, Britain, and North Africa

1351: Black Death reaches much of northern Europe

1320–30: Mongol armies help spread plague throughout China

1346: Plague reaches coast of Black Sea

1349: Black Death arrives in central Europe

TRADING IN HUMAN LIVES

The use of slaves seems to have been endemic in many human societies. Normally taken as prisoners of war, slaves were also acquired as a form of tribute. The establishment of European colonies and overseas empires between the 16th and 19th centuries saw the creation of a slave trade on an industrial scale, a commerce which laid the foundations for pan-global trading networks. Trading concerns such as the English and Dutch East India companies developed trade on a larger scale than ever before; but it was the need to supply labor for the plantations of the Americas which led to the greatest movement of peoples across the face of the earth.

Slaves in the New World

The great plantation systems and mining concerns that arose in the New World from the 16th century onward demanded large reservoirs of labor. Though the Spanish and Portuguese initially used enslaved indigenous people, they soon required a more reliable source of labor. The Portuguese began bringing African slaves to the Caribbean and Brazil in the early 16th century. The cotton plantations of the southern U.S., which boomed in the early 19th century, were a key factor in sustaining the Atlantic trade.

The Atlantic slave trade

From the late 15th to the early 19th century, European merchants—especially the British and Portuguese—carried on a massive trade in African slaves across the Atlantic. As well as utilizing the established sources of slaves from the Central and West African kingdoms, they also raided coastal areas of West Africa for additional supplies of slaves. European manufactured goods, especially guns, were exchanged for slaves destined to work as agricultural laborers on plantations in the Caribbean and the tropical Americas. Slaves transported to the western hemisphere may have numbered 12 million or more.

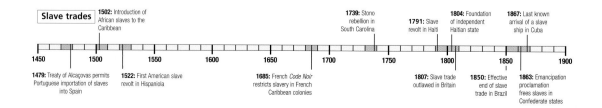

Other slave trades

By the 9th and 10th centuries, a number of complex slave-trading routes were in existence in Europe and the Near East. Viking and Russian merchants traded in slaves from the Balkans who were often sold to harems in southern Spain and North Africa. The Baghdad Caliphate drew slaves from western Europe via the ports of Venice, Prague, and Marseille, and Slavic and Turkic slaves from eastern Europe and Central Asia. In the 13th century, the Mongols sold slaves at Karakorum and in the Volga region. There was long-standing commerce in African slaves—primarily from East Africa before European mariners entered the slave trade. Between the 9th and 19th centuries Muslim merchants may have transported as many as 14 million across the Sahara by camel caravan and through East African ports, principally to destinations in the Indian Ocean basin.

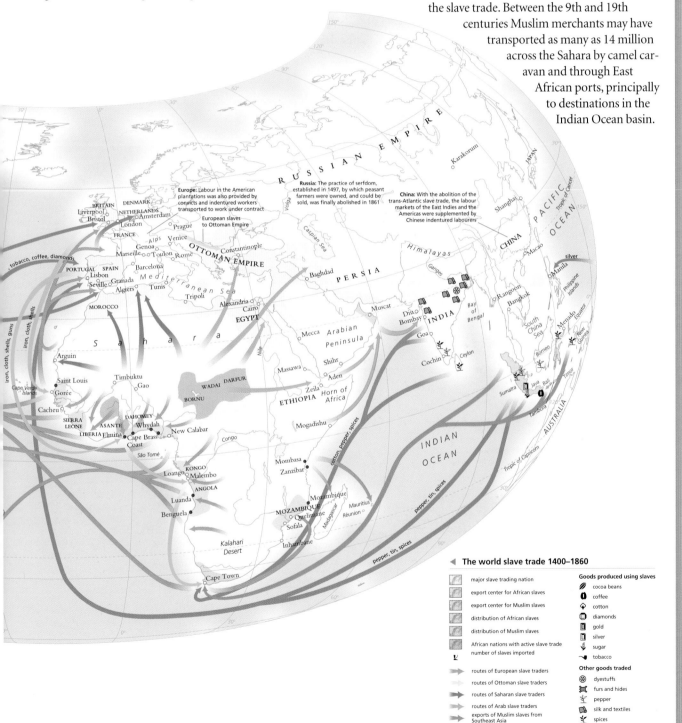

Europe: Labour in the American plantations was also provided by convicts and indentured workers transported to work under contract

European slaves to Ottoman Empire

Russia: The practice of serfdom, established in 1497, by which peasant farmers were owned, and could be sold, was finally abolished in 1861

China: With the abolition of the trans-Atlantic slave trade, the labour markets of the East Indies and the Americas were supplemented by Chinese indentured labourers

◀ **The world slave trade 1400–1860**

		Goods produced using slaves	
	major slave trading nation		cocoa beans
	export center for African slaves		coffee
	export center for Muslim slaves		cotton
	distribution of African slaves		diamonds
	distribution of Muslim slaves		gold
	African nations with active slave trade		silver
	number of slaves imported		sugar
			tobacco

routes of European slave traders

routes of Ottoman slave traders

routes of Saharan slave traders

Other goods traded

routes of Arab slave traders — dyestuffs

exports of Muslim slaves from Southeast Asia — furs and hides

goods exported in exchange for slaves — pepper

goods exported for slaves — silk and textiles

European exports to Africa — spices

— tin

slave factory

Goods imported for slaves

— salt cod

THE INDUSTRIAL REVOLUTION AND THE SPREAD OF TECHNOLOGY

In the first half of the 19th century, world trade and industry was dominated by Britain; by the 1870s, the industrial balance was shifting in favor of other nations, especially Germany, France, Russia, and the U.S., with rapid industrialization occurring throughout most of Europe by the end of the century. A stable currency, a standard (for example, the price of gold) against which the currency's value could be measured, and an effective private banking system were seen as essential to the growth and success of every industrializing nation. The major industrial nations also began to invest heavily overseas. Their aims were the discovery and exploitation of cheaper raw materials, balanced by the development of overseas markets for their products.

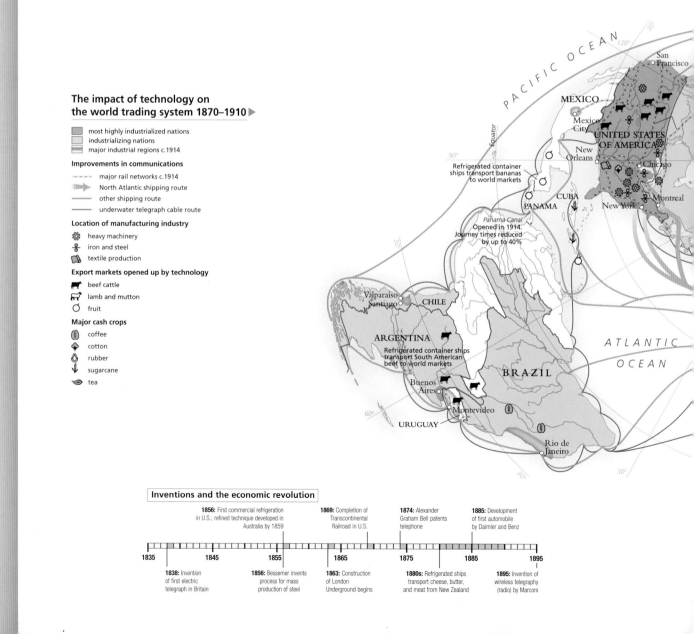

The impact of technology on the world trading system 1870–1910 ▶

- ▨ most highly industrialized nations
- ▢ industrializing nations
- ▨ major industrial regions c.1914

Improvements in communications
- ‑‑‑‑ major rail networks c.1914
- ▦▦▶ North Atlantic shipping route
- ——— other shipping route
- ——— underwater telegraph cable route

Location of manufacturing industry
- ⚙ heavy machinery
- ⚒ iron and steel
- 🧵 textile production

Export markets opened up by technology
- 🐂 beef cattle
- 🐑 lamb and mutton
- ○ fruit

Major cash crops
- ◉ coffee
- ♠ cotton
- ◐ rubber
- ↓ sugarcane
- 🍃 tea

Refrigerated container ships transport bananas to world markets

Panama Canal Opened in 1914. Journey times reduced by up to 40%

Refrigerated container ships transport South American beef to world markets

PACIFIC OCEAN

San Francisco

MEXICO

Mexico City

UNITED STATES OF AMERICA

New Orleans

Chicago

Montreal

New York

CUBA

PANAMA

Valparaiso
Santiago
CHILE

ARGENTINA

BRAZIL

Buenos Aires

Montevideo

URUGUAY

Rio de Janeiro

ATLANTIC OCEAN

Equator

Inventions and the economic revolution

1856: First commercial refrigeration in U.S.; refined technique developed in Australia by 1859

1869: Completion of Transcontinental Railroad in U.S.

1874: Alexander Graham Bell patents telephone

1885: Development of first automobile by Daimler and Benz

| 1835 | 1845 | 1855 | 1865 | 1875 | 1885 | 1895 |

1838: Invention of first electric telegraph in Britain

1856: Bessemer invents process for mass production of steel

1863: Construction of London Underground begins

1880s: Refrigerated ships transport cheese, butter, and meat from New Zealand

1895: Invention of wireless telegraphy (radio) by Marconi

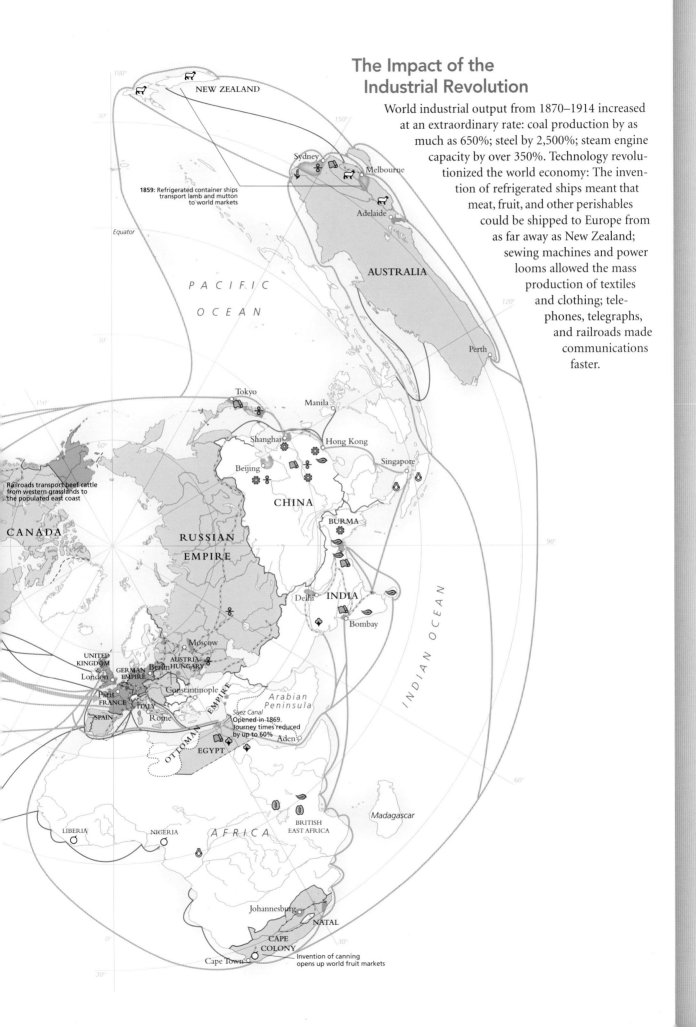

The Impact of the Industrial Revolution

World industrial output from 1870–1914 increased at an extraordinary rate: coal production by as much as 650%; steel by 2,500%; steam engine capacity by over 350%. Technology revolutionized the world economy: The invention of refrigerated ships meant that meat, fruit, and other perishables could be shipped to Europe from as far away as New Zealand; sewing machines and power looms allowed the mass production of textiles and clothing; telephones, telegraphs, and railroads made communications faster.

NEW ZEALAND

Sydney
Melbourne

1859: Refrigerated container ships transport lamb and mutton to world markets

Adelaide

Equator

AUSTRALIA

PACIFIC OCEAN

Perth

Tokyo

Manila

Shanghai
Hong Kong

Beijing
Singapore

CHINA

BURMA

Railroads transport beef cattle from western grasslands to the populated east coast

CANADA

RUSSIAN EMPIRE

Delhi
INDIA

Bombay

INDIAN OCEAN

Moscow

UNITED KINGDOM
AUSTRIA-HUNGARY
GERMAN Berlin
London EMPIRE
Paris Constantinople
FRANCE
ITALY
SPAIN Rome

Arabian Peninsula

Suez Canal
Opened in 1869.
Journey times reduced by up to 60%

Aden

OTTOMAN EMPIRE

EGYPT

LIBERIA
NIGERIA
AFRICA

BRITISH EAST AFRICA

Madagascar

Johannesburg

NATAL

CAPE COLONY

Cape Town

Invention of canning opens up world fruit markets

WESTERN IMPERIALISM

Imperialism is as old as the state. Even before Classical Greece and Imperial Rome, there was imperialism, in ancient Mesopotamia, India, and elsewhere. Other imperialist states included the Phoenician, Chinese, Ottoman, Russian, Spanish, and Portuguese empires, to name but a few. The last twenty years of the 19th century saw unprecedented competition by the major European nations for control of territory overseas. The balance of imperial power was changing: having lost their American empires, Spain and Portugal were no longer preeminent. From the 1830s, France began to build a new empire, and Britain continued to acquire new lands throughout the century. Newly unified Italy and Germany sought to bolster their nation status from the 1880s with their own empires. Africa was the most fiercely contested prize in this race to absorb the non-industrialized world, but much of Southeast Asia and Oceania was also appropriated in this period. Even the U.S., historically the champion of anticolonial movements, began to expand across the Pacific.

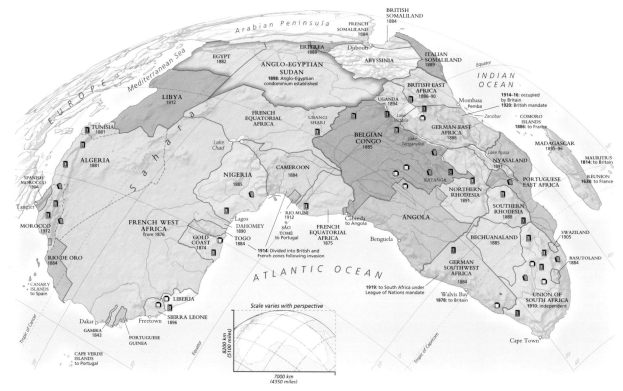

The scramble for Africa

The race for European political control in Africa began in the early 1880s. The Berlin Conference of 1884–85, convened to discuss rival European claims to Africa, was the starting point for the "scramble." Some governments worked through commercial companies; elsewhere, land was independently annexed by these companies; sometimes Africans actually invited Europeans in. In most cases, however, European political control was directly imposed by conquest. By 1914, Africa was fully partitioned along lines that bore little relation to cultural or linguistic traditions.

▲ **Imperialism in Africa, 1880–1920**

Territory controlled by European nations by 1914

Belgium	Portugal	
Britain	Spain	
France	nominally Ottoman, under British control	
Germany	1882 date of taking	
Italy	control borders in 1914	

Important mineral deposits

- coal
- copper
- diamonds
- gold

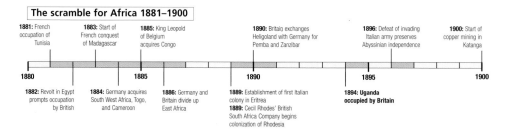

The scramble for Africa 1881–1900

1881: French occupation of Tunisia

1883: Start of French conquest of Madagascar

1885: King Leopold of Belgium acquires Congo

1890: Britain exchanges Heligoland with Germany for Pemba and Zanzibar

1896: Defeat of invading Italian army preserves Abyssinian independence

1900: Start of copper mining in Katanga

1880 · 1885 · 1890 · 1895 · 1900

1882: Revolt in Egypt prompts occupation by British

1884: Germany acquires South West Africa, Togo, and Cameroon

1886: Germany and Britain divide up East Africa

1889: Establishment of first Italian colony in Eritrea
1889: Cecil Rhodes' British South Africa Company begins colonization of Rhodesia

1894: Uganda occupied by Britain

Imperialism in Southeast Asia

Though the Dutch East Indian Empire had existed since the early 17th century, much of Southeast Asia was not colonized until the mid-19th century. Moving east from India, British ambitions concentrated on Burma, the Malay Peninsula, and north Borneo. Renewed French interest in empire-building began in earnest with the capture of Saigon in 1858 following a concerted naval effort. By 1893, France controlled Tongking, Laos, Annam, and Cambodia, collectively known as Indochina.

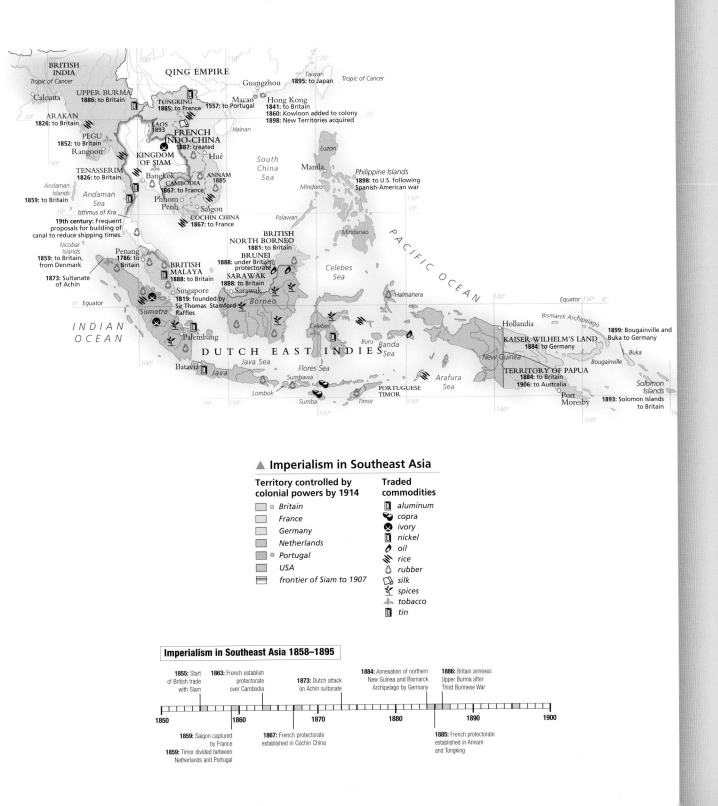

▲ **Imperialism in Southeast Asia**

Territory controlled by colonial powers by 1914
- Britain
- France
- Germany
- Netherlands
- Portugal
- USA
- frontier of Siam to 1907

Traded commodities
- aluminum
- copra
- ivory
- nickel
- oil
- rice
- rubber
- silk
- spices
- tobacco
- tin

Imperialism in Southeast Asia 1858–1895

1855: Start of British trade with Siam
1863: French establish protectorate over Cambodia
1873: Dutch attack on Achin sultanate
1884: Annexation of northern New Guinea and Bismarck Archipelago by Germany
1886: Britain annexes Upper Burma after Third Burmese War

1850 — 1860 — 1870 — 1880 — 1890 — 1900

1859: Saigon captured by France
1859: Timor divided between Netherlands and Portugal
1867: French protectorate established in Cochin China
1885: French protectorate established in Annam and Tongking

MIGRATION IN THE 19TH CENTURY

The technical innovations of the Industrial Revolution made the 19th-century world a much smaller place. Railroads could quickly transport large human cargoes across continents, the Suez and Panama canals reduced travel times—sometimes by as much as 50%, and ships became larger, faster, and more seaworthy. The mechanization and centralization of industry required the concentration of labor on a scale never seen before. At the same time, the European imperial powers were exploiting their tropical possessions for economic benefit. Cash crops, grown on large plantations, needed a plentiful supply of labor as well. Political upheaval, wars, and economic hardship provided the most dramatic impetus to emigration—especially in the Russian Empire and Central Europe, and in southeastern China.

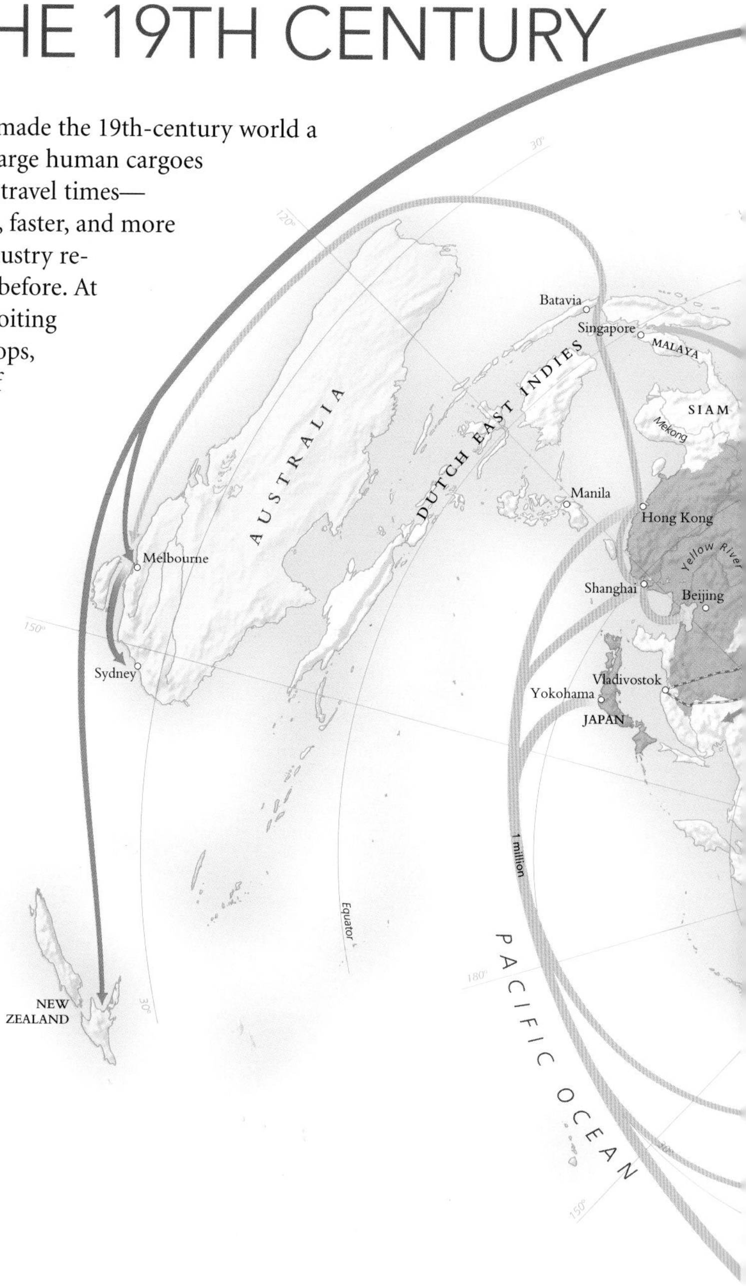

Batavia
Singapore MALAYA
AUSTRALIA
DUTCH EAST INDIES
SIAM
Mekong
Manila
Hong Kong
Yellow River
Melbourne
Shanghai Beijing
Sydney
Vladivostok
Yokohama
JAPAN
Equator
NEW ZEALAND
1 million
PACIFIC OCEAN

Migration in the 19th century

More than 80 million people emigrated from their country of origin during the 19th and early 20th centuries. Over half of them moved across the Atlantic to North and South America. The end of the American Civil War in 1865, and the opening up of Native American land to settlers saw the greatest period of immigration to the U.S. and Canada. In the Russian Empire, movement was eastward from European Russia into Siberia and the Caspian region. Europeans moved south and east to take up employment in the colonies, while indentured laborers traveled to the Americas, Africa, and Southeast Asia.

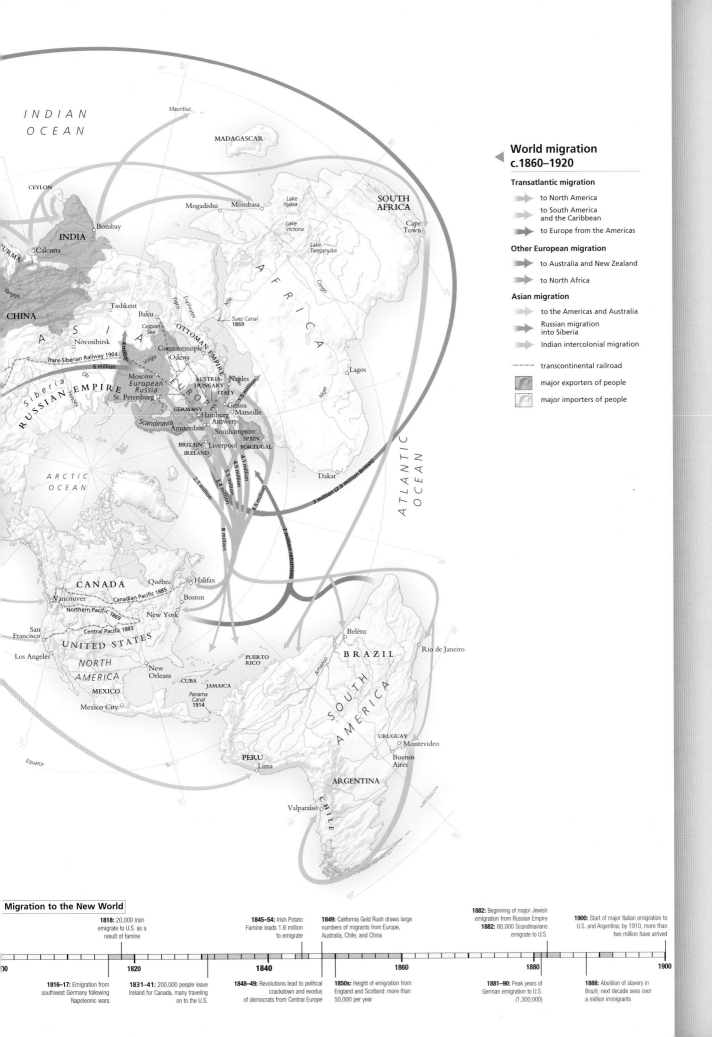

INDIAN
OCEAN

CEYLON

Mauritius

MADAGASCAR

Mogadishu   Mombasa
Bombay   Lake
INDIA   *Nyasa*
Calcutta   Lake
                          Victoria   SOUTH
URMA   AFRICA
                         Lake
Yangtze   *Tanganyika*   Cape
                                             Town
CHINA   Tashkent   A   F   R   I   C   A
             Baku   *Tigris*
Caspian   *Euphrates* *Nile*
Novosibirsk *Sea*   Suez Canal
  A S I A   1869   Congo
Trans-Siberian Railway 1904   *Congo*
         6 million Moscow Constantinople
Kenisey *Volga* Odessa OTTOMAN EMPIRE
Siberia   European AUSTRIA- Naples   Lagos
RUSSIAN EMPIRE Russia HUNGARY *Niger*
          St. Petersburg ITALY
                    GERMANY Genoa
          Scandinavia Hamburg Marseille
             Amsterdam Antwerp
ARCTIC   BRITAIN Liverpool SPAIN
OCEAN   IRELAND Southampton PORTUGAL
                  4.1 million
             2.1 million Dakar
        3.4 million 5.5 million
                  4.5 million
                  4.5 million
           8 million
        7 million returnees
                              3 million (2.5 million British)

CANADA   Québec   Halifax
Vancouver Canadian Pacific 1885
  Northern Pacific 1869 Boston
San   Central Pacific 1883 New York
Francisco
         UNITED STATES
Los Angeles NORTH   Belém
         AMERICA New   BRAZIL   Rio de Janeiro
    MEXICO Orleans PUERTO
         CUBA   RICO *Amazon*
    JAMAICA
MEXICO CITY Panama   SOUTH
         Canal   AMERICA
         1914
              PERU
              Lima   URUGUAY
                         Montevideo
              ARGENTINA Buenos
                         Aires
         Valparaíso CHILE

Equator

ATLANTIC
OCEAN

World migration
c.1860–1920

Transatlantic migration

→ to North America

→ to South America
  and the Caribbean

→ to Europe from the Americas

Other European migration

→ to Australia and New Zealand

→ to North Africa

Asian migration

⇢ to the Americas and Australia

→ Russian migration
  into Siberia

→ Indian intercolonial migration

---- transcontinental railroad

▨ major exporters of people

▢ major importers of people

Migration to the New World

00   1820   1840   1860   1880   1900

BIOLOGICAL EXCHANGES

European expansion had a profound biological impact. Travelers transported numerous species of fruits, vegetables, and animals from the Americas to Europe. At the same time, settlers introduced European species to the Americas and Oceania. Horses, pigs, and cattle were transported to the western hemisphere where, without natural predators, their numbers increased spectacularly. The settlers consciously introduced food crops, such as wheat, grapes, apples, peaches, and citrus fruits. Some plants, such as nettles,

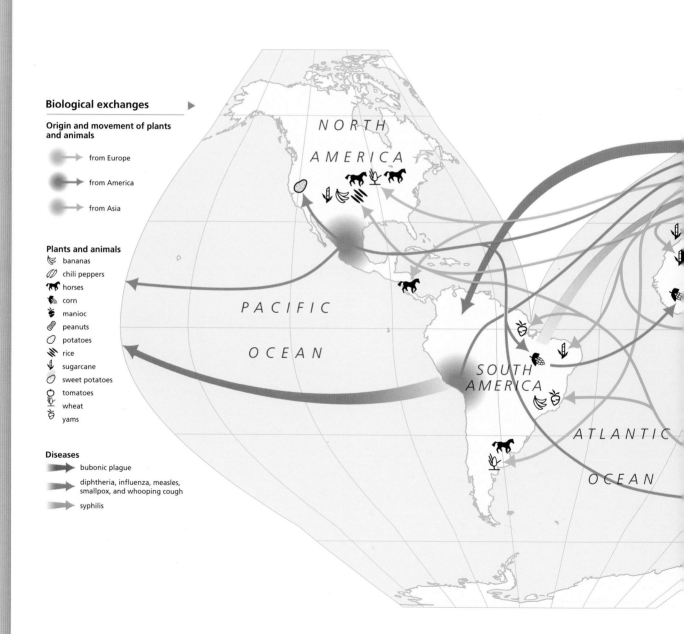

Biological exchanges ▶

Origin and movement of plants and animals

- → from Europe
- → from America
- → from Asia

Plants and animals
- bananas
- chili peppers
- horses
- corn
- manioc
- peanuts
- potatoes
- rice
- sugarcane
- sweet potatoes
- tomatoes
- wheat
- yams

Diseases
- → bubonic plague
- → diphtheria, influenza, measles, smallpox, and whooping cough
- → syphilis

dandelions, and other weeds were inadvertently dispersed by the winds or on the coats of animals. European expansion also led to a spread of European diseases. Vast numbers of indigenous American peoples died from measles and smallpox, which broke out in massive epidemics among populations with no natural or acquired immunity. During the 16th century, syphilis—thought now to be the result of the fusion of two similar diseases from Europe and the New World—killed a million Europeans.

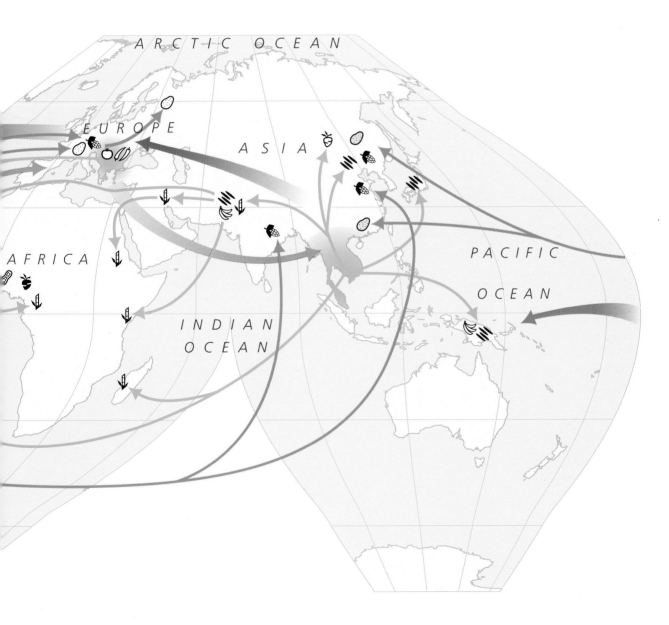

EUROPEAN EXPANSION IN THE 16TH CENTURY

The 16th century saw the expansion of several of the great European nations far beyond their continental limits. Explorers searching for new sources of luxury goods and precious metals began to open up new territories which monarchs such as Philip II of Spain quickly built up into great empires in the "New World." The Spanish and Portuguese, inspired by the voyages of Columbus and da Gama, led the way, closely followed by the Dutch and the English. The explorers were aided by technological advances in shipbuilding, navigational equipment, and cartography. At the start of the 16th century, the Americas were virtually unknown to Europeans; by 1700, outposts of a greater European empire had been established almost everywhere the explorers landed.

Spain and Portugal were the leaders of world exploration in the 16th century. In search of maritime trade routes to Asia, the Portuguese found sea lanes through the Atlantic and Indian oceans to India. By 1512, fortified trading posts were in place at Goa and Malacca, and they had reached the "Spice Islands" of the Moluccas in eastern Indonesia. The Spanish, taking a westward route, found the Caribbean islands and the Americas instead. Magellan's three-year global circumnavigation revealed a western route through the Strait of Magellan and across the Pacific Ocean. English and French mariners sought northern passages to Asian markets and their voyages paved the way for the establishment of European settlements in North America.

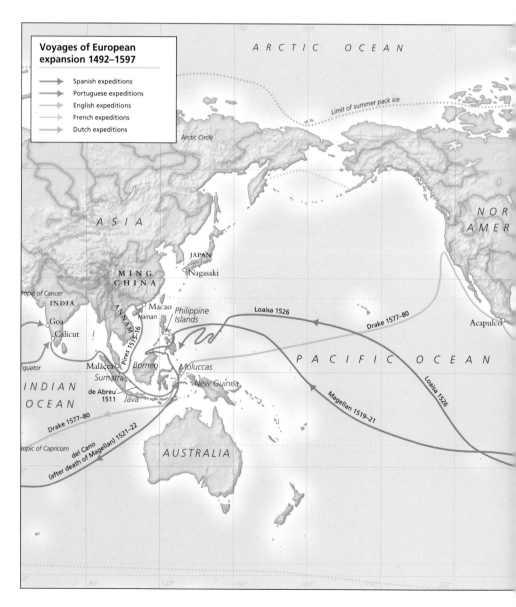

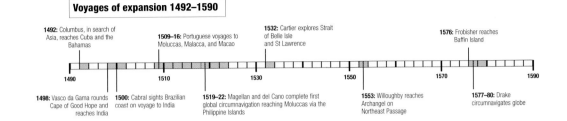

1492: Columbus, in search of Asia, reaches Cuba and the Bahamas

1509–16: Portuguese voyages to Moluccas, Malacca, and Macao

1532: Cartier explores Strait of Belle Isle and St Lawrence

1576: Frobisher reaches Baffin Island

1490 1510 1530 1550 1570 1590

1498: Vasco da Gama rounds Cape of Good Hope and reaches India

1500: Cabral sights Brazilian coast on voyage to India

1519–22: Magellan and del Cano complete first global circumnavigation reaching Moluccas via the Philippine Islands

1553: Willoughby reaches Archangel on Northeast Passage

1577–80: Drake circumnavigates globe

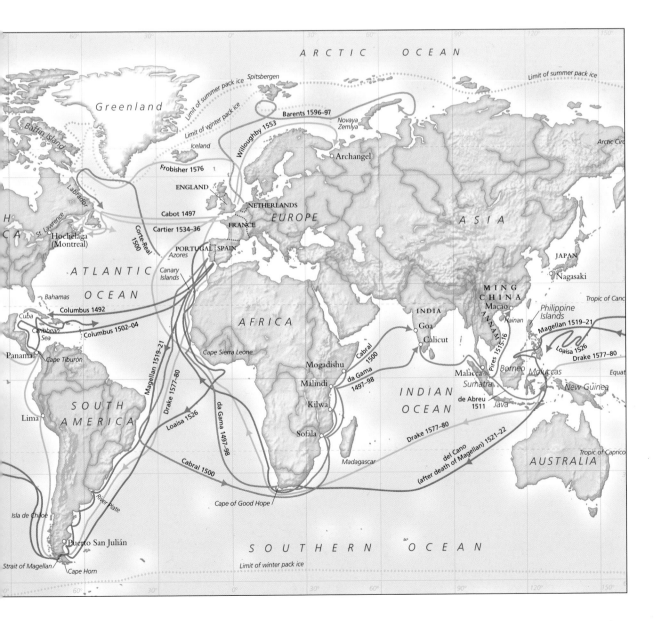